DSM-III-R
CASEBOOK

A Learning Companion to the
Diagnostic and Statistical Manual
of Mental Disorders (Third Edition, Revised)

Robert L. Spitzer, M.D.
Miriam Gibbon, M.S.W.
Andrew E. Skodol, M.D.
Janet B. W. Williams, D.S.W.
Michael B. First, M.D.

Columbia University
and the
New York State Psychiatric Institute

American Psychiatric Press, Inc.

1400 K St., N.W.
Washington, DC 20005

Copyright © 1989 American Psychiatric Press, Inc.
ALL RIGHTS RESERVED
Manufactured in the United States of America
93   92   91
10   9   8   7   6   5   4

The paper used in this publication meets the minimum requirements of the American National Standard for Information Sciences—Permanence of Paper for Printed Library Materials ANSI Z39.48-1984. ∞

Library of Congress Cataloging-in-Publication Data

DSM-III-R casebook : a learning companion to the Diagnostic and
    statistical manual of mental disorders (third edition, revised) /
    Robert L. Spitzer . . . [et al.].
        p.   cm.
    Rev. ed. of: DSM-III case book. 1st ed. 1981.
    Includes index.
    ISBN 0-88048-161-7 (alk. paper). ISBN 0-88048-283-4 (soft : alk.
paper)
    1. Mental illness—Diagnosis—Case studies. 2. Mental illness—
Classification. 3. Diagnostic and statistical manual of mental disorders.
I. Spitzer, Robert L. II. Diagnostic and statistical manual of mental
disorders. III. DSM-III case book. IV. Title: DSM-III-R case book.
    [DNLM: 1. Mental Disorders—diagnosis—case studies. WM 15 D536
1987 Suppl.]
RC455.2.C4A48 1980 Suppl. 2
616.89′075—dc19
DNLM/DLC
for Library of Congress   88-26257
                                                                CIP

Contents

Acknowledgments

We gratefully acknowledge the contributions of case material supplied by our colleagues listed below.

Contributors of Cases from English Speaking Countries

Gene Abel, M.D.
Henry David Abraham, M.D.
Hagop Akiskal, M.D.
Nancy Andreasen, M.D., Ph.D.
Rena Appel, M.D.
Robert Arnstein, M.D.
Lorian Baker, Ph.D.
Stephen Bauer, M.D.
Robert Benjamin, M.D.
Fred S. Berlin, M.D., Ph.D.
Joan Brennan, Ph.D.
Allan Burstein, M.D.
Dennis Cantwell, M.D.
Mark Chalem, M.D.
Paula J. Clayton, M.D.
David E. Comings M.D.
Anthony J. Costello, M.D.
George C. Curtis, M.D.
Carlo C. DiClemente, Ph.D.
Robert L. Custer, M.D.
Park Elliott Dietz, M.D., M.P.H., Ph.D.
Norman Greenspan Doidge, M.D.
Armando R. Favazza, M.D.
Leslie M. Forman, M.D.
Allen J. Frances, M.D.
Richard Friedman, M.D.
Abby J. Fyer, M.D.
Martha Gay, M.D.
Paul H. Gebhard, Ph.D.

Yonkel Goldstein, Ph.D.
Donald Goodwin, M.D.
Arthur H. Green, M.D.
Richard Green, M.D.
Stanley I. Greenspan, M.D.
John G. Gunderson, M.D.
Katherine Hamli, M.D.
Roger Harman, Ph.D.
Joseph A. Himle, A.C.S.W.
Steven Hyler, M.D.
Helene A. Jackson, M.S.W.
Richard L. Jenkins, M.D.
Edwin E. Johnstone, M.D.
David Kahn, M.D.
Helen S. Kaplan, M.D., Ph.D.
Sandra J. Kaplan, M.D.
Kenneth S. Kendler, M.D.
Otto Kernberg, M.D.
Robert Kertzner, M.D.
Donald Klein, M.D.
Rachel Klein, Ph.D.
Richard Kluft, M.D.
Robert S. Lampke, M.D.
Jerome H. Liebowitz, M.D.
Harold I. Lief, M.D.
Thomas F. Liffick, M.D.
John Lion, M.D.
Z. J. Lipowski, M.D.
Joseph LoPiccolo, Ph.D.
Roger A. MacKinnon, M.D.

Salvatore Mannuzza, Ph.D.
Lynn Martin, R.N., M.S.N.
Gary J. May, M.D.
George J. McAfee, M.D.
Patrick McKeon, M.D.
Heino F.L. Meyer-Bahlburg, Dr. rer. nat.
John Money, Ph.D.
J. Lawrence Moodie, M.D.
Alistair Munro, M.D.
Philip Muskin, M. D.
Kathi Nader, M.S.W.
Yehuda Nir, M.D.
Arlene Novick, A.C.S.W.
Barbara Parry, M.D.
Roger Peele, M.D.
Judith A. Perry, M.D.
Ethel S. Person, M.D.
Gerald C. Peterson, M.D.
Harrison G. Pope, Jr., M.D.
Michael Popkin, M.D.
Lloyd J. Price, M.D.
Joaquim Puig-Antich, M.D.
Robert Pynoos, M.D.
Pamela Raizman, R.N., M.S.W.
Judith L. Rapaport, M.D.
Quentin R. Regestein, M.D.
Phillip J. Resnick, M.D.
Richard Ries, M.D.
Norman E. Rosenthal, M.D.

Neal D. Ryan, M.D.
Diana Sandberg, M.D.
Phillip Schlobohm, M.D.
Benjamin Seltzer, M.D.
Sally K. Severino, M.D.
David Shaffer, M.D.
Arthur Shapiro, M.D.
Elaine Shapiro, Ph.D.
Lawrence Sharpe, M.D.
Michael Sheehy, M.D.
Meriamne Singer, M.D.
Stephan Sorrell, M.D.
David A. Soskis, M.D.
Laurie Stevens, M.D.
Alan Stone, M.D.
Richard P. Swinson, M.D.
Ludwik S. Szymanski, M.D.
Donn L. Tippet, M.D.
William M. Valverde, M.D.
Fred R. Volkmar, M.D.
Timothy B. Walsh, M.D.
Arnold M. Washton, Ph.D.
Betsy P. Weiner, M.D.
Katherine Whipple, Ph.D.
Ronald Winchel, M.D.
Lorna Wing, M.D.
George Winokur, M.D.
Ken Winters, Ph.D.
Kenneth J. Zucker, Ph.D.

Contributors of International Cases

The following clinicians contributed cases to the International Cases chapter. They are listed along with the country in which their cases were seen.

Renato D. Alarcon, M.D., M.P.H., Peru
Paul Cosyns, M.D., Belgium
Alv A. Dahl, M.D., Norway
Joop T. V. M. de Jong, M.D., Ph.D, West Africa
Ovidio A. deLeon, M.D., Panama

Peter M. Ellis, FRANZCP, New Zealand
Yutaka Honda, M.D., Japan
S. T. C. Ilechukwu, M.D., Nigeria
Arthur Kleinman, M.D., People's Republic of China
Carlos A. Leon, M.D., Colombia

Werner Mombour, M.D., Federal
 Republic of Germany
Vernon M. Neppe, M.D., Ph.D,
 South Africa
Charles Pull, M.D., Luxembourg
Nils Retterstol, Dr. Med., Norway
Hsien Rin, M.D., Taiwan,
 Republic of China
Shekhar Saxena, M.D., India
Michael von Bose, M.D., Federal
 Republic of Germany

Hans Ulrich Wittchen, Ph.D.,
 Federal Republic of Germany
Xu Youxin, M.D., People's
 Republic of China
DerSon Young, M.D., People's
 Republic of China
Michael Zaudig, M.D., Federal
 Republic of Germany
Boris Zoubok, M.D., U.S.S.R.

Thanks are due to Betty Appelbaum, copy editor for DSM-III, DSM-III-R, and the original *Case Book*, for her meticulous copy editing of this book. We also thank Cheryl S. Cohen for reviewing the manuscript, and Sheila Renert and Harriet Ayers for typing the many revisions.

Introduction

This collection of cases grew out of our experience in teaching both DSM-III and DSM-III-R. We have found that these descriptions of real patients, edited to focus on information relevant to differential diagnosis, are the most effective (and painless) way for clinicians and students to get experience in applying DSM-III-R principles of differential diagnosis to a wide range of patients.

We have chosen focused, edited descriptions of patients since our experience has been that with the use of standard case summaries, discussions of diagnosis are often bogged down in a swamp of details not relevant to the purpose of establishing a diagnosis. (Such nondiagnostic information, however, is obviously necessary in actual clinical records.) In addition, routine case summaries often inadvertently omit crucial diagnostic information, whereas these cases, for the most part, have been prepared to ensure that all available information relevant to making a diagnosis has been included.

These cases have been drawn from our own experience and from the practices of a large number of clinicians, among them many well-known experts in particular areas of diagnosis and treatment. The identities of the patients have been disguised by altering such details as age and occupation and, occasionally, locale. Often we needed to go back to the contributors of the cases to obtain diagnostically crucial information; we avoided the temptation to manufacture the missing details. Sometimes, as in the real world, this led to diagnoses that had to be made provisionally or noted as "rule-outs" (R/O).

Following Freud's example, we have provided titles for each case in order to make them easier to refer to. These titles are listed in Appendix A (Index of Case Names). We have included a number of historical cases from the writings of such great nosologists as Emil Kraepelin, Eugen Bleuler, and Sigmund Freud himself. We have made no effort to disguise the identity of these historical patients; we have, however, taken the liberty of providing appropriate names for those who lacked them.

Each case is followed by a discussion of our diagnosis, made according to the diagnostic criteria in the revised third edition of the American Psychiatric Association's *Diagnostic and Statistical Manual of Mental Disorders* (DSM-III-R). These discussions include important diagnostic considerations, such as the rationale for making each particular diagnosis, other disorders to be considered in formulating each diagnosis, and, in some cases, recognition of diagnostic uncertainty because of inadequate information, ambiguity in the clinical features, or problems in the classification itself. Each discussion concludes with the DSM-III-R diagnosis and its code number. Where appropriate, we have often, but not invariably, followed the recommendation in DSM-III-R of noting the severity of the current disorder as either mild, moderate, severe, in partial remission, or residual state. To aid the reader we have noted in parentheses the page number of the diagnostic criteria in the DSM-III-R manual.

Despite the increase in reliability made possible by the use of diagnostic criteria, some degree of ambiguity is still inevitable. The reader, who may not always agree with our assessment, should understand that we sometimes disagreed with each other about the correct diagnosis. Usually these disagreements were resolved, often by changing our initial diagnosis. We trust that the reader will seriously consider our formulations, but not regard them as infallible.

These cases can be used for a variety of purposes. They should be of value to experienced clinicians, facilitating their understanding of the concepts and terminology in DSM-III-R. All clinicians, regardless of their level of experience and training, may benefit from reading descriptions of cases that are examples of diagnostic categories rarely seen in treatment settings. Teachers and students of abnormal psychology in the disciplines of psychology, psychiatry, social work, and psychiatric nursing will find these cases useful as illustrations of various types of psychopathology. Similarly, other professionals, such as primary care physicians, internists, and attorneys, may find them instructive. These cases should prove helpful to professionals studying for specialty examinations, such as the psychiatry boards: they can serve as a means of testing one's knowledge of diagnosis. Research investigators can use them to assess the level of diagnostic expertise and the reliability with which members of their staff can make diagnostic assessments. Finally, these cases provide a historical point of reference as illustrations of diagnostic concepts in the United States in the late 1980s and, by means of the historical cases, a comparison with diagnostic concepts of the past.

There are four chapters dealing, respectively, with adults, children and adolescents, international cases, and historical cases. For the sake of variety, cases with similar diagnoses or from similar settings are not grouped together in the first two chapters. The international cases are grouped by geographic region, and the historical cases, by their authors. Readers may consult the various appendices to find cases of particular diagnoses or of special interest (e.g., forensic cases, cases with a multiaxial assessment, cases with a difficult differential diagnosis, cases with a physical disorder in the differential diagnosis).

Most of the cases in this book do not include reference to treatment considerations or discussions of alternative classification systems, although they may serve as useful points of departure for discussions of such subjects. (We acknowledge that the kind of information included in these cases is a function of the diagnostic system used; alternative systems of classification are likely to require other kinds of information.) For some of the cases, we have been able to obtain follow-up information, which usually includes response to treatment. Often the follow-up information confirms the original diagnosis; occasionally, it raises doubts or leads to a change in diagnosis.

The original *DSM-III Case Book* was published in 1981, a year after the publication of DSM-III. In this revised version, we have included over a hundred new cases, many of them somewhat longer than those in our original book. We have eliminated over a third of the original cases, and completely revised the discussions of those remaining to conform to the DSM-III-R diagnostic criteria.

All of the more than thirty new diagnostic categories that were added to DSM-III-R, including Sleep Disorders and the "controversial" categories, are illustrated by new cases. For example, there are now cases of Sleep-Wake Schedule Disorder, Cocaine Dependence, Body Dysmorphic Disorder, Trichotillomania, Self-Defeating and Sadistic Personality Disorders, and Late Luteal Phase Dysphoric Disorder. Adding new cases has enabled us to expand the coverage of disorders so that we now have at least one example of virtually every diagnostic category in DSM-III-R. Moreover, we have obtained 28 cases from colleagues in non-English-speaking countries to illustrate the usefulness, as well as the limitations, of DSM-III-R in diagnosing patients from widely divergent cultures.

Robert L. Spitzer, M.D.
Miriam Gibbon, M.S.W.
Andrew E. Skodol, M.D.
Janet B. W. Williams, D.S.W.
Michael B. First, M.D.

MENTAL DISORDERS IN ADULTS

CHAPTER ONE

MENTAL DISORDERS IN ADULTS

The Procrastinator

FORTY-NINE-YEAR-OLD Roger comes to a Montreal psychiatric outpatient clinic, saying that his family thinks he needs help. He does not have any specific complaints, but acknowledges that because of "perfectionism and immobility," he has been unable to work for about seven years.

Roger was reared in a professional family in a small city in British Columbia. He had "a happy childhood" and did well in school. However, his wife (whom he met in Grade 6) claims he was "methodical and slow" even in his teens. He graduated from the university, but was a semester late because he was unable to complete written assignments on time.

Roger worked for a small company in an administrative capacity for four years, then left to join a medium-sized real estate development company. Initially he did well; but as time went on, he found it increasingly difficult to get to work on time, primarily because, while getting dressed, articles of clothing had to be arranged in a special way before he could put them on. He began to miss deadlines for reports. He had no difficulty starting the reports, but often was unable to complete them because he wanted them to be "perfect." In addition, he had difficulty keeping up with opening the mail at home and paying bills. He was aware that they had to be paid, but he somehow could not get around to doing it.

In his early thirties, Roger settled into a routine of getting up later than he intended. Even though he knew he would be late for work, he insisted that he have exactly the same breakfast of orange juice, cereal, and eggs every day; while eating, he read the paper, and then took a shower, shaved, and dressed. No matter how late he was, he was unable to shower in less than 45 minutes or to dress in less than 30 minutes. Frequently he was not ready to leave the house until noon or later. Nevertheless, when he was at work he generally did a good job, except for his difficulty with finishing reports.

His wife reports that he has gradually become slower in completing tasks. He was able to run his own real estate company for a few years after losing his position at the development company; but after a very large deal fell through, he stayed at home most of the time, and finally lost his business and source of income. At the time of the interview, he was facing disciplinary proceedings from the real estate board in his city because he had completed a deal for a friend, but had not gotten around to paying his real estate broker license fee.

When Roger came for help, he had tasks to complete that went back 14 years. He had mail that had been unopened for over ten years that he refused to allow anyone else to touch because they would "not do it properly." His wife decided that she would deal with any accounts that she could identify in the mail and leave the rest of the mail to him. For the first month following delivery, the letters would remain in the hallway; then they would be moved to the dining-room table and, after about a year, to a steadily growing pile in the basement for "proper sorting." Roger's car, which was rusted out, remained in the driveway for seven years before he got around to calling someone to tow it away.

Roger's wife has gone back to work to support the family. Roger is left alone in the house in the morning, and has an unvarying daily routine. He wakes up at 7:00 AM, but is unable to shower and get dressed before 11:00 or 12:00. He then makes his standard breakfast and reads the paper. These activities usually take until 4:00 to 5:00 PM. After accomplishing nothing during the day, he watches television in the evening, and eventually goes to bed at 2:00 or 3:00 AM. In contrast to his inability to initiate or complete tasks on his own, he is able to help others in writing reports and is often helpful to neighbors with real estate problems.

Roger denies ever having any checking rituals or other typical compulsions, such as repetitively washing his hands. Although he denies having a depressed mood and symptoms commonly seen in Depressive Disorders, he describes his thinking as "sticky."

Discussion of "The Procrastinator"

There is no doubt that Roger is in deep trouble, and it all seems to be a consequence of his slowness. But why is Roger so slow? It is hard to know exactly what goes on, for example, when it takes him several hours to get dressed. One possibility is that he is spending a lot of time performing repetitive, stereotyped behaviors (compulsions), such as tying and untying his shoes, but neither he nor his wife report this. Perhaps he is preoccupied with recurrent senseless and intrusive ideas (obsessions); but again, neither he nor his wife report this. We suspect that what actually happens is a mixture of two things. First, he probably spends a lot of time thinking about whether he should take the next step (indecisiveness) rather than simply taking it. Second, he probably spends an inordinate amount of time adjusting each article of clothing and personal grooming until he has the sense that it is "just right."

Maybe we ourselves are exhibiting obsessive thinking when we question whether Roger's perfectionist behavior meets the definition of a compulsion. Our problem is that we do not know whether he performs his routines "in response to an obsession, or according to certain rules or in a stereotyped fashion." In any case, although Roger's maddening slowness is quite different from the typical compulsions seen in Obsessive Compulsive Disorder, we think it is not stretching the rules too much to regard his illness as a variant of that disorder. In fact, some clinicians have suggested the need for a subtype of Obsessive Compulsive Disorder for handling such cases as Roger's, in which the slow, painstaking, methodical, unvarying manner of performing even the simplest task is the predominant symptom.

Some readers may wonder why Roger's problems cannot adequately be explained as being due to a particularly malignant form of Obsessive Compulsive Personality Disorder. Five of the nine criteria are required for the diagnosis, and the case provides evidence for at least four of them: he is a perfectionist, preoccupied with details, indecisive, and unable to discard worthless objects. We suspect that his wife, if asked, would provide evidence for several other symptoms, such as lack of generosity and restricted expression of affection. Since this pattern has been apparent all his life, we make the additional provisional diagnosis of Obsessive Compulsive Personality Disorder.

DSM-III-R Diagnosis:

Axis I: 300.30 **Obsessive Compulsive Disorder (p. 247)**
Axis II: 301.40 **Obsessive Compulsive Personality Disorder (Provisional) (p. 356)**

The Journalist with Uncertain News

MARVIN, A 35-YEAR-OLD JOURNALIST, went to his internist because of fatigue, sore throat, and headaches. These symptoms had developed three months earlier, a few weeks after he learned that he was HIV positive (i.e., his blood test indicated the presence of antibodies to the AIDS virus). He was given a complete physical examination and was told that he was in good health, except for mild allergies that accounted for his sore throat, and that the routine laboratory examinations of blood and urine were all negative. Nevertheless, he worried that his symptoms of fatigue, sore throat, and headaches might be the prodrome of AIDS. He began to have frequent and intrusive thoughts about dying and had recurrent fantasies of cancerous disfigurement, protracted illness, and complete dependence on others. Having followed the news coverage about AIDS, he understood that a positive test did not indicate that he would necessarily get AIDS, but this did not prevent him from ruminating about a painful and prolonged death. His internist suggested that he see a psychiatrist.

Marvin describes his physical symptoms to the psychiatrist and relates them to his constant and increasing anxiety. He says that he is now having trouble concentrating at work. He has begun to question the value of his career compared to the pursuit of other interests. He has become increasingly concerned about the possible debilitating effects of job-related stress and worries that such stress may itself compromise his immune system. He contemplates quitting his job and retiring to his country home, where life would be simpler.

Last week his anxiety escalated when he heard that two acquaintances had recently been diagnosed as having AIDS. He now finds that he avoids reading anything in the newspaper about AIDS and any social situation in which this topic is likely to be discussed.

When he is in a situation that takes his mind off of his problems, such as an engrossing movie or concert, Marvin can experience pleasure. His appetite and sleep have remained unchanged except for the recurrence of a nightmare in which he has a mysterious illness and is left alone to die in a hospital.

Marvin has never sought psychiatric help before, and says that until now he always regarded himself as a happy person, proud of his professional achievements, and fulfilled in his long-term relationship with his male lover. He hopes that therapy will help reduce "stress," which will "help my immune system fight off AIDS."

Discussion of "The Journalist with Uncertain News"

Like most people who are told that they are HIV positive, Marvin has become increasingly anxious and preoccupied with thoughts of his illness and death. In his case the anxiety is severe enough to interfere with his occupational functioning.

Marvin's nightmares and intrusive thoughts about illness and death suggest Post-traumatic Stress Disorder, in which a traumatic event is reexperienced in a number of ways. What is the event in this case? His nightmares and intrusive thoughts are of what he fears will happen (becoming ill and dying), and are not about being told or knowing that he is HIV positive. Therefore, he is not reexperiencing a traumatic event.

Marvin is depressed and anxious, but the full clinical picture of Major Depression or an Anxiety Disorder (such as Generalized Anxiety Disorder) is not present. Thus, we are left with the residual category of Adjustment Disorder with Mixed Emotional Features. If the symptoms persist more than six months, the diagnosis of Adjustment Disorder must be changed to another diagnosis—in this case, perhaps Generalized Anxiety Disorder or Depressive Disorder Not Otherwise Specified.

In an individual with evidence of HIV infection, it is important to exclude a physical cause of psychiatric symptoms, such as central nervous system infections or tumor. This distinction is often difficult since HIV related illnesses may present with psychiatric symptoms. In addition, mental disorders may coexist with, and be exacerbated by, HIV related physical illness. In this case there is no evidence of active HIV related physical illness although his symptoms of fatigue and headache will need periodic medical reevaluation.

DSM-III-R Diagnosis:

Axis I: **309.28 Adjustment Disorder with Mixed Emotional Features (p. 330)**

Memories

ZELDA PADLEVNER, a 59-year-old, married, Orthodox Jewish woman is referred to a psychiatrist for an evaluation in preparation for an appeal to the board that had previously denied her claim for Workmen's Compensation. Zelda's problems began six months earlier, following a fire in the dress factory where she had been employed as a seamstress for 15 years. The fire was minor and easily contained, but the synthetic fabrics that burned produced an extremely acrid smell. After the fire, Zelda developed abdominal pains, nausea, and palpitations. She was hospitalized in an intensive care unit for a week because her doctor suspected asthma or a heart condition. A thorough medical evaluation revealed no evidence of physical illness.

Zelda went home, but felt depressed, and so frightened about leaving her apartment that she was unable to go to work. Her symptoms persisted and intensified when her compensation claim was rejected two months ago. She has been staying at home, cooking and cleaning with no interest in doing anything else.

In the psychiatric interview she appears mildly depressed, and says that whatever the decision of the appeal board, she cannot bring herself to go back to work. She feels comfortable and safe at home; but whenever she has to go out, she becomes apprehensive, though she cannot say exactly what she is afraid of. She feels more comfortable when her husband accompanies her to stores in the neighborhood; but when she has to travel to a different neighborhood (e.g., to go to a doctor's office), she feels uncomfortable despite his presence, afraid that his long side-burns and ethnic garments will attract hostile attention from non-Jews. She has trouble sleeping because of recurrent nightmares of her experiences in a concentration camp over forty years ago and finds herself dwelling on these memories during the day and unable to concentrate on reading.

Zelda has always been an active and competent person, and she does not understand why she has developed all of these problems since the fire and why she now feels that "I am a dead person." Although she would not describe herself as a particularly "happy" person before the fire, she believes that she was "content." She has always thought about how she would have been a very different person were it not for the war, but she claims this was not a thought that preoccupied her.

The psychiatrist asks her to talk about her experiences in the concentration camp and learns that she was in Auschwitz in 1943, at the age of 17. Having been young and healthy, she was selected by Dr. Mengele, the sadistic camp doctor, to be part of the work force. After the selection, she and hundreds of other women were told to undress and wait for instructions. As the camp was extremely overcrowded, they were shoved into a strange-looking empty hall without windows. The place had a peculiar odor. When they were transferred a few hours later, she found out that she and the other women had been temporarily kept in a gas chamber. She began to cry as she realized that the smell in the factory fire had brought back the memory of the gas chamber.

Discussion of "Memories"

This is an example of the Delayed Type of Post-traumatic Stress Disorder. The fire in the factory in which Zelda worked triggered a reliving of her experience in Auschwitz, even though she was not aware of the connection until she spoke with the psychiatrist. Why such a relatively minor event could trigger such an extreme response after so many years is a mystery.

The characteristic symptoms of Post-traumatic Stress Disorder are apparent: The stress of being in a concentration camp is certainly outside the range of usual human experience. The trauma is reexperienced in the form of nightmares and distressing recollections. Esther avoids situations that remind her of the trauma (going back to work). She has lost interest in her usual activities, has a restricted range of affect (feels "dead"), and has difficulty sleeping and concentrating.

In making a multiaxial assessment, we note on Axis IV the severity of the psychosocial stress as catastrophic. Ordinarily, the psychosocial stressor noted on Axis IV must have occurred within the year before the evaluation. An exception, as in this case, is for a stressor associated with Post-traumatic Stress Disorder.

DSM-III-R Diagnosis:

Axis I: **309.89 Post-traumatic Stress Disorder, Delayed Type, Severe (p. 250)**
Axis II: **V71.09 No Diagnosis or Condition**
Axis III: **None**
Axis IV: **Psychosocial stressor: concentration camp incarceration Severity: 6–Catastrophic (acute event)**
Axis V: **Current GAF: 45 Highest GAF past year: 85**

Follow-up

The psychiatrist sent his report to the Workmen's Compensation Board. At the hearing, the presiding officer said that he did not want to hear the story again and agreed to full compensation. Zelda has been in treatment for six months. She is still afraid to go to work, but is less depressed. Her therapist says she is dealing with the feeling that her life stopped when she was 17.

Twisted Sister

A 19-YEAR-OLD YOUTH sporting a punk-style haircut and T-shirt with "Twisted Sister" written across the front is brought, by ambulance, at midnight to a hospital emergency room in Baltimore. He is accompanied by a 23-year-old male friend who called the ambulance because he was afraid his companion "was going to die like that basketball player."

The patient is agitated and argumentative, his breathing is irregular and rapid, his pulse is rapid, and his pupils are dilated. Reluctantly, the patient's friend admits they used a lot of cocaine that evening.

In addition to attending to the patient, the medical staff attempts to contact the patient's parents. As often happens at this inner-city hospital, the patient is not carrying any identifying information. The friend is hesitant to say anything, but he finally provides the patient's name and home phone number. The patient's mother, sounding groggy and confused on the phone, has difficulty understanding the seriousness of her son's predicament, and only after a lengthy discussion does she finally agree to come to the hospital. Worried about her state of mind, the hospital sends a police car to pick her up.

By the time the mother arrives, the patient's condition has improved somewhat, although he creates a commotion in the emergency room with his loud singing and gesticulations. The mother, looking disheveled and smelling of alcohol, is distraught and tearful. She tells a disorganized story about her son's problems at home: he is disobedient to and resentful of authority, unwilling to take part in family activities, and violently argumentative when confronted about his carrying on and partying at all hours of the night. She reports that he has been arrested twice for shoplifting and once for driving while intoxicated, and that he spends almost all of his time with an older crowd. "They drag race a lot and hang out in the streets."

Divorced for almost 15 years, the mother admits that not having a stable father figure in the household makes disciplining quite difficult. She suspects that her son uses drugs because she has heard him talk to his friends about drugs, but she does not have any direct evidence. She claims that her son is not all bad, that he is a fairly good student and even a star member of the basketball team. (In fact, the son is quite successful in deceiving his non-vigilant mother into believing that he is a good student and star basketball player. Actually, the patient never completed high school, had poor or failing grades, and never played on the school's basketball team.) When asked about her own drinking habits, the mother becomes defensive and claims she drinks only occasionally and in small amounts.

Within 24 hours the patient is physically well and quite willing to talk. He states, almost boastfully, that he has been using alcohol and other drugs regularly since the age of 13. Initially, his drug use was limited to alcohol and marijuana, particularly because alcohol was readily available in his home and marijuana was commonly sold in the neighborhood. Once he reached high school, however, he began to associate with an older and more experienced drug-using group. Choice and level of drug use were largely a function of availability and price. By the time the patient had reached the age of 17, he was regularly using various combinations of alcohol, marijuana, speed pills, and cocaine, no one drug predominating. After about one year of this pattern of mixing several drugs, he settled on a preference for cocaine.

He tells of repeated instances in which he and his friends have each consumed an entire case of beer in a day ("I can drink a lot before I feel anything—We call ourselves the 'Andre the Giant Club'") in addition to using other drugs. These drug orgies have often included a dangerous game called "hurricane drag racing," in which intoxicated contestants engage in drag racing on side roads until somebody "chickens out" to avoid an oncoming car. During this heavy drug use, it is common for him to skip school because of the drug activity; when he has to be in school, he typically is intoxicated. To help support his drug involvement, he has devised various schemes for acquiring money, such as "borrowing" money from friends that will never be repaid, or stealing car radios from the student parking lot—plus blatant stealing of money from his mother.

This behavior is justified by a "Robin Hood" attitude: "I take from people who have a lot of money anyway."

Despite the patient's admission of heavy drug involvement, he stops short of admitting that he has a real problem. In response to a question about his ability to control drug use, he replies, hostilely, "Of course I could. No problem. I just don't see any damn good reason to stop."

Somewhat fidgety and restless, the patient says he is finished with the interview. Before the interviewer has an opportunity to press him further about seeking treatment, the patient begins to roam around the hospital unit, looking for someone who has an extra cigarette.

Discussion of "Twisted Sister"

This young man comes into the hospital suffering from the acute effects of Cocaine Intoxication. He is agitated and argumentative and has a rapid pulse and dilated pupils. From what we know of his recent use of cocaine, we can say only that it causes serious social problems (he steals money and lies to his mother). Although we suspect that he probably has other symptoms of loss of control of his cocaine use that would justify the diagnosis of Cocaine Dependence, we give him the benefit of the doubt and diagnose Cocaine Abuse.

The patient's indiscriminate use of many drugs when he was younger follows the pattern of a polydrug-user. During this period he spent a great deal of time "doing drugs," used drugs when it was dangerous to do so ("drag racing"), and skipped school to use drugs. All of these symptoms of loss of control over his drug use and the pattern of indiscriminate use of many drugs indicate a past diagnosis of Polysubstance Dependence.

In addition to his problems with drugs, this young man exhibits considerable antisocial behavior, not all of which is directly associated with his dependence on drugs (e.g., he is disobedient and resentful of all authority). He fulfills the adult criteria for Antisocial Personality Disorder in that he does not go to school regularly or hold a job, he fails to conform to social norms with respect to lawful behavior, he repeatedly fails to honor financial obligations, and he has no regard for the truth. Although we do not know at what age he began to lie, steal, and skip school, we suspect that this behavior began before he was 15. Therefore, we make a provisional diagnosis of Antisocial Personality Disorder.

DSM-III-R Diagnosis:

Axis I: 305.60 Cocaine Intoxication (p. 142)

305.60 Cocaine Abuse (p. 177)
301.70 Antisocial Personality Disorder (Provisional)
        (p. 344)
304.90 Polysubstance Dependence (p. 185) [past]

My Fan Club

DURING THE COURSE of a routine physical examination, Nick, a 25-year-old single black man, unexpectedly started crying and blurted out that he was very depressed, and was thinking about a suicide attempt he had made when he felt this way as a teen-ager. His doctor referred him for a psychiatric evaluation.

Nick is tall, bearded, muscular, and handsome. He is meticulously dressed in a white suit and has a rose in his lapel. He enters the psychiatrist's office, pauses dramatically, and exclaims, "Aren't roses wonderful this time of year?" When asked why he has come for an evaluation, he replies laughingly that he has done it to appease his family doctor, "who seemed worried about me." He has also read a book on psychotherapy, and hopes that "maybe there is someone very special who can understand me. I'd make the most incredible patient." He then takes control of the interview and begins to talk about himself, after first remarking, half jokingly, "I was hoping you would be as attractive as my family doctor."

Nick pulls out of his attaché case a series of newspaper clippings, his resume, photographs of himself, including some of him with famous people, and a photostat of a dollar bill with his face replacing George Washington's. Using these as cues, he begins to tell his story.

He explains that in the last few years he has "discovered" some now-famous actors, one of whom he describes as a "physically perfect teen-age heartthrob." He volunteered to coordinate publicity for the actor, and as part of that, posed in a bathing suit in a scene that resembled a famous scene from the actor's hit movie. Nick, imitating the actor's voice, laughingly, and then seriously, describes how he and the actor had similar pasts. Both were rejected by their parents and peers, but overcame this to become popular. When the actor came to town, Nick rented a limousine and showed up at the gala "as a joke," as though he were the star himself. The actor's agent expressed annoyance at what he had done, causing Nick to fly into a rage. When Nick cooled down, he realized that he was "wasting my time promoting others, and that it was time for me to start promoting myself." "Someday," he said, pointing to the picture of the actor, "he will want to be president of my fan club."

Nick has had little previous acting experience of a professional nature, but he is sure that success is "only a question of time." He pulls out some promotional material he has written for his actors and says, "I should write letters to God—He'd love them!" When the psychiatrist is surprised that some materials are signed by a different name than the one Nick has given the receptionist, Nick pulls out a legal document explaining the name change. He has dropped his family name and taken as his new second name his own middle name.

When asked about his love life, Nick says he has no lover, and this is because people are just "superficial." He then displays a newspaper clipping in which he had letterset his and his ex-lover's names in headlines that read: "The relationship is over." More recently he has dated and adored a man with the same first name as his own; but as he became disenchanted, he realized that the man was ugly, and was an embarrassment since he dressed so poorly. Nick then explains that he owns over a hundred neckties and about thirty suits, and is proud of how much he spends on "putting myself together." He has no relationships with other homosexual men now, describing them as "only interested in sex." He considers heterosexual men as "mindless and without aesthetic sense." The only people who have understood him are older men who have suffered as much he has. "One day, the mindless, happy people who have ignored me will be lining up to see my movies."

Nick's father was very critical, an alcoholic who was rarely around, and had many affairs. His mother was "like a friend." She was chronically depressed about her husband's affairs and turned to her son, often kissing him good night, until he was 18, when she started an affair of her own. Nick then felt abandoned and made his suicide gesture. He described a tortured childhood, being picked on by his peers for looking odd, until he began body building.

At the end of the interview, Nick is referred to an experienced clinician associated with the clinic, who charges a minimal fee (ten dollars), which he can afford. However, Nick requests a referral to someone who would offer him free treatment, seeing no reason for paying anyone since the therapist "would be getting as much out of it as [I] would."

Discussion of "My Fan Club"

What is remarkable about Nick is his unabashed grandiosity and preoccupation with unrealistic fantasies of success. Ironically, for one so "self-assured," he reacts to criticism with rage or sulking. He believes that he is so special that he is entitled to be treated gratis. He is preoccupied with envy of the stars that he emulates. He seems to require constant attention and admiration, and we strongly suspect that he is unable to recognize and experience how others feel (lack of empathy). He can adore and flatter others if they are of use to him, but he quickly changes his mind if they are not, coldly devaluing them and pointing out their flaws. This pervasive pattern of grandiosity and hypersensitivity to the evaluation of others indicates Narcissistic Personality Disorder.

Nick almost certainly also meets the criteria for Histrionic Personality Disorder. He is overly concerned with physical attractiveness, expresses emotions with inappropriate exaggeration, is uncomfortable in situations in which he is not the center of attention, and undoubtedly displays rapidly shifting and shallow expressions of emotions. We also suspect that he has little tolerance for the frustration of delayed gratification.

In addition, there are many suggestions of the pervasive pattern of instability of mood, interpersonal relationships, and self-image that is characteristic of Borderline Personality Disorder. However, we do not count enough symptoms to meet the criteria for that disorder.

DSM-III-R Diagnosis:

Axis I: V71.09 No Diagnosis or Condition
Axis II: 301.81 Narcissistic Personality Disorder (p. 351)
          301.50 Histrionic Personality Disorder (Provisional)
                  (p. 349)

No Joke*

A WOMAN HEARD A MAN shouting for help and went to his apartment door. Calling through the door, she asked the man inside if he needed help. "Yes," he said. "Break the door down."

"Is this a joke?"

"No."

The woman returned with her two sons, who broke into the apartment. They found the man lying on the floor, his hands tied behind him, his legs bent back, his ankles secured to his hands. A mop handle had been placed behind his knees. He was visibly distraught, sweating, and short of breath, and his hands were turning blue. He had defecated and urinated in his trousers. In his kitchen the woman found a knife and freed him.

When police officers arrived and questioned the man, he stated that he had returned home that afternoon, fallen asleep on his couch, and awakened an hour later only to find himself hopelessly bound. The officers noted that the apartment door had been locked. There were no signs of forced entry. The man continued his story. As far as he knew, he had no

*From Dietz, P.E., Burgess, A.W., and Hazelwood, R.R.: Autoerotic asphyxia, the paraphilias, and mental disorder, pp. 83-85. In: Hazelwood, R.R., Dietz, P.E., and Burgess, A.W.: *Auto-erotic Fatalities*. Lexington, MA: Lexington Books, 1983.

enemies, and certainly no friends capable of this kind of practical joke. The officers questioned him about the rope. The man explained that, because he had considered moving in the near future, he kept a bag of rope in his bedroom. Near the couch lay a torn bag, numerous short lengths of thin rope, and a steak knife.

When the officers filed their report, they noted that "this could possibly be a sexual deviation act." Interviewed the next day, the man confessed to binding himself in the position in which he was found.

A month later, police were called back to the same man's apartment. A building manager had discovered him face down on the floor in his apartment. A paper bag covered his head like a hood. When the police arrived, the man was breathing rapidly with a satin cloth stuffed in his mouth. Rope was stretched around his head and mouth and wrapped his chest and waist. Several lengths ran from his back to his crotch, and ropes at his ankles had left deep marks. A broom handle locked his elbows behind his back. Once freed, the man explained, "While doing isometric exercises, I got tangled up in the rope."

Police interviewed the man's employer, and the employer subsequently advised him to seek counseling. When the man agreed to follow through on a referral to a private psychiatrist, his boss supported his assertion that the incident, while unfortunate, had been unique, and would not recur.

Two years passed, and the man moved on to another job. He failed to appear for work one Monday morning. A fellow employee found him dead in his apartment.

During their investigation, police were able to reconstruct the man's final minutes. On the preceding Friday, he had bound himself in the following manner: sitting on his bed and crossing his ankles, left over right, he had bound them together with twine. Fastening a tie around his neck, he then secured the tie to an 86-inch pole behind his back. Aligning the pole with his left side, the upper end crossing the front of his left shoulder, he placed his hands behind his bent legs and there, leaving his wrists four inches apart, secured them with a length of rope. He then tied the rope that secured his wrists to the pole and to an electric cord girdling his waist. Thus bound, he lay on his bed on his back and stretched his legs. By thus applying pressure to the pole, still secured to the tie around his neck, he strangled himself. In order to save himself, he might have rolled over onto his side and drawn up his legs; but the upper end of the pole pressed against the wall. He was locked into place.

Discussion of "No Joke"

This man aroused himself sexually by depriving himself of oxygen while masturbating, thereby risking death. Such bizarre sexual behavior has to be regarded as a Paraphilia, a Sexual Disorder in which the person is aroused by stimuli that are not part of normative arousal-activity patterns and that in varying degrees may interfere with the capacity for reciprocal, affectionate sexual activity.

This particular Paraphilia, Hypoxyphilia (hypoxy = lack of oxygen), is not common enough to be included as a specific Paraphilia in DSM-III-R and therefore is coded as a Paraphilia Not Otherwise Specified. This case was chosen because it is one of the few that has come to psychiatric attention before the death of the patient. When people with the disorder seek treatment, it is usually for depression, and they are unlikely to reveal their sexual practices unless a therapist takes a very careful sexual history. The most commonly associated Paraphilias are Sexual Masochism and Transvestic Fetishism.

An estimated 500–1,000 people die annually in the United States from autoerotic asphyxiation; almost all (96%) are male. Deaths occur among persons from adolescence through the seventies, the greatest frequency being in the twenties. A complication of Hypoxyphilia, other than death, is anoxic brain damage.

DSM-III-R Diagnosis:

Axis I: 302.90 **Paraphilia Not Otherwise Specified, Severe (Hypoxyphilia) (p. 290)**

The Radiologist

A 38-YEAR-OLD RADIOLOGIST is evaluated after returning from a 10-day stay at a famous out-of-state diagnostic center to which he had been referred by a local gastroenterologist after "he reached the end of the line with me." He reports that he underwent extensive physical and laboratory examinations there, X-ray examinations of the entire gastrointestinal tract, esophagoscopy, gastroscopy, and colonoscopy. Although he was told that the results of the examinations were negative for significant physical disease, he appears resentful and disappointed rather than relieved at the findings. He was seen briefly for a "routine" evaluation by a psychiatrist at the diagnostic center, but had difficulty relating to the psychiatrist on more than a superficial level.

On further inquiry concerning the patient's physical symptoms, he describes occasional twinges of mild abdominal pain, sensations of "fullness," "bowel rumblings," and a "firm abdominal mass" that he can sometimes feel in his left lower quadrant. Over the last few months he has gradually become more aware of these sensations and convinced that they may be due to a carcinoma of the colon. He tests his stool for occult blood weekly and spends 15 to 20 minutes every 2-3 days carefully palpating his abdomen as he lies in bed at home. He has secretly performed several X-ray studies on himself in his own office after hours.

Although he is successful in his work, has an excellent attendance record, and is active in community life, the patient spends much of his leisure time at home alone in bed. His wife, an instructor at a local school of nursing, is angry and bitter about this behavior, which she describes as "robbing us of what we've worked so hard and postponed so much for." Although she and the patient share many values and genuinely love each other, his behavior causes a real strain on their marriage.

When the patient was 13 years old, a heart murmur was detected on a school physical exam. Since a younger brother had died in early childhood of congenital heart disease, the patient was removed from gym class until the murmur could be evaluated. The evaluation proved the murmur to be benign, but the patient began to worry that the evaluation might have "missed something" and considered the occasional sensations of "skipping a beat" as evidence that this was so. He kept his fears to himself, and they subsided over the next two years, but never entirely left him.

As a second-year medical student he was relieved to share some of his health concerns with his classmates, who also worried about having the diseases they were learning about in pathology. He realized, however, that he was much more preoccupied with and worried about his health than they were. Since graduating from medical school, he has repeatedly experienced a series of concerns, each following the same pattern: noticing a symptom, becoming increasingly preoccupied with what it might mean, and having a negative physical evaluation. At times he returns to an "old" concern, but is too embarrassed to pursue it with physicians he knows, as when he discovered a "suspicious" nevus only one week after he had persuaded a dermatologist to biopsy one that proved to be entirely benign.

The patient tells his story with a sincere, discouraged tone, brightened only by a note of genuine pleasure and enthusiasm as he provides a detailed account of the discovery of a genuine, but clinically insignificant, urethral anomaly as the result of an intravenous pyelogram he had ordered himself. Near the end of the interview, he explains that his coming in for evaluation now is largely at his own insistence, precipitated by an encounter with his nine-year-old son. The boy had accidentally walked in while he was palpating his own abdomen for "masses" and asked, "What do you think it is this time, Dad?" As he describes his shame and anger (mostly at himself) about this incident, his eyes fill with tears.

Discussion of "The Radiologist"

It is apparent that this doctor's symptoms are not due to any physical disorder. Preoccupation with physical symptoms without an organic basis can be seen in psychotic disorders such as Schizophrenia or Major Depression with Psychotic Features, but there is no evidence of any psychotic features in this case. This suggests, therefore, a Somatoform Disorder—a mental disorder with physical symptoms suggesting physical disorder, but for which there is positive evidence, or a strong presumption, that the symptoms are linked to psychological factors.

A variety of physical symptoms without organic basis is seen in Somatization Disorder. In this case the symptoms are few, whereas in Somatization Disorder there are a large number of different symptoms that appear in many different organ systems. Furthermore, in Somatization Disorder the preoccupation is generally with the symptoms themselves. In this case the disturbance is preoccupation with the fear of having a serious disease resulting from an unrealistic interpretation of physical signs or sensations. The persistence of this irrational fear for more than six months, despite medical reassurance, indicates Hypochondriasis.

DSM-III-R Diagnosis:

Axis I: 300.70 Hypochondriasis, Moderate (p. 261)

Dr. Jekyll and Ms. Hyde

TWENTY-EIGHT-YEAR-OLD Brenda Wilkens sought admission to the hospital because: "I don't know what else to do. I'm afraid I'll hurt my kids or myself. Life seems futile. I feel on the verge of losing it, of going crazy. One minute I'm angry at the whole world for no reason and I yell at my husband, and the next minute I feel guilty, worthless, and I cry uncontrollably. I'm tired all the time, but feel revved up inside. I can't concentrate. It takes me an hour to do a 20-minute report. I don't want to be around people. I don't sleep right or eat right, and I ache all over."

Ms. Wilkens reported she had been feeling this way for the past week and a half. She has had five episodes like this in the last six months, and each of them stopped abruptly. The episodes became problematic starting the year after the birth of her second child, four years ago.

She is the mother of two, and a part-time student. Though she had exams this week, other things in her life have been going well. She had one episode of severe depression, a few months after the birth of her first child. During that episode, which lasted approximately six months, she didn't feel like getting out of bed in the morning and felt she was a terrible mother. The episodes she now has seem different from that six-month episode. She is much more angry and irritable, and yells at her husband and kids. She thinks about getting a divorce and dropping out of school.

She also gets the feeling that people are going out of their way to annoy her. The episodes come periodically and "out of the blue." During the episodes she feels as though she is a totally different person, "like Dr. Jekyll and Mr. Hyde." Sometimes they get so bad she thinks about killing herself, but she has never actually hurt herself. Then, for no reason, the episode suddenly subsides, and she feels back to her "old self again."

The patient reports she has been in good physical health. She does not abuse alcohol or drugs, though she tends to drink more during these "episodes" in order to "calm my nerves." She thinks these episodes are associated with her menstrual cycle and believes they are getting worse with age. She is worried that she may become incapacitated like her mother, who had lengthy periods of severe depression. She has been told it's "all in your head" and to just "shape up," but she feels she has no control over the episodes. She wonders if anything can be done, because they are "ruining my life."

Ms. Wilkens was admitted to the hospital. On the third day she reported that she was remarkably calm and "back to my old self." Her remission of symptoms coincided with the onset of menses.

Discussion of "Dr. Jekyll and Ms. Hyde"

Ms. Wilkens's description of her current difficulties suggests a Major Depressive Episode. She has depressed mood and feels tired, guilty, and worthless. She can't concentrate, and she has suicidal thoughts. However, the clear pattern of onset of these dysphoric episodes during the late luteal phase of her menstrual cycle and remission with the onset of menses, and the presence of such symptoms as irritability and affective lability suggest the (unofficial) diagnosis of Late Luteal Phase Dysphoric Disorder. In order to confirm this provisional diagnosis, it would be necessary to have Ms. Wilkens make daily ratings of her mood and behavior for at least two menstrual cycles.

DSM-III-R Diagnosis:

Axis I: 300.90 Unspecified Mental Disorder (Late Luteal Phase Dysphoric Disorder, Provisional) (p. 369)

Rx Florida

IN THE WINTER OF 1982, John Redland, a 42-year-old physician, married with two children, applied to a special depression treatment program of the National Institute of Mental Health. He stated that over the last few weeks, he felt he was again slipping into a depression.

John says his first depression occurred at age 21 after he had moved to the Washington, D.C., metropolitan area from Florida, where he had lived until that time. Depressions recurred the next four winters, while he was in college and early in medical school. During the last of these episodes, John was hospitalized and told that, because of his recurrent depressions, he was unlikely ever to succeed in becoming a physician, which had been his lifelong goal. He remained depressed and in the hospital for the next year, during which time he was treated with psychotherapy alone. His depression remitted in the spring; and he remained free of depressions for several years, during which he completed medical school and his internship. However, the winter depressions had returned each year for the nine years before he applied to the NIMH treatment program.

John now realizes that all of his depressive episodes seem to follow the same pattern. They start around the first of December (plus or minus three weeks) and begin to lift by April. In most years the onset of depression is gradual, but sometimes it occurs more precipitously, apparently in response to some environmental stress. When depressed, John is lethargic, apathetic, irritable, and pessimistic. His mood is worse in the morning. He cannot sleep through the night. He craves carbohydrates (bread, cake, cookies) and gains weight. He has noticed that his winter clothes are often two sizes larger than his summer ones. He recalls feeling much better during a winter vacation in Bermuda, the mood improvement occurring a few days after he arrived there. However, he relapsed a few days after returning to the North. He also recalls one particularly difficult winter when he worked in Syracuse, New York. These associations between latitude, the weather, and his mood make him wonder whether the climate may actually be influencing his mood changes.

John has been treated for several years with psychotherapy and a tricyclic antidepressant, Norpramin, 175 mg/day, both of which he has found to be "quite helpful."

Discussion of "Rx Florida"

There can be little doubt that John suffers from Major Depression, Recurrent. He has had numerous episodes of persistent depressed mood, disturbed sleep, increased appetite and weight gain, decreased energy, and loss of interest in usual activities. As he is once again "slipping into a depression," we note the current severity as mild, although in the past his depressions have been severe.

What is unusual about John's depressions is that they apparently all began in the winter and remitted in the spring. Recurrent mood disorders that regularly begin and end during a particular period of the year have been called "Seasonal Affective Disorders." John's case illustrates the most common pattern, in which depression begins in fall or winter and ends in spring. Less common patterns involve recurrent depressions or Manic Episodes that begin in the summer and remit in the fall or winter. In DSM-III-R, the concept of Seasonal Affective Disorder is expressed with the specification "Seasonal Pattern."

John's weight gain and craving for carbohydrates are typical of cases with Seasonal Affective Disorder. In other ways John's case is atypical; most patients with Seasonal Affective Disorder are women, and most complain of increased sleeping (hypersomnia) rather than of disturbed sleep (insomnia).

DSM-III-R Diagnosis:

Axis I: 296.31 **Major Depression, Recurrent, Mild, Seasonal Pattern (p. 230)**

Follow-up

When John entered the NIMH treatment program, he was maintained on Norpramin and entered a light treatment research protocol involving exposure for 3 hours, twice a day, morning and evening, to 2,500 lux of full-spectrum light. The light treatments involved his sitting 3 feet in front of a standard 2-foot by 4-foot metal light fixture containing six 40-watt Powertwist Vitalite (R®) tubes, and glancing at the light for a few seconds every minute or two. After one week of treatment, he became much less depressed, and his Hamilton Depression Rating Scale score fell from 21 to 8.

After the formal light treatment study was over, John's Norpramin was increased to 250 mg/day. He was maintained on light treatment during the day and in the evening hours and remaind free of depression on the combination of light and Norpramin. John has used lights each winter since then, and remains on Norpramin 250 mg/day during the winter months. He has been virtually free of depression for the last four years and is not currently in psychotherapy.

Like many patients with Seasonal Affective Disorder, during the summer John is able to reduce the dose of antidepressant medication and discontinue the light treatment; but in the winter he is unable to stop the light treatment for more than a few days without suffering a return of his depressive symptoms.

Sam Schaefer

A PSYCHIATRIST WAS ASKED by the court to evaluate a 21-year-old man arrested in a robbery since his lawyer raised the issue of his compe-

tence to stand trial. During the course of a two-and-a-half-hour evaluation, the patient acknowledged frequent run-ins with the law since about
the age of 11 and incarceration in various institutions for criminal offenses, but was reluctant to provide details about them.

During the interview he appeared calm and in control, sat slouched
in the chair, and had good eye contact. His affect showed a good range.
His thought processes were logical, sequential, and spontaneous even
when he was describing many difficulties with his thinking. He seemed
guarded in his answers, particularly to questions about his psychological
symptoms. He gave the impression of thoughtfully considering hi answers
before responding and seemed to be pretending a reluctance to talk
about symptoms suggesting psychosis when, in fact, he apparently enjoyed elaborating the details of presumably psychotic experiences.

He claims to have precognition on occasion, knowing, for instance,
what is going to be served for lunch in the jail; that people hear his
thoughts, as if broadcast on the radio; and that he does not like narcotics
because Jeane Dixon doesn't like narcotics either, and she is in control of
his thoughts. He states that he has seen a vision of General Lee in his cell,
and that his current incarceration is a mission in which he is attempting to
be an undercover agent for the police, although none of the local police
realize this. He says that "Sam Schaefer" is his "case name." He feels that
the Communists are taking over and are locking up those who would
defend the country. Despite the overtly psychotic nature of these
thoughts as described, the patient does not seem to be really engaged in
these ideas; he seems to be simply reciting a list of what appears crazy
rather than recounting actual experiences and beliefs.

He was asked about the processes and procedures of a trial, and stated
that there was a jury, which he thought consisted of eight to ten friends.
He also thought there was a judge present, who asked for money and
made decisions about the procedure. He described the prosecuting attorney as someone who pointed out all your faults and tried to make the jury
think that you were bad, and the defense attorney as someone who tried
to point out your good points. He saw no particular reason why he could
not cooperate with his attorney. When asked the date, he said that it was
June 28, either 1970 or 1985. He then saw the inconsistency in the dates
he gave for the year and said that this therefore must be 1978, since he
was 20 and was born in 1958. When asked where he was, he said it was a
Communist control center in Austin, Texas. He reported that he graduated from high school in 1976. When asked to do serial 7 subtractions
from 100, his responses were 88, 76. Asked to do additions, he responded: 4+6 = 10, 4+3 = 7, 4+8 = 14. Asked to recall Presidents, he
mentioned Ford and said that Agnew was President before him.

When asked the color of the red rug in the room, he said it was
orange; his blue and white striped shirt he said was white on white. When
presented with some questions from an aphasia screening test, he copied
a square faithfully except for rounding the corners; a cross was copied as a
capital "I." When shown a picture of a clock, he said he did not know

what it was, but it looked familiar. A dinner fork was identified as a "pitchfork."

When asked whether he thought he was competent to stand trial, he replied "yes," and said he did not think there was anything wrong with him mentally. When told that the examiner agreed with his assessment, he thought for several seconds and then, somewhat angered, protested that he probably couldn't cooperate with his attorney because he couldn't remember things very well, and therefore was incompetent to stand trial.

Discussion of "Sam Schaefer"

This gentleman is in trouble, and apparently he has concluded that his best chance of avoiding prosecution is to prove that he is crazy and therefore not competent to stand trial. He goes about trying to prove this by claiming to have a variety of unrelated bizarre beliefs and by giving responses to questions that would suggest severe cognitive impairment. However, he presents the responses in a manner that is inconsistent with the disorganization of psychological functioning that would be expected if the symptoms were genuine. Furthermore, some of his responses to the questions testing cognitive functioning, although clearly wrong, indicate that he knows the correct response (e.g., rounding the corners of a square indicates appreciation that a square has four sides). If there is any doubt about his motivation, it is eliminated when he becomes angry with the examiner for agreeing that he is sane and competent to stand trial.

There is little question that in this case the "psychotic" symptoms are under voluntary control. The differential diagnosis is therefore between a Factitious Disorder and Malingering. Since the goal this fellow hopes to achieve is obviously motivated by external incentives (avoiding prosecution) and there is no evidence of an intrapsychic need to maintain the sick role, what is involved is an act of malingering, which in DSM-III-R is given a V code for a Condition Not Attributable to a Mental Disorder That Is a Focus of Attention.

Thi clinical picture has some of the features of what has been referred to as Ganser's syndrome—the giving of "approximate" answers to questions, commonly associated with other symptoms such as amnesia, disorientation, perceptual disturbances, fugue, and conversion symptoms. The full picture of Ganser's syndrome is classified in DSM-III-R as a Dissociative Disorder Not Otherwise Specified. Since there is no evidence of dissociative symptoms in this case, a diagnosis of a Dissociative Disorder is not made.

From the history there is a strong suggestion of Antisocial

Personality Disorder—a diagnosis that needs to be ruled out, but that will be of no help to this man in avoiding prosecution. Even if there were sufficient evidence to warrant a diagnosis of Antisocial Personality Disorder, it would still be appropriate to note Malingering on Axis I. Lying is a common symptom of Antisocial Personality Disorder; but when it is elaborated to create the impression of a mental disorder, then it should be identified in its own right as the V code Malingering.

DSM-III-R Diagnosis:

Axis I: V65.20 Malingering (p. 360)
Axis II: R/O Antisocial Personality Disorder

Close to the Bone*

A 23-YEAR-OLD WOMAN FROM ARKANSAS wrote a letter to the head of a New York research group after seeing a television program in which he described his work with patients with unusual eating patterns. In the letter, which requested that she be accepted into his program, the woman described her problems as follows:

Several years ago, in college, I started using laxatives to lose weight. I started with a few and increased the number as they became ineffective. After two years I was taking 250-300 Ex-Lax® pills at one time with a glass of water, 20 per gulp. I would lose as much as 20 pounds in a 24-hour period, mostly water and some food, dehydrated so that I couldn't stand, and could barely talk. I ended up in the university infirmary several times with diagnoses of food poisoning, severe gastrointestinal flu, etc., with bland diets and medications. I was released within a day or two. A small duodenal ulcer appeared and disappeared on X-rays in 1975.

I would not eat for days, then would eat something, and, overcome by guilt at eating, and *hunger*, would eat-eat-eat. A girl on my dorm floor told me that she occasionally forced herself to vomit so that she wouldn't gain weight. I did this every once in a while and discovered that I could consume large amounts of food, vomit, and still lose weight. This was spring of 1975. I lost nearly 50 pounds over a few months, to 90 pounds. My hair started coming out in handfuls, and my teeth were loose.

I never felt lovelier or more confident about my appearance: physically liberated, streamlined, close-to-the-bone. I was flat everywhere except my stomach when I binged, when I would be full-blown and distended. When I bent over, each rib and back vertebra was outlined. After vomiting my stomach was once more flat, empty. The more I lost, the more I was afraid of getting fat. I was afraid to drink water for days at a time because it would add

*From Spitzer R.L., Skodol A.E., Gibbon M. and Williams J.B.W.: Psychopathology: A Case Book. McGraw-Hill, Inc. New York, 1983.

pounds on the scale and make me miserable. Yet I drank (or drink; perhaps I should be writing this all in the *present* tense) easily a half-gallon of milk and other liquids at once when binging. I didn't need the laxatives as much to get rid of food and eventually stopped using them altogether (although I am still chronically constipated, I become nauseous whenever I see them in the drugstore).

I exercised for hours each day to tone my figure from the weight fluctuations, and joined the university track team. I wore track shoes all the time and ran to classes and around town, stick-legs pumping. I went to track practice daily after being sick, until I was forced to quit; a single lap would make me dizzy, with cramps in my stomach and legs.

At some point during my last semester before dropping out I came across an article on anorexia nervosa. It frightened me; my own personal obsession with food and bodyweight was shared by other people. I had not menstruated in two years. So, I forced myself to eat and digest healthy food. Hated it. I studied nutrition and gradually forced myself to accept a new attitude toward food—vitalizing—something needed for life. I gained weight, fighting panic. In a rigid, controlled way I have maintained myself nutritionally ever since: 105-115 pounds at 5'6". I know what I need to survive and I eat it—a balanced diet with the fewest possible calories, mostly vegetables, fruits, fish, fowl, whole grain products, etc. In five years I have not eaten anything like pizza, pastas or pork, sweets, or anything fattening, fried or rich without being very sick. Once I allowed myself an ice cream cone. But I am usually sick if I deviate as much as one bite.

It was difficult for me to face people at school, and I dropped courses each semester, collecting incompletes but finishing well in the few classes I stayed with. The absurdity of my reclusiveness was even evident to me during my last semester when I signed up for correspondence courses, while living only two blocks from the correspondence university building on campus. I felt I would only be able to face people when I lost 'just a few more pounds.'

Fat. I cannot stand it. This feeling is stronger and more desperate than any horror at what I am doing to myself. If I gain a few pounds I hate to leave the house and let people see me. Yet I am sad to see how I have pushed aside the friends, activities, and state of energized health that once rounded my life.

For all of this hiding, it will surprise you to know that I am by profession a model. Last year when I was more in control of my eating-vomiting, I enjoyed working in front of a camera, and I was doing well. Lately I've been sick too much and feel out-of-shape and physically unable to cope with the discipline involved. I keep myself supported during this time with part-time secretarial work and whatever unsolicited photo bookings my past clients give me. For the most part, I do the secretarial work. And I can't seem to stop being sick all the time.

The more I threw-up when I was in college, the longer it took, and the harder it became. I needed to use different instruments to induce vomiting. Now I double two electrical cords and shove them several feet down into my throat. This is preceded by 6-10 doses of ipecac [an emetic]. My knees are calloused from the time spent kneeling sick. The eating-vomiting process takes usually 2-3 hours, sometimes as long as 8. I dread the gagging and pain and sometimes my throat is very sore and I procrastinate using the ipecac and cords. I sit on the floor, biting my nails, and pulling the skin off around my nails with tweezers. Usually I wear rubber gloves to prevent this somewhat.

After emptying my stomach completely I wash thoroughly. In a little while I will hydrate myself with a bottle of diet pop, and take a handful of lasix 40mg [a diuretic] (which I have numerous prescriptions for). Sometimes I am faint, very cold. I splash cool water on my face, smooth my hair, but my hands are shaking some. I will take aspirin if my hands hurt sharply ... so I can sleep later. My lips, fingers are bluish and cold. I see in the mirror that blood vessels are broken. There are red spots over my eyes. They always fade in a day or two. There is a certain relief when it is over, that the food is gone, and I am not horribly fat from it. And I cry often ... for some rest, some calm. It is foolish for me to cry for someone, someone to help me; when it is only me who is hiding and hurting myself.

Now there is a funny new split in my behavior. This honesty about my illness. Hopefully it will bring me more help than humiliation. Sometimes I feel a hypocrisy in my actions, and in the frightened, well-ordered attempts to seek out help. All the while I am still sick, night after night after night. And often days as well.

Two sets of logic seem to be operating against each other, each determined, each half-canceling the effects of the other. It is the part of me which forced me to eat that I'm talking about ... which cools my throat with water after hours of heaving, which takes potassium supplements to counteract diuretics, and aspirin for torn hands. It is this part of me, which walks into a psychiatrist's office twice weekly and sees the liability of hurting myself seriously, which makes constant small efforts to repair the tearing-down.

It almost sounds as if I am being brutalized by some unrelenting force. Ridiculous to feel this way, or to stand and cry, because the hands that cool my throat and try to make small repairs only just punched lengths of cord into my stomach. No demons, only me.

For your consideration, I am

Gratefully yours,

Nancy Lee Duval

Ms. Duval was admitted to the research ward for study. Additional history revealed that her eating problems began gradually during her adolescence, and had been severe for the past three to four years. At age 14 she weighed 128 pounds and had reached her adult height of 5'6". She felt "terribly fat" and began to diet without great success. At age 17 she weighed 165 pounds and began to diet more seriously for fear that she would be ridiculed, and went down to 130 pounds over the next year. She recalled feeling very depressed, overwhelmed, and insignificant. She began to avoid difficult classes so that she would never get less than straight A's, and began to lie about her school and grade performance for fear of being humiliated. She had great social anxiety in dealing with boys, which culminated in her transferring to a girls' school for the last year of high school.

When she left for college, her difficulties increased. She had trouble deciding how to organize her time, whether to study, to date, or to see friends. She became more desperate to lose weight and began to use laxatives, as she describes in her letter. At age 20, in her sophomore year of college, she reached her lowest weight of 88 pounds (70% of ideal body weight) and stopped menstruating.

As Ms. Duval describes in her letter, she recognized that there was a problem and eventually forced herself to gain weight. Nonetheless, the overeating and vomiting she had begun the previous year worsened. As she was preoccupied with her weight and her eating, her school performance suffered, and she dropped out of school midway through college at age 21.

Ms. Duval is the second of four children and the only girl. She comes from an upper-middle-class professional family. From the patient's description, it sounds as though the father has a history of alcoholism. There are clear indications of difficulties between the mother and the father, and between the boys and the parents; but no other family member has ever had psychiatric treatment.

Discussion of "Close to the Bone"

Ms. Duval is suffering from a disorder that was first described nearly three hundred years ago, and was named Anorexia Nervosa in 1968. Although theories about the cause of the disorder have come and gone, the essential features have remained unchanged. Ms. Duval poignantly describes these features.

She had an intense and irrational fear of becoming obese, even when she was emaciated. Her body image was disturbed in that she perceived herself as fat when her weight was average and "never lovelier" when, to others, she must have appeared grotesquely thin. She lost about 30% of her body weight by relentless dieting and exercising, self-induced vomiting, and use of cathartics and diuretics. She has not menstruated for the past three years.

Significantly, Ms. Duval's dieting takes place despite persistent hunger; thus, the anorexia (loss of appetite) in the name of the disorder is a misnomer. In fact, she also has recurrent episodes of binge eating—rapid, uncontrolled consumption of high-caloric foods. These binges are followed by vomiting and remorse. When this pattern of binge eating and purging occurs at least twice a week for three months, and there is persistent overconcern with body weight and shape, the additional diagnosis of Bulimia Nervosa is made.

When an emaciated patient with Anorexia Nervosa insists that she is fat, this suggests the presence of a somatic delusion, as might be seen in Schizophrenia or Major Depression. However, such a patient is generally not considered to have a delusion because she is describing how she experiences herself, rather than disputing the facts of her weight.

DSM-III-R Diagnosis:

Axis I: 307.10 Anorexia Nervosa, Severe (p. 67)
            307.51 Bulimia Nervosa, Severe (p. 68)

Follow-up

Ms. Duval remained in the research ward for several weeks, during which time she participated in research studies, and, under the structure of the hospital setting, was able to give up her abuse of laxatives and diuretics. After her return home, she continued in treatment with a psychiatrist in psychoanalytically oriented psychotherapy twice a week, which she had begun six months previously. That therapy continued for approximately another six months, when her family refused to support it. The patient also felt that while she had gained some insight into her difficulties, she had been unable to change her behavior.

Two years after leaving the hospital, she wrote that she was "doing much better." She had returned to college, and was completing her course work satisfactorily. She had seen a nutritionist, and felt that form of treatment was useful for her in learning what a normal diet was and how to maintain a normal weight. She was also receiving counseling from school guidance counselors, but she did not directly relate that to her eating difficulties. Her weight was normal, and she was menstruating regularly. She continued to have intermittent difficulty with binge eating and vomiting, but the frequency and severity of these problems were much reduced. She no longer abused diuretics or laxatives.

Under Surveillance

MR. SIMPSON IS A 44-YEAR-OLD, single, unemployed, white man brought into the emergency room by the police for striking an elderly woman in his apartment building. His chief complaint is, "That damn bitch. She and the rest of them deserved more than that for what they put me through."

Mr. Simpson had been continuously ill since the age of 22. During his first year of law school, he gradually became more and more convinced that his classmates were making fun of him. He noticed that they would snort and sneeze whenever he entered the classroom. When a girl he was dating broke off the relationship with him, he believed that she had been "replaced" by a look-alike. He called the police and asked for their help to solve the "kidnapping." His academic performance in school declined dramatically, and he was asked to leave and seek psychiatric care.

Mr. Simpson got a job as an investment counselor at a bank, which he held for seven months. However, he was getting an increasing number of distracting "signals" from co-workers, and he became more and more suspicious and withdrawn. It was at this time that he first reported hearing voices. He was eventually fired, and soon thereafter was hospitalized for the first time, at age 24. He has not worked since.

Mr. Simpson has been hospitalized 12 times, the longest stay being eight months. However, in the last five years he has been hospitalized only once, for three weeks. During the hospitalizations he has received various antipsychotic drugs. Although outpatient medication has been prescribed, he usually stops taking it shortly after leaving the hospital. Aside from twice-yearly lunch meetings with his uncle and his contacts with mental health workers, he is totally isolated socially. He lives on his own and manages his own financial affairs, including a modest inheritance. He reads the *Wall Street Journal* daily. He cooks and cleans for himself.

Mr. Simpson maintains that his apartment is the center of a large communication system that involves all three major television networks, his neighbors, and apparently hundreds of "actors" in his neighborhood. There are secret cameras in his apartment that carefully monitor all his activities. When he is watching TV, many of his minor actions (e.g., getting up to go to the bathroom) are soon directly commented on by the announcer. Whenever he goes outside, the "actors" have all been warned to keep him under surveillance. Everyone on the street watches him. His neighbors operate two different "machines"; one is responsible for all of his voices, except the "joker." He is not certain who controls this voice, which "visits" him only occasionally, and is very funny. The other voices, which he hears many times each day, are generated by this machine, which he sometimes thinks is directly run by the neighbor whom he attacked. For example, when he is going over his investments, these "harassing" voices constantly tell him which stocks to buy. The other machine he calls "the dream machine." This machine puts erotic dreams into his head, usually of "black women."

Mr. Simpson describes other unusual experiences. For example, he recently went to a shoe store 30 miles from his house in the hope of getting some shoes that wouldn't be "altered." However, he soon found out that, like the rest of the shoes he buys, special nails had been put into the bottom of the shoes to annoy him. He was amazed that his decision concerning which shoe store to go to must have been known to his "harassers" before he himself knew it, so that they had time to get the altered shoes made up especially for him. He realizes that great effort and "millions of dollars" are involved in keeping him under surveillance. He sometimes thinks this is all part of a large experiment to discover the secret of his "superior intelligence."

At the interview, Mr. Simpson is well-groomed, and his speech is coherent and goal-directed. His affect is, at most, only mildly blunted. He was initially very angry at being brought in by the police. After several weeks of treatment with an antipsychotic drug failed to control his psychotic symptoms, he was transferred to a long-stay facility with the plan to arrange a structured living situation for him.

Discussion of "Under Surveillance"

Mr. Simpson's long illness apparently began with delusions of reference (his classmates making fun of him by snorting and sneezing when he entered the classroom). Over the years his delusions have become increasingly complex and bizarre (his neighbors are actually actors; his thoughts are monitored; a machine puts erotic dreams in his head). In addition, he has prominent hallucinations of different voices that harass him.

Bizarre delusions and prominent hallucinations are the characteristic psychotic symptoms of Schizophrenia. The diagnosis is confirmed by the marked disturbance in his work and social functioning and the absence of a sustained mood disturbance and of any known organic factor that can account for the disturbance.

All of Mr. Simpson's delusions and hallucinations seem to involve the single theme of a conspiracy to harass him. This systematized persecutory delusion, in the absence of incoherence, marked loosening of associations, flat or grossly inappropriate affect, or catatonic or grossly disorganized behavior, indicates the Paranoid Type. Schizophrenia, Paranoid Type, is further specified as Stable Type if, as in this case, all past and present active phases of the illness have been Paranoid Type. The prognosis for the Stable Paranoid Type is expected to be better than the prognosis for the Disorganized and Undifferentiated Type. Mr. Simpson has in fact done remarkably well despite a chronic psychotic illness, in that over the past five years he has been able to take care of himself.

DSM-III-R Diagnosis:

Axis I: 295.32 Schizophrenia, Stable Paranoid Type, Chronic
                  (p. 194)

Dear Doctor

MYRNA FIELD, A 55-YEAR-OLD woman, was a cashier in a hospital coffee shop three years ago when she suddenly developed the belief that a physician who dropped in regularly was intensely in love with her. She fell passionately in love with him, but said nothing and became increasingly distressed each time she saw him. Casual remarks that he made were interpreted as cues to his feelings, and she believed he gave her significant glances and made suggestive movements, though he never declared his feelings openly. She was sure this was because he was married.

After more than two years of this, she became so agitated that she had to give up her job; she remained at home, thinking about the physician incessantly. She had frequent, intense abdominal sensations, which greatly frightened her. (These turned out to be sexual feelings, which she did not recognize as she had never been orgasmic before.) Eventually she went to her family doctor, who found her so upset he referred her to a male psychiatrist. She was too embarrassed to confide in him, and it was only when she was transferred to a female psychiatrist that she poured forth her story.

Myrna was an illegitimate child whose subsequent stepfather was excessively strict. She was a slow learner and was always in trouble at home and at school. She grew up anxious and afraid, and during her adult life consulted many doctors because of hypochondriacal concerns. She was always insecure in company.

Myrna married; but the marriage was asexual, and there were no children. Although her husband appeared long-suffering, she perceived him as overly critical and demanding. Throughout their married life she had periodically abused alcohol and, during the past three years, had been drinking more heavily and steadily to try to cope with her distress. She could not confide in her husband about her "love" affair.

When she was interviewed, Myrna was very distressed, and talked under great pressure. Her intelligence was limited, and many of her ideas appeared simple; but the only clear abnormality was the unshakeable belief that her physician "lover" was passionately devoted to her. She could not be persuaded otherwise.

Discussion of "Dear Doctor"

Mrs. Field's only symptom is a delusion that she is loved by a doctor whom she barely knows. Although her belief seems false, it is certainly possible that a doctor could fall in love with her; thus, it is a nonbizarre delusion. This kind of delusion, in the absence of prominent hallucinations, bizarre behavior, a mood syndrome, or any specific organic factor to account for it, indicates a diagnosis of Delusional Disorder. The content of the delusion, that the person is loved by someone (usually of higher status), makes it the Erotomanic Type.

Since we think that Alcohol Abuse is very likely, we note it as a provisional diagnosis.

DSM-III-R Diagnosis:

Axis I: 297.10 Delusional Disorder, Erotomanic Type (p. 202)
          305.00 Alcohol Abuse (Provisional) (p. 173)

Follow-up

Mrs. Field readily accepted medication, and pimozide, an anti-psychotic drug, was prescribed, eventually in a daily dose of 2 mg. Over a period of three to four weeks, she became much calmer, the delusion became less insistent, and she reduced her alcohol consumption considerably. She developed an episode of depression, which responded to a tricyclic antidepressant that was temporarily added to her antipsychotic medication.

Three years later, Mrs. Field remains well and rarely drinks. She and her husband appear content with their marriage, which remains platonic. She occasionally thinks of the physician with some nostalgia and still believes he loves her, but is no longer distressed about this. She continues to take her antipsychotic medication.

Mr. Macho*

HANK ALLEN WAS CHARGED with the murder of ten women. His wife, Jody, who eventually testified against him, had worked as his partner, luring victims to their deaths.

Wanting to further her husband's fantasy of finding the "perfect lover," Jody had accompanied him to shopping centers or county fairs and talked young girls into climbing into their customized van. Once inside, the victims were confronted by her husband, who held a handgun and bound them with adhesive tape. Most were teen-agers, though two of the final victims were adults; the youngest was 13. The oldest victim, 34, was a bartender who closed up late one night, went out to her car, then rolled down her window to talk to the couple, who had been inside drinking and who now approached her. The Allens kidnapped her and drove her back to their own residence. While Jody sat inside watching an old movie on television, Hank assaulted his victim in the back of the van, scripting her to play the role of his teen-age daughter. When he was through, Jody rejoined him, and they drove away in the early morning hours, the radio blaring to drown out the sounds of Hank in the back of the van, strangling his victim to death. That evening they celebrated his birthday at a restaurant.

*From Dietz, P.E., Harry, B., Hazelwood, R.R.: Detective magazines: Pornography for the sexual sadist? *Journal of Forensic Sciences*, 31:197-211, 1986.

Most of Hank's victims were petite blonds like Jody and Hank's own daughter. All were sexually abused, then shot or strangled to death; several were buried in shallow graves. One, a pregnant 21-year-old hitch-hiker (Jody was also pregnant at the time), was raped, strangled, and buried alive in sand.

Hank rated the sexual performance of each of his victims, and always made sure that Jody knew she was never number-one. Jody tried to redeem herself in the eyes of her difficult husband by submitting to his every demand. Even when she finally separated from him, she was unable to say "no." They had been apart for several months when Hank called her, asking that they get together one more time. She agreed, and that day they claimed their ninth and tenth victims.

Hank's violence was a legacy from his father. When he was born, his father, 19, was serving a prison sentence for auto theft and passing bad checks. A later conviction earned him a term for second-degree robbery, but he escaped. In an ensuing saga of recapture, escape, recapture, and escape, he killed a police officer and a prison guard, blinding the latter by tossing acid into his face before beating him to death. A short time before he was executed, his father wrote: "When I killed this cop, it made me feel good inside. I can't get over how good it did make me feel, for the sensation was something that made me feel elated to the point of happiness. . . . "

Often told that he was going to be just like his father when he grew up, Hank was 16 when he learned that his father had been captured and executed in a gas chamber after his mother betrayed his hiding place. Hank later confessed to the police: "Sometimes I [think] about blowing her head off. . . . Sometimes I wanta put a shotgun in her mouth and blow the back of her head off. . . . "

In a forensic psychiatric evaluation, Hank revealed that his mother was the object of his most intense sexual fantasy:

> "I was gonna string her up by her feet, strip her, hang her up by her feet, spin her, take a razor blade, make little cuts, just little ones, watch the blood run out, just drip off her head. Hang her up in the closet, put airplane glue on her, light her up. Tattoo 'bitch' on her forehead. . . . "

Hank's mother had beaten and mocked her son, a bed-wetter until age 13, calling him "pissy pants" in front of guests. One of her husbands punished him mercilessly, forcing him to drink urine and burning a cigar coal into his wrist. When his mother tried to intervene, his stepfather smashed her head into a plaster wall. From that point on, she joined in the active abuse of her children. As far back as he could remember, Hank had nightmares of being smothered by nylon stocking material and being strapped to a chair in a gas chamber as green gas floated into the room.

Hank began to burglarize with an older brother at age 7, and at age 12 was put on probation. A year later he was sent to the California Youth Authority for committing "lewd and lascivious acts" with a six-year-old girl. As a teen-ager he faced charges of armed robbery and auto theft. A habitual truant, he was suspended from high school at 17 with F's in five academic subjects and F's in five categories of "citizenship." That same year he married for the first time.

Often knocked unconscious in fights, he was comatose twice, briefly at age 16, and for over a week at age 20. A computerized tomography brain scan revealed "abnormally enlarged sulci and slightly enlarged ventricles." A Halstead-Reitan neuropsychological battery and a Luria-Nebraska neuropsychological battery showed "damage to the right frontal lobe."

Hank married seven times. He beat each of his wives, sometimes badly. Most of the marriages lasted no more than a few months. One wife described him as "dominant," and said "he's got to be in control." Another, who had had clumps of hair yanked from her head, called him "a Jekyll and Hyde." Yet another said he was "vicious." When she told him she wanted out, he took revenge by beating her parents. His first marriage ended when he beat his wife with a hammer. When she left him, she replaced his mother in his central fantasy. They had married five days after the birth of a baby daughter, and a custody battle ensued. In spite of his lengthy record of assaults, thefts, and parole violations, Hank won.

When he was 23, Hank went on a crime spree that eventually covered five states. Stealing license plates and cars, holding up bars and drugstores, he eluded capture until caught and convicted for the armed robbery of a motel. Sent to prison for five years to life, he molested his six-year-old daughter for the first time during a conjugal visit.

Upon release, Hank went to live with his mother, who had not visited him during his three and a half years in prison. While there, he got involved with a woman whom he impregnated and whom he once kicked out of bed, literally, when she refused him anal intercourse. He chose not to marry her, she later recalled, as "he didn't want the responsibility." Thirteen days after she gave birth, he married another woman, his fifth wife. He was 28-years-old.

Hank and his fifth wife separated when he was released from parole. He took up residence with his 13-year-old daughter, whom he soon impregnated. She had an abortion. His daughter had, by this time, replaced his first wife in his favorite fantasy, and he often raped her in the back of the van to which he and Jody would later lure victims. For the next six years, Hank assaulted her at least once a week. When a friend of hers arrived for a two-week visit, he also raped her.

He was 30 years old, and his divorce from his fifth wife had not been finalized when he moved in with Jody. By the time they met, Hank had been arrested on 23 separate occasions. The following summer Hank was fired from his job as a driver. He had been fired often, and it was an event that usually left him sexually impotent. An employer at the time termed him "inadequate." A week earlier he had celebrated his birthday by sodomizing his 14-year-old daughter. When his daughter finally informed authorities of the 6 years of abuse, felony charges were filed against Hank for incest, unlawful sexual acts, sodomy, and oral copulation. Hank responded by changing his name. Using the stolen driver's license of a state police officer, he obtained a new birth certificate and Social Security number, and he and Jody moved to another town.

Shortly before his final arrest, Hank, a gun enthusiast, owned a semi-automatic assault rifle, an automatic pistol, two revolvers, and a derringer. He was working as a bartender. A co-worker described him as a ladies' man, and said that women called him at work at all hours. After hanging up, he would rate them. Several women referred to him as "Mr. Macho." He was also a heavy drinker. Jody once cautioned him as he drank and drove that the combination was illegal. "Fuck the law," he answered. For his crimes, he eventually received multiple death sentences.

Discussion of "Mr. Macho"

Hank Allen's terrible behavior has been punished by the criminal justice system, and many readers may wonder about the appropriateness of trying to assess his behavior from the perspective of psychiatric diagnosis. This case provides vivid examples of extremely antisocial behavior that is symptomatic of several mental disorders.

Perhaps the most frightening aspect of this man's behavior is that the link between sexual arousal and sadistic behavior is so extreme that it involves killing his victims. Such behavior is a symptom of Sexual Sadism, a Paraphilia in which the person is sexually excited by the psychological or physical suffering of a victim.

Hank Allen's sadism is not only in the service of sexual excitement, as in Sexual Sadism. He also demonstrates a lifelong pattern of cruel, demeaning, and aggressive behavior. He has been physically cruel in order to establish dominance in relationships, he humiliates and demeans other people, he gets other people to do what he wants by intimidating them, and he is fascinated by violence and weapons. This personality pattern indicates the nonofficial diagnosis of Sadistic Personality Disorder.

Finally, Hank Allen demonstrates a lifelong pattern of irresponsible and antisocial behavior, beginning with stealing and truancy as a child and, as an adult, robbery, assault, and murder. This pattern indicates Antisocial Personality Disorder.

It is hard to know how to interpret the abnormal findings on the brain scan and on the neuropsychological and neuropsychiatric tests. We are not sure whether they are merely the result of his frequent head trauma or whether they reflect an underlying brain abnormality that itself is a factor in the development of his pathological behavior.

One could discuss at some length the childhood experiences

that undoubtedly were a factor in the evolution of Hank Allen's psychopathology and criminal behavior. As is often the case in people who physically victimize others, he was himself psychologically and physically abused as a child.

DSM-III-R Diagnosis:

Axis I: 302.84 **Sexual Sadism (p. 288)**
Axis II: 301.90 **Personality Disorder Not Otherwise Specified**
                   (Sadistic Personality Disorder) (p. 371)
           301.70 **Antisocial Personality Disorder (p. 344)**

Follow-up

"Mr. Macho" decided to represent himself in several of the murder trials. He was sentenced to death in more than one state. Five years after his arrest, he now awaits execution.

Hardworking Businessman

D ANIEL FARBER, A 49-YEAR-OLD businessman, reluctantly comes for evaluation at the insistence of his wife of 20 years. During the first session, only the following information emerges:

The couple has four children. Ms. Farber's complaint is that because of her husband's behavior, the marriage is in danger and she is thinking of leaving him, although she still loves him and does not want to break up the marriage, for her own sake as well as for the children's. Mr. Farber says that there is nothing wrong in the marriage that they cannot sort out themselves, and he does not think his behavior is wrong under the circumstances.

Over the past ten years, the couple has advanced from being poor and hardworking shopkeepers to affluence and an income in excess of $200,000 annually. Both of them left school at the age of 17. Four years ago, Ms. Farber decided to go to college, and her husband reluctantly agreed, although he could see no reason why she would want to do so. After the first year in college, he asked her to stop going; but she insisted on continuing to take part-time courses. He then restricted her contacts with her college friends and refused to allow her to bring them to their house or to entertain them socially. At the same time, he insisted that she accompany him to many business meetings and all social activities connected with his business. Over the past year there have been increasing arguments about his demands and her wishes to pursue social contacts apart from him; and on each occasion, the argument has led to physical violence, Mr. Farber getting so angry that he storms around the house and breaks furniture.

The referral was precipitated by Mr. Farber's arguing with his wife at a social function in the neighborhood because she was wearing a blouse that was too revealing, and his demanding that she return home to change it. She refused to do so, and he physically lifted her and tried to carry her to their car. This altercation was witnessed by everyone at the party. When they got home, Mr. Farber became abusive, and his wife threatened to leave. He locked himself in the bathroom and threatened to shoot himself. This led to his wife's calling his brother. Finally, Mr. Farber came out of the bathroom and handed over a gun. His wife promised not to leave, and he agreed to seek psychiatric help.

Discussion of "Hardworking Businessman"

Does this man have a mental disorder or only a marital problem? DSM-III-R recognizes that not all difficulties between spouses are symptoms of a mental disorder. If their difficulties had been limited to conflict over the wife's changing goals, we should see no need to infer the presence of a mental disorder. However, the extent of Mr. Farber's narcissism, reflected in his inability to allow his wife to grow as an independent person and culminating in his locking himself in the bathroom and threatening to kill himself, and his inability to control his temper strongly suggest a pervasive maladaptive pattern of relating to other people—that is, a Personality Disorder.

It is true that there is no evidence that such behavior has caused Mr. Farber problems in the past. It is conceivable that his narcissistic traits were accommodated by his wife and that the equilibrium was disturbed only when she decided to develop herself. Nevertheless, the diagnosis of a Personality Disorder seems appropriate even in cases in which special environmental circumstances minimize the expression of the underlying pathology.

Since, on the basis of the available information the full criteria for Narcissistic Personality Disorder are not met, the diagnosis is Personality Disorder Not Otherwise Specified (Provisional), R/O Narcissistic Personality Disorder

DSM-III-R Diagnosis:

Axis II: 301.90 **Personality Disorder Not Otherwise Specified (Provisional) (p. 358)**
R/O Narcissistic Personality Disorder

Junior Executive

A 28-YEAR-OLD JUNIOR EXECUTIVE was referred by a senior psychoanalyst for "supportive" treatment. She had obtained a master's degree in business administration and moved to California a year and a half earlier to begin work in a large firm. She complained of being "depressed" about everything: her job, her husband, and her prospects for the future.

She had had extensive psychotherapy previously. She had seen an "analyst" twice a week for three years while in college, and a "behaviorist" for a year and a half while in graduate school. Her complaints were of persistent feelings of depressed mood, inferiority, and pessimism, which she claims to have had since she was 16 or 17 years old. Although she did reasonably well in college, she consistently ruminated about those students who were "genuinely intelligent." She dated during college and graduate school, but claimed that she would never go after a guy she thought was "special," always feeling inferior and intimidated. Whenever she saw or met such a man, she acted stiff and aloof, or actually walked away as quickly as possible, only to berate herself afterward and then fantasize about him for many months. She claimed that her therapy had helped, although she still could not remember a time when she didn't feel somewhat depressed.

Just after graduation, she married the man she was going out with at the time. She thought of him as reasonably desirable, though not "special," and married him primarily because she felt she "needed a husband" for companionship. Shortly after their marriage, the couple started to bicker. She was very critical of his clothes, his job, and his parents; and he, in turn, found her rejecting, controlling, and moody. She began to feel that she had made a mistake in marrying him.

Recently she has also been having difficulties at work. She is assigned the most menial tasks at the firm and is never given an assignment of importance or responsibility. She admits that she frequently does a "slipshod" job of what is given her, never does more than is required, and never demonstrates any assertiveness or initiative to her supervisors. She views her boss as self-centered, unconcerned, and unfair, but nevertheless admires his success. She feels that she will never go very far in her profession because she does not have the right "connections," and neither does her husband; yet she dreams of money, status, and power.

Her social life with her husband involves several other couples. The man in these couples is usually a friend of her husband. She is sure that the women find her uninteresting and unimpressive, and that the people who seem to like her are probably no better off than she.

Under the burden of her dissatisfaction with her marriage, her job, and her social life, feeling tired and uninterested in "life," she now enters treatment for the third time.

Discussion of "Junior Executive"

This woman's marriage and occupational functioning are severely affected by her chronically depressed mood, low self-esteem, and pessimism. Although she now complains also of loss of interest and energy, it is unlikely that this represents a significant change from her usual condition. Since her depression is not severe enough to meet the criteria for a Major Depressive Episode, and the mood disturbance and associated symptoms have persisted for more than two years, the diagnosis of Dysthymia is considered. Since this woman's depression did not begin with a Major Depressive Episode, and there is no evidence of a Manic or Hypomanic Episode, the diagnosis of Dysthymia would be made. In this case, the onset of the mood disturbance in adolescence would be noted as "early onset," and the absence of a relationship to any preexisting Axis I or Axis III disorder would be noted as "primary type."

Many clinicians would regard this patient's depressive symptoms as an expression of a Personality Disorder rather than a Mood Disorder. They would argue that it is impossible to separate her depressive symptoms from the characteristic and persistent way in which she relates to the world and to herself and that treatment should be focused on her characterological style as well as on the affective symptoms. However, in classifying Dysthymia under the broad rubric of Mood Disorders, DSM-III-R makes no assumption that the optimal treatment is necessarily biological or should be directed merely at symptom relief.

This woman exhibits several features that suggest symptoms of the unofficial DSM-III-R diagnosis of Self-Defeating Personality Disorder. Does she choose people and situations that lead to disappointment, incite rejecting responses from others, fail to accomplish tasks crucial to her objectives, and reject people who are interested in her? Even if the answer to these questions is yes, the diagnosis of Self-Defeating Personality Disorder requires a judgment that the self-defeating behaviors do not occur only when the person is depressed. In this case, it seems as if she is always depressed, so it would be very difficult to make this judgment with any degree of certainty.

DSM-III-R Diagnosis:

Axis I: **300.40 Dysthymia, Primary Type, Early Onset (p. 232)**

No Fluids

ANN, A 32-YEAR-OLD medical secretary in Dublin, is referred to a clinic for treatment of depression. She confides that the reason she is depressed is that for the last five months she has been afraid that she will urinate in public. She has never actually done this, and in the safety of her own home she considers the idea that it will actually happen to her to be nonsensical.

When Ann is away from home, the fear dominates her thinking, and she takes precautions to prevent its happening. She always wears sanitary napkins, never travels far from home, limits her intake of fluids, has stopped drinking alcohol, and has had her desk at work relocated near a toilet. For the two weeks before the consultation, she has been unable to go to work because the fear has become more intense.

She vaguely recalls that her deceased father also had a fear of urinating in public. Before leaving for work each day, he urinated several times and avoided taking any fluids. Her younger sister has been successfully treated for a cleansing ritual.

Ann had psychiatric treatment ten years ago when she began to fear that she had contracted syphilis, even though there was no clinical or laboratory evidence of infection. Prior to five months ago, she never feared that she would urinate in public. Apart from these specific fears, she has always been an anxious, insecure person, considered by her family to be overly cautious and perfectionistic. For the past year she has been upset about her boyfriend's impending return to his home country, after completing his medical studies in Ireland. She was divorced five years previously, and is now living with her seven-year-old-son and mother. Her mother disapproves of her boyfriend, and Ann has felt increasing pressure to end the relationship. She believes that the onset of her current difficulties coincided with the stress of her relationship with her mother and the threat of her boyfriend's departure from the country.

When interviewed, Ann is anxious and agitated. She remarks that she has been feeling despondent about her problems. She has trouble sleeping and has no energy during the day. Although her appetite is poor, she has not lost any weight.

Discussion of "No Fluids"

Ann has markedly restricted her usual activities because of a fear that she will involuntarily urinate in public. The fear of being in situations from which escape might be difficult in the event of developing an embarrassing or incapacitating symptom is called Agoraphobia. Usually Agoraphobia is a complication of Panic Disorder, in which the person associates having an unexpected panic attack with particular situations, which he or she then avoids. Much more rarely, there is no history of Panic Disorder, and the fear is of developing some specific symptom such as loss of bladder control (as in Ann's case), vomiting, or cardiac distress. In such cases the diagnosis is Agoraphobia without History of Panic Disorder.

A reader may wonder why Ann's condition is not diagnosed as a Social Phobia: a persistent fear of a situation in which she is exposed to possible scrutiny by others and fears that she may do something (e.g., urinate) that will be humiliating or embarrassing. Although in the course of answering this question we realized that the DSM-III-R criteria do not make it clear, in a Social Phobia the person is attempting to accomplish a voluntary activity (e.g., speaking, eating, writing, urinating) and fears that the normal activity will be impaired by signs of anxiety (e.g., be unable to speak, choke while eating, tremble while writing, be unable to urinate). In contrast, in Agoraphobia without History of Panic Disorder, the person is afraid of suddenly developing a symptom that is unrelated to the activity that he or she is trying to accomplish (e.g., cardiac distress while shopping, involuntary urination when away from home, dizziness while crossing the street).

Ann is also depressed and has several symptoms of the depressive syndrome, including poor appetite, insomnia, and decreased energy. We suspect a Major Depressive Episode; but since there is inadequate information to determine if the full criteria are met, we note Depressive Disorder Not Otherwise Specified.

DSM-III-R Diagnosis:

Axis I: **300.22 Agoraphobia without History of Panic Disorder, Severe (p. 241)**
             311.00 Depressive Disorder Not Otherwise Specified (p. 233)

Follow-up

Ann was treated with an antidepressant, clomipramine, initially at a dose of 10 mg daily, increasing over two weeks to 125 mg daily. Her fear that she might urinate in public lessened after ten days of treatment, and a behavioral program was then instituted to correct her repertoire of avoidance behavior. Before her boyfriend left the country, Ann and her son moved away from her mother; and she was able to lead a more independent life. Her medication was phased out after two months, and the fear that she would urinate in public did not return. The psychiatrist attributed her initial improvement to the medication and her continued improvement to the behavioral program, and the changes that she made in her life circumstances, particularly moving away from her mother.

Joe College

A 19-YEAR-OLD COLLEGE FRESHMAN spends an afternoon drinking beer with fraternity brothers. After eight or ten glasses, he becomes argumentative with one of his larger companions and suggests that they step outside and fight. Normally a quiet, unaggressive person, he now speaks in a loud voice and challenges the larger man to fight with him, apparently for no good reason. When the fight does not develop, he becomes morose and spends long periods looking into his beer glass. He seems about to cry. After more beers, he begins telling long, indiscreet stories about former girl friends. His attention drifts when others talk. He tips over a beer glass, which he finds humorous, laughing loudly until the bartender gives him a warning look. He starts to get up and say something to the bartender, but trips and falls to the floor. His friends help him to the car. Back at the fraternity house, he falls into a deep sleep, awaking with a headache and a bad taste in his mouth. He is again the quiet, shy person his friends know him to be.

Discussion of "Joe College"

Although intoxication in the physiologic sense occurs in social drinking, maladaptive behavior is required for the mental-disorder diagnosis of a Psychoactive Substance-induced Intoxication. In this case there is evidence of disinhibition of aggressive impulses (picking a fight), impaired judgment (telling indiscreet stories), mood lability (argumentative, then crying and morose), and physiologic signs (incoordination and unsteady gait) of intoxication. This is therefore Alcohol Intoxication, since obviously alcohol is the offending substance.

The diagnosis of Alcohol Idiosyncratic Intoxication is not made unless such marked behavioral changes occur after the ingestion of an extremely small amount of alcohol, an amount that would be insufficient to cause intoxication in most people. This fellow has apparently drunk enough to "do in" anyone.

We are not told if this kind of behavior occurs repeatedly. If it did, the diagnosis of a Psychoactive Substance Use Disorder, Alcohol Abuse, or even Alcohol Dependence, would need to be considered.

DSM-III-R Diagnosis:

Axis I: 303.00 Alcohol Intoxication (p. 128)

High-strung

JANE BERENSON, A 36-YEAR-OLD vice-president of a Detroit department store, responded to an advertisement describing a new clinic specializing in the treatment of sleep problems. Ever since college she has had difficulty falling asleep most nights. She feels "mentally hyperactive" at bedtime, and is unable to stop thinking about significant experiences of the day, particularly her interactions with dissatisfied customers. When she feels she has accomplished too little during a particular day, she feels she does not "deserve" to go to bed. Any evening excitement, e.g., an interesting movie or a lively party, leaves her unable to simmer down for hours thereafter. Occasionally, in the middle of the night, she awakens feeling wide awake and again finds herself ruminating about the day's events. When she sleeps poorly, she feels "high-strung" and tense the following day. The insomnia has worsened during the past year, coincident with more stress at work. She notes that she has not read a novel in over a year, an activity she previously enjoyed.

Her business involves occasionally "wining and dining" other executives, but she finds that late meals or alcohol intake aggravates the insomnia. She has noticed that on days when she has cocktails with dinner, she invariably awakens in the middle of the night, feeling wide awake and slightly sweaty. Business travel also worsens her sleep. She finds herself in a state of unrelieved overstimulation when her job requires "running from city to city" for extended periods.

Ms. Berenson was divorced three years ago after ten years of marriage. She has a wide circle of friends and enjoys socializing with them. Relaxing alone, however, has long been considered "dead time."

Both of her parents and a sister have had problems with alcohol. She is the only one in her family to be steadily employed.

During the last year she has been in once-a-week psychotherapy to try to understand "why I am so driven." This has not helped her insomnia. She has also tried sleeping pills, which leave her "hung over" the following day.

Discussion of "High-strung"

This woman has a long-standing problem in falling asleep at night and frequently awakening during the night and being unable to return to sleep. The frequency and severity of the disturbance exceed the minimal requirements for an Insomnia Disorder (insomnia occurring at least three times a week for at least a month and resulting in significant daytime fatigue or some other symptom attributable to the sleep disturbance). Although there is a suggestion of obsessive compulsive personality traits (excessive devotion to work and productivity to the exclusion of leisure activities and friendships), since there is no other mental or physical disorder or use of medication that can account for the disturbance, the diagnosis is Primary Insomnia.

This case demonstrates a frequently associated feature of Primary Insomnia: that the person is hyperalert in the evening and ruminates about the day's activities.

DSM-III-R Diagnosis:

Axis I: 307.42 Primary Insomnia (p. 301)
Axis II: V71.09 No diagnosis on Axis II
           Obsessive compulsive personality traits
Axis III: None
Axis IV: Psychosocial stressors: Stressful job
           Severity: 3 - Moderate (predominantly enduring circumstances)
Axis V: Current GAF: 58
           Highest GAF past year: 65

Follow-up

The patient was taught by the sleep clinic to use various meditation procedures, to avoid stimulating evening activities, and to take hot soaks at bedtime. She was told to discontinue any use of alcohol, which, although it might make it easier for her to fall asleep, would make it harder for her to stay asleep. She was able to decrease her night-work obligations. With this regimen her sleep greatly improved, although she occasionally still had trouble sleeping when she traveled.

Ashamed

A 27-YEAR-OLD ENGINEER requested consultation because of irresistible urges to exhibit his penis to female strangers.

The patient, an only child, had been reared in an orthodox Jewish environment. Sexuality was strongly condemned by both parents as being "dirty." His father, a schoolteacher, was authoritarian and punitive, but relatively uninvolved in the home. His mother, a housewife, was domineering, controlling, and intrusive. She was preoccupied with cleanliness and bathed the patient until he was ten years old. The patient remembers that he feared he might have an erection in his mother's presence during one of his baths; however, this did not occur. His mother was opposed to his meeting and dating girls during his adolescence. He was not allowed to bring girls home; according to her, the proper time to bring a woman home was when she was "your wife, and not before." Despite his mother's antisexual values, she frequently walked about the house partially disrobed in his presence. To his shame, he found himself sexually aroused by this stimulation, which occurred frequently through-out his development.

As an adolescent the patient was quiet, withdrawn, and studious; teachers described him as a "model child." He was friendly, but not intimate, with a few male classmates. Puberty occurred at 13, and his first ejaculation occurred at that age during sleep. Because of feelings of guilt, he resisted the temptation to masturbate, and between the ages of 13 and 18 orgasms occurred only with nocturnal emissions.

He did not begin to date women until he moved out of his parents' home, at the age of 25. During the next two years he dated from time to time, but was too inhibited to initiate sexual activity.

At age 18, for reasons unknown to himself, during the week before final exams, he first experienced an overwhelming desire to engage in the sexual activity for which he now sought consultation. He sought situations in which he was alone with a woman he did not know. As he would approach her, he became sexually excited. He would then walk up to her and display his erect penis. He found that her shock and fear further stimulated him, and usually he would then ejaculate. At other times he fantasized past encounters while masturbating.

He felt guilty and ashamed after exhibiting himself and vowed never to repeat it. Nevertheless, the desire often overwhelmed him, and the behavior recurred frequently, usually at periods of tension. He felt desperate, but was too ashamed to seek professional help. Once, when he was 24, he had almost been apprehended by a policeman, but managed to run away.

For the last three years, the patient has managed to resist his exhibitionistic urges. Recently, however, he met a young woman, who has fallen in love with him and is willing to have intercourse with him. Never having had intercourse before, he felt panic lest he fail in the attempt. He likes and respects his potential sexual partner, but also condemns her for being willing to engage in premarital relations. He has once again started to exhibit himself and fears that, unless he stops, he will eventually be arrested.

Discussion of "Ashamed"

One could discuss at great length the childhood experiences that may have contributed to the development of this disorder in this patient. Regarding the diagnosis, however, there can be little speculation. Recurrent intense sexual urges and sexually arousing fantasies involving the exposure of one's genitals to a stranger, acted upon or causing marked distress, establishes the diagnosis of Exhibitionism.

Many clinicians would assume that there is also a coexisting personality disorder, but without more information about the patient's personality functioning, such a diagnosis cannot be made.

DSM-III-R Diagnosis:

Axis I: 302.40 Exhibitionism, Mild (p. 282)

Radar Messages

ALICE DAVIS, A 24-YEAR-OLD copy editor who has recently moved from Colorado to New York, comes to a psychiatrist for help in continuing her treatment with a mood stabilizer, lithium. She describes how, three years previously, she was a successful college student in her senior year, doing well academically and enjoying a large circle of friends of both sexes. In the midst of an uneventful period in the first semester, she began to feel depressed; experienced loss of appetite, with a weight loss of about ten pounds; and had both trouble falling asleep and waking up too early.

After about two months of these problems, they seemed to go away; but she then began to feel increasingly energetic, requiring only two to five hours' sleep at night, and to experience her thoughts as "racing." She started to see symbolic meanings in things, especially sexual meanings, and began to suspect that innocent comments on television shows were referring to her. Over the next month, she became increasingly euphoric, irritable, and overtalkative. She started to believe that there was a hole in her head through which radar messages were being sent to her. These messages could control her thoughts or produce emotions of anger, sadness, or the like, that were beyond her control. She also believed that her thoughts could be read by people around her and that alien thoughts from other people were intruding themselves via the radar into her own head. She described hearing voices, which sometimes spoke about her in the third person and at other times ordered her to perform various acts, particularly sexual ones.

Her friends, concerned about Alice's unusual behavior, took her to an emergency room, where she was evaluated and admitted to a psychiatric unit. After a day of observation, Alice was started on an antipsychotic, chlorpromazine, and lithium carbonate. Over the course of about three weeks, she experienced a fairly rapid reduction in all of the symptoms that had brought her to the hospital. The chlorpromazine was gradually reduced, and then discontinued. She was maintained thereafter on lithium carbonate alone. At the time of her discharge, after six weeks of hospitalization, she was exhibiting none of the symptoms reported on admission; but she was noted to be experiencing some mild hypersomnia, sleeping about ten hours a night, and loss of appetite and some feeling of being "slowed down," which was worse in the mornings. She was discharged to live with some friends.

Approximately eight months after her discharge, Alice was taken off lithium carbonate by the psychiatrist in the college mental health clinic. She continued to do fairly well for the next few months, but then began to experience a gradual reappearance of symptoms similar to those that had necessitated her hospitalization. The symptoms worsened, and after two weeks she was readmitted to the hospital with almost the identical symptoms that she had had when first admitted.

Alice responded in days to chlorpromazine and lithium; and, once again, the chlorpromazine was gradually discontinued, leaving her on lithium alone. As with the first hospitalization, at the time of her discharge, a little more than a year ago, she again displayed some hypersomnia, loss of appetite, and the feeling of being "slowed down." For the past year, while continuing to take lithium, she has been symptom free and functioning fairly well, getting a job in publishing and recently moving to New York to advance her career.

Alice's father, when in his 40s, had had a severe episode of depression, characterized by hypersomnia, anorexia, profound psychomotor retardation, and suicidal ideation. Her paternal grandmother had committed suicide during what also appeared to be a depressive episode.

Discussion of "Radar Messages"

Alice was functioning at a high level before the development of a depressive episode, followed shortly by an episode with characteristic manic symptoms: euphoric and irritable mood, decreased need for sleep, pressured speech, and the subjective experience that her thoughts were racing. At the height of the illness, she developed bizarre delusions (her emotions and thoughts were being controlled by radar messages sent through a hole in her head) and auditory hallucinations (both command hallucinations and voices speaking about her in the third person). These psychotic symptoms are characteristic of the active phase of Schizophrenia, but in this case are considered part of a psychotic mood disorder since they occur exclusively during the manic mood disturbance.

In the absence of any evidence of a specific organic factor that could have initiated and maintained the mood disturbance, such as the use of a stimulant, this disturbance is considered a Manic Episode. The occurrence of a single Manic Episode, even in the absence of any Major Depressive Episodes, is sufficient for a diagnosis of Bipolar Disorder.

The most recent episode of mood disturbance, which necessitated Alice's second hospitalization, was also a Manic Episode, so the current subtype is Manic. Finally, the current severity of the disorder, which is coded in the fifth digit, is "in Full Remission," in that she has been essentially free of symptoms for the past six months (even though taking lithium prophylactically).

There is no evidence of any Personality Disorder (Axis II) or of a physical disorder (Axis III) that is relevant to the Axis I diagnosis. Since there has been no recurrence of Alice's disorder in the past year, no psychosocial stressors are specified. Finally, because she has been functioning well in the past year without recurrences, both her current and "highest past year" GAFs are rated 80.

DSM-III-R Diagnosis:

Axis I: 296.46 Bipolar Disorder, Manic, in Full Remission (p. 226)
Axis II: V71.09 No Diagnosis or Condition
Axis III: None
Axis IV: Psychosocial stressors: none
             Severity: 1 - none
Axis V: Current GAF: 80
             Highest GAF past year: 80

Follow-up

In the last seven years, Alice has had two Manic Episodes, one requiring hospitalization, and one managed as an outpatient. Currently she continues to take lithium, and is pursuing a Ph.D. in creative writing at a New England university.

Peaceable Man

THE PATIENT IS A 20-YEAR-OLD MAN who was brought to the hospital, trussed in ropes, by his four brothers. This is his seventh hospitalization in the last two years, each for similar behavior. One of his brothers reports that he "came home crazy" late one night, threw a chair through a window, tore a gas heater off the wall, and ran into the street. The family called the police, who apprehended him shortly thereafter as he stood, naked, directing traffic at a busy intersection. He assaulted the arresting officers, escaped them, and ran home screaming threats at his family. There his brothers were able to subdue him.

On admission, the patient was observed to be agitated, his mood fluctuating between anger and fear. He had slurred speech and staggered when he walked. He remained extremely violent and disorganized for the first several days of his hospitalization, then began having longer and longer lucid intervals, still interspersed with sudden, unpredictable periods in which he displayed great suspiciousness, a fierce expression, slurred speech, and clenched fists.

After calming down, the patient denied ever having been violent or acting in an unusual way ("I'm a peaceable man") and said he could not remember how he got to the hospital. He admitted using alcohol and marijuana socially, but denied phencyclidine (PCP) use except for once, experimentally, three years previously. Nevertheless, blood and urine tests were positive for phencyclidine, and his brother believes "he gets dusted every day."

According to his family, the patient was perfectly normal until about three years before. He made above-average grades in school, had a part-time job and a girl friend, and was of a sunny and outgoing disposition. Then, at age 17, he had his first episode of emotional disturbance. This was of very sudden onset, with symptoms similar to the present episode. He quickly recovered entirely from that first episode, went back to school, and graduated from high school. From subsequent episodes, however, his improvement was less and less encouraging.

After three weeks of the current hospitalization, the patient is sullen and watchful, and quick to remark sarcastically on the smallest infringement of the respect due him. He is mostly quiet and isolated from others, but is easily provoked to fury. His family reports that "This is as good as he gets now." He lives and eats most of his meals at home, and keeps himself physically clean, but mostly lies around the house, will do no housework, and has not held a job for nearly two years. The family does not know how he gets spending money, or how he spends his time outside the house.

Discussion of "Peaceable Man"

The hospitalization was occasioned by acute effects of PCP on the central nervous system: violence, bizarre and disorganized behavior, psychomotor agitation, emotional lability, slurred speech, and ataxia. This is a typical picture of Phencyclidine Intoxication.

In addition, there is a history of regular use of PCP, resulting in many similar episodes of disturbed behavior. This patient is frequently intoxicated when he would be expected to be working (lies around the house, does no work); he spends a great deal of time recovering from the effects of PCP use, continues to use PCP despite knowledge that it causes him to get into trouble over and over again, and has given up important social and occupational activities because of PCP use. These behaviors indicate the additional diagnosis of Phencyclidine Dependence. Although we count only four of the required symptoms for PCP Dependence, we suspect that additional information would confirm that he has more symptoms.

Moreover, the two criteria referring to withdrawal symptoms probably do not apply to PCP. Certainly there is extreme impairment in the patient's social and occupational functioning, and we note the severity of the Dependence as Severe.

DSM-III-R Diagnosis:

Axis I: 305.90 Phencyclidine (PCP) Intoxication (p. 155)
            304.50 Phencyclidine (PCP) Dependence, Severe (p. 183)

First Baby

LINDA BRIAR, AGE 28, was looking forward to the birth of her first child. Linda had been married for five years and had worked for most of that time as an advertising copywriter. She had never had any particular emotional problems and had always been physically well.

The delivery of a healthy, seven-pound baby girl was without complications, and Linda was tired but happy for the first three days after the delivery. She left the hospital in good spirits and all was well for the first week at home. Then, rather suddenly, she became anxious and unable to sit still. She started to think that someone was trying to harm the baby. She recognized that this was ridiculous, but could not stop thinking that someone was trying to poison the baby or break into the house. She began to upset her husband by saying strange things, such as that they had twin boys rather than a baby girl.

Sometimes she would feel perfectly normal, while at other times she was agitated and preoccupied with her strange ideas. Over the next week she became so upset and preoccupied that she could not take care of the baby, and eventually could not even get out of bed in the morning. She felt guilty about "everything," could not sleep at night, and had no appetite. She was often confused, not knowing where she was or what was happening to her. She became almost mute.

At that point her husband took her to see her obstetrician, who immediately referred her for psychiatric care. By the time she saw the psychiatrist, she was afraid she would harm herself or her baby.

Discussion of "First Baby"

In discussing the diagnosis for this case, it is necessary to deal with two issues: the first is the symptom picture that Linda presents; the second is the relationship of this disturbance to the recent childbirth.

The most prominent symptoms are delusions (someone will harm the baby; she has had twins), agitation, confusion, guilt, and inability to take care of the child or herself. There is no evidence of sustained depressed mood, thus ruling out either a psychotic Major Depression or Schizoaffective Disorder. The diagnosis of a Delusional Disorder is ruled out by the marked disturbance in her behavior not accounted for by the delusions. Schizophreniform Disorder is ruled out by the absence of bizarre delusions or hallucinations.

The symptom picture in this case is similar to that seen in Brief Reactive Psychosis (delusions, disorganized behavior, and emotional turmoil). The appearance of the symptoms in response to a markedly stressful event (childbirth certainly is markedly stressful) in a person who has no prodromal symptoms of Schizophrenia also suggests this diagnosis. The key issue is the exclusion criterion that rules out this diagnosis if it can be established that an organic factor initiated and maintained the disturbance.

Since we cannot prove that the organic factor of childbirth initiated this psychotic disturbance, if we follow the criteria strictly, we are obliged to give the diagnosis of Brief Reactive Psychosis. However, we are uncomfortable with that diagnosis, because we think of the stressor involved in Brief Reactive Psychosis as being purely psychosocial, rather than biological, as is likely (we think) in this case. Therefore, we shall bend the rules and diagnose Psychotic Disorder Not Otherwise Specified.

DSM-III-R does not recognize the diagnosis that many clinicians and researchers would like to apply in this case: Postpartum Psychosis. They would argue that this case shows its typical features: sudden emergence of delusions, agitation, confusion, and disorientation shortly after childbirth. DSM-III-R also does not recognize the concept of Postpartum Depression. Such cases would be diagnosed as Major Depression, and the clinician would have to note on Axis IV the presence of childbirth as a stressor that may have contributed to the development of the depression.

It is estimated that Postpartum Psychosis occurs in one in a thousand deliveries; but once a woman has had a previous episode, her risk for a subsequent episode after her next delivery is one in three to one in four. It is estimated that approximately 10% of women who give birth develop postpartum Major Depressions. (As many as 50% to 80% of women develop a mild and transient postpartum condition known as "baby blues," characterized by crying, irritability, mild dysphoria, and labile mood.)

DSM-III-R Diagnosis:

Axis I: 298.90 Psychotic Disorder Not Otherwise Specified (p. 211)

Follow-up

The patient was prescribed small doses of an antipsychotic medication. Her symptoms, particularly her paranoid ideation and agitation, gradually subsided over the next one to two weeks. However, a few months later, she again began to be bothered by symptoms of suspiciousness, guilt, and unworthiness. She was again treated with small doses of antipsychotic medication, and at one year postpartum, is off of all medication, and has been well for the last six months.

Wealthy Widow

A WEALTHY, 72-YEAR-OLD WIDOW is referred by her children, against her will, as they think she has become "senile" since the death of her husband 6 months previously. After the initial bereavement, which was not severe, the patient had resumed an active social life and become a volunteer at local hospitals. The family encouraged this, but over the past three months have become concerned about her going to local bars with some of the hospital staff. The referral was precipitated by her announcing her engagement to a 25-year-old male nurse, to whom she planned to turn over her house and a large amount of money. The patient's three sons, by threat and intimidation, have made her accompany them to this psychiatric evaluation. While one of her sons is talking to the psychiatrist, the patient is heard accusing the other two of trying to commit her so they can get their hands on her money.

Initially in the interview the patient is extremely angry at her sons and the psychiatrist, insisting that they don't understand that for the first time in her life she is doing something for herself, not for her father, her husband, or her children. She then suddenly drapes herself over the couch and asks the psychiatrist if she is attractive enough to capture a 25-year-old man. She proceeds to elaborate on her fiancé's physique and sexual abilities and describes her life as exciting and fulfilling for the first time. She is overtalkative and repeatedly refuses to allow the psychiatrist to interrupt her with questions. She says that she goes out nightly with her fiancé to clubs and bars and that although she does not drink, she thoroughly enjoys the atmosphere. They often go on to an after-hours place and end up breakfasting, going to bed, and making love. After only three or four hours' sleep, she gets up, feeling refreshed, and then goes shopping. She spends about $700 a week on herself and gives her fiancé about $500 a week, all of which she can easily afford.

The patient agrees that her behavior is unusual for someone of her age and social position, but states she has always been conventional and now is the time to change, before it is too late. She refuses to participate in formal testing, saying, "I'm not going to do any stupid tests to see if I am sane." She has no obvious memory impairment, and is correctly oriented in all areas. According to the family, she has no previous history of emotional disturbance.

Discussion of "Wealthy Widow"

As the story unfolds, many readers will wonder, as we did, whether this poor lady is suffering only from avaricious children rather than a mental disorder. It does seem, however, that her alternately irritable and expansive mood, pressure of speech, decreased need for sleep, and poor judgment (signing her house over to someone she has met only recently) represent more than a new start in life for someone who has been too "conventional." In fact, all of these symptoms, in the absence of an Organic Mental Disorder or a psychotic disorder unrelated to a mood disorder (e.g., Schizophrenia), are quite characteristic of a Manic or Hypomanic Episode. In a Manic Episode there is "marked impairment in occupational functioning, or usual activities or relationships with others"; in a Hypomanic Episode this degree of impairment, if any, is not present. We believe that, even though she is wealthy, the Widow's plan to sign her house over to her new lover does represent marked impairment in her relationship with others (she would not agree). Thus, the diagnosis is Bipolar Disorder, Manic, without Psychotic Features.

Bipolar Disorder first appearing at age 72 is certainly uncommon. One would want to be careful to rule out the possibility of a physical disorder, such as a brain tumor or degenerative central nervous system disorder, that might be causing an Organic Mood Syndrome. Since the workup to rule out a physical disorder has not yet been done, the qualifying term "Provisional" is added to this diagnosis.

DSM-III-R Diagnosis:

Axis I: 296.42 Bipolar Disorder, Manic, without Psychotic
                    Features, Mild (Provisional) (p. 217)

The Jerk

LEON IS A 45-YEAR-OLD POSTAL EMPLOYEE who was evaluated at a clinic specializing in the treatment of depression. He claims to have felt constantly depressed since the first grade, without a period of "normal" mood for more than a few days at a time. His depression has been accompanied by lethargy, little or no interest or pleasure in anything, trouble concentrating, and feelings of inadequacy, pessimism, and resentfulness. His only periods of normal mood occur when he is home alone, listening to music or watching TV.

On further questioning, Leon reveals that he cannot ever remember feeling comfortable socially. Even before kindergarten, if he was asked to speak in front of a group of family friends, his mind would "go blank." He felt overwhelming anxiety at children's social functions, such as birthday parties, which he either avoided or, if he went, attended in total silence. He could answer questions in class only if he wrote down the answers in advance; even then, he frequently mumbled and couldn't get the answer out. He met new children with his eyes lowered, fearing their scrutiny, expecting to feel humiliated and embarrassed. He was convinced that everyone around him thought he was "dumb" or "a jerk."

As he grew up, Leon had a couple of neighborhood playmates, but he never had a "best friend." His school grades were good, but suffered when oral classroom participation was expected. As a teen-ager, he was terrified of girls, and to this day has never gone on a date or even asked a girl for a date. This bothers him, although he is so often depressed that he feels he has little energy or interest in dating.

Leon attended college and did well for a while, then dropped out as his grades slipped. He remained very self-conscious and "terrified" of meeting strangers. He had trouble finding a job because he was unable to answer questions in interviews. He worked at a few jobs for which only a written test was required. He passed a Civil Service exam at age 24, and was offered a job in the post office on the evening shift. He enjoyed this job since it involved little contact with others. He was offered, but refused, several promotions because he feared the social pressures. Although by now he supervises a number of employees, he still finds it difficult to give instructions, even to people he has known for years. He has no friends and avoids all invitations to socialize with co-workers. During the past several years, he has tried several therapies to help him get over his "shyness" and depression.

Leon has never experienced sudden anxiety or a panic attack in social situations or at other times. Rather, his anxiety gradually builds to a constant high level in anticipation of social situations. He has never experienced any psychotic symptoms.

Discussion of "The Jerk"

Leo comes to the clinic complaining of lifelong depression. Indeed, he has been depressed and has experienced only limited interest and enjoyment ever since he was a child. Although his depressed mood has been associated with pessimism, low energy, and difficulty concentrating, other symptoms of a Major Depressive Episode, such as appetite and sleep disturbance, have not been present. This chronic mild depression is diagnosed as Dysthymia, which is further qualified as Primary Type (since it is not related to a preexisting Axis I or Axis III disorder) and of Early Onset (before age 21).

In addition, Leon has lifelong social anxiety that makes it difficult for him to maintain even the most minimal social contact. His fear is that he will have nothing to say and will be thought of as "a jerk." This fear seems to be independent of his Dysthymia and therefore justifies the additional diagnosis of Social Phobia, Generalized Type (including most social situations).

This patient illustrates a frequent problem in diagnosing the Axis I disorder of Social Phobia, Generalized Type, in that the symptoms overlap considerably with those of Avoidant Personality Disorder. Leon has certainly displayed a pervasive pattern of social discomfort, fear of negative evaluation, and timidity throughout his life. He has no close friends, avoids activities that involve significant interpersonal contact, and is reticent in social situations. He undoubtedly is also easily hurt by disapproval and is probably unwilling to become involved with people unless he is certain of being liked. Therefore, we make the diagnosis of Avoidant Personality Disorder on Axis II and hope that DSM-IV will clarify the boundaries of these two disorders.

DSM-III-R Diagnosis:

Axis I: 300.40 Dysthymia, Primary Type, Early Onset (p. 232)
            300.23 Social Phobia, Generalized Type (p. 243)
Axis II: 301.82 Avoidant Personality Disorder (p. 352)

The Director

A 36-YEAR-OLD FILM DIRECTOR had had frequent difficulty falling asleep since early childhood. He went to bed between 11:30 PM and 3:30 AM and arose at irregular times before 1:00 PM. His sleep was lighter at the beginning of the night, when he was easily disturbed by random noise or his wife's shifting in bed. Later in the night he slept more soundly, and felt his deepest sleep came at about 8:00 AM. He felt groggy for half an hour or longer upon first arising and was not able to function well in the early part of the day.

The patient was currently free of scheduled work obligations except for a morning meeting once a week. This further lessened his motivation to get out of bed in the morning. In the evening, however, he experienced a surge of productive energy. His mind was enjoyably active, and he delayed bedtimes to capitalize on his high work capacity. On fishing trips he would arise at 5:00 AM and take a nap at 9:00 AM. The discrepancy between his and others' sleep schedules on weekends and other social inconveniences caused by his sleep schedule motivated his seeking help.

The patient drank two to five cups of coffee daily, more during occasional work crises. He had a frequently stuffed nose, and occasionally used pseudoephedrine for stimulation, as well as a nasal decongestant (such medications often have long lasting stimulant effects).

Both of the patient's parents and two brothers had alcoholism. He had survived a childhood full of severe physical and emotional trauma. Further, his mother abused sedatives, and had had a two-year depressive episode during which she remained in bed. His mother, sister, and one brother had made near-lethal suicide attempts, and his father had killed himself. Despite this background, the patient had graduated with high marks from a prestigious university and had done well in graduate school and in his subsequent work. His history revealed that in college he frequently had been unable to get to morning classes.

The patient lived with his wife, who was a writer, and his young daughter. He thought his major problems were indecisiveness and being too ready to please during contract negotiations, to the detriment of his

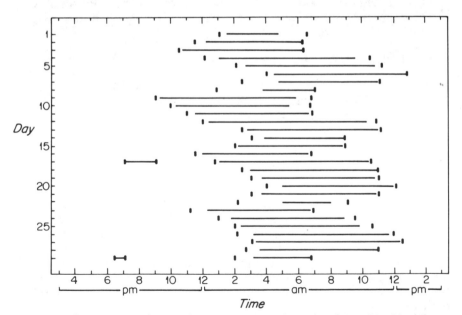

Figure 1. The Director's Sleep-Wake Pattern   Day (Y axis) and time (X axis) of sleep. First vertical mark on each line indicates when he first tried to sleep, horizontal line when he estimated he slept, and subsequent vertical line when he arose from bed. Note 2½ to 3 hour periods between bedtime and sleep onset, days 8 and 22, and evening naps, days 17 and 29.

own interests. He thought his childhood misfortunes had diminished his self-confidence.

At the evaluation, the man was casually dressed, ingratiating, and friendly. Despite professions of self-doubt, he was forward, frank, and engaging. The psychiatrist recommended that he keep a sleep chart for one month.

The sleep chart revealed bedtimes that were progressively delayed from 9:00 or 10:00 PM until about 3:15 AM over five-to-seven-day cycles. Arising times were even less regular in pattern, generally becoming later at the end of three cycles. Usually some obligation required the patient to get up even after a late bedtime, causing him to take an afternoon nap or to retire at around 10:00 PM. Thereafter he would fail to fall asleep for some hours. After one or two such days, the cycle would begin again. (See Figure 1.)

Discussion of "The Director"

This patient shows the characteristic features of Sleep-Wake Schedule Disorder, Delayed Type. There is a mismatch between his normal circadian sleep-wake pattern and the sleep-wake schedule for his environment. The mismatch is that his preferred sleep onset and offset are several hours later than those of people he works and socializes with, i.e., his sleep schedule is delayed relative to the conventional societal sleep-wake schedule. The patient's sleep chart suggests that his normal underlying circadian rhythm, which is somewhat longer than 24 hours, is not reset by external cues that ordinarily induce a 24-hour sleep-wake rhythm.

The lack of regular work hours, the "night person" pattern of greater evening productivity, and the subjectively deeper sleep later in the night are all typical of patients with this problem. The lack of scheduled work obligations removed an important pacemaker for the sleep-wake schedule, unmasking the delaying tendency. The patient's use of stimulants contributed to his evening productivity and to difficulty in falling asleep earlier.

DSM-III-R Diagnosis:

Axis I: 307.45 **Sleep-Wake Schedule Disorder, Delayed Type**
                    (p. 307)

Follow-up

The patient was treated first by withdrawal of stimulants and establishment of a regular arising hour of 7:00 AM daily. This lessened both his morning impairment and his evening sense of arousal.

However, within a few weeks he gradually drifted back to late bedtimes and late arising times, and was again using caffeine-containing beverages during work crises. He was then treated with triazolam, 0.25 mg at 11:30 PM. (This short-acting benzodiazepine can reportedly resynchronize circadian rhythms that have been displaced, e.g., by jet lag.) He subsequently fell asleep regularly and, unexpectedly, awoke about 6:00 AM with a feeling of great alertness. He kept a regular schedule and reported that he accomplished more, despite the lessening of his evening energy surge.

The patient's fear of insomnia and work impairment disappeared. He gradually reduced his drug dosage, but a decrease from 0.25 mg to 0.125 mg of triazolam caused a sense of decreased concentration the following afternoon. On the reduced dose he slept slightly longer each night and continued to function well.

The Sailor

P SYCHIATRIC CONSULTATION IS REQUESTED by an emergency-room physician on an 18-year-old male who has been brought into the hospital by the police. The youth appears exhausted and shows evidence of prolonged exposure to the sun. He identifies the current date incorrectly, giving it as September 27 instead of October 1. It is difficult to get him to focus on specific questions, but with encouragement he supplies a number of facts. He recalls sailing with friends, apparently about September 25, on a weekend cruise off the Florida coast, when bad weather was encountered. He is unable to recall any subsequent events and does not know what became of his companions. He has to be reminded several times that he is in a hospital, since he expresses uncertainty as to his whereabouts. Each time he is told, he seems surprised.

There is no evidence of head injury or dehydration. Electrolytes and cranial nerve examination are unremarkable. Because of the patient's apparent exhaustion, he is permitted to sleep for six hours. Upon awakening, he is much more attentive, but is still unable to recall events after September 25, including how he came to the hospital. There is no longer any doubt in his mind that he is in the hospital, however; and he is able to recall the contents of the previous interview and the fact that he had fallen asleep. He is able to remember that he was a student at a southern college, maintained a B average, had a small group of close friends, and has a good relationship with his family. He denies any previous psychiatric history and says he has never abused drugs or alcohol.

Because of the patient's apparently sound physical condition, a sodium amytal interview is performed. During this interview he relates that neither he nor his companions were particularly experienced sailors capable of coping with the ferocity of the storm they encountered. Although he had taken the precaution of securing himself to the boat with a life jacket and tie line, his companions had failed to do this and had been washed overboard in the heavy seas. He completely lost control of the boat and felt he was saved only by virtue of good luck and his lifeline. He had been able to consume a small supply of food that was stowed away in the cabin over a three-day period. He never saw either of his sailing companions again. He was picked up on October 1 by a Coast Guard cutter and brought to shore, and subsequently the police had brought him to the hospital.

Discussion of "The Sailor"

The differential diagnosis of acute memory loss begins with a consideration of an Organic Mental Disorder, such as Delirium, Dementia, or Amnestic Syndrome, which may be due to head trauma, cerebrovascular accidents, or drug use. The normal physical and neurological examination and the absence of a history of drug use rule out these possibilities in this patient. With the amytal interview it becomes clear that the amnestic period developed following a particularly traumatic and life-threatening experience. Amnesia (an episode of sudden inability to recall important personal information that is too extensive to be considered "forgetfulness") that is not due to an Organic Mental Disorder, justifies the diagnosis Psychogenic Amnesia. In this case, the circumscribed nature of the amnesia and the perplexity and disorientation during the amnestic period, all following a traumatic event, are quite characteristic of the diagnosed disorder.

DSM-III-R Diagnosis:

Axis I: 300.12 Psychogenic Amnesia (p. 275)

Cry Me a River

A 38-YEAR-OLD CLERICAL WORKER described to a psychiatrist how she has been suffering from a disabling sleep problem for a year and a half. She usually goes to bed at 6:00 PM, and sleeps straight through until 7:00 AM. The reason that she comes for help now is that last month her driver's license was suspended after she fell asleep while driving her car out of a parking lot, and hit a telephone pole. As a result, she now has to arise at 6:00 AM to use public transportation to arrive in time for work at 8:15 AM. Upon arising she typically feels groggy and "out of it." During the day she remains sleepy. She frequently falls asleep on buses, missing her stop. She recently took a sales job after work, from 6:00 PM until 10:00 PM two nights a week, in an attempt to remain on her feet at least some of the time that she is away from her office job. On weekends she remains in bed, asleep all day, arising only to go to the toilet or for meals, except on an occasional Saturday when she does her routine chores.

The patient does not believe that she snores during sleep (as would be likely in sleep apnea); and she denies nightmares (as in Dream Anxiety Disorder), sleepwalking (as in Sleepwalking Disorder), or sudden loss of muscle tone (cataplexy) or feelings of paralysis upon awakening, both symptoms of the neurologic disorder narcolepsy.

Before the onset of her sleep problem, the patient generally required only six to seven hours of sleep a night. During the first year of her "sleepiness" she began to treat herself with caffeine, drinking up to ten cups of coffee and one to two liters of cola daily.

In addition to the sleepiness, the patient has had severe, recurrent periods of depression since approximately age 13. For several months before the evaluation, she was having crying spells in her office. These sometimes would come on so suddenly that she had no time to run to the restroom to hide them. She acknowledged trouble concentrating on her job and noted that she was getting little pleasure from her work, something she used to enjoy. She had been harboring angry and pessimistic feelings for the past several years, and noted that these were more severe recently as she had allowed her diabetes and weight to get out of control. She felt guilty that she was physically damaging herself and slowly dying in this way. She sometimes thought that she deserved to be dead.

She had been treated from age 18 to age 33 with psychotherapy, during which time her depression gradually worsened. More recently she had been given trials of antidepressants, including imipramine, desipramine, and protriptyline, which had each made improvements in mood and wakefulness that lasted several months. She tended to fall asleep during evening group psychotherapy sessions.

The patient's diabetes was diagnosed at age 11. She first lost control of her weight and her blood sugar during her teen-age years, regained it, but has frequently lost control since then. At this evaluation she weighed about 30% above her ideal weight, was on 52 units of insulin daily, but neither kept regular mealtimes nor tested her urine. Results of recent random blood sugar determinations were abnormally high. Significant diabetic retinopathy had developed, compelling her to use a magnifying glass for reading. She had mild hypertension without apparent diabetic kidney disease, and took one diuretic tablet daily.

The patient had done poorly in high school, and had gone to business school for four years, but had failed to graduate. She had had some hope of a romantic relationship, but never had a steady boyfriend. She lives at home with her mother and has no close friends outside her family. On close questioning, it became apparent that the onset of the sleep problems and the beginning of the most recent period of depression had coincided.

The patient's family history revealed that one of her five siblings took a nap each afternoon, and slept seven hours nightly. Otherwise, there was no history of Sleep Disorder, diabetes, or treatment for depression in her family.

As the patient described her problem to the psychiatrist, she gazed continually downward and conversed in a low monotone. She answered questions dutifully, but without elaboration. She shed copious tears.

The patient was admitted to the hospital for studies. Nursing observations documented that the patient slept 12 to 15 hours daily. She was much impaired in tests of vigilance, which involved her pushing a button whenever the letter "X" appeared in a series of letters visually presented at one per second; she averaged 4% correct responses during two trials, compared with a normal score of 66%–78%. She had an average multiple sleep latency (i.e., onset of sleep after lights out) of 8.5 minutes during four polygraphically recorded daytime naps, a result consistent with only mild sleepiness. Nocturnal sleep monitoring revealed an abnormally short REM latency of 2 minutes and an abnormal increase (42%) in the amount of REM sleep. (This increased REM activity occurs in states of presumed central catecholamine depletion such as in depression, narcolepsy, use of catecholamine-blocking drugs, and stimulant withdrawal states.) The nocturnal sleep monitoring revealed no other abnormality. The patient had only 2% wakefulness, much less than expected in a prolonged recording; this was consistent with her daytime sleepiness. She continued to sleep for 9½ hours, until she had to be awakened so the laboratory could be used for daytime purposes.

Discussion of "Cry Me a River"

Although this patient suffers from recurrent periods of depression, her predominant complaints are of excessive daytime sleepiness (falls asleep on buses, remains in bed all day on weekends) and prolonged transition to the fully awake state (feels groggy and "out of it" on awakening). The sleep laboratory findings (prolonged sleep, impaired vigilance, short REM latency, increased REM activity) confirm her complaints of hypersomnia.

In this case there is no evidence of a specific organic factor (such as narcolepsy or sleep apnea) to account for the disturbance. The magnitude of her excessive sleepiness is compatible with that seen in Primary Hypersomnia. However, since the onset of her sleep disturbance seems to have coincided with the most recent recurrence of her depression, it seems reasonable to conclude that the hypersomnia is related to the Mood Disorder. Therefore, the principal diagnosis is Hypersomnia Related to Another Mental Disorder (Nonorganic). The recurrent episodes of depression warrant the additional Axis I diagnosis of Major Depression, Recurrent.

The reason a separate diagnosis is given for the sleep disturbance caused by the Mood Disorder is that the hypersomnia constitutes the *predominant* complaint. Otherwise, it would be considered merely a symptom of the Major Depression, and would not require a separate diagnosis.

DSM-III-R Diagnosis:

Axis I: **307.44 Hypersomnia Related to Another Mental Disorder (Nonorganic) (p. 303)**
             296.32 Major Depression, Recurrent, Moderate (p. 230)
Axis III: **Diabetes and diabetic retinopathy**
             Obesity
             Mild hypertension

Perpetual Patient

IN 1945, AT THE AGE OF 18, the patient became apprehensive about leaving home to go to an out-of-state college for her freshman year. One day in September, while with her mother shopping for college clothes, she began to have episodes in which she would stop walking and become stiff for a few moments without explanation, then proceed to talk and act appropriately. The next day she became more silent. Sometimes she made inappropriate remarks, but at other times she acted and talked quite normally. Silences, refusal to eat, and inappropriate comments such as "Daddy, kill me" precipitated a consultation, and then hospitalization, almost on the day that the patient was to have been admitted to college.

In the early days of hospitalization, the patient vaguely suggested that she might be having auditory hallucinations, and at times gave "confused" or silly answers that were out of keeping with her 121 IQ score on psychological testing. When by herself, she would write coherent letters and short stories that were regarded as publishable. Partly because of the "lack of progress" and the bizarreness of her behavior at times, she was diagnosed as having "Catatonic Dementia Praecox."

Early in her hospitalization the patient received individual psychotherapy four times a week. She continued to receive psychotherapy in and out of the institution, with a series of nine therapists, for the next 20 years. From the beginning of her hospitalization, she was frequently negativistic, precipitated physical fights, mutilated herself in many minor ways, and self-induced vomiting. These behaviors contributed to her receiving a great deal of attention in a public institution with limited staff. She stated that she wanted to try every form of therapy there was, "even lobotomy," and her wishes were carried out, except for the lobotomy. She received a dozen electroconvulsive treatments, four dozen insulin subcoma treatments, dance therapy, occupational therapy, recreational therapy, psychodrama (loved it), group psychotherapy, and art therapy, in addition to individual psychotherapy and lots of attention from ministers and priests.

After the first three stormy years of her hospitalization, the patient was transferred to the care of a woman psychiatrist, became much calmer, registered at a local university, and did well at her studies. Nevertheless, "hysterical" vomiting, violence, and other bizarre acts would take place whenever discharge from the institution was mentioned. In two more years, working primarily with women therapists, she held a job and acted appropriately, and eventually accepted discharge to a female psychotherapist as "recovered" at age 24.

One evening, after six uneventful years and satisfactory occupational functioning, the patient appeared at the hospital, distraught at being unable to reach her therapist by phone, and asked to be readmitted. She was admitted despite the difficulties in determining the genuineness of her behavior and of her statements about suicide and "confusion." A series of many forms of psychotherapies, including individual psychotherapy, commenced immediately, and lasted nearly a decade.

When the patient was 40, a change in the approach to her evaluation and treatment was initiated when it was decided that she had an "hysterical personality." For the next five years, a series of efforts to place her in the community was blocked by negativism, threats, minor self-mutilations, self-induced vomiting, occasional inappropriate comments, and other attention-getting behavior, none of which was "rewarded," however, with individual therapy, psychodrama, etc. Eventually, when she was in her mid-40s, she was discharged, despite complaints that she was not ready. When told that the discharge was being carried out, over her objections, the patient vomited; but the therapist stated that she would be discharged nevertheless. She pulled down her pants and defecated in the office, but was still discharged. In the decade since, she has continued to function outside the institution, usually with the support of a boarding home.

Discussion of "Perpetual Patient"

This woman was able to engage the attention of countless dedicated mental health professionals over many years. Her remarkable illness persisted despite a trial of nearly every known treatment. The pattern of her symptoms, from the start, did not correspond to any recognizable illness, and she seemed able to produce them at will (e.g., defecation in public when her discharge was imminent). Over the years her behavior seems to have been designed to achieve one goal: continuing to be treated as a psychiatric patient.

In the past such a case might have been called "hysteria"

because of the exaggerated, self-dramatizing nature of the symptoms. These histrionic features were also noted by the hospital personnel who took care of this patient. In DSM-III-R the voluntary production of psychological symptoms for the purpose of assuming the patient role (and the absence of external incentives for the behavior, as in Malingering) is called Factitious Disorder with Psychological Symptoms.

In addition to the factitious production of symptoms, this woman's long-term functioning is characterized by excessive emotionality and attention-seeking; in her relationships with people she is vain, demanding, and dependent. These features suggest the additional diagnosis of Histrionic Personality Disorder. However, there is insufficient information about other symptoms of the disorder, such as inappropriate seductiveness and overconcern about physical attractiveness, to make this diagnosis. We therefore would add the diagnosis of Personality Disorder Not Otherwise Specified (with histrionic features).

DSM-III-R Diagnosis:

Axis I: 300.16 **Factitious Disorder with Psychological Symptoms**
                 (p. 319)
Axis II: 301.90 **Personality Disorder Not Otherwise Specified**
                 (p. 358)

I Am Vishnu

MR. NEHRU IS A 32-YEAR-OLD, single, unemployed man who migrated from India to the United States when he was 13. His brother brought him to the emergency room of an Atlanta, Georgia, hospital after neighbors complained that he was standing in the street harassing people about his religious beliefs. To the psychiatrist he keeps repeating, "I am Vishnu. I am Krishna."

Mr. Nehru has been living with his brother and sister-in-law for the past seven months, attending an outpatient clinic. During the last four weeks, his behavior has become increasingly disruptive. He awakens his brother at all hours of the night to discuss religious matters. He often seems to be responding to voices that only he hears. He neither bathes nor changes his clothes.

Mr. Nehru's first episode of emotional disturbance was five years ago. Medical records are not available; but from the brother's account, it seems to have been similar to the present episode. There have been two other similar episodes, each requiring hospitalization for a few months. Mr. Nehru admits that, starting about five years ago and virtually continuously since then, he has been troubled by "voices" that he hears throughout the day. There are several voices, which comment on his behavior and discuss him in the third person. They usually are either benign ("Look at him now. He is about to eat.") or insulting in content ("What a fool he is. He doesn't understand anything!").

Between episodes, according to both his outpatient psychiatrist and his brother, Mr. Nehru is a quiet, somewhat withdrawn person, but popular in his neighborhood because he helps some of his elderly neighbors with shopping and yard work. At these times his mood is unremarkable. However, he claims that because of the voices, he cannot concentrate sufficiently to hold a job. He sometimes reads books, but watches little TV, because he hears the voices coming out of the television and is upset that the television shows often refer to him.

For the past six weeks, with increasing insistence, the voices have been telling Mr. Nehru that he is the new Messiah, Jesus, Moses, Vishnu, and Krishna, and should begin a new religious epoch in human history. He has begun to experience surges of increased energy, "so I could spread my gospel," and needs very little sleep. According to his brother, he has become more preoccupied with the voices and disorganized in his daily activities.

When interviewed, Mr. Nehru is euphoric, and his speech is rapid and hard to follow. He paces up and down the ward and, upon seeing a doctor, grabs his arm, puts his face within two inches of the doctor's, and talks with great rapidity and enthusiasm about his religious "insights." In the middle of a speech on his new religion, he abruptly compliments the doctor on how well his shirt and tie match. When limits are placed on his behavior, he becomes loud and angry. In addition to his belief that he is the Messiah, he feels that the hospital is part of a conspiracy to suppress his religious message. Although he seems to enjoy his "voices," he sometimes complains about them and makes references to "those damned voices." He states that he feels that his religious insights, euphoria, and energy have been put into him by God.

Discussion of "I Am Vishnu"

Mr. Nehru suffers from a chronic illness characterized by prominent hallucinations that are so intrusive that he cannot concentrate enough to be able to work. These hallucinations seem to have been persistently present, since his illness began five years ago. In addition, there have been four episodes (including the current one) with symptoms that fulfill the criteria for a Manic Episode: he is euphoric, grandiose, and irritable, and has pressured speech and increased energy.

If we did not know that between these Manic Episodes Mr. Nehru was continuously hearing voices, we would have no trouble in making the diagnosis of Bipolar Disorder. However, the diagnosis of Bipolar Disorder excludes cases in which there are delusions or hallucinations for as long as two weeks in the absence of prominent mood symptoms. Thus, the continuous voices during the times when Mr. Nehru was not manic rule out the diagnosis of Bipolar Disorder.

If we were diagnosing Mr. Nehru's condition between these episodes, we would note that the prominent hallucinations, with no apparent relation to depression or elation, fulfill the symptomatic criteria for Schizophrenia. We would then have to consider the differential diagnosis with Schizoaffective Disorder. The key question is whether the total duration of all of the episodes of a mood syndrome (in his case, Manic Episodes) has been brief relative to the total duration of the whole illness. We do not know exactly how long each of Mr. Nehru's Manic Episodes lasted; but it is unlikely that the total time is more than six months compared to the five years total duration of the psychotic illness. Is this brief? Since DSM-III-R does not provide more precise guidelines, we are inclined to give more weight to the prominent manic symptoms that seem to have been present with each exacerbation of his psychotic illness. We therefore diagnose Schizoaffective Disorder, Bipolar Type and note the need to rule out Schizophrenia.

DSM-III-R Diagnosis:

Axis I: 295.70 **Schizoaffective Disorder, Bipolar Type (p. 210)**
                    (Provisional, R/O Schizophrenia)

Agitated Businessman

THIS AGITATED 42-YEAR-OLD businessman was admitted to the psychiatric service after a two-and-one-half-month period in which he found himself becoming increasingly distrustful of others and suspicious of his business associates. He was taking their statements out of context, "twisting" their words, and making inappropriately hostile and accusatory comments; he had, in fact, lost several business deals that had been "virtually sealed." Finally, the patient fired a shotgun into his backyard late one night when he heard noises that convinced him that intruders were about to break into his house and kill him.

One and one-half years previously, the patient had been diagnosed as having narcolepsy (episodes of sleep attacks, i.e., a sudden, irresistible urge to fall asleep, and cataplexy, i.e., sudden loss of muscle tension, such as jaw drop, head drop, weakness of the knees, or paralysis of all skeletal muscles) and had been placed on an amphetaminelike stimulant, methylphenidate. He became asymptomatic and was able to work quite effectively as the sales manager of a small office-machine company and to participate in an active social life with his family and a small circle of friends. In the four months before admission he had been using increasingly large doses of methylphenidate to maintain alertness late at night because of an increasing amount of work that could not be handled during the day.

Discussion of "Agitated Businessman"

The primary symptoms are persecutory delusions about coworkers, delusions of reference (the patient believed that noises indicated the presence of intruders who were about to kill him), and psychomotor agitation. Because of the temporal relationship between the increasing doses of methylphenidate and the development of these symptoms, it is reasonable to assume that the disturbance represents an Organic Delusional Syndrome, more specifically, Methylphenidate-induced Delusional Disorder.

Since there is no evidence of any personality problems, the code on Axis II is V71.09, No Diagnosis or Condition.

The narcolepsy, a neurologic disorder, is noted on Axis III. The increased demands at work are noted as a mild psychosocial stressor on Axis IV, and are considered to be a predominantly acute event since the duration of the increased demand at work has lasted less than six months. At his best, in the preceding year, the patient's functioning in both work and social relations was apparently very good. His highest GAF in the past year is therefore rated 80; his current GAF would be rated at 20, in that he appears to be potentially dangerous to others as evidenced by his firing a shotgun outside his house in response to his delusions.

DSM-III-R Diagnosis:

Axis I: 292.11 Methylphenidate-induced Delusional Disorder
           (p. 138)
Axis II: V71.09 No Diagnosis or Condition
Axis III: Narcolepsy
Axis IV: Psychosocial stressors: increased demands at work
           Severity: 2 - Mild (predominantly acute events)
Axis V: Current GAF: 20
           Highest GAF past year: 80

I Could Be Dying

A 52-YEAR-OLD WHOLESALE DISTRIBUTOR of automobile parts awoke in the middle of the night, gasping for breath, sweating, shaking, and with palpitations. He felt his pulse; it was 120. He again had the thought: "I could be dying." It was his third attack of the week, and at least his tenth that month, that had awakened him from sleep. The problem, which had begun two years previously, was getting much worse: not only was he having trouble staying asleep because of similar attacks, but after such nights he felt tired all day. He decided to take a friend's advice and seek help from a psychiatrist who specialized in sleep problems.

The psychiatrist elicited this additional history. Attacks of panic occurring during the day had begun at age 12 and had recurred every few months since that time. They did not begin to occur during sleep until the patient turned 50, two years earlier. A few months ago the attacks had become much rarer, after the patient had discontinued drinking the eight to ten beers he had periodically drunk every weekend for most of his adult life. His weight had fallen from 227 pounds to a mildly overweight 181 pounds, and the mild hypertension he had had for several years disappeared.

In addition to the recurrent attacks, for most of his life the patient had also felt anxious in anticipation of particular situations, including being shut inside airplanes or elevators or traveling in the middle lane of a road. On a turnpike he counted the exits until he could leave, fearing that he would have a panic attack.

He described a fear of falling apart if he ever got too far from his "support system," his term for a beer cooler, which he carried with him always, although he rarely drank the beer. In anticipation of an airplane flight, however, he would drink six to eight beers. He almost always had a company employee, his son, or a friend accompany him, and particularly disliked plane flights when he was not accompanied by a familiar person. The night after he drank, the anxiety attacks occurred, awakening him from sleep.

The patient ran a successful business and consulted for several others. Recently, however, anxiety had prevented his accepting a huge government contract to set up an international distribution system for retail stores on military bases. He felt he would be too exposed to scrutiny and would therefore fail. He also worried that some long plane flights would be unavoidable.

At interview the patient was highly verbal, informative, cheerful, friendly, and engaging. He talked about uncomfortable subjects frankly and productively. He had two sisters and two daughters who suffered from "agoraphobia"; one of the daughters was housebound.

Initially, the patient was thought to have sleep apnea (recurrent periods of not breathing during sleep), on the basis of the loud snoring that he reported and the awakening provoked by drinking alcohol, relieved by weight loss, and the presence of mild hypertension. (These symptoms are commonly seen in sleep apnea, and are presumably related to the pulmonary hypertension that develops from insufficient breathing and oxygen desaturation. No evidence for this emerged from results of sleep laboratory recording, upper airway examination, or daytime vigilance testing.)

Discussion of "I Could Be Dying"

This case is unusual from two perspectives. First of all, it is unusual for patients with Panic Disorder to have panic attacks at night. Secondly, insomnia is rarely caused by panic attacks that awaken the patient. When persistent insomnia is the predominant symptom and is apparently due to a mental disorder, the diagnosis is Insomnia Related to Another Mental Disorder (Nonorganic). In this case, we should also note the mental disorder, Panic Disorder, and its subtype, with Agoraphobia (his enduring, with distress, situations in which he fears he will have a panic attack).

DSM-III-R Diagnosis:

Axis I: **300.21 Panic Disorder with Agoraphobia, Panic Attacks Severe, Agoraphobic Avoidance Mild (p. 237)**
           307.42 Insomnia Related to Another Mental Disorder (Nonorganic) (p. 300)

Follow-up

The Panic Disorder was treated with a short-acting benzodiazepine, alprazolam, 0.5 mg three times a day. His panic attacks disappeared, and his sleep returned to normal.

Superstitions

A 20-YEAR-OLD JUNIOR at a Midwestern college complained to his internist that he was having difficulty studying because, over the last six months, he had become increasingly preoccupied with thoughts that he could not dispel. He now spent hours each night "rehashing" the day's events, especially interactions with friends and teachers, endlessly making "right" in his mind any and all regrets. He likened the process to playing a videotape of each event over and over again in his mind, asking himself if he had behaved properly and telling himself that he had done his best, or had said the right thing every step of the way. He would do this while sitting at his desk, supposedly studying; and it was not unusual for him to look at the clock after such a period of rumination and note that, to his surprise, two or three hours had elapsed. His declining grades worried him.

The patient admitted, on further questioning, that he had a two-hour grooming ritual when getting ready to go out with friends. Here again, shaving, showering, combing his hair, and putting on his clothes all demanded "perfection." In addition, for several years he had been bothered by certain "superstitions" that, it turned out, dominated his daily life. These included avoiding certain buildings while walking on campus, always sitting in the third seat in the fifth row in his classrooms, and lining up his books and pencils in a certain configuration on his desk before studying.

Discussion of "Superstitions"

Obsessions are recurrent ideas that are not experienced as voluntarily produced, but rather as thoughts that invade consciousness and are experienced as senseless (ego-dystonic). Certainly this patient does not experience his rumination about the day's events as under his voluntary control. It is less evident that he regards the *content* of these thoughts as senseless, although he clearly attempts to ignore or suppress them. This ambiguity about whether such thoughts represent true obsessions or merely obsessional brooding could be of diagnostic importance in distinguishing Obsessive Compulsive Disorder from Obsessive Compulsive Personality Disorder or Generalized Anxiety Disorder, in which rumination is often present. In this case, however, there are also clear signs of compulsions—repetitive behavior performed according to certain rules or in a stereotyped fashion that serves no useful function, is not pleasurable in itself, and is generally experienced as senseless (the patient's grooming rituals and "superstitions").

Obsessive Compulsive Personality Disorder is frequently, but not invariably, associated with Obsessive Compulsive Disorder. However, in this case there is no evidence to justify that additional diagnosis.

DSM-III-R Diagnosis:

Axis I: 300.30 Obsessive Compulsive Disorder, Moderate
                   (p. 247)

Something Happened

A 25-YEAR-OLD WOMAN was admitted to a psychiatric unit after being brought to the emergency ward by police officers. She reported that she had been shopping in an exclusive boutique when "Something happened." She said that she had no recollection of events between that time and an hour later, when she was arrested for shoplifting in a nearby department store. She protested her innocence and became so agitated, belligerent, and profane that the arresting officers took her to the hospital. At the hospital she reported that two years previously, she had been arrested for shoplifting and had had amnesia for the act. The charges against her were then dropped because she explained that both the shoplifting and the amnesia were due to her forgetting to eat after taking her insulin. However, her blood-sugar level on testing in the emergency ward was actually elevated.

The patient rapidly calmed down after admission, and appeared asymptomatic for two days. When she learned that her discharge was planned for the next day and that the charges against her would not be dropped, she became extremely agitated, angry, and abusive to the staff. Shortly thereafter, she complained of a headache and said she had no recollection of her abusive behavior. Later that evening she accosted a nurse angrily. When the nurse responded and addressed the patient by name, "Elaine," the patient said that her name was "Leslie," and that she would not allow herself to be called "Elaine," whom she described as a "wimp and a loser."

"Leslie's" voice and movement were somewhat different from those of "Elaine." She claimed that she had done the shoplifting, and stepped back so that "Elaine" could be caught and humiliated, that if she had wanted to, she could have evaded detection easily. For the next two days, the patient had many apparent switches of personality, accompanied by conspicuous changes in dress, makeup, and deportment. On several occasions "Leslie" was disruptive, and twice "Elaine" reported to nurses that she had found things belonging to other patients in her possession.

There were no consistent differences in blood sugar levels in the different personalities or changes at the time of the shifts. A neurologic workup with extensive EEG studies proved unremarkable. The patient began to complain that her behavior was out of her control, and that she could not be held accountable for it. Each day's progress notes revealed further details of the differences between "Elaine" and "Leslie."

A consultant with considerable experience with Multiple Personality Disorder (MPD) was asked to see the patient. He observed the presence of both "Elaine" and "Leslie" and documented their polarized and clear-cut differences. The personalities were detailed and elaborate as they discussed issues relating to the patient's current legal difficulties. He learned that the patient had an extensive history of discrepant behaviors that she had "forgotten," to which many witnesses would attest, and that her family often remarked that she was "like two different people." He found that these episodes had usually occurred when the patient had engaged in behavior that brought adverse personal consequences upon her. He noted that the patient was on a unit that, by coincidence, had three patients suffering from MPD and that, beginning the day the patient learned that the charges against her would not be dropped, she had begun to associate with those patients. He learned that she was aware of a case in which the consultant had appeared as a defense witness for a man with MPD arrested under similar circumstances.

An extensive history, taken over several days, and ancillary sources failed to reveal the typical childhood history of a patient with MPD, i.e., there was no indication that the patient had suffered child abuse or any other overwhelming traumatic events. Furthermore, the history indicated that the patient, despite the apparently classic nature of her two personalities, had never shown or complained of the wide variety of symptoms suggestive of other mental disorders that is characteristic of MPD and often delays recognition of the diagnosis.

The interviewer also noted that the "Elaine" he was interviewing was somewhat different from the "Elaine" with whom her family and friends were familiar. The usual "Elaine" was pleasant and mild-mannered unless "crossed," at which times she became angry and bellicose: she was not unfailingly mild and good. He also found that the patient was not very hypnotizable, which is quite unusual in patients with MPD. He undertook a prolonged interview in which he covered a wide range of topics over several hours. As the interview proceeded, "Leslie," who was completely consistent in her presentation during her discussion of matters related to the shoplifting and disruptive events on the ward, began to become inconsistent in her voice and manner. She complained that the consultant disbelieved her and was trying to "trick" her. As "Leslie" seemed unable to maintain her presentation, "Elaine" vehemently reproached the consultant for doubting the account offered by "Leslie," for whose past behaviors and current interactions with the consultant she had consistently maintained she had amnesia. At these angry moments her behavior was indistinguishable from "Leslie's." After another hour's interviewing, during which the patient made several efforts to convince the consultant that she had MPD, she ceased to display behaviors typical of the disorder.

Discussion of "Something Happened"

The psychiatrist who consulted on this case provided the following discussion:

This case illustrates that distinguishing MPD from Malingering can be difficult. Patients with true MPD often do not have the stereotypical features of the disorder, such as polarization of the personalities and clear boundaries and amnestic barriers between and among them. Elaine demonstrates that it is easy to mimic classic MPD behaviors around a unified theme for circumscribed bits of time, but exceedingly difficult to simulate the full spectrum of symptoms in a wide range of contexts over a long period of time.

People motivated to represent themselves as having MPD in order to achieve an understandable goal (in Elaine's case, to have the authorities drop charges against her) generally draw upon lay sources of information and stress those aspects of the disorder that are obvious and can be made public and be used as "evidence" for the reality of the condition. Usually this is the dramatization of a small number of polarized "personalities" related to the issue that has prompted the evaluation.

Anticipating (correctly) that Elaine could mobilize herself to offer a convincing portrayal of "personalities" with regard to the shoplifting offense, the consultant focused on exploring the presence or absence of the plethora of associated features of the disorder, such as high hypnotizability, relative consistency of the different "personalities," history of the "personalities" before the current difficulties, and a history of being abused in childhood. Elaine had none of these characteristics, and her MPD-like behavior invariably occurred in situations in which she sought to escape the consequences of illegal or inappropriate actions. She dramatized the manifestations of the "personalities" to create a public record of their behaviors. The consultant became increasingly convinced that she was malingering.

The consultant considered the likelihood of Antisocial Personality Disorder or Borderline Personality Disorder. He documented strong evidence suggesting both of these conditions, but noted that Elaine, in her efforts to represent herself as a good person intruded upon by "Leslie," minimized her personality difficulties. Therefore, although he suspected that either or both personality disorders might be present, there was insufficient information to document either of them.

DSM-III-R Diagnosis:

Axis I: V65.20 Malingering (p. 360)
Axis II: 799.90 Diagnosis Deferred

Follow-up

Elaine was placed on probation and never again showed signs of having more than one personality. On one occasion she deliberately manipulated her blood sugar to create the alibi of hypoglycemia for a shoplifting episode that she realized had been observed, but she was unable to escape the consequences of her actions, and has not shoplifted again.

Subsequent psychotherapists have made the diagnosis of Borderline Personality Disorder and have been divided as to whether Elaine merited the additional diagnosis of Antisocial Personality Disorder. There has, however, been increasing stability in her life, and she has been steadily employed for the past three years.

Ulcers

A 42-YEAR-OLD TRIAL LAWYER, married and the mother of two children, is referred for consultation by her gastroenterologist following her third hospitalization for duodenal ulcer disease. Her ulcer disease was first diagnosed four years ago, but an upper gastrointestinal series at that time showed evidence both of an active ulcer and of scarring secondary to previously healed ulcers. The gastroenterologist has requested the consultation for help in considering the possibility of surgery, prompted by the seriousness of the bleeding episode that precipitated the patient's last admission and by the fact that she seems to "ignore pain." His referral note indicates that he sees no clear connection between the bleeding episodes and the patient's highly stressful occupation.

The patient appears exactly on time for her appointment; she is neatly and conservatively dressed. She presents an organized, coherent account of her medical problem and denies any past or immediate family history of significant mental or physical disorder. She appears genuinely worried by her recent hospitalization, frightened by the prospect of surgery, and doubtful that speaking to a psychiatrist will produce any meaningful help. As she points out, "Ulcers are supposed to be related to stress, and that just isn't true with me." She then produces a detailed, written outline of her professional life over the past five years together with a chronology of her ulcer attacks. Indeed, there seems to be no temporal relationship between her attacks and several dramatic and highly taxing court cases in which she has appeared.

During the second evaluation session, the patient discusses her background. She is the oldest of four children and the clear favorite of her father, also an attorney. He had, and communicated, a strong expectation that she would become a lawyer and that she would succeed in this profession. The patient experiences herself as having fulfilled this expectation admirably, and displays a rare smile while describing several of her more dramatic courtroom triumphs. There is no evidence that she herself experiences these difficult cases as stressful; in fact, she seems to enjoy them.

She married a law-school classmate, who is also quite successful and who works noncompetitively in an unrelated legal field. Their marriage seems sound. As she begins to talk about her two sons, aged eight and four, the patient becomes noticeably more tense, and appears much more concerned and upset than usual while describing minor crises they have experienced with friends or in school. With great surprise, she discovers that the chronology of these crises corresponds clearly to five of her seven ulcer attacks, including all of those that resulted in hospitalization. She admits that despite being upset by her sons' problems, she finds it difficult to share her concerns about parenting with her husband or friends. At the end of the session, she comments: "You'd have made a good lawyer. I'm glad I'm not arguing against you." She herself suggests that some further sessions may be in order.

Discussion of "Ulcers"

In the past, certain disorders, such as duodenal ulcer, were assumed to be caused by emotional factors and were classified as Psychophysiologic Disorders. In DSM-III-R the corresponding category is called Psychological Factors Affecting Physical Condition, but this diagnosis is to be used only in cases in which a relationship between psychologically meaningful environmental stimuli and the initiation or exacerbation of a physical disorder can be demonstrated. This case attests to the fact that it is often difficult to demonstrate the role of psychological factors and that the precise nature of the psychologically meaningful stimuli frequently is not obvious.

The dramatic demonstration of the relationship between her children's minor crises and the exacerbations of this woman's ulcer justify the Axis I diagnosis of Psychological Factors Affecting Physical Condition. The presence of the duodenal ulcer is noted on Axis III.

DSM-III-R Diagnosis:

Axis I: 316.00 Psychological Factors Affecting Physical Condition (p. 334)

Axis III: Duodenal ulcer

Minister's Daughter

THE 22-YEAR-OLD DAUGHTER of a fundamentalist minister was brought for treatment by her parents because of their concern that over the last three years "she has become a different person." Although always somewhat "shy and quiet," their daughter apparently was "completely normal" and had gotten "O.K." grades in high school. Her troubles seemed to begin when she dropped out of college after the first semester and came home to live. Since that time she has held several jobs, but each for only a few weeks. Recently she has just been sitting at home, wanting only to go shopping, using her parents' money. She has no goals, has gained considerable weight, and insists on dressing like a little girl. On several occasions she has been verbally abusive to her parents, at least once to the extent that they had her jailed for a week when she threatened her father.

On examination, the patient was found to have flat affect, with occasional inappropriate smiling. She avoided eye contact. She rarely answered questions with more than "yes" or "no," but did admit to feeling "unhappy," which she said was only because "they won't give me what I want." There was no evidence of delusions, hallucinations, catatonic behavior, loosening of associations, or incoherence.

Discussion of "Minister's Daughter"

This clinical picture does not correspond to any specific DSM-III-R diagnosis, but strongly suggests the prodromal phase of Schizophrenia. The diagnosis of Schizophrenia cannot now be made since only one of the "A" criteria of Schizophrenia has been present, namely, flat affect. There is no clear evidence of psychotic features, although the patient may be experiencing delusions or hallucinations that she is not revealing.

In this ambiguous situation, we should recommend noting both Unspecified Mental Disorder (Nonpsychotic) and a statement that Schizophrenia needs to be ruled out. Perhaps in subsequent interviews the patient will acknowledge having psychotic symptoms, thus confirming the diagnosis of Schizophrenia.

Although schizoid and eccentric features are prominent in this patient, a diagnosis of Schizotypal Personality Disorder would not seem appropriate because this diagnosis implies enduring patterns of behavior rather than a marked change, which seems to be present in this case.

DSM-III-R Diagnosis:

Axis I: 300.90 Unspecified Mental Disorder (Nonpsychotic)
                    (p. 363)
                    R/O Schizophrenia

Back to Bed

MR. WINCHELL, A 49-YEAR-OLD unemployed account clerk, comes to a sleep clinic complaining of "falling asleep when I should be awake." For many years, two or three times a day, he suddenly feels overwhelmed by the need to go to sleep. This happens in "ridiculous" situations, such as in the midst of putting on his coat to go out. On these occasions he finds the nearest bed or couch on which he can lie down and fall asleep for a few hours. On awakening, he generally feels refreshed and alert for several hours. However, most of the time he feels tired and lethargic.

Because of these attacks of sleepiness, Mr. Winchell is unable to get through any lengthy social occasion. For instance, he left his granddaughter's birthday party after a few minutes, so that he could lie down and sleep. In the mornings his wife attempts to get him up before she goes to work, but often he feels too sleepy to get up and so remains in bed and quickly falls asleep again. Last month he lost his job because he was making so many mistakes and working so slowly, and this led to his now seeking help.

Mr. Winchell's wife reports that when he falls asleep, his whole body sometimes jerks. He is not aware of this. Neither Mr. Winchell nor his wife reports any other disturbance during his sleep, such as restlessness of his legs (as would be seen in the neurologic disorder myoclonus), or snoring (a common symptom of sleep apnea, i.e., recurrent periods of not breathing during sleep).

Family history reveals that his father once was markedly depressed, and also suffered from daytime sleepiness.

A previous consultation attributed his sleep difficulties to "depression." However, adequate trials of various antidepressants, including imipramine, amitriptyline, protriptyline, phenylzine, methylphenidate, and tranylcypromine, all failed to relieve his symptoms. He is now taking no drugs, but is taking megadoses of vitamins.

In the office Mr. Winchell looks much older than 49. He is unkempt and malodorous. He occasionally stops talking abruptly and looks down. He provides abundant answers, but fails to organize them into a coherent history. The interviewer is impressed with an undercurrent of hopelessness, which Mr. Winchell denies.

A month's chart of time spent in bed reveals that Mr. Winchell goes to bed any time between 4:00 PM and 4:00 AM and gets up any time from 6:00 AM to 2:00 PM. He sleeps for varying lengths of time. Most days he has a major sleep period of six hours or more, plus two sleep periods of shorter length. The major sleep periods shift randomly throughout the 24-hour day, but never occur between 2:00 PM and 4:00 PM, although there may be occasional naps during these hours.

Discussion of "Back to Bed"

Mr. Winchell suffers from a Sleep-Wake Schedule Disorder, a mismatch between the normal sleep-wake schedule that is induced by time cues from the person's environment controlling the person's circadian (circa = about, dies = day) rhythm. Because Mr. Winchell has a random or capricious pattern of sleep and wake times, in which there is no daily major sleep period, his Sleep-Wake Schedule Disorder is the Disorganized Type. This type of Sleep-Wake Schedule Disorder is seen in people who, for whatever reason, schedule their sleep hours haphazardly and snatch moments of sleep throughout the 24 hours. Some of these people may be unemployed, bedridden, or without scheduled obligations and nap off and on throughout the day.

The reader may suspect, as we do, that Mr. Winchell also suffers from a personality disturbance, but since we do not have any relevant information, we defer an Axis II diagnosis.

DSM-III-R Diagnosis:

Axis I: 307.45 **Sleep-Wake Schedule Disorder, Disorganized Type (p. 307)**
Axis II: 799.90 **Diagnosis Deferred**

Follow-up

Treatment consisted of supportive, informative, and directive discussions over a four-year period. The patient felt that regularly scheduled obligations would induce a regular arising time. Since he had been overwhelmed by the obligations of a daily job, he began hospital volunteer work two days a week, beginning at 9:00 AM. Over a two-year period this gradually expanded to four days a week. He attempted to do private contract work, e.g., to set up a new bookkeeping system for a store-owner, but found he often could not complete work that he started. He began to do the office work of a small automobile body shop, but was fired after three months for making many mistakes. Examination of this difficulty led to his getting a hearing aid, which enabled him to better understand telephone conversations.

Gradually the range of the patient's bedtimes narrowed to between 10:00 PM and noon. He quit napping at other times of day, and his diurnal sleepiness attacks stopped. Subsequently, his in-bed periods settled to times between midnight and 8:00 AM, with late sleeping on an occasional weekend morning.

Mr. Winchell got a regular half-time job with a billing company. During a six-month period, he arrived late or missed work on only six days. The company offered him a full-time job, but he felt that the fatigue he had previously suffered might return, and continued to work half time.

Barber's Daughter

MIMI, A 25-YEAR-OLD SINGLE WOMAN, came to the dermatology clinic of a university hospital with the complaint of increasing baldness of the crown of her scalp. Because no dermatologic disease could be identified, she was referred to the psychiatry department. She reported to the psychiatrist that since childhood, she had pulled out single hairs from the top of her head after "twirling" the strand of hair on a finger. The behavior was described as usually occurring when she was alone, tired, unoccupied, and ruminating over some unpleasant, stressful interaction. After plucking out the hair, she commonly inspected it and ran it across her lips. This pattern of hair-pulling was often repeated for several minutes at a time; Mimi did not find it painful—in fact, it often produced a sense of "relief." By wearing her hair up, Mimi had always managed to hide the bald area, but this had now become almost impossible. She indicated that seeing a woman with a wig at work had prompted her to seek medical attention; she feared her problem might soon require that she wear a wig.

Mimi complained of long-standing problems with her temper, drinking too much, and a series of unsatisfying relationships. She had had no previous psychiatric treatment and had never been hospitalized for any physical reason. She traced the hair-pulling to her childhood and associated it with absences of her mother from the home.

Further sessions revealed that the patient had sustained a series of traumatic events in her first decade, foremost among these being the death of her father from a malignancy. Despite her young age, she had a series of vivid recollections of him, especially associated with his illness. It was only after many sessions that she mentioned to the psychiatrist that her father had been a barber!

The patient regarded herself as a "clean, orderly person" who denied cleaning or compulsive rituals. She smoked a pack of cigarettes a day, and had tried speed and marijuana, but found that they each made her "paranoid." She had been working long hours in a family business, and was considering changing jobs.

Discussion of "Barber's Daughter"

Stroking and "fiddling with" the hair are common parts of the repertoire of social primates. In Mimi's case, however, hair-pulling had escalated to the point of marked alopecia. She was unable to control the impulse to pull out her own hair and achieved a sense of release by engaging in the behavior. This behavior meets the requirements for the diagnosis of Trichotillomania, a Disorder of Impulse Control Not Elsewhere Classified.

This diagnosis is a new entity in DSM-III-R; it is characterized by specific histopathologic changes of the hair follicle, which can be demonstrated by biopsy and distinguished from other causes of alopecia. The disorder usually begins in childhood, and commonly is associated with Mental Retardation and possibly with Schizophrenia, although not in this case.

DSM-III-R Diagnosis:

Axis I: 312.39 Trichotillomania (p. 328)

Follow-up

After an initial behavioral treatment program failed to modify the hair-pulling, the patient was seen in weekly therapy sessions that focused on her childhood trauma. In addition, she was given lithium carbonate, which is sometimes effective in the treatment of disorders of impulse control. With this treatment, the hair-pulling gradually stopped, and within ten months, Mimi had sufficient regrowth of hair so that she no longer needed to hide the crown area. The lithium was then discontinued without recurrence of the hair-pulling.

The Workaholic

THE PATIENT IS A 45-YEAR-OLD LAWYER who seeks treatment at his wife's insistence. She is fed up with their marriage: she can no longer tolerate his emotional coldness, rigid demands, bullying behavior, sexual disinterest, long work hours, and frequent business trips. The patient feels no particular distress in his marriage, and has agreed to the consultation only to humor his wife.

It soon develops, however, that the patient is troubled by problems at work. He is known as the hardest-driving member of a hard-driving law firm. He was the youngest full partner in the firm's history, and is famous for being able to handle many cases at the same time. Lately, he finds himself increasingly unable to keep up. He is too proud to turn down a new case, and too much of a perfectionist to be satisfied with the quality of work performed by his assistants. Displeased by their writing style and sentence structure, he finds himself constantly correcting their briefs, and therefore unable to stay abreast of his schedule. People at work complain that his attention to details and inability to delegate responsibility are reducing his efficiency. He has had two or three secretaries a year for 15 years. No one can tolerate working for him for very long because he is so critical of any mistakes made by others. When assignments get backed up, he cannot decide which to address first, starts making schedules for himself and his staff, but then is unable to meet them and works 15 hours a day. He finds it difficult to be decisive now that his work has expanded beyond his own direct control.

The patient discusses his children as if they were mechanical dolls, but also with a clear underlying affection. He describes his wife as a "suitable mate" and has trouble understanding why she is dissatisfied. He is punctilious in his manners and dress and slow and ponderous in his speech, dry and humorless, with a stubborn determination to get his point across.

The patient is the product of two upwardly mobile, extremely hardworking parents. He grew up feeling that he was never working hard enough, that he had much to achieve and very little time. He was a superior student, a "bookworm," awkward and unpopular in adolescent social pursuits. He has always been competitive and a high achiever. He has trouble relaxing on vacations, develops elaborate activities schedules for every family member, and becomes impatient and furious if they refuse to follow his plans. He likes sports, but has little time for them and refuses to play if he can't be at the top of his form. He is a ferocious competitor on the tennis courts and a poor loser.

Discussion of "The Workaholic"

Although the marital problem is the entry ticket, it is clear that this fellow has many personality traits that are quite maladaptive. He is cold, rigid, excessively perfectionistic, and preoccupied with details. He is indecisive, but insists that others do things his way; his interpersonal relationships suffer because of his excessive devotion to work. It is hard to imagine a more prototypic case of Obsessive Compulsive Personality Disorder! The additional notation of the V code Marital Problem is not made in this case since the patient's marital problems are clearly symptomatic of his mental disorder.

DSM-III-R Diagnosis:

Axis I: V71.09 No Diagnosis or Condition
Axis II: 301.40 Obsessive Compulsive Personality Disorder,
                  Moderate (p. 356)

Follow-up

The patient has been seen by a psychotherapist off and on for several years. He usually has come back into treatment when there was a crisis at work or at home, and dropped out after the crisis was resolved. He has made considerable progress in learning how to play, e.g., he now plays squash, and has bought a vacation home, where he spends frequent weekends. His relationships with his children have improved, and he is generally happier and more relaxed. Moreover, he has been extremely successful at work, and has made a great deal of money.

The Outdoorsman

A 78-YEAR-OLD, RETIRED lumber-company president sought help for the onset of a series of episodic attacks in which he experienced marked apprehension, restlessness, and the need to be outdoors to relieve his sense of discomfort. He described the most recent event as having occurred at 3:00 AM a week earlier: he awoke from sleep and felt "the walls were caving in" on him. He denied that this was related to dreaming and said that he was fully awake at the time. He arose, dressed, and went outside in subzero weather; once outside, he noted gradual improvement (but not full resolution) of his symptoms. Complete resolution took a full day.

In response to pointed questioning, the patient denied dyspnea, palpitations, choking sensations, paresthesias, and nausea. He reported trembling and some sweating, together with intermittent dizziness. He imagined that he would die (or lose consciousness) if he could not "escape" from his house. He spoke of a need "to be active."

On questioning, the patient recalled a similar series of attacks almost thirty years earlier following eye surgery for an injury. He described bilateral patching of his eyes and being confined to bed for days, with his head sandbagged to preclude movement. Once ambulatory, he had experienced these attacks for more than a year.

The patient denied recent sleep dysfunction, change in appetite or weight, crying spells, or decreased energy. He had been taking Valium, 5 to 10 mg, for approximately two months for feelings of increased nervousness and tension. He had noted mild memory problems of late.

Further inquiry established a problem with balance and intermittent pain in the right arm. The patient had stopped gardening the past summer because of his balance problem. On examination he was found to have a "beefy" red tongue (which he said was painful), difficulty with tandem gait and rapid alternating motion, and a mild intention tremor. He denied urinary incontinence.

Laboratory studies revealed a macrocytic anemia, and vitamin B_{12} deficiency. The patient was given B_{12} replacement, and his attacks did not recur.

Discussion of "The Outdoorsman"

This patient describes fairly typical, unexpected panic attacks, suggesting a diagnosis of Panic Disorder. However, careful physical examination and laboratory findings indicate the characteristic features of vitamin B_{12} deficiency. Since the panic attacks disappeared with treatment of the vitamin deficiency, it is reasonable to assume that the correct diagnosis is Organic Anxiety Disorder.

What is puzzling is the history of similar episodes of panic many years ago. In the absence of any known organic cause at that time, we assume that he then had Panic Disorder. The current Organic Anxiety Disorder may be a manifestation of an underlying vulnerability to panic attacks.

DSM-III-R Diagnosis:

Axis I: 294.80 Organic Anxiety Disorder (p. 114)
Axis II: V71.09 No Diagnosis or Condition
Axis III: Vitamin B$_{12}$ deficiency
Axis IV: Severity: 1 - None
Axis V: Current GAF: 0 (Inadequate information)
           Highest GAF past year: 0 (Inadequate information)

Supply Sergeant*

THE PATIENT, A BLACK MAN, was a supply sergeant in the military during the late 1950s. He was caught by the military police stealing a deodorant stick from the post exchange. The army, which had reason to suspect the sergeant of other thefts and was undeterred by constitutional restraints on search and seizure, went to his home and reclaimed every piece of army property the sergeant could not account for. The pile of supplies—uniforms, blankets, picks and shovels, cartons of canned goods, mess kits, etc.—could have filled a trailer truck. It was all photographed on the sergeant's front lawn, and that photo became part of his army medical file.

The army was determined to court-martial the sergeant; but he had been examined by a civilian psychiatrist, who decided that much of what was stolen was of no use to him and, on the basis of an understanding of the sergeant's psychodynamics, had diagnosed him as having Kleptomania. This civilian psychiatrist was prepared to testify at a courtmartial that the stealing was due to unconscious and irresistible impulses. Unhappy with the civilian psychiatrist's report, the army sent this man to be evaluated at an army hospital. There he was told repeatedly that anything he said could be used against him at the court-martial. The sergeant took the warning rather impassively, and the army psychiatrist set to work gathering a detailed history.

The sergeant, a very intelligent man, got caught up in telling the story of his life. He had grown up in a southern city during the days of racial segregation. A good and serious student from a deeply religious family, he had done well in school and had gone on to a small college, where he had studied literature. After graduation, despite his hopes and dreams, he had found no appropriate work, and eventually was drafted during the Korean War. After the war, seeing no alternatives, he became increasingly bitter. He was convinced that life had cheated him because he was black and that the army, in the work and position it gave him, continued to discriminate against him. Out of this sense of being cheated grew a sense of

---

*Taken from Stone A: (Presidential address): Conceptual ambiguity and morality in modern psychiatry. Am J Psychiatry 137:887-894, 1980.

entitlement, and he came to feel that he was justified in taking whatever he could, whenever he could. He had no sense of being impulsively driven to steal army property; instead, he stole with a sense of entitlement and reparation in protest against the racist world that had deprived him of his hopes.

It is not clear why, despite being warned, the sergeant told all this to the army psychiatrist. At any rate, he did; and the army psychiatrist, after puzzling over the diagnostic possibilities, which included Paranoid Personality and Depression, concluded that the sergeant did not have Kleptomania or any other mental disorder that might excuse him from responsibility. Subsequently, the army psychiatrist, trying to avoid the sergeant's eyes, testified to this at the court-martial. The sergeant sat there in his dress uniform with his medals, his wife, and their small children. He was sentenced to five years at hard labor.

Discussion of "Supply Sergeant"

This poignant case illustrates that some maladaptive behavior is not encompassed by the concept of mental disorder offered in standard classifications such as DSM-III-R. Although stealing by an adult may occur in many disorders (e.g., Schizophrenia, Dementia, Bipolar Disorder), there are only two in which it is likely to be the predominant symptom: Antisocial Personality Disorder and Kleptomania.

The civilian psychiatrist attempted to make a case for the diagnosis of Kleptomania. The army psychiatrist had no difficulty in demonstrating the absence of the characteristic signs of the disorder: Kleptomania is an Impulse Control Disorder in which the stealing represents a failure to resist an impulse; it is always preceded by an increasing sense of tension and is followed by the experience of pleasure or release. In this case the sergeant "had no sense of being impulsively driven to steal army property; instead, he stole with a sense of entitlement and reparation in protest against the racist world that had deprived him of his hopes." A diagnosis of Antisocial Personality Disorder would make no sense in view of the absence of any childhood history of antisocial behavior, the sergeant's good work and family functioning in adulthood, and the lack of a pervasive pattern of adult antisocial behavior.

There is a suggestion that this man stole some things that he did not need and that the extent of his stealing probably invited his being caught. In addition, once caught, he made no attempt to protect himself either by distorting his story to lend credence to the diagnosis of Kleptomania or by refusing to cooperate with the army psychiatrist. All this indicates a self-destructive, and therefore maladaptive, aspect to his behavior.

Does the maladaptive nature of his behavior indicate a mental disorder—albeit unspecified—since it does not correspond to any of the specific mental disorders included in the DSM-III-R classification? To classify it as such would so broaden the concept of mental disorder that virtually all criminal acts (murder, rape, grand larceny) could be interpreted as symptoms of mental disorder. There is no doubt that careful psychological study of any person who has engaged in a criminal act would reveal the psychological origins of the maladaptive behavior—in this case, the sergeant's sense of entitlement as a reaction to his life in a racist society.

DSM-III-R does provide a code for indicating that antisocial behavior in an adult is the focus of attention, but is not due to a mental disorder—the V code Adult Antisocial Behavior.

DSM-III-R Diagnosis:

Axis I: V71.01 Adult Antisocial Behavior (p. 359)

Threatening Voices

A 44-YEAR-OLD UNEMPLOYED MALE who lived alone in a single-room-occupancy hotel was brought to the emergency room by police, to whom he had gone for help, complaining that he was frightened by hearing voices of men in the street below his window talking about him and threatening him with harm. When he looked out the window, the men had always "disappeared."

The patient had a 20-year history of almost daily alcohol use, was commonly "drunk" each day, and often had experienced the "shakes" on awakening. On the previous day he had reduced his intake to one pint of vodka, because of gastrointestinal distress. He was fully alert and oriented on mental status examination.

Discussion of "Threatening Voices"

Vivid auditory hallucinations that develop shortly after the reduction in heavy ingestion of alcohol in a person who apparently has Alcohol Dependence indicate Alcohol Hallucinosis. This is distinguished from Alcohol Withdrawal Delirium by the absence of a disturbance in attention.

The additional diagnosis of Alcohol Dependence is made because of a long pattern of daily heavy alcohol use, inability to work because of alcohol use, and frequent withdrawal symptoms (experiencing morning "shakes"). Alcohol Hallucinosis apparently develops only in people with a long history of Alcohol Dependence.

DSM-III-R Diagnosis:

Axis I: 291.30 Alcohol Hallucinosis (p. 132)
           303.91 Alcohol Dependence, Severe (p. 167)

Fleas

MR. WALLACE, A FIT-LOOKING MAN of 70, consulted a dermatologist, complaining of being infested with fleas for about a year. The dermatologist found no evidence of infestation and referred him for psychiatric consultation. Although very angry about this, the patient followed through on the referral and gave the following history.

About a year previously, he had bought a canary and soon noticed that it had fleas. He applied an insecticide, but the fleas "attacked" him and "invaded" his house. He washed his clothes repeatedly, applied many lotions, and saw a number of physicians, but nothing helped. He insisted he could see the fleas. He was distressed and too ashamed to see his friends, so he had become almost completely isolated.

Mr. Wallace had enjoyed good health until two years before, when he had had a severe myocardial infarction. He had made a good recovery, and kept himself active. He had given up heavy pipe-smoking at that time. He had always been a moderate drinker. There was no personal or family history of emotional problems. He had married as a young man, but his wife had deserted him, and he had lived alone for many years.

When interviewed, Mr. Wallace looked considerably younger than his stated age and was alert and friendly, though he became angry when talking about the "incompetent" doctors who had failed to cure him and bristled when asked if the infestation could possibly be due to his imagination. His sensorium and cognitive functions were normal; his mood was essentially normal except for some anxiety and, at times, anger. His basic personality appeared stable. His conviction about the infestation was unshakeable, but there was no evidence of other false beliefs.

Discussion of "Fleas"

It was unclear whether the insects Mr. Wallace "saw" were the result of delusional misinterpretations of normal visual stimuli or visual hallucinations with a delusional explanation. In any case, his primary symptom is a somatic delusion. Since it is actually possible to be infested with fleas, the delusion is not bizarre. The persistence of nonbizarre somatic delusions in the absence of other psychotic symptoms (e.g., prominent hallucinations, incoherence), a mood syndrome, or a known organic cause indicates Delusional Disorder, Somatic Type.

DSM-III-R Diagnosis:

Axis I: 297.10 Delusional Disorder, Somatic Type (p. 202)

Follow-up

Mr. Wallace reluctantly agreed to take an antipsychotic medication, pimozide, though at one point he accused the psychiatrist of "only wanting to dope me to make me forget the fleas." His condition gradually improved, but it became apparent that he was only partially complying with treatment. He was subsequently admitted to a hospital, where he was stabilized and became symptom free on 4 mg of pimozide daily. He remained on that dose for six months, then insisted on stopping the drug because he saw no reason to continue taking it. One year later, he remained cheerful and symptom free.

Bruised

A 25-YEAR-OLD FEMALE GRADUATE STUDENT asked for a consultation because of depression and marital discord. The patient had been married for five years, during which time both she and her husband were in school. During the past three years, her academic performance had been consistently better than his, and she attributed their frequent, intense arguments to this. She noted that she experienced a feeling of sexual excitement when her husband screamed at her or hit her in a rage. Sometimes she would taunt him until he had sexual intercourse with her in a brutal fashion, as if she were being raped. She experienced the brutality and sense of being punished as sexually exciting.

One year before the consultation, the patient had found herself often ending arguments by storming out of the house. On one such occasion she went to a "singles bar," picked up a man, and got him to slap her as part of their sexual activity. She found the "punishment" sexually exciting and subsequently fantasized about being beaten during masturbation to orgasm. The patient then discovered that she enjoyed receiving physical punishment at the hands of strange men more than any other type of sexual stimulus. In a setting in which she could be whipped or beaten, all aspects of sexual activity, including the quality of orgasms, were far in excess of anything she had previously experienced.

This sexual preference was not the reason for the consultation, however. She complained that she could not live without her husband, yet could not live with him. She had suicidal fantasies stemming from the fear that he would leave her.

She recognized that her sexual behavior was dangerous to herself and felt mildly ashamed of it. She was unaware of any possible reasons for its emergence and was not sure she wished treatment for "it," because it gave her so much pleasure.

Discussion of "Bruised"

Fantasies of being humiliated, beaten, bound, or otherwise made to suffer may increase sexual excitement for some people whose sexual life is in all other respects unremarkable. However, when sexually arousing fantasies of this kind are acted out (as in this case) or are markedly distressing, the diagnosis of Sexual Masochism is made.

With the limited information available, it is not possible to determine if this patient's marital problem is primarily: (1) a symptom of the Sexual Masochism (Does she provoke arguments in order to be sexually aroused?); (2) a symptom of a Personality Disorder; or (3) a problem unrelated to a mental disorder for which the V code Marital Problem would be appropriate.

DSM-III-R Diagnosis:

Axis I: 302.83 Sexual Masochism, Mild (p. 287)

The Wreck

THE PATIENT IS A 40-YEAR-OLD, married carpenter who, approximately two years previously, was involved in a motor vehicle accident that "totalled" his car. He sustained no head trauma or loss of consciousness. He was hospitalized for one day with a diagnosis of cervical strain and inflammation of the spinal nerve to the trapezius muscle. A course of physical therapy and anti-inflammatory medication was prescribed.

In the months that followed the accident, the patient experienced occasional involuntary thoughts of it, had trouble falling asleep, irritability, anxious mood, impaired concentration, and increased appetite, with a 30 lb weight gain. These symptoms tended to wax and wane over the subsequent months. The patient suffered no avoidance behavior, numbing of general responsiveness, or loss of sexual interest, and he continued to socialize with his friends. He drove an automobile and was comfortable as a passenger in a car. However, there was some transient anxiety when he drove past the accident site.

The patient's orthopedic injuries prevented him from returning to work as a carpenter, but he continued to work actively at various "side" businesses. His marital life began to deteriorate as he became increasingly irritable at home. Despite these difficulties, he was able to enjoy himself on a three-day camping trip with some friends.

After approximately two years of physical therapy, it was decided that surgery was necessary. The patient tolerated the surgery well, but the procedure left him with a temporary disability (a restriction in range of motion and loss of strength) in his right shoulder and arm. As soon as he returned home, his emotional status changed dramatically. In addition to concerns about the ultimate outcome of the surgery, he began thinking about the accident continually, despite efforts to avoid such thoughts. He was unable to sleep, in large part because of terrifying dreams that would awaken him and leave him unable to return to sleep for one to two hours. He lost interest in sex and reported that he now "did not care about anybody or anything." He developed an exaggerated startle response to loud noises, such as the honking of a horn or the slamming of a door.

The patient's postsurgery disability prevented him from driving. When he was a passenger in a car, he became acutely anxious, broke out in a sweat, felt nauseated, and often gave vent to abusive verbal outbursts. He had a similar response when passing an accident on the road. He was unable to concentrate on his side businesses. His marital situation deteriorated, because of an increasing sense of emotional isolation from his wife, to the point of a planned divorce. "I am a wreck," he reported.

Discussion of "The Wreck"

In considering the diagnosis in this case, it is necessary to distinguish the symptoms the patient experienced in the months following the trauma of the accident from the more dramatic symptoms that developed immediately following surgery two years after the accident. In the months following the accident, the patient exhibited many nonspecific anxiety symptoms, such as occasional thoughts of the accident, trouble sleeping, and impaired concentration. A depressive disorder is apparently ruled out by the absence of depressed mood or loss of interest or pleasure.

For reasons that are not clear, following the surgery the patient developed symptoms of reexperiencing the trauma of the accident (thinking about the accident continually, having terrifying dreams of the accident, and distress at being a passenger in a moving car), avoidance of stimuli associated with the accident (trying not to think about it), numbing of general responsiveness (loss of interest in everything and feeling estranged from his wife), and symptoms of increased arousal (difficulty staying asleep, exaggerated startle response, difficulty concentrating, outbursts of anger). This clinical picture following a traumatic event that is outside the range of usual human experience and that would be markedly distressing to almost anyone is characteristic of Post-traumatic Stress Disorder. What is unusual in this case is that the full clinical picture did not develop immediately or soon after the trauma. For that reason, it is specified as Delayed Onset.

DSM-III-R Diagnosis:

Axis I: 309.89 Post-traumatic Stress Disorder, Delayed Onset (p. 250)

Follow-up

After six weeks of symptoms, the patient sought assistance from his orthopedic surgeon, who made a psychiatric referral. The psychiatrist treated the patient with an antidepressant, imipramine (175 mg/day), and supportive psychotherapy, which resulted in prompt control of his symptoms. During the next two months, his postsurgical disability resolved so that he had full range of motion and nearly full strength. Attempts were made to reduce the dosage of imipramine, but the dreams, sleep disturbances, and high level of anxiety promptly returned.

Sickly

A 38-YEAR-OLD MARRIED WOMAN came to a mental health clinic with the chief complaint of depression. In the last month she had been feeling depressed, suffered from insomnia, frequently wept, and been aware of poor concentration and diminished interest in activities.

The patient relates that she was sickly as a child, and has been depressed since childhood because her father deserted the family when she was approximately ten. Apparently, she was taken to a doctor for this, and the family doctor recommended that her mother give the patient a little wine before each meal. Her adolescence was unremarkable, although she describes herself as having been shy. She graduated from high school at age 17 and began working as a clerk and bookkeeper at a local department store. She married at about the same time, but the marriage was not a success: she had frequent arguments with her husband, in part related to her sexual indifference and pain during intercourse.

At age 19 she began to drink heavily, with binges and morning shakes, which she would relieve by having a drink as soon as she got up in the morning. She felt guilty that she was not caring adequately for her children because of her drinking. At 21 she was admitted to a local mental hospital, where she was diagnosed as suffering from alcoholism and depression. She was treated with antidepressants. After discharge, she kept drinking almost continually; when she was 29, she was again hospitalized, this time on the alcohol treatment unit. Since then she has remained abstinent. She has subsequently been admitted to psychiatric hospitals for a mixture of physical and depressive symptoms, and once was treated with a course of electroconvulsive therapy, which produced little relief.

The patient describes nervousness since childhood; she also spontaneously admits being sickly since her youth with a succession of physical problems doctors often indicated were due to her nerves or depression. She, however, believes that she has a physical problem that has not yet been discovered by the doctors. Besides nervousness, she has chest pain, and has been told by a variety of medical consultants that she has a "nervous heart." She often goes to doctors for abdominal pain, and has been diagnosed as having a "spastic colon." She has seen chiropractors and osteopaths for backaches, for pains in the extremities, and for anesthesia of her fingertips. Three months ago, she experienced vomiting, chest pain, and abdominal pain, and was admitted to a hospital for a hysterectomy. Since the hysterectomy she has had repeated anxiety attacks, fainting spells that she claims are associated with unconsciousness that lasts more than thirty minutes, vomiting, food intolerance, weakness, and fatigue. She has had surgery for an abscess of the throat.

The patient is one of five children. She was reared by her mother after her father left. Her father was said to have been an alcoholic, who died at age 53 of liver cancer. Despite a difficult childhood financially, the patient graduated from high school and worked two years. She tried to work a second time, but was forced to quit because of her sickliness. Her husband is said to be an alcoholic who has had some periods of work instability. They have argued about sex and finances. They have five children, ranging in age from 2 to 20.

The patient currently admits to feeling depressed, but thinks that it is all because her "hormones were not straightened out." She is still looking for a medical explanation for her physical and psychological problems.

Discussion of "Sickly"

It is first necessary to separate the immediate problem that prompted the patient's current consultation (depression) from her long-standing problems (physical symptoms and excessive use of alcohol). She is apparently now having a recurrence of a Major Depressive Episode (one month of depressed mood, accompanied by diminished interest, insomnia, and poor concentration). Note that although the patient is one short of the required number of criteria for a Major Depressive Episode (i.e., four instead of the required five), this disturbance is considered to be a current Major Depressive Episode since there have apparently been several previous Major Depressive Episodes, some severe enough to require hospitalization. The mood disturbance is therefore diagnosed as Major Depression, Recurrent, Mild.

Nearly all of the patient's many physical symptoms that have plagued her for so many years are apparently without an organic basis. This is consistent with the two "physical" diagnoses mentioned: "nervous heart" and "spastic colon." This suggests a Somatoform Disorder, and the large number of symptoms involving multiple organ systems suggests Somatization Disorder. The cardinal feature of this disorder, which this patient has, is a belief that one is sickly, beginning before the age of 30 and persisting for at least several years. In addition, the diagnosis requires 13 symptoms that the patient reports cause her to see a physician, take medicine, or otherwise alter her life pattern. Let us count them: sexual indifference, pain during intercourse, chest pain, abdominal pain, backaches, extremity pain, vomiting, periods of "unconsciousness," food intolerance, weakness, and diarrhea (colitis). Since we count only 11, the diagnosis is provisionally made, on the assumption that the patient almost certainly had others not noted, since the characteristic picture of Somatization Disorder is clearly present.

The patient has also had periods of heavy alcohol consumption, accompanied by "morning shakes," which she treated by drinking more alcohol, and difficulty functioning as a mother. Since it is mentioned that she was unable to care for her children because of her drinking, we can infer that she had frequent intoxication or withdrawal symptoms when expected to fulfill her role obligations as a mother but continued to use alcohol despite the problems it caused. These problems, plus evidence of withdrawal, all indicate a diagnosis of Alcohol Dependence. Since the patient is apparently not currently having difficulties attributable to alcohol use, the course is noted as "in Remission." (We prefer "in Remission" to not noting the history of Alcohol Dependence because of the high probability of relapse in this case.) The order in which these diagnoses have been discussed indicates their order as listed on Axis I and reflects their relative importance as factors determining the current evaluation.

On Axis II we are tempted to note Personality Disorder Not

Otherwise Specified (Provisional) to indicate our suspicion that the patient's pattern of relating to herself and others (apart from the Axis I diagnoses) is maladaptive. However, the chronic and pervasive psychopathology described in this case can be entirely accounted for by her Axis I diagnoses. Therefore, we note "Diagnosis deferred" on Axis II.

On Axis III we should list those current physical symptoms of the Somatization Disorder that might require clinical attention or treatment in their own right, such as vomiting and fainting. (The DSM-III-R discussion of Axis III does not include listing physical symptoms that are part of the Axis I diagnosis. Nevertheless, we think it will prove clinically useful to note such symptoms according to the above principle, despite the apparent redundancy.)

This woman's life situation has probably always been associated with considerable stress. Arguments with her husband and his alcoholism and work instability are mentioned, indicating the presence of some enduring stressors. In addition, she is noted to have had a hysterectomy three months earlier, which may well have played a role in precipitating a recurrence of her Major Depression. Since this acute stressor appears to be the predominant factor associated with the Major Depression, this stressor is listed on Axis IV, with a severity rating of 4—Severe. (A serious physical illness is given as an example of a rating of 5—Extreme, but this seems too high a rating in this case, given the patient's history of chronic physical illness.)

Owing to her inability to work because of her "sickliness" and the interpersonal problems with her husband, a GAF rating of 50 is given on Axis V for both current functioning and the highest level of functioning in the past year, to indicate serious impairment in her occupational functioning. Note that her depressive symptoms would put her in the 51-60 range, but her poor occupational functioning because of her Somatization Disorder warrants a score in the next lower range.

DSM-III-R Diagnosis:

Axis I: **296.31 Major Depression, Recurrent, Mild (p. 222)**
          300.81 Somatization Disorder (Provisional) (p. 263)
          303.90 Alcohol Dependence, in Remission (p. 167)
Axis II: **799.90 Diagnosis deferred**
Axis III: **Vomiting, fainting**
Axis IV: **Psychosocial stressors: recent hysterectomy**
          Severity: 4 - Severe (predominantly acute event)
Axis V: **Current GAF: 50**
          Highest GAF past year: 50

Coffee Break

A 35-YEAR-OLD SECRETARY sought consultation for "anxiety attacks." A thorough history revealed that the attacks occurred in mid-to-late afternoon, when she became restless, nervous, and easily excited and sometimes was noted to be flushed, sweating, and, according to co-workers, "talking a mile a minute." In response to careful questioning, she acknowledged drinking five or six cups of coffee each day before the time the attacks usually occurred.

Discussion of "Coffee Break"

The temporal association of heavy coffee drinking and the anxiety symptoms indicates the etiological significance of caffeine. In the literature this has been referred to as Caffeinism. In DSM-III-R this organic brain syndrome is diagnosed when symptoms such as restlessness, nervousness, flushed face, rambling speech, and excitability are present because of the effect of recent ingestion of caffeine, usually in excess of 250 mg (a single cup of coffee has 100–150 mg; tea is about half as strong; a glass of cola is about a third as strong).

Although the symptoms suggest an Anxiety Disorder, such a diagnosis is not made when the disturbance is due to a known specific organic factor.

DSM-III-R Diagnosis:

Axis I: 305.90 Caffeine Intoxication (p. 139)

Paranoid and Dangerous

T RACY SHAW, AGE 32, OVERWEIGHT and wild-looking, was brought to the psychiatric emergency room by the police after she had furiously pushed a chair into a full-length mirror in the principal's office of her child's school, shattering it. The psychiatrist who examined her described her as "paranoid and dangerous to others" and recommended immediate hospitalization by two-physician certification, if she refused to admit herself voluntarily.

Ms. Shaw refused voluntary admission. She stated that her suspicions concerning her child's unfair treatment in school were well founded and that she would harm no one. She acknowledged that she was particularly irritable and angry because she was premenstrual. Her husband supported her decision and assumed responsibility for her and for bringing her back to see the psychiatrist the next day. That evening her menses began.

When Ms. Shaw saw the psychiatrist the next day, she appeared to be a "different" person. She was relaxed, her anger and irritability had dissipated, and she displayed a sense of humor. However, her conviction that the school principal owed her an explanation of his unfair treatment of her child remained.

Ms. Shaw gave a history of monthly premenstrual symptoms beginning at menarche, but worsening since her twenties. The symptoms were not the same every month. Some months she would become depressed, with thoughts of suicide; other months she would crave chocolate and gain 5–10 pounds in one week; some months she would break out in hives; and there were months when she was symptom-free. The symptoms were always predictable in their timing, occurring the week before her menses and remitting with their onset.

Ms. Shaw was the oldest daughter of a chronically depressed and fearful mother and an alcoholic businessman father. Before marriage, she was the caretaker of her family. Her mother recovered significantly during Ms. Shaw's adolescence, only to fail rapidly and die when her daughter left home and married after high school.

Currently, Ms. Shaw is the mother of four grade-school children and, in addition, has primary responsibility for a sibling with alcoholism who is dying of cancer, as well as for her handicapped husband, who has been severely depressed and vocationally incapacitated since surgery one and a half years ago. She lives with her in-laws. Both her husband and his parents have significant alcohol problems.

Ms. Shaw is still the family caretaker. "I can't live with myself unless I do it all. I feel guilty if I do something for myself." She can cope with the demands of her life and is not usually depressed, except during her premenstruum, when "the whole world closes in" and she feels "pulled down."

Discussion of "Paranoid and Dangerous"

The uncontrolled behavior that led to Ms. Shaw's psychiatric evaluation suggested to the psychiatrist that she was psychotic and potentially dangerous to others and therefore in need of involuntary hospitalization. Fortunately, Ms. Shaw was able to convince the psychiatrist that she was not psychotic, but that she suffered from episodic difficulties that always occurred in the few days before her menses and remitted within a few days after their onset. Her symptoms vary from cycle to cycle and include depression, anger, irritability, and overeating. Between episodes she is apparently completely free of such symptoms.

This pattern of recurrent dysphoric episodes beginning in the premenstrual phase and remitting with the onset of menses suggests Late Luteal Phase Dysphoric Disorder, a diagnosis that is not in the official classification, but is included in an appendix to DSM-III-R. In order to confirm this diagnosis, it would be necessary to have Ms. Shaw make daily ratings of her mood and behavior for at least two cycles in order to confirm her impression that the changes are always associated with the menstrual cycle. In addition, it would be necessary to establish that at least five associated symptoms, such as decreased interest in usual activities, marked lack of energy, sleep disturbance and other physical symptoms, have been present for most of the time during each symptomatic late luteal phase.

DSM-III-R Diagnosis:

Axis I: 300.90 **Unspecified Mental Disorder (Late Luteal Phase Dysphoric Disorder) (Provisional) (p. 369)**

Car Salesman

A 29-YEAR-OLD CAR SALESMAN was referred by his current girl friend, a psychiatric nurse, who suspected he had a Mood Disorder, even though the patient was reluctant to admit that he might be a "moody" person. According to him, since the age of 14 he has experienced repeated alternating cycles that he terms "good times and bad times." During a "bad" period, usually lasting four to seven days, he oversleeps 10-14 hours daily, lacks energy, confidence, and motivation—"just vegetating," as he puts it. Often he abruptly shifts, characteristically upon waking up in the morning, to a three-to-four-day stretch of overconfidence, heightened social awareness, promiscuity, and sharpened thinking—"Things would flash in my mind." At such times he indulges in alcohol to enhance the experience, but also to help him sleep. Occasionally the "good" periods last seven to ten days, but culminate in irritable and hostile outbursts, which often herald the transition back to another period of "bad" days. He admits to frequent use of marijuana, which he claims helps him "adjust" to daily routines.

In school, A's and B's alternated with C's and D's, with the result that the patient was considered a bright student whose performance was mediocre overall because of "unstable motivation." As a car salesman his performance has also been uneven, with "good days" canceling out the "bad days"; yet even during his "good days," he is sometimes perilously argumentative with customers and loses sales that appeared sure. Although considered a charming man in many social circles, he alienates friends when he is hostile and irritable. He typically accumulates social obligations during the "bad" days and takes care of them all at once on the first day of a "good" period.

Discussion of "Car Salesman"

This patient has had numerous periods during the last two years in which he has had some symptoms characteristic of both the depressive and the manic syndromes. Characteristic of the "good days" are overconfidence, increased activity, and poor judgment (promiscuity). These periods come perilously close to meeting the criteria for Manic Episodes, but they are not sufficiently severe to cause *marked* impairment in social or occupational functioning, which is required for the diagnosis of a manic episode. Similarly, the "bad days," characterized by oversleeping and lack of energy, confidence, and motivation, are not of sufficient severity and duration to meet the criteria for a major depressive episode. Moreover, the brief cycles follow each other irregularly though chronically. Therefore, the appropriate diagnosis is Cyclothymia.

If there were, in addition, a history of a clear-cut Manic Episode, the *additional* diagnosis of superimposed Bipolar Disorder would be made. If there were a clear history of a Major Depressive Episode, then the *additional* diagnosis of Bipolar Disorder Not Otherwise Specified would be made because the presence of hypomanic episodes would preclude a diagnosis of a depressive disorder.

Additional diagnoses of Alcohol Abuse and Cannabis Abuse are suspected, but insufficient information is available to make them.

DSM-III-R Diagnosis:

Axis I: 301.13 Cyclothymia, Severe (p. 227)

Follow-up

This patient was stabilized on lithium, married the nurse, and did well for a year. He then ceased taking the lithium on his own and had several extramarital affairs that led to his separation and divorce. He was then forced to seek psychiatric help upon his ex-wife's insistence that resumption of treatment with lithium be a precondition for reconciliation. When next seen the patient was in the midst of a moderately severe Major Depressive Episode. Lithium was reinstituted. The couple remarried three months later, and the patient did reasonably well when last seen.

Unfaithful Wife

A WOMAN IN HER LATE FORTIES took an overdose of drugs. When she recovered, she confided to her family doctor that during the previous 18 months, her husband had become increasingly jealous and accusatory. Recently his accusations had become totally irrational, and he was saying that she had multiple lovers, that she got out of bed at night to go to them, and that she was communicating with them by lights and mirrors. Wrong-number telephone calls were "evidence" that men were contacting her, and he believed that cars passing the house at night flashed their headlights as a signal to her. He put tape on the windows and doors, nailed doors shut, and closely measured the location of every piece of furniture. Any change resulted in a tirade about her unfaithfulness. He refused to accept any food or cigarettes from her. During this time her husband did not physically assault her, and their sexual activity remained at its usual level; but he appeared increasingly distressed and haggard, and had lost 15 pounds.

The wife was so wretched about her husband's behavior that she considered leaving him, but was afraid he might become violent. She admitted her overdose was a "cry for help."

The husband was referred for psychiatric assessment and complied willingly. He gave an account similar to his wife's, but with total conviction about her infidelity. Despite his vehemence and his belief in all the various pieces of "evidence," he seemed to have some awareness that something was wrong with him. An interview with a daughter who lived at home corroborated her mother's innocence and her father's irrationality.

The marriage had been stable until onset of this disorder, though the patient had drunk heavily as a young man and sometimes assaulted his wife. His heavy drinking and violent behavior had ceased in his mid-thirties and he had generally been a good husband and provider. He had never used street drugs at any time. His wife described him as always being "pig-headed," but he was not normally unduly argumentative and had never previously evinced jealousy. The patient had attended school up to grade 7; he was probably of low average intelligence. His family history included many relatives with alcoholism, but no other mental disorders.

Discussion of "Unfaithful Wife"

All of this man's difficulties stem from his unfounded belief that his wife has been unfaithful. It hardly needs to be stated that this is not a bizarre delusion. The persistence of a nonbizarre delusion of jealousy, in the absence of other psychotic symptoms (e.g., prominent hallucinations, incoherence), a mood disorder, or a known organic cause, makes the diagnosis Delusional Disorder, Jealous Type.

DSM-III-R Diagnosis:

Axis I: 297.10 Delusional Disorder, Jealous Type (p. 202)

Follow-up

The patient was unexpectedly compliant with treatment and started on a neuroleptic antipsychotic drug, pimozide, which he continues to take three years later. On two occasions this drug has been withdrawn; but after a week or two he reports, "I'm beginning to get funny ideas about the wife again," and he voluntarily resumes the medication. Not long after commencing treatment with the neuroleptic, he had an episode of postpsychotic depression, which responded to a tricyclic antidepressant in addition to the pimozide. The antidepressant was subsequently withdrawn, and the mood disorder has not recurred.

Fraulein Von Willebrand

A 29-YEAR-OLD FEMALE laboratory technician was admitted to the medical service via the emergency room because of bloody urine. The patient said she was being treated for lupus erythematosus by a physician in a different city. She also mentioned that she had had Von Willebrand's disease (a rare hereditary blood disorder) as a child. On the third day of her hospitalization, a medical student mentioned to the resident that she had seen this patient several weeks before at a different hospital in the area, where the patient had been admitted for the same problem. A search of the patient's belongings revealed a cache of anticoagulant medication. When confronted with this information, she refused to discuss the matter and hurriedly signed out of the hospital against medical advice.

Discussion of "Fraulein Von Willebrand"

The circumstances (bloody urine, possession of anticoagulants, history of repeated hospitalizations, leaving the hospital when confronted) strongly suggest that this patient's symptoms were intentionally produced and were not genuine symptoms of a physical order.

The differential diagnosis of simulated illness is between Factitious Disorder and Malingering. From what is known of this case, it would appear that there are no external incentives for the behavior, and that the woman's goal is only to assume the patient role. Therefore, the diagnosis is Factitious Disorder with Physical Symptoms.

If the facts had suggested, for example, that her goal was primarily to get disability payments, this would have indicated the act of malingering (coded in section V, Codes for Conditions Not Attributable to a Mental Disorder That Are a Focus of Attention or Treatment) rather than a mental disorder.

DSM-III-R Diagnosis:

**Axis I: 301.51 Factitious Disorder with Physical Symptoms
                   (p. 318)**

Martial Arts

MR. MARSHALL, A 32-YEAR-OLD, single, white man, was referred for psychiatric evaluation by juvenile court prior to termination of his parental rights for his 7-year-old son, Richard. Mr. Marshall had been involved with child protective services and in dependency and neglect proceedings for seven years. During that time he had one charge of physical abuse of children other than his son, and two charges of spouse abuse brought against him. He has had no other legal involvement.

Child protective services initially worked with Mr. and Mrs. Marshall when their son was living with them. However, by the time he was three, Richard was afraid of water, not toilet-trained, extremely withdrawn, unable to play, and had bilateral optic nerve damage, which was thought to be related to repeated, severe shaking as an infant. He is now legally blind. At the age of three, Richard was placed in foster care. It was discovered that his father had locked him in closets for long periods of time and had prevented his mother from caring for him.

Since Richard has been in foster care, his father has been assessed for child support. Mr. Marshall is regularly employed, but has paid none of the child support and has not bought any gifts for his son at any time. He is known to have some discretional income, which he tends to use to buy magazines, such as *Soldier of Fortune*, or to otherwise indulge his continuing interest in the martial arts. He is fascinated by guns, knives, and other weapons, which he describes as "tools of status." He enjoys these "toys" and finds that they "make his adrenaline flow." He fantasizes becoming a mercenary and joining the Foreign Legion.

Mr. Marshall freely admits beating up two children, aged six and seven, for whom he was babysitting, and giving them bruises and a black eye. He believes this was justified because one of the two children lied to him. He addresses his son as "brat" or "rug rat" during visits. In front of Richard he describes in great detail his own abusive upbringing and plays with sharp knives during these discussions. When he was sent to parenting classes to improve his relationship with Richard, he distracted the class by telling long, dramatic stories about various devious deeds, such as breaking the necks of geese in the city park. He was eventually asked to leave parenting classes.

Mr. Marshall met his common-law wife when she was working in a massage parlor. She attempted to leave him at various times, but he followed her whenever she moved out and caused such a disruption at her new place of residence that she was evicted. He also harassed her at work and threatened repeatedly that if she left him, he would get her fired. He did, in fact, precipitate her being fired on several occasions. He would call her workplace, telling her boss that he was a detective investigating her for embezzlement, fraud, or child abuse (all of these allegations were untrue). Shortly after she left him for the last time, Mr. Marshall called her workplace, leaving a message that he was a representative of the foster home where their son was staying and that Richard had been mortally injured in an auto accident (untrue). Mrs. Marshall eventually filed spouse abuse charges against him.

Mr. Marshall met a new girl friend at parenting class. He became abusive of this woman soon after moving in with her, and she filed charges against him. He continued to harass her, following her to work, calling her there, and being very disruptive. On one occasion he followed her into her workplace, cornered her in a room without windows, and "karate-chopped" at various supplies, saying that he would do the same to her. He did not actually touch her.

Mr. Marshall is the eldest of six step-siblings. He had no contact with his natural father. His stepfather was a career military man, and the family therefore moved frequently during Mr. Marshall's childhood. He denies observing any spouse abuse in his own home when he was growing up, but says that his stepfather had a violent temper and sometimes beat him for no reason. These beatings frequently resulted in bruises and cuts. Mr. Marshall became interested in karate at the age of 14, as a means of defending himself against his father.

Mr. Marshall obtained a B average in high school, and was involved in various sports activities. Nevertheless, he never felt he won acknowledgment or praise from his father. Following high school, Mr. Marshall attended college for two years, studying police science.

Mr. Marshall does not have a drug or alcohol problem, and there is no family history of drug or alcohol abuse. He is not aware of having been depressed at any time in his life, and has made no suicidal gestures. He feels unjustly treated by the child protective services and juvenile court. Although Social Services reports that he frightens the homemaker, the homemaker's supervisor, the social worker, and his own grandmother, he perceives himself as being picked on by child protective services.

He believes that the allegations against him are insignificant or false, and that he will eventually get custody of his son. He laughs when he describes being told that his son has significant visual problems and will never see well enough to drive.

During the interview, Mr. Marshall was somewhat demanding, attempting to manipulate meeting times for evenings or weekends. He was demeaning of the Social Services worker in this case and of his ex-wife, but not of the interviewer. Formal mental status testing indicated normal cognition, abstractions, concentration, and fund of general information, with poor judgment.

Discussion of "Martial Arts"

Mr. Marshall's long-standing pattern of cruel and aggressive behavior suggests the diagnosis of Antisocial Personality Disorder. However, there is no evidence of the childhood antecedents of that disorder—e.g., truancy, fighting, stealing, and conduct problems at school—that are required for the diagnosis.

As an adult, Mr. Marshall is physically cruel, humiliates and demeans people, uses harsh discipline, lies for the purpose of harming others, and is fascinated by weapons and violence. When this kind of behavior is directed toward many other people and is not for the purpose of sexual arousal (as in Sexual Sadism), the diagnosis of Sadistic Personality Disorder is appropriate.

Mental health professionals rarely encounter people with Sadistic Personality Disorder except when they are referred, as in this case, because of court proceedings in which they are accused of abusing a wife (in almost all cases they are men) or child. In forensic settings the condition is not rare, particularly among perpetrators of violent crimes against people. This diagnosis is not included in the official classification, but appears in an appendix to DSM-III-R.

DSM-III-R Diagnosis:

Axis I: V71.09 No Diagnosis or Condition on Axis I
Axis II: 301.90 Personality Disorder Not Otherwise Specified
          (Sadistic Personality Disorder) (p. 371)

Bridge Boy

A N 18-YEAR-OLD HIGH-SCHOOL SENIOR was brought to the emergency room by police after being picked up wandering in traffic on the Triborough Bridge. He was angry, agitated, and aggressive and talked of various people who were deliberately trying to "confuse" him by giving him misleading directions. His story was rambling and disjointed, but he admitted to the police officer that he had been using "speed." In the emergency room he had difficulty focusing his attention and had to ask that questions be repeated. He was disoriented as to time and place and was unable to repeat the names of three objects after five minutes. The family gave a history of the patient's regular use of "pep pills" over the past two years, during which time he was frequently "high" and did very poorly in school.

Discussion of "Bridge Boy"

The history of regular use of "pep pills" immediately raises the question of the presence of an Organic Brain Syndrome caused by amphetamine. Although persecutory delusions are present, the disorientation, attention disturbance, and increased psychomotor activity indicate a Delirium, which, because it involves a global cognitive disturbance, takes precedence over the diagnosis of an Amphetamine-induced Organic Delusional Disorder. For the same reason, a diagnosis of Amphetamine Intoxication is not made.

Although we do not have much information about his pattern of use of amphetamine, his regular use during the school day undoubtedly contributed to his poor school performance. Thus we make a provisional diagnosis of Amphetamine Dependence.

DSM-III-R Diagnosis:

Axis I: 292.81 Amphetamine-induced Delirium (p. 137)
          304.40 Amphetamine Dependence (Provisional) (p. 167)

On Stage

H ARRY IS A 33-YEAR-OLD MAN who lives in Seattle with his wife. He has been employed as a salesperson for an insurance company since graduating from college, where he majored in mathematics. He came to a private psychiatrist, recommended by a friend, complaining of "anxiety at work."

Harry describes himself as having been outgoing and popular

throughout his adolescence and young adulthood, with no serious problems until his third year of college. He then began to become extremely tense and nervous when studying for tests and writing papers. His heart would pound; his hands would sweat and tremble. Consequently, he often did not write the required papers and, when he did, would submit them after the date due. He could not understand why he was so nervous about doing papers and taking exams when he had always done well in these tasks in the past. As a result of his failure to submit certain papers and his late submission of others, his college grades were seriously affected.

Soon after graduation, Harry was employed as a salesperson for an insurance firm. His initial training (attending lectures, completing reading assignments) proceeded smoothly. However, as soon as he began to take on clients, his anxiety returned. He became extremely nervous when anticipating phone calls from clients. When his business phone rang, he would begin to tremble, and sometimes would not answer. Eventually, he avoided becoming anxious by not scheduling appointments and by not contacting clients whom he was expected to see.

When asked what it was about these situations that made him nervous, he said that he was concerned about what the client would think of him. "The client might sense that I am nervous and might ask me questions that I don't know the answers to, and I would feel foolish." As a result, he would repeatedly rewrite and reword sales scripts for telephone conversations because he was "so concerned about saying the right thing. I guess I'm just very concerned about being judged."

Although never unemployed, Harry estimates that he has been functioning at only 20% of his work capacity, which his employer tolerates because a salesman is paid only on a commission basis. For the last several years, Harry has had to borrow large sums of money to make ends meet.

Although financial constraints have been a burden, Harry and his wife entertain guests at their home regularly and enjoy socializing with friends at picnics, parties, and formal affairs. Harry lamented, "It's just when I'm expected to do something. Then, it's like I'm on stage, all alone, with everyone watching me."

Discussion of "On Stage"

Harry's problem is crippling anxiety whenever he feels that he is performing. In college this happened when he had to write papers or take exams. At work it happens whenever he has to talk to clients, either on the phone or face to face. What he fears is that people will observe his anxiety and make him "feel foolish." Significantly, he has no anxiety in social situations that he does not define as "being on stage," and he has never experienced sudden attacks of panic in situations that he did not expect to cause him anxiety (as in the panic attacks of Panic Disorder).

A persistent fear of one or more situations in which the person is exposed to possible scrutiny by others and fears that he or she may do something or act in a way that will be humiliating or embarrassing is the essential feature of Social Phobia. Social Phobias may be limited to a specific phobic stimulus (as in this case) or may be generalized to almost all social situations. The most common specific Social Phobia is fear of public speaking. Usually fear of public speaking is limited to formal presentations and does not include, as in this case, fear of talking on the telephone. Less common specific Social Phobias are fear of eating in public, fear of writing in public, and fear of using public lavatories. In the generalized type of Social Phobia the phobic situation includes most social situations (see "Mail Sorter," p. 125).

DSM-III-R Diagnosis:

Axis I: 300.23 Social Phobia, Severe (p. 243)

Trapped

A 30-YEAR-OLD MALE CHEMIST was referred by his internist because he wanted to talk to someone about his shaky marriage. During five years of courtship and two years of marriage, there have been numerous separations, usually precipitated by his dissatisfaction. Although he and his wife share many interests and, until recently, have had a satisfactory sexual relationship, he thinks that his wife is basically a cold and self-centered person who has no real concern about his career or feelings. His dissatisfaction periodically builds up to a point that leads to fights, which often result in temporary separations. He then feels lonely and comes "crawling back" to her. Their relationship currently is one of "icy separateness," and the patient seems to be seeking support to make a permanent break. Although he is in extreme distress because of his marital situation, frequently choking back tears, there is no evidence that he has difficulties with other interpersonal relationships. He has many good friends, functions well in his job, and denies symptoms other than distress about his marital situation.

Discussion of "Trapped"

Although this man is very upset about his marital situation and is apparently not able to resolve it as well as he might, his reaction to the situation appears to be well within normal and expectable limits. Therefore, a diagnosis of a mental disorder, such as Adjustment Disorder, is not appropriate.

Despite the fact that the designation of the V code Marital Problem implies that the patient's difficulties are not due to a mental disorder, it might nonetheless be appropriate to offer some form of professional help.

DSM-III-R Diagnosis:

Axis I: V61.10 Marital Problem (p. 360)

Underground Sex

C HARLES WAS 45 when he was referred for psychiatric consultation by his parole officer following his second arrest for rubbing up against a woman in the subway. According to Charles, he had a "good" sexual relationship with his wife of 15 years when he began, 10 years ago, to touch women in the subway. A typical episode would begin with his decision to go into the subway to rub against a woman, usually in her twenties. He would select the woman as he walked into the subway station, move in behind her and wait for the train to arrive at the station. He would be wearing plastic wrap around his penis so as not to stain his pants after ejaculating while rubbing up against his victim. As riders moved on to the train, he would follow the woman he had selected. When the doors closed, he would begin to push his penis up against her buttocks, fantasizing that they were having intercourse in a normal non-coercive manner. In about half of the episodes, he would ejaculate and then go on to work. If he failed to ejaculate, he would either give up for that day, or change trains and select another victim. According to Charles, he felt guilty immediately after each episode, but would soon find himself ruminating about and anticipating the next encounter. He estimated that he had done this about twice a week for the last ten years, and thus had probably rubbed up against approximately a thousand women.

During the interview, Charles expressed extreme guilt about his behavior and often cried when talking about fears that his wife or employer would find out about his second arrest. However, he had apparently never thought about how his victims felt about what he did to them.

His personal history did not indicate any other obvious mental problems other than being rather inept and unassertive socially, especially with women.

Discussion of "Underground Sex"

The recurrent touching and rubbing up against a nonconsenting person for the purpose of sexual arousal and gratification is called Frotteurism, and is classified in DSM-III-R as one of the Paraphilias. In some classical textbooks Frotteurism (rubbing) is distinguished from Toucherism (fondling), but both are included in the DSM-III-R category of Frotteurism. No cases of the disorder have ever been reported in females.

Charles's behavior is typical of that seen in this disorder. A crowded place where there is a wide selection of victims is selected (e.g., subway, sports event, mall). In such a setting the initial rubbing of the woman may not be immediately noticed; the victim usually does not protest because she is not absolutely sure what has happened. This probably explains why Charles has only been arrested twice.

What we do not know is the kind of sexual fantasies that Charles had for years before he actually engaged in the acts of Frotteurism. However, as is common in the disorder, while he engaged in the act he fantasied about a loving sexual relationship with the victim.

The psychiatrist who contributed this case tells us that this condition is underdiagnosed in smaller cities because psychiatrists do not ask patients if they commit these kinds of sex acts in crowded situations.

DSM-III-R Diagnosis:

Axis I: 302.89 Frotteurism, Severe (p. 284)

Stubborn Psychiatrist

A 34-YEAR-OLD PSYCHIATRIST is 15 minutes late for his first appointment. He had recently been asked to resign from his job in a mental health center because, according to his boss, he had frequently been late for work and meetings, missed appointments, forgot about assignments, was late with his statistics, refused to follow instructions, and seemed unmotivated. The patient was surprised and resentful—he thought he had been doing a particularly good job under trying circumstances and experienced his boss as excessively obsessive and demanding. Nonetheless, he reported a long-standing pattern of difficulties with authority.

The patient had a childhood history of severe and prolonged temper tantrums that were a legend in his family. He had been a bossy child who demanded that other kids "play his way" or else he wouldn't play at all.

With adults, particularly his mother and female teachers, he was sullen, insubordinate, oppositional, and often unmanageable. He had been sent to an all-boys' preparatory school that had primarily male teachers, and he gradually became more subdued and disciplined. He continued, however, to stubbornly want things his own way and to resent instruction or direction from teachers. He was a brilliant but erratic student, working only as hard as he himself wanted to; and he "punished" teachers he didn't like by not doing their assignments. He was argumentative and self-righteous when criticized, and claimed that he was not being treated fairly.

The patient is unhappily married. He complains that his wife does not understand him and is a "nitpicker." She complains that he is unreliable and stubborn. He refuses to do anything around the house and often fails to complete the few tasks he has accepted as within his responsibility. Tax forms are submitted several months late; bills are not paid. The patient is sociable and has considerable charm, but friends generally become annoyed at his unwillingness to go along with the wishes of the group (for example, if a restaurant is not his choice, he may sulk all night or "forget" to bring his wallet).

Discussion of "Stubborn Psychiatrist"

Whenever this patient feels that demands are being made on him, either socially or occupationally, he passively resists through such characteristic maneuvers as procrastination (e.g., tax returns are late, bills are not paid), forgetfulness (e.g., forgets errands for wife and assignments at work), and sulking when asked to do something he doesn't want to do. His behavior has resulted in impaired work performance and marital difficulties. Such a long-standing pattern of resistance to demands for adequate performance in role functioning is a prototype of Passive-Aggressive Personality Disorder.

Although passive-aggressive behavior is quite common in situations in which assertive behavior is not encouraged or is actually punished (e.g., in the military service), the diagnosis is made only if the behavior occurs in situations in which more assertive behavior is possible.

This case demonstrates that neither a high IQ nor membership in a mental health profession conveys immunity to this disorder!

DSM-III-R Diagnosis:

Axis I: V71.09 No Diagnosis or Condition
Axis II: 301.84 Passive-Aggressive Personality Disorder,
          Moderate (p. 357)

> **Follow-up**
>
> The patient was treated once a week, for five years, with psychotherapy that was in part behavioral and in part psychodynamic. The behavior therapy aspect of his treatment consisted of assertiveness training and specific assignments, e.g., an instruction to do his monthly report the minute it appeared on his desk, and then use the therapy session to discuss the feelings engendered by having done it. When he stopped treatment, the patient was doing very well professionally, and reported being much happier.

Parental Rights

CLARA COLE, A 34-YEAR-OLD, black mother of three children, aged 13, 11, and 5, was referred by a juvenile court for psychiatric evaluation pending termination of her parental rights for her two oldest children, Tyrone and Tanya.

Ms. Cole described her Tyrone as a difficult child who had been hyperactive from birth. She had trouble toilet training him and difficulty disciplining him. When he was two and a half, Tyrone was treated for second-degree burns on his ankles, posterior calves, buttocks, and penis. Ms. Cole was alone with him at the time, but claimed this was an accidental injury that could have happened to anyone. She explained that he had turned on the hot water by himself when she was out of the room.

Since that injury there have been many other multiple injuries to all three children. Each of them has been observed to have bruises, welts, and marks consistent with their stories that they were hung upside down and beaten with rubber hoses. The youngest child, Winnie, has been treated for ongoing hallucinations of a female voice telling her to hit other children. Both of the two older children are in residential treatment facilities at this time because of the severity of their behavior problems. When each of these children entered residential treatment, they were frightened, particularly of adult women. Both Tyrone and Tanya have said that their mother threatened further physical abuse if they told anyone what was going on at home.

Ms. Cole is insulted that the juvenile court is involved in her case. She says her children were abused in the past by her ex-husband, who was also physically and emotionally abusive of her. She denies she has ever abused them and cannot explain why the children appear to be selectively frightened of women. Ms. Cole acknowledges that she disciplined her children by whipping them with a belt, but denies that she has ever hung them upside down. She believes that her oldest son began making up stories about how she mistreated them to get back at her for setting limits on him. She does not believe that the younger two children verified his stories (which they did). Ms. Cole says that recently, when she understood that her parental rights were to be terminated, she stopped spanking her youngest child for fear of losing custody of her as well. Ms. Cole admits disciplining the children to the point of leaving bruises and welts on them for infractions such as talking back to her, not coming home immediately after school, not getting grades as good as she expected, and being disrespectful.

Ms. Cole's parents were both alcoholic, but she has never had any problems with drugs or alcohol. Her mother beat her frequently without telling her what she had done wrong. She recalls being frightened that her mother would "get weird on me and hit me with whatever was handy." At times, she needed stitches from injuries caused by her mother. These were taken care of at home, as her family was too poor to afford medical help. Her mother accused her of being the root of all of her problems, the reason for her divorce, and of being responsible for the misbehavior of her siblings. She recalls that by the time she was in high school, she was so hostile toward women that she was assigned only male teachers. Nevertheless, she obtained good grades and was active in the Reserve Officers Training Corps.

Ms. Cole is steadily employed as a supervisor in a shipping department, a job she has held for three years. She has had two promotions during this time. She is a large, attractive, neatly dressed woman. On formal mental status exam, she appears to be of above-average intelligence, is fully oriented, and has no difficulty with concentration or abstractions. Although she is very hostile, and critical of the child protective services and juvenile court, she is calm and pleasant with the examiner.

Ms. Cole's ex-husband is frightened of her. He says it is true that he has a bad temper, but she was the one who instigated the physical fights that they had when they were married. He would like to have custody of the children, but will not seek custody unless her parental rights have already been terminated.

Ms. Cole does not see any need for psychiatric intervention. She does not believe that she has a problem for which she needs treatment. She also says that although Tyrone has had multiple behavior problems for a number of years, if his custody were returned to her, she would stop his psychotherapy. She believes his problems would be resolved by placing him back in her care. If that proves not to be the case, she is prepared to give custody back to Social Services.

Discussion of "Parental Rights"

This unhappy woman inflicts the same abuse on her children that she experienced as a child from her own mother. She uses unnecessary physical cruelty, disciplines her children harshly, undoubtedly intimidates them into doing what she wants them to do, and restricts their autonomy (insists that they come home immediately after school). This pattern of cruel and aggressive behavior justifies the unofficial DSM-III-R diagnosis of Sadistic Personality Disorder, a condition that is practically never seen in women.

Some people with Sadistic Personality Disorder also suffer from Antisocial Personality Disorder. However, in this case, there is no mention of the childhood antecedents of Antisocial Personality Disorder, such as truancy, fighting, and stealing.

DSM-III-R Diagnosis:

Axis I: V71.09 No Diagnosis or Condition
Axis II: 301.90 Personality Disorder Not Otherwise Specified
          (Sadistic Personality Disorder) (p. 371)

House Painter

A 46-YEAR-OLD HOUSE PAINTER is admitted to the hospital with a history of 30 years of heavy drinking. He has had two previous admissions for detoxification, but his family states that he has not had a drink in several weeks, and he shows no signs of alcohol withdrawal. He looks malnourished, however, and on examination is found to be ataxic and to have a bilateral sixth-cranial-nerve palsy. He appears confused and mistakes one of his physicians for a dead uncle.

Within a week the patient walks normally, and there is no longer any sign of a sixth-nerve palsy. He seems less confused and can now find his way to the bathroom without direction. He remembers the names and birthdays of his siblings, but has difficulty naming the past five U.S. presidents. More strikingly, he has great difficulty in retaining information for longer than a few minutes. He can repeat a list of numbers immediately after he has heard them, but a few minutes later does not recall being asked to perform the task. Shown three objects (keys, comb, ring), he cannot recall them three minutes later. He does not seem worried about this. Asked if he can recall the name of his doctor, he replies, "Certainly," and proceeds to call the doctor "Dr. Masters" (not his name), whom, he claims, he first met in the Korean War. He tells a long untrue story about how he and "Dr. Masters" served as fellow soldiers.

The patient is calm, alert, and friendly. Because of his intact immediate memory and spotty but sometimes adequate remote memory, one can be with him for a short period and not realize he has a severe memory impairment. His amnesia, in short, is largely anterograde. Although treated with high doses of thiamine, the short-term memory deficit persists and appears to be irreversible.

Discussion of "House Painter"

Confusion, ataxia, and sixth-nerve palsy, with a history of heavy alcohol use, are diagnostic of the neurological disorder Wernicke's Encephalopathy, noted on Axis III. As is often the case, when this responds to treatment with thiamine, the patient is left with an Amnestic Syndrome, Alcohol Amnestic Disorder. This is characterized by short-term (rather than immediate or long-term) memory impairment. In an effort to mask the memory impairment, the person may confabulate, i.e., fabricate facts or events in response to questions about situations that are not recalled.

If a generalized loss of intellectual functioning rather than memory loss were the predominant disturbance, then a diagnosis of Dementia Associated with Alcoholism would be appropriate.

The history of years of heavy drinking and two admissions for detoxification make the additional diagnosis of Alcohol Dependence extremely likely.

DSM-III-R Diagnosis:

Axis I: 291.10 Alcohol Amnestic Disorder, Severe (p. 133)
          303.91 Alcohol Dependence, Severe (p. 167)
Axis III: Wernicke's Encephalopathy

Latin American Businessman

M R. ZEIGLER IS A 55-YEAR-OLD married Latin American businessman who is hospitalized with an eight-month history of diarrhea, fatigue, and weight loss. He has sought help from several institutions both in the United States and Europe, but his illness remains undiagnosed. A psychiatric consultation is requested because both the patient and his physician think he is depressed and wonder what role this might play in his weight loss and overall condition.

Mr. Zeigler gives a detailed history of his family's emigration from Europe when he was a child, his personal success in business, and the progressive difficulty he he has been experiencing because of his weight loss and fatigue. He has lost 85 pounds over the 8 months and now has to force himself to eat. In the past, eating had been a great pleasure for him, and he considered himself a gourmet. Although he complains of some difficulty with his memory and concentration, he continues to manage a multinational business and to conduct complex financial deals. He says he feels sad, but is hopeful the diagnosis can be made quickly. He conducts himself in the same autocratic manner in the hospital that he is accustomed to displaying in business and with his family. He has many interests, including an active sex life, which he wishes to resume once he regains his strength.

Mrs. Zeigler confirms her husband's history and speaks of his complete control of his business and of all of the family's financial affairs. She describes how this has created conflicts with her sons, who resent their father's unyielding control, even though they work in the family company. It is her opinion that her husband is depressed and that this is the cause of most of his symptoms. In response to questions about his activities, she agrees that his fatigue seems the only obstacle to pursuing his interests. She cannot answer any questions about his sex drive because she stopped having sex with him ten years before this illness. He accepted this, and she presumed he frequented prostitutes.

Over the next few days Mr. Zeigler's condition deteriorates markedly, and he is thought to have suffered a stroke, because of some slurred speech and a slight weakness of the right side of his body. He then becomes short of breath, and is admitted to the intensive care unit. A chest X-ray suggests pneumocystis carinii pneumonia, which is confirmed by bronchoscopy. He does not respond to trimethoprim/sulfamethoxazole and is started on pentamidine. While in the intensive care unit Mr. Zeigler is delirious, frequently hallucinating, and often incoherent in both Spanish and English. His children fly to the United States, as he is not expected to survive. This prediction proves to be incorrect, and his pneumonia resolves after several weeks of treatment. A computerized tomography scan of the brain is suggestive of a central nervous system infection with toxoplasmosis, and examination of the stomach by endoscopy leads to the diagnosis of gastrointestinal isospora. Surprisingly, all of these infections respond to treatment.

It is now clear that Mr. Zeigler has Acquired Immune Deficiency Syndrome (AIDS), and his physician presents this diagnosis to him along with an inquiry about his sexual experiences. Mr. Zeigler is enraged by his doctor's "implication" of homosexuality and adamantly denies any homosexual activity. He discusses his adaptation to his wife's decision to cease sexual activity with him. He has frequented prostitutes in the Far East, where he traveled regularly on business. It seems impossible to him that he might have AIDS, although he admits to having contracted syphilis four years before his current illness. On discharge, Mr. Zeigler is given the diagnosis of AIDS, with the only clear risk factor his sexual contact with prostitutes.

Six months later Mr. Zeigler and his wife return to the United States for further evaluation of his mental status. His wife is concerned that he has become depressed because he is no longer able to handle his financial affairs. She feels his personality has undergone a radical change, as he no longer seems to care about anything, in spite of the fact that his appetite has returned to normal and he has regained much of his lost weight. Much of his time is now spent sitting idly in their garden.

When examined, Mr. Zeigler appears to be in good physical health. However, his mental condition has obviously deteriorated, and it is not possible to conduct an interview in English, whereas previously he had spoken several languages fluently. He smiles pleasantly, but is both disoriented and confused, even in Spanish. This surprises his wife, since she had not been aware of this change in his cognitive functioning. He has poor short-term memory, and cannot perform simple calculations. His remote memory is intact, although his wife feels that he has confused some historical events. Mr. Zeigler seems unaware that there are any deficits in his intellectual functioning. Medical evaluation does not reveal any active infections.

Discussion of "Latin American Businessman"

This sad case illustrates one aspect of the current epidemic of human immunodeficiency virus (HIV) infection. In retrospect, when Mr. Zeigler first presented with diarrhea, fatigue, and weight loss, he was already suffering from AIDS-related Complex (ARC). His loss of memory and difficulty concentrating were most likely the early manifestations of neuropsychological impairment due to HIV infection. On his last visit, his impairment in memory and abstract thinking and his personality change (apathy), severe enough to interfere with his work, were evidence of AIDS dementia.

Because many of the symptoms of Major Depression can be seen in patients with physical disorders (fatigue, impaired appetite and weight loss, insomnia), this differential diagnosis is often difficult. The possible diagnosis of Major Depression on Mr. Zeigler's first visit was suggested by his admitted sadness, fatigue, weight loss, and disturbed concentration. However, the magnitude of the weight loss (85 pounds) in the absence of profound depressed mood and anhedonia is not what one would expect in Major Depression.

DSM-III-R Diagnosis (when last evaluated):

Axis I: 294.10 Dementia, Moderate (p. 107)
Axis III: AIDS

Follow-up

Mr. Zeigler returned to his country, where he died of an unknown infection several months later.

Frieda

A 42-YEAR-OLD WOMAN, accompanied by her husband, sought psychiatric consultation, primarily at the husband's request. She described a number of marital difficulties of an unexceptional nature and appeared to lapse into periods of daydreaming during the evaluation. Independently, her husband reported that on occasion she would leave the house suddenly, dressed in a manner quite different from her customary sedate appearance, and not return for 12 to 36 hours. At other times, after some minor family argument, she would withdraw into a corner of the room, sit on the floor, curl up, and talk as if she were a young girl. Her husband found that he could not bring her out of these episodes easily. His subsequent attempts to discuss them with her were fruitless, as she refused to talk about them.

Initially the patient claimed to have no awareness of these incidents; but under hypnosis she acknowledged them openly, giving a highly detailed, vivid, and emotional account. She had been born in 1938 in Poland, shortly before the German invasion. During the war she lived in a variety of orphanages, as her father was killed during the hostilities and her mother fled the country to live in Italy with relatives. The orphanages were run by nuns, who provided institutional care and strong discipline. Food supplies were meager, friendships marginal, and moves frequent, necessitated by wartime conditions.

The patient described a make-believe female companion of the same age with whom she engaged in lengthy reveries from about the age of four. In the face of wartime privation, she would retreat with this companion and imagine playing in a sunny peaceful field with dolls. The girls would run there to get away from family chores. They would dress up in their parents' clothes and impersonate grown-ups, flaunting the staid customs of their rural village. These reveries continued and, in fact, increased in frequency when she was a young adolescent, especially after she was sexually molested by two Soviet occupation soldiers stationed in Poland after the war.

The patient never saw either of her parents again. She was angry at her mother, whom she perceived as having selfishly abandoned her. Her perception of her father was more complex. She imagined that he had collaborated with German occupation forces as an informant and was killed by residents of his village in retaliation. She felt that her antipathy toward him characterized her relationships with nearly all men, especially since having been molested in adolescence.

After emigrating to the United States, she had married, but was sexually indifferent to her husband. The couple had difficulty resolving disagreements about money, vacation schedules, and child discipline. When disputes arose, producing clear signs of emotional withdrawal in her husband, the patient would retreat to the bedroom, dress in flamboyant clothes, and leave the house without a word. During these episodes she would experience herself as Frieda, the girl friend of the Soviet soldier who had molested her. She would meet a man at a nearby bar and propose a sexual liaison, only to belittle his masculinity before any physical involvement occurred.

The other incidents, in which she appeared to her husband to curl up on the floor and talk as if she were a young girl, occurred after arguments with her children over issues of discipline, especially their failure to keep their room clean and complete their homework on time. At these times the patient would reexperience, as real, her wartime reveries with her imaginary companion.

Following completion of the interview under hypnosis, the patient had no memory of Frieda.

Discussion of "Frieda"

Sudden and dramatic changes in behavior can occur in a variety of mental disorders, such as Schizophrenia, Psychogenic Amnesia, and Psychogenic Fugue. In this case, however, there is no evidence of psychotic symptoms; and there are repeated shifts of both identity and complex behavior patterns, neither of which are present in Psychogenic Amnesia or Fugue. The presence of several distinct personalities, each of which at some time determines the patient's behavior, is characteristic of Multiple Personality Disorder.

DSM-III-R Diagnosis:

Axis I: 300.14 Multiple Personality Disorder (p. 272)

Perfect Relationship

JIM HEALY IS A 35-YEAR-OLD social-science researcher who has just received multiple sentences of life imprisonment after his third conviction for a series of rapes.

Jim was reared in a chaotic family. His father was physically abusive toward his mother and toward women in general. Both parents were sexually promiscuous, sometimes in his presence. On at least one occasion as a child, he was sodomized by his father. Growing up, often feeling alone and unloved, he began fantasizing about a "perfect relationship" with an ideal woman whom he could "sweep off her feet." As time passed, such fantasies and urges began to develop an eroticized, obsessional quality. Initially, he would imagine himself coercing an unwilling woman into sexual activities that she would then come to enjoy. He would then fantasize a continuing caring relationship. Often he would masturbate while having these fantasies.

Although Jim understood that the scenario in his fantasies was unlikely, he nevertheless began to be preoccupied with sexually exciting urges to act upon these fantasies. When he was 16, he committed his first rape. After each rape, he would promise himself "never again," but in time, as his preoccupations and urges were rekindled, he would repeat the cycle.

Although he would often threaten women with a knife to obtain their compliance, he never physically hurt them and used the minimal amount of force necessary. Any obvious signs of suffering or anguish would diminish rather than enhance his erotic arousal. During the course of each rape, he would invariably throw away his weapon, and assure the woman that he did not intend to injure her or cause her harm.

When reading magazines or watching movies depicting scenes of females in positions of subjugation or bondage, he would become erotically aroused, fantasizing that they were enjoying the experience, but he would not become thus aroused if the women seemed to be suffering or to be in genuine distress.

When tested in prison with a penile plethysmograph, Jim developed an erection when presented with stimuli depicting females in positions of subjugation or bondage, but his arousal was diminished if they seemed to be suffering. Laboratory testing of his blood revealed an elevated level of serum testosterone.

Apart from his convictions for rape, Jim has never been convicted or even accused of any other type of criminal activity. He has no history of outpatient or inpatient psychiatric treatment. He has a stable work history. He has never abused alcohol or any other drugs.

Discussion of "Perfect Relationship"

Jim has committed repeated rapes. Rape is by definition a coercive act and a traumatic experience for the person who is raped. Recognizing that rape is an antisocial and criminal act should not preclude an investigation of the motivation or mental state of the rapist. Most rapes are probably committed by men with quite ordinary (nonparaphilic) sexual preferences, many of whom would meet the criteria for Antisocial Personality Disorder. More rarely, rape is committed by men with Mental Retardation, a psychotic disorder, drug intoxication, or Multiple Personality Disorder. However, some rapists, particularly serial rapists, suffer from an aberrant sexual drive, a Paraphilia, a disorder in which there are intense sexual urges and sexually arousing fantasies involving either nonhuman objects, the suffering or humiliation of oneself, one's partner, children, or other nonconsenting persons.

Jim showed no evidence of other antisocial behavior. Although he had raped often, he had never engaged in any other criminal acts. He had a reasonably stable work and social history, and the other criteria necessary to make a diagnosis of Antisocial Personality Disorder were absent. His acts of rape could not be explained as a function of Mental Retardation, drug intoxication, a psychotic disorder, or Multiple Personality Disorder.

Jim experienced recurrent eroticized urges and fantasies about coercing women sexually. Such fantasies and urges had been present for many years, and he had repeatedly acted upon them. Unlike a person with Sexual Sadism, he was not erotically aroused by inflicting pain, humiliation, or suffering; in fact, his erotic arousal was inhibited by any signs of anguish or distress in the victim. His rape behavior can best be understood as a manifestation of a specific Paraphilia. The term Paraphilic Coercive Disorder has been suggested for this particular kind of Paraphilia, but the category is not recognized by DSM-III-R. Therefore, Jim's disorder would be coded as a Paraphilia Not Otherwise Specified.

DSM-III-R Diagnosis:

Axis I: 302.90 **Paraphilia Not Otherwise Specified, Severe
              (Paraphilic Coercive Disorder) (p. 290)**

Follow-up

While in prison, Jim was treated with behavioral therapy utilizing masturbatory satiation, in which he was required to masturbate repeatedly to the fantasies of coercive situations that he had previously found sexually arousing. He was also given pharmacologic treatment with a testosterone-lowering medication, medroxyprogesterone acetate. This combined therapy diminished his aberrant erotic arousal pattern, as evidenced both by less time spent fantasizing rape situations and diminished physiologic arousal as measured by the penile plethysmograph.

When last seen in prison, two years after his incarceration, Jim was still receiving the medication and reported that, at least for now (in prison), he was free of both fantasies and urges to rape.

Mystery Mastery

D ONNA, A 28-YEAR-OLD LAWYER, described her problems to a psychiatrist. She frequently felt anxious and upset around bedtime. On these nights it would take her an hour or more to fall asleep. She dreaded going to bed, and would engross herself in reading murder mysteries until late hours. Her bedtimes varied from 7:00 PM to 2:00 AM. On awakening in the morning, she felt groggy and incapacitated, hardly able to crawl out of bed. Some mornings she missed work completely. She slept until noon on weekends. Worry about her tardiness getting to work motivated her to seek a consultation.

Donna had had bronchial asthma since the age of 18 months. Her mother had constantly worried that Donna would die during the night. As a teen-ager Donna used epinephrine inhalers to remain awake until 1:00 to 3:00 AM, reading. She remembers her father screaming at her to turn out the lights. She always considered the late night hours, when everyone else was asleep, a "safe time," free from interference by others.

Donna was particularly prone to nocturnal asthma attacks, which typically occurred around 4:00 AM. Wheezing at night led to feelings of terror and fear of dying—"I feel out of control." The current treatment for her asthma was aminophyllin 400 mg daily plus 2 puffs on a beclomethasone inhaler twice daily. She also used an albuterol inhaler irregularly, sometimes at bedtime. About once a year, an exacerbation of asthma would require a short course of systemic steroids.

Donna drank five to eight cups of coffee daily. Alcoholic beverages precipitated wheezing and aggravated the delay in onset of sleep. Short-acting sedatives at bedtime caused a noticeable decrease in her ability to concentrate on work the following day. Evening relaxation exercises precipitated fears of being alone with a breathing problem and made her feel like "a skeleton with a pair of lungs."

During the consultation, Donna was articulate, smiling, cheerful, and had a full range of affect. She seemed to enjoy her own idiosyncrasies. She was quite talkative, organized, and informative, and easily able to discuss her feelings. She noted that it was ironic that she feared death so much yet loved to read about murders in fiction. "I guess it's been my way of feeling some sense of control."

Ascultation of the heart revealed a systolic click. Twenty-four-hour electrocardiographic monitoring revealed significant ventricular ectopic activity. These findings are consistent with prolapsed mitral valve syndrome (which is presumed to involve hypersensitivity to circulating catacholamines and is occasionally associated with increased insomnia).

Discussion of "Mystery Mastery"

The fear of asthma, the effects of drugs, and the possible effects of prolapsed mitral valve syndrome all contribute to this patient's difficulty falling asleep at reasonable times. Xanthines, beta-agonists, and steroids all exert long-lasting stimulation effects likely to interfere with good sleep quality. After an initial sedative effect, alcohol often lightens sleep five or six hours following ingestion.

Because of the many specific organic factors that contribute to the insomnia in this case, the diagnosis is Insomnia Related to Known Organic Factors.

DSM-III-R Diagnosis:

Axis I: 780.50 Insomnia Related to Known Organic Factors
                    (p. 301)

Axis III: Asthma
            Mitral valve prolapse
            Use of stimulant drugs (xanthines, beta-agonists,
            steroids)

Binoculars

A 25-YEAR-OLD MALE business executive requests psychiatric consultation because of his repeated need to peep at women undressing or engaging in sexual activity. The patient was apprehended for this activity in the past, and the personnel office at his place of work found out about it. He was advised that treatment of his problem was mandatory, and that he would lose his job if the behavior were repeated. He did not seek professional assistance and continued to engage in voyeuristic activity. Recently, he was almost caught again, and because of this now seeks a consultation.

The patient is an articulate, handsome man who has no difficulty attracting sexual partners. He dates frequently and has sexual intercourse once or twice a week with a variety of partners. In addition, however, he is frequently drawn to certain types of situations he finds uniquely arousing. He owns a pair of high-powered binoculars and uses these to peep into neighboring apartments. Sometimes he is rewarded for his efforts, but more frequently is not. He then leaves his apartment and goes to rooftops of large apartment buildings, where he searches with his binoculars until he finds a woman undressing or engaging in sexual activity. He has no desire to enter the apartments he peeps into, and he denies experiencing impulses to rape. If he finds a scene in which he can watch a woman undressing or engaging in sexual activity, he masturbates to orgasm while watching, or immediately afterward, and then returns home. He experiences the voyeuristic situation, in its entirety, as uniquely pleasurable, despite the fact that he sometimes encounters potentially hazardous situations. On more than one occasion he has been nearly apprehended by building staff or police, who took him to be a potential burglar or assailant; once he was chased from a "lovers' lane" by an irate man wielding a tire iron; another time he was discovered peeping into a bedroom window in a rural area and barely escaped being shot.

The patient was reared in a family that included three older sisters. His father was puritanical, religious, and generally punitive in his attitudes toward the patient. The patient's mother was allegedly warm, expressive, and flirtatious toward men, but not toward the patient. He felt he was his mother's favorite child and wondered whether he would ever fall in love with a woman who measured up to her. He had never been in love, nor had he experienced a durable, deep attachment to a woman.

The patient's family was sexually puritanical. Family members did not disrobe in front of each other, for example; and the parents avoided open displays of activity that could be interpreted as erotic. Still, the patient recalls that, between the ages of seven and ten, he watched his mother and sisters undress "as much as possible."

The patient began "peeping," along with many other boys, at the age of ten, while at summer camp. He is unable to explain why this particular stimulus subsequently had a unique appeal for him whereas other boys seemed to become less interested in peeping as they became more interested in sexual intercourse. He has used binoculars to search for erotically stimulating scenes since he was 11, but did not leave his home to do so until age 17.

The patient notices some relationship between presumed psychological stress and his voyeuristic activity; for example, at times of major life change, such as moving out of his parents' home or finishing a college semester, the activity increased. He is not, however, aware of any relationship between anxiety about having sexual intercourse and the desire to engage in voyeuristic activity. He feels that anxiety is often present in the voyeuristic situation, but it is only a fear of being apprehended. He feels no guilt or shame about his voyeurism and considers it harmless. He is concerned, however, that he might one day go to jail unless he alters his sexual behavior, and for that reason seeks help.

Discussion of "Binoculars"

There is no question that this patient repeatedly engages in voyeuristic activities for the purpose of achieving sexual excitement. According to DSM-III-R, when a person acts on recurrent and intense voyeuristic urges or is markedly distressed by them, the diagnosis of Voyeurism is made.

Many people have voyeuristic impulses, but no clinician would consider making a diagnosis of Voyeurism in someone who occasionally was sexually aroused by observing an unsuspecting neighbor disrobe, or by watching pornography, in which the actors pretend to be unaware that they are being observed. In this case, however, the impulses are recurrent and intense, and even the patient is able to recognize the potentially disastrous consequences of his continued voyeuristic behavior.

This case illustrates that people with Paraphilias may also get pleasure from nonparaphilic heterosexual intercourse.

DSM-III-R Diagnosis:

Axis I: 302.82 Voyeurism, Severe (p. 290)

Contract On My Life

MR. POLSEN, A 42-YEAR-OLD, married, black postal worker and father of two, is brought to the emergency room by his wife because he has been insisting that "there is a contract out on my life."

According to Mr. Polsen, his problems began four months ago, when his supervisor at work accused him of tampering with a package. Mr. Polsen denied that this was true and, because his job was in jeopardy, filed a protest. At a formal hearing, he was exonerated and, according to him, "This made my boss furious. He felt he had been publicly humiliated."

About two weeks later, Mr. Polsen noticed that his co-workers were avoiding him. "When I'd walk toward them, they'd just turn away like they didn't want to see me." Shortly thereafter, he began to feel that they were talking about him at work. He never could make out clearly what they were saying, but he gradually became convinced that they were avoiding him because his boss had taken out a contract on his life.

This state of affairs was stable for about two months, until Mr. Polsen began noticing several "large white cars," new to his neighborhood, driving up and down the street on which he lived. He became increasingly frightened and was convinced that the "hit men" were in these cars. He refused to go out of his apartment without an escort. Several times, when he saw the white cars, he would panic and run home. After one such incident, his wife finally insisted that he accompany her to the emergency room.

Mr. Polsen was described by his wife and brother as a basically well-adjusted, outgoing man who enjoyed being with his family. He had served with distinction in Vietnam. He saw little combat there, but was pulled from a burning truck by a buddy seconds before the truck blew up.

When interviewed, Mr. Polsen was obviously frightened. Aside from his belief that he was in danger of being killed, his speech, behavior, and demeanor were in no way odd or strange. His predominant mood was anxious. He denied having hallucinations and all other psychotic symptoms except those noted above. He claimed not to be depressed; and although he noted that he had recently had some difficulty falling asleep, he said there had been no change in his appetite, sex drive, energy level, or concentration.

Discussion of "Contract On My Life"

Mr. Polsen's anxiety stems from his belief that his boss has a contract out on his life. There is no reason to believe this; thus, we must conclude that he has a delusion. Since contract killers *are* sometimes hired in real life, the delusion is nonbizarre. Mr. Polsen has no auditory or visual hallucinations, no manic or depressive syndrome, and no evidence of an organic factor that initiated and maintained the disturbance. His behavior, apart from the delusion and its ramifications, is not odd or bizarre. These are the characteristics of Delusional Disorder. Since the content of his delusion involves the theme of being malevolently treated in some way, the disorder is specified as Persecutory Type.

Often people with the Persecutory Type of Delusional Disorder are reluctant to seek help. Mr. Polsen, however, was apparently frightened enough to be persuaded to seek help.

DSM-III-R Diagnosis:

**Axis I: 297.10 Delusional Disorder, Persecutory Type
             (p. 202)**

Follow-up

Mr. Polsen was hospitalized. During the first week of hospitalization, he received an antipsychotic drug, thioridazine. However, he remained delusional and, in fact, became convinced that several of the other patients on the ward with Italian names were part of the "hit team" sent to kill him. Over the ensuing three weeks, with continued treatment, these beliefs faded. At discharge, one month after admission, he stated: "I guess my boss has called off the contract. He couldn't get away with it now without publicity."

Mr. Polsen was followed up over a period of 18 months, during which time he had two relapses into more active delusions, all with the same content, and each occurring after he stopped taking his medication. Both episodes resolved relatively rapidly with outpatient treatment with an antipsychotic drug.

Blood Is Thicker Than Water

MATTHEW IS A 34-YEAR-OLD single man who lives with his mother and works as an accountant. He seeks treatment because he is very unhappy after having just broken up with his girl friend. His mother had disapproved of his marriage plans, ostensibly because the woman was of a different religion. Matthew felt trapped and forced to choose between his mother and his girl friend, and since "blood is thicker than water," he had decided not to go against his mother's wishes. Nonetheless, he is angry at himself and at her and believes that she will never let him marry and is possessively hanging on to him. His mother "wears the pants" in the family, and is a very domineering woman who is used to getting her way. Matthew is afraid of her and criticizes himself for being weak, but also admires his mother and respects her judgment—"Maybe Carol wasn't right for me after all." He alternates between resentment and a "Mother knows best" attitude. He feels that his own judgment is poor.

Matthew works at a job several grades below what his education and talent would permit. On several occasions he has turned down promotions because he didn't want the responsibility of having to supervise other people or make independent decisions. He has worked for the same boss for ten years, gets on well with him, and is, in turn, highly regarded as a dependable and unobtrusive worker. He has two very close friends, whom he has had since early childhood. He has lunch with one of them every single workday and feels lost if his friend is sick and misses a day.

Matthew is the youngest of four children and the only boy. He was "babied and spoiled" by his mother and elder sisters. He had considerable separation anxiety as a child—difficulty falling asleep unless his mother stayed in the room, mild school refusal, and unbearable homesickness when he occasionally tried "sleepovers." As a child he was teased by other boys because of his lack of assertiveness and was often called a baby. He has lived at home his whole life except for one year of college, from which he returned because of homesickness. His heterosexual adjustment has been normal except for his inability to leave his mother in favor of another woman.

Discussion of "Blood Is Thicker Than Water"

This patient has allowed his mother to make the important decision as to whether he should marry his girl friend, and this seems to be merely one instance of a pattern of subordinating his own needs and wishes to those of his domineering mother. At work he demonstrates lack of initiative and reluctance to rely on his own judgment and abilities by avoiding promotions and working below his potential. He apparently feels uncomfortable when he is alone, and has always worried about being abandoned. This dependent and submissive behavior is severe enough to interfere significantly with his social and occupational functioning and therefore justify the diagnosis Dependent Personality Disorder.

DSM-III-R Diagnosis:

Axis I: V71.09 No Diagnosis or Condition
Axis II: 301.60 Dependent Personality Disorder, Mild (p. 354)

Follow-up

   Matthew's therapist treated him with a combination of behavior therapy and psychodynamic psychotherapy for several years. He was also seen in group therapy. After a year of therapy, he moved out of his mother's house and married his girl friend. When last heard from, he said he was fairly happy in his marriage.

Mail Sorter

ANDY, A 25-YEAR-OLD single man, lives with his mother and brother. He works as a mail sorter at the post office, a job he has had since he dropped out of college after two years. He came to a local clinic complaining of "nervousness." He says that right now he is "just going through the motions" and wants "to lead a normal life and go back to college."

During his adolescence and young adulthood, Andy had no close friends and usually preferred to be by himself. When he entered college, he formed several close friendships, but became "super self-conscious" when speaking to strangers, classmates, and sometimes even friends. He would feel nervous, and his face would become so "stiff" that he had difficulty speaking. He had a "buzzing" in his head, felt as if he was "outside [his] body," had hot flashes, and perspired. These "panic attacks" (his term) came on suddenly, within seconds, and only when he was with people. When a classmate spoke to him, he sometimes "couldn't hear" what the classmate was saying because of his nervousness.

Outside class, Andy began to feel increasingly uncomfortable in social situations. "I think that I was afraid of saying or doing something stupid." He began to turn down invitations to parties and to withdraw from other social activities, e.g., a bowling league. Eventually, he dropped out of college entirely.

Andy explains that the reason he chose to work at the post office is that the job does not require him to deal with people. When asked about other things that make him nervous, he says he tries to avoid using public lavatories, and feels more comfortable in a public bathroom when the lights are dim, when there are few people present, and when he can use a stall rather than a urinal.

Andy has two long-standing "best" friends with whom he socializes regularly and feels completely comfortable. However, he hasn't dated since college, and he totally avoids group settings, such as weddings and dances. He has no problem with authority figures, and even welcomes constructive criticism from his supervisor at the post office. "My problem is nervousness, not obstinacy."

Discussion of "Mail Sorter"

Andy says that he has "panic attacks," and it is true that he gets sudden attacks of intense anxiety. However, these always occur in situations that he knows are frightening to him. Thus, the attacks are quite different from the unexpected attacks of panic that occur in Panic Disorder. Andy's anxiety occurs in a variety of different social situations in which he fears that he will do something or act in a way that will be humiliating or embarrassing. This is the hallmark of a Social Phobia, Generalized Type. This diagnosis is given only, as in Andy's case, when the fear interferes with occupational functioning or with usual social activities or there is marked distress about having the fear.

The diagnosis of Social Phobia is given only when the fear is unrelated to another disorder. For example, the diagnosis would not be given to a patient with Panic Disorder who was afraid of having a panic attack in public, or to a patient with Parkinson's disease who was afraid of trembling in public.

In many cases it is difficult to differentiate Social Phobia, Generalized Type from the Axis II Avoidant Personality Disorder. According to DSM-III-R, when the criteria for both disorders are met, both diagnoses should be given. We count only two items from Avoidant Personality Disorder (four are required): Andy avoids social or occupational activities that involve significant interpersonal contact and is reticent in social situations because of a fear of saying something inappropriate or foolish. There is no evidence that he meets other criteria such as being easily hurt by criticism; fearing being embarrassed by blushing, crying, or showing signs of anxiety in front of other people; or exaggerating potential difficulties in ordinary activities. Furthermore, he does have close friends.

DSM-III-R Diagnosis:

Axis I: 300.23 Social Phobia, Generalized Type, Moderate
           (p. 243)

Professor

A 33-YEAR-OLD COLLEGE PROFESSOR presented with the complaint that he had never been able to ejaculate while making love. He had no trouble in attaining and maintaining an erection and no difficulties in stimulating his partner to her orgasm, but he could never be stimulated himself to ejaculation and would finally give up in boredom. He has always been able to reach ejaculation by masturbation, which he does about twice a week; but he has never been willing to allow a partner to masturbate him to orgasm. Previously he resisted all of his girl friend's attempts to persuade him to seek medical or psychological help, as he felt that intravaginal ejaculation was unimportant unless one wanted children.

The patient's current relationship is in jeopardy because his girl friend is eager to marry and have children. He has never wanted to have children and is reluctant to become a father, but the pressures from his girl friend have forced him to seek therapy. Throughout the interview his attitude toward the problem is one of distance and disdain. He describes the problem as though he were a neutral observer, with little apparent feeling.

Discussion of "Professor"

This professor has an unusual sexual problem. He is able to have an erection without any difficulty, has no problem in sustaining the erection during intercourse (as would be the case in Male Erectile Disorder), but is unable to have an orgasm during intercourse. Significantly, he has no trouble having an orgasm when he masturbates, which excludes the possibility that a physical disorder accounts for the problem. Persistent inhibition of the male orgasm phase not caused exclusively by an organic factor (such as a side effect of certain antidepressants) is called Inhibited Male Orgasm. We note the condition is psychogenic (not associated with an Axis III disorder), lifelong (not acquired after a period of normal functioning) and generalized (not limited to a specific situation).

There is a suggestion of coldness and hyperintellectualization, traits often present in men with this disorder. Perhaps on the basis of more information a diagnosis of Obsessive Compulsive Personality Disorder might also be warranted.

DSM-III-R Diagnosis:

Axis I: 302.74 Inhibited Male Orgasm, Psychogenic Only, Lifelong, Generalized (p. 295)

Cocaine

A L SANTINI, A 39-YEAR-OLD restaurant owner, is referred by a marriage counselor to a private outpatient substance abuse treatment program for evaluation and treatment of a possible "cocaine problem." According to the counselor, attempts to deal with the couple's marital problems have failed to produce any signs of progress over the past six or seven months. The couple continues to have frequent, explosive arguments, some of which have led to physical violence. Fortunately, neither spouse has been seriously injured, but the continuing chaos in their relationship has led to a great deal of tension at home and appears to be contributing to the acting-out behavior and school problems of their two children, aged 9 and 13.

Several days ago the patient admitted to the counselor and to his wife that he has been using cocaine "occasionally" for at least the past year. The wife became angry and tearful, stating that if her husband failed to obtain treatment for his drug problem, she would separate from him and inform his parents of the problem. He reluctantly agreed to seek professional help, insisting that his cocaine use was "not a problem," and that he felt capable of stopping his drug use without entering a treatment program.

During the initial evaluation interview, Al reports that he is currently using cocaine, intranasally, three to five days a week, and that this pattern has been continuing for at least the past two years. On average, he consumes a total of 1 to 2 grams of cocaine weekly, for which he pays $80 per gram. Most of his cocaine use occurs at work, in his private office or in the bathroom. He usually begins thinking about "coke" while driving to work in the morning. When he arrives at work, he finds it nearly impossible to avoid thinking of the cocaine vial in his desk drawer. Although he tries to distract himself and postpone using it as long as possible, he usually snorts his first "line" within an hour of arriving at work. On some days he may snort another two or three lines over the course of the entire day. On other days, especially if he feels stressed or frustrated at work, he may snort a line or two every hour from morning through late afternoon. His cocaine use is sometimes fueled by offers of the drug from his business partner, whom the patient describes as a more controlled, infrequent user of the drug.

Al rarely uses cocaine at home, and never in the presence of his wife or children. Occasionally he snorts a line or two on weekday evenings or weekends at home when everyone else is out of the house. Al denies current use of any other illicit drug, but reports taking 10 to 20 mg of an antianxiety drug, diazepam (prescribed by a physician friend), at bedtime on days when cocaine leaves him feeling restless, irritable, and unable to fall asleep. When diazepam is unavailable, he drinks two or three beers instead.

He first tried cocaine five years ago at a friend's party. He enjoyed the energetic, euphoric feeling and the absence of any unpleasant side effects, except for a slightly uncomfortable "racing" feeling in his chest. For nearly three years thereafter he used cocaine only when it was offered by others, and never purchased his own supplies or found himself thinking about the drug between episodes of use. He rarely snorted more than four or five lines on any single occasion of use. During the past two years his cocaine use escalated to its current level, coincident with a number of significant changes in his life. His restaurant business became financially successful; he bought a large home in the suburbs; he had access to large sums of cash; and the pressures of a growing business made him feel entitled to the relief and pleasures offered by cocaine.

He denies any history of alcohol or drug abuse problems. The only other drug he has ever used is marijuana, which he smoked infrequently in college, but never really liked. He also denies any history of other emotional problems and, except for marriage counseling, reports that he has never needed help from a mental health professional.

During the interview, Al remarks several times that although he thinks that his cocaine use "might be a problem," he does not consider himself to be "addicted" to it, and is still not sure that he really requires treatment. In support of this view, he lists the following evidence: (1) His current level of cocaine use is not causing him any financial problems or affecting his standard of living. (2) He is experiencing no significant drug-related health problems that he is aware of, with the possible exception of feeling lethargic the next day following a day of heavy use. (3) On many occasions he has been able to stop using cocaine on his own, for several days at a time. (4) When he stops using the drug, he experiences no withdrawal syndrome and no continuous drug cravings. On the other hand, he does admit that: (1) He often uses much more cocaine than intended on certain days. (2) The drug use is impairing his functioning at work because of negative effects on his memory, attention span, and attitude toward employees and customers. (3) Even when he is not actively intoxicated with cocaine, the aftereffects of the drug cause him to be short-tempered, irritable, and argumentative with his wife and children, leading to numerous family problems, including a possible breakup of his marriage. (4) Although he seems able to stop using cocaine for a few days at a time, somehow he always goes back to it. (5) As soon as he starts to use cocaine again, the craving and the preoccupation with the drug are immediately as intense as before he stopped using it.

At the end of the interview, Al agrees that although he came for the evaluation largely under pressure from his wife, he can see the potential benefits of trying to stop using cocaine on a more permanent basis. With a saddened expression, he explains how troubled and frightened he feels about the problems with his wife and children. He says that although marital problems existed before he started snorting cocaine, his continuing drug use has made them worse; and he now fears that his wife might leave him. He also feels extremely guilty about not being a "good father." He spends very little time with his children, and often is distracted and irritable with them because of his cocaine use.

Discussion of "Cocaine"

Al, like many people with a serious drug problem, does not like to think of himself as "addicted." However, Al's use of cocaine illustrates the core concept of psychoactive substance dependence: a cluster of cognitive, behavioral, and physiologic symptoms indicating that the person has impaired control of psychoactive substance use and continues use of the substance despite adverse consequences. Al cannot stop himself from using the first hit of cocaine in the morning; he continues to use it despite the adverse consequences for his marriage; he keeps returning to it after stopping for a few days; he uses it more often than he plans to; he is frequently intoxicated while at work; he experiences withdrawal symptoms (lethargy); and he has reduced important social activities with his family because of mood changes due to taking cocaine.

We note the severity of the dependence as moderate since Al is still able to function effectively in his job, and his social relationships, although impaired, are still relatively intact.

DSM-III-R Diagnosis:

Axis I: 304.20 Cocaine Dependence, Moderate (p. 167)

Follow-up

Al entered the outpatient treatment program. His treatment included individual, group, and marital counseling combined with supervised urine screening and participation in a self-help group (Cocaine Anonymous). He initially had difficulty in fully acknowledging and accepting the seriousness of his drug dependency problem. He harbored fantasies about returning to "controlled" cocaine use and disputed the program's requirement of total abstinence from all mood-altering substances, arguing that since he had never experienced problems with alcohol, he saw no reason to deny himself an occasional drink with dinner or at social gatherings. During the first three months of treatment, he had two short "slips" back to taking cocaine, one of which was precipitated by drinking a glass of wine, which led to intense craving for cocaine.

Subsequently, Al remained completely abstinent for the duration of the program (12 months) and became increasingly committed to maintaining a drug-free life style. His relationship with his wife and children improved considerably. The violent arguments had stopped immediately with the cessation of cocaine use, and spending more time with his children became much easier without the negative influence of cocaine on his mood and mental state.

Three years later Al was still abstinent. He was no longer in treatment, but continued to attend Cocaine Anonymous meetings at least two to three times every week.

Draftsman

A 65-YEAR-OLD ARCHITECTURAL DRAFTSMAN began to have difficulty remembering details necessary for performing his job. At home he was having problems keeping accurate financial records and, on several occasions, forgot to pay bills. It became increasingly difficult for him to function properly at work, and eventually he was forced to retire. Intellectual deterioration continued, and behavioral problems appeared. He became extremely stubborn and, when thwarted, was verbally and physically abusive.

When seen by a neurologic consultant five years after the problem began, the patient was fully alert and cooperative, but obviously anxious and fidgety. He thought he was at his place of employment and the year was "1960 or something" (it was actually 1982). He could not remember any one of six objects after an interval of ten minutes, even when prompted by multiple-choice answers. He knew his birthplace and high school, but not the names of his parents or siblings. He said he had two children, whereas in fact he had only one. Although he insisted he was still working, he could not describe his job. He did not know the current President and could not explain the resignation of President Nixon or remember the assassination of President Kennedy. His speech was well-articulated, but vague and circuitous, with many empty, meaningless phrases. He had difficulty naming common objects and repeating sentences. He could not do even the simplest arithmetic calculations. He could not write a proper sentence, copy a two- or three-dimensional figure, or draw a house. He interpreted proverbs concretely and had difficulty finding similarities between related objects.

An elementary neurologic examination revealed nothing abnormal. All laboratory studies were normal, including B$_{12}$, folate, T4 levels, and serology; but a computerized tomography (CT) scan showed marked cortical atrophy.

Discussion of "Draftsman"

The difficulties with short- and long-term memory, abstract thinking (difficulty finding similarities between related objects), and other higher cortical functions (e.g., inability to name common objects, to do arithmetic calculations, or copy a figure), all severe enough to interfere with social and occupational functioning, occurring in a clear state of consciousness, and not accounted for by a nonorganic mental disorder (such as Major Depression) indicate a Dementia.

The insidious onset with a generally progressive deteriorating course, the absence of focal neurological signs, the absence of a history of trauma or a stroke, the normal blood tests, and the cortical atrophy evident from the CT scan add up to the diagnosis of Primary Degenerative Dementia of the Alzheimer Type. Because there are no psychotic features or mood disturbance, the diagnosis is noted to be Uncomplicated. The severity of the Dementia is noted to be moderate because the patient requires some supervision.

DSM-III-R Diagnosis:

Axis I: 290.00 **Primary Degenerative Dementia of the Alzheimer Type, Senile Onset, Uncomplicated, Moderate (p. 121)**

Follow-up

Shortly after the time of his neurological consultation, the patient's behavior problems became so severe that his family could no longer cope with him at home. He was admitted to the hospital for a long-term stay. A progressive deterioration in his intellectual and physical status continued, but his aggressive behaviors were controlled, more or less, with antipsychotic drugs.

Eventually, he was transferred to another chronic disease hospital to be closer to his family. Word was received that he died three years later, at age 74, 8 years after the initial symptoms. No autopsy was done.

Age Lines

S ALLY IS A HAPPILY MARRIED, 23-year-old investment counselor who reluctantly agrees to see a psychiatrist, an old friend of her husband, Joe. She tells the psychiatrist that she doesn't think she needs to see a psychiatrist, because her problem is "these ugly lines on my forehead." The psychiatrist asks, "What lines?" Sally points to the frown lines above her nose, which to the psychiatrist seem no more pronounced than they are on the foreheads of most people Sally's age.

Sally continues. "It's horrible, isn't it? I mean, I don't have to be the most gorgeous girl on earth, but I also don't want to be disfigured."

The psychiatrist asks, "What makes you think it looks so awful? Everyone has those lines."

"C'mon. I appreciate your trying to make me feel better but I can see what I look like."

"What *do* you look like?"

"It's horrible. Everybody notices. They make me look so old. I'm sure

Joe is turned off. I don't know what I would ever do if he left me. I have started to wear all this heavy makeup to hide them, but try to hide something like this."

"Let me ask you this. Most of us are sensitive about our appearance, and sometimes we exaggerate some minor imperfection. Do you think you might be doing that?"

Sally sighed. "Joe has been saying the same thing. I think about that, and sometimes I can convince myself that I am too concerned about something that is really very minor. But then I go to the mirror, and there it is. Can't you help me convince Joe that I should see if a plastic surgeon can do something about it?"

"Before we get into that, how long have you been bothered by the lines?"

"I'm not sure, but I didn't pay any attention to it until a few months ago. A friend at work mentioned that she had seen a doctor for a bad sunburn and told me I had better be careful because my skin was so fair. I began looking in the mirror and kept noticing the lines."

The psychiatrist asked about other problems in Sally's life and learned that her concern with her appearance was not affecting her ability to work, but that she had started to avoid social situations because she didn't want people looking at her blemish. Sally acknowledged being upset and unhappy about her problem, but denied having a persistently depressed mood or any associated symptoms of depression.

Discussion of "Age Lines"

Sally looks perfectly normal, but is preoccupied with a defect in her appearance that she grossly exaggerates. Her belief is not of delusional intensity (as in Delusional Disorder, Somatic Type), in that she can acknowledge the possibility that she may be exaggerating the extent of the defect.

Sally, like many people with a condition of this nature, avoids social situations, but the essential feature of the disorder is not phobic avoidance. Therefore, the original term for this condition, Dysmorphophobia, is incorrect. The more accurate, descriptive, new name is Body Dysmorphic (dysmorphic = abnormal shape) Disorder.

The most common complaints in Body Dysmorphic Disorder involve facial flaws, such as wrinkles, spots on the skin, excessive facial hair, swelling of the face, and shape of nose, mouth, jaw, or eyebrows. More rarely the complaint involves the appearance of the feet, hands, breasts, back, or some other part of the body.

In some cases, such as Sally's, no physical anomaly is actually present. In other cases there may be a minor physical anomaly, but the person's concern is grossly excessive.

DSM-III-R Diagnosis:

Axis I: 300.70 Body Dysmorphic Disorder, Moderate (p. 256)

Follow-up

Sally consulted a psychiatrist who treated her with an antidepressant. She did not like the side effects and discontinued treatment. Gradually, her preoccupation with her wrinkles disappeared. She entered therapy, apparently for issues unrelated to her former concern with her wrinkles. When last seen three years after her initial evaluation, she appeared happy and generally satisfied with her life.

Too Far from Home

THIS 32-YEAR-OLD, white, married housewife comes to the clinic because of fear of losing her balance and either falling or fainting. (She has, in fact, never fallen or fainted.) The current difficulties began one year ago, shortly after she and her family moved away from her mother's neighborhood. Her husband went into his own business, which kept him away from home much of the time. Before the move, she could walk to her mother's and sister's houses; now she lives so far from them that she knows they can't come over immediately if she needs them. At first she avoided going out of her new house, but she eventually could go alone to small neighborhood stores and supermarkets if they were not crowded. Two months ago a man of 41, who was her friend, died of a brain cyst. Since then she has been continuously anxious, unable to go out, and comfortable at home only when she is with her husband.

The patient's present condition is a recurrence of symptoms she first experienced 12 years ago, immediately after her marriage. She began to fear losing her balance and falling. The more frightened she became, the more unsteady she felt. She became unable to go anywhere. She remembers thinking, "Now that I don't want to die, God is going to answer my childhood prayers, and I will die." At that time she consulted an internist, who was unable to help her; then a psychiatrist, whom she saw three times, with no improvement; and finally, a hypnotist. Following hypnosis, her symptoms subsided.

She denies ever having such symptoms as palpitations or chest pain, sweating, or difficulty breathing.

Discussion of "Too Far from Home"

This woman is terrified of leaving her house because of a fear that she may fall or faint. This fear has kept her housebound, and she is also afraid of being alone, even at home. This marked constriction of activity from a fear of being in places or situations from which escape might be difficult (or embarrassing) or in which help might not be available in the event of suddenly developing a symptom(s) that could be incapacitating or extremely embarrassing is called Agoraphobia.

In clinical settings, Agoraphobia is almost always preceded by panic attacks, which the patient associates with being in certain places or situations. More rarely, as in this case, there is no such history. Therefore, the diagnosis is Agoraphobia without History of Panic Disorder. According to DSM-III-R, when a person with this disorder has a single or small number of symptoms, such as feeling unsteady (this case), or attacks of depersonalization, loss of bladder or bowel control, or cardiac distress, this should be noted as part of the diagnosis with the specification: with Limited Symptom Attacks.

DSM-III-R Diagnosis:

Axis I: **300.22 Agoraphobia without History of Panic Disorder, Severe, with Limited Symptom Attacks (p. 241)**

Child Psychiatrist

D R. CRONE IS A 35-YEAR-OLD, single child psychiatrist. He has been arrested and convicted of fondling several neighborhood boys, ages 6 to 12. Friends and colleagues were shocked and dismayed, as he had been considered by all to be particularly caring and supportive of children. Not only had he chosen a profession involving their care but he had been a Cub Scout leader for many years and also a member of the local Big Brothers.

Dr. Crone is from a stable family. His father, who had also been a physician, was described as a workaholic, spending little time with his three children. Dr. Crone never married and, when interviewed by a psychiatrist as part of his presentence investigation, admitted that he experienced little, if any, sexual attraction toward females, either adults or children. He also denied sexual attraction toward adult men. In presenting the history of his psychosexual development, he reported that he had become somewhat dismayed as a child when his boyfriends began expressing rudimentary awareness of an attraction toward girls. His "secret" at the time was that he was attracted more to other boys and, in fact, during childhood, often played "doctor" with other boys, eventually progressing to mutual masturbation with some of his boyfriends.

His first sexual experience was at the age of 6, when a 15-year-old male camp counselor performed fellatio on him several times over the course of the summer—an experience that he had always kept to himself. As he reached his teen-age years, he began to suspect that he was homosexual. As he grew older, he was surprised to notice that the age range of males that attracted him sexually did not change, and he continued to have recurrent erotic urges and fantasies about boys between the ages of 6 and 12. Whenever he masturbated, he would fantasize about a boy in that age range, and on a couple of occasions over the years had felt himself to be in love with such a youngster.

Intellectually, Dr. Crone knew that others would disapprove of his many sexual involvements with young boys. He never believed, however, that he had ever caused any of these youngsters harm, feeling instead that they were simply sharing pleasurable feelings together. He yearned to be able to experience the same sort of feelings toward women, but he never was able to do so. He frequently prayed for help, and that his actions would go undetected. He kept promising himself that he would stop, but the temptations were such that he could not. He was so fearful of destroying his reputation, his friendships, and his career that he had never been able to bring himself to tell anyone else about his problem.

Discussion of "Child Psychiatrist"

Dr. Crone experiences recurrent intense sexual urges and sexually arousing fantasies involving sexual activity with prepubescent boys. He has acted on these fantasies and urges on many occasions. This alone is sufficient to make the diagnosis of Pedophilia. The diagnosis would also be made if Dr. Crone had never acted on these fantasies and urges, but was markedly distressed by them.

In DSM-III the diagnosis of Pedophilia required that the deviant sexual behavior be the preferred source of sexual arousal. In DSM-III-R this is not required, since in many cases of people who act on pedophilic (and other paraphilic) impulses, the deviant behavior may alternate with other paraphilic or with more ordinary sexual behavior. In Dr. Crone's case, we note that his deviant behavior is directed toward the same sex. This has prognostic significance in that the recidivism rate for people with Pedophilia involving a preference for the same sex may be roughly twice that of those who prefer the opposite sex. We also note that he is exclusively aroused by young boys and, as is usually the case, boys within a relatively narrow age range.

Dr. Crone, like many other men with Pedophilia who do not also have Sexual Sadism, has a genuine interest in children, and justified his behavior with the rationalization that he was not harming them in any way.

DSM-III-R Diagnosis:

Axis I: 302.20 Pedophilia, Same Sex, Exclusive Type, Severe
                   (p. 285)

Emilio

EMILIO IS A 40-YEAR-OLD MAN who looks 10 years younger. He is brought to the hospital, his 12th hospitalization, by his mother because she is afraid of him. He is dressed in a ragged overcoat, bedroom slippers, and a baseball cap and wears several medals around his neck. His affect ranges from anger at his mother—"She feeds me shit . . . what comes out of other people's rectums"—to a giggling, obsequious seductiveness toward the interviewer. His speech and manner have a childlike quality, and he walks with a mincing step and exaggerated hip movements. His mother reports that he stopped taking his medication about a month ago, and has since begun to hear voices and to look and act more bizarrely. When asked what he has been doing, he says "eating wires and lighting fires." His spontaneous speech is often incoherent and marked by frequent rhyming and clang associations.

Emilio's first hospitalization occurred after he dropped out of school at 16, and since that time he has never been able to attend school or hold a job. He lives with his elderly mother, but sometimes disappears for several months at a time, and is eventually picked up by the police as he wanders in the streets. There is no known history of drug or alcohol abuse.

Discussion of "Emilio"

The combination of a chronic illness with marked incoherence, inappropriate affect, auditory hallucinations, and bizarre behavior leaves little doubt that the diagnosis is Chronic Schizophrenia, with an acute exacerbation. The presence of marked loosening of associations and grossly inappropriate affect, and the absence of prominent catatonic symptoms, indicate the Disorganized Type.

DSM-III-R Diagnosis:

Axis I: 295.14 Schizophrenia, Disorganized Type, Chronic with
           Acute Exacerbation (p. 194)

Follow-up

Emilio has been hospitalized five more times in the ten years following this admission to the hospital. During each of his hospitalizations, he was treated with high doses of antipsychotic drugs, and within a few weeks began to behave appropriately and to be able to ignore the voices of his auditory hallucinations. During the first hospitalization he was able to establish a relationship with a therapist and talk thoughtfully and with a full range of appropriate affect about his unhappy life, his inability to do any work because "nobody wants me," and his desire to be taken care of. However, soon after leaving the hospital, Emilio stopped taking his medication, failed to keep clinic appointments, and within a few months was again grossly disorganized and psychotic.

Emilio's last psychiatric hospitalization was two years ago, when he was 48. His mother was now too feeble to care for him, and arrangements were made for him to live in an adult home after he left the hospital, supported by welfare, and with medication managed by the staff of the institution. In that setting he does fairly well.

Worms

M S. GREEN IS A 62-YEAR-OLD retired librarian who complains to her doctor that "The worms are still at it."

Four years ago, when taking a bath, Ms. Green noted what she thought were lots of "little worms" floating in the bath water. Soon thereafter she began to experience the feeling of these worms "digging under my skin." Multiple visits to doctors, to whom she brought samples of the "worms," could uncover no evidence of parasites. She received symptomatic treatment for itching. To her exasperation, the doctors persisted in telling her that her samples were only "flakes of dry skin." She refused a psychiatric consultation. She soon began to feel that her co-workers and friends avoided her because of her worms. She reduced her previously rather numerous social activities. She became so upset by the worms that she eventually decided to take early retirement from her job, which she had held for over thirty years. She denied symptoms of depression during this time.

Ms. Green's condition was apparently unchanged until nine months ago when, in church, she noticed that all the rosaries within a few yards of her were rotating in a clockwise direction. She began to see other evidence that she was giving off a "magnetic field." She explains that this is a result of the worms entering her spinal cord and traveling up and down, which "creates a magnetic current."

Ms. Green is a pleasant, articulate woman with full range of affect and coherent goal-directed speech. She denies other unusual experiences, such as hearing voices, or any symptoms of depression. She has become more socially isolated recently as she feels the "magnetic field" makes other people uncomfortable. Otherwise, she maintains active correspondence with several people, likes to knit and to read, and continues to volunteer her time at her old library, where they say her work continues to be of high quality.

Discussion of "Worms"

Had we seen Ms. Green early in her illness, when she was complaining only of being infested with "worms," we would have concluded that she had a nonbizarre delusion, and made a diagnosis of Delusional Disorder. Seeing her now, however, we have to take into account that her delusion now involves phenomena that her culture would regard as totally implausible: the worms create a magnetic current that causes the rosaries to rotate. She now has a prominent bizarre delusion, so the diagnosis of Delusional Disorder is no longer appropriate.

The chronic bizarre delusion and the absence of a mood disturbance suggest Schizophrenia. However, Schizophrenia is an illness that invariably involves marked disturbance in social and occupational functioning. Ms. Green did reduce her social activities, but is still described as functioning well in her work and maintaining social contact, at least by mail. We are therefore more comfortable with the diagnosis of Psychotic Disorder Not Otherwise Specified.

DSM-III-R Diagnosis:

**Axis I: 298.90 Psychotic Disorder Not Otherwise Specified
             (p. 211)**

Evening Shift

A 30-YEAR-OLD WAREHOUSE WORKER had experienced episodes of poor sleep for the preceding five years whenever he had to work on the evening shift. Every two weeks he alternated between working evenings (3:00 PM to 11:00 PM) and working the day shift (7:00 AM to 3:00 PM).

When he worked the evening shift, he would go to bed about two hours after work, around 1:00 AM. About half the time it would take him an hour or two to fall asleep. When this happened, he typically would awaken at 5:00 AM, his normal time for getting up to go to work the day shift. He would have a snack, and then return to bed and drift in and out of sleep until arising between 8:30 AM and 11:00 AM. On weekends and holidays, however, he would revert to his normal bedtime, approximately 10:00 PM, when he would fall into bed exhausted.

When the patient slept poorly at night, he felt sleepy the next day; if he slept well, he felt alert. When he worked the day shift, and on vacations, he slept well and felt alert the next day.

Discussion of "Evening Shift"

Sleep, like most biologic functions, follows a rhythm over a period that lasts about twenty-four hours (circadian rhythm). The sleep rhythm induced by daytime work in this patient persists when he works the evening shift. At these times the mismatch between his circadian rhythm and the demands of his work schedule result in insomnia (trouble falling asleep and staying asleep). His biologic clock causes sleepiness at 10:00 PM and awakening at about 5:00 AM. When he works the evening shift, he is forced to stay awake hours beyond his usual bedtime and he initially awakens at his usual arising time.

If the patient were able to stay on the evening shift for several months and maintain the same sleep times, his biologic clock would gradually be reset, so that his sleep schedule would harmonize with the hours of his work day. It is because the hours of his shift keep changing, and he is apparently particularly intolerant of the mismatch between his circadian rhythm and his daily work schedule, that he cannot sleep during desirable hours.

Sleep problems resulting from a mismatch between the normal sleep-wake schedule for the person's environment and his or her circadian sleep-wake pattern are diagnosed as Sleep-Wake Schedule Disorder. When the disorder is apparently due to frequently changing sleep and waking times, such as changes in work shifts or time zones, the Frequently Changing Type is specified. The diagnosis is confirmed, as in this case, by normal sleep and daytime alertness when the internal sleep schedule conforms again to environmental demands.

DSM-III-R Diagnosis:

Axis I: 307.45 Sleep-Wake Schedule Disorder, Frequently
                  Changing Type (p. 307)

Follow-up

The patient was advised to gradually discontinue eating at night, in order to stop reinforcing nocturnal appetite and wakefulness. In addition, he was advised to arise at 8:30 AM when he worked the evening shift, no matter how tired he felt. In this way it was hoped that he would feel tired enough at 1:00 AM to fall asleep immediately and then have a full night's sleep.

After trying the program, the patient reported that he could not stick to it. He said he became "like a madman" during the night, searching everywhere for his favorite snacks after his wife, with his consent, had hidden them. Nor could he remain awake until 1:00 AM on the weekend between the two weeks of the evening shift.

The patient did not return for another appointment, but called several months later to report that he had been able to convince his employer to take him off the evening work shift permanently, which completely relieved his sleep problem.

The Socialite

DOROTHEA CABOT, A 42-YEAR-OLD socialite, has never had any mental problems before. A new performance hall is to be formally opened with the world premiere of a new ballet; and Dorothea, because of her position on the cultural council, has assumed the responsibility for coordinating that event. However, construction problems, including strikes, have made it uncertain whether finishing details will meet the deadline. The set designer has been volatile, threatening to walk out on the project unless the materials meet his meticulous specifications. Dorothea has had to calm this volatile man while attempting to coax disputing groups to negotiate. She has also had increased responsibilities at home since her housekeeper has had to leave to visit a sick relative.

In the midst of these difficulties, her best friend has been decapitated in a tragic auto crash. Dorothea herself is an only child, and her best friend had been very close to her since grade school. People have often commented that the two women were like sisters.

Immediately following the funeral, Dorothea becomes increasingly tense and jittery, and able to sleep only two to three hours a night. Two days later she happens to see a woman driving a car just like the one her friend had driven. She is puzzled, and after a few hours she becomes convinced that her friend is alive, that the accident had been staged, along with the funeral, as part of a plot. Somehow the plot is directed toward deceiving her, and she senses that somehow she is in great danger and must solve the mystery to escape alive. She begins to distrust everyone except her husband, and begins to believe that the phone is tapped and that the rooms are "bugged." She pleads with her husband to help save her life. She begins to hear a high-pitched, undulating sound, which she fears is an ultrasound beam aimed at her. She is in a state of sheer panic, gripping her husband's arm in terror, as he brings her to the emergency room the next morning.

Discussion of "The Socialite"

Our initial impression was that this was a rather straightforward example of Brief Reactive Psychosis. A severe psychosocial stressor (the death and funeral of her friend) preceded the development of psychotic symptoms (persecutory delusions and, later, auditory hallucinations) in a thus far short-lived illness. On further reflection, however, we realized that there was no evidence of emotional turmoil—that is, rapid shifts from one dysphoric affect to another without the persistence of any one affect—or of overwhelming perplexity or confusion. These features are required for a diagnosis of Brief Reactive Psychosis.

Since the predominant symptoms are persecutory delusions, Delusional Disorder needs to be considered; but that diagnosis requires a duration of illness of at least one month. We recognize that some clinicians would regard the patient's delusion of an "ultrasound beam" aimed at her as bizarre, which would suggest Schizophreniform Disorder. However, ultrasound does exist, and her major delusion (i.e., that the death of her friend was staged) is not bizarre, so we rule out Schizophreniform Disorder. We are therefore left with the residual category of Psychotic Disorder Not Otherwise Specified.

DSM-III-R Diagnosis:

Axis I: 298.90 Psychotic Disorder Not Otherwise Specified
                          (p. 211)

Lovely Rita

A 36-YEAR-OLD LONDON METER MAID was referred for psychiatric examination by her solicitor. Six months previously, moments after she had written a ticket and placed it on the windshield of an illegally parked car, a man came dashing out of a barbershop, ran up to her, swearing and shaking his fist, swung, and hit her in the jaw with enough force to knock her down. A fellow worker came to her aid and summoned the police, who caught the man a few blocks away and placed him under arrest.

The patient was taken to the hospital, where a hairline fracture of the jaw was diagnosed by X-ray. The fracture did not require that her jaw be wired, but the patient was placed on a soft diet for four weeks. Several different physicians, including her own, found her physically fit to return to work after one month. The patient, however, complained of severe pain and muscle tension in her neck and back that virtually immobilized her. She spent most of her days sitting in a chair or lying on a bedboard on her bed. She enlisted the services of a solicitor since the Workmen's Compensation Board was cutting off her payments and her employer was threatening her with suspension if she did not return to work.

The patient shuffled slowly and laboriously into the psychiatrist's office and lowered herself with great care into a chair. She was attractively dressed, well made up, and wore a neck brace. She related her story with vivid detail, and with considerable anger directed at her assailant (whom she repeatedly referred to as that "bloody foreigner"), her employer, and the compensation board. It was as if the incident had occurred yesterday. Regarding her ability to work, she said that she wanted to return to the job, would soon be severely strapped financially, but was physically not up to even the lightest office work.

She denied any previous psychological problems and initially described her childhood and family life as storybook perfect. In subsequent interviews, however, she admitted that as a child she had frequently been beaten by her alcoholic father, and had once suffered a broken arm as a result, and that she had often been locked in a closet for hours at a time as punishment for misbehavior.

Discussion of "Lovely Rita"

In this case the first question is: Can this woman's pain be entirely accounted for by the nature of her very real physical injury? Evidently, the answer is no, given the extensive assessment by several physicians. The next question is: Is this woman *simply* attempting to get continued financial support from Workmen's Compensation so that she will no longer have to earn a living? If the answer to this is yes, this would be an instance of Malingering, that is, the voluntary production and presentation of false symptoms in pursuit of external incentives. The apparent genuineness of her suffering and her desire to return to work make this unlikely. This leaves us with the possibility of undiagnosed physical pain or Somatoform Pain Disorder, a diagnosis that is made only when there is a preoccupation with pain and appropriate evaluation uncovers no organic cause that can entirely account for the pain.

In DSM-III, this diagnosis was called Psychogenic Pain Disorder and required positive evidence of the role of psychological factors in the development of the pain, such as a temporal relationship between an environmental stimulus related to a psychological conflict and the initiation of the pain. In this case such evidence would be the history of the patient's having been physically abused by her father as a child, which probably produced psychological conflict that was revived by the assault. This might account for the continuation of the pain beyond what would be accounted for by her injury. In DSM-III-R positive evidence of the role of psychological factors in the development of the pain is no longer required, because often such evidence cannot be found, and specialists in the treatment of chronic pain argued that the treatment approach was the same regardless of whether or not such factors were evident.

DSM-III-R Diagnosis:

Axis I: 307.80 Somatoform Pain Disorder, Severe (p. 266)

Nightmares

MARTHA, A 35-YEAR-OLD WOMAN, has suffered from nightmares every night, beginning in her early teen-age years. She comes to a sleep specialist at the insistence of her husband who is fed up with her behavior, both while sleeping and while awake. One to four times a night, she awakens out of a dream, the content of which is always disturbing. Often she dreams of yelling at other people or of menacing confrontations. In the dreams she feels angry and frustrated. Typically, she awakes from the dreams feeling extremely tense.

During the day Martha often has uncontrollable outbursts of temper. These can be precipitated by minor frustrations, such as a delay in finding her eyeglasses. In the midst of an outburst she may feel that it is wrong to behave thus, that her outburst is unwarranted, but she is powerless to stop it. After the outburst she apologizes for it.

Martha sleeps excessively, sometimes 12 or 13 hours consecutively on weekends, and often takes 3-4-hour naps. She is sleepy while driving on the turnpike, but manages to stay awake by having the temperature cold and the radio "blasting."

She denies having sudden, irresistible attacks of sleepiness, cataplexy (sudden loss of motor power), hypnogogic hallucinations (hallucinations while awakening), or sleep paralysis (motor weakness and brief inability to move upon sudden awakening), all of which are characteristic of narcolepsy. She denies feeling confused or disoriented when she awakens from her dreams (as might be found in impaired arousal states, such as in episodes associated with temporal lobe dysfunction). Her

husband notes that she has greatly increased eyelid flutter and eye movements shortly after she has fallen asleep (which might mean abnormally
early onset of REM sleep, as is seen in Major Depression and drug withdrawal states). She always sleeps restlessly and occasionally hits him
suddenly in the middle of the night (a common symptom of Parasomnias).

At the initial evaluation, Martha appeared downcast, but did not cry.
She was organized and informative. She made three mistakes on serial
sevens, but her sensorium was otherwise intact. She described her work
as a registrar in a small college, which she considered enjoyable and her
"salvation." Her 4½-year-old daughter was bright and well.

Martha had smoked a pack of cigarettes a day for 25 years, and drank
a cup of chocolate and 48 ounces of cola beverages daily. She took
alcohol only a few times per year.

Electroencephalography showed a somewhat slowed background
rhythm intermixed with slower frequencies. There were intermittent
bursts of high-voltage, 4-6 per second sharp theta-waves, moderately
increased by hyperventilation. There were no significant asymmetries.
(These nonspecific cerebral dysrhythmias suggest that a central nervous
system abnormality may underlie her sleep disturbance.)

All-night sleep recording revealed 9 hours of sleep continually interrupted by 10–30-second arousals that frequently began with a K-complex
(an arousal pattern) and were mostly unassociated with prior body movements. These happened about 35 times per hour in sleep stages I and II
and during REM sleep, but only 4 times per hour during deep sleep.
Otherwise, REM latency (the time spent before the initial appearance of
REM sleep), density, and amount were normal, and other stages, although
interrupted, were of normal pattern and percentage. However, there
were no reports of nightmares during the night. (The constant arousals
were unusual, and possibly related to the abnormalities noted on the
electroencephalogram.)

Discussion of "Nightmares"

Martha's recurrent nightmares are a form of Parasomnia, a
group of Sleep Disorders in which the predominant symptom is an
abnormal event that occurs either during sleep or at the threshold
between wakefulness and sleep. Martha suffers from Dream Anxiety
Disorder, sometimes called Nightmare Disorder. In Dream Anxiety
Disorder there are repeated awakenings from sleep with detailed
recall of frightening dreams. These dreams are typically vivid and
quite extended and usually include threats to survival, security, or
self-esteem. The dreams occur during periods of REM sleep, and
thus are more likely to appear toward the end of the night.

Martha also suffers from unusually prolonged sleep and day-time sleepiness (hypersomnia). Since the cause of the hypersomnia is neither a known organic factor (as in hypersomnia caused by sleep apnea) nor another mental disorder (such as Major Depression), the diagnosis of Primary Hypersomnia is made.

It is hard to know how to explain Martha's irritability and temper outbursts. The psychiatrist who treated her suspected that these symptoms might have been manifestations of hypomania.

DSM-III-R Diagnosis:

Axis I: 307.47 Dream Anxiety Disorder (p. 310)
            780.54 Primary Hypersomnia (p. 305)

Follow-up

Treatment has included psychotherapy; attempts to control dream content through a lucid dreaming routine (in which the dreamer directs the events of the dream or attempts to converse with the characters in it); and trials of an antidepressant, imipramine, 200 mg daily for 6 weeks, and of an anticonvulsant, carbamazepine, 800 mg daily for 4 weeks, neither of which helped. A trial of lithium significantly lessened the temper outbursts for a period of two weeks, but they then returned, despite dosage increases.

After being seen for eight months, the patient became discouraged and angry with the therapist and refused further treatment.

Smoke Rings

BETH IS A 42-YEAR-OLD ACTRESS who had been smoking two packs of cigarettes daily for over twenty-two years. Still touting the great pleasures of smoking, she came to a clinic hoping to stop. Over the past decade, she has had behavioral treatment, hypnosis, and acupuncture, all with only short-lived success. She estimated that she had tried to stop smoking on her own over thirty times. Typically, she manages to abstain from smoking through the morning (painful and slow as it may be), but "gives in" at lunch time, immediately relieved by the second drag of her cigarette. Recurrent bouts of bronchitis, two pregnancies, and periodic pleas from her husband have been motivators for her attempts to quit smoking.

Entering the office for her first appointment, she asked: "Would it be all right if I smoke while we talk? Just the thought of preparing to quit makes me want to smoke more!"

Discussion of "Smoke Rings"

For many years it has been recognized that the clinical features of dependence on substances such as opioids and alcohol apply as well to dependence on substances containing nicotine. Beth demonstrates the same lack of control over her smoking of cigarettes as a person addicted to heroin displays over the use of heroin. She has tried to stop smoking many times, but has not succeeded. She spends a great deal of time smoking and continues to smoke despite realizing that it exacerbates a physical problem (bronchitis). Therefore, the diagnosis of Nicotine Dependence is made.

Because of the availability of cigarettes and the absence of a clinically significant nicotine intoxication syndrome (one does not ordinarily get "stoned" on cigarettes), impairment in occupational or social functioning is not necessary for a rating of severe Nicotine Dependence. We suspect that Beth would agree with us that her dependence on cigarettes is severe.

DSM-III-R Diagnosis:

Axis I: 305.10 Nicotine Dependence, Severe (p. 167)

Follow-up

Beth's treatment included supportive and educational sessions with a therapist in conjunction with clonidine, a medication believed to reduce withdrawal symptoms during smoking cessation. As her past attempts to quit smoking had lasted only a few hours, it was only now, when she stopped smoking for an extended time, that the characteristic symptoms of Nicotine Withdrawal (craving, irritability, restlessness, anxiety, and difficulty concentrating) could be seen.

During the first two days without cigarettes, Beth thought of nothing but smoking and found relief only in going to sleep. Mostly anxious, restless, and irritable during this time, she occasionally lapsed into feeling listless, "fuzzy-headed," and apathetic.

In the week that followed, the craving became intermittent, and the anxiety turned into "butterflies in the stomach" and severe headaches. By her third week without cigarettes, although these acute symptoms were much rarer, Beth was frequently insomniac, still irritable, and unable to focus her attention on anything requiring even minimal concentration. Her joy about her success was tempered by her disbelief that it could last. But, by her sixth week free of cigarettes, she was feeling only occasional cravings, usually associated with enjoying coffee, studying a script, or having an argument; and by her sixth *month*, the craving was limited to infrequent evenings when she watched a friend blowing smoke rings after dinner.

Antique Dealer

A N INTERNIST REQUESTED consultation on a 59-year-old antique dealer who had been admitted to the hospital for workup of severe hypertension. On the third hospital day he appeared "depressed." The consultant found the patient dozing in his bed; it was apparent that he had spilled some of his lunch on the sheets. The patient was difficult to arouse; and although he responded to his name and looked at the consultant, he did not appear to understand simple questions such as where he was or what the date was. He mumbled incoherently and, when tested, had obvious weakness in his right arm and leg. A neurological consultation confirmed the diagnosis of a stroke.

Discussion of "Antique Dealer"

Reduced ability to maintain attention (the patient did not appear to understand simple questions), disorganized thinking (incoherent speech), reduced level of consciousness (he dozed in bed and was difficult to arouse), and disorganized thinking (his speech was incoherent), in the presence of evidence of an organic etiology (right-sided weakness), indicate the Organic Mental Syndrome Delirium. Although in the past the term *delirium* had the connotation of an agitated or excited confusional state, more recently the essence of the syndrome is thought to be a disturbance in attention and goal-directed thinking. Other common symptoms of Delirium, which this patient did not display, include perceptual disturbances (misinterpretations, illusions, or hallucinations), increased psychomotor activity, and memory impairment.

Although neurologists would generally agree that, technically, this patient had a Delirium when he was seen by the psychiatric consultant, they would very likely not note it in their own diagnostic formulation, as they would focus diagnostically on the etiologic process, the cerebrovascular accident (stroke).

In DSM-III-R, Delirium is coded from the section of the Organic Mental Disorders associated with Axis III physical disorders or conditions or whose etiology is unknown, since the etiology (cerebrovascular accident) is outside the mental disorders section of the ICD-9-CM classification. The physical disorder (etiology) is noted on Axis III.

DSM-III-R Diagnosis:

Axis I: 293.00 Delirium (p.103)
Axis III: Cerebrovascular accident

Paul and Petula

PAUL AND PETULA have been living together for the last six months and are contemplating marriage. Petula describes the problem that has brought them to the sex therapy clinic.

"For the last two months he hasn't been able to keep his erection after he enters me."

The psychiatrist turns to Paul and asks him how he sees the problem. Paul, embarrassed, agrees with Petula and adds, "I just don't know why."

The psychiatrist learns that Paul, 26 years old, is a recently graduated lawyer, and that Petula is 24 and a successful buyer for a large department store. They both grew up in educated, middle-class, suburban families. They met through mutual friends, and started to have sexual intercourse a few months after they met and recall no real problems at that time.

Two months later, Paul moved from his family home into Petula's apartment. This was her idea, and Paul was unsure that he was ready for such an important step. Within a few weeks, Paul noticed that although he continued to be sexually aroused and wanted intercourse, as soon as he entered his partner, he began to lose his erection and could not stay inside. They would try again, but by then his desire had waned, and he was unable to achieve another erection.

After the first few times this happened, Petula became so angry that she began punching him in the chest and screaming at him. Paul, who weighs 200 pounds, would simply walk away from his 98-pound lover, which would infuriate her even more.

The psychiatrist learned that sex was not the only area of contention in the relationship. Petula complained that Paul did not spend enough time with her, and preferred to go to baseball games with his male friends. Even when he was home, he would watch all the sports events that were available on TV, and was not interested in going to foreign movies, museums, or the theater with her. Despite these differences, Petula was eager to marry Paul and was pressuring him to set a date.

Physical examination of the couple revealed no abnormalities, and there was no evidence that either partner was persistently depressed.

Discussion of "Paul and Petula"

Paul and Petula have many problems that a family-oriented clinician would want to focus on, such as Paul's ambivalence about committing himself to a relationship with Petula and her frantic efforts to obtain that commitment. The effect of these problems on Paul's sexual functioning is clear: he is unable to maintain his erection until the completion of sexual activity.

When there is no evidence that the disturbance is caused exclusively by organic factors (such as by diabetic neuropathy or certain medications), the diagnosis of Male Erectile Disorder is made. (An erectile dysfunction caused exclusively by organic factors would be coded as a physical disorder on Axis III.) We note that the disorder is acquired (recent onset), and not lifelong.

DSM-III-R Diagnosis:

Axis I: 302.72 Male Erectile Disorder, Psychogenic Only, Acquired (p. 294)

Follow-up

Neither partner was willing to discuss nonsexual problems. They were treated with Masters and Johnson's sensate focus exercises over the next several months. In these exercises, the couple explored nongenital ways of giving physical pleasure to each other without the psychological demands of demonstrating sexual competence. Petula continually pressured Paul to translate the therapy into action. She saw herself as a therapist and teacher, and Paul as patient and pupil. Paul passively avoided doing the exercises on many occasions; but over a period of eight months, Paul's problem with maintaining an erection was gradually resolved. They were married within three months after treatment ended.

Paul and Petula sought treatment twice more over the next eight years. On both occasions the underlying issue was again Paul's ambivalence about further committing himself to the relationship (buying a house, having children). Paul had a recurrence of erectile problems and, in addition, a complaint of premature ejaculation on the rare occasions when he could maintain an erection intravaginally. During the treatment greater attention was given to their relationship rather than simply focusing on the sexual problem. At last report they had two children, had bought a house in the suburbs, and the sexual problem had again been resolved.

The Bully

J. P. IS A MUSCULAR, 24-YEAR-OLD MAN who presented himself to the admitting office of a state hospital. He told the admitting physician that he had taken 30 200-mg tablets of Thorazine in the bus on the way over to the hospital. After receiving medical treatment for the "suicide attempt," he was transferred to the inpatient ward.

On mental status examination the patient told a fantastic story about his father's being a famous surgeon who had a patient die in surgery and whose husband then killed his father. J.P. then stalked his father's murderer several thousand miles across the United States and, when he found him, was prevented from killing him, at the last moment, by the timely arrival of his 94-year-old grandmother. He also related several other intriguing stories involving his $64,000 sports car, which had a 12-cylinder diesel engine, and about his children, two sets of identical triplets. All these stories had a grandiose tinge, and none of them could be confirmed. The patient claimed that he was hearing voices, as on the TV or in a dream. He answered affirmatively to questions about thought control, thought broadcasting, and other Schneiderian first-rank symptoms; he also claimed depression. He was oriented and alert and had a good range of information except that he kept insisting that it was the Germans (not the Russians) who had invaded Afghanistan. There was no evidence of any associated features of mania or depression, and the patient did not seem either elated, depressed, or irritable when he related these stories.

It was observed on the ward that the patient bullied the other patients and took food and cigarettes from them. He was very reluctant to be discharged, and whenever the subject of his discharge was brought up, he renewed his complaints about "suicidal thoughts" and "hearing voices." It was the opinion of the ward staff that the patient was not truly psychotic, but merely feigned his symptoms whenever the subject of further disposition of his case came up. They thought that he wanted to remain in the hospital primarily so that he could bully the other patients and be a "big man" on the ward.

Discussion of "The Bully"

Although this patient would have us believe that he is psychotic, his story, almost from the start, seems to conform to no recognizable psychotic syndrome. That his symptoms are not genuine is confirmed by the observation of the ward staff that he seemed to feign his symptoms whenever the subject of discharge was brought up.

Why does this fellow try so hard to act crazy? His motivation is not to achieve some external incentive, such as avoiding the draft, as would be the case in Malingering; his goal of remaining a patient is understandable only with knowledge of his individual psychology (the suggestion that he derives satisfaction from being the "big man" on the ward). The diagnosis is, therefore, Factitious Disorder with Psychological Symptoms.

DSM-III-R Diagnosis:

Axis I: 300.16 Factitious Disorder with Psychological Symptoms
                 (p. 319)

Gloria

THE PATIENT IS AN ATTRACTIVE, well-dressed, 43-year-old woman who became acutely psychotic about one month before admission to the hospital. Before that time she had been working with her husband in a mail order gift business. After completing the Christmas catalog, under considerable pressure because of the printer's deadlines, the patient began to have vague fears that her husband would hurt her. She felt an "evil presence" in the building in which they lived and ran away to a friend's house. There she tried to write a letter to her husband, but felt that the electric typewriter she was using was "canceling people out" and that she might be the last person left on earth. On the street she felt that people were not who they seemed to be, and that they were giving her messages by "clicking" their eyes. Intermittently she heard a voice saying, "Gloria is nuts" and telling her not to smoke.

On admission, Gloria spoke in a rambling, tangential manner. She was quite labile—she appeared frightened when she spoke about her husband, cried frequently, but then brightened and said that she felt something "wonderful" was going to happen.

There had been no changes in her sleep or appetite, although in the last few weeks she had become somewhat preoccupied with the necessity of eating "healthy" food.

The patient first had psychiatric treatment at age nine, after being picked up for shoplifting. She spent her senior year of high school in a "residential community" because of conflicts with her aged grandmother, who had reared her. At 27 she had an acute psychotic episode during which she was confused and self-referential, and was hospitalized for 9 months. Shortly after leaving the hospital, she married her long-time boyfriend, to whom she is still married. Between the ages of 33 and 43, the patient experienced two brief psychotic episodes, which were treated with Mellaril and outpatient psychotherapy. After each episode she apparently recovered completely, with no residual symptoms. She worked successfully as a secretary, traveled with her husband to select items for their import business, kept the books for the company, and had an active social life.

Discussion of "Gloria"

If there were no history of previous psychotic episodes in this case, there would be no difficulty in diagnosing the current episode. This apparently began one month previously and was characterized by bizarre delusions (the electric typewriter was "cancelling people out"), delusions of reference (people were giving her messages by "clicking their eyes"), and auditory hallucinations ("a voice saying, 'Gloria is nuts' "). In the absence of a known organic factor or a mood syndrome, the diagnosis would be Schizophreniform Disorder rather than Schizophrenia, because the duration of the illness is less than six months.

The diagnosis becomes less certain when we learn of several previous episodes, apparently also of brief duration, with similar symptoms and with complete recovery. Theoretically, it is possible to have recurrent episodes of Schizophreniform Disorder, but the occurrence of many episodes makes full recovery increasingly unlikely. The first psychotic episode, during which the patient was hospitalized for nine months, causes even more diagnostic confusion. If psychotic or residual signs of the illness persisted for the full nine months, then the diagnosis of that episode would have been Schizophrenia! The apparent period of complete recovery would then become Schizophrenia in Remission.

Because the very concept of Schizophrenia in Remission (as distinct from Residual Type) is dubious, DSM-III-R offers no guidelines for characterizing the course of a new psychotic episode following Schizophrenia in Remission. On the other hand, there is the possibility that despite a nine-month hospitalization, the psychotic illness may have been much briefer. Perhaps Gloria had largely recovered from the psychotic illness after a few months, but remained in the hospital because she was "a good psychotherapy patient" or because it took several months to work out suitable living arrangements in the community.

Because of the uncertainty about the nine-month episode and the apparently complete recovery from two other brief psychotic episodes, we prefer the less ominous provisional diagnosis of Schizophreniform Disorder. Because of the acute onset of psychotic symptoms, good premorbid social and occupational functioning, and the absence of blunted affect, the diagnosis is further specified as with good prognostic features. We should not quarrel with a clinician who preferred to make a provisional diagnosis of Psychotic Disorder Not Otherwise Specified and delayed making a more definitive diagnosis until after records of her nine-month hospitalization had been obtained.

DSM-III-R Diagnosis:

Axis I: 295.40 Schizophreniform Disorder, with Good Prognostic Features (Provisional) (p. 208)
R/O Chronic Schizophrenia with Acute Exacerbation

Toughing It Out

MINDY MARKOWITZ IS AN ATTRACTIVE, stylishly dressed, 25-year-old art director for a trade magazine who comes to an anxiety clinic after reading about the clinic program in the newspaper. She is seeking treatment for "panic attacks" that have occurred with increasing frequency over the past year, often two or three times a day. These attacks begin with a sudden intense wave of "horrible fear" that seems to come out of nowhere, sometimes during the day, sometimes waking her from sleep. She begins to tremble, is nauseated, sweats profusely, feels as though she is gagging, and fears that she will lose control and do something crazy, like run screaming into the street.

Mindy remembers first having attacks like this when she was in high school. She was dating a boy her parents disapproved of, and had to do a lot of "sneaking around" to avoid confrontations with them. At the same time, she was under a lot of pressure as the principal designer of her high-school yearbook, and was applying to Ivy League colleges. She remembers that her first panic attack occurred just after the yearbook went to press and she was accepted by Harvard, Yale, and Brown. The attacks lasted only a few minutes, and she would just "sit through them." She was worried enough to mention them to her mother; but because she was otherwise perfectly healthy, she did not seek treatment.

Over the eight years since her first attack, Mindy has had them intermittently, sometimes not for many months, sometimes, as now, several times a day. There have also been extreme variations in the intensity of the attacks, some being so severe and debilitating that she had to take a day off from work.

Apart from her panic attacks and a brief period of depression at 19, when she broke up with a boyfriend, Mindy has always functioned extremely well, in school, at work, and in her social life. She is a lively, friendly person who is respected by her friends and colleagues both for her intelligence and creativity and for her ability to mediate disputes.

Even during the times that she was having frequent, severe attacks, Mindy never limited her activities. She might stay home from work for a day because she was exhausted from multiple attacks, but she never associated the attacks with particular places. She says, for example, that she is as likely to have an attack at home in her own bed as on the subway, so there is no point in avoiding the subway. Whether she has an attack in the subway, in a supermarket, or at home by herself, she says, "I just tough it out."

Discussion of "Toughing It Out"

Mindy describes classic unexpected panic attacks. They hit her unpredictably with a sudden burst of fear and the characteristic symptoms of autonomic arousal: sweating, trembling, nausea, and gagging, all severe enough to make her fear she will lose control. Unlike most patients who have such severe panic attacks (see "Reluctant Home Buyer," p. 213), she has never associated particular situations, such as crowded places or public transportation, with having the attacks. Therefore, she does not show any symptoms of agoraphobic avoidance. Thus, the diagnosis is Panic Disorder without Agoraphobia. The current severity of the panic attacks is noted as severe.

DSM-III-R Diagnosis:

**Axis I: 300.01 Panic Disorder without Agoraphobia, Panic
                    Attacks Severe (p. 239)**

Toy Designer

A 45-YEAR-OLD TOY DESIGNER was admitted to the hospital following a series of suicidal gestures culminating in an attempt to strangle himself with a piece of wire. Four months before admission, his family had observed that he was becoming depressed: when at home he spent long periods sitting in a chair, he slept more than usual, and he had given up his habits of reading the evening paper and puttering around the house. Within a month he was unable to get out of bed in the morning to go to work. He expressed considerable guilt, but could not make up his mind to seek help until forced to do so by his family. He had not responded to two months of outpatient antidepressant drug therapy, and had made several half-hearted attempts to cut his wrists before the serious attempt that precipitated the admission.

Physical examination revealed signs of increased intracranial pressure, and a computerized tomographic (CT) scan showed a large frontal-lobe tumor.

Discussion of "Toy Designer"

Depressed mood, suicidal gestures, increased sleep, loss of interest, and guilt all suggest a Major Depressive Episode. Although the patient's symptoms are identical with those seen in a Major Depressive Episode, it is reasonable to infer that the disturbance is caused by the frontal-lobe tumor; thus, the diagnosis is Organic Mood Disorder.

Some clinicians might prefer to consider this diagnosis "provisional," pending the results of surgery. If the depression lifts after removal of the brain tumor, the diagnosis of an Organic Mood Disorder would be supported. If the depression persists following surgery, the diagnosis would remain equivocal, since there would be no way to definitely rule out a Major Depression that developed coincidentally.

The frontal-lobe tumor, of course, is noted on Axis III.

(Minor point: It is helpful to specify that the Organic Mood Disorder, in this case, was "depressed.")

DSM-III-R Diagnosis:

Axis I: 293.83 Organic Mood Disorder, Depressed (p.112)
Axis III: Frontal-lobe tumor

Follow-Up

The patient underwent surgery, and the tumor was removed. Two years following surgery, his wife described to the surgeon how hopeful she initially was following surgery since his depression seemed to lift. However, he never regained interest in returning to work, and has spent all of his time at home. Although the patient makes few complaints, his wife describes him as lacking his former enthusiasm and "spark." In addition, he seems to have trouble concentrating while reading the paper.

The diagnosis at follow-up is changed from the original diagnosis of Organic Mood Syndrome. The predominant disturbance now is a marked change in personality, as manifested by the patient's apathy and indifference. Personality changes are common in Dementia; but in this patient, despite some difficulty in concentrating, there is no evidence of a global deterioration in intellectual functioning. Thus, the follow-up Axis I diagnosis is Organic Personality Syndrome Disorder (p. 115). The physical condition, postsurgical removal of the frontal-lobe tumor, is noted on Axis III.

Freaking Out

IN THE MIDDLE OF A RAINY October night in 1970, a family doctor in a Chicago suburb was awakened by an old friend who begged him to get out of bed and come quickly to a neighbor's house, where he and his wife had been visiting. The caller, Lou Wolff, was very upset because his wife, Sybil, had smoked some marijuana and was "freaking out."

The doctor, extremely annoyed, arrived at the neighbor's house to find Sybil lying on the couch looking quite frantic, unable to get up. She said she was too weak to stand, that she was dizzy, having palpitations, and could feel her blood "rushing through [her] veins." She kept asking for water because her mouth was so dry she could not swallow. She was sure there was some poison in the marijuana. Sybil was relieved to see the doctor, because she had believed the neighbors would not let her husband call him for fear of being arrested for possession of marijuana, and she was sure that without medical help, she would die.

Sybil Wolff, age 42, is the mother of three teen-age boys. She works as a librarian at a university. She is a very controlled, well-organized woman who prides herself on her rationality. She has smoked marijuana, a small amount, only once before, and the only reaction she detected was that it made her feel "slightly mellow." It was she who asked the neighbors to share some of their high-quality homegrown marijuana with her, because marijuana was now a big thing with the students, and she "wanted to see what all the fuss was about."

Her husband says that she took four or five puffs of a joint and then wailed, "There's something wrong with me. I can't stand up." Lou and the neighbors tried to calm her, telling her she should just lie down and she would soon feel better; but the more they reassured her, the more convinced she became that something was really wrong with her, and that her husband and neighbors were just trying to cover it up.

The doctor examines her. The only positive findings are that her heart rate is increased and her pupils are dilated. Adopting his best bedside manner, he says to her, "For Christ's sake, Sybil, you're just a little stoned. Go home to bed and stop making such a fuss." Sybil seems reassured. He then walks into another room and tells Lou, "If that doesn't work, we'll have to take her to the emergency room."

Discussion of "Freaking Out"

Sybil's bad experience with marijuana (cannabis) includes characteristic physical symptoms such as dry mouth and increased heart rate. It is the psychological symptoms, however, that caused her husband to seek help. Sybil became extremely anxious and had paranoid ideation (that the marijuana was poisoned and that her neighbors would not let her husband call the doctor). This maladaptive reaction to the recent use of cannabis indicates Cannabis Intoxication.

In diagnosing this case, we considered whether Sybil's paranoid ideation could justify a diagnosis of Cannabis Delusional Disorder; we decided the answer was no. First of all, the neighbors might well have been reluctant to call the doctor since they would have had to admit that they were smoking an illegal substance. Secondly, Sybil *was* reassured by the doctor that the marijuana did not contain poison, whereas, by definition, a delusion is a false belief that is firmly held, even despite evidence to the contrary.

DSM-III-R Diagnosis:

Axis I: 305.20 Cannabis Intoxication (p. 140)

Follow-up

Sybil was helped into her car by Lou (she still couldn't stand up) and went home to bed. She stayed in bed for two days, feeling "spacey" and weak, but no longer terribly anxious. She realized that since the marijuana was homegrown, there was no reason to think that it contained any poison. However, she still believed her neighbors did not want to call the doctor because they were afraid of the police. She vowed never to smoke marijuana again.

Charles

A 25-YEAR-OLD PATIENT, called Charles, requested a "sex change operation." Charles had for three years lived socially and been employed as a man. For the last two of these years, Charles had been the housemate, economic provider, and husband-equivalent of a bisexual woman who had fled from a bad marriage. Her two young children regarded Charles as their stepfather, and there was a strong affectionate bond between them.

In social appearance the patient passed as a not very virile man whose sexual development in puberty might be conjectured to have been extremely delayed or hormonally deficient. Charles' voice was pitched low, but not baritone. Bulky clothing was worn to camouflage tightly bound, flattened breasts. A strap-on penis produced a masculine-looking bulge in the pants; it was so constructed that, in case of social necessity, it could be used as a urinary conduit in the standing position. Without success the patient had tried to obtain a mastectomy so that in summer only a T-shirt could be worn while working outdoors as a heavy construction machine operator. Charles had also been unsuccessful in trying to get a prescription for testosterone, to produce male secondary sex characteristics and suppress menses. The patient wanted a hysterectomy and oophorectomy, and as a long-term goal looked forward to obtaining a successful phalloplasty.

The history was straightforward in its account of progressive recognition in adolescence of being able to fall in love only with a woman, following a tomboyish childhood that had finally consolidated into the transsexual role and identity.

Physical examination revealed normal female anatomy, which the patient found personally repulsive, incongruous, and a source of continual distress. The endocrine laboratory results were within normal limits for a female.

Discussion of "Charles"

The diagnosis of Transsexualism is certainly suggested by the first sentence, which indicates that the person desperately wants to get rid of her primary sex characteristics and acquire the characteristics of the other sex. This case also demonstrates the other characteristic features of the disorder: persistent discomfort and sense of inappropriateness about one's assigned sex, persistent preoccupation for at least two years with getting rid of one's primary and secondary sex characteristics and acquiring the sex characteristics of the other sex. As is almost always the case, there is no evidence of physical intersex or genetic abnormality.

The diagnosis is further specified with regard to the predominant history of sexual orientation, in this case relationships with persons of the same anatomic sex. This is noted as "homosexual," although such people, because of their gender identity, do not perceive it as such.

People who develop Transsexualism almost invariably report having had a gender identity problem in childhood, although the onset of the full syndrome is (as with Charles) most often in late adolescence or early adult life. For that reason, Transsexualism and the other Gender Identity Disorders are listed in the childhood disorders section of the DSM-III-R classification.

DSM-III-R Diagnosis:

Axis I: 302.50 Transsexualism, with Homosexual History of Sexual Orientation (p. 76)

Cat Naps

NORA, A 24-YEAR-OLD GRADUATE STUDENT, complained of episodes of severe sleepiness that forced her to take naps. Sometimes when she attempted to stay awake, she was unable to do so, and had fallen asleep at the dinner table and even when walking. She had trouble staying alert enough to get off at the right bus stop. In fact, she was unable to remain seated without becoming sleepy, slept through classes, and failed her courses in graduate school.

Nora is bothered by frequent cataplexy, in which she becomes limp and briefly unable to move after sudden emotional arousal. This had occurred, for example, when she discovered that her cat had urinated on her rug, and when she had become enraged with her roommate; it was a serious problem when she was driving and another driver did something that annoyed her.

As she falls asleep at night, Nora sees vivid scenes that seem real, and feels that someone else is in the room. She still feels awake, however, and knows that really there is no one there. Her sleep is frequently punctuated by nightmares. She then wakes up feeling very hungry and has a snack.

Extremely bothersome to Nora is her continual automatic behavior, in which she suddenly discovers that she has accomplished very little after a lengthy period of work on a task. For example, she spent two hours unsuccessfully trying to fix her glasses and was unaware of this until her roommate interrupted her and pointed it out. The automatic behavior makes it difficult for her to change from one task to another, so it sometimes takes her two hours to get out of the house in the morning or to get ready for bed at night. Delays in getting to bed prevent her from getting a good night's sleep, which further aggravates her daytime sleepiness. Her roommates grew weary of her undependability and she had to move back to her parents' home.

Previous treatment with a drug regime consisting of an antidepressant, a stimulant, and a bedtime sedative was unsuccessful.

Discussion of "Cat Naps"

Nora's problem of sleep attacks and excessive daytime sleepiness is an example of hypersomnia. Her daytime sleep attacks, cataplexy, hypnogogic (when falling asleep) hallucinations, automatic behavior, nightmares, and disturbed sleep are the characteristic features of the neurologic disorder of narcolepsy. Thus, on Axis I we diagnose Hypersomnia Related to a Known Organic Factor, and on Axis III, narcolepsy.

DSM-III-R Diagnosis:

Axis I: 296.44 Bipolar Disorder, Manic, with Psychotic
                   Features (Mood-congruent) (p. 226)
Axis III: Narcolepsy

Follow-up

Nora was instructed to keep records of her in-bed times, nap times, cataplexy attacks, episodes of night eating, and automatic behavior. Psychotherapy was focused on examining the details of her failure to adhere to prescribed bedtimes, forgetting to take medication, and other behaviors that worsened her situation. She was withdrawn from the sedative, and her treatment with an antidepressant, protriptyline, and a stimulant, dextroamphetamine, was empirically adjusted on the basis of the record she kept of her behavior.

Nora's symptoms gradually disappeared, and she was able to move out of her parents' house, get a job, reestablish a social life, and return to graduate school.

A Praying Athlete

R ICHARD GRAMM, A 24-YEAR-OLD black man, was, when brought to the emergency room, mute and rigid. The friends who had brought him stated that he was playing basketball with them at the student athletic building when he suddenly put his head down on the floor, made sounds as if he were praying, and had then become "catatonic." When interviewed an hour later, Richard would only say, "I am communicating directly with God."

According to his friends, Richard had been getting "hyper" recently, but they emphatically denied that he either used drugs or drank to excess. A call to his girl friend, whose name and number were provided by his friends, revealed the following.

Richard had been doing well, with no evidence of unusual behavior, up until one week prior to admission. He had been living with his girl friend, going to school, and working at a part-time job. One week before admission, he began to say "odd" things, usually of a religious nature. He also stopped sleeping at night and became sexually demanding of his girl friend. He had begun working out even more than usual at the gym in order to "burn off excess energy." His girl friend said that he had had similar symptoms when he was hospitalized one year previously. At that time he left the hospital against medical advice, and had become increasingly depressed for about three months. He did not seek professional help. He withdrew from social activities at school, and would spend up to 14 hours a day sleeping. Just when his girl friend had decided to break up with him, he spontaneously returned to his normal self. She described him as a friendly, outgoing, energetic young man interested in school and athletics, who performed well both academically and at work.

Toxicology screening in the emergency room was negative, as were other medical tests. Physical examination revealed an extremely healthy, athletic young man who was largely mute and held his body in a rigid posture. The hospital chart noted one previous psychiatric admission a year before. The diagnosis was "Atypical Psychosis, rule out some kind of organic or drug psychosis." Richard had been in the hospital only four days, during which time he was observed to have auditory hallucinations and a delusion that he was communicating directly with God.

During the first few days of the current hospitalization, Richard was observed to alternate between "rigid posturing" and "mild hyperactivity." He would spontaneously become "unstuck" and begin pacing actively around the unit, talking about his new-found faith in religion to "anyone he could corral."

Discussion of "Praying Athlete"

The bizarre behavior (becoming mute and rigid) that is the reason for Richard's admission to the hospital is a catatonic symptom. Traditionally, catatonic symptoms have been understood to be evidence of either Schizophrenia or unusual forms of a central nervous disorder. Now it is recognized that catatonic symptoms are also seen in Manic Episodes of Bipolar Disorder.

Richard continues to have catatonic symptoms (rigid posturing) when he is in the hospital, but at other times he has the classic symptoms of a Manic Episode: his mood is expansive (we suspect that is what was meant by his friends' describing him as "hyper," "talking to anyone he could corral" about his religious ideas, and his girl friend's description of him as sexually demanding); he is grandiose (communicates with God), hyperactive (paces), and does not sleep. In addition, there is a history of what seems to be a Major Depressive Episode: he was extremely depressed, socially withdrawn, and slept 14 hours a day.

Also characteristic of Bipolar Disorder is the rapid development of the Manic Episode and the full return to usual functioning between episodes of mood disturbance. Richard's delusion of communicating with God is a typical mood-congruent, grandiose delusion. Therefore, we diagnose Bipolar Disorder, Manic, with Mood-congruent Psychotic Features.

DSM-III-R Diagnosis:

**Axis I: 296.44 Bipolar Disorder, Manic, with Psychotic
              Features (Mood-congruent) (p. 226)**

Follow-up

An antipsychotic, thiothixene, and a mood stabilizer, lithium carbonate, were prescribed, and Richard's lithium level rapidly increased to therapeutic levels over the next 5 days. During this time his catatonic episodes became less frequent, and his hyperactivity between episodes decreased in amplitude. Twelve days after admission, Richard's medical status was essentially normal, without hallucinations or active delusions. He was discharged, with follow-up through the university clinic. Richard had a mild depression about one month after discharge from the hospital. This was managed by increasing his lithium dose. During the year of follow-up, no further psychotic symptoms or depressive or manic episodes occurred.

Useful Work

AN 85-YEAR-OLD MAN is seen by a social worker at a senior citizens' center for evaluation of health-care needs for himself and his bedridden wife. He is apparently healthy, with no evidence of impairment in thinking or memory. He has been caring for his wife, but has been reluctantly persuaded to seek help because her condition has deteriorated, and his strength and energy have decreased with age.

A history is obtained from the subject and his daughter. He has never been treated for mental illness, and in fact has always claimed to be "immune to psychological problems" and to act only on the basis of "rational" thought. He had a moderately successful career as a lawyer and businessman. He has been married for 60 years, and his wife is the only person for whom he has ever expressed tender feelings, and is probably the only person he has ever trusted. He has always been extremely careful about revealing anything of himself to others, assuming that they are out to take something away from him. He refuses obviously sincere offers of help from acquaintances because he suspects their motives. He never reveals his identity to a caller without first questioning him as to the nature of his business. Throughout his life there have been numerous occasions on which he has displayed exaggerated suspiciousness, sometimes of almost delusional proportions (e.g., storing letters from a client in a secret safe deposit box so that he could use them as evidence in the event that the client attempted to sue him for mismanagement of an estate).

He has always involved himself in "useful work" during his waking hours, and claims never to have time for play, even during the 20 years he has been retired. He spends many hours monitoring his stock-market investments, and has had altercations with his broker when he suspected that an error on a monthly statement was evidence of the broker's attempt to cover up some fraudulent deal.

Discussion of "Useful Work"

This gentleman demonstrates a pervasive and unwarranted tendency to interpret the actions of people as deliberately threatening. He expects to be exploited or harmed by others (assuming others are out to take something from him; first questioning callers before revealing his identity). He is easily slighted and quick to counterattack (has had altercations with his broker when he suspected a cover-up of a fraudulent deal). He questions the loyalty or trustworthiness of others (his wife is the only person he has ever trusted). He is reluctant to confide in others (has always been extremely careful about revealing anything about himself). These lifelong features, in the absence of any evidence of persistent persecutory delusions or any other psychotic symptoms, characterize Paranoid Personality Disorder.

This case illustrates the ego-syntonic nature of the disturbance. For this reason, treatment is rarely sought. It also demonstrates the frequently associated feature of inability to relax (never has time for recreation) and restricted affectivity (e.g., pride in being "rational").

This patient has several schizoid features, but not enough to warrant the additional diagnosis of Schizoid Personality Disorder.

DSM-III-R Diagnosis:

Axis I: V71.09 No Diagnosis or Condition
Axis II: 301.00 Paranoid Personality Disorder, Moderate (p. 339)

Music Lessons

GARY AND NORMA CAME to a sexual disorder clinic a few weeks after Norma had attended the funeral of her uncle. At the funeral she suddenly recalled childhood experiences with her uncle that made her think there might be a psychological basis for her sexual problems.

Gary and Norma were having sex approximately once every one to two months, and only at Gary's insistence. Their sexual activity consisted primarily of Gary stimulating Norma to orgasm by manually caressing her genitals while he masturbated himself to orgasm. The couple had discontinued attempts at penile-vaginal intercourse in the recent past because Norma often had spasms of her vagina that made entry of the penis painful and difficult, if not impossible.

There were other problems in the marriage. Gary worked long hours and spent much of his free time visiting his widowed mother and doing errands or household chores for her. He also had a compulsive gambling problem, and went to the race track three or four times a week. As their income was not large, Gary's gambling losses caused severe financial problems.

Norma had always had a strong aversion to looking at or touching her husband's penis. During the interview she explained that she had had no idea of the origin of this aversion until her uncle's recent funeral. At the funeral she was surprised to find herself becoming angry as the eulogy was read. Her uncle had been a world-famous concert musician, and was widely respected and admired. As Norma became angrier, she suddenly recalled having been sexually molested by him when she was a child. From the ages of 9 to 12, her uncle had been her music teacher. The lessons included "teaching [her] rhythm" by having her caress his penis in time with the beating of the metronome. This repelled her, but she was too frightened to tell her parents about it. She finally refused to continue lessons at age 12, without ever telling her parents why. At some point during her adolescence, she said, she "forgot what he did to me."

Discussion of "Music Lessons"

Norma's traumatic sexual experiences with her uncle when she was a child apparently made it impossible for her as an adult to experience sexual activity as pleasurable. Norma is repelled by male genitalia and avoids sexual activity with her husband. Since, in Norma's case, this is not a symptom of another Axis I disorder, such as Major Depression, the diagnosis of Sexual Aversion Disorder is made. In addition, she has persistent, involuntary spasms of the vaginal muscles, so severe that coitus is impossible. This indicates a diagnosis of Vaginismus.

DSM-III-R Diagnosis:

Axis I: **302.79 Sexual Aversion Disorder, Psychogenic Only, Lifelong (p. 293)**
           306.51 Vaginismus, Psychogenic Only, Lifelong (p. 295)

Loan Sharks

A 48-YEAR-OLD MALE ATTORNEY was interviewed while he was being detained awaiting trial. He had been arrested for taking funds from his firm, which he stated he had fully intended to return after he had a "big win" at gambling. He appeared deeply humiliated and remorseful about his behavior, although he had a previous history of near-arrests for defrauding his company of funds. His father had provided funds to extricate him from these past financial difficulties, but refused to assist him this time. The patient had to resign his job under pressure from his firm. This seemed to distress him greatly since he had worked diligently and effectively at his job, although he had been spending more and more time away from work in order to pursue gambling.

The patient had gambled on horse racing for many years. He spent several hours each day studying the results of the previous day's races in the newspaper. He had been losing heavily recently and had resorted to illegal borrowing in order to increase his bets and win back his losses (called "chasing" in gambling circles). He was now being pressured by "loan sharks" for payment. He stated that he embezzled the money to pay off these illegal debts because the threats of the "loan sharks" were so frightening to him that he could not concentrate or sleep. He admitted to problems with his friends and wife since he had borrowed from them. They were now alienated and giving him little emotional support since they no longer had any faith in his repeated promises to limit his gambling. His wife had decided to leave him and live with her parents.

During the interview the patient was tense and restless, at times having to stand up and pace. He said he was having a flare-up of a duodenal ulcer. He was somewhat tearful throughout the interview, and said that although he realized his problems stemmed from his gambling, he still had a strong urge to gamble.

Discussion of "Loan Sharks"

This man is preoccupied with gambling, which has led to his being arrested for embezzlement, defaulting on debts, and the disruption of his marriage. This is clearly beyond the bounds of "recreational gambling" and, with his inability to limit his gambling behavior, indicates a disturbance in impulse control, Pathological Gambling. The essential features of this disorder parallel the features of dependence on a psychoactive substance. In both cases the person who is addicted has impaired control over the behavior and continues it despite severe adverse consequences.

Although this patient has engaged in antisocial behavior, a diagnosis of Antisocial Personality Disorder is not appropriate because the antisocial behavior is limited to attempts to obtain money to pay off gambling debts, and there is neither a childhood history of antisocial behavior nor evidence of impaired occupational and interpersonal functioning other than that associated with his gambling.

A complete diagnostic assessment would also make note of the duodenal ulcer (recorded on Axis III), which is apparently being exacerbated by the stress associated with his out-of-control gambling (recorded on Axis I as Psychological Factors Affecting Physical Condition).

DSM-III-R Diagnosis:

Axis I: 312.31 Pathological Gambling (p. 325)
           316.00 Psychological Factors Affecting Physical
                   Condition (p. 334)
Axis III: Duodenal ulcer

A Man Who Saw the Air

A 20-YEAR-OLD UNDERGRADUATE presented with a chief complaint of "see-ing the air." The visual disturbance consisted of perception of white pinpoint specks in both the central and peripheral visual fields too nu-merous to count. They were constantly present, and were accompanied by the perception of trails of moving objects left behind as they passed through the patient's visual field. Attending a hockey game was difficult, since the brightly dressed players left streaks of their own images against the white of the ice for seconds at a time. The patient also described the false perception of movement in stable objects, usually in his peripheral visual fields; halos around objects; and positive and negative afterimages. Other symptoms included mild depression, daily bitemporal headache, and a loss of concentration in the last year.

The visual syndrome had gradually emerged over the past 25 months, following experimentation with the hallucinogenic drug LSD-25 on three separate occasions in the preceding 3 months. He feared he had suffered some kind of "brain damage" from the drug experience. He denied use of any other agents, including amphetamines, phencyclidine, narcotics, or alcohol, to excess. He had smoked marijuana twice a week for a period of 7 months at age 17.

The patient had consulted two ophthalmologists, both of whom confirmed that the white pinpoint specks were not vitreous floaters (di-agnostically insignificant particulate matter floating in the vitreous hu-mour of the eye that can cause the perception of "specks"). A neurolo-gist's examination also proved negative. A therapeutic trial of an anticonvulsant, clonazepam, resulted in a 50% improvement in the pa-tient's visual symptoms and remission of his depression.

Discussion of "A Man Who Saw the Air"

This young man is experiencing a variety of visual disturbances that are presumably similar to those that he experienced when he was intoxicated with the hallucinogen LSD. (For a description of the typical perceptual disturbances seen with LSD Intoxication, see "Dr. Hofmann," p. 483.) Mild and transient perceptual disturbances that occur long after cessation of use of a hallucinogen may be common. When the perceptual disturbance is severe enough to cause marked distress, as in this patient, it is called Posthallucinogen Perception Disorder. Usually such perceptual disturbances last for just a few seconds. More rarely, as in this patient, they are experienced throughout the day for long periods of time. The symptoms are often triggered by emergence from a dark environment or use of cannabis or of a phenothiazine. They can sometimes be brought on by intention.

DSM-III-R Diagnosis:

Axis I: 292.89 Posthallucinogen Perception Disorder (p. 148)

Leather

A 35-YEAR-OLD MARRIED WRITER sought consultation because he feared he might kill someone by acting upon sexually sadistic impulses.

The patient has been married for 15 years, and during the last year has had sexual intercourse with his wife approximately every other week. The patient's fantasy life is predominantly homosexual, however, and has been so since age nine. He has felt sexually attracted to males since childhood, but resisted acting on these impulses until mid-adulthood, long after he married. Before that, he felt sexually aroused by homosexual pornography (to which he was exposed from mid-adolescence), particularly by pornography with sadistic content. Although somewhat responsive to heterosexual pornography, his interest in it was much less than in homosexual pornography, and he was never excited by heterosexual pornography with sadistic content.

The patient had married for reasons of social propriety, and also because he consciously hoped that initiation into regular heterosexual activity would lead to diminution of his sadistic homosexual impulses. This was not the case, however. These impulses continued periodically to form the basis of the patient's masturbation fantasies. Typical masturbation fantasies were of a man bound, tortured, and killed. Sometimes the men in his fantasies were people he knew, such as colleagues or teachers, and sometimes movie stars or strangers. These fantasies were more intense at certain times than at others. The patient recalls, for example, that he was "wildly" aroused when he read about the activities of a homosexual lust murder as described in a detective magazine. Immediately following this, he masturbated many times a day, always with sadistic homosexual fantasies. After a few weeks, this period of intense arousal subsided, but the patient used the scenario of the events described in this magazine in subsequent masturbation fantasies.

About eight years ago, the patient went to a gay bar with an associate from his office. At the time, he was under much pressure, and his work was being closely supervised by an aggressive, demanding male superior. The patient's associate was openly homosexual, and the patient allegedly went to the bar with him "as a lark." En route to the particular bar they visited, they passed other bars that, the patient's friend told him, were for "the leather crowd who like S and M." The patient had a brief homosexual encounter with someone he picked up in the bar they visited, following which he "put sex out of [his] mind."

Some months later, however, following a week of intense work at his office, the patient impulsively sought out one of the "S and M" bars he had previously walked past. There he met a man who was sexually aroused by being beaten, and the patient engaged in pleasurable sadistic activity with the understanding that the severity of the beating, administered with a belt, was under the control of his masochistic partner. That incident, occurring when he was 28 years old, was the first episode in a series of sexually sadistic activities, ultimately leading to his consultation. About once a month the patient would frequent a homosexual sadomasochistic bar. He would dress in a leather jacket and wear a leather cap. Once in the bar, he would seek out a masochistic partner and engage in a variety of activities, all of which the patient experienced as sexually exciting. The activities included binding the partner with ropes, whipping him, threatening to burn him with cigarettes, forcing him to drink urine, forcing him to "beg for mercy." The patient would experience orgasm during these activities, usually by "forcing" his partner to commit fellatio.

During the year before the consultation, the patient's wife had become progressively dissatisfied with their marriage. She was unaware of her husband's homosexual interest and of his sadistic tendencies. She felt, however, that his sexual involvement with her was desultory, and she wondered whether he had a mistress. She became confronting and also more hostile and demanding toward the patient. He realized that he "needed" his wife, and he did not wish the relationship to end, yet he felt unable to deal with her dissatisfactions directly. He avoided her as much as possible and argued with her when she insisted on talking to him. The patient's work pressures increased; and he found, to his dismay, that the intensity of his sadistic impulses also increased.

On one occasion the patient convinced a partner to agree to being burned. Afterward, he felt guilty and ashamed. Just before the consultation, he bound a partner and cut the man's arm. At the sight of blood he experienced a powerful desire to kill his partner. He restrained himself and, alarmed that his sadistic impulses were out of control, sought psychiatric consultation.

Discussion of "Leather"

This man had first been aroused by sadistic homosexual fantasies in mid-adolescence. These intense sexually arousing fantasies persisted, and eventually he began to act on them. He married, hoping that marriage would be an antidote to his sadistic homosexual impulses, but found that this was not the case. He now enters treatment fearful that the sadistic impulses may become so strong that he will lose control and kill a sexual partner.

This is a fairly typical history of a person with severe Sexual Sadism. This man was treated in 1978, before the AIDS epidemic. If he were seen now, one would certainly be concerned about his HIV status and whether his sexual activities were putting other people at risk for the infection.

DSM-III-R Diagnosis:

Axis I: 302.84 Sexual Sadism, Severe (p. 288)

Fix It

S ANDRA IS A 27-YEAR-OLD single woman who is admitted to a Chicago hospital after running away from a nearby halfway house because she saw "devils" there and was afraid of being killed. When interviewed she is tense, suspicious of the interviewer, and guarded about revealing her symptoms. She does acknowledge that she is still hearing voices and needs to protect herself from people at the halfway house. She will not elaborate on how they might harm her.

Sandra is more open in talking about her history. She has been ill much of the time since she dropped out of college eight years ago. At that time she needed to arrange her clothes and shoes in the closet so they were "perfect," and to open and close her drawers many times, and eventually was unable to leave her room because she couldn't get things "fixed right." Her feeling was that she could not face people if things were not "perfect" in her room.

During the following year she was hospitalized off and on because of her rituals and was given many medications, which did not help. About six years ago she began to hear voices of unknown people ordering her to "fix it" or accusing her of "not fixing it right," and telling her she could not go out and face people until she fixed her room perfectly. (On questioning by the psychiatrist, she insists that she has actually heard these voices, and can hear them now.)

Five years previously, for reasons that are not clear, she lost her job as a secretary. She then began to believe that her roommate wanted to kill her, and kept asking her, "Why do you want to kill me?" She moved back into her parents' house in the suburbs, where she stayed in her room for two months doing nothing, until her parents finally hospitalized her. Since that time she has either been hospitalized or in day-hospital and work programs, but has not been able to support herself.

Discussion of "Fix It"

Sandra's first symptoms, eight years ago, were a variety of compulsions (arranging clothes and shoes, opening and closing doors), all in response to obsessions that she had to "fix" her room perfectly. Because the obsessions and compulsions were sufficiently severe to interfere with her functioning, the diagnosis of Obsessive Compulsive Disorder would have been made.

What complicates the case is the development of hallucinations two years later (voices telling her to "fix it right"), followed by persecutory delusions (her roommate wanted to kill her; devils pursue her in the halfway house). The presence of the hallucinations and delusions, along with the marked impairment in functioning, justifies the additional diagnosis of Schizophrenia. The type is Undifferentiated because the voices and delusions do not seem to be related to a single theme.

In the past, a diagnosis of Schizophrenia would preempt a diagnosis of Obsessive Compulsive Disorder. In DSM-III-R, this diagnostic hierarchy has been removed, so it is possible to give both diagnoses if the criteria for both disorders are met, even if both disorders occurred during the same period. In Sandra's case, once the symptoms of Schizophrenia developed, the obsessions and compulsions seemed to diminish, and currently there is no mention of any symptoms of Obsessive Compulsive Disorder. Therefore, we first diagnose Schizophrenia, and then note Obsessive Compulsive Disorder (Past).

Suppose Sandra's only psychotic symptom had been prominent hallucinations of voices telling her to "fix it," that is, limited to the content of the Obsessive Compulsive Disorder. Although some clinicians have argued that this would merely be a psychotic form of Obsessive Compulsive Disorder, DSM-III-R does not recognize this concept, and even these hallucinations (because they are prominent and unrelated to a mood disturbance) would justify the additional diagnosis of Schizophrenia.

DSM-III-R Diagnosis:

Axis I: **295.92 Schizophrenia, Undifferentiated Type, Chronic (p. 198)**
300.30 Obsessive Compulsive Disorder (Past) (p. 247)

New Face

THE PATIENT, A SINGLE, UNEMPLOYED, 19-year-old male was referred for psychiatric evaluation before undergoing orthognathous surgery for a protruding mandible. The procedure was to create a new facial look and improve both function and aesthetics. The evaluation was requested to determine if there were any psychiatric contraindications to surgery.

The patient says that his jaw has been protruding since childhood: he feels it may have protruded because as a child he frequently stuck his tongue out, and "maybe this stretched my jaw." He knows his molars are in place, but the teeth on the side are "pointed." His friends don't tease him about his jaw, but they do say, "You got a mug," and this upsets him. He describes himself as shy and feels it is partly from his self-consciousness about his jaw. He has difficulty talking and eating, as his teeth underbite and his tongue protrudes; thus, he cannot bite, but has to tear, his food. He has wanted to have his jaw fixed for a long time, but was "too shy" to ask about it. He says that, as a result, he hasn't seen a dentist for the last four years. He is aware that some teeth will have to be removed and that he will have his jaw wired for six weeks and will be on a liquid diet. He is uneasy about being unable to eat solid food. He hopes the surgery will correct his chewing problem, and that he will feel better about his face and become more comfortable with other people.

The patient did well in school until he reached high school, then he started to cut classes and dropped out of the tenth grade. He worked for two years as a security guard. He is now unemployed, but wants to go back to school and become an auto mechanic.

The patient is the third in a family of eight children. His parents separated when he was 14 years old. He lives with his mother and siblings. He argues with his siblings about doing household chores and, as a result, doesn't spend much time with his family; he just comes and goes and spends time with friends. He restrains himself from telling his friends not to comment on his "mug," preferring to "keep it inside." He hopes that if the operation is successful, his friends will stop remarking on his looks.

When examined, the young man was noted to have mild acne and a very visibly protruding jaw with an underbite. His manner was somewhat awkward. There were no gross abnormalities of thinking, perception, or overt behavior. He denied ever having any problems with mood, sleeping, eating, or in the use of alcohol or other drugs.

Discussion of "New Face"

The complaint of a defect in some aspect of one's physical appearance requires a clinical judgment about whether the complaint is out of proportion to any actual physical abnormality that may exist. A gross discrepancy suggests the possibility of Body Dysmorphic Disorder, or what has sometimes been referred to in the literature as "Dysmorphophobia." In this case, however, the interviewer notes the visibly protruding jaw and underbite, ruling out such a diagnosis.

The next question is whether or not the patient's reaction to his physical appearance is maladaptive, leading, for example, to marked social withdrawal, preoccupation, or depression. This does not appear to be the case. The young man is shy, and sensitive to his friends' comments about his appearance, but this hardly indicates significant psychopathology.

On the basis of the limited information provided, there is no reason to suspect a mental disorder. Thus, the appropriate notations on Axes I and II are "No Diagnosis." His protruding jaw and underbite *may* be recorded on Axis III as relevant to understanding this young man, but the intent of Axis III is really to facilitate the recording of physical conditions relevant to a person with a mental disorder, which does not apply in this case.

DSM-III-R Diagnosis:

Axis I: V71.09 No Diagnosis or Condition (p. 363)
Axis II: V71.09 No Diagnosis (p. 363)

Clairvoyant

THE PATIENT IS A 32-YEAR-OLD unmarried, unemployed woman on welfare who complains that she feels "spacey." Her feelings of detachment have gradually become stronger and more uncomfortable. For many hours each day she feels as if she were watching herself move through life, and the world around her seems unreal. She feels especially strange when she looks into a mirror. For many years she has felt able to read people's minds by a "kind of clairvoyance I don't understand." According to her, several people in her family apparently also have this ability. She is preoccupied by the thought that she has some special mission in life, but is not sure what it is; she is not particularly religious. She is very self-conscious in public, often feels that people are paying special attention to her, and sometimes thinks that strangers cross the street to avoid her. She has no friends, feels lonely and isolated, and spends much of each day lost in fantasies or watching TV soap operas.

The patient speaks in a vague, abstract, digressive manner, generally just missing the point, but she is never incoherent. She seems shy, suspicious, and afraid she will be criticized. She has no gross loss of reality testing, such as hallucinations or delusions. She has never had treatment for emotional problems. She has had occasional jobs, but drifts away from them because of lack of interest.

Discussion of "Clairvoyant"

Although the patient's symptoms have become more distressing to her recently, they are manifestations of a long-standing maladaptive pattern that suggests a Personality Disorder rather than the new development of an Axis I disorder. Her symptoms include unusual perceptual experiences, such as depersonalization (feelings of detachment and feeling as if she were watching herself) and derealization ("... the world ... seems unreal"), odd beliefs or magical thinking (clairvoyance), ideas of reference (strangers cross the street to avoid her), no close friends, odd speech (vague, abstract, digressive), and suspiciousness. These are the hallmarks of Schizotypal Personality Disorder.

Is her belief in her ability to read people's minds a delusion, rather than merely magical thinking, which indicates a psychotic disorder? Her statement that she herself "doesn't understand" the process suggests that it is probably not a belief that is firmly held, as in a delusion.

The clinician might be concerned about the likelihood of a previous psychotic episode in this patient, in which case the current symptoms would be indicative of the residual phase of Schizophrenia. In the absence of such a history, however, a diagnosis of Schizotypal Personality Disorder is most appropriate.

DSM-III-R Diagnosis:

Axis I: V71.09 No Diagnosis or Condition (p. 363)
Axis II: 301.22 Schizotypal Personality Disorder, Severe (p. 341)

Follow-up

The patient was first treated with an antipsychotic drug, Haldol. This helped her feelings of detachment, but was discontinued because she could not tolerate the side effects. She has been treated with supportive psychotherapy and no medication for eight years, during which time she has seen two therapists. Her sessions are infrequent (once every two to three weeks); and although the content is minimal, she apparently has a strong attachment to her current therapist, and often becomes upset during his vacations. Her life is little changed from how it was at intake. She has never needed to be hospitalized.

Goody Two Shoes

MARYANN IS AN ATTRACTIVE, 35-year-old single woman, originally from San Diego, now working as a magazine editor and living by herself in a deteriorating Boston neighborhood. She was referred for psychotherapy by her female family doctor, who suggested she needed to work on problems in her relationships with men. Maryann resisted following through on the referral for a year, saying, "I don't like getting help. I like giving it."

When interviewed, Maryann appeared to be highly intelligent; she was affable and articulate and spoke in a breathy, girlish voice. She had metal-black hair, was dressed all in black—leather skirt and jacket and black top—and wore "punkish" glasses. She said, at the beginning of the interview, that she didn't want a male therapist because she was mistrustful of men, who, in her experience, wanted only to exploit women. However, with the exception of her family doctor, she had no close women friends.

Her story was that she had just extricated herself from a "destructive" relationship with a man, "my outlaw love," who was a heroin addict; and she was fighting her wish to return to him. Once, four years earlier, he had hit her and made her cry, but she told him that if he did that again, she'd leave, and it never recurred. She claimed she was not frightened of him, and actually blamed herself for his attacking her. "I often tell him things he should know about himself, and he gets furious. I only do it to motivate him. I hit his soft spot."

Her lover's addiction persisted, and Maryann continued to support him financially whenever he needed help. She said she received many indications that this relationship could not make her happy. The man had gone out with other women while dating Maryann, served a brief jail sentence for selling drugs, and never wanted to engage in mutually entertaining activities, except sex, which was enjoyable. Maryann had gone to a university, but her lover had never completed high school. She felt that he was like a little child who needed mothering. He would tell her to get lost when she insisted he stop using drugs, but she continued to call him regularly in spite of his ungrateful behavior. She felt resentful and embittered because of all she had done for him, but always helped him when he, typically, came back to her, late at night, asking for money or assistance. As a result, she said she felt "more like a Mother Theresa than a girl friend."

Maryann is now seeing another "exciting" man, also a substance abuser. Although she considers herself "left-wing," her new friend is a collector of Nazi memorabilia. She knew that he treated his previous girl friend cruelly by being unfaithful and abusive, but didn't think about whether this might happen to her. She has seen this man on and off for a year. He insisted he wanted a close relationship, but did not tell her he was seeing one of her acquaintances on the side. When she found out about this she was very upset but continues to have an intense interest in him. A number of nicer men who had monogamous intentions have frequently tried to date her, but she has avoided them because they all seemed "boring."

In her other relationships, Maryann always gives help, but never asks for it, even when she is in real need. Most of her friends and ex-boyfriends have been drug addicts, or ex-addicts. She herself has never abused drugs. She often visits these people in jail and offers to help them; but when they are released, they hardly ever visit her.

At her job Maryann is hardworking and good at solving disputes, but she has sometimes gotten into trouble with her boss for arranging to use the magazine's resources to raise money for needy groups. She feels that her female colleagues "gang up on her" because of envy of her abilities and capacity for hard work, in spite of all the benefits that she has helped them obtain.

Maryann is the oldest of four children, and often had to grudgingly care for her young sibs. She became a "Goody Two Shoes," while her younger brothers were permitted to "act up." In church and school she did well and won many awards, until, in her teens, she rebelled and left home. Her parents predicted she would "go to hell." She went through a period of "sexual liberation" during which she had about fifty lovers, often in one-night stands, which she rarely enjoyed "because I didn't love those guys." As a young adult she was always involved in some worthy cause for the underprivileged, the poor or the politically disadvantaged.

Discussion of "Goody Two Shoes"

Maryann seems to have gone through life playing the role of martyr. She has repeatedly been attracted to and chosen boyfriends who are inappropriate and mistreat her. She does not like to take help from others, and this has delayed her seeking treatment, even though she has realized for a long time that her relationships with people are harmful to her. She incites angry responses from others and then feels hurt when she is rejected (telling her boyfriend his failings). She is not interested in boyfriends who treat her well because they are "boring," and she engages in excessive self-sacrifice that is unsolicited by the recipients (visiting people in jail).

Behavior which appears to an outside observer as "self-defeating" may be observed when a person is in a situation in which he or she is afraid of being psychologically or physically abused, or when a person is depressed. In Maryann's case, however, it seems to be a pervasive personality pattern that expresses itself in many situations and relationships of her own choosing, thus justifying the unofficial diagnosis of Self-defeating Personality Disorder.

Flashbacks

A 23-YEAR-OLD VIETNAM VETERAN was admitted to the hospital one year after the end of the Vietnam War, at the request of his wife, after he began to experience depression, insomnia, and "flashbacks" of his wartime experiences. He had been honorably discharged two years previously, having spent nearly a year in combat. He had only minimal difficulties in returning to civilian life, resuming his college studies, and then marrying within six months after his return. His wife had noticed that he was always reluctant to talk about his military experience, but she wrote it off as a natural reaction to unpleasant memories.

The patient's current symptoms began, however, at about the time of the fall of Saigon. He became preoccupied with watching TV news stories about this. He then began to have difficulty sleeping, and at times would awaken at night in the midst of a nightmare in which he was reliving his past experiences. His wife became particularly concerned one day when he had a flashback experience while out in the back yard: as a plane flew overhead, flying somewhat lower than usual, the patient threw himself to the ground, seeking cover, thinking it was an attacking helicopter. The more he watched the news on TV, the more agitated and morose he became. Stories began to spill out about atrocities that he had seen and experienced, and he began to feel guilty that he had survived while many of his friends had not. At times he also seemed angry and bitter, feeling that the sacrifices he and others had made were all wasted.

The veteran's wife expressed concern that his preoccupation with Vietnam had become so intense that he seemed uninterested in anything else, and was emotionally distant from her. When she suggested that they try to plan their future, including having a family, he responded as if his life consisted completely of the world of events experienced two years earlier, as if he had no future.

Discussion of "Flashbacks"

This veteran has become totally preoccupied with his painful year in Vietnam. His combat experience was obviously a stressor that is generally outside the range of usual human experience and that would evoke significant symptoms of distress in almost anyone. He reexperiences this trauma through dreams and flashbacks. His responsiveness to his current environment is diminished (he is uninterested in things, emotionally distant from his wife, and living almost completely in a "world of events experienced two years earlier"). In addition, he has symptoms of increased arousal (disturbed sleep, outbursts of anger, and exaggerated startle response). This is the full picture of Post-traumatic Stress Disorder. The disorder is further subclassified as "Delayed" to indicate that the onset of the symptoms occurred at least six months after the trauma.

This patient displays a common symptom seen in people who experience a life-threatening trauma shared with others: a sense of guilt that they have survived when others have not.

DSM-III-R Diagnosis:

Axis I: 309.89 Post-traumatic Stress Disorder, Delayed Onset, Severe (p. 250)

The Fat Man

G REGORY, A 43-YEAR-OLD THEATRICAL MANAGER, was evaluated at an eating disorders clinic in San Francisco. Although he had lost 58 pounds in the last 5 months, dropping from 250 to 192 pounds on a 6'1" frame, he was still terrified of getting fat.

Gregory first began to diet five months earlier when his wife told him he was "a fat slob" and implied that she might be considering a divorce. This terrified him and started him on a strict dietary regimen: an omelet and bran for breakfast, coffee for lunch, and salad and shrimp or chicken for dinner. His original goal was to lose about fifty pounds. When dieting did not result in sufficiently rapid loss of weight, he started sticking his finger down his throat to induce vomiting after meals.

Gregory is now "obsessed" with food. Before he goes to a restaurant, he worries about what he will order. He has done a study of what he eats in terms of what is easiest to purge, and he knows all the bathrooms in the areas he frequents. He cannot bear feeling full after eating and worries that his stomach is "fat." Three or four times a week he is unable to resist the urge to "binge." At those times he may gobble down three hamburgers, two orders of french fries, a pint of ice cream, and two packages of Oreo® cookies. He always induces vomiting after a binge. He has never used laxatives, diuretics, or diet pills to lose weight.

Gregory is also preoccupied with being thin. He has progressively revised downward his original goal in dieting, first to 190, and then to 185 pounds. He has begun to exercise, walking at least an hour a day and, more recently, working out with weights several times a week. He believes that women look at him differently now: when he was heavy, they glanced at him casually; now their response is "admiring."

Gregory has always been somewhat heavy, turning to food in times of stress; but he never worried about his weight until his wife criticized his appearance. He can no longer enjoy any meals and feels he has lost control of this area of his life since he cannot stop dieting, even though his wife has told him he is now too thin. He therefore recently saw his internist who found no physical problems and referred him for psychiatric evaluation.

Discussion of "The Fat Man"

Gregory's eating disorder began, as is often the case, with a reasonable attempt to lose some weight. He soon became preoccupied with losing weight and continued to view his body as "fat" even though others did not. This preoccupation with losing weight and distorted body image suggest Anorexia Nervosa, but this diagnosis cannot be made since Gregory has not let his weight go far below the normal minimum for his size.

The binges (rapid consumption of a large amount of food in a discrete period of time) two or three times a week, that Gregory describes, his lack of control over his eating behavior, his regular self-induced vomiting, and his persistent overconcern with his weight indicate Bulimia Nervosa. This case is unusual in that the disorder is far more common in women than in men.

DSM-III-R Diagnosis:

Axis I: 307.51 Bulimia Nervosa (p. 68)

Saturday Night Fever

A 19-YEAR-OLD FEMALE SECRETARY was transferred from the medical clinic to the psychiatric inpatient service. At age 16 she had first been diagnosed as having systemic lupus erythematosus and had begun steroid treatment. About three months before her current admission, she developed kidney complications, and her cortisone was gradually increased to 70 mg/day. One month before admission, her mother reported a change in the patient's usual shy and cooperative disposition. She had started staying out very late at night, often "clubbing" until early morning; she dressed in wild and inappropriate costumes.

On the day of admission, the patient paced the clinic, could not wait for the doctor, was alternately abusive and seductive to male staff, and talked incessantly about a range of loosely related topics: her future as a go-go dancer, how she was going to marry George Michael (a rock star), and the lack of style in the dress of the female employees.

Discussion of "Saturday Night Fever"

The patient presents with a manic syndrome: poor judgment (wearing wild and inappropriate clothing), pressure of speech (talks incessantly), physical restlessness (pacing), and grandiosity (talk of marrying a rock star). One can infer that her mood is alternately irritable and expansive.

In view of the temporal association between the increased dose of cortisone and the behavioral changes, it is reasonable to assume that steroids have caused an Organic Mood Syndrome. Since steroids are not listed as a specific substance class in DSM-III-R, the diagnosis is Other (or Unspecified) Psychoactive Substance Mood Disorder, but the name of the specific substance is substituted for "Other."

DSM-III-R Diagnosis:

Axis I: 292.84 Steroid Organic Mood Disorder (Manic) (p. 112)

Fire Setter

MR. RODRIGUEZ, A 52-YEAR-OLD, Cuban-born president of a successful family business in Miami, was brought to a hospital by his wife after he told her that he had suddenly remembered setting several major fires when he was a child and murdering a man 30 years previously.

Mr. Rodriguez tells the following story. He has been "on edge" recently because he has been having a lot of financial problems in his business. A few weeks ago he became enraged with a long-time employee of whom he had been very fond, yelled at him for misspending a considerable amount of the firm's money, and almost threw an ashtray at him. He was stunned by the violence of his impulses and began to realize how angry and hateful he has always been, particularly in relation to his wife and children.

Later, at home, when thinking about the events of the day, "the curtains were opened and I was flooded with memories of acts that had previously been cut off from my conscious mind." He recalled having set fire to a woman's house while she was inside. This occurred when he was five years old, at his father's urging. He also recalled having set fires in doctors' offices and libraries. He was convinced that, at age 19, he had shot a man for having assaulted his wife. There were many other similar "memories" of violent acts, which he had never had before.

For two weeks Mr. Rodriguez stayed home from work. He sat, inactive, sometimes tearful about the damage he thought he had done, ruminating about what a terrible father he had been. Although his thoughts were painful, he actually "enjoyed the pleasure of knowing and discovering" and denied being persistently depressed. He also denied having experienced any change in weight, appetite, sleep, or psychomotor activity. He admitted to poor concentration, beginning about one month previously, when the financial pressures at work had begun to escalate. Sometimes he thought of killing himself.

The day before, he had had another sudden "revelation." He "remembered" for the first time that his father had beaten and sodomized him. He now understood that his destructiveness was caused by his father's abuse. With this realization, he no longer felt guilty about the terrible things that he had done. Nevertheless, he had agreed today to his wife's request that he come to the hospital.

Mr. Rodriguez is a tall, slender, neatly dressed man with a piercing gaze, poised demeanor, and polished manners. He smokes constantly throughout the session. He is quick-witted and playful, even while talking about the serious crimes he claims to have committed. He does well on tests of cognitive functioning. When told that his wife and others maintain that his memories cannot be accurate, he remarks, "Their facts do contradict my recollections. I can't explain the discrepancy. All I know is I set those fires." When asked to explain how he could have no police record, he replies that this is because he was so "quick and wily" that no one could catch him. He accounts for his wife's refusal to believe his stories by asserting that "she must have blocked the memories of the events because they are so upsetting to her."

On admission, physical examination of Mr. Rodriguez, including a neurologic evaluation, revealed no abnormality. All laboratory examinations were also negative.

Discussion of "Fire Setter"

There is no reason to believe that Mr. Rodriguez's "memories" are of actual events. We therefore conclude that he has many delusions about his past behavior. These delusions are not bizarre in that they involve situations that occur in real life, such as setting fires and committing violent crimes. Although Mr. Rodriguez is at first somewhat upset and depressed upon realizing what he has done, he does not have the full depressive syndrome, so the diagnosis of a psychotic Mood Disorder is ruled out. We therefore diagnose a Delusional Disorder. The theme of Mr. Rodriguez's delusion, that he has done something terrible, is quite uncommon in Delusional Disorder, and is not described by any of the specified types.

DSM-III-R Diagnosis:

Axis I: 297.10 Delusional Disorder, Unspecified Type (p. 202)

Follow-up

Mr. Rodriguez was treated with an antipsychotic drug. Over the next few days the delusions became more and more vague. He said that he still *felt* as though he had set the fires, but acknowledged nonetheless that these events had never really taken place. Five days after medications were begun, he submitted a sign-out letter because he could "no longer stand the hospital." He did not appear to present any danger to himself or others, agreed to seek follow-up in Miami, and was discharged.

The Heiress

A WEALTHY AND BEAUTIFUL 34-year-old woman presented with a "marital problem." She was an heiress of a wealthy European family, and her husband was the president of a small importing company. She felt he was being insensitive and demanding; and he, apparently, accused her of being self-centered, impulsive, and a "compulsive" liar. Over the course of their ten-year marriage, each had had numerous affairs, most of which eventually came out into the open. Both would resolve to deal with their marital frustrations and to stop having affairs, and a brief period of reconciliation would follow; but soon one or the other would again surreptitiously begin an affair.

The patient also described a special problem that worried her and that she had never disclosed to her husband. Periodically she experienced the urge to walk into one of the more elegant department stores in the city and steal an article of clothing. Over the course of the previous three or four years she had stolen several blouses, a couple of sweaters, and a skirt. Since her husband's income alone was over $250,000 a year and her investments worth many times that, she recognized the "absurdity" of her acts. She also indicated that what she stole was rarely very expensive and sometimes not even enough to her liking for her to wear.

The patient would become aware of the desire to steal something several days before she actually did so. The thoughts would increasingly occupy her mind until, on impulse, she would walk into a store, pluck an item off the rack, and stuff it under her coat or into a bag she happened to be carrying. Once out the door, she would experience a sense of relaxation and satisfaction; but at home she would feel anxious and guilty when she realized what she had done. She was caught on one occasion, but gave a long, involved story about intending to pay after she had gone elsewhere in the store and then "forgetting" to do so. She was released by the store security officers with a warning and suspiciously raised eyebrows.

She spent considerable time describing her own accomplishments, talents, and abilities. Her affairs, she said, proved that she was indeed beautiful and of superior "stock." She thought that she and her husband, who was handsome, aggressive, and successful, should be a perfect match. According to her, the problems with her husband stemmed from the little attention he paid her and the expectations he seemed to have that she should be at his beck and call. The frequent arguments they had upset her greatly, and thus it was her idea that they seek professional help. Regarding the charge that she was a compulsive liar, she admitted that she often found it easier to tell "white lies" than to face up to something "stupid" that she had done.

Discussion of "The Heiress"

Although not the reason for seeking treatment, the stealing this woman describes has the classic features of Kleptomania. She has recurrent failure to resist impulses to steal objects she does not like and does not need. There is a mounting sense of tension that builds until she gives in to the impulse to steal; this is followed by a feeling of pleasure. Typically, this is followed by remorse at what she has done. The act of stealing is not committed to express anger or vengeance.

Her marital problem, which is the reason for her seeking professional help, is apparently unrelated to the Kleptomania. It may be related to certain narcissistic personality traits, such as her exaggerated sense of her own importance (belief that she is of superior stock), her disregard of the rights of others (her lying), and her apparent lack of empathy (totally blaming her husband for their marital problems). Her need to have affairs may be because she requires constant admiration and attention. Although she displays many characteristics of Narcissistic Personality Disorder, in the absence of clear evidence of other features of the disorder (e.g., reacting to criticism with indifference or rage, preoccupation with envy), we prefer only to note narcissistic personality *traits* on Axis II.

Since the marital problem is the focus of attention, rather than the Kleptomania, and it is related to the narcissistic personality traits, the V code Marital Problem is the first condition noted on Axis I.

DSM-III-R Diagnosis:

Axis I: V61.10 Marital Problem (p. 360)
          312.32 Kleptomania (p. 323)
Axis II: Narcissistic personality traits

Sex Is a Nasty Business

CLARA, A 33-YEAR-OLD SECRETARY, was referred by her gynecologist to a clinic specializing in sexual problems. The immediate reason for the referral was that he had been unable to conduct a pelvic examination because of extreme contractions of her perivaginal muscles.

At the first clinic visit Clara was visibly uncomfortable as she discussed her sexual problems. Since the birth of her son, two years ago, she has been unable to have sexual intercourse because of vaginal spasms that are so extreme that neither her husband's nor her own little finger can be inserted into the vagina. She never looks forward to sexual contact with her husband and actively discourages his advances. Recently her husband has been pressuring her to become pregnant again. She would like to become pregnant both to please him and because she herself wants another child.

The onset of the perivaginal muscle spasms had been at an earlier time. Virginal at the time of her marriage, eight years previously, Clara had not been able to allow vaginal penetration for the first year. After a year of an "unconsummated marriage," she and her husband had seen a marriage counselor, who had helped them considerably so that they were able to have intercourse, at least episodically, over the next five years. Clara had always had some anxiety about vaginal penetration and didn't really like it, although she could be orgastic, albeit rarely, with appropriate sexual stimulation.

Clara was unable to get pregnant during the first five years of her marriage, apparently because of chronic endometriosis. When she finally gave birth, the baby was premature, weighing only three pounds, and was delivered about eleven weeks early. Clara felt guilty about having possibly caused the premature birth by taking estrogen for the endometriosis. Since the birth, she has been extremely fearful of becoming pregnant again and possibly delivering another premature child.

Clara recalled the difficulty that her mother had in talking to her about menstruation and sex. Clara's religious upbringing precluded any discussion of premarital sex, birth control, and abortion, which were all considered sinful. She knew nothing about the use of a condom as a birth-control device. She acknowledged not knowing where her clitoris was, and was unable to identify it on a model. She had never masturbated, and indeed had learned about masturbation only recently. She expressed an aversion toward her husband's licking or sucking parts of her body, describing this as "yucky." She described a lifelong fear of bathtub water getting into her vagina and "infecting" her. She recalled dreams in which large and frightening objects penetrated her body.

Discussion of "Sex Is a Nasty Business"

Clara has a number of Sexual Dysfunctions, but her major difficulty at the present time is contraction of her perivaginal muscles, demonstrated, as it often is, during a pelvic examination. Recurrent or persistent involuntary spasm of the musculature of the outer third of the vagina that interferes with coitus is called Vaginismus and is classified as a Sexual Pain Disorder.

Clara also has a lifelong aversion to anything connected with sex. Her avoidance of almost all genital sexual activity justifies the diagnosis of Sexual Aversion Disorder. On the rare occasions when she does have sexual intercourse, she undoubtedly also has difficulty becoming sexually aroused and having an orgasm. However, diagnosing Female Sexual Arousal Disorder and Inhibited Female Orgasm would seem to be superfluous at the present time since she now so rarely has sexual intercourse.

DSM-III-R Diagnosis:

Axis I: 306.51 Vaginismus, Psychogenic Only, Acquired (p. 295)
302.79 Sexual Aversion Disorder, Lifelong (p. 293)

Follow-up

Treatment involved a combination of conjoint sessions to deal with the husband's frustration, anger, and impatience and secure his cooperation in exercises that were designed to focus on sensual pleasure without intercourse (sensate focus exercises). Clara also had individual sessions, and was given an antianxiety agent, alprazolam, 0.5 mg, two or three times a day.

The main focus of treatment, however, was on vaginal dilatation, Clara using her own fingers in a tub of warm water. Her progress with vaginal dilatation was slow, and went through a series of gradual steps in which she could introduce the tip of one finger at the beginning and, gradually, two or three fingers. When the sensate focus exercises were added to the dilatation, she disliked her husband's sucking, licking, and kissing; she had to spend a great deal of time trying to achieve some comfort with her own body. This was later enhanced by group therapy for inorgasmic women.

Seen at first weekly, and then monthly, Clara slowly made

progress, allowing penetration during intercourse to occur. She was still frightened of pregnancy, even when her husband used a condom, expressing marked fear that the condom would break or slip off. After several more months of therapy, her fear of pregnancy diminished, so that intercourse could take place without birth control.

Traction

THE PATIENT IS A PREVIOUSLY HEALTHY 32-year-old carpenter from Nevada who was involved in a motor vehicle accident as he was returning from a three-month trip to Mexico. He was found by the state police and taken to the hospital. On admission, he was revealed to have multiple fractures involving his pelvis, toes on his right foot, and several ribs on his left side. He also sustained two small cuts on his head that required stitches. The patient reported that he had had a period of amnesia of about fifteen minutes and that he had lost consciousness during the accident, but this was not witnessed. He was alert and complained of severe back pain; he was not disoriented. He was treated with a narcotic, Demerol, 125 mg IM every 3 hours; a hypnotic, Seconal, 100 mg PO at bedtime; and a preanesthetic, Phenergan, 25 mg IM every 3 hours. The following day his back pain was unimproved, and his pain medication was changed to morphine and Phenergan.

Two days later he spiked a fever and was sweaty and tremulous. Because a history of drinking five to six beers a day had been elicited, the diagnosis of Alcohol Withdrawal was considered, and a minor tranquilizer, Valium, 5 mg PO every 6 hours, was added to his daily medication regimen, which at this time included Tylox, a narcotic and an analgesic, 1 or 2 capsules PO every 3-4 hours, and Seconal, 100 mg at bedtime.

The next day he was described as anxious, agitated, and constantly scratching. Two days later he was still febrile. Blood cultures, urinalysis, and chest X-ray were negative. Atarax, an antihistamine, 25 PO four times a day, was given to relieve itching.

The next day, one week after admission, the patient was noted to be disoriented. He complained that it took him some time to realize where he was upon awakening. His temperature was still elevated. He was receiving morphine, 3-10 mg every 3 hours for pain; Valium, a muscle relaxant, 5 mg PO every 6 hours ; and Dalmane, a hypnotic, 30 mg PO at bedtime. The next day, his pain medication was again changed, this time to Percodan, a narcotic, 1-2 tablets every 3 hours, and Demerol, 75 mg IM every 4 hours.

One day later the patient underwent an open reduction for a fractured left acetabulum. The surgery, done under general anesthesia, was tolerated well; but immediately following the procedure, the patient was disoriented to time and place and was noted to be picking at things in the air. His temperature was still elevated, and there was no documented source of infection. At this time the patient was taking Demerol, 75-100 mg IM every 4 hours; Atarax, 75 mg every 3 hours; and Tylenol, every 4 hours.

Over the next few days the patient's mental status improved, although he was still disoriented at times and confessed, "You know, sometimes I can't pay attention to what you're saying." His temperature was still moderately elevated. Medication consisted of a synthetic opioid, Dilaudid, 2-4 mg every 3-4 hours. The continuing periods of disorientation disturbed his doctors, and a psychiatric consultation was requested.

Upon initial interview, now 17 days after the accident, the patient was alert, fully oriented, and in good spirits. Results of mental status testing were normal. The patient admitted having had difficulties in thinking and "hallucinations" at times during the previous couple of weeks. He described them as "opiate dreams," caused by his pain medication.

Over the next few days his condition was generally improved during the daytime hours, but at night he was frequently found to be taking his traction apparatus apart. When discovered, he would sometimes talk incoherently about the "traction thingamajig." If questioned the next day, he always denied having dismantled the equipment. At this time he was taking Tylox, two capsules every 6 hours, for pain. He often complained of severe pain, many times arguing with his doctors in an attempt to persuade them to give him Tylox more often. The psychiatrist was called in again to help, and the Tylox dose was given more frequently. It was felt that his addiction potential was not very high at that time.

Several days later the patient was observed to be playing with fecal matter in his bed and once again dismantling his traction apparatus. When discovered, he admitted to these acts, was so upset that he could not sleep that night, and asked to see a psychiatrist. When interviewed, he appeared anxious and angry. He stated that he did not understand what was happening to him and was very upset about his behavior. He said he had not been sleeping more than two to three hours a night for at least two weeks. He was very frightened by the thought that his mind was doing things he was not aware of and could not control. He asked for a "game plan" to stop this behavior and even suggested stopping all pain medication if necessary. Over the next few days, pain medication was reduced. The patient now appeared alert and oriented, and there were no further episodes of disturbed behavior at night.

Discussion of "Traction"

Beginning with the second day of hospitalization and continuing for several weeks, this man intermittently had reduced ability to maintain attention to external stimuli ("I can't pay attention to what you are saying") and disorganized thinking (he talked incoherently). He also had a reduced level of consciousness (it took him some time to realize where he was upon awakening), visual hallucinations (he picked at things in the air and had "opiate dreams"), and disturbance of his sleep-wake cycle (he had trouble sleeping). These are the characteristic features of a Delirium; and in this case there is no difficulty in identifying several physical factors that could have contributed to the development of the disturbance. The difficulty is in deciding the relative roles of infection and fever and the large number of analgesics and sedatives that the patient received. (It is not clear from the case record why his medications were so often changed.) We note the Delirium on Axis I, and on Axis III, the physical factors that we think caused or contributed to the Delirium. An equally plausible alternative formulation would be to note on Axis I a Psychoactive Substance-induced Delirium, but there is no single diagnosis that describes the cumulative effects of the multiple drugs that were probably involved in this case.

DSM-III-R Diagnosis:

Axis I: 293.00 Delirium (p. 103)
Axis III: Fever of unknown origin

Former Pilot

A 46-YEAR-OLD FORMER PROFESSIONAL PILOT, Harold Riley, sought treatment for a fear of flying that had interrupted his career. Eight years earlier, after flying professionally for over twenty years, he suddenly felt intensely anxious one morning during an uneventful solo flight. For over an hour, his heart beat rapidly, he felt a smothering sensation, he sweat profusely, trembled, was nauseated, and felt faint. His symptoms stopped only after he landed. Thirty minutes later he took off again, but immediately began to experience the same symptoms, which forced him to fly at a low altitude with the windows open. He landed the plane as soon as possible.

Harold attempted several flights in the days following this incident, but the symptoms always recurred. He then began to fear that he might faint while at the controls of the plane, although this had never happened. He had no fear flying in a plane if someone else were at the controls. Finally, after several medical evaluations were negative, he stopped flying for a year. He then made another attempt to fly with an instructor, but again discontinued flying after the symptoms returned.

Initially Harold denied any history of other mental symptoms or of any irrational anxiety other than while flying. However, on close questioning he described two brief, sudden, and unexpected episodes of anxiety while driving an automobile. The first had occurred shortly after his first episode in the air, and the other, several years later.

Disussion of "Former Pilot"

Because this man's fear is focused on a circumscribed situation, flying an airplane, the reader may consider the diagnosis of a Simple Phobia. That diagnosis, however, is made only when the fear does not involve that of having a panic attack. This former pilot is afraid of flying only because he fears he will have another attack like the first one he experienced, an attack that included sudden anxiety accompanied by the characteristic symptoms of a panic attack: rapid heartbeat, sweating, nausea, faintness, and fear of loss of control.

Ordinarily, the diagnosis of Panic Disorder is made when a person has at least four unexpected panic attacks during a four-week period. Our pilot has had only one clear panic attack and two additional possible attacks. The diagnosis is also made if a single attack is followed by a period of at least a month of persistent fear of having another attack, but this would not seem to apply to Mr. Riley, who was afraid only when he was at the controls of an airplane.

What about Agoraphobia without History of Panic Disorder? Mr Riley is afraid of developing symptoms, in this case a panic attack, that would be incapacitating; and he has never had Panic Disorder. His avoidance, however, is limited to the specific situation of piloting an airplane, and he does not restrict his travel in any other way.

Since this case does not meet the criteria for any specific Anxiety Disorder in DSM-III-R, we are left with the not very satisfactory diagnosis of Anxiety Disorder Not Otherwise Specified.

DSM-III-R Diagnosis:

Axis I: 300.00 Anxiety Disorder Not Otherwise Specified (p. 253)

Food for Thought

MR. GRIM IS 46, an advertising salesman and writer for a small magazine. During 15 years of marriage, his wife had noticed loud snoring and episodes, lasting 10 to 15 seconds, during which he did not breathe. "Then he takes a giant breath, exhales, inhales one to four or five times, then he stops breathing for another one of these silences." During longer, "not-breathing" periods, as she called them, "He is very restless. He can dish out quite a kick or punch if I haven't moved far enough out of the way." After nights full of such events, Mr. Grim groggily drags himself out of bed, suffering from a headache.

Mr. Grim is usually sleepy during the day, especially while driving the turnpikes around New England, which his work requires. To remain vigilant, he munches on coin-machine sandwiches, washed down by gallons of Coca-Cola®. Any alcoholic beverages make him want to fall asleep.

As a result of his snacks, Mr. Grim has 280 pounds packed onto his 5'8" frame. He is able to diet and lose weight only temporarily. Recently he has developed a hiatus hernia—associated with stomach pain and indigestion—mild diabetes, and high blood pressure, all complications of the obesity.

When he was a child, the patient's mother constantly berated him for being too fat, and he feared she would starve him. It was then that he developed a habit of stopping for food whenever he was out of the house.

Nasal stuffiness during the ragweed season worsened his snoring, the nocturnal "struggles," and the morning headaches. Just before his first interview about his sleep problems, he had cleaned out an old barn and attic, both full of dust and pigeon droppings, and had had a severe allergy attack. It was for this reason that he now came for help.

Physical examination disclosed a deviated nasal septum, enlargement and thickening of pharyngeal structures, and collapse of his pharyngeal walls into the airway upon taking a deep breath with his nose blocked.

A daytime continuous performance test was administered. The test involved his pushing a button whenever he saw certain letters presented at a rate of one per second. He scored 44% correct compared with a normal rate of 66% to 78%, indicating moderate impairment in concentration, which was worse in the morning. Laboratory sleep monitoring revealed recurrent 15- to 66-second periods of not breathing (sleep apnea) associated with decreased oxygen saturation (frequently below 50%) and decreased heart rate (50 to 55 beats per minute), followed by increased rates (to about 90 per minute). No normal periods of deep sleep were recorded on the polysomnograph. These findings indicated severe sleep apnea, which interfered with the quality of his nocturnal sleep and caused his daytime sleepiness and impaired daytime arousal. The clinician decided that Mr. Grim's obesity and the structural and functional impairment of his upper airway were the cause of the apnea.

Discussion of "Food for Thought"

Mr. Grim's primary problem is chronic excessive daytime sleepiness (hypersomnia). In his case the hypersomnia is not a symptom of another mental disorder, such as Major Depression, but is due to organic factors that cause recurrent periods of sleep apnea, which in turn results in sleep that is adequate in amount, but not restful. On Axis I we note the sleep problem as Hypersomnia Related to a Known Organic Factor. On Axis III we note the organic factors: Sleep Apnea associated with obesity, deviated nasal septum, and other upper airway obstructions. We also note the hypertension, hiatus hernia, and diabetes.

The cluster of symptoms that Mr. Grim has—loud snoring, respiratory pauses, upper airway problems, obesity, and hypertension—is commonly seen in people with the chief complaint of hypersomnia who present at sleep disorders centers. In fact, 85% of cases of hypersomnia seen at sleep disorders centers are diagnosed as Hypersomnia Related to a Known Organic Factor, and 50% of these are associated with sleep apnea.

DSM-III-R Diagnosis:

Axis I: **780.50 Hypersomnia Related to a Known Organic Factor (p. 304)**
Axis III: **Sleep Apnea associated with obesity, deviated nasal septum, and other upper airway obstructions**
Hypertension
Hiatus hernia
Mild diabetes

Follow-up

Treatment of the sleep apnea was by continuous positive airway pressure, a technique in which the pressure of the inspired air is increased by a machine connected to the patient with a tube and face mask at night, which helps overcome the airway obstruction. The patient's snoring and sleepiness were rapidly relieved, and he was now motivated, for the first time, to stay on a diet. Within 6 months he lost 80 pounds. He said he felt "like I have gotten my youth back."

Empty Shell

THE PATIENT IS A 23-YEAR-OLD veterinary assistant admitted for her first psychiatric hospitalization. She arrived late at night, referred by a local psychiatrist, saying "I don't really need to be here."

Three months before admission, the patient learned that her mother had become pregnant. She began drinking heavily, ostensibly in order to sleep nights. While drinking she became involved in a series of "one-night stands." Two weeks before admission, she began feeling panicky and having experiences in which she felt as if she were removed from her body and in a trance. During one of these episodes she was stopped by the police while wandering on a bridge late at night. The next day, in response to hearing a voice repeatedly telling her to jump off a bridge, she ran to her supervisor and asked for help. Her supervisor, seeing her distraught and also noting scars from a recent wrist-slashing, referred her to a psychiatrist, who then arranged for her immediate hospitalization.

At the time of the hospitalization, the patient appeared as a disheveled and frail, but appealing waif. She was cooperative, coherent, and frightened. Although she did not feel hospitalization was needed, she welcomed the prospect of relief from her anxiety and depersonalization. She acknowledged that she had had feelings of loneliness and inadequacy and brief periods of depressed mood and anxiety since adolescence. Recently she had been having fantasies that she was stabbing herself or a little baby with a knife. She complained that she was "just an empty shell that is transparent to everyone."

The patient's parents divorced when she was three, and for the next five years she lived with her maternal grandmother and her mother, who had a severe drinking problem. The patient had night terrors during which she would frequently end up sleeping with her mother. At age six she went to a special boarding school for a year and a half, after which she was withdrawn by her mother, against the advice of the school. When she was eight, her maternal grandmother died; and she recalls trying to conceal her grief about this from her mother. She spent most of the next two years living with various relatives, including a period with her father, whom she had not seen since the divorce. When she was nine, her mother was hospitalized with a diagnosis of Schizophrenia. From age ten through college, the patient lived with an aunt and uncle, but had ongoing and frequent contacts with her mother. Her school record was consistently good.

Since adolescence she has dated regularly, having an active but rarely pleasurable sex life. Her relationships with men usually end abruptly after she becomes angry with them when they disappoint her in some apparently minor way. She then concludes that they were "no good to begin with." She has had several roommates, but has had trouble establishing a stable living situation because of her jealousy of sharing her roommates with others and her manipulative efforts to keep them from seeing other people.

Since college she has worked steadily and well as a veterinary assistant. At the time of admission, she was working a night shift in a veterinary hospital and living alone.

Discussion of "Empty Shell"

In the last three months, since hearing of her mother's pregnancy, this young woman has begun drinking heavily, has had several episodes of what appears to be depersonalization, and has been anxious, depressed, and suicidal. In addition, she briefly had auditory hallucinations telling her to kill herself. In the absence of a previous history of significant psychopathology, these symptoms would suggest one or more Axis I diagnoses, such as Major Depression with Psychotic Features, Alcohol Abuse, or even Adjustment Disorder. However, the long-standing history of interpersonal difficulties and a variety of other symptoms, such as loneliness, depression, feelings of inadequacy, etc., suggests that she has a Personality Disorder and that the current disturbance merely represents an exacerbation of this, not a separate illness.

In fact, this patient demonstrates enough of the characteristic features of Borderline Personality Disorder to warrant that diagnosis. She clearly has a pattern of unstable mood, interpersonal relationships, and self-image. Her relationships with men have been intense and unstable, the relationships ending when she becomes angry and devalues them. Affective instability is suggested by the reference to her having brief periods of depressed mood and anxiety since adolescence. She reports that she is an "empty shell," evidence of chronic feelings of emptiness. In addition, at least during the present episode, she demonstrates impulsivity (drinking and sex) and physically self-damaging acts (slashing her wrists). It is quite likely that these chacteristics have also been present during periods of stress in the past.

The diagnosis of a psychotic disorder, such as Psychotic Disorder Not Otherwise Specified, for the current episode is not warranted since the brief hallucination and her reaction to it as egodystonic are an example of the transient psychotic experiences that are often a feature of Borderline Personality Disorder.

DSM-III-R Diagnosis:

Axis I: V71.09 No Diagnosis or Condition
Axis II: 301.83 Borderline Personality Disorder, Severe (p. 347)

Follow-up

When she left the hospital, the patient resumed work and saw a woman therapist on a twice-weekly schedule. Her therapist felt that it was a tenuous relationship in which the patient sometimes seemed to seek nurturance or special favors and at other times was belligerent and viewed therapy as useless. After three months, the patient became involved with a new boyfriend and soon thereafter quit therapy, with the complaint that her therapist didn't really care or understand her.

Househusband

TOM KAPLAN IS A 35-YEAR-OLD, married, white male architect, who recently became a salaried partner in a large urban architectural firm. He lives with his 30-year-old wife and 3-year-old son in an older suburban house, which they have renovated. He was referred for psychiatric evaluation by his wife's psychiatrist when, during a series of joint sessions, he complained of feelings of fatigue, restlessness, and irritability, associated with their marital quarrels. These complaints have increased over the past year, during which time his wife has been a first-year law student.

Tom is a tall, handsome man, but round-shouldered and stooped, with an obviously pained, worried expression. His affect is somber, and he begins the initial interview by complaining that the time is terribly inconvenient for him, although he willingly accepted it when the appointment was made.

He launches into a long, whining story of how his life is overburdened with work and he is perpetually behind. He has to prepare most of the meals and takes care of all household chores, in addition to working 70 hours a week at his job. He has just been made a partner in the firm, and feels that he cannot disappoint the senior partners by taking life easier. His partnership was delayed by several years, probably because of his tendency to keep his creative ideas to himself. In fact, he is always worried that he is not "truly creative" and that if he shows his drawings, his partners will be disappointed. These doubts about himself kept him from applying to the most prestigious architectural firms, which would have been appropriate for him given his academic accomplishments.

Tom denies feeling depressed and claims that his chronic exhaustion is because he is sleeping only five hours a night. He jokes that he could not survive were it not for the 24-hour supermarket and the shopping center that is open Sundays. He is resentful of his wife, who is barely able to cope with law school and be in treatment at the same time. As the story unfolds, it becomes clear that he had actually encouraged her to enter law school, although she had been reasonably satisfied with her job as a paralegal aide. They have had baby-sitter expenses, plus those of her psychiatric sessions and law-school tuition.

At his job, Tom frequently takes time from his own work to help younger associates with their assignments, the end result being that he completes his own projects at home, late at night and on weekends, while his wife studies. (This same pattern prevailed in college: he helped his roommates with their work while putting off his own.) He believes this behavior is essential to being liked. When he asks, "Would you believe that I haven't had a vacation for three years?" it is in a tone of voice suggesting pride.

Tom has no close male friends, although other men have made friendly overtures toward him. His typical response when someone suggests that they get together for some social activity such as a drink or playing chess (which he likes) is to refuse politely in a sad tone on the grounds that he has too much work to do. After two or three such refusals, people usually lose interest.

Tom believes that people are lazy and too self-indulgent and has, from time to time, alienated his co-workers with comments such as "Don't you feel guilty going on vacation when you have work left behind?" Most frequently it is his wife who is the recipient of his resentful remarks, and she states that his critical and self-righteous attitude is the cause of most of their fights.

Before his marriage Tom was involved with a series of relatively uneducated girls. Invariably, he would find himself in a messy break-up of the relationship. His wife was his first girl friend who was his intellectual peer.

Other sources of conflict involve the religious holidays. Tom's mother acts hurt if he and his family do not always come to her home, rather than alternating with his wife's family. Tom feels like an innocent victim caught between the conflicting pressures of two demanding women. This increases his predominant feeling that "Whatever I do, it will be wrong. I just can't please everybody."

Discussion of "Househusband"

During the controversy regarding the inclusion of Self-defeating Personality Disorder in DSM-III-R, critics of the category expressed concern that the diagnosis would be given only to women. This case was submitted as an example of this unofficial diagnosis in a man.

Tom has a pervasive pattern of choosing people (girl friends) and situations (jobs) that lead to disappointment. He rejects opportunities for pleasure (turns down social invitations) and fails to accomplish tasks that are crucial to his own personal objectives (helps colleagues, but fails to show his own work). He engages in excessive self-sacrifice, and we suspect that he rejects the offers of others to help him. These are the characteristic features of the unofficial diagnosis Self-defeating Personality Disorder, which is coded as Personality Disorder Not Otherwise Specified.

DSM-III-R Diagnosis:

Axis I: V71.09 No Diagnosis or Condition
Axis II: 301.90 Personality Disorder Not Otherwise Specified
                  (Self-defeating Personality Disorder) (p. 373)

Fear of Flying

LOLA, A 25-YEAR-OLD FEMALE laboratory technician, has been married to a 32-year-old cabdriver for 5 years. The couple has a two-year-old son, and the marriage appears harmonious.

The presenting complaint is Lola's lifelong inability to experience orgasm. She has never achieved orgasm, although during sexual activity she has received what should have been sufficient stimulation. She has tried to masturbate, and on many occasions her husband has manually stimulated her patiently for lengthy periods of time. Although she does not reach climax, she is strongly attached to her husband, feels erotic pleasure during lovemaking, and lubricates copiously. According to both of them, the husband has no sexual difficulty.

Exploration of her thoughts as she nears orgasm reveals a vague sense of dread of some undefined disaster. More generally, she is anxious about losing control over her emotions, which she normally keeps closely in check. She is particularly uncomfortable about expressing any anger or hostility.

Physical examination reveals no abnormality.

Discussion of "Fear of Flying"

Lola's sexual difficulties are limited to the orgasm phase of the sexual response cycle (she has no difficulty in desiring sex or in becoming excited). During lovemaking there is what would ordinarily be an adequate amount of stimulation. The report of a "vague sense of dread of some undefined disaster" as she approaches orgasm is evidence that her inability to have orgasms represents a pathological inhibition. There is no suggestion of any other Axis I disorder or any physical disorder that could account for the disturbance. Thus, the diagnosis is of a Sexual Dysfunction Orgasm Disorder, Inhibited Female Orgasm.

If with treatment it became apparent that the fear of loss of control were a symptom of a Personality Disorder, such as Obsessive Compulsive Personality Disorder, the diagnosis of a Sexual Dysfunction would still be made. However, if the sexual dysfunction occurred exclusively during the course of another Axis I disorder, such as Major Depression, then the sexual disturbance would be assumed to be a symptom of the Axis I disorder, and the diagnosis of a Sexual Dysfunction would not be made.

DSM-III-R Diagnosis:

Axis I: 302.73 Inhibited Female Orgasm, Psychogenic Only, Lifelong, Generalized (p. 294)

False Rumors

BOB, A 21-YEAR-OLD MAN, comes to the psychiatrist's office, on the advice of his college counselor, accompanied by his parents. He begins the interview by announcing that he has no problems. His parents are always overly concerned about him, and it is only to get them "off my back" that he has agreed to the evaluation. "I am dependent on them financially, but not emotionally."

The psychiatrist was able to obtain the following story from Bob and his parents. Bob had apparently spread malicious and false rumors about several of the teachers who had given him poor grades, implying that they were having homosexual affairs with students. This, as well as increasingly erratic attendance at his classes over the past term, following the loss of a girl friend, prompted the school counselor to suggest to Bob and his parents that help was urgently needed. Bob claimed that his academic problems were exaggerated, his success in theatrical productions was being overlooked, and that he was in full control of the situation. He did not deny that he spread the false rumors, but showed no remorse or apprehension about possible repercussions for himself.

Bob is a tall, stylishly dressed young man with a dramatic wave in his hair. His manner is distant, but charming, and he obviously enjoys talking about a variety of intellectual subjects or current affairs. However, he assumes a condescending, cynical, and bemused manner toward the psychiatrist and the evaluation process. He conveys a sense of superiority and control over the evaluation.

Accounts of Bob's development were complicated by his bland dismissal of its importance and by the conflicting accounts about it by his parents. His mother was an extremely anxious, immaculately dressed, outspoken woman. She described Bob as having been a beautiful, joyful baby, who was always extremely gifted and brilliant. She recalled that after a miscarriage, when Bob was one year old, she and her husband had become even more devoted to his care, giving him "the love for two." The father was a rugged-looking, soft-spoken, successful man. He recalled a period in Bob's early life when they had been very close, and he had even confided in Bob about very personal matters and expressed deep feelings. He also noted that Bob had become progressively more resentful with the births of his two siblings. The father laughingly commented that Bob "would have liked to have been the only child." He recalled a series of conflicts between Bob and authority figures over rules, and that Bob had expressed disdain for his peers at school, and for his siblings.

In his early school years, Bob seemed to play and interact less with other children than most others do. In fifth grade, after a change in teachers, he became arrogant and withdrawn and refused to participate in class. Nevertheless, he maintained excellent grades. In high school he had been involved in an episode similar to the one that had led to the current evaluation. At that time he had spread false rumors about a classmate with whom he was competing for a role in the school play.

In general, it became clear that Bob had never been "one of the boys." He liked dramatics and movies, but had never shown an interest in athletics. He always appeared to be a loner, though he did not complain of loneliness. When asked, he professed to take pride in "being different" from his peers. He also distanced himself from his parents and often responded with silence to their overtures for more communication. His parents felt that behind his guarded demeanor was a sad, alienated, lonely, young man. Though he was well known to classmates, the relationships he had with them were generally under circumstances in which he was looked up to for his intellectual or dramatic talents.

Bob conceded that others viewed him as cold or insensitive. He readily acknowledged these qualities, and that he had no close friends; but he dismissed this as unimportant. This represented strength to him. He went on to note that when others complained about these qualities in him, it was largely because of their own weakness. In his view, they envied him and longed to have him care about them. He believed they sought to gain by having an association with him.

Bob had occasional dates, but no steady girl friends. Although the exact history remains unclear, he acknowledged that the girl whose loss seemed to have led to his escalating school problems had been someone whom he cared about. She was the first person with whom he had had a sexual relationship. The relationship had apparently dissolved after she had expressed an increasing desire to spend more time with her girl friends and to go to school social events.

Discussion of "False Rumors"

This case was supplied as an example of Narcissistic Personality Disorder, and the reader will certainly be struck by Bob's grandiosity and insensitivity to others (lack of empathy). In identifying behavior that justifies three additional criteria for the disorder, we make some inferences from the limited case material that is presented. For example, we assume that the reason Bob has had trouble with authorities about conforming to school rules is that he does not believe the rules should apply to him, and this behavior is an indication of entitlement. We interpret his spreading rumors about teachers and peers as evidence that he is interpersonally exploitative. Finally, his extreme jealousy of his siblings, his spreading rumors about a student with whom he was competing, and his belief in others' envy of him are evidence of preoccupation with feelings of envy. His need for constant attention and admiration is suggested by his dramatic presentation. We have no evidence that he is preoccupied with fantasies of unlimited success, but we suspect it to be true.

DSM-III-R Diagnosis:

Axis I: V71.09 No Diagnosis or Condition
Axis II: 301.81 Narcissistic Personality Disorder (Provisional)
          (p. 351)

Thunderstorms

S HEILA, A 28-YEAR-OLD HOUSEWIFE, sought psychiatric treatment for a fear of storms that had become progressively more disturbing to her. Although frightened of storms since she was a child, the fear seemed to abate somewhat during adolescence, but had been increasing in severity over the past few years. This gradual exacerbation of her anxiety, plus the fear that she might pass it on to her children, led her to seek treatment.

She is most frightened of lightning, but is uncertain about the reason for this. She is only vaguely aware of a fear of being struck by lightning, and recognizes that this is an unlikely occurrence. When asked to elaborate on her fears, she imagines that lightning could strike a tree in her yard; the tree might fall and block her driveway, thus trapping her at home. This frightens her, but she is quite aware that her fear is irrational. She also recognizes the irrational nature of her fear of thunder. She begins to feel anxiety long before a storm arrives. A weather report predicting a storm later in the week can cause her anxiety to increase to the point that she worries for days before the storm. Although she does not express a fear of rain, her anxiety increases even when the weather becomes overcast because of the increased likelihood of a storm.

During a storm, she does several things to reduce her anxiety. Since being with another person reduces her fear, she often tries to make plans to visit friends or relatives or go to a store when a storm is threatening. Sometimes, when her husband is away on business, she stays overnight with a close relative if a storm is forecast. During a storm she covers her eyes or moves to a part of the house far from windows, where she cannot see lightning should it occur.

Sheila has three young children. She describes her marriage as a happy one and states that her husband has been supportive of her when she is frightened and has encouraged her to seek psychiatric treatment. She is in good physical health, and at the time she entered treatment there were no unusually stressful situations in her life or other emotional difficulties. Her parents separated shortly after she began treatment. Although she found this distressing, she felt her personal supports were adequate and that this occurrence did not necessitate psychiatric attention.

She describes her past history as generally unremarkable in terms of any obvious psychiatric problems, except for her fear of storms. She feels that she may have "learned" this fear from her grandmother, who also was frightened of storms. She denies panic attacks, or any other unusual or incapacitating fears.

Discussion of "Thunderstorms"

Many people feel uncomfortable during thunder and lightning storms; but this woman's persistent fear of this circumscribed stimulus is clearly excessive, causes her considerable distress, and is acknowledged by her to be irrational. Furthermore, the fear and the avoidant behavior frequently significantly interfere with her normal routine. These features indicate the presence of a phobia. Although she is afraid of being alone during storms, there is apparently no fear of developing a panic attack or some other incapacitating or embarrassing symptom when alone or in public places away from home, as in Agoraphobia without History of Panic Disorder. Her fear of storms does not involve a fear of humiliation or embarrassment in certain social situations, as in Social Phobia, and it is not related to the content of the obsessions of Obsessive Compulsive Disorder. Therefore, by exclusion, the diagnosis is Simple Phobia.

DSM-III-R Diagnosis:

Axis I: 300.29 Simple Phobia, Mild (p. 244)

Worthless Wife

CONNIE, A 33-YEAR-OLD HOMEMAKER and mother of a 4-year-old son, Robert, is referred by her general practitioner to a psychiatric outpatient program because of her complaint that she has been depressed and unable to concentrate ever since she separated from her husband 3 months previously.

Connie left her husband, Donald, after a five-year marriage. Violent arguments between them, during which Connie was beaten by her husband, had occurred for the last four years of their marriage, beginning when she became pregnant with Robert. There were daily arguments during which Donald hit her hard enough to leave bruises on her face and arms. During their final argument, about Connie's buying an expensive tricycle for Robert, her husband had held a loaded gun to Robert's head and threatened to shoot him if she didn't agree to return the tricycle to the store. Connie obtained a court order of protection that prevented Donald from having any contact with her or their son. She took Robert to her parents' apartment, where they are still living.

Connie is an only child, and a high school and secretarial school graduate. She worked as an executive secretary for six years before her marriage and for the first two years after, until Robert's birth. Before her marriage Connie had her own apartment. She was close to her parents, visiting them weekly and speaking to them a couple of times a week. Connie had many friends whom she also saw regularly. She still had several friends from her high school years. In high school she had been a popular cheerleader and a good student. In the office where she had worked as a secretary, she was in charge of organizing office holiday parties and money collections for employee gifts. She had no past history of depression; and there was no family history of violence, mental illness, or substance abuse. Her parents had been happily married for 25 years.

Connie met Donald at work, where he was an accountant. They married after a three-month courtship, during which time Connie observed Donald using cocaine twice at parties. When she expressed concern, he reassured her that he was only "trying it to be sociable," and denied any regular use.

Donald, a college graduate, is the oldest of three siblings. His father drank a pint of bourbon each night and often beat Donald's mother. Donald's two younger brothers both have histories of substance abuse.

During their first year of marriage, Donald became increasingly irritable and critical of Connie. He began to request that Connie stop calling and seeing her friends after work, and refused to allow them or his in-laws to visit their apartment. Connie convinced Donald to try marital therapy, but he refused to continue after the initial two sessions.

Despite her misgiving about Donald's behavior toward her, Connie decided to become pregnant. During the seventh month of the pregnancy, she developed thrombophlebitis and had to stay home in bed. Donald began complaining that their apartment was not clean enough and that Connie was not able to shop for groceries. He never helped Connie with the housework. He refused to allow his mother-in-law to come to the apartment to help. One morning when he couldn't find a clean shirt, he became angry and yelled at Connie. When she suggested that he pick some up from the laundry, he began hitting her with his fists. She left him and went to live with her parents for a week. He expressed remorse for hitting her and agreed to resume marital therapy.

At her parents' and Donald's urging, Connie returned to her apartment. No further violence occurred until after Robert's birth. At that time, Donald began using cocaine every weekend and often became violent when he was high.

In the three months since she left Donald, Connie has become increasingly depressed. Her appetite has been poor, and she has lost ten pounds. She cries a lot and often wakes up at five in the morning, unable to get back to sleep. Ever since she left Donald, he has been calling her at her parents' home and begging her to return to him. One week before her psychiatric evaluation, Connie's parents took her to their general practitioner. Her physical examination was normal, and he referred her for psychiatric treatment.

When seen by a psychiatrist in the outpatient clinic, Connie is pale and thin, dressed in worn-out jeans and dark blue sweater. Her haircut is unstylish, and she appears older than she is. She speaks slowly, describing her depressed mood and lack of energy. She says that her only pleasure is in being with her son. She is able to take care of him physically, but feels guilty because her preoccupation with her own bad feelings prevents her from being able to play with him. She now has no social contacts other than with her parents and her son. She feels worthless and blames herself for her marital problems, saying that if she had been a better wife, maybe Donald would have been able to give up the cocaine. When asked why she stayed with him so long, she explains that her family disapproved of divorce and kept telling her that she should try harder to make her marriage a success. She also thought about what her life would be like trying to take care of her son while working full time and didn't think she could make it.

Discussion of "Worthless Wife"

When Connie comes to treatment, she has all of the characteristic symptoms of a Major Depression. Her mood is persistently depressed, she feels worthless, has trouble concentrating, has lost weight, and has difficulty sleeping. This picture is not unusual in someone who has recently left a marriage.

The question that many readers may ask is whether Connie has a personality disturbance that has kept her in a relationship with a man who has been psychologically and physically abusive. As is typically the case, there is no evidence that Connie has chosen someone because he is abusive or that she gets any particular gratification from being victimized. Instead, what has kept her in the marriage is a combination of her low self-esteem and social pressures against leaving her husband. In more extreme cases of physical abuse, the wife may actually fear for her life or the lives of her children if she leaves her abusive husband.

DSM-III-R Diagnosis:

Axis I: 296.22 Major Depression, Single Episode, Moderate
            (p. 229)
Axis II: None
Axis III: None
Axis IV: Psychosocial stressor: spouse abuse
            Severity: 5 - Extreme (predominantly enduring
            circumstances)
Axis V: Current GAF: 45
            Highest GAF Past Year: 75

Follow-up

Connie received medication and individual psychotherapy for her depression. She also participated in group therapy with other women who had been abused by their spouses.

After six months of therapy, Connie was no longer depressed. She bought new clothes and had her hair cut in a more flattering and youthful style. She found employment as an executive secretary and placed Robert in a day-care center, where she participated in parent programs. She reported that she and Robert had fun together in the evening and on weekends. She again began seeing her friends. With financial assistance from her parents, she began divorce proceedings against Donald and requested sole custody of Robert.

Vertigo

A 46-YEAR-OLD HOUSEWIFE was referred by her husband's psychiatrist for consultation. In the course of discussing certain marital conflicts that he was having with his wife, the husband had described "attacks" of dizziness that his wife experienced that left her quite incapacitated.

In consultation, the wife described being overcome with feelings of extreme dizziness, accompanied by slight nausea, four or five nights a week. During these attacks, the room around her would take on a "shimmering" appearance, and she would have the feeling that she was "floating" and unable to keep her balance. Inexplicably, the attacks almost always occurred at about 4:00 PM. She usually had to lie down on a couch and often did not feel better until 7:00 or 8:00 PM. After recovering, she generally spent the rest of the evening watching TV; and more often than not, she would fall asleep in the living room, not going to bed in the bedroom until 2:00 or 3:00 in the morning.

The patient had been pronounced physically fit by her internist, a neurologist, and an ENT specialist on more than one occasion. Hypoglycemia had been ruled out by glucose tolerance tests.

When asked about her marriage, the patient described her husband as a tyrant, frequently demanding and verbally abusive of her and their four children. She admitted that she dreaded his arrival home from work each day, knowing that he would comment that the house was a mess and the dinner, if prepared, not to his liking. Recently, since the onset of her attacks, when she was unable to make dinner he and the four kids would go to McDonald's or the local pizza parlor. After that, he would settle in to watch a ball game on TV in the bedroom, and their conversation was minimal. In spite of their troubles, the patient claimed that she loved and needed her husband very much.

Discussion of "Vertigo"

This woman complains of a variety of physical symptoms (dizziness, nausea, visual disturbances, loss of balance) that all suggest a physical disorder; but thorough examinations by a number of medical specialists have failed to detect a physical disorder that could account for the symptoms. With a specific physical disorder ruled out, the differential diagnosis is between undiagnosed physical symptoms and a mental disorder.

The context in which these symptoms occur suggests the role of psychological factors in their development: they recur at virtually the same time each day, closely associated with the husband's arrival home from work; the husband's angry tirades and verbal abuse are undoubtedly very stressful. Since there is no evidence that the patient is conscious of intentionally producing the symptoms (e.g., taking a drug that would induce such symptoms or claiming to have the symptoms when they are not present), a diagnosis of a Factitious Disorder, or Malingering, are ruled out. Although the symptoms resemble those of a panic attack, there is no evidence that they occur unexpectedly, thus ruling out Panic Disorder. The disorder, therefore, is a Somatoform Disorder—a mental disorder with physical symptoms that suggest a physical disorder.

Since the patient's complaints are not part of a long-standing polysymptomatic disturbance involving many organ systems, Somatization Disorder is excluded. The symptoms are limited to an alteration in physical functioning; hence, the diagnosis is Conversion Disorder.

DSM-III-R Diagnosis:

Axis I: 300.11 Conversion Disorder (p. 259)

Stay Healthy

MR. MICHAELS, A 28-YEAR-OLD computer programmer, seeks treatment because of fears that prevent him from visiting his terminally ill father-in-law in the hospital. He explains that he is afraid of any situation even remotely associated with bodily injury or illness. For example, he cannot bear to have his blood drawn, or to see or even hear about sick people. These fears are the reason he has avoided consulting a doctor even when he is sick, avoids visiting sick friends or family members, or even listening to descriptions of medical procedures, physical trauma, or illness. He became a vegetarian five years ago in order to avoid thoughts of animals' being killed.

The patient dates the onset of these fears to the age of nine, when his Sunday school teacher gave a detailed account of a leg operation she had undergone. As he listened, he began to feel anxious and dizzy, to sweat profusely, and finally he fainted. He recalls great difficulty receiving immunizations and being subjected to other routine medical procedures through the rest of his school years, as well as numerous fainting and near-fainting episodes throughout his teen and adult years whenever he witnessed the slightest physical trauma, heard of an injury or illness, or saw a sick or disfigured person. He recently saw someone in a store in a wheelchair. He started wondering if the person was in pain and became so distressed that he fainted and fell to the floor, and was greatly embarrassed, when he regained consciousness, by the crowd of people surrounding him.

Mr. Michaels denies any other emotional problems. He enjoys his work, seems to get along well with his wife, and has many friends.

Discussion of "Stay Healthy"

Mr. Michaels is afraid of thinking about or being near a situation involving bodily illness or injury. He recognizes that his fear is irrational, but nevertheless avoids such situations. Although the fear and avoidance behavior apparently do not interfere with his normal routine or social activities, he is quite distressed about having the fear, which is the reason he now seeks treatment.

Because his fear is unrelated to Obsessive Compulsive Disorder (e.g., an obsession involving being infected with germs) or to the trauma of Post-traumatic Stress Disorder (e.g., having witnessed mutilation on the battlefield), the diagnosis of a Simple Phobia is made.

Mr. Michaels has a particular kind of Simple Phobia, referred to as a blood-injury phobia. Like many people with this type of phobia, he feels faint in the presence of the phobic stimulus. This symptom is rarely seen in other forms of Simple Phobia, such as fear of flying or of animals, or in Social Phobia or Agoraphobia.

DSM-III-R Diagnosis:

Axis I: 300.29 Simple Phobia (p. 244)

Panties

A 32-YEAR-OLD, SINGLE, MALE, free-lance photographer presented with the chief complaint of "abnormal sex drive." The patient related that although he was somewhat sexually attracted by women, he was far more attracted by "their panties."

To the best of the patient's memory, sexual excitement began at about age seven, when he came upon a pornographic magazine and felt stimulated by pictures of partially nude women wearing "panties." His first ejaculation occurred at age 13 via masturbation to fantasies of women wearing panties. He masturbated into his older sister's panties, which he had stolen without her knowledge. Subsequently he stole panties from her friends, and from other women he met socially. He found pretexts to "wander" into the bedrooms of women during social occasions, and would quickly rummage through their possessions until he found a pair of panties to his satisfaction. He later used these to masturbate into, and then "saved them" in a "private cache." The pattern of masturbating into women's underwear had been his preferred method of achieving sexual excitement and orgasm from adolescence until the present consultation.

The patient first had sexual intercourse at age 18. Since then he had had intercourse on many occasions, and his preferred partner was a prostitute paid to wear panties, with the crotch area cut away, during the act. On less common occasions when sexual activity was attempted with a partner who did not wear panties, his sexual excitement was sometimes weak.

The patient felt uncomfortable dating "nice women" since he felt that friendliness might lead to sexual intimacy and that they would not understand his sexual needs. He avoided socializing with friends who might introduce him to such women. He recognized that his appearance, social style, and profession all resulted in his being perceived as a highly desirable bachelor. He felt anxious and depressed because his social life was limited by his sexual preference.

He sought consultation shortly after his mother's sudden and unexpected death. Despite the fact that he complained of loneliness, he admitted that the pleasure he experienced from his unusual sexual activity made him unsure about whether or not he wished to give it up.

Discussion of "Panties"

This man's first remembered sexual arousal was in response to pictures of women wearing "panties." Ever since that time he has had recurrent, intense, sexual urges and sexually arousing fantasies, which he has acted on, involving the use of nonliving objects by themselves (panties, alone or worn by a woman). These are the features of Fetishism.

Fetishism should not be confused with Transvestic Fetishism, in which a heterosexual male is sexually aroused by dressing like a woman. Whereas in Fetishism the nonliving object (in this case, a female garment) is sexually arousing in and of itself, in Transvestic Fetishism, the female garment is sexually stimulating not by itself, but by virtue of the person's having the experience of cross-dressing.

As is generally the case with the Paraphilias, the deviant sexual act itself gives only pleasure, and it is the secondary consequences (humiliation, fear of exposure or criminal prosecution) that cause the person to seek treatment.

DSM-III-R Diagnosis:

Axis I: 302.81 Fetishism, Severe (p. 283)

Sitting by the Fire

PADDY O'BRIEN IS A 26-YEAR-OLD BACHELOR, living with his mother and two older brothers on the family farm in the west of Ireland. He is interviewed as part of a family study of mental disorders being conducted in Ireland.

Paddy is described by his mother as having been a "normal" youngster up until the age of 14. He was average to slightly below average in his schoolwork. He had friends he played with after school, and he helped his brothers and father with the chores around the farm. When he was 14, he began to "lose interest" in his schoolwork. His teacher noted that he was "staring into space" while in class, and rarely followed the work. Soon thereafter, his mother noticed that he no longer played with his friends after school, but would just come home and sit in front of the turf fire. It also became harder and harder to get him to do the farm chores. Sometimes he would come in and say the work was finished. Only hours later would they notice that only some of the cows had been milked, or only some of the eggs collected.

When he was 16, because his condition had become progressively worse, Paddy was withdrawn from school and was admitted to the county psychiatric hospital. The hospital records indicate that he was socially withdrawn and had a flat affect. It was not possible to interest him in ward activities. No psychotic symptoms could be elicited. Paddy has been in psychiatric care intermittently ever since that time. For the last year and a half, Paddy has been attending the local day center two days a week.

When interviewed by the research team, Paddy is observed to be an obese, rather disheveled young man. He replies to most questions with a "yes," "no," or "could be." He denies any psychotic symptoms, feelings of depression or elation, or difficulty with appetite or energy. He does, however, admit to unspecified problems with his "nerves," and problems in sleeping. On probing, he admits to feeling uncomfortable around "people," except his family. Eye contact is poor: he looks at the floor during most of the interview. His affect is flat. Despite all attempts, the interviewer is unable to establish rapport with him.

According to Paddy's family, when he is not at the day center, he sits all day in front of the fire at home. Occasionally, he can be encouraged to help with a farm chore, but he usually stops after about 15 minutes and returns to his chair by the fire. Unless prompted, he will not wash or change his clothes. He refuses to attend any social functions, and his childhood friends have long ago stopped calling at the house for him.

At the day center, Paddy sometimes works for brief periods of time at simple tasks in occupational therapy, but then soon quits and goes to sit by himself in the day room. Both the family and staff note that he is quite aware of what is going on around him, as reflected by an occasional perceptive comment. Neither his family nor any of the psychiatric staff who care for Paddy has ever been able to elicit any psychotic symptoms.

Discussion of "Sitting by the Fire"

Paddy certainly has the pervasive pattern of deficits in interpersonal relatedness and peculiarities of ideation, appearance, and behavior that is characteristic of Schizotypal Personality Disorder. He is socially anxious, unkempt and odd in appearance, and has no friends or confidants. His speech is odd, and his affect is constricted. However, his clinical picture is so typical of the residual symptoms of chronic Schizophrenia, the negative symptoms and social impairment are so profound, and the deterioration from a previous level of functioning so clear that his illness is not what is ordinarily thought of as a "personality disorder."

The narrow definition of Schizophrenia in DSM-III and DSM-III-R does not permit the diagnosis in cases in which there have never been psychotic symptoms. However, Paddy's illness corresponds to the traditional Bleulerian concept of Simple Schizophrenia in that the primary symptoms of autism, loose associations or other "thought disorder," and affective blunting are present in the absence of any secondary psychotic symptoms (delusions or hallucinations), and the disturbance represents a marked deterioration from a previous level of functioning.

We think that the diagnostic concept of Simple Schizophrenia should be considered as a possible addition to DSM-IV (perhaps called Simple Deteriorative Disorder, not a subtype of Schizophrenia). According to DSM-III-R, we would have to diagnose Schizotypal Personality Disorder, Severe, although the marked change in functioning that Paddy experienced when he was about 14 is certainly not characteristic of personality disorders.

DSM-III-R Diagnosis:

Axis I: V71.09 No Diagnosis or Condition
Axis II: 301.22 Schizotypal Personality Disorder, Severe (p. 341)

Mr. and Ms. B.

MR. AND MS. B. HAVE BEEN MARRIED for 14 years and have three children, aged 8 through 12. They are both bright and well educated. Both are from Scotland, from which they moved ten years ago because of Mr. B.'s work as an industrial consultant. They present with the complaint that Ms. B. has been able to participate passively in sex "as a duty," but has never enjoyed it since they have been married.

Before their marriage, although they had intercourse only twice, Ms. B. had been highly aroused by kissing and petting and felt she used her attractiveness to "seduce" her husband into marriage. She did, however, feel intense guilt about their two episodes of premarital intercourse; and during their honeymoon, she began to think of sex as a chore that could not be pleasing. Although she periodically passively complied with intercourse, she had almost no spontaneous desire for sex. She never masturbated, had never reached orgasm, thought of all variations such as oral sex as completely repulsive, and was preoccupied with a fantasy of how disapproving her family would be if she ever engaged in any of these activities.

Ms. B. is almost totally certain that no woman she respects in any older generation has enjoyed sex, and that despite the "new vogue" of sexuality, only sleazy, crude women let themselves act like "animals." These beliefs have led to a pattern of regular, but infrequent, sex that at best is accommodating and gives little or no pleasure to her or her husband. Whenever Ms. B. comes close to having a feeling of sexual arousal, numerous negative thoughts come into her mind, such as "What am I, a tramp?"; "If I like this, he'll just want it more often"; or "How could I look myself in the mirror after something like this?" These thoughts almost inevitably are accompanied by a cold feeling and an insensitivity to sensual pleasure. As a result, sex is invariably an unhappy experience. Almost any excuse, such as fatigue or being busy, is sufficient for her to rationalize avoiding intercourse.

Yet, intellectually Ms. B. wonders, "Is something wrong with me?" She is seeking help to find out if she is normal or not. Her husband, although extraordinarily tolerant of the situation, is in fact very unhappy about their sex life and is very hopeful that help may be forthcoming.

Discussion of "Mr. and Ms. B."

This couple seeks help for the wife's long-standing sexual problem. Clearly this woman's sexual difficulties are due to her many negative attitudes toward sexuality, and cannot be accounted for by a nonsexual Axis I disorder, such as Major Depression. The diagnosis of Sexual Aversion Disorder needs to be considered. Although she certainly has a persistent extreme aversion to genital sexual contact and might like to avoid sexual activity, she does, in fact, have regular though infrequent intercourse. The persistent absence of sexual fantasies and desire for sexual activity justify the diagnosis of Hypoactive Sexual Desire Disorder. When she does have sexual intercourse, she probably does not become sexually excited, so the additional diagnosis of Female Sexual Arousal Disorder should be considered. The diagnosis of Inhibited Female Orgasm would be added only if there were many occasions when during sexual activity she failed to have an orgasm, but had no disturbance in sexual excitement—extremely unlikely in this case.

The absence of any significant complaint on the part of the husband is reflected in the notation No Diagnosis or Condition on Axis I for him.

DSM-III-R Diagnosis:

Wife:
Axis I: 302.71 Hypoactive Sexual Desire Disorder, Psychogenic
                Only, Lifelong, Generalized (p. 293)
                R/O Female Sexual Arousal Disorder
Husband:
Axis I: V71.09 No Diagnosis or Condition

Hungarian Opera Singer

EVA, A 39-YEAR-OLD Hungarian opera singer, is readmitted to a psychiatric hospital after keeping her family awake for several nights with a prayer and song marathon. She is flamboyantly dressed in a floor-length red skirt and peasant blouse, and is adorned with heavy earrings, numerous necklaces and bracelets, and medals pinned to her bosom. She speaks very rapidly and is difficult to interrupt as she talks about her intimate relationship with God. She often breaks into song, explaining that her beautiful singing voice is a special gift that God has given her to compensate for her insanity. She uses it to share the joy she feels with others who are less fortunate.

Eva has had at least ten admissions to this hospital in the past 20 years, some because of serious suicide attempts made when she was depressed, some because she was manic, and some, in her words, "just because I was crazy." Although she does have a lovely voice, she has not been able to organize herself to work professionally during the past 15 years, and has spent much of her time at the local community mental health center. She has seen the same therapist weekly for many years, and believes that he communicates with her through a local radio station, giving her instructions on how to conduct her life between therapy sessions. She also receives illuminations from Kahlil Gibran and Adele Davis, whose conversations she is able to overhear.

Discussion of "Hungarian Opera Singer"

There should not be much difficulty recognizing that this woman is currently in a Manic Episode. She displays an expansive mood (singing, flamboyant dress), with pressure of speech (difficult to interrupt), decreased need for sleep, and grandiosity (intimate relationship with God). In the past she has had similar episodes, as well as depressions with suicide attempts. There have also been other periods when she was neither depressed nor manic, in which she apparently had psychotic symptoms (delusions and hallucinations). She describes this as "just crazy"; in fact, she has had persistent delusions of reference in between her episodes of mood disturbance (e.g., her therapist gives her messages via the radio).

A history of Manic Episodes (whether or not there is also a history of Depressive Episodes) and persistent psychotic symptoms when the mood disturbance is not present are the defining features of Schizoaffective Disorder, Bipolar Type.

DSM-III-R Diagnosis:

Axis I: 295.70 Schizoaffective Disorder, Bipolar Type (p. 210)

Follow-up

Eva has been hospitalized many times in the seven years following the admission described here. She has been treated with an antipsychotic drug, haloperidol, and a mood stabilizer, lithium; but her psychotic symptoms and her extreme mood swings have been poorly controlled. She is often agitated, yelling and screaming nonstop and referring to bizarre delusions and hallucinations of "voices saying crude things about people's genitals." Most of the time she is psychotic, but neither manic nor depressed.

Eva was living with her mother and her son. As her son became an adolescent, his resentment of her behavior led him to taunt and provoke her. Eva's mother found it increasingly difficult to maintain the peace as she became older. After Eva's last hospital admission she refused to take her daughter back, which necessitated transferring Eva to a state hospital. The state hospital refused to keep her for more than a few weeks; when last contacted, she was again creating havoc in her mother's home.

Painkillers

L EE, A 27-YEAR-OLD black man, comes to the emergency room of a city hospital. He points to an abscess on his right forearm and tells the receptionist that it is very painful. She notices that he is wearing sunglasses and rocks back and forth while waiting for the physician. As she takes his history, he becomes impatient and starts yelling at her for asking so many irrelevant questions, such as his mother's maiden name. Eventually he sees the doctor and readily admits that he had been "shooting six to eight ten-dollar bags" of heroin until about eight hours earlier, when he began "to shake so bad I couldn't get a hit." His arm started hurting so much that he came to the emergency room so he could get "some antibiotics and painkillers."

Lee has been using heroin daily for about twenty months, since he was released from prison, where he served six months for drug possession. He also occasionally uses cocaine intravenously, plus Valium, Ativan, and alcohol. He smokes two packs of cigarettes a day. Lee denies having used anything except heroin and tobacco in the last two weeks.

When he is examined, Lee is noted to have difficulty sitting still, and to be sweating profusely and yawning frequently. His pupils are dilated. He has "goose pimples" (piloerection), his eyes are tearing (lacrimation), and his nose is running (rhinorrhea). His pulse rate is elevated. His hands are tremulous, and his arms have the characteristic scars of intravenous drug use, with evidence of blood clots in the veins of the forearm and a large abscess on his right forearm. The physical examination is frequently interrupted, first by pleas, then by demands for opioid analgesics.

Lee is given a local anesthetic, and the abscess is drained and irrigated. Oral antibiotics are prescribed, and he is referred to both a local methadone and a drug-free chemical dependency treatment program. He is given only aspirin for the pain. As he leaves the emergency room, he is overheard muttering to himself about the lousy treatment he has just received.

Discussion of "Painkillers"

Lee has been taking lots of heroin (an opioid) intravenously for twenty months. When he came to the emergency room, he had not had a shot for eight hours and was showing the characteristic symptoms of Opioid Withdrawal: craving for the drug (he could not ask for heroin, but asked for an opioid analgesic), yawning, lacrimation, rhinorrhea, pupillary dilation, piloerection, and sweating. Other symptoms frequently seen in Opioid Withdrawal include nausea and vomiting, muscle aches, diarrhea, fever, and insomnia.

Lee has been in jail for possession of heroin and almost certainly has a long history of Heroin Dependence. Because the details are not known, we make this diagnosis provisionally.

DSM-III-R Diagnosis:

Axis I: 292.00 Opioid Withdrawal (p. 153)
**   304.00 Opioid Dependence, Severe (Provisional) (p. 167)**

Reluctant Home Buyer

A 30-YEAR-OLD ACCOUNTANT was referred by his internist to a psychiatric consultant because of a 6-month history of recurrent bouts of extreme fear of sudden onset, accompanied by sweating, shortness of breath, palpitations, chest pain, dizziness, numbness in his fingers and toes, and the thought that he was going to die. His internist had given him a complete physical, an EKG, and glucose tolerance and other blood tests, and had found no abnormalities.

The patient has been married for five years; he has no children. He went to night school, while working, to get a master's degree in business administration and was quite successful and well liked at his firm. He and his wife, a teacher, generally get along well and have several couples with whom they enjoy going out.

Because of the attacks, which occurred unexpectedly and in a variety of situations several times each week, the patient started to avoid driving his car and going into department stores, lest he have an attack in these situations. He began to coax his wife to accompany him on errands; and during the last month, he had felt comfortable only at home with his wife. Finally, he could not face the prospect of leaving home to go to work, and took a medical leave of absence. When at home, he experienced only "twinges" of chest pain and slight numbness in his fingers, but no full-blown attacks.

When asked about circumstances surrounding the onset of his attacks, the patient said that he and his wife had been discussing buying a house and moving from their apartment. He admitted that the responsibilities of home ownership intimidated him and related the significance of the move to similar concerns his mother had had that prevented his parents from ever buying a house.

Discussion of "Reluctant Home Buyer"

Recurrent, unexpected bouts of extreme fear of sudden onset, with sweating, shortness of breath, palpitations, chest pain, dizziness, numbness, and thoughts of being about to die, in the absence of an organic cause, indicate Panic Disorder.

As is often the case, Agoraphobia developed as the patient increasingly constricted his normal activities (he could not face the prospect of leaving home to go to work) because of a fear of being in situations from which escape might be difficult or embarrassing or in which help might not be available in the event of a panic attack (he avoided driving his car or going into department stores).

In Panic Disorder with Agoraphobia, the current severity of the agoraphobic avoidance *and* of the panic attacks can be specified. In this case, the Agoraphobia is severe, since the patient became virtually housebound. The panic attacks are noted as mild, because the patient has experienced only limited symptom attacks (fewer than four characteristic symptoms) since developing Agoraphobia.

DSM-III-R Diagnosis:

Axis I: **300.21 Panic Disorder with Agoraphobia, Panic Attacks Mild, Agoraphobic Avoidance Severe (p. 238)**

Beasts

A WHITE MALE IN HIS MID-THIRTIES, in prison for molesting prepubescent girls, volunteered for an interview with a sex researcher. He had been reared in a rural area by lower-middle-class parents with grammar-school educations. His mother, who was extremely prudish, frightened her son with tales of venereal disease and the dire consequences of masturbation, and impressed upon him that all sexual activity was nasty and that men were "beasts." He therefore felt guilty about his heterosexual urges and his preadolescent heterosexual play, and with puberty at age 12 ceased all heterosexual activity. Masturbation had begun a year before puberty and ceased a year after puberty, evidently because of the maternal warnings. During adolescence he was shy and fearful of females, although desiring them. Girls accused him of being "tied to his mother's apron strings."

He had always been sexually aroused by the sight of stallions and mares copulating and sometimes fantasized animal contact while masturbating. He had heard of animal contact from his peer group; and as a substitute for masturbation, he engaged in coitus with cows, almost daily from ages 13 to 18. Some affectional component developed, such as one might have for a pet animal. However, he never found the idea of sexual activity with an animal as exciting as the idea of sexual activity with a girl.

When he was 18, an epidemic of brucellosis appeared among the farm animals in the region, and the young man associated this mentally with venereal disease—concerning which he had a deep horror, instilled by his mother. He therefore terminated his animal contacts. Lacking any adult heterosexual activity, afraid to masturbate or engage in animal contacts, the young man reverted to his preadolescent pattern (which had been very gratifying) and began seeking contact with prepubescent girls. This led to his arrest and imprisonment.

Discussion of "Beasts"

The Institute for Sex Research at Indiana University, founded by Alfred C. Kinsey, was asked to submit a case for this book of Zoophilia, a specific Paraphilia recognized by DSM-III-R. A computer search of their extensive files of thousands of people interviewed between 1938 and 1963 revealed 96 cases involving intensive sexual activity with animals, but in not a single case was the animal contact or the fantasy of contact with animals the *preferred* source of achieving sexual excitement. Unlike the other Paraphilias, sexual activity with animals may always be a second choice, as it was in this case. Apparently there are no cases in which the idea of sexual activity with an animal is more exciting than the idea of sexual activity with a human.

The behavior that led to this young man's incarceration involved sexual activity with prepubescent girls. Therefore, the most likely diagnosis at the time of his arrest is: Pedophilia, Opposite Sex, with a history of Paraphilia Not Otherwise Specified (Zoophilia).

DSM-III-R Diagnosis:

**Axis I: 302.20 Pedophilia, Opposite Sex, Severe (Provisional)
(p. 285)**

Burt Tate

THE PATIENT IS A 42-YEAR-OLD white male who was brought to the emergency room by the police. He was involved in an argument and fight at the diner where he is employed. When the police arrived and began to question the patient, he gave his name as Burt Tate, but had no identification. "Burt" had drifted into town several weeks earlier and begun working as a short-order cook at the diner. He could not recall where he had worked or lived before his arrival in this town. There were no charges against him, but the police convinced him to come to the emergency room for an examination.

When questioned in the emergency room, "Burt" knew what town he was in and the current date. He admitted that it was somewhat unusual that he could not recall the details of his past life, but he did not appear very upset about this. There was no evidence of alcohol or drug abuse, and a physical examination revealed no head trauma or any other physical abnormalities. He was kept overnight for observation.

When the police ran a description check on the patient, they found that he fit the description of a missing person, Gene Saunders, who had disappeared a month before from a city 200 miles away. A visit by Mrs. Saunders confirmed the identity of the patient as Gene Saunders. Mrs. Saunders explained that for 18 months before his disappearance, her husband, who was a middle-level manager at a large manufacturing company, had been having considerable difficulty at work. He had been passed over for a promotion, and his supervisor had been very critical of his work. Several of his staff had left the company for other jobs, and the patient found it impossible to meet production goals. Work stress made him very difficult to live with at home. Previously an easygoing, gregarious person, he became withdrawn and critical of his wife and children. Immediately preceding his disappearance, he had had a violent argument with his 18-year-old son. The son had called him a "failure" and stormed out of the house to live with some friends who had an apartment. It was two days after this argument that the patient disappeared.

When brought into the room where his wife was waiting, the patient stated that he did not recognize her. He appeared noticeably anxious.

Discussion of "Burt Tate"

The police brought this man to the emergency room because of his amnesia concerning where he had previously lived and worked. Although this impairment in memory suggests an Organic Mental Disorder, ordinarily in such a disorder the disturbance in memory is more marked for recent than for remote events. The lack of any disturbance in attention or orientation also weighs against the presence of an Organic Mental Disorder.

The critical role of psychological factors in the patient's amnesia becomes more apparent when we learn that just before the development of his symptoms, on top of increasing difficulties at work, he had a violent argument with his son. The additional features of sudden, unexpected travel away from his home and the assumption of a new identity justify the diagnosis of Psychogenic Fugue.

DSM-III-R Diagnosis:

Axis I: 300.13 Psychogenic Fugue (p. 273)

Eggs

KEVIN IS A 19-YEAR-OLD white male who, until admission, was working in a mailroom while waiting to apply to college. The onset of his illness is not clear. According to him, he has not been "the same" since his mother died of a cerebral hemorrhage nine months before his admission. According to his father, however, he exhibited a normal mourning response to his mother's death and changed only three months earlier.

At that time, shortly after his girl friend had rejected him for another man, he began to think that male co-workers were making homosexual advances toward him. He began to fear that he was homosexual and that his friends believed he was homosexual. He finally developed the conviction that he had a disorder of the reproductive system—that he had one normal testicle that produced sperm and that his other testicle was actually an ovary that produced eggs. He thought that this was evidence that a "woman's body resides inside my man's body." He began to gamble, and was convinced that he had won $400,000 and was not paid by his bookie, and that he was sought after by talk-show hosts to be a guest on their shows and tell his unusual story (all not true). He claimed that he had a heightened awareness, an "extra sense," and that sounds were unusually loud. He had difficulty sleeping at night, but no appetite disturbance.

On admission, Kevin's speech was somewhat rapid, and he jumped from topic to topic. His affect was neither irritable, euphoric, nor expansive. He said he was now seeking treatment because "there is a war between my testicles, and I prefer to be male."

When he was ten, his pediatrician became concerned that he had an undersized penis. This led to a complete endocrine workup and examinations of his genitals every four months for the next four years. At that time it was concluded that there were no significant abnormalities.

During high school Kevin had been a poor student, with poor attendance. He claims always to have had many friends. He has never received psychiatric treatment. He admits to occasional marijuana and phencyclidine use in the past, but denies any use of hallucinogens.

Kevin is the oldest child in a family of six children. His parents met when they were both patients in a psychiatric hospital.

Discussion of "Eggs"

The significant features of Kevin's illness include bizarre somatic delusions, grandiose delusions, and disorganization in his speech (he jumped from topic to topic). Although the grandiose delusions and pressured speech suggest the possibility of a Manic Episode, this is ruled out by the absence of either an elevated, expansive, or irritable mood.

When did his illness begin? Although he says he has not been the same since his mother died nine months ago, he does not describe any change in himself that is out of keeping with normal bereavement. Furthermore, his father claims that his abnormal behavior began only three months ago. Giving the patient the benefit of the doubt, we date the onset of the illness at three months before admission. The presence of the characteristic symptoms of Schizophrenia in an illness of less than six months' duration indicates Schizophreniform Disorder. His affect is not blunted or flat. However, because it is unclear whether the onset of the illness was rapid (he and his father give different accounts), we are unable to subtype the disorder as to With or Without Good Prognostic Features.

DSM-III-R Diagnosis:

Axis I: 295.40 Schizophreniform Disorder (p. 208)

Follow-up

Kevin was treated in the hospital with lithium and chlorpromazine and was soon well enough to go home. He returned to college the following fall and finished the semester with A's and B's. The following year he stopped taking his medication and again became very disturbed. He was irritable, loud, angry, and verbally abusive. He talked incessantly, did not sleep, and ran naked into the street. He expressed bizarre ideas about "time running backward," and again believed that he had an ovary. There were several such episodes requiring hospitalization over a period of three years. Finally, he became convinced that he could avoid such episodes only if he kept taking medication. For the past year, he has been taking lithium alone and has been well. He has his own apartment, an active social life, and has just passed a licensing examination to become a plumber.

The clinical picture of Manic Episodes subsequent to his first hospitalization certainly suggests the need to change the diagnosis to Bipolar Disorder. In retrospect, there was a suggestion of expansive mood during his initial presentation, but it was not marked enough to warrant the diagnosis of a Manic Episode at that time.

The Fashion Plate

MR. A., A 65-YEAR-OLD security guard, formerly a fishing-boat captain, is distressed about his wife's objections to his wearing a nightgown at home in the evening, now that his youngest child has left home. His appearance and demeanor, except when he is dressing in women's

clothes, are always appropriately masculine, and he is exclusively heterosexual. Occasionally, over the past five years, he has worn an inconspicu-
ous item of female clothing even when dressed as a man—sometimes a
pair of panties, sometimes an ambiguous pinkie ring. He always carries a
photograph of himself dressed as a woman.

His first recollection of an interest in female clothing was putting on
his sister's bloomers at age 12, an act accompanied by sexual excitement.
He continued periodically to put on women's underpants—an activity
that invariably resulted in an erection, sometimes a spontaneous emis-
sion, sometimes masturbation, but never accompanied by fantasy. Although he occasionally wished to be a girl, he never fantasized himself as
one. He was competitive and aggressive with other boys and always
acted "masculine." During his single years he was always attracted to
girls, but was shy about sex. Following his marriage at 22, he had his first
heterosexual intercourse.

His involvement with female clothes was of the same intensity even
after his marriage. Beginning at age 45, after a chance exposure to a
magazine called *Transvestia*, he began to increase his cross-dressing activity. He learned there were other men like himself, and he became more
and more preoccupied with female clothing in fantasy and progressed to
periodically dressing completely as a woman. More recently he has become involved in a transvestite network, writing to other transvestites
contacted through the magazine and occasionally attending transvestite
parties. Cross-dressing at these parties has been the only time that he has
cross-dressed outside his home.

Although still committed to his marriage, sex with his wife has dwin-
dled over the past 20 years as his waking thoughts and activities have
become increasingly centered on cross-dressing. Over time this activity
has become less eroticized and more an end in itself, but it still is a source
of some sexual excitement. He always has an increased urge to dress as a
woman when under stress; it has a tranquilizing effect. If particular circumstances prevent him from cross-dressing, he feels extremely frustrated.

The patient's parents belonged to different faiths, a fact of some
importance to him. He was the eldest of three children, extremely close
to his mother, whom he idolized, and angry at his "whoremaster, alcoholic" father. The parents fought constantly. He is tearful, even now at
age 65, when he describes his mother's death when he was 10. He was
the one who found her dead (of pleurisy), and he says he has been "not
the same from that day . . . always [having] the feeling something's not
right." The siblings were reared by three separate branches of the family
until the father remarried. When the patient was 20, his father died, a
presumed suicide; but Mr. A. believes he may have been murdered, since
he could not figure out a suicide motive. His brother also died traumati-
cally, drowned in his teens.

Because of the disruptions in his early life, the patient has always
treasured the steadfastness of his wife and the order of his home. He told

his wife about his cross-dressing practice when they were married, and she was accepting so long as he kept it to himself. Nevertheless, he felt guilty, particularly after he began complete cross-dressing, and periodically he attempted to renounce the practice, throwing out all his female clothes and makeup. His children served as a barrier to his giving free rein to his impulses. Following his retirement from fishing, and in the absence of his children, he finds himself more drawn to cross-dressing, more in conflict with his wife, and more depressed.

Discussion of "The Fashion Plate"

This man demonstrates the characteristic development and course of Transvestic Fetishism. Over a long period of time, Mr. A, a heterosexual male, has acted upon recurrent intense sexual urges and sexually arousing fantasies involving cross-dressing. He is never in doubt about his gender identity as a male (as in Transsexualism or as in Gender Identity Disorder of Adolescence or Adulthood, Nontranssexual Type).

Characteristically, his urge to cross-dress increases under stress, and the cross-dressing has a calming effect. If the behavior is prevented, he feels intensely frustrated. Frequently, as in this case, as the person becomes more involved in cross-dressing, the practice becomes less eroticized and more an end in itself. If the cross-dressing is no longer a source of any sexual excitement and there is a persistent sense of inappropriateness about being a male, the diagnosis should be changed to Gender Identity Disorder of Adolescence or Adulthood, Nontranssexual Type.

DSM-III-R Diagnosis:

Axis I: 302.30 Transvestic Fetishism, Severe (p. 289)

Three Voices

A 23-YEAR-OLD MAN was admitted to the hospital. He was almost totally mute. His parents reported that he had been apparently well until about four years previously when he broke off with his girl friend. Since then he had been living at home, spending much time by himself, holding various odd jobs, and unable to pursue any long-term goals. About four months before his hospital admission, he decided to go to California to find a new job and change his environment. However, shortly after he arrived there, his parents received a telephone call from him in which he "sounded bad." His father flew to California and found him vigilant, paranoid, and frightened, having seemingly not eaten for several days. The father brought his son home, where he saw a neurologist, and was found to be essentially normal neurologically. Shortly thereafter he saw a psychologist, who recommended admission to a psychiatric hospital.

On admission the patient was sleeping 10-12 hours a night, had little appetite, and had lost perhaps 20 pounds in weight over the last couple of months. He reported a profound loss of energy and did not speak except to give occasional monosyllabic answers to the interviewer's questions. During his first few days in the hospital, the patient showed virtually no interest or pleasure in any activities and spent most of the time sitting on his bed and staring into space. On questioning he did not complain of any specific feelings of worthlessness, self-reproach, or guilt, nor did he mention thoughts of death or suicide, although it was difficult to be certain about any of these points because of his paucity of speech.

In the hospital the patient was seen daily by a medical student who took a great interest in him and gradually gained his trust. Eventually the patient revealed to the student that he was hearing three distinct voices—the voice of a child, the voice of a woman, and the voice of a man impersonating a woman. The three voices talked among themselves and sometimes talked to him directly. At times they spoke about him in the third person, and on some occasions they seemed to echo his thoughts. The voices spoke about many different subjects and did not focus on any specific depressive themes, such as guilt, sin, or death.

On the second day after admission to the hospital, the patient was started on a regimen of an antipsychotic, molindone, 50 mg/day, and an antidepressant, imipramine, at a dose that was gradually increased to 150 mg/day. For the first two weeks there was virtually no improvement. However, by the second week the patient displayed some increased restlessness. The dose of molindone was reduced to 25 mg/day, and was eventually stopped entirely by about the third week. On the 23rd hospital day, the patient began to experience a marked improvement in his energy level; and by the end of the fourth week, he was smiling, talkative, sleeping and eating well, and able to reminisce about the hallucinations, which he stated had now completely disappeared. A week later he was discharged home, on a maintenance regimen of imipramine, 150 mg/day, but no other psychotropic medication.

Approximately eight months after his discharge the patient ran out of imipramine and did not obtain more from his pharmacy. His symptoms reappeared rapidly over the course of a few days. After a phone call from his parents to his doctor, the imipramine treatment was hastily resumed, and the patient again reverted essentially to normal after another week or so.

The patient's mother had had a postpartum depressive episode of about a year's duration that had gradually remitted spontaneously without treatment. In addition, the mother's sister had had a "nervous breakdown" when she was in her forties that had required her to be hospitalized; she had received a course of 12 electroconvulsive treatments. Since that time the aunt had had a complete remission, and was described as functioning normally.

Discussion of "Three Voices"

This young man apparently had a four-year period during which he had some nonspecific difficulties (social withdrawal and inability to pursue long-term goals), followed by an episode of illness with paranoid behavior, bizarre auditory hallucinations, loss of interest and pleasure, anorexia and a 20-pound weight loss, hypersomnia, loss of energy, and psychomotor retardation (paucity of speech and spending most of his time sitting on the bed staring into space).

In the past this might well have been diagnosed as Schizophrenia, the four-year period being viewed as prodromal to the acute psychotic phase. The loss of interest and pleasure and the other nonpsychotic symptoms would have been considered merely associated features. According to DSM-III-R, the loss of interest and pleasure and other nonpsychotic symptoms actually constitute a full major depressive syndrome. Since the psychotic symptoms apparently have been present only when the patient had a major depressive syndrome, they are considered a psychotic feature of a Major Depressive Episode. This is true in spite of the fact that the content of the delusions and hallucinations is not consistent with such usual depressive themes as personal inadequacy, guilt, or deserved punishment. Thus, on admission the diagnosis would be Major Depression, Single Episode, with Mood-incongruent Psychotic Features, a diagnosis that is certainly supported by the good response to an antidepressant and the family history of Mood Disorder.

What are we to make of the four-year period reported by his parents? Did this represent mild depressive symptoms or identity problems? Either would be consistent with our recommended diagnosis. If mild depressive symptoms were present for more than two years, the additional diagnosis of Dysthymia would be made. On the other hand, if closer examination revealed more malignant symptoms, such as ideas of reference or bizarre behavior that preceded the depressive symptoms, this would seem to indicate that the psychotic disturbance was not just a feature of Major Depression, and would suggest the eventual diagnosis of a primary psychotic disorder such as Schizoaffective Disorder or Schizophrenia.

Another question raised by this case is the appropriate subclassification of Major Depression at the time of the reappearance of the depressive syndrome when medication was discontinued. Should this be regarded as Major Depression, Recurrent, or as the continuation of the Major Depression, Single Episode, the symptoms of which had been suppressed by medication? DSM-III-R considers a six-month period with no symptoms of the disturbance to be the minimal amount of time needed to consider a recurrence a different episode. Because this patient's symptoms reappeared after eight months, we note Recurrent Episode, although we recognize that many clinicians might regard the rapid development of symptoms following discontinuation of the medication as suggesting the diagnosis of a Single Episode.

DSM-III-R Diagnosis:

Axis I: **296.24 Major Depression, Recurrent Episode, Severe, with Psychotic Features (Mood-incongruent) (p. 222)**

The Cold War

A BEAUTIFUL, SUCCESSFUL, 34-year-old interior designer is brought to the clinic by her 37-year-old husband, a prominent attorney. The husband laments that for the past three years his wife has made increasingly shrill accusations that he is unfaithful to her. He declares that he has done everything in his power to convince her of his innocence, but there is no shaking her conviction. A careful examination of the facts reveals that there is actually no evidence that the man has been unfaithful. When his wife is asked what her evidence is, she becomes vague and mysterious, declaring that she can tell such things by a faraway look in his eye.

She is absolutely sure that she is right, and feels highly insulted by the suggestion that she is imagining the disloyalty. Her husband reports that for the past year, she has been increasingly bitter, creating a kind of "cold war" atmosphere in the household. Militantly entrenched against her husband, she refuses to show him any affection except at social gatherings. She seems intent on giving the impression socially that they have a good relationship; but when they are alone, the coldness reenters the picture. She has physically assaulted her husband on occasion, but her account obscures the fact that she initiated the assaults; her description of the tussles actually begins at the point at which the husband attempted to interrupt her assault by holding her arms. She declares that she will never forgive him for holding her down and squeezing her arms, and her account makes it appear that she was unfairly restrained.

The patient experiences no hallucinations; her speech is well organized; she interprets proverbs with no difficulty; she seems to have a good command of current events and generally displays no difficulty in thinking aside from her conviction of the infidelity. She describes herself as having a generally full and effective life, with a few close friends and no problems except those centering on her experiences of unhappiness in the marriage. The husband reports that his wife is respected for her skills, but that she has had difficulties for most of her life in close relationships with friends. She has lost a number of friends because of her apparent intolerance of differences in opinion. The patient reports that she does not want to leave the marriage, nor does she want her husband to leave her; instead, she is furious about the "injustice," and demands that it be confessed and redeemed.

Discussion of "The Cold War"

Not all complaints of infidelity are unfounded, but in this case the evidence supports the notion that the wife's jealousy is delusional. Delusional jealousy may be seen in Schizophrenia; but in the absence of the characteristic psychotic symptoms of Schizophrenia, such as bizarre delusions, hallucinations, or disorganized speech, it is a symptom of a Delusional Disorder. As is commonly the case in Delusional Disorder, this woman's impairment because of her delusion does not involve her daily functioning apart from her relationship with her husband.

DSM-III-R Diagnosis:

Axis I: 297.10 Delusional Disorder, Jealous Type (p. 202)

Thunderbird

A 43-YEAR-OLD DIVORCED CARPENTER is examined in the hospital emergency observation ward. The patient's sister is available to provide some information. The sister reports that the patient has consumed large quantities of cheap wine daily for over five years. He had a reasonably stable home life and job record until his wife left him for another man five years previously. The sister indicates that the patient drinks more than a fifth of wine a day, and that this has been an unvarying pattern since the divorce. He often has had blackouts from drinking and has missed work; consequently, he has been fired from several jobs. Fortunately for him, carpenters are in great demand, and he has been able to provide marginally for himself during these years. However, three days ago he ran out of money and wine and had to beg on the street to buy a meal. The patient has been poorly nourished, eating perhaps one meal a day and evidently relying on the wine as his prime source of nourishment.

The morning after his last day of drinking (three days earlier), he felt increasingly tremulous, his hands shaking so grossly that it was difficult for him to light a cigarette. Accompanying this was an increasing sense of inner panic, which had made him virtually unable to sleep. A neighbor became concerned about the patient when he seemed not to be making sense and clearly was unable to take care of himself. The neighbor contacted the sister, who brought him to the hospital.

On examination, the patient alternates between apprehension and chatty, superficial warmth. He is quite keyed up and talks almost constantly in a rambling and unfocused manner. At times he recognizes the doctor, but at other times he gets confused and thinks the doctor is his older brother. Twice during the examination he calls the doctor by his older brother's name and asks when he arrived, evidently having lost track entirely of the interview up to that point. He has a gross hand tremor at rest, and there are periods when he picks at "bugs" he sees on the bed sheets. He is disoriented for time and thinks that he is in a supermarket parking lot rather than in a hospital. He indicates that he feels he is fighting against a terrifying sense that the world is ending in a holocaust. He is startled every few minutes by sounds and scenes of fiery car crashes (evidently provoked by the sound of rolling carts in the hall). Efforts at testing memory and calculation fail because his attention shifts too rapidly. An electroencephalogram indicates a pattern of diffuse encephalopathy.

Discussion of "Thunderbird"

This carpenter, with a long history of heavy alcohol use, develops severe withdrawal symptoms after he stops drinking. He has the characteristic symptoms of a Delirium: difficulty sustaining attention, disorganized thinking (rambling), perceptual disturbances (he sees scenes of car crashes provoked by the sound of rolling carts in the hall), disorientation to place and person (mistakes the doctor for his brother and the hospital for a parking lot), and disturbance of his sleep-wake cycle (insomnia). The appearance of a Delirium, with marked autonomic hyperactivity (hand tremors) shortly after cessation or reduction of heavy alcohol ingestion indicates Alcohol Withdrawal Delirium.

Although the treatment will initially be directed at the Alcohol Withdrawal Delirium, the additional diagnosis of Alcohol Dependence can be assumed from the information that he has been a heavy daily user of alcohol for more than five years, has lost jobs because of his alcohol use, and has been poorly nourished. The Alcohol Dependence is severe because he almost certainly has many of the symptoms of dependence and they interfere markedly with his occupational and social functioning.

DSM-III-R Diagnosis:

Axis I: 291.00 Alcohol Withdrawal Delirium (p. 131)
            303.90 Alcohol Dependence, Severe (p. 167)

Fidgety

A 32-YEAR-OLD MOTHER OF FOUR presented at the clinic with complaints of anxiety, irritability, temper outbursts, and concentration problems. She wept continuously throughout the first interview, claiming that her life had brought her little happiness. She had come to the clinic on the recommendation of a child psychiatrist, who, while evaluating one of her sons for a learning problem, had observed emotional difficulties in her.

Although she recalls that her mother described her as a "difficult" child, the patient had no substantial problems until she entered elementary school. During the first two years, she did well in arithmetic, but reading and spelling were problems. She remembers being so "fidgety" in the first and second grades that she could not stay seated for long, and the teacher had to turn the pages of books, since she would get too distracted to do so. She daydreamed frequently and failed to complete classwork unless closely supervised. She had difficulty organizing both her schoolwork and her chores at home (the latter improved with constant supervision) and had the problem, which continues to the present day, of speaking before thinking. She recalls her mother telling her to stop talking so much. As she grew older, her academic problems worsened, and she developed behavioral problems (fighting with other children, disrupting the class); in the third grade she was placed in a special school for children with learning difficulties (her IQ in adulthood was 115). Despite the transfer, she continued to have difficulties, not only academically, but with her peers, because of her quick temper and her inability to wait her turn.

There was some improvement in high school, where the patient began to have friends. Reading continued to be difficult, and she avoided it as much as possible. She attributes her reading problems to continuing difficulty in attention. She stated that it was difficult for her to keep her mind on movies or TV programs unless they were unusually spellbinding. Although she participated in many social activities, she had the nagging feeling that she derived less pleasure from them than other people did. She made and severed interpersonal relations impulsively.

She had married her husband after a few weeks' courtship when she was 22, and they had frequently argued from the very beginning. Their problems had been compounded by the birth of four children in rapid succession. These children displayed behavioral difficulties similar to those the patient had had as a child; and their problems were aggravated by their mother's inability to set reasonable limits, be consistent, and maintain a relatively even temper. Since their marital problems persisted, both she and her husband began psychotherapy. Despite intermittent individual and couple therapy over a ten-year period, there had been little improvement in their marital relationship. The severity of the problem had diminished somewhat since her husband had learned the efficacy of leaving her alone when she became angry, since arguments only made things worse.

Discussion of "Fidgety"

This woman demonstrates that even when diagnosing an adult case, one should consider the possibility of a residual form of a disorder that usually is seen in children. As a child this woman often was fidgety, could not stay seated, had difficulty waiting her turn, and often talked too much and spoke out in class impulsively. She also had difficulty organizing her work and failed to complete her classwork. All of these characteristics suggest the hyperactivity, impulsivity, and inattention associated with Attention-deficit Hyperactivity Disorder. According to DSM-III-R, this diagnosis is given if at least eight of a list of 14 characteristic symptoms are present. We count six symptoms, but are quite sure that if she had been evaluated as a child, there would have been evidence of several additional symptoms.

During adolescence many of the patient's childhood difficulties persisted, and as an adult she continues to be impulsive (temper outbursts) and to have attentional difficulties (trouble concentrating). When, as in this case, there is a childhood history of Attention-deficit Hyperactivity Disorder and many of the characteristic childhood symptoms persist into adult life and cause some social or occupational impairment, the diagnosis of Attention-deficit Hyperactivity Disorder, Residual State, is made.

DSM-III-R Diagnosis:

Axis I: 314.01 Attention-deficit Hyperactivity Disorder, Residual State (Provisional) (p. 52)

Better Living Through Chemistry

T WENTY-TWO-YEAR-OLD RAY brings his 17-year-old brother, Danny, to the emergency room at 3:00 AM on a Sunday morning. Upon returning home from a date, Ray found Danny stumbling about their parents' basement den crying and mumbling, "Everything is blurry and double." Ray says that Danny cursed him out on the way to the hospital. He says that his brother drinks alcohol and smokes both tobacco and marijuana, but he doesn't know of any other drug use.

The examining physician notes that Danny is wearing an earring and a T-shirt that bears the inscription "Better Living Through Chemistry." Around his neck on a chain is a coke spoon hanging outside his shirt. His breath has an odor suggestive of an organic solvent. There is a symmetrical erythematous rash about his mouth and nose. His pupils are symmetrical and responsive to light although the whites of his eyes are markedly inflamed. Close inspection reveals transparent viscous material just inside both nostrils.

On questioning Danny, the doctor notes that he has an extremely short attention span. His speech is slurred, and his manner at one moment is apathetic and disinterested, and at the next, belligerent and abusive. Neurologic examination reveals no localized signs. Danny appears intoxicated, with slurred speech and unsteady, staggering gait. Reflexes are bilaterally depressed, his muscular strength is generally diminished, and there is an intentional tremor (a tremor of the hand when it is extended), and horizontal and vertical nystagmus (involuntary rapid movements of the eyeballs). Examination of the oral and pharyngeal mucosa reveals diffuse irritation. Several times during the examination, Danny attempts to leave, and once takes the reflex hammer and starts testing the doctor. The physical examination is otherwise unremarkable.

Over the 45-minute course of the examination, Danny comments that the blurring of his vision and double vision have disappeared. Over the same period, it was observed that his reflexes had become more vigorous. Despite these changes, Danny's affect continues to vacillate between apathy and hostility.

A urine specimen is collected for a drug toxicology screening, and Danny is placed in a holding area while a psychiatric consultant is called. He waits a short while and then, against medical advice, leaves the hospital. All attempts to reach his parents are unsuccessful. Subsequently, the urine drug toxicology screen revealed aromatic inhalants.

Discussion of "Better Living Through Chemistry"

Ray says that his brother uses only marijuana and alcohol, but the doctor smells an organic solvent on his breath, notices a rash around his nose and mouth, and therefore wonders whether he may be intoxicated from inhaling a volatile substance such as gasoline, glue, paint, or paint thinner. The doctor's suspicion of Inhalant Intoxication is confirmed by the urine drug test.

Aromatic substances are inhaled, sometimes by soaking a rag

with the substance, which is then applied to the mouth and nose and the vapors breathed in, or the substance may be inhaled directly from containers or from aerosols. The inhalants quickly reach the lungs and bloodstream and cause an acute intoxication state. Danny's visual symptoms, slurred speech, unsteady gait, lethargy, depressed reflexes, tremor, and muscle weakness are characteristic of Inhalant Intoxication. The diagnosis is made when these symptoms are accompanied by maladaptive behavioral changes, such as, in this case, belligerence alternating with apathy.

We assume that this is not the first time that Danny has used an inhalant. Therefore, we make a provisional diagnosis of Inhalant Abuse.

The most serious complication of recurrent Inhalant Intoxication is brain damage, which, when severe, takes the form of a Dementia. It is not possible to know whether some of the symptoms that Danny was showing, such as short attention span, may have been symptoms of incipient Dementia.

DSM-III-R Diagnosis:

Axis I: 305.90 Inhalant Intoxication (p. 149)
           305.90 Inhalant Abuse (Provisional) (p. 169)
                   R/O Psychoactive Substance-induced Dementia

Mr. and Ms. Albert

MR. AND MS. ALBERT ARE AN ATTRACTIVE, gregarious couple, married for 15 years, who present in the midst of a crisis over their sexual problems. Mr. Albert, a successful restaurateur, is 38. Ms. Albert, who since marriage has devoted herself to child-rearing and managing the home, is 35. She reports that throughout their marriage she has been extremely frustrated because sex has "always been hopeless for us." She is now seriously considering leaving her husband.

The difficulty is the husband's rapid ejaculation. Whenever any lovemaking is attempted, Mr. Albert becomes anxious, moves quickly toward intercourse, and reaches orgasm either immediately upon entering his wife's vagina or within one or two strokes. He then feels humiliated, recognizes his wife's dissatisfaction, and they both lapse into silent suffering. He has severe feelings of inadequacy and guilt, and she experiences a mixture of frustration and resentment toward his "ineptness and lack of concern." Recently, they have developed a pattern of avoiding sex, which leaves them both frustrated, but which keeps overt hostility to a minimum.

Mr. Albert has always been a perfectionist, priding himself on his ability to succeed at anything he sets his mind to. As a child, he had always been a "good boy," in a vain effort to please his demanding father. His inability to control his ejaculation is a source of intense shame, and he finds himself unable to talk to his wife about his sexual "failures." Ms. Albert is highly sexual, easily aroused by foreplay, but has always felt that intercourse is the only "acceptable" way to reach orgasm. Intercourse with her husband has always been unsatisfying, and she holds him completely responsible for her sexual frustration. Since she cannot discuss the subject without feeling rage, she usually avoids talking about it. As a result, they have developed other techniques for pleasing each other, and sex has always been a disaster.

In other areas of their marriage, including rearing of their two children, managing the family restaurant, and socializing with friends, the Alberts are highly compatible. Despite these strong points, however, they are near separation because of the tension produced by their mutual sexual disappointment.

Discussion of "Mr. and Ms. Albert"

This couple presents with a sexual problem that is threatening their marriage. Since DSM-III-R does not include a classification of disturbed dyadic units, it is necessary, when focusing on this type of diagnostic problem, to consider each marital partner separately. (This does not preclude the clinician's focusing on the relationship when considering both how the problem arose and its possible treatment.)

The husband's sexual difficulty is that he lacks a reasonable degree of voluntary control over ejaculation, so that he invariably ejaculates almost immediately upon penetration during intercourse. As a result, his wife is never sexually satisfied, and he feels extremely inadequate. Since the lack of control is not limited to novel situations and does not occur only after long periods of abstinence, the Axis I diagnosis of Premature Ejaculation is made. Because the husband's "perfectionism" is mentioned and this might be related to either the development or the perpetuation of the sexual problem, obsessive compulsive personality traits are noted on Axis II.

There is little information about the wife's difficulties, other than that she clearly has a marital problem. With this limited information, the V code Marital Problem is appropriate; it should be understood, however, that with more information it may need to be changed to, for example, a Personality Disorder. The husband, of course, does not receive the V code Marital Problem since his marital problem apparently is due to his Axis I mental disorder.

Some clinicians might consider the diagnosis of Adjustment

Disorder for either the husband, the wife, or both. In the husband's case, the diagnosis would not be made since the distress he is experiencing seems to be an associated feature of the Premature Ejaculation rather than a separate illness. In the wife's case, an Adjustment Disorder diagnosis would imply that her reaction to her husband's sexual problem (her rage and threatening separation) is excessive and indicates significant psychopathology. This might be the case, but such a judgment would require more information than is available.

DSM-III-R Diagnosis:

Husband:
Axis I: **302.75 Premature Ejaculation, Psychogenic Only, Lifelong, Generalized (p. 295)**
Axis II: **Obsessive Compulsive Personality Traits**

Wife:
Axis I: **V61.10 Marital Problem (p. 360)**

Embarrassed

A 46-YEAR-OLD MARRIED MALE was referred for evaluation in 1966 because of unremitting tics. At age 13 he had developed a persistent eye blink, soon followed by lip-smacking, head-shaking, and barking-like noises. Despite these symptoms, he functioned well academically, and eventually graduated from high school with honors. He was drafted during World War II. While in the army his tics subsided significantly, but were still troublesome, and eventually resulted in a medical discharge. He married, had two children, and worked as a semiskilled laborer and foreman. At the age of 30 his symptoms included tics of the head, neck, and shoulders, hitting his forehead with his hand and various objects, repeated throat-clearing, spitting, and shouting out "Hey, hey, hey; la, la, la." Six years later, noisy coprolalia started: he would emit a string of profanities, such as "Fuck you, you cocksucking bastard" in the middle of a sentence and then resume his conversation.

From 1951 to 1957, various treatments, all without benefit, were tried: insulin shock therapy, electroshock treatment, and administration of various phenothiazines and antidepressants. The patient's social life became increasingly constricted because of his symptoms. He was unable to go to church or to the movies because of the cursing and noises. He worked at night to avoid social embarrassment. His family and friends became increasingly intolerant of his symptoms, and his daughters refused to bring friends home. He was depressed because of his enforced isolation and the seeming hopelessness of finding effective treatment. At the age of 46, he sought a prefrontal lobotomy; but after psychiatric evaluation, his request was denied. This led to the 1966 referral.

Discussion of "Embarrassed"

This patient has the characteristic features of Tourette's Disorder: onset before age 21, multiple motor and one or more vocal tics (involuntary cursing or shouting), the tics occurring many times a day (usually in bouts), nearly every day or intermittently throughout a period of more than one year, and changes over time in the anatomic location, number, frequency, complexity, and severity of the tics.

It is largely for historical reasons that this disorder is classified as a mental rather than a neurologic disorder. Originally the coprolalia and other bizarre symptoms were thought to represent pregenital conversion symptoms. Now, most investigators believe that the etiology of the disorder is organic and that whatever psychological disturbance may be present is best understood as a reaction to the chronic, incapacitating symptoms. In this case, when the symptoms of Tourette's Disorder were brought under control, the patient was no longer depressed.

When the patient was evaluated, he was described as being "depressed over his enforced isolation and the seeming hopelessness of finding effective treatment." This raises the question of Adjustment Disorder with Depressed Mood or of a Major Depression. The concept of Adjustment Disorder generally does not include situations in which the patient is distressed because of the consequences of the symptoms of, or the reaction of others to, his or her mental disorder. Such distress is commonplace in chronic illnesses and is better thought of as an associated feature of the illness rather than as Adjustment Disorder. On the other hand, if the depression were so severe as to meet the criteria for a Major Depressive Episode, then the additional diagnosis of Major Depression would be appropriate. In this case there is no information about the other features of a depressive syndrome that would be necessary to make such a diagnosis.

DSM-III-R Diagnosis:

Axis I: 307.23 Tourette's Disorder, Severe (p. 80)

Follow-up

The patient was given a new experimental drug, haloperidol, 1 mg/day, which eliminated 99% of his symptoms. He resumed a normal social life and was no longer depressed. When last seen, 18 years later, he continues to do well on the same maintenance dosage of haloperidol.

Hurting

A 26-YEAR-OLD UNEMPLOYED WOMAN was referred for admission to a hospital by her therapist because of intense suicidal preoccupation and urges to mutilate herself by cutting herself with a razor.

The patient was apparently well until her junior year in high school, when she became preoccupied with religion and philosophy, avoided friends, and was filled with doubt about who she was. Academically she did well; but later, during college, her performance declined. In college she began to use a variety of drugs, abandoned the religion of her family, and seemed to be searching for a charismatic religious figure with whom to identify. At times massive anxiety swept over her, and she found it would suddenly vanish if she cut her forearm with a razor blade.

Three years ago she began psychotherapy, and initially rapidly idealized her therapist as being incredibly intuitive and empathetic. Later, she became hostile and demanding of him, requiring more and more sessions, sometimes two in one day. Her life became centered on her therapist, to the exclusion of everyone else. Although her hostility toward her therapist was obvious, she could neither see it nor control it. Her difficulties with her therapist culminated in many episodes of cutting her forearm and threatening suicide, which led to the referral for admission.

Discussion of "Hurting"

This is a textbook case of Borderline Personality Disorder. Characteristic of the patient's long-term functioning is a pervasive pattern of instability of mood, interpersonal relationships, and self-image. There is impulsivity (use of drugs and self-mutilation), unstable and intense interpersonal relations (idealization followed by devaluation of her therapist), inappropriate, intense anger (hostility toward the therapist), identity disturbance (doubt about who she was), affective instability (episodes of massive anxiety), and recurrent self-mutilating behavior (cutting self with a razor). The only characteristic symptoms of the disorder that are not clearly described in this case are chronic feelings of emptiness or boredom (which may have been present) and frantic efforts to avoid real or imagined abandonment (which may have been involved in her insatiable demands for more time with her therapist).

Although this woman is suicidal, there is no description of other depressive symptoms that would justify a diagnosis of Dysthymia or Major Depression.

DSM-III-R Diagnosis:

Axis I: **V71.09 No Diagnosis or Condition**
Axis II: **301.83 Borderline Personality Disorder, Severe (p. 347)**

Foggy Student

A 20-YEAR-OLD MALE COLLEGE STUDENT sought psychiatric consultation because he was worried that he might be going insane. For the past two years he had experienced increasingly frequent episodes of feeling "outside" himself. These episodes were accompanied by a sense of deadness in his body. In addition, during these periods he was uncertain of his balance and frequently stumbled into furniture; this was more apt to occur in public, especially if he was somewhat anxious. During these episodes he felt a lack of easy, natural control of his body; and his thoughts seemed "foggy" as well, in a way that reminded him of having received intravenous anesthetic agents for an appendectomy some five years previously.

The patient's subjective sense of lack of control was especially troublesome, and he would fight it by shaking his head and saying "stop" to himself. This would momentarily clear his mind and restore his sense of autonomy, but only temporarily, as the feelings of deadness and of being outside himself would return. Gradually, over a period of several hours, the unpleasant experiences would fade. The patient was anxious, however, about their return, since he found them increasing in both frequency and duration.

At the time the patient came for treatment, he was experiencing these symptoms about twice a week, and each incident lasted from three to four hours. On several occasions the episodes had occurred while he was driving his car and was alone; worried that he might have an accident, he had stopped driving unless someone accompanied him. Increasingly he had begun to discuss this problem with his girl friend, and eventually she had become less affectionate toward him, complaining that he had lost his sense of humor and was totally self-preoccupied. She threatened to break off with him unless he changed, and she began to date other men.

The patient's college grades remained unimpaired—they had, in fact, improved over the past six months, since the patient was spending more time studying than had previously been the case. Although discouraged by his symptoms, the patient slept well at night, had noted no change in appetite, and had experienced no impairment in concentration. He was neither fatigued nor physically "edgy" because of his worry.

Because a cousin had been hospitalized for many years with severe mental illness, the patient had begun to wonder if a similar fate might befall him, and sought direct reassurance on the matter.

Discussion of "Foggy Student"

Depersonalization—that is, alteration in the perception or experience of the self so that the usual sense of one's own reality is lost—can be a symptom of a variety of mental disorders, such as Schizophrenic, Anxiety, Mood, Personality, and Organic Mental Disorders. Mild depersonalization, without functional impairment, occurs at some time in a large proportion of young adults, and does not by itself warrant diagnosis as a mental disorder. When, as in this case, the symptom of depersonalization occurs in the absence of a more pervasive disorder and is sufficiently severe and persistent to cause marked distress, the diagnosis Depersonalization Disorder is made.

DSM-III-R Diagnosis:

Axis I: 300.60 Depersonalization Disorder (p. 276)

Disabled Vet

THE PATIENT IS A 32-YEAR-OLD MAN who admits himself to a mental hospital in 1982, after attempting suicide by taking sleeping pills. He says that nothing in particular prompted this attempt, but that he has been very depressed, with only minor fluctuations, ever since he returned from Vietnam ten years earlier.

He describes a reasonably normal childhood and adolescence. "I never in my life felt like this before I got to Nam." He had friends throughout high school, always got at least average grades, and never was in trouble with the law or other authorities. He has had many girl friends, but has never married. After high school, he went to technical school, was trained as an electrician, and was working in this occupation when he was drafted for military service in Vietnam. He loathed the violence there; but on one occasion, evidently swept away by the group spirit, he killed a civilian "for the fun of it." This seems to him totally out of keeping with his character. The memory of this incident continues to haunt him, and he is wracked with guilt. He was honorably discharged from the army, and has never worked since, except for three weeks when an uncle hired him. He has been living on various forms of government assistance.

In the army the patient began to drink heavily and to use whatever drugs he could get his hands on, abusing most of them; but in the last few years, he has turned to alcohol almost exclusively. He has been drinking very heavily and nearly continually for the past 10 years, with blackouts, frequent arrests for public intoxication, and injuries in barroom brawls. He has acquaintances, but no friends. Whenever he "dries out," he feels terribly depressed (as he also does when he drinks); he has made four suicide attempts in the last seven years. For the month before his latest suicide attempt, he had been living in an alcohol-treatment residence, the longest dry period he can remember, all previous attempts at cutting down on his drinking having failed.

The patient presents as a very sad, thoughtful, introspective man with a dignified bearing, and in informal conversation appears to be of at least normal intelligence. He is not interested in anything and confides that when he sees others enjoying themselves, he is so jealous he wants to hit them; this urge is never evident from his unfailingly courteous behavior. There is no evidence of delusions, and no history of hallucinations except during several bouts of Alcohol Withdrawal Delirium in the past. His appetite is normal, as is his sex drive, "but I don't enjoy it." He has trouble falling asleep or staying asleep without medication. He is not psychomotorically slow. He complains of "absentmindedness."

After two weeks, the patient still had trouble finding his way around the ward. He seemed very well motivated to cooperate with neuropsychological testing, and was extremely distressed by his disabilities. Testing revealed impaired immediate and long-term memory, apraxias, agnosias, peripheral neuropathy, and constructional difficulties; his IQ measured 66.

The patient has not responded to antidepressant medication. He is sorry that his suicide attempt did not succeed, and he says that if things aren't going to get any better, he definitely wants to die.

Discussion of "Disabled Vet"

What occasioned this patient's hospital admission was a suicide attempt, a symptom of his long-standing depression. A ten-year period of depressed mood and anhedonia, with such associated symptoms as sleep difficulties and recurrent suicidal acts, suggest a chronic Major Depressive Episode. Because one more symptom is required for the diagnosis, and we are unsure whether his "absent-mindedness" is a symptom of depression or of dementia, we make a provisional diagnosis of chronic Major Depression.

There is a long history of heavy drinking, with frequent periods of intoxication when expected to fulfill major role obligations, unsuccessful efforts to cut down on alcohol use, and continued drinking despite knowledge of recurrent problems caused by alcohol use (blackouts, frequent arrests, and injuries in barroom brawls). These, together with the history of episodes of withdrawal (Alcohol Withdrawal Delirium), indicate the presence of Alcohol Dependence. Since the patient has not been drinking for the past month, the severity is noted as "In Partial Remission," although with such a brief period of remission, the likelihood of relapse is extremely high.

Furthermore, the patient has severe memory loss and evidence of impairment of higher cortical functioning (apraxias, agnosias, constructional difficulties) and a decrement in intellectual abilities (IQ of 66) that interferes with functioning. Since this is apparently due to the long history of Alcoholism and is not limited to memory loss (as in Alcohol Amnestic Disorder), the diagnosis of Dementia Associated with Alcoholism is given. Because this diagnosis is more relevant to his current condition than the Alcohol Dependence, in Partial Remission, it is listed as the second diagnosis.

DSM-III-R Diagnosis:

Axis I: 296.22 Major Depression, Single Episode (Chronic), Moderate (p. 229)
291.20 Dementia Associated with Alcoholism (p. 134)
303.90 Alcohol Dependence, in Partial Remission (p. 167)

Miriam and Esther

M IRIAM WAS HOSPITALIZED after her mother called the police because she feared Miriam might hurt both of them. Miriam claimed she was 56 years of age and lived with her 76-year-old "assumed" or "estranged" mother, Esther, and her 12-year-old daughter, Alice. She described Esther as a family friend who had given her and her daughter a room some years ago, but who had increasingly angered her by acting as a mother and a grandmother, invading her privacy, attacking her in her sleep, and jealously turning Alice against her.

According to the patient, domestic squabbling had threatened to become violent on the night of admission, causing Esther to send her to the hospital "for hygiene." The patient expected to leave as soon as the ward social worker could relocate her and Alice in a "condominium or other suitable environment in which to rear my own child, who is coming of age as a young lady." She admitted to a recent sense of confusion, but denied sleep and appetite changes, mood disturbance, and hallucinations. However, she did describe a "whooshing" sound in her "cranium" intermittently over the past several years, which she felt resulted from fluid in her ear; at other times she had felt "very aware" of her own thoughts, but denied hearing voices.

Miriam gave a vague but complex past history, as follows: She was born 56 years ago in Italy, on November 15, 1924. Her "biologic parents" (as she put it), Louise and William, were wealthy from oil. They took her to their country house in Mt. Vernon, New York, where she spent her childhood. Esther, a family friend, visited often. Miriam recalled people driving Packards and Rolls Royces. She stated she later lived in Europe and North Africa, and was present in Hiroshima when the atom bomb was dropped. This event left her with a steel plate in her head and an "atom brain." She lived with Louise and William from 1957 to 1968. She said that she had had three husbands and seven children. Her youngest, Alice, fathered by her last husband, was born in 1968, four years after his death. When asked how this could be, she explained that a "tubal infection" had delayed the baby's conception in a "technical way."

According to Miriam, after the birth of Alice, she moved in with Esther and enrolled in Hunter College in a special program for middle-aged students, where she excelled in Romance languages. She became an alcoholic, consuming up to a pint of whiskey daily. Once when she didn't drink, she became shaky and broke into a sweat. Following the death in 1973 of her "biologic mother," Louise, Miriam became depressed and lost weight. A "nervous breakdown" landed her in a state mental hospital for three months, where she stopped drinking and improved with medication. For several years thereafter, a local "mental hygiene" clinic gave her medication for "stability," including Prolixin (an antipsychotic), which made her hair fall out. Since then, she had worked steadily, first for the Board of Education, and then as a home health aide. For the past year she had remained home to care for her child.

Miriam's mother, Esther, related a quite different history, corroborated by family members and clinic staff. Miriam is actually 30 years old, and was born October 8, 1950. Esther is 56 and is, in fact, her biologic mother. When Miriam was seven, her father walked out on the family. The next year she and her older sister were sent, probably for financial reasons, to Mt. Vernon to live with Esther's middle-class Aunt Louise and Uncle William. Esther visited on weekends.

Miriam was a good student, but had few friends and kept to herself. In 1968, at 17 years of age, she became pregnant by a cousin from Trinidad, whom she never saw again. She finished high school but, ashamed, returned to her mother's home to have the baby. Esther cared for them both and took responsibility for rearing her granddaughter, Alice. Miriam attended night classes in business skills for two years at Hunter College, but did poorly. She then worked for a year as a home health aide, but quit because she thought people were against her. She began to hear voices that commented about her actions, and was finally admitted to a state hospital in 1973, where she improved with medication. The voices ceased several months after discharge. She lived at home and worked occasionally as a secretary, but failed a stenography and typing course.

In 1977, her mother paid for Miriam to have her own apartment. Miriam mismanaged her money, and was evicted after a year. The stress apparently caused her to become psychotic again (details are not known). She moved back to her mother's, and improved greatly on antipsychotics. She worked inconsistently for a year, again as a home health aide, but then stopped her medication and quit work. She began to call her mother "Esther," rather than "Mother," and began to say she was not her real mother. Friction developed because of Esther's disappointment in Miriam and Miriam's jealousy of the continued mothering role taken by Esther toward Miriam's child. The child clearly preferred Esther.

Miriam spent more time alone in her room, friendless, venturing out only for shopping trips, during which she would spend her disability check on expensive clothes. Relatives say she was often belligerent when talking about her mother. She became unkempt and unable to help with the household chores. She began yelling at imaginary people to leave her alone and not touch her. On several occasions, by the time police had been summoned, Miriam had calmed down. However, the night of admission she was out of control, threatening to throw herself and her mother out the window, and was forcibly handcuffed and brought to the hospital.

Miriam's mental status in numerous interviews was characterized by calm, socially appropriate behavior. She was obese and homely, but tastefully dressed. Speech and movement were of normal tempo and quantity. Her affect was constricted, although at times she seemed pedantic and slightly haughty. Contained anger and sarcasm were apparent during a joint interview with her mother. Thought processes were slightly loose, vague, and circumstantial. Most striking was her odd language, ranging from idiosyncratic usage—"my assumed mother," "my estranged mother"—to neologisms ("Medicine makes me incognizant . . . I am not correlative enough . . . My mother does not accreditize me . . . The hospital will have my records if they are consortive; they must have a litigation department . . . My cousin was a devasive schizoid").

When confronted with inconsistencies in her account of her life, Miriam only smiled or giggled. While hospitalized she admitted neither to currently hearing the "whooshing" sound nor to any hallucinations. Nurses reported that when unknowingly observed, she acted as if she were aware of nonexistent beings.

Discussion of "Miriam and Esther"

This woman clearly has an illness with prominent psychotic features, the most notable being a delusion that the woman who claims to be her mother is actually only a family friend. (This delusion seems to be a variant of the Capgras syndrome, in which the person believes that one or more people in his or her environment are actually imposters who either look exactly or almost exactly like the people whose roles they have assumed.) Other bizarre delusions include the belief that the conception of her youngest child was delayed several years beyond the death of the biologic father and that she was in Hiroshima when the atom bomb was dropped, leaving her with a steel plate in her head.

Although she denies hallucinations, the sound in her head probably is an auditory hallucination; her mother claims that she has heard voices in the past.

The absence of a known organic factor that could account for the symptoms, the deterioration in functioning over several years, and the bizarre delusions and hallucinations clearly establish the diagnosis as Schizophrenia. Preoccupation with one or more systematized delusions and the absence of such features as incoherence, marked loosening of associations, and flat or inappropriate affect indicate the Paranoid Type. The course of her illness is characterized as chronic (ill for more than two years) with a current acute exacerbation (reemergence of prominent psychotic symptoms).

An unusual feature of this case is what is sometimes referred to as *pseudologia fantastica*, the presentation of fantastic and elaborate details about oneself that are completely false, but that the patient appears to believe. In Miriam's case this is illustrated by her account of her past history, being born in Italy, growing up with wealthy parents, later living in Europe and North Africa, and her claim of having had a serious alcohol problem (which her family denied).

DSM-III-R Diagnosis:

Axis I: **295.34 Schizophrenia, Paranoid Type, Chronic with Acute Exacerbation (pp. 194, 197)**

The Men's Room

N ICK, A 26-YEAR-OLD, single, male grocery clerk complained: "I have a problem with shit." He was referred to a mental health clinic by a pastoral counselor who had been seeing him for the past six months for interpersonal problems.

Over the past three to four years, during periods of low sexual activity, Nick has become sexually frustrated and gone to public restrooms, where he turns off the water to the toilets and then waits for a man whom he finds sexually attractive to enter. He waits until this person uses a toilet and then "retrieves" the feces and takes them home in a plastic bag. He warms the feces by placing the bag in boiling water and subsequently plays with the feces, which sexually excites him. He then masturbates to orgasm. This behavior has occurred about once a month. He admits to a great deal of guilt and concern over his habit because "it is not socially acceptable."

Nick is homosexual, but is extremely reluctant to frequent "gay" bars. When he does, he stays only a short time; if he is not approached within the first 15 to 20 minutes, he leaves. He shares an apartment with a roommate, but is not emotionally involved with him. He has a limited circle of friends.

He has had an attraction for restrooms since early adolescence. Some of his earliest sexual contacts occurred in restrooms. Once he was excited by urine; however, this is not currently the case.

Nick recalls having been a "loner" throughout his childhood. At an early age he realized that his sexual attraction to other boys made him different from his peers. This led him to be socially isolated. His first sexual activity occurred at age ten with group masturbation. At age 11 he began engaging in homosexual activity. This has continued throughout his life, and he has had no history of heterosexual arousal or activity.

Nick is short, stocky, rather masculine, and meticulously dressed and groomed. During the interview he is tense and stiff, especially when describing his sexual behavior. His affect is constricted. He complains of feeling depressed, but he has no associated symptoms of depression. His speech is overinclusive and circumstantial. There is no evidence of psychotic symptoms.

Discussion of "The Men's Room"

How should the use of feces for achieving sexual excitement be classified? In DSM-III-R, Coprophilia is given as an example of Paraphilia Not Otherwise Specified. In Coprophilia the person is excited by observing the act of defecation or by being defecated upon. In this case, however, it is the feces themselves that serve as the stimulus. Therefore, it seems to us no different from the use of other nonliving objects by themselves, such as female undergarments, for sexual excitement, and as such should be classified as Fetishism. (We cannot claim that classifying this disorder as Fetishism rather than as a Paraphilia Not Otherwise Specified has profound treatment implications.)

In view of the history of social isolation and inability to initiate relationships with people, it seems reasonable to give an Axis II diagnosis of Personality Disorder Not Otherwise Specified (Provisional), R/O Schizoid Personality Disorder.

Note: This case was submitted before the AIDS epidemic, and no follow-up information is available.

DSM-III-R Diagnosis:

Axis I: 302.81 Fetishism, Severe (p. 283)
Axis II: 301.90 Personality Disorder Not Otherwise Specified
           (Provisional) (p. 358)
           R/O Schizoid Personality Disorder

Sex Problem

MS. B. IS A 43-YEAR-OLD HOUSEWIFE who entered the hospital in 1968 with
a chief complaint of being concerned about her "sex problem"; she
stated that she needed hypnotism to find out what was wrong with her
sexual drive. Her husband supplied the history: he complained that she
had had many extramarital affairs, with many different men, all through
their married life. He insisted that in one two-week period she had had as
many as a hundred different sexual experiences with men outside the
marriage. The patient herself agreed with this assessment of her behavior,
but would not speak of the experiences, saying that she "blocks" the
memories out. She denied any particular interest in sexuality, but said that
apparently she felt a compulsive drive to go out and seek sexual activity
despite her lack of interest.

The patient had been married to her husband for over twenty years.
He was clearly the dominant partner in the marriage. The patient was
fearful of his frequent jealous rages, and apparently it was he who suggested that she enter the hospital in order to receive hypnosis. The
patient maintained that she could not explain why she sought out other
men, that she really did not want to do this. Her husband stated that on
occasion he had tracked her down, and when he had found her, she
acted as if she did not know him. She confirmed this and believed it was
due to the fact that the episodes of her sexual promiscuity were blotted
out by "amnesia."

When the physician indicated that he questioned the reality of the
wife's sexual adventures, the husband became furious and accused the
doctor and a ward attendant of having sexual relations with her.

Neither an amytal interview nor considerable psychotherapy with
Ms. B. was able to clear the "blocked out" memory of periods of sexual
activities. The patient did admit to a memory of having had 2 extramarital
relationships in the past: one, 20 years before the time of admission, and
the other just a year before admission. She stated that the last one had
actually been planned by her husband, and that he was in the same house
at the time. She continued to believe that she had actually had countless
extramarital sexual experiences, though she remembered only two of
them.

Discussion of "Sex Problem"

One's first impression is that an Amnestic Syndrome, either psychogenic or organic, should be considered. However, the plot thickens as evidence accumulates that the husband, the chief informant, has delusional jealousy, believing that his wife is repeatedly unfaithful to him. Apparently, under his influence, his wife has accepted this delusional belief, explaining her lack of memory of the events by believing that she has "amnesia." It would seem that she has adopted his delusional system and does not really have any kind of "amnesia." Before the onset of her becoming delusional, there was no indication of any preexisting psychotic disorder or that she had any of the prodromal symptoms of Schizophrenia. Because her delusional system developed as a result of a close relationship with another person who had an already established delusion, i.e., her husband, and because her delusions are similar in content to his delusions, the diagnosis is Induced Psychotic Disorder, formerly called *Folie à deux*. An interesting twist to this case is that it is the patient who, by virtue of her alleged extramarital activity, is the source of the husband's distress. It is more common in an Induced Psychotic Disorder for the person who has adopted the other's delusional system to believe that he or she is also being harmed.

DSM-III-R Diagnosis:

Axis I: 297.30 Induced Psychotic Disorder (p. 211)

*The Heavenly Vision**

A N OBESE 34-YEAR-OLD WOMAN was brought to a local hospital by the police. She had removed her clothing and, standing naked beside her car in a gas station, had ostentatiously engaged in fellatio with her five-month-old son. She later claimed that she did this in response to a vision: "I felt I had been instructed to step out of the car, remove my clothes as a sort of shocking, attention-getting episode depicting the stripping that this nation is going to be going through soon." She explained that the depiction of oral sex was in order to draw attention to the abuse of children in vile ways in this country, as in prostitution and pornography. She described her own behavior as a "bizarre act" and understood that it

---

*Adapted from Spitzer RL, Gibbon M, Skodol A, Williams JBW, Hyler S: The heavenly vision of a poor woman: A down-to-earth discussion of the DSM-III differential diagnosis. J Operational Psychiatry 11 (2):169-172, 1980.

was viewed as evidence of a "mental aberration." But in her own words, "There's method to my madness."

The patient had apparently, for the past 20 years, been having "different levels of visionary states" during which she both saw and heard God. Recently she had been receiving religious and political messages from God and believed that "The Communist Party and the Nazi Party have joined hands and will be occupying the country . . . the strike of the invasion point will come over Canada down through the Midwest to the point of St. Louis."

The patient's description of her visionary experiences and her history was coherent and articulate and delivered in a matter-of-fact manner, although with many vivid and startling details.

Records from a previous hospitalization noted that the patient had a completely positive review of physical symptoms. Her presenting complaint at the time was migraine headaches; but as each physician examined her, the symptom list grew longer and longer. Records from a psychiatric outpatient evaluation nine years before the current admission noted that she complained of extreme shakiness, which had gone on for a number of years; of a painful "knot" growing at the lower part of the back of her head; and of blackout spells. After these spells she said she frequently went into a deep sleep. Several electroencephalograms (EEGs) were negative. A neurologist who examined her did not think she had epilepsy and recommended that she see a psychiatrist.

During her current hospitalization, the patient had some physical complaints, particularly back pain, which she attributed to a fall at age 18 and to arthritis of the lower spine. She had difficulty walking, and had consulted many doctors about this. She had a 100% disability rating for "nerves and arthritis."

On physical examination the patient was noted to be overweight. She had several small lipomas on her back and arm. Palpation of her abdomen revealed a poorly localized right quadrant tenderness. She complained of polymenorrhea. A Pap smear and endometrial biopsy were normal. An electrocardiogram (EKG) showed a right bundle branch block and left ventricular hypertrophy. Radiological examination of her skull revealed microcephaly (greater than two standard deviations below the lower limits of normal) and osteosclerosis. A rheumatology consultant diagnosed mechanical low back pain exacerbated by obesity.

Her personal history was obtained from the patient alone. She reported that her father was a fundamentalist Christian minister, and she had been deeply involved in the church from an early age. She was baptized at 12, and was "speaking in tongues." At that age she "felt a call to the ministry." She completed high school with above-average grades. At 18, after a broken engagement (which she describes very dramatically, as she does every event in her history), she joined the WACs, against her parents' wishes; and she has been alienated from her family ever since. She claims to have been raped while in the service, and later to have fallen down, hit her head on concrete, and been "unconscious for nine days," after which she was "very weak" and had "bouts of amnesia." She left the WACs after 13 months and married a man who turned out to be a bigamist. She lived with him for 12 years, had 4 children, and separated from him when she discovered that he had molested her daughters. She has worked sporadically since then.

After her marital separation, the patient left town with her children because she was being "harassed" by gossiping neighbors. She moved to another town, but the harassment continued. At one point she took the children to Israel, with no money and no plans other than to settle there, claiming that she had traced a "Jewish bloodline" in her ancestry. She gives the impression of having been "on the road" a good deal of the time since her separation (four years ago). For at least part of that time, she placed her children in state foster homes.

Fourteen months before admission, she had slept with a stranger in a motel. She claims that this was her only sexual contact in four years; it resulted in the birth of her son, five months previously.

During her hospital stay the patient was quite verbal, and the staff noted her to be "hostile and histrionic." She held firmly to her religious beliefs, and referred to many prophecies that, she claimed, had come true. She produced tape cassettes from various people throughout the country who shared her religious beliefs. In these tapes she was generally praised for her steadfast faith and her gift of prophecy. In some tapes "speaking in tongues" was prominent. The staff had the impression that she experienced brief psychotic episodes, which centered on feelings of persecution by the government.

The patient was discharged after a month. She refused any follow-up care and told a few people that she was heading west in the hope of matriculating in an evangelist training school. Her children remained in the custody of the appropriate state social service agency. Several days after her discharge, she was sought by law-enforcement officials because she had allegedly written about $650 in bad checks and had apparently stolen the car she had been driving before admission.

Discussion of "The Heavenly Vision"

The central question in the differential diagnosis in this case is whether or not the visions, voices, unusual beliefs, and bizarre behavior are symptoms of a true psychotic disorder—a disorder in which there is gross impairment in reality testing. By definition, a delusion is a belief that is not ordinarily accepted by other members of the person's culture or subculture. This patient has a long history of association with fundamentalist religious sects in which such experiences as speaking in tongues and having visions of God are not uncommon. Can this woman's unusual perceptual experiences and strange notions be entirely accounted for by her religious beliefs? We think not. It is true that receiving messages from God and instructions to do various things to carry out God's will are common among such groups. However, this patient's elaborate notions of a combined invasion by Communist and Nazi forces and her instructions to reveal the sexual depravity of this country seem to us well beyond the range of even extreme fundamentalist beliefs. Thus, we doubt that this woman's behavior is merely the reflection of a culture-bound pattern of beliefs and behavior and without psychopathologic significance.

Having ruled out subcultural identifications as an explanation for her "symptoms," we must ask whether the symptoms are genuine (i.e., true delusions and hallucinations) or in some way intentionally produced, or whether they are on a point along a genuine–fake continuum. There is some evidence that at least some of the symptoms, particularly the bizarre behavior that occasioned her admission to the psychiatric hospital, were produced for dramatic effect. The patient seemed particularly aware of the likely reactions to what she was saying and doing. Such awareness is generally not seen in a person who is currently in a psychotic state.

In the interview itself, the patient described events in her life that strained credulity and suggested that many of them might be at least consciously exaggerated or outright fabrications (*pseudologia fantastica*). Was she unconscious for nine days? Were her children sexually molested by her husband? Did she trace her lineage back to a Jewish ancestor? Did she conceive during a single occasion of intercourse?

Further evidence suggesting that this woman's "psychotic" symptoms may not be genuine is the long history of physical complaints that appear not to be symptomatic of genuine physical illness. The patient has had episodes of amnesia with blackout "spells," yet her EEGs were negative. She has been noted to have a completely positive review of physical symptoms, many of which presumably cannot be traced to organic pathology. Finally, both the interviewer and the ward staff are apparently impressed with her histrionic manner and presentation.

The DSM-III-R concept of Factitious Disorder is meant to encompass the murky area between the act of malingering to achieve an easily understandable goal (e.g., feigning illness to avoid military duty) and a genuinely psychotic experience over which the person has no control whatever. The two critical judgments involved in making a diagnosis of a Factitious Disorder are that the "symptoms" are intentionally produced and that the motivation is not for an easily understandable goal. Since the sense of intentionally producing a symptom is subjective and can only be inferred by an outside observer, what circumstances would favor such a judgment? Examples would include the "patient" who appears to be hallucinating only when he believes that he is being observed, or the "patient" who claims to have a cluster of symptoms that generally do not coexist (e.g., a severe Dementia with systematized persecutory delusions).

The judgment that the motivation is not for an easily understandable goal is based on the assumption that in a Factitious Disorder the "patient" is motivated to achieve some benefit that is subsumed within the concept of the patient role. This might be the obvious benefit of treatment and being taken care of in a hospital, or the less obvious benefit of being absolved of certain responsibilities that are normally a part of adult life, such as having to work for a living, even though it means being a "patient" for life.

What evidence do we have that this patient's crazy behavior is motivated by the desire to assume some benefits of the patient role? There is the possibility that she realized that her sexual behavior with her infant son would result in her being hospitalized in a mental hospital. Furthermore, whether or not she deliberately sought to have her children removed from her care, this did occur, divesting her of the responsibility for their care and making it possible for her to take off more easily on her own pursuits. We regard this "evidence" as equivocal.

If one accepts the authenticity of the delusions and hallucinations in this case, then the following specific DSM-III-R categories need to be considered: Schizophrenia (or Schizophreniform Disorder), Bipolar Disorder, and Delusional Disorder. Schizophrenia (and Schizophreniform Disorder) requires marked impairment in functioning in such areas as work, social relations, and self-care that is markedly below the highest level achieved before onset of the disturbance. There is no evidence of this in our patient. Furthermore, such common features of Schizophrenia as flat affect and loosening of associations are not present. A Delusional Disorder is ruled out by the prominent hallucinations. Although the patient is grandiose and expansive, none of the other characteristic symptoms of the manic syndrome were noted by either the interviewer or the ward staff; therefore, the diagnosis of Bipolar Disorder seems unlikely.

In DSM-III-R the diagnosis of Psychotic Disorder Not Otherwise Specified may be used when the clinician judges that the patient has a psychotic disorder but the clinical picture does not conform to any of the specific mental disorders. Thus, in this case, we are left with either a diagnosis of Factitious Disorder with Psychological Symptoms (if one judges the psychotic symptoms to be factitious) or Psychotic Disorder Not Otherwise Specified (if one judges the psychotic symptoms to be genuine).

Although this woman has real physical illness, it is unlikely that this accounts for her amnesia, menstrual symptoms, and probable conversion seizures, reported during a previous hospitalization. This suggests the need to rule out Somatization Disorder, an illness characterized by recurrent and multiple somatic complaints that apparently are not due to any physical disorder, but for which medical attention is sought. In this case we count only about 9 symptoms, whereas 13 are required to make the diagnosis. However, we make the diagnosis at a provisional level since we strongly suspect that the other symptoms have been present.

In view of the long history of disturbed interpersonal relationships, a diagnosis of a Personality Disorder would certainly seem appropriate. The patient's history reveals prominent histrionic features and a suggestion of significant antisocial traits (car theft, passing bad checks, possible abandonment of children). In the absence of more information, a diagnosis of Personality Disorder Not Otherwise Specified with Histrionic and Antisocial Traits seems appropriate.

DSM-III-R Diagnosis:

Axis I: 298.90 **Psychotic Disorder Not Otherwise Specified (p. 211) (Provisional) R/O Factitious Disorder with Psychological Symptoms**
           300.81 **Somatization Disorder (Provisional)**
Axis II: 301.90 **Personality Disorder Not Otherwise Specified (p. 358) with Histrionic and Antisocial Traits**

Slim and Trim

A VERY SLIM, ATTRACTIVE, articulate, 22-year-old graduate student consulted a counseling service about an eating problem. Since age 17 she has been preoccupied with her weight. Between the ages of 17 and 21, she dieted and reduced her weight from 127 to 94 pounds. Her weight has been stable for the past year.

The patient is not afraid of becoming obese, but feels angry and guilty if she gains a few pounds. She often goes on what she calls "binges," during which she typically consumes two or three sandwiches and a salad, and then feels guilty. During the late afternoons or early mornings, she becomes ravenous, and has gone into classrooms searching through trash cans for any leftover food, which she will eat. At times she has experienced excitement at the thought that she might be seen doing this. When she was finally "caught" by a classmate, she was very embarrassed; this was the incentive for seeking treatment.

The patient denies persistent anxiety or depression, and has always functioned well both academically and interpersonally. She has not used laxatives or excessive exercise to lose weight, and has never been amenorrheic, although her periods have often been irregular.

Discussion of "Slim and Trim"

This young woman has a problem with food. There are suggestions of both Anorexia Nervosa and Bulimia Nervosa, but she does not have the full syndrome of either disorder. She does not have the fear of becoming obese or the disturbed body image that is characteristic of Anorexia Nervosa. She refers to her loss of control of the impulse to eat as a "binge," but she apparently does not consume enormous amounts of food in a short period of time, as in a true binge. What she does have is preoccupation with her weight and her eating behavior, and a morbid thrill at the prospect of being seen eating garbage. The residual diagnosis of Eating Disorder Not Otherwise Specified is therefore appropriate.

DSM-III-R Diagnosis:

Axis I: 307.50 Eating Disorder Not Otherwise Specified (p. 71)

Man's Best Friend

JOHN IS A 50-YEAR-OLD retired policeman who seeks treatment a few weeks after his dog has been run over and died. Since that time he has felt sad, tired, and has had trouble sleeping and concentrating.

John lives alone, and has for many years had virtually no conversational contacts with other human beings beyond a "Hello" or "How are you?" He prefers to be by himself, finds talk a waste of time, and feels awkward when other people try to initiate a relationship. He occasionally spends some time in a bar, but always off by himself and not really following the general conversation. He reads newspapers avidly, and is well informed in many areas, but takes no particular interest in the people around him. He is employed as a security guard, but is known by fellow workers as a "cold fish" and a "loner." They no longer even notice or tease him, especially since he never seemed to notice or care about their teasing anyway.

John floats through life without relationships except for that with his dog, which he dearly loved. At Christmas he would buy the dog elaborate gifts and, in return, would receive a wrapped bottle of scotch that he bought for himself as a gift from the dog. He believes that dogs are more sensitive and loving than people, and he can, in return, express toward them a tenderness and emotion not possible in his relationships with people. The loss of his pets are the only events in his life that have caused him sadness. He experienced the death of his parents without emotion, and feels no regret whatever at being completely out of contact with the rest of his family. He considers himself different from other people, and regards emotionality in others with bewilderment.

Discussion of "Man's Best Friend"

This man's intense reaction to the death of his dog would not be regarded as abnormal if the deceased were a family member or close friend. In such a case the V code Uncomplicated Bereavement would probably apply. However, the facts that the deceased is a dog and that the patient's symptoms have lasted several weeks and are severe enough to make him seek treatment indicate that this reaction is in excess of what would be considered normal. Thus, we are dealing with a mental disorder. (Clinicians with particular fondness for "man's best friend" may disagree with this conclusion and prefer instead the designation Uncomplicated Bereavement.) Since a full major depressive syndrome is not present, the diagnosis is Adjustment Disorder with Depressed Mood rather than Major Depression.

The patient's long-standing pattern of not wanting or enjoying close relationships with other people, including his family, always choosing solitary activities, and only rarely experiencing strong emotions, coupled with an absence of oddities and eccentricities of behavior, speech, or thought, is indicative of Schizoid Personality Disorder. It is the presence of the Schizoid Personality Disorder that has made him particularly vulnerable to the stress of his pet's death.

If there were evidence of unusual perceptions or thinking, such as recurrent illusions or ideas of reference, the diagnosis Schizotypal Personality Disorder would have to be considered.

DSM-III-R Diagnosis:

Axis I: 309.00 Adjustment Disorder with Depressed Mood (p. 330)
Axis II: 301.20 Schizoid Personality Disorder (p. 340)

Follow-up

After a year of supportive psychotherapy, John's therapist moved to a different city. John continued to call the therapist once a week for several years. The content of these calls was minimal from the therapist's point of view, but obviously the contact was very important to John. He got another dog, and his life continued much as it had before his first dog died.

Inhibited

A 24-YEAR-OLD WOMAN was referred by her therapist to a sexual dysfunction clinic because she was no longer able to achieve orgasm. She has been married for five years, and previously was able to reach orgasm and enjoyed a regular, sexually satisfying relationship with her husband.

Two years ago she had a classic Major Depression with melancholic and psychotic features, which was successfully treated with antidepressant drugs, Tofranil and Parnate. She now has no associated symptoms of the depressive syndrome, such as loss of appetite or trouble sleeping, yet she still feels "down" and does not think she has fully recovered her normal, healthy ebullience. For this reason her therapist has continued to give her Parnate, 15 mg, 3 times a day.

The patient often initiates sexual encounters, finds pleasure in sexual activities, and claims her husband is a "good and satisfactory lover." However, she has to use a lubricant as she finds she does not lubricate enough for him to penetrate without causing her discomfort; and, more disturbingly, she has been unable to have an orgasm since her depression. She has tried to masturbate herself to orgasm without success.

Discussion of "Inhibited"

According to the history, this woman had a Major Depressive Episode from which she has recovered, but not entirely. The issue is whether her difficulty with sexual excitement (does not lubricate enough) and orgasm should be regarded as residual symptoms of the Major Depressive Episode or side effects from her medication. Since MAO inhibitors, such as Parnate, are known to cause both impairment in sexual arousal and, more commonly, difficulty in orgasm, it is more practical to regard these symptoms first as drug side effects (noted on Axis III), since reducing the dose somewhat might alleviate the sexual symptoms. A diagnosis of a Sexual Dysfunction is not given in this case because of the absence of evidence of a psychogenic component.

On Axis I we would diagnose Major Depression, Single Episode, in Partial Remission, as there are still some residual symptoms of the disturbance (still feels "down" and not her normal, healthy, ebullient self).

DSM-III-R Diagnosis:

Axis I: 296.26 Major Depression, Single Episode, in Partial Remission (p. 229)

Axis III: Impaired sexual excitement and orgasm secondary to Parnate

Fits of Rage

A 38-YEAR-OLD MOTHER of 4 was referred to a psychiatrist by her priest, to whom she had confided that every few months she was subject to intense fits of rage in which she struck her children and threw things at her husband, sometimes needing to be physically restrained. The children had learned to run off to their rooms and lock the doors when she began to rant "Did you do your homework?" or "Look at this messy house!" She had overheard them referring to her to their father as "crazy Mommy" and "looney." Her husband would not talk to her for several days after such an incident. The patient herself felt very guilty and ashamed.

Detailed questioning revealed that each episode was apparently associated with the patient's sneaking only "a swallow or two" from a bottle of bourbon she kept hidden from her husband in the trunk of her car.

Discussion of "Fits of Rage"

This case was submitted as an example of Alcohol Idiosyncratic Intoxication. The clinician accepted (as we did initially) his patient's claim that each episode was initiated by only "a swallow or two" of bourbon. If this were the case, the maladaptive behavior would be seen as the effect on the central nervous system of an amount of alcohol insufficient to cause intoxication in most people, and the diagnosis would be Alcohol Idiosyncratic Intoxication.

On further reflection, it seemed to us that a person experiencing such an extreme reaction would very quickly learn to avoid alcohol. Why, then, is she hiding the bottle of bourbon? We suspect that she minimizes the amount of alcohol she actually uses and that, in all likelihood, the more prosaic diagnosis of Alcohol Abuse is appropriate. The patient's outbursts and the problems that they cause with her husband and her children surely are the kind of recurrent social problems that indicate a maladaptive pattern of alcohol use.

DSM-III-R Diagnosis:

Axis I: 305.02 Alcohol Abuse, Provisional (p. 167)

Masters and Johnson

A 33-YEAR-OLD STOCKBROKER sought treatment because of "impotence." Five months previously, a close male friend had died of a coronary occlusion, and within the following week the patient developed anxiety about his own cardiac status. Whenever his heart beat fast because of exertion, he became anxious that he was about to have a heart attack. He had disturbing dreams from which he would awaken anxious and unable to get back to sleep. He stopped playing tennis and running.

The patient began to avoid sexual intercourse, presumably because of his anxiety about physical exertion. This caused difficulties with his wife, who felt that he was deliberately depriving her of sexual outlets and was also preventing her from becoming pregnant, which she very much desired. In the past month, although no longer worried about his heart, the patient had avoided sexual intercourse entirely. He claimed to still have some desire for sex; but when the situation arose, he could not bring himself to do it. He became so upset about his sexual difficulties that he began to have trouble concentrating at work. He felt himself to be a failure both as a husband and as a man.

Before his marriage, the patient had had no sexual experience, and had masturbated by rubbing his penis against the bedclothes, without ever manually touching it. Four years previously, at the age of 29 and after 3 years of marriage, he had presented himself for treatment with the complaint that he had never attempted to have sexual intercourse with his wife. Sexual activity consisted of his obtaining an erection without either his wife or himself touching his penis, and ejaculation occurred by rubbing his penis on his wife's abdomen. He was unable to touch his wife's genitalia with his hands or allow his penis to be placed anywhere near his wife's genitalia.

Treatment had consisted of two weeks of intensive couples therapy, using the techniques developed by Masters and Johnson, with dramatic success. Sexual activity became frequent, with vaginal penetration and ejaculation. The husband began to display flirtatious sexuality toward other females, which led to some embarrassing social situations, but not to promiscuity. His wife's anxiety about her own sexuality and the adoption of a more passive role led her to seek treatment in her own right. After one year of psychotherapy, her anxieties were allayed; and sexual intercourse and interpersonal relationships between the patient and his wife had been at a satisfactory level until the present problem arose.

Discussion of "Masters and Johnson"

This man's reaction to the death of his friend five months previously involved severe anxiety and restriction in his physical activities because of fear that he might have a heart attack; and had he been evaluated at that time, an appropriate diagnosis would have been Adjustment Disorder with Anxious Mood. His anxiety affected his sexual functioning, and it is the sexual symptoms that have persisted and occasioned this evaluation.

His current sexual problem is a recurrence of the problem that caused him to seek sex therapy four years earlier: avoidance of sexual intercourse because of the anxiety associated with it. Although he refers to his problem as "impotence," the diagnosis of Male Erectile Disorder presumes that there is sexual activity during which a man fails to attain or maintain an erection and lacks a subjective sense of excitement and pleasure. What this man demonstrates is avoidance of sexual intercourse. Persistent or recurrent extreme aversion to, and avoidance of, all or almost all genital sexual contact with a partner is diagnosed as Sexual Aversion Disorder.

DSM-III-R Diagnosis:

Axis I: 302.79 Sexual Aversion Disorder, Psychogenic Only, Acquired, Generalized (p. 293)

Wash Before Wearing

A 41-YEAR-OLD MAN WAS REFERRED to a community mental health center's activities program for help in improving his social skills. He had a lifelong pattern of social isolation, with no real friends, and spent long hours worrying that his angry thoughts about his older brother would cause his brother harm. He had previously worked as a clerk in civil service, but had lost his job because of poor attendance and low productivity.

On interview the patient was distant and somewhat distrustful. He described in elaborate and often irrelevant detail his rather uneventful and routine daily life. He told the interviewer that he had spent an hour and a half in a pet store deciding which of two brands of fish food to buy, and explained their relative merits. For two days he had studied the washing instructions on a new pair of jeans—Did "Wash before wearing" mean that the jeans were to be washed before wearing the first time, or did they need, for some reason, to be washed each time before they were worn? He did not regard concerns such as these as senseless, though he acknowledged that the amount of time spent thinking about them might be excessive. When asked about his finances, he could recite from memory his most recent monthly bank statement, including the amount of every check and the running balance as each check was written. He knew his balance on any particular day, but sometimes got anxious if he considered whether a certain check or deposit had actually cleared.

He asked the interviewer whether, if he joined the program, he would be required to participate in groups. He said that groups made him very nervous, and he was unsure if he could "stand" participating in them.

Discussion of "Wash Before Wearing"

This man's long-standing maladaptive pattern of behavior indicates a Personality Disorder. Prominent symptoms include the absence of close friends or confidants, magical thinking (worrying that his angry thoughts would cause his brother harm), constricted affect (observed to be "distant" in the interview), odd speech (providing elaborate and often irrelevant details), and social anxiety. These features are characteristic of Schizotypal Personality Disorder.

Although the absence of close friends or confidants is also characteristic of Schizoid Personality Disorder, this patient's eccentricities of thought and speech preclude that diagnosis. There are many similarities between Schizotypal Personality Disorder and the symptoms seen in the Residual Type of Schizophrenia, but the absence of a history of overt psychotic symptoms rules out that diagnosis.

The patient's concerns with choosing the best brand of fish food and understanding the instructions for washing his jeans suggest obsessions, but the ego-syntonic nature of the concerns indicates that they are not true obsessions, but rather examples of indecisiveness and perfectionism. Since these are traits of Obsessive Compulsive Personality Disorder, we have noted them. (The full criteria for Obsessive Compulsive Personality Disorder are not met.)

DSM-III-R Diagnosis:

Axis I: V71.09 No Diagnosis or Condition
Axis II: 301.22 Schizotypal Personality Disorder (p. 341)
          Obsessive Compulsive Traits

Foster Mother

CHERYL JONES, A 44-YEAR-OLD MOTHER of 3 teen-agers, is hospitalized for treatment of depression. She gives the following history: One year previously, after a terminal argument with her lover, she became acutely psychotic. She was frightened that people were going to kill her and heard voices of friends and strangers talking about killing her, sometimes talking to each other. She heard her own thoughts broadcast aloud and was afraid that others could also hear what she was thinking. Over a three-week period she stayed in her apartment, had new locks put on the doors, kept the shades down, and avoided everyone but her immediate family. She was unable to sleep at night because the voices kept her awake, and unable to eat because of a constant "lump" in her throat. In retrospect, she cannot say whether she was depressed, denies being elated or overactive, and remembers only that she was terrified of what would happen to her. The family persuaded her to enter a hospital, where, after six weeks of treatment with Thorazine, the voices stopped. She remembers feeling "back to normal" for a week or two, but then she seemed to lose her energy and motivation to do anything. She became increasingly depressed, lost her appetite, and woke at 4:00 or 5:00 every morning and was unable to get back to sleep. She could no longer read a newspaper or watch TV because she couldn't concentrate.

Ms. Jones's condition persisted for nine months. She has done very little except sit in her apartment, staring at the walls. Her children have managed most of the cooking, shopping, bill-paying, etc. She has continued in outpatient treatment, and was maintained on Thorazine until before this admission. There has been no recurrence of the psychotic symptoms since the medication was discontinued; but her depression, with all the accompanying symptoms, has persisted.

In discussing her past history, Ms. Jones is rather guarded. There is, however, no evidence of a diagnosable illness before last year. She apparently is a shy, emotionally constricted person who "has never broken any rules." She has been separated from her husband for ten years, but in that time has had two enduring relationships with boyfriends. In addition to rearing three apparently healthy and very likable children, she cared for a succession of foster children full time in the four years before her illness. She enjoyed this, and was highly valued by the agency she worked for. She has maintained close relationships with a few girl friends and with her extended family.

Discussion of "Foster Mother"

During her initial period of illness, this patient demonstrated such characteristic schizophrenic symptoms as bizarre delusions (people could hear what she was thinking) accompanied by auditory hallucinations (voices of friends and strangers talking to each other). There was deterioration in functioning to the point that she was unable to take care of her house. With treatment, after about nine weeks the psychotic symptoms remitted, but she remembers being "back to normal" for only about a week. She then developed the characteristic symptoms of a Major Depressive Episode, with depressed mood, poor appetite, insomnia, lack of energy, loss of interest, and poor concentration. The depressive period has lasted for about nine months.

Are the two periods of illness two separate disorders, or a single illness? If they represent two separate disorders, they could be characterized as either Schizophreniform Disorder (because the duration is less than six months) followed by Major Depression, or Schizophrenia (the period after the psychotic phase being considered a residual phase of Schizophrenia) with a superimposed depression (for the second period of illness). If there is a single disorder, it is hard to know what to call it (Schizophrenia with depressive features?).

This case would seem to be an example of an instance in which it is difficult to make a differential diagnosis with any degree of certainty between a Mood Disorder and Schizophrenia or Schizophreniform Disorder. Many clinicians would want to call it Schizoaffective Disorder. This diagnosis, according to DSM-III-R criteria, cannot be made because there is apparently no temporal overlap of the patient's psychotic symptoms and her depression. Because of the uncertainty about the "real" diagnosis, we prefer to make the dual diagnoses of Psychotic Disorder Not Otherwise Specified and Depressive Disorder Not Otherwise Specified.

DSM-III-R Diagnosis:

Axis I: 298.90 Psychotic Disorder Not Otherwise Specified
                     (p. 211)
              311.00 Depressive Disorder Not Otherwise Specified
                     (p. 233)

Follow-up

Ms. Jones was treated with an antidepressant drug, desipramine, and a stimulant, dexadrine. She recovered within a few months, went back to school to get her General Education Diploma, and began working as a homemaker for the welfare department. A year later she returned to the hospital, depressed and anxious, and with psychotic symptoms. She was treated with a combination of antidepressant and antipsychotic drugs, and she recovered within a few months.

With this follow-up information, indicating an episode in which psychotic and depressive symptoms co-occurred, the correct diagnosis would seem to be Schizoaffective Disorder, Depressed Type.

The Basketball Player

M S. GUNDERSON, THE MOTHER OF an 18-year-old boy, requested help from the Visiting Nurse Association. Her son Brad, a recent high-school graduate with no previous medical history, had suffered a myocardial infarction 16 days previously. After being released from the hospital, he was told to remain in bed, with only bathroom privileges, for one week, until his next appointment with the cardiologist. When seen at home by the visiting nurse two days after leaving the hospital, the boy was playing basketball in the back yard. He acknowledged that he had had a "heart attack," but said he now felt "fine" and therefore saw no need to further restrict his activities. He was planning to begin a full-time job in a local factory in two weeks and was unwilling to consider the possible effect of his physical condition on his plans.

Brad had been popular, a high-school football hero, with many friends and a series of steady girl friends. He had gotten average grades and never been in any trouble. His use of alcohol had been moderate, and he had smoked marijuana only a few times. He was not interested in talking about plans beyond the next year, but guessed he would probably go into the army at some point. His relationship with his family was distant, but harmonious. Ms. Gunderson had stopped trying to enforce the regimen prescribed by his doctor after her son had reassured her that he would go to bed if he felt any pain.

Discussion of "The Basketball Player"

By not following standard medical advice, this patient may kill himself. Why does he persist in acting as if he does not have a life-threatening illness? It is certainly not because he has rationally considered the pros and cons of the prescribed treatment, as might be the case, for example, with a patient with lung cancer who has chosen not to undergo postoperative chemotherapy recommended by a surgeon in view of the controversy surrounding the effectiveness of the treatment. One can only conclude that our patient is now demonstrating massive denial, a lesser degree of which may have served him well up to now. Apparently, it is only in this unusual situation that his denial may cause him serious problems.

Although his noncompliance with medical treatment is maladaptive and represents psychopathology (broadly defined), it may not be sufficient to make the diagnosis of a mental disorder. We therefore would note the V code Noncompliance with Medical Treatment. The V codes are "for conditions not attributable to a mental disorder that are [nevertheless] a focus of attention or treatment." Hence, using a V code to characterize this problem does not preclude offering treatment.

We should not quarrel with a clinician who, wishing to emphasize the seriousness of the psychological problem, preferred the diagnosis Unspecified Mental Disorder (Nonpsychotic).

DSM-III-R Diagnosis:

Axis I: V15.81 Noncompliance with Medical Treatment (p. 360)
Axis III: Status post myocardial infarction

Triple Divorcée

J O ELLEN, A 37-YEAR-OLD, thrice divorced woman, was hospitalized in a private psychiatric facility because of an attempt to end her life by putting her head into the oven and turning on the gas. When the acute effects of central nervous system depression had worn off, she complained of hopelessness and uselessness, inordinate fatigue, guilt about having abandoned her five-year-old daughter, and total anhedonia; she displayed marked psychomotor retardation and slept 12-14 hours a night.

This was Jo Ellen's sixth episode of this kind. The first episode, at the age of 23, had been triggered by marital separation; but she could suggest no explanation for subsequent episodes—"I just seem to sink into a gloomy despair." She has received individual psychotherapy and small doses of all kinds of psychotropic drugs except, ironically, the tricyclic antidepressants. During the present episode she was given increasing doses of the tricyclic antidepressant desipramine; and in ten days, at a daily dosage level of 200 mg, her mood became elated, flirtatious, and overconfident, and she did not sleep more than four to five hours a night. This mood receded in four days with a downward adjustment of her tricyclic dose.

Detailed questioning revealed that Jo Ellen had had one previous "high period," which had occurred at the tail end of her second depressive episode, when she was on no medication. It had lasted for two weeks. She recalls "being on Cloud 9," having an overabundance of energy and a decreased need for sleep, keeping the house immaculate, arranging and rearranging the furniture two or three times a day, and kissing the children every time they passed by. She denies having racing thoughts or inflated self-esteem, and there is no evidence of poor judgment or serious impairment in functioning.

Discussion of "Triple Divorcée"

The current episode of illness has all the features of a Major Depressive Episode, with disturbances in mood, sleep, psychomotor activity, energy level, and feelings of hopelessness and guilt. While being treated pharmacologically with a tricyclic antidepressant, the patient developed symptoms suggesting a Manic Episode; but the disturbance was too mild and too brief to be considered a Manic Episode of Bipolar Disorder.

Tricyclic-induced hypomanic episodes are not rare. Because there is some evidence that most people in whom this occurs have a family history of Bipolar Disorder, DSM-III-R classifies such an episode as a manifestation of Bipolar Disorder Not Otherwise Specified rather than as an Organic Mood Syndrome. In this particular case, there is a history of a similar hypomanic episode not associated with pharmacologic treatment, which further supports the diagnosis. A history of one or more Major Depressive Episodes with one or more hypomanic (but no manic) episodes has been referred to as Bipolar II.

DSM-III-R Diagnosis:

**Axis I: 296.70 Bipolar Disorder Not Otherwise Specified
            (p. 228)**

Sleepy

A 55-YEAR-OLD BUSINESSMAN had suffered from excessive sleepiness since age 21, which he had described to his new family physician, who then referred him to a sleep specialist. Typically, he slept regularly from 10:15 PM to 6:30 AM. He also took half-hour to three-quarter-hour naps between 9 and 10:15 AM, and 1:30 and 2:00 PM, and napped irregularly between 4:30 and 8:30 PM. When napping at work, on his office floor, he deferred all calls. He awoke temporarily refreshed. Delaying his naps caused overwhelming fatigue. He had no sudden loss of muscle tone (as in cataplexy) or other symptoms suggesting narcolepsy, and neither snored nor had any other symptoms suggesting recurrent periods of sleep apnea (not breathing during sleep).

The patient owned a television station in Birmingham, Alabama. He was spared obligatory hard work since his staff could run the operation. Nevertheless, he was an organized, motivated person. He was in good health, and jogged four to five miles daily. He lived with his wife and youngest son. He enjoyed socializing with his married children and their families and dabbling in local politics. He would take a longer afternoon nap in anticipation of any evening activity, which he always left early in favor of his regular bedtime.

His father had taken a nap daily after lunch, and his paternal grandfather had been excessively sleepy. During childhood the patient had had some nightmares, but no other sleep problem. He had been athletic, and spontaneously ran along his paper route.

The patient drank about two beers a week, but avoided additional alcohol, caffeine, and other drugs. Previous physical exams had revealed good health, with a resting heart rate maintained in the 50s, blood pressures that ran around 110-105/70 mm Hg, normal thyroid function, and normal glucose tolerance.

When interviewed, the patient was friendly, informative, and self-assured. He denied depressed mood or loss of interest or pleasure. He regarded his sleepiness as a difficulty with which he had come to terms, but would be grateful for further relief.

Tests of daytime vigilance indicated impaired arousal. He had an average interval to sleep onset of 11 minutes, during 5 polygraphically recorded naps, which is within the normal range. During a nighttime polygraphic recording, he had normal-appearing sleep that continued uninterrupted for 9-1/2 hours until he had to be awakened.

Discussion of "Sleepy"

In most patients with a chief complaint of excessive daytime sleepiness (hypersomnia) sufficiently severe to cause the person to seek help at a sleep disorders center, an organic factor is found to cause the disturbance. This case illustrates the relatively uncommon situation in which neither an organic factor nor another mental disorder (such as Major Depression) can account for the disturbance. The diagnosis is therefore Primary Hypersomnia. Primary Hypersomnia is usually associated, as in this case, with normal sleep latency and patterns as measured by the polysomnograph.

DSM-III-R Diagnosis:

Axis I: 780.54 Primary Hypersomnia (p. 305)

Follow-up

Treatment with pemoline, a long-acting stimulant, caused severe headaches. Amphetamines and caffeine-containing beverages did not help, since their initial stimulation was followed by increased sleepiness. Moderate doses of protriptyline, a stimulating anti-depressant, helped alleviate evening sleepiness, but did not prevent daytime naps and caused severe side effects.

Since the patient speculated that psychotherapy might shed light on his problem and pose fewer disadvantages, he began a course of weekly sessions. However, after two years of this treatment with a psychoanalyst, his sleep pattern was unchanged, and he continued to manage his sleepiness with regular naps.

The Reporter

MICHAEL DODGE, A 29-YEAR-OLD newspaper reporter, had been a heavy drinker for 10 years. One evening after work, having finished a feature article, he started drinking with friends and continued to drink through the evening. He fell asleep in the early morning hours. Upon awakening he had a strong desire to drink again and decided not to go to work. Food did not appeal to him, and instead he had several Bloody Marys. Later he went to a local tavern and drank beer throughout the afternoon. He met some friends and continued drinking into the evening.

The pattern of drinking throughout the day persisted for the next seven days. On the eighth morning, Michael tried to drink a cup of coffee and found his hands were shaking so violently he could not get the cup to his mouth. He managed to pour some whiskey into a glass and drank as much as he could. His hands became less shaky, but now he was nauseated and began having "dry heaves." He tried repeatedly to drink, but could not keep alcohol down. He felt ill and intensely anxious and decided to call a doctor friend. The doctor recommended hospitalization.

When evaluated on admission, Michael is alert; he has a marked resting and intention tremor of the hands, and his tongue and eyelids are tremulous. He has feelings of "internal" tremulousness. Lying in the hospital bed, he finds the noises outside his window unbearably loud and begins seeing "visions" of animals and, on one occasion, a dead relative. He is terrified and calls a nurse, who gives him a tranquilizer. He becomes quieter, and his tremor, less pronounced. At all times he realizes that the visual phenomena are "imaginary." He always knows where he is and is otherwise oriented. He has no memory impairment. After a few days, the tremor disappears, and Michael no longer hallucinates. He still has trouble sleeping, but otherwise feels normal. He vows never to drink again.

When questioned further about his history of drinking, Michael claims that although during the last ten years he has developed the habit of drinking several scotches each day, his drinking has never interfered with his work or relations with colleagues or friends. He denies having aftereffects of drinking other than occasional mild hangovers; ever going on binges before this one; and needing to drink every day in order to function adequately. He admits, however, that he has never tried to reduce or stop drinking.

Discussion of "The Reporter"

This heavy drinker markedly increases his amount of drinking for a week and then stops drinking as he becomes sick with nausea and vomiting. He then develops visual hallucinations; tremor of the hands, tongue, and eyelids; and anxiety. Significantly, he realizes that the hallucinations are imaginary; and he remains alert, fully oriented, and without memory impairment. These symptoms, associated with the reduction in heavy alcohol use, indicate Uncomplicated Alcohol Withdrawal.

Many clinicians might conclude that this was Alcohol Withdrawal Delirium (Delirium Tremens) because of the visual hallucinations. Delirium, however, requires reduced ability to maintain attention to external stimuli, disorganized thinking, and other symptoms such as disorientation and memory impairment, in addition to whatever perceptual disturbances may be present. The visual hallucinations with intact reality testing that Michael experienced are rather common in Uncomplicated Alcohol Withdrawal.

Does the presence of Alcohol Withdrawal invariably indicate the presence of Alcohol Dependence? This is controversial. In developing the DSM-III-R criteria for Alcohol Dependence, a decision was made to give the diagnosis only if there were other cognitive and behavioral symptoms that indicate that the person has impaired control of psychoactive substance use. This was done because some heavy recreational use of alcohol might result in tolerance or withdrawal without any impaired control of alcohol use. In such cases it was thought not appropriate to make a diagnosis of Dependence. In this case the patient denies impaired control of his drinking and claims that his drinking does not interfere with his work or social relations. If this is actually true (we doubt it), he would not have the additional diagnosis of Alcohol Dependence (or even Abuse). We note the need to rule out this diagnosis, but are skeptical about Michael's ability to stop drinking, as he has vowed to do.

DSM-III-R Diagnosis:

**Axis I: 291.80   Uncomplicated Alcohol Withdrawal (p. 130)
            R/O Alcohol Dependence**

Cough Medicine

A 42-YEAR-OLD EXECUTIVE in a public relations firm was referred for psychiatric consultation by his surgeon, who discovered him sneaking large quantities of a codeine-containing cough medicine into the hospital. The patient had been a heavy cigarette smoker for 20 years and had a chronic, hacking cough. He had come into the hospital for a hernia repair, and found the pain from the incision unbearable when he coughed.

An operation on his back five years previously had led his doctor to prescribe codeine to help relieve the incisional pain at that time. Over the intervening five years, however, the patient had continued to use codeine-containing tablets and had increased his intake to 60-90 5-mg tablets daily. He stated that he often "just took them by the handful—not to feel good, you understand, just to get by." He had spent considerable time and effort developing a circle of physicians and pharmacists to whom he would "make the rounds" at least three times a week to obtain new supplies of pills. He had tried several times to stop using codeine, but had failed. During this period he lost two jobs because of lax work habits, and was divorced by his wife of 11 years.

Discussion of "Cough Medicine"

Spending a great deal of time obtaining a supply of a substance, repeated unsuccessful efforts to cut down use, tolerance (markedly increased amounts are needed to achieve the desired effect: his taking 60-90 tablets a day), use of the substance to avoid withdrawal symptoms, and use despite multiple problems secondary to taking the substance all indicate Psychoactive Substance Dependence. The diagnosis is coded as Opioid Dependence, because codeine is classified as an opioid. However, the name of the specific substance, codeine, rather than the class of substance, opioid, is recorded. The severity is specified as severe since there are many symptoms in excess of those required to make the diagnosis, and they have markedly interfered with the patient's functioning and relationships with others.

Although the criteria for Psychoactive Substance Abuse are also met in this case (a maladaptive pattern of use indicated by continued use despite knowledge of consequent social and occupational impairment), the diagnosis of Psychoactive Substance Dependence takes precedence.

DSM-III-R Diagnosis:

Axis I: 304.00 Codeine Dependence, Severe (p. 167)

Edgy Electrician

A 27-YEAR-OLD, MARRIED ELECTRICIAN complains of dizziness, sweating palms, heart palpitations, and ringing of the ears of more than eighteen months' duration. He has also experienced dry mouth and throat, periods of uncontrollable shaking, and a constant "edgy" and watchful feeling that has often interfered with his ability to concentrate. These feelings have been present most of the time over the previous two years; they have not been limited to discrete periods.

Because of these symptoms the patient had seen a family practi-

tioner, a neurologist, a neurosurgeon, a chiropractor, and an ENT specialist. He had been placed on a hypoglycemic diet, received physiotherapy
for a pinched nerve, and told he might have "an inner ear problem."

He also had many worries. He constantly worried about the health of
his parents. His father, in fact, had had a myocardial infarction two years
previously, but was now feeling well. He also worried about whether he
was "a good father," whether his wife would ever leave him (there was no
indication that she was dissatisfied with the marriage), and whether he
was liked by co-workers on the job.

For the past two years the patient has had few social contacts because of his nervous symptoms. Although he has sometimes had to leave
work when the symptoms became intolerable, he continues to work for
the same company he joined for his apprenticeship following high-school
graduation. He tends to hide his symptoms from his wife and children, to
whom he wants to appear "perfect," and reports few problems with them
as a result of his nervousness.

Discussion of "Edgy Electrician"

Although this man has consulted numerous physicians for his
symptoms, the absence of preoccupation with fears of having a
specific physical disease precludes a diagnosis of Hypochondriasis.
He has symptoms of motor tension (uncontrollable shaking), autonomic hyperactivity (dizziness, sweating palms, heart palpitations,
dry mouth), and vigilance and scanning ("a constant 'edgy' and
watchful feeling"). He is also constantly worrying about his father's
illness, his marriage, and whether he is a good father. The combination of excessive worry about two or more life circumstances and
the physical symptoms suggest Generalized Anxiety Disorder. The
diagnosis is made (as in this case) when the disturbance has been
present for at least six months, the focus of the worry is not related
to another Axis I disorder (e.g., worrying about having a panic attack, as in Panic Disorder, or being embarrassed in public, as in
Social Phobia), and the symptoms do not occur only during the
course of a mood or psychotic disorder.

DSM-III-R Diagnosis:

Axis I: 300.02 Generalized Anxiety Disorder (p. 252)

Alice

ALICE IS A 20-YEAR-OLD, SINGLE, white female, a junior in a southern college,
who came to the student health clinic with complaints of "turbu-

lence" in her life, which she experienced as vague feelings of anxiety, depression, and worries about the uncertainty of her future. She felt confused and directionless, and these feelings often interfered with her ability to concentrate on her schoolwork.

Alice had looked forward to attending college in her freshman year, and when she arrived, was excited by the diversity of people she met. Sometimes she enjoyed being with her "arty, more way-out, and kind of radical" friends, and at other times she felt more comfortable with her "traditional, more moderate, preppie" friends. In the past year, however, she had increasingly had the feeling that she did not fit into any one group of friends, and was confused about who she "really was." She experienced this not only with regard to her friends but in her academic studies as well: a second-semester junior, she still did not have a clear idea of what she really wanted to study or, in a larger sense, what she wanted to do with her life after finishing college. At the end of her sophomore year she had decided on chemistry, but then had changed to sociology at the beginning of her junior year, and more recently had changed to art history; yet she was not completely happy with her choice—"It's as if I wanted to do everything and yet I don't really want to do anything in particular."

Discussion of "Alice"

Many adolescents or young adults are troubled about the choices they must make regarding careers, life-styles, group loyalties, and other issues relating to a sense of identity. In this case Alice's uncertainty about issues related to identity (choice of career, choice of friends, not knowing who she "really was") is sufficiently severe to cause not only subjective distress but impairment in academic functioning. Since this disturbance has been apparent for more than three months and is not due to another mental disorder, such as a Mood Disorder or a disorder with psychotic features, the diagnosis of Identity Disorder is made.

Some clinicians doubt that Identity Disorder is a valid diagnosis, believing that it merely describes nonspecific developmental problems that many adolescents and young adults experience in our society.

Because the patient is over 18, the diagnosis of Borderline Personality Disorder might be considered; but there is no evidence of this more pervasive disorder, such as affective instability, impulsivity, and intense and unstable interpersonal relationships.

DSM-III-R Diagnosis:

Axis I: 313.82 Identity Disorder (p. 90)

Burned

A PSYCHIATRIST WAS CALLED to see a 28-year-old woman one week after she had been admitted to the Burn Unit. She had incurred burns over 28% of her body in a house fire in which her children, aged three and five, had also been injured and her husband had been killed. The circumstances of the injury had been quite traumatic in that she was trapped, found it difficult to escape, and risked her own life to save her children.

On examination the patient was alert and oriented, but quite fearful and anxious. She was noted by the nurses to awaken repeatedly during the night, and she reported recurrent nightmares in which she relived the experience of escaping from her home. During the day she was emotionally labile, at times seemingly inappropriately cheerful, given her recent experiences, and at other times responding fearfully to slight noises, such as traffic. The consultation was requested because the nursing staff had become concerned that she seemed almost "numb" to her husband's death. She would not talk about her husband. She discussed her children's conditions unemotionally, and she seemed to forget many of the important details of the tragedy. The nurses concluded that she did not appear to be "working through" her grief appropriately.

Discussion of "Burned"

In response to an overwhelming stress, this woman is reexperiencing the trauma (in recurrent dreams), exhibiting symptoms of increased arousal (exaggerated startle response and sleep disturbance), avoiding stimuli associated with the trauma (will not talk about husband's death), and shows a numbing of responsiveness to the environment (amnesia for aspects of the trauma, lack of emotion when discussing her children).

This constitutes the well-recognized syndrome of Post-traumatic Stress Disorder. This diagnosis takes precedence over Adjustment Disorder, which is a residual category for disturbances that are not severe enough to meet the criteria for a more serious disorder.

DSM-III-R Diagnosis:

Axis I: 309.89 Post-traumatic Stress Disorder (p. 250)

The Boards

A 29-YEAR-OLD, MARRIED WOMAN was presented as the neurology patient at the examination of a young psychiatrist for his specialty certification in psychiatry. Six months previously she had been riding in a car, driven by her husband, that was involved in a minor traffic accident. She was thrown forward, but was kept from hitting the window or dashboard by her seat belt. Three days later she began to complain of a stiff neck and sharp pains radiating down both arms, her spine to the small of her back, and both legs. Because an orthopedic consultation failed to uncover the cause of the pain, she was referred to the neurology clinic.

The patient was an attractive, statuesque woman in obvious distress who described her injury and her symptoms in vivid detail, tracing the course of her pains down her arms and legs with her hands. She smiled frequently at the young psychiatrist and at the two examiners who were observing him. She performed each test of neurologic function with precision and appeared to relish the attention. The neurologic examination findings were totally normal.

The psychiatrist inquired into the patient's past history and present life. There was no previous history of emotional disturbance. The patient currently worked as a computer programmer. She had been married four years and had no children. Until recently her marriage had been smooth, except that her husband sometimes complained that they were "mismatched" sexually. He seemed considerably more interested in frequent and "imaginative" sex, while she seemed satisfied with weekly intercourse without variation or much foreplay.

Two weeks before the accident, the patient had discovered a woman's phone number in her husband's wallet. When she confronted him with it, he admitted that he had seen several women over the preceding year, mainly for "sexual release." The patient was bitterly hurt and disappointed for several days, then began to get angry and attacked him for his "hang-ups." At the time of the accident, they had been arguing in the car on the way to a friend's house for dinner. After the accident they decided to try harder to please each other in their marriage, including sexually; but because of the pains that the patient was experiencing, they had not been able to have any sexual contact.

The young psychiatrist passed the exam.

Discussion of "The Boards"

The absence of physical findings and the apparent genuineness of the symptoms rule out a physical disorder, Malingering, and a Factitious Disorder. This leaves us with the pain as an undiagnosed physical symptom or Somatoform Pain Disorder. The Somatoform Pain Disorder diagnosis is made when there are no signs of organic pathology (as in this case) or pathophysiologic mechanism to account for the pain or, when there is related organic pathology, the complaint of pain and resulting impairment is in excess of what would be expected.

It is difficult to escape the conclusion that this woman's pain serves the function of enabling her to avoid an activity that is noxious to her: having to deal with both her husband's increasing sexual demands and their apparent sexual incompatibility. Further positive evidence of the role of psychological factors is the temporal relationship between the onset of the symptoms and the discovery and argument about the husband's extramarital sexual activity. Although it is common to find evidence of psychological factors that are etiologically involved in the development of pain, there are cases in which there is no direct evidence of such factors. Thus, the DSM-III term *Psychogenic Pain Disorder* was changed in DSM-III-R to *Somatoform Pain Disorder.*

DSM-III-R Diagnosis:

Axis I: 307.80 Somatoform Pain Disorder (p. 266)

The Hiker

A T THE AGE OF 61, a high-school science department head, an experienced and enthusiastic camper and hiker, became extremely fearful while on a trek in the mountains. Gradually, over the next few months, he lost interest in his usual hobbies. Formerly a voracious reader, he stopped reading. He had difficulty doing computations and made gross errors in home financial management. On several occasions he became lost while driving in areas that were formerly familiar to him. He began to write notes to himself so that he would not forget to do errands. Very abruptly, and in uncharacteristic fashion, he decided to retire from work, without discussing his plans with his wife. Intellectual deterioration gradually progressed. He spent most of the day piling miscellaneous objects in one place and then transporting them to another spot in the house. He became stubborn and querulous. Eventually he required assistance in shaving and dressing.

When examined six years after the first symptoms had developed, the patient was alert and cooperative. He was disoriented with respect to place and time. He could not recall the names of four of five objects after a five-minute interval of distraction. He could not remember the names of his college and graduate school or the subject in which he had majored. He could describe his job by title only. In 1978 he thought that Kennedy was President of the United States. He did not know Stalin's nationality. His speech was fluent and well articulated, but he had considerable difficulty finding words and used many long, essentially meaningless phrases. He called a "cup" a "vase," and identified the rims of glasses as "the holders." He did simple calculations poorly. He could not copy a cube or draw a house. His interpretation of proverbs was concrete, and he had no insight into the nature of his disturbance.

An elementary neurologic examination revealed nothing abnormal, and routine laboratory tests were also negative. A computerized tomography (CT) scan, however, showed marked cortical atrophy.

Discussion of "The Hiker"

Although the life circumstances of this patient are quite different from those of "Draftsman," (p. 131), the diagnostic considerations are similar. This patient also has memory impairment, impairment in abstract thinking (concrete interpretation of proverbs), other disturbances in higher cortical functioning (aphasia), and personality changes (becoming stubborn and querulous). These signs of global cognitive impairment, severe enough to interfere significantly with work and social activities, and not occurring exclusively during the course of Delirium, indicate a Dementia. There is an insidious onset, beginning before age 65, with a generally progressive, deteriorating course and no specific cause. Thus, the diagnosis is Primary Degenerative Dementia of the Alzheimer Type, Presenile Onset. Because some degree of supervision is necessary, the severity of the Dementia is noted as Moderate. We note the presence of the neurologic disease, Alzheimer's disease, on Axis III.

DSM-III-R Diagnosis:

Axis I: 290.10 Primary Degenerative Dementia of the Alzheimer
                 Type, Presenile Onset, Uncomplicated,
                 Moderate (p. 121)
Axis III: Alzheimer's disease

Follow-up

This man's condition progressed, and he required admission to the hospital within a year of his initial assessment. Over the next year, he became essentially mute, and mental status testing was virtually impossible. He had a tendency to pace back and forth constantly in the ward; on one occasion he managed to get out of the locked ward, and was found some miles from the hospital.

His retained physical appearance was in striking contrast to his devastated intellectual capacities for a long time, but eventually he began to lose weight, took to bed, and developed contractures (permanent muscular contractions).

He died at age 72 of pneumonia. Autopsy revealed cerebral atrophy and, microscopically, the plaques and tangles diagnostic of Alzheimer's disease.

End Times

MR. P., A 25-YEAR-OLD MAN from Arkansas indicted for the murder of an 8-year-old girl, was interviewed by a forensic psychiatrist on court order to determine his sanity at the time of the crime. The following is excerpted from the psychiatrist's report.

The defendant says that on the day of the crime, he smoked his usual six to seven pipe bowls of marijuana. He used no alcohol or other drugs that day. During the day he watched television. His mood was normal. His girl friend was around all day until she left for her father's birthday party at about 6:30 or 7:00 PM; she returned about 9:30 PM.

After his girl friend left the house, Mr. P. went to sit on the porch. About half an hour later, he saw some neighborhood children running around the house. Three youngsters, including the victim, asked if they could see his pet tarantula. He said they must come in one at a time. The girl's younger brother and another boy left. She then asked if she could come in to see the spider. She looked at the spider and started to walk back out of the house. No one else was around. The defendant grabbed her around her chest. He said he made up his mind to "do it" as she was walking out since, he thought, this was a possible chance to obtain a dead body.

The defendant reports that he ran into the bathroom with the victim, and turned on the bathtub water. "She just stood there and looked like she didn't know what was going on." Once he had sufficient water in the tub to submerge her face, he did so. She kicked and struggled, and screamed briefly. He never said a word to her. He was panicky and nervous. "I didn't believe I was actually doing it." After holding her face under water for three or four minutes, he pulled her up. She tried to catch her breath and he realized that he had "pulled her up too quickly." He was fearful that her brother might come looking for her, so he ran with her to a large crawl space under a floor board in a closet on the first floor. He was fearful that if her brother came back, he would tell their parents and they would "catch us," and then he would be unable to fulfill his fantasy of having sex with her dead body.

In the crawl space he hit her on the head with a brick he found there. She appeared to lose consciousness after the first blow. He struck her head many more times with the brick. He claims that he was crying and that it was "horrible, much harder than the drowning." He then put her body under a piece of plastic, closed off the crawl space, and straightened up the things he had knocked over. He turned on the television set.

A short time later, the victim's brother, who was about five years old, walked in the door and asked if his sister was there. Mr. P. said, "No." He instructed the boy to get out, and the youngster left. About half an hour later, the police came and asked to see his spider and permission to look around. Mr. P. was nervous, but he did not think they would find the crawl space. They did not in their first 15-minute search.

The next morning, after his girl friend went to work, police detectives came again, and this time found the crawl space but didn't notice the body in the dark. He felt that they would be unlikely to search the house again. Later that morning, he went back into the crawl space and took the clothes off the victim's body. He put Vaseline on her anus and inserted his penis, while he placed his finger in her vagina. He was so scared that he had only a partial erection, but he did ejaculate. He felt he had to do it because otherwise "it all would have been for nothing." He wrapped the body in the plastic, put it farther back against a slope in the crawl space, and pushed dirt over it. He hoped he would be able to go back for additional sexual activity with the corpse, but at that point was more concerned about not being detected.

The police returned the next day, used a better light to search the crawl space, and found the body. Mr. P. was down there with them. He felt terror and could not stop sweating. "I was more or less in shock." He said, "That's her" when they found the body. At that point he felt the "jig was up": there was no way that he could say he didn't kill the child.

In response to my questions, Mr. P. stated that when he grabbed the victim, it was for the purpose of carrying out his sexual fantasy. He was willing to take an "allowable minor risk" of getting caught if the risk was very small. He reports that his urge to grab her was sufficient to outweigh a small risk, but not sufficient to outweigh a substantial risk of getting caught. "Once I started, I felt I couldn't stop. All I was thinking about was carrying out my fantasy." He says he knew his actions were "wrong in the eyes of the law." The only justification he felt was that "It was in my destiny, something I needed to experience. It was for the purpose of knowing what all kinds of sex were like." When I asked for clarification of the issue of his "destiny," he indicated that his destiny was "to have sex with a dead body, not necessarily to kill." The decision to kill rather than steal a dead body was his own. In his fantasy, however, he reports there was the "killing part" because of his inability to obtain an already dead body.

Past history revealed bed-wetting until age six and cruelty to animals as a child. As an adolescent, Mr. P. cut the legs off frogs and put firecrackers in their mouths. He put a small dog on top of the refrigerator and watched it fall off.

His sexual history indicated that when he was four years old, an adult man in the neighborhood had him perform oral sex and performed oral sex on him. Between the ages of 12 and 14, he had homosexual relationships with 2 boys his age. Although Mr. P. had a regular girl friend from age 16 on, he also commonly had sex with prostitutes and masturbated frequently, usually with the fantasy that he was having anal sex with a woman. He says that he was preoccupied with sex; it was the strongest of all his feelings.

When he was 18, he became interested in more unusual sexual objects, including women's underwear and sexual devices, such as a rubber penis, a rubber vagina, and a blow-up doll, with which he had all varieties of intercourse. He performed fellatio on a dog and trained it to insert its penis into his anus. He killed another dog and then performed sex on it. He became interested sexually in the urine and feces of attractive women and finally got the idea of having sex with a dead human female body. Before the incident that led to his arrest, the fantasy of having sex with a dead body occurred to him every time he masturbated.

His necrophiliac fantasy became more clearly defined over time. It involved drowning a woman, taking her to the crawl space in his house, undressing her, and then doing "all kinds of mutilation." The fantasy included "eating her feces, drinking urine, anal sex, biting her ear," and "scratching her back with my nails." He also had thoughts of "licking eyeballs, opening the abdomen" and putting his hand in. He thought of removing the uterus and inserting it in his anus. He thought of "chewing on an ear, nose or tongue while raping the body." Fantasies included eating various body parts, such as the "breasts, vulva, nose, and tongue." He thought of eating the clitoris and labia raw, or after cooking them. While masturbating with these fantasies, he took pleasure in fantasizing about both mutilating the body and using the body parts. His fantasies were more like an "explosion of ideas" than methodical plans. He took pleasure in the idea that any thought he had at the time he would actually be able to carry out. All the fantasies were sexually exciting. The most exciting involved the anus of the dead body. He thought of putting his hand in the anus and eating the anus, either raw or cooked.

As a teen-ager Mr. P. became interested in Satan. He enjoyed reading both the Old and New Testaments, particularly the books "Revelation" and "The Prophets." He felt that he could relate passages in the Bible to current events and concluded that we were living in the "end times." He reports that while a teen-ager, at times he felt he was "the Antichrist." He believed that he would eventually rise to power and rule things in the "end times." He felt he knew things that others did not know. By referring to passages in the Bible, he thought he could understand some events going on now and in the future. He reports he was able to convince many people that they were living in the "end times" and that Armageddon would be here by the year 2000.

Mr. P. made predictions about comets, the Israeli invasion of Lebanon, and certain natural disasters before they occurred. He felt he had a gift for prediction. He used the writings of Nostradamus for his predictions.

When he was 15, Mr. P. was unsure about whether he was the prophet Elijah or the Antichrist. He looked at his eyes in a mirror and felt that they looked strange, especially when he was on drugs. He felt he should know something he had not yet been told, that he was on the verge of acquiring new knowledge. He reports that the uncertainty as to whether he was a prophet or the Antichrist persisted until the killing. He felt that if he were the prophet, he could predict things; if he were the Antichrist, he would do things to increase his power so that he would eventually be able to rule the world. He usually preferred to be the prophet, but at other times being the Antichrist was more appealing. When he was close to people he knew, he wanted to do good; when he was alone, he wanted to do bad sexual things.

I questioned Mr. P. closely to try and clarify the length and degree of certainty he felt regarding his ideas of being an Antichrist. He repeated that since he had begun to have the idea at age 15, he alternated in believing that he was either the Antichrist or the prophet Elijah. He was certain that he was going to be "something big religiously." When he engaged in perverse sexual activity, it would be as the Antichrist. When he spoke with friends about religion, it would be as a prophet. Once he was arrested after the body had been found, he immediately gave up the idea that he would be something great religiously because he thought that a criminal record would preclude success as a religious person. When I questioned the likelihood of his becoming a great prophet, in view of his work and school attainment, he replied that Hitler and Einstein had done poorly in school. When I asked whether he had prepared himself for exercising great power by taking courses in political science, he replied that he had not.

Discussion of "End Times"

Running through the story of Mr. P.'s life are three themes: extremely intense uncontrollable sexual impulses, violent fantasies, and a tenuous relationship to reality. The sexual impulses have been paraphilic, first involving nonhuman objects and body parts (female undergarments, sexual toys, dogs, urine, feces), and later focusing on anal intercourse with a dead body. As a child, he tortured animals; and when he was an adolescent, his violent impulses became intertwined with overpowering sexual impulses.

Since adolescence Mr. P. has had two opposing grandiose fantasies: either he is the Antichrist (bad, violent, and sexual) or the prophet Elijah (a powerful religious leader). His grandiosity has apparently never been of delusional intensity; rather, he has entertained the possibility that he might be either of these figures.

There is no doubt about the diagnosis of Mr. P.'s deviant sexual behavior. Like many people with paraphilic disorders, his choice of deviant sexual stimuli has changed over time. He has a history of Fetishism (nonhuman objects), and his current diagnosis is the rare disorder Necrophilia (erotic attraction to corpses), classified as a Paraphilia Not Otherwise Specified.

The diagnosis of Mr. P.'s long-term problems in perceiving, relating to, and thinking about the environment and himself is more difficult. His odd beliefs about himself and his magical thinking (that he can foretell the future) suggest Schizotypal Personality Disorder, but the case material does not describe other features of the disorder. He tortured animals as a child, but has none of the other features of either Antisocial Personality Disorder or the unofficial diagnosis of Sadistic Personality Disorder. Because his personality is so obviously pathological, we use the residual and not very descriptive diagnosis of Personality Disorder Not Otherwise Specified.

DSM-III-R Diagnosis:

Axis I: 302.90 **Paraphilia Not Otherwise Specified, Severe (Necrophilia) (p. 290)**

Axis II: 301.90 **Personality Disorder Not Otherwise Specified with Schizotypal Traits (p. 358)**

Follow-up

The defense lawyers planned to argue for an insanity defense by presenting expert psychiatric testimony that Mr. P. suffered from Schizotypal Personality Disorder, and because of that, was unable to refrain from the homicide. The prosecution expert, who prepared this case, concurred in the diagnosis of Schizotypal Personality Disorder but did not believe that this qualified for an insanity defense. At some point in his trial Mr. P. accepted a plea bargain in order to avoid the possibility of a death sentence. He is now serving a life term.

MENTAL DISORDERS IN CHILDREN AND ADOLESCENTS

MENTAL DISORDERS IN CHILDREN AND ADOLESCENTS

Saigon Pete from Grosse Point

O N THE DAY BEFORE PETE'S 16TH BIRTHDAY, he was admitted to the psychiatric unit of a general hospital in the wealthy Detroit suburb in which he lives. He had slashed his wrist with a butcher knife, severing nerves and tendons in his left hand, and drifted in and out of consciousness during the night, finally calling a friend's mother for help in the morning.

Pete is the son of a Vietnamese mother and an American serviceman. He lived with his mother in Saigon until he was two, when he came to the United States to be adopted by an American family through an agency specializing in adoption of Vietnamese children. He was apparently abused (burned and beaten) in this family, removed to a foster home for a brief period, and, at two and a half, placed with his current adoptive parents.

Although always somewhat reserved and uncommunicative with his adoptive parents, Pete initially did well in his new surroundings. He was a bright and quite beautiful little boy who was sought out by other children from the time he started school. He always got along well with his friends, but his relationship with his parents was stormy, and they describe him as the most difficult of the four children they have adopted.

By the time he was in junior high, Pete was hanging out with a group of long-haired, counterculture kids who skipped school to smoke marijuana and considered nihilism as a philosophy of life, shoplifted beer from the local supermarket, and disparaged the values of their parents and teachers. His grades dropped, and he got into trouble for shooting at squirrels with his BB gun, blowing up mailboxes with firecrackers, and fighting with the "jocks" from his school.

When Pete was 14, his parents separated; he elected to stay with his father rather than move with his mother and siblings to another state. His misdemeanors escalated. He and his friends were picked up for "borrowing" the car of a vacationing neighbor to go joy-riding. By age 15 he was truant more days than he was in school, and was using any drug he and his friends could get hold of—mostly LSD, mescaline, glue, and marijuana. His parents sent him away to military school, but he had been expelled the month before his admission to the hospital because he never attended classes.

On admission Pete is described as an immensely appealing, waiflike young man who was immediately adored by every adolescent girl on the ward. He says that he did not intend to kill himself when he slashed his wrist. When pressed, he finally tells the following story: He was dropping acid with some friends. After they left, he thought he heard a police siren. Thinking to save himself from being arrested, he slashed his wrist, and then lost consciousness. He denies being depressed, but says his life is pointless and it makes no difference whether he lives or dies.

Discussion of "Saigon Pete from Grosse Point"

Although Pete's ticket of admission to a psychiatric hospital seemed to be a suicide attempt, he later tells us that it was a clever way of avoiding being arrested. Whether or not he was also depressed and did intend to kill himself, there does not seem to be evidence of a full depressive syndrome that would justify the diagnosis of a Major Depression. Nor do we have enough information to make a positive diagnosis of Dysthymia, although his feeling that life is pointless suggests that this is likely.

In any case, there can be little doubt that Pete has a history of a chronic pattern of antisocial behavior in which the basic rights of others and age-appropriate societal norms are violated. He has stolen, been truant, broken into someone's car, been cruel to animals, and has initiated physical fights.

Pete's pattern of antisocial behavior exemplifies the Group Type of Conduct Disorder. Practically all of Pete's antisocial behavior occurs as a group activity. Although the prognosis for Pete does not look very good, generally the prognosis for the Group Type is better than for the Solitary Aggressive Type. Because Pete does not cause considerable harm to others or engage in extensive vandalism or theft, we note the severity as moderate.

Pete certainly has abused various drugs. We do not have sufficient information to know whether he was ever dependent on any of them. We do know that he has used marijuana extensively during times when he was supposed to be in school. Therefore, we shall make the minimal diagnosis of Cannabis (Marijuana) Abuse, with the realization that careful questioning would probably reveal abuse of other drugs.

DSM-III-R Diagnosis:

Axis I: 312.20 Conduct Disorder, Group Type, Moderate (p. 55)
           305.20 Cannabis Abuse (p. 169)

Don't Worry

A WORRIED PSYCHIATRIST and his wife were referred to a speech therapist for a consultation on their three-year-old son, Aaron. The psychiatrist explained that he and his wife had first noticed several months previously that at times Aaron had been "stuttering." When this happened, he would get stuck on words or initial syllables, often repeating them many times until he was finally able to finish the sentence. Sometimes he was unable to finish the sentence and just gave up. Initially these periods were rare; but in the last few weeks, they had become much more frequent and now Aaron was visibly upset when they occurred. A few days earlier he had become so frustrated that he began striking his head with his fist in an effort to get the words out.

Aaron's parents knew that transient stuttering, particularly among boys, was common. However, they now wondered if something needed to be done to make sure that the problem did not become chronic. They had consulted their pediatrician, who tried to reassure them; but the pediatrician's own slight but noticeable stuttering was disconcerting, to say the least.

The speech therapist told the parents that it was important to maintain their own composure during Aaron's episodes of distress and not to complete his sentences for him. She sympathized with their concern, but said that most likely the stuttering would go away and would not leave any permanent emotional scars.

Discussion of "Don't Worry"

Although Aaron's father was a psychiatrist, any lay person would have had little trouble making the diagnosis. Stuttering is a marked impairment in speech fluency characterized by frequent repetitions (as in Aaron's case) or prolongations of sounds or syllables. The extent of the disturbance varies from situation to situation and is more severe when there is special pressure to communicate.

DSM-III-R Diagnosis:

Axis I: 307.00 Stuttering (p. 88)

Follow-up

The speech therapist was correct. Over the next few months, the stuttering gradually resolved; and Aaron, now four, is a happy and articulate child without any trace of speech difficulty.

Roman

R ONALD, AGED 17, WAS BROUGHT by the police to a psychiatric emergency room in London. He had been found naked, covered in red paint, standing in a fixed posture in the middle of a busy road, with consequent disruption of the traffic. When asked for an explanation, he made no reply, but bit the policeman who addressed him.

Ronald was the last of four children, the rest being intelligent and well adjusted. Unlike the others, he had a difficult birth and had some episodes of cyanosis in the first 48 hours. He was somewhat delayed in motor and language development, but not enough to cause his parents to ask for advice. He was a quiet, self-contained baby and child, but presented no obvious problems. The sibship was close-knit, and Ronald fitted in as the passive member of the group: he never initiated play, but did what he was told. In retrospect, his parents remembered that he never seemed to engage in imaginative pretend play, but they did not worry about this at the time. He tended to be poorly coordinated in large movements and was somewhat slower than his siblings in learning to dress himself and perform other motor tasks. He spoke very little and then mostly in response to questioning, but his speech was grammatical and his vocabulary was adequate. His intonation was always rather odd; he used few or no gestures when talking, and tended to avoid eye contact; but none of these abnormalities seemed sufficient to warrant referral for help.

Ronald went to the same schools as his siblings. He coped with schoolwork, because of his good rote memory and reading skills, but he was poor at arithmetic, and did less well in all subjects in later school years, as understanding of more abstract ideas was demanded. He was naive and immature, which tempted some classmates to tease him; but he was protected from serious bullying by his popular and lively older siblings. He never developed any real friendships.

Ronald learned to read before starting school, probably from watching TV commercials. By the age of about seven years, he had begun to read books on the ancient Romans and the archaeological remains found in England. He had amassed a prodigious number of facts on this subject, which he could produce on questioning; but he could not enter into any discussion of theories relevant to the subject. He spent all his spare time in this pursuit, except when pulled into games with his siblings.

As a teen-ager Ronald remained a loner, with no interest in girls. He decided that he wanted to be an archaeologist, working on Roman remains. He managed to pass some school examinations at age 16 and stayed on to take the higher exams at age 18. By this time, all his siblings had left the school, and Ronald missed their protection. He had great difficulty in working for the higher exams. From being rather silent, he began to talk more and more about Roman remains, regardless of the evident boredom of his unwilling audience. He seemed sure that he was destined to become a world-famous archaeologist.

Over the course of a few weeks, the pressure of his talk increased, and it became more and more incoherent, though still focused on ancient Rome. When he heard an item on the radio concerning the possibility of museums charging entrance fees, he became excited and agitated and ran out of the house. To his parents' alarm, he did not return for some hours. Eventually, they were informed of his admission to a psychiatric hospital, following the episode in the busy road described above.

Within a few days, with medication, Ronald's bizarre behavior lessened. When he began to reply to questions, he said that after he had heard the radio announcement, he had decided to protest against the charging of entrance fees to any museum that exhibited Roman remains. He had some vague idea that this was his special mission and duty. He had rushed out of the house to find the red paint he knew was in the garden shed. After that, his recollection of events was confused. In the hospital, he returned to his former quiet, passive self, but retained his interest in Roman remains and his determination to become an archaeologist. He was still indignant about the idea of museums' charging entrance fees, but showed no desire to undertake any dramatic action in protest.

Discussion of "Roman"

Ronald was admitted to the hospital after several weeks of increasingly incoherent and pressured speech and grandiosity, which culminated in the catatonic-like, bizarre behavior that led to his being picked up by the police. These symptoms suggest a manic episode, but there is no description of a persistently elevated or irritable mood. We are reluctant to make a separate diagnosis for this episode of strange behavior, and instead see it as a complication of a chronic disorder that began in childhood.

The long history of oddities of social behavior, beginning in early childhood, suggests a Pervasive Developmental Disorder. The DSM-III-R criteria for the only specific disorder in this diagnostic class, Autistic Disorder, require two of five symptoms of impairment in reciprocal social interaction. Of the five, we find evidence only for gross impairment in ability to make peer friendships. We see no evidence of lack of awareness of the existence of feelings of others, abnormal seeking of comfort at times of distress, impaired imitation, or absence of normal social play. Therefore, we cannot make a diagnosis of Autistic Disorder. However, since Ronald does have several of the other characteristic features of Autistic Disorder, such as impairment in imaginative play and a markedly restricted range of interests, a diagnosis of Pervasive Developmental Disorder Not Otherwise Specified is appropriate.

Some readers may wonder why the diagnosis of Schizophrenia is not appropriate. His childhood difficulties could be regarded as prodromal symptoms, and his current catatonic symptoms and incoherence as fulfilling the requirements for the characteristic psychotic symptoms of the active phase of the illness. However, the diagnosis of Schizophrenia excludes cases that have a history of Autistic Disorder (we stretch this to include Pervasive Developmental Disorder Not Otherwise Specified) unless there are prominent delusions or hallucinations. Although Ronald's attempt to protest the new museum policy is inappropriate and bizarre, we would regard it as evidence of an overvalued idea, rather than a delusion.

The British psychiatrist who submitted this case noted that Ronald's disorder has been referred to as Asperger's syndrome, a condition that resembles Autistic Disorder but is milder in that gross impairment in language and communication is not present. She also noted that brief episodes of catatonic posturing and manic-like symptoms are common in adolescents with Pervasive Developmental Disorders.

In making a multiaxial assessment, we note that an event (an announcement about charging admission to museums) apparently precipitated the current episode of bizarre behavior. However, DSM-III-R instructs the clinician that the rating on Axis IV should be based on the stress that an "average person" would experience in such a circumstance. It is clear that most people would not be very stressed by the new museum policy, and that this was a stressor for Ronald only because of the special meaning that museums have for him, which is a symptom of his Axis I disorder. Therefore, we rate the severity of the stressor as 1 - None.

DSM-III-R Diagnosis:

Axis I: 299.80 Pervasive Developmental Disorder Not Otherwise Specified (p. 39)

Axis II: V71.09 No Diagnosis or Condition
Axis III: None
Axis IV: Severity: 1 - None
Axis V: Current GAF: 25
          Highest GAF past year: 45

Sniper

L EAH, AGE SEVEN, WAS REFERRED by her teacher for evaluation because of her tearfulness, irritability, and difficulty concentrating in class. Three months earlier Leah had been among the children pinned down by sniper fire on her school playground. Over a period of 15 minutes, the sniper killed one child and injured several others. After the gunfire ceased, no one moved until the police stormed the sniper's apartment and found that he had killed himself. Leah did not personally know the child who was killed, or the sniper.

According to her teacher, before the shooting, Leah was shy but vivacious, well behaved, and a good student. Within a few days after the incident, there was a noticeable change in her behavior. She withdrew from her friends. She began to bicker with other children when they spoke to her. She seemed uninterested in her schoolwork and had to be prodded to persist in required tasks. The teacher noticed that Leah jumped whenever there was static noise in the public address system and when the class shouted answers to flashcards.

Leah's parents were relieved when the school made the referral, because they were uncertain about how to help her. Leah was uncharacteristically quiet when her parents asked her about the sniping incident. At home she had become moody, irritable, argumentative, fearful, and clinging. She was apprehensive about new situations and fearful of being alone, and insisted that someone accompany her to the bathroom. Leah regularly asked to sleep with her parents. She slept restlessly and occasionally cried out in her sleep. She appeared always to be tired, complained of minor physical problems, and seemed more susceptible to minor infections. Her parents were especially worried after Leah nearly walked in front of a moving car without being aware of it. Although she seemed less interested in many of her usual games, her parents noticed that she kept engaging her siblings in nurse games, in which she was often bandaged.

When asked about the incident in the interview, Leah said that she had tried desperately to hide behind a trash can when she heard the repeated gunfire. She had been terrified of being killed, and was "shaking all over," her heart pounding and her head hurting. She vividly told of watching an older child fall to the ground, bleeding and motionless. She ran to safety when there was a pause in the shooting.

Leah described a recurring image of the injured girl lying bleeding on the playground. She said that thoughts of the incident sometimes disrupted her attention, though she would try to think about something else. Lately, she could not always remember what was being said in class. She no longer played in the area where the shooting had occurred during recess or after school. She avoided crossing the playground on her way home from school each day and avoided the sniper's house and street. She was particularly afraid at school on Fridays, the day the shooting had occurred. Although her mother and father had comforted her, she did not know how to tell them what she was feeling.

Leah continued to be afraid that someone would shoot at her again. She had nightmares about the shooting and dreams in which she, or a family member, was being shot at or pursued. She ran away from any "popping noises" at home or in the neighborhood. Although she said that she had less desire to play, when asked about new games, she reported frequently playing a game in which a nurse helped an injured person. She began to watch television news about violence, and recounted news stories that demonstrated that the world was full of danger.

Discussion of "Sniper"

Leah's experience was clearly outside the range of usual human experience. Within a few days of the trauma, she began to exhibit the characteristic symptoms of a severe Post-traumatic Stress Disorder.

Although adults sometimes have "flashback" experiences in which they actually experience the situation as if it were currently happening, children rarely reexperience trauma in this way. As is typical for her age, Leah reexperienced the trauma in the form of recurrent, intrusive images and recollections of the event and recurrent, distressing dreams about it. She also incorporated themes from the event into repetitive themes in play.

Leah attempted to avoid thoughts and feelings associated with the trauma and places that reminded her of the event. This formerly vivacious little girl exhibited numbing of general responsiveness. She became apathetic and uninterested in her schoolwork and detached from her former friends. She displayed persistent symptoms of increased arousal, including exaggerated startle reaction (to loud noises), irritability, difficulty concentrating, and sleep disturbance.

In making a multiaxial assessment, we rate the severity of the stress of witnessing a murder and being in danger of being killed as Extreme. Because of the impairment in her social relationships and schoolwork, we assign a current GAF of 45.

DSM-III-R Diagnosis:

Axis I: 309.89 Post-traumatic Stress Disorder (p. 250)
Axis II: V71.09 No Diagnosis or Condition
Axis III: None
Axis IV: Psychosocial stressors: witnessing a killing and in danger
           of being killed
           Severity: 5 - Extreme (acute event)
Axis V: Current GAF: 45
           Highest GAF past year: 85

Shoelaces

G EORGE IS A 16-YEAR-OLD who was admitted to the hospital from a juvenile detention center following a serious suicide attempt. He had, in some way, wrapped shoelaces and tape around his neck, causing respiratory impairment. When found, he was cyanotic and semiconscious. He had been admitted to the detention center earlier that day; it had been noted there that he was quite withdrawn.

On admission, George was reluctant to speak, except to say that he would kill himself, and nobody could stop him. He did, however, admit to a two-week history of depressed mood, difficulty sleeping, decreased appetite, decreased interest, guilt feelings, and suicidal ideation.

According to his parents, George had had no emotional difficulties until, at age 13, he became involved in drugs, primarily LSD, marijuana, and nonopioid sedatives. His grades dropped drastically, he ran away from home on several occasions after arguments with his parents, and he made a suicide gesture by overdosing on aspirin. A year later, following an argument with the principal, he was expelled from school. Unable to control his behavior, his parents had him evaluated in a mental health clinic, and a recommendation was made for placement in a group home. He apparently did well in the group home, and his relationship with his parents improved immensely with family counseling. He was quite responsible in holding a job and attending school and was involved in no illegal activities, including use of drugs.

Six months before admission to the hospital, however, he again became involved in drugs and, over a course of two weeks, engaged in ten breaking-and-enterings, all of which he did alone. He remembers being depressed at this time, but cannot recall whether the mood change was before or after reinvolvement with drugs. He was then sent to the juvenile detention center, where he did so well that he had been discharged to his parents' care three weeks previously. One day after returning home, he impulsively left with his buddies in a stolen car for a trip to Texas. His depression began shortly thereafter; and, according to him, his guilt about what he had done to his parents led to his suicide attempt.

Discussion of "Shoelaces"

The serious suicide attempt that occasioned admission to the hospital is clearly a symptom of a Major Depressive Episode. There is a two-week history of depressed mood with many of the characteristic symptoms of the depressive syndrome. Although there is mention of the patient's being depressed six months previously, it is not clear whether at that time he had the full depressive syndrome. There is also a reference to his having made a suicide gesture by overdosing on aspirin at age 13, but it is unclear whether that represented a Major Depressive Episode. Thus, the first-listed diagnosis would be Major Depression, Single Episode, Severe, without Psychotic Features.

Since age 13, the patient has displayed a repeated and persistent pattern of conduct in which the basic rights of others or major age-appropriate societal norms or rules have been violated. This has included behavior leading to expulsion from school, purchasing illegal drugs, and running away from home, culminating in the ten breaking-and-enterings and the stealing of a car. This pattern of antisocial behavior justifies the diagnosis of a Conduct Disorder. Since some of his antisocial behavior is done alone (the spree of breaking and entering) and some of it is done with peers (running away from home in a stolen car with his buddies) the Conduct Disorder cannot be adequately subtyped as either Group Type or Solitary Aggressive Type. Therefore, it is diagnosed as Undifferentiated Type.

There have been many episodes of maladaptive use of substances, including LSD, marijuana, and sedatives. With the little information available, it is not possible to determine if the criteria for Psychoactive Substance Dependence were ever met; therefore, the diagnosis of Psychoactive Substance Abuse is indicated. DSM-III had a category, Mixed Substance Abuse, that would have been appropriate for this case. DSM-III-R does not have this category, so it is necessary to note each specific drug of abuse.

DSM-III-R Diagnosis:

Axis I: 296.23 Major Depression, Single Episode, Severe, without Psychotic Features (p. 229)
            312.90 Conduct Disorder, Undifferentiated Type, Severe (p. 55)
            305.20 Cannabis Abuse (p. 176)
            305.30 Hallucinogen Abuse (p. 179)
            305.40 Sedative Abuse (p. 184)

Chubby

MARY IS A GAUNT 15-YEAR-OLD high-school student evaluated at the insistence of her parents, who are concerned about her weight loss. She is 5′ 3″, and obtained her greatest weight of 100 pounds a year ago. Shortly thereafter, she decided to lose weight to be more attractive. She felt chubby and thought she would be more appealing if she were thinner. She first eliminated all carbohydrate-rich foods and gradually increased her dieting until she was eating only a few vegetables a day. She also started a vigorous exercise program. Within six months she was down to 80 pounds. She then became preoccupied with food and started to collect recipes from magazines and prepare gourmet meals for her family, never eating the food that she prepared herself. She had difficulty sleeping and was irritable and depressed, having several crying spells each day. Her menses started last year, but she has had no periods in the last four months.

Mary has always obtained high grades in school and has spent a great deal of time studying. She has never been active socially and has never dated. She is conscientious and a perfectionist in everything she undertakes. She has never been away from home as long as a week. Her father is a business manager. Her mother is a housewife who, for the past two years, has had a problem with hypoglycemia and has been on a low-carbohydrate diet.

During the interview Mary said she felt fat even though she weighed only 80 pounds, and described a fear of losing control and eating so much food that she would become obese. She did not feel she was ill and thought hospitalization unnecessary.

Discussion of "Chubby"

This patient demonstrates the characteristic clinical features of Anorexia Nervosa: the refusal to maintain body weight over a minimal normal weight for age and height (weighing only 80 pounds on a 5′ 3″ frame); intense fear of gaining weight or becoming fat, even though underweight; disturbance in the way in which one's body weight, size, or shape is experienced (feeling fat when actually gaunt); and (in females) absence of at least three consecutive menstrual cycles when otherwise expected to occur.

This case also demonstrates such frequently associated features as vigorous exercise in order to lose weight, preoccupation with the preparation of food, and obsessive compulsive personality traits, such as perfectionism.

Although there are some features of the depressive syndrome, such as crying spells, difficulty sleeping, and depressed and irritable mood, the criteria for the full major depressive syndrome are not met. There is no evidence of binge eating or purging, behavior commonly associated with Anorexia Nervosa. If there were, the additional diagnosis of Bulimia Nervosa might be justified.

DSM-III-R Diagnosis:

Axis I: 307.10 Anorexia Nervosa (p. 67)

Ed Hates School

ED, NINE AND A HALF YEARS OLD, is failing in school, as evidenced by extensive school reports from his teacher and from a school psychologist. The teacher reports that he is failing in arithmetic, spelling, and science, and that he is doing average work in reading, art, history, and sports. She states that he does not work well on his own, but that he tries.

The psychologist reports that Ed has been tested frequently over the past several years with the Wechsler Intelligence Scale for Children, and was given the Stanford Achievement Test in the third grade (intelligence score of 95, reading achievement score of grade level 3.0, and math achievement score of grade level 1.0); the Wide-Range Achievement Test in the fourth grade (grade-level scores of 4.4 for reading, 3.9 for spelling, and 2.8 for arithmetic); and, two months ago, in the fifth grade, the Peabody Individual Achievement Test (with age-level scores of 10 years, 3 months, for reading; 8 years, 6 months, for math; and 9 years, 2 months, for spelling). There is no evidence of any hearing problem or of any neurologic disorder that could account for his difficulties.

Examination revealed a quiet but personable boy who expressed concern about his schoolwork and "just really hates to go to school."

Discussion of "Ed Hates School"

Why is Ed failing in school? He has normal intelligence, no physical problems that could interfere with his abilities, adequate motivation, and there is no evidence that his schooling is inadequate.

The extensive achievement testing consistently reveals that he has the most difficulty with arithmetic, and it is only in this one area that both his school performance and test results indicate a level of achievement significantly below expected levels. This suggests a diagnosis of Developmental Arithmetic Disorder.

Although the teacher reports that the boy is failing in spelling and science as well, an additional diagnosis of Specific Developmental Disorder Not Otherwise Specified is not appropriate since achievement tests indicate that the boy is not performing significantly below the expected level in spelling.

DSM-III-R Diagnosis:

Axis I: V71.09 No Diagnosis or Condition
Axis II: 315.10 Developmental Arithmetic Disorder (p. 42)

Compulsions

A LAN, A TEN-YEAR-OLD BOY, is brought for a consultation by his mother because of "severe compulsions." The mother reports that the child at various times has to run and clear his throat, touch the doorknob twice before entering any door, tilt his head from side to side, rapidly blink his eyes, and touch the ground with his hands suddenly by flexing his whole body. These "compulsions" began two years ago. The first was the eye-blinking, and then the others followed, with a waxing and waning course. The movements occur more frequently when the patient is anxious or under stress. The last symptom to appear was the repetitive touching of the doorknobs. The consultation was scheduled after the child began to make the middle finger sign while saying "fuck."

When examined, Alan reported that he did not know most of the time when the movements were going to occur except for the touching of doorknobs. Upon questioning, he said that before he felt he had to touch a doorknob, he got the thought of doing it and tried to push it out of his head, but he couldn't because it kept coming back until he touched the doorknob several times; then he felt better. When asked what would happen if someone did not let him touch the doorknob, he said he would just get mad, and that his father had tried to stop him and he had had a temper tantrum.

During the interview the child grunted, cleared his throat, turned his head, and rapidly blinked his eyes several times. At other times he tried to make it appear as if he had voluntarily been trying to perform these movements.

Past history and physical and neurologic examination were totally unremarkable except for the abnormal movements and sounds. The mother reported that her youngest uncle had had similar symptoms when he was an adolescent, but she could not elaborate any further. She stated that she and her husband had always been "very compulsive," by which she meant only that they were quite well organized and stuck to routines.

Discussion of "Compulsions"

The mother describes Alan's difficulties as "compulsions," and Alan's description of what goes on in his mind before he touches doorknobs seems to describe a compulsion. He first gets the senseless thought of touching the doorknob. He tries to resist the thought, but is unable to do so; in response to this obsession, he then touches the doorknob twice. He acknowledges that if he resisted the compulsion to touch doorknobs, he would be extremely uncomfortable. However, this obsession and compulsion are only a symptom, and are not persistent and disruptive enough to justify the diagnosis of Obsessive Compulsive Disorder.

Alan has both complex motor tics (e.g., tilting his head from side to side, touching the doorknob twice, blinking his eyes and flexing his whole body) and verbal tics (clearing throat, and saying "fuck"). The combination of motor and verbal tics with a duration of over one year establishes the diagnosis of Tourette's Disorder. Obsessions and compulsions are often seen, as in this case, in people who have Tourette's Disorder.

DSM-III-R Diagnosis:

Axis I: 307.23 Tourette's Disorder (p. 80)

The Enigma

A PSYCHIATRIST SPECIALIZING in patients with Mental Retardation received a call from a pediatric colleague referring 17-year-old Libby. She was described as "cured from depression" and needing only follow-up medication.

Libby's arrival created a commotion in the waiting room. She was a small, slender person, markedly agitated and restless, who screamed unintelligibly in a high-pitched voice, while her anxious parents tried to calm her. She looked far from being cured.

The parents provided the following history. When Libby was under one year of age, she was diagnosed as having severe Mental Retardation. Extensive diagnostic evaluations failed to determine the etiology of the retardation. She has always been physically healthy. Libby is an only child, was reared at home, and attended special classes in public schools. She was cheerful, friendly, and affectionate. She was nonverbal, but managed to communicate through gestures and vocalizations. She learned some household tasks and liked to help her mother around the house.

Libby had never been separated from her parents until six months ago, when the parents went to Europe for a week and left Libby with a housekeeper. On their return, they found her agitated, unresponsive to their requests, and uninterested in her usual activities. She cried frequently, slept poorly, ate little, and spent most of the time roaming around the house aimlessly. The parents felt guilty about having gone away and tried to make amends by spending all their time with Libby and trying to do things with her that would make her happy.

Libby's parents wondered if she might be physically ill, but an examination and tests by her pediatrician were negative. The pediatrician gave her an antianxiety drug, diazepam, 2 mg three times a day, but it had no effect. The school psychologist thought that Libby's behavior was an attention-getting device, reinforced by her parents' indulgence; suggested setting firm limits; and referred them to a child guidance clinic, where they were informed by the child psychiatrist that Libby was punishing them for abandoning her when they went on their vacation. He suggested giving Libby unlimited attention and affection.

When this regimen only made matters worse, another psychiatrist was consulted. He thought that Libby might be depressed and started her on an antidepressant, imipramine. Libby did not improve. In desperation, the parents called every psychiatric hospital in the area, trying to have Libby admitted, but none were willing to take her. As one admitting social worker explained, psychiatric hospitals generally have no experience treating retarded, nonverbal patients. Libby was finally hospitalized on a pediatric ward, where an extensive medical evaluation failed to disclose the cause of her condition.

Libby's pediatrician decided to treat her in the hospital for a "psychotic depression." He therefore increased the imipramine to 100 mg a day and added an antipsychotic drug, thioridazine, 100 mg a day. Libby started to eat better, slept throughout the night, and was somewhat less agitated. She was discharged, but soon suffered a relapse. She again became irritable and agitated, slept poorly, and experienced a decrease in appetite.

During the diagnostic interview with the specialist, Libby was extremely agitated. She screamed often, in a high-pitched voice, would not sit in one place, and tugged at her mother's arm, indicating she wanted to go home.

Discussion of "The Enigma"

This case illustrates the difficulty in diagnosing people with severe Mental Retardation who are unable to describe their subjective experiences. Libby seems depressed and agitated, but cannot tell us about a persistent depressed mood. It seems reasonable to make a provisional diagnosis of Major Depression, based on her crying, being uninterested, and having decreased appetite, insomnia, and psychomotor agitation, even though she has not consistently responded to antidepressant medication. Her pediatrician diagnosed a "psychotic depression," but we see no evidence of psychotic symptoms and assume that the antipsychotic medication was intended primarily to control her psychomotor agitation.

DSM-III-R Diagnosis:

Axis I: 296.23 Major Depression, Single Episode, Severe (p. 229)
Axis II: 318.10 Severe Mental Retardation (p. 31)

Follow-up

The dosage of imipramine was gradually decreased and eventually discontinued. For the next three months, Libby's mood and behavior varied. For several weeks she was calmer, and then she would again start to scream and become extremely agitated, aggressive, and very distractible.

Detailed family history disclosed that a maternal aunt suffered from "depression" and responded well to maintenance treatment with a mood stabilizer, lithium. Therefore, Libby was started on lithium, 300 mg daily, which was increased to 600 mg daily, until her serum level was between 0.5 and 0.7 meq/l. She improved steadily and gradually, and within a few months was her "old self" again. Her improvement continued even after the thioridazine was gradually (over several months) discontinued.

The specialist who treated this patient noted the following, with which we concur:

Patients like Libby are often dismissed as cases of nonspecific behavior disorders peculiar to retarded persons, or as exhibiting "attention-getting behaviors" due to parental overprotection as a compensation for their guilt feelings. In fact, Libby's case was seen by some as an example of such a mechanism.

Libby's clinical presentation was in marked contrast to her usual condition. It was dominated by irritable mood, agitation, distractibility, regression in adaptive skills, eating and sleep disturbance, all of which are included in the diagnostic criteria for a Manic Episode. Her screaming could be seen as an equivalent of pressured speech. Symptoms such as grandiosity, flight of ideas, and excessive involvement in pleasurable activity could not, of course, be described by a severely retarded and nonverbal person. The clinical presentation was cyclic, and the periods of crying, decrease in activities, and loss of weight, suggest a Major Depressive Episode. The family history was positive for a lithium-responding "depression." It is possible that Libby was in a Major Depressive Episode when she was put on imipramine, and she improved at first, but then developed a Manic Episode, possibly triggered by the medication. Her good response to lithium suggests that the most likely diagnosis is Bipolar Disorder.

Omnivorous George

G EORGE, A THIN, PALE five-year-old, was admitted to the hospital for a nutritional anemia that seemed to be due to his ingestion of paint, plaster, dirt, wood, and paste. He had had numerous hospitalizations under similar circumstances, beginning at 19 months of age, when he had ingested lighter fluid.

George's parents subsisted on welfare, and were described as immature and dependent. He was the product of an unplanned but normal pregnancy. His mother began eating dirt when she was pregnant, at 16 years of age. His father periodically abused drugs and alcohol.

Discussion of "Omnivorous George"

Eating non-nutritive substances, such as paint, plaster, string, hair, or cloth, may be seen in Autistic Disorder, Schizophrenia, or the neurologic disorder Klein-Levin syndrome. When not symptomatic of such a disorder, the diagnosis of Pica is made. As in this case, it is commonly associated with a similar history in the mother and low socioeconomic status.

DSM-III-R Diagnosis:

Axis I: 307.52 Pica (p. 69)

Miserable Molly

T EN-MONTH-OLD MOLLY was brought by her mother, at the suggestion of her pediatrician, for a consultation with a specialist in infant development. Her mother was most concerned because "Molly is not responding to me. She often won't look at me. She looks in the opposite direction. She won't smile, won't play, and bangs her hand on the table, looking angry. She throws toys on the floor. When I talk to her, she closes her eyes." Her mother also reported that her little girl was waking up three or four times each night and refusing to go back to sleep unless she stayed with her in the room, either holding her or stroking her back.

The current problems seemed to begin two months earlier when Molly's mother, a busy attorney, went back to work full time. The father, also an attorney, was quite angry at her for returning to work. He had wanted her to give up her career and stay at home. For the first month after she returned to work, Molly was cared for by a baby-sitter, who eventually was fired after a neighbor reported that the baby-sitter was frequently drunk and left Molly in her crib, with a bottle of formula, ignoring her cries. Although Molly's mother had suspected that the baby-sitter was far from ideal, she did not realize how bad she was until she heard about it from the neighbor. For the past month, Molly's care has been arranged on a day-to-day basis, and she has had six different baby-sitters.

During the last two months, because of sleepless nights and feeling overwhelmingly guilty about Molly's distress, yet at the same time feeling compelled to return to work or else "lose my status in my firm," Molly's mother has been "a nervous wreck." Now she blames herself for all of Molly's difficulties, saying, "I've done a terrible thing. Now, not only my husband doesn't love me but Molly doesn't love me either."

Molly weighed eight pounds at birth and was in good health. The pregnancy was unremarkable. The pediatrician's report revealed that Molly had slightly increased motor tone bilaterally, with no asymmetries, and tended to be overly sensitive to touch. For example, her mother reported that when she tried to bathe Molly, the child would often scream, and that she had to hold her with soft cotton blankets in order for her to feel comfortable. Molly was also very sensitive to loud noises, turning red, and becoming rigid. She often cried if lights were too bright.

Molly had displayed social responsiveness by the fourth month, but only if her parents worked very hard and found just the right rhythm of sound and "funny faces." By six months she was able to reach for objects, but her parents reported that if they handed her something, she would often try to knock it out of their hands rather than grab it.

Molly has always been a fussy eater, but nonetheless is gaining adequate weight, and is in the 80th percentile for size and weight. Her pediatrician says that her overall physical health is good and that, in terms of motor milestones, she is doing fine.

During the evaluation, the impression of Molly as physically healthy was confirmed. Her gross and fine motor functioning were age-appropriate. Observation of parent-infant interaction revealed an infant who held her body stiffly, looked away from her parents' eyes, and reacted to their vocalization by arching her back. When offered interesting objects, she would usually grab another object or knock the offered object away. Her facial expression looked angry and tense. Her mother appeared depressed, and her interaction with Molly had a mechanical quality. Molly's father was impatient and abrupt with her.

Discussion of "Miserable Molly"

Molly's mother's description of the problem, that Molly "is not responding to me," suggests the possibility of Autistic Disorder. However, there is no description of the stereotyped body movements or marked distress over trivial changes in the environment that one would expect to see in a child with Autistic Disorder, even at ten months.

Molly had a number of worrisome characteristics at birth, such as sensitivity to touch, sound, and bright lights, and slightly increased motor tone, and was described as extremely fussy and difficult to console. A marked change in her behavior seemed to coincide with her mother's return to work and her receiving grossly inadequate care from her baby-sitter. It was at this time that her failure to respond to social interaction became obvious—lack of reciprocal play, failure to respond to her mother's smiles, and turning away from her mother.

In the absence of Mental Retardation or a Pervasive Developmental Disorder, such as Autistic Disorder, the presumption is that the change in Molly's behavior is the result of the grossly pathogenic care she was given. Thus, we diagnose Reactive Attachment Disorder of Infancy or Early Childhood.

DSM-III-R Diagnosis:

Axis I: 313.89 Reactive Attachment Disorder of Infancy or Early Childhood (p. 93)

Follow-up

Treatment included helping Molly's mother deal with her depression and anxiety and finding a pattern of work and home life that was more comfortable for her. She was able to arrange a half-time position at work for the following year, which was consistent with what she viewed as her own interest. This also enabled her to take more time in finding appropriate help to care for Molly. She was able to find a warm and nurturing person to come in during the day and help her with Molly and to be there during the times she was working.

The mother was also helped to understand Molly's sensitivity to touch and loud noises as a variation in her maturation, one that would be helped by special patterns of handling and would improve with time. The mother ceased interpreting Molly's reactions as a rejection of her and tried different, gentle ways of "wooing" her. As the relationship with Molly improved, the infant became considerably more engaging, initiating closeness with her mother and responding to her mother's overtures for closeness. By 12 months of age, Molly was a competent toddler who was just beginning to walk. She could frequently be seen toddling up to her mother or father, giving them a big hug and kiss, and often taking them by the hand to point to toys she wanted to play with. She could even bang on the refrigerator door when she was hungry. Her sleeping improved, so that she would wake up only once or twice a night, and then could be reassured by her mother's presence for a few minutes and return to sleep. Molly was able to be assertive without being negative, indicating her wants and desires with intentional behaviors and vocalizations.

This response to intervention confirms the diagnosis of Reactive Attachment Disorder of Infancy or Early Childhood.

Broken Home

D ON, 3 YEARS AND 7 MONTHS OLD, has a complicated early medical history, including having been born 11 weeks prematurely with hyaline membrane disease and later having undergone bilateral hernia repairs. He began sitting up at 6 months, crawling at 10 months, walking at 13 months, and saying words at 12 months. At three years his parents noted that his speech seemed far less well developed than that of his many playmates, although most of them were younger than he. Don did not attend nursery school, and had been subjected to a number of moves because of parental problems and divorce.

During examination, Don was slow to warm up. He was extremely difficult to understand, and had to augment most of his utterances with gestures to make himself understood. Most of his sentences consisted of single words that were mispronounced—for example, "gun" was "dub," "scissors" was "duhduh," and "fish" was "pet." The boy could follow commands such as "Get the red book and bring it to the table"; could point out body parts and objects in the room; and could produce drawings that seemed quite sophisticated for his age. Scores on several standardized tests of language development, such as the Carrow Elicited Language Inventory (CELI) and the Illinois Test of Psycholinguistic Abilities (ITPA), were significantly lower than expected, as was the verbal IQ from the Stanford-Binet Intelligence Scale. In contrast, Don's performance IQ was only slightly below average.

Discussion of "Broken Home"

Normal developmental milestones and near-average performance IQ rule out Mental Retardation as an explanation for Don's speech difficulties. Similarly, Pervasive Developmental Disorder is ruled out by the lack of impairment in developing reciprocal social relationships. Significantly, Don's speech difficulties are not in articulating certain speech sounds, but rather in finding the proper words to express himself. This rules out Developmental Articulation Disorder. His substantially lower than expected scores on several standardized measures of expressive language (compared with his performance IQ) and the significant impairment caused by this disability (others have great difficulty understanding him) suggest a Developmental Language Disorder. The fact that he apparently has no difficulty understanding language (as evidenced by his ability to follow verbal instructions) indicates an Expressive Type of Developmental Language Disorder. (The two subtypes, Expressive and Receptive, have the same code.)

DSM-III-R Diagnosis:

Axis I: V71.09 No Diagnosis or Condition
Axis II: 315.31 Developmental Expressive Language Disorder
           (p. 47)

A Perfect Checklist

B ILLY, A SEVEN-YEAR-OLD black child, was brought to a mental health clinic by his mother because "he is unhappy and always complaining about feeling sick." He lives with his parents, his younger brother, and his grandmother. His mother describes Billy as a child who has never been very happy and never wanted to play with other children. From the time he started nursery school, he has complained about stomachaches, headaches, and various other physical problems. They are most intense in the morning when he is getting ready to go to school. In the last few months, his somatic complaints have escalated, prompting a complete medical examination, including a neurologic examination and electroencephalogram, all of which were normal.

Billy did well in first grade, but in second grade he is now having difficulty completing his work. He takes a lot of time to do his assignments and frequently feels he has to do them over again so that they will be "perfect." Because of Billy's frequent somatic complaints, it is hard to get him off to school in the morning. If he is allowed to stay home, he worries that he is falling behind in his schoolwork. When he does go to school, he often is unable to do the work, which makes him feel hopeless about his situation. In order to get through the day, he carries a note that he has instructed his mother to write for him: "You are not getting out of school early today. If you feel that you have to do your papers over and over again, please just do the best you can. Do not think about the time of day and it will go quickly."

His worries have expanded beyond school, and frequently he is clinging and demanding of his parents. He is fearful that if his parents come home late or leave and go somewhere without him that something may happen to them. For the past two weeks he has insisted that his little brother sleep with him because he is afraid to go to sleep at night alone.

Although Billy's mother acknowledges that he has never been really happy, in the last six months, she feels, he has become much more depressed. He frequently lies around the house, saying that he is too tired to do anything. He has no interest or enjoyment in playing. His appetite has diminished. He has trouble falling asleep at night and often wakes up in the middle of the night or early in the morning. Three weeks ago, he talked, for the first time, about wanting to die, and said that maybe he would shoot himself.

Billy's mother became pregnant two months after she was married. She did not feel ready for a child. She was hypertensive during the pregnancy and was emotionally upset. Delivery was complicated because of increasing hypertension. At the time of delivery, Billy reportedly went into cardiac arrest. During the first week of his life, he developed projectile vomiting, which persisted for two weeks. He had nocturnal enuresis until a year ago.

During the assessment, Billy allowed his mother to go to another room to be interviewed; but after 20 minutes, he became very upset, began crying, and insisted on being taken to her. He then was willing to sit outside the room where his mother was, as long as the door was open and he could see her.

Billy was unable to finish a symptom checklist (designed for children his age) given at the time of the evaluation. He felt that he had to have a perfect checklist and requested that he be allowed to take the papers home so that he could finish them. He became very worried about not being able to complete the list; and although he was told that it was not necessary for him to take the papers home, he insisted upon doing so.

Discussion of "A Perfect Checklist"

This case was submitted as an example of Dysthymia in a child with a recent superimposed Major Depression. There is little doubt about the latter, since Billy is clearly depressed, has lost interest and enjoyment in playing, and has trouble sleeping, poor appetite, low energy, and suicidal thoughts. In cases such as this, in which there has been a long history of depressed mood before the onset of a full depressive syndrome, the question is whether to regard the chronically depressed mood as a prodrome of the Major Depression, or to make another diagnosis of Dysthymia. The DSM-III-R rule is that in a child, a one-year period of sustained depressed mood accompanied by at least two symptoms of the depressive syndrome justifies an additional diagnosis of Dysthymia. In Billy's case, however, we do not have enough information about specific symptoms before the recent episode of Major Depression to justify the diagnosis of Dysthymia.

Billy has many other symptoms, including perfectionism, somatic complaints, and anxiety about being separated from his mother. The perfectionism raises the question of Obsessive Compulsive Personality Disorder or Obsessive Compulsive Disorder. He is too young to consider a personality disorder diagnosis and there is no evidence of frank obsessions or compulsions.

The diagnosis of Separation Anxiety Disorder requires at least three of eight symptoms of excessive anxiety concerning separation from those to whom the child is attached. We count at least four: unrealistic worry about possible harm befalling major attachment figures, reluctance to go to school, avoidance of being alone (including clinging), and complaints of physical symptoms on school days.

The many somatic complaints suggest Undifferentiated Somatoform Disorder, but a more parsimonious approach is to regard these symptoms as a manifestation of the Separation Anxiety Disorder.

DSM-III-R Diagnosis:

Axis I: **296.22 Major Depression, Single Episode, Moderate (p. 229)**
309.21 Separation Anxiety Disorder, Mild (p. 60)

Echo

RICHARD, AGED THREE AND A HALF, a firstborn child, was referred at the request of his parents because of his uneven development and abnormal behavior. Delivery had been difficult, and he had needed oxygen at birth. His physical appearance, motor development, and self-help skills were all age-appropriate; but his parents had been uneasy about him from the first few months of life because of his lack of response to social contact and the usual baby games. Comparison with their second child, who, unlike Richard, enjoyed social communication from early infancy, confirmed their fears.

Richard appeared to be self-sufficient and aloof from others. He did not greet his mother in the mornings, or his father when he returned from work, though, if left with a baby-sitter, he tended to scream much of the time. He had no interest in other children and ignored his younger brother. His babbling had no conversational intonation. At three years he could understand simple practical instructions. His speech consisted of echoing some words and phrases he had heard in the past, with the original speaker's accent and intonation; he could use one or two such phrases to indicate his simple needs. For example, if he said, "Do you want a drink?" he meant he was thirsty. He did not communicate by facial expression or use gesture or mime, except for pulling someone along and placing his or her hand on an object he wanted.

He was fascinated by bright lights and spinning objects, and would stare at them while laughing, flapping his hands, and dancing on tiptoe. He also displayed the same movements while listening to music, which he had liked from infancy. He was intensely attached to a miniature car, which he held in his hand, day and night; but he never played imaginatively with this or any other toy. He could assemble jigsaw puzzles rapidly (with one hand because of the car held in the other), whether the picture side was exposed or hidden. From age two he had collected kitchen utensils and arranged them in repetitive patterns all over the floors of the house. These pursuits, together with occasional periods of aimless running around, constituted his whole repertoire of spontaneous activities.

The major management problem was Richard's intense resistance to any attempt to change or extend his interests. Removing his toy car, disturbing his puzzles or patterns, even retrieving, for example, an egg whisk or a spoon for its legitimate use in cooking, or trying to make him look at a picture book precipitated temper tantrums that could last an hour or more, with screaming, kicking, and the biting of himself or others. These tantrums could be cut short by restoring the *status quo*. Otherwise, playing his favorite music or a long car ride were sometimes effective.

His parents had wondered if Richard might be deaf, but his love of music, his accurate echoing, and his sensitivity to some very soft sounds, such as those made by unwrapping a chocolate in the next room, convinced them that this was not the cause of his abnormal behavior. Psychological testing gave him a mental age of 3 years in non-language-dependent skills (fitting and assembly tasks), but only 18 months in language comprehension.

Discussion of "Echo"

Richard demonstrates marked impairment in reciprocal social interaction and in verbal and nonverbal communication, and a markedly restricted repertoire of activities, all beginning in the first few months of life. He doesn't seem interested in other children, and never wanted to play "baby games" with his parents. His speech is limited and peculiar (echoing words and phrases of others), and his play is abnormal in that he never engages in imaginative play. His interests are markedly restricted and stereotyped (doing puzzles and making patterns with kitchen utensils), and he becomes wildly upset if anyone interferes with his routines. These behaviors, beginning in infancy (much more rarely in childhood), are the characteristic signs of Autistic Disorder.

DSM-III-R Diagnosis:

Axis I: 299.00 Autistic Disorder (p. 38)

Zombie

A N 11-YEAR-OLD GIRL asked her mother to take her to a psychiatrist because she feared she might be "going crazy." Several times during the last two months she has awakened confused about where she is until she realizes she is on the living-room couch or in her little sister's bed, even though she went to bed in her own room. When she recently woke up in her older brother's bedroom, she became very concerned and felt quite guilty about it. Her younger sister says that she has seen the patient walking during the night, looking like a "zombie," that she didn't answer when she called her, and that the patient has done that several times, but usually goes back to her bed. The patient fears she may have "amnesia" because she has no memory of anything happening during the night.

There is no history of seizures or of similar episodes during the day. An electroencephalogram (EEG) and physical examination are normal. The patient's mental status is unremarkable except for some anxiety about her symptom and the usual early-adolescent concerns. School and family functioning are excellent.

Discussion of "Zombie"

This girl is not "going crazy," but rather is experiencing the characteristic features of Sleepwalking Disorder: episodes of arising from bed during sleep and walking about, appearing unresponsive during the episodes, experiencing amnesia for the episode upon awakening, and exhibiting no evidence of impairment in consciousness several minutes after awakening. Psychomotor epileptic seizures are ruled out by the normal EEG and the absence of any seizurelike behavior during the waking state.

Although the process of dissociation is involved in Sleepwalking Disorder, since the disturbance begins during sleep, it is classified as a Sleep Disorder rather than as a Dissociative Disorder.

DSM-III-R Diagnosis:

Axis I: 307.46 Sleepwalking Disorder (p. 313)
Axis II: V71.09 No diagnosis on Axis II
Axis III: None
Axis IV: Severity: 1 - None
Axis V: Current GAF: 65
            Highest GAF past year: 90

Slow Learner

JANET, 13 YEARS OLD, has a long history of school problems. She failed first grade, supposedly because her teacher was "mean," and was removed from a special classroom after she kept getting into fights with the other children. Currently in a normal sixth-grade classroom, she is failing reading, barely passing English, arithmetic, and spelling, but doing satisfactory work in art and sports. Her teacher describes Janet as a "slow learner with a poor memory" and states that she doesn't learn in a group setting and requires a great deal of individual attention.

Janet's medical history is unremarkable except for a tonsillectomy at age five and an early history of chronic otitis. She sat up at 6 months, walked at 12 months, and began talking at 18 months. Examination revealed an open and friendly girl who was very touchy about her academic problems. She stated that she was "bossed around" at school, but had good friends in the neighborhood. Intelligence testing revealed a full-scale intelligence quotient of 97; and wide-range achievement testing produced grade-level scores of 4.8 for reading, 5.3 for spelling, and 6.3 for arithmetic.

Discussion of "Slow Learner"

The differential diagnosis of academic problems includes consideration of poor schooling, Mental Retardation, Attention-deficit Hyperactivity Disorder, Oppositional Defiant Disorder, Conduct Disorder, and Specific Developmental Disorders. In this case, because other children in her class are apparently passing when she is not, it is reasonable to rule out inadequate schooling as an explanation for Janet's academic difficulties. Her average intelligence rules out a diagnosis of Mental Retardation. Although there is a mention of "fights with other children" and inability to "learn in a group setting," there is certainly no description of other behaviors that would justify a diagnosis of either Attention-deficit Hyperactivity Disorder, Oppositional Defiant Disorder, or Conduct Disorder.

There is positive evidence suggesting a Specific Developmental Disorder: she not only seems to have particular difficulty with reading in school but also performs significantly below her expected level on a reading achievement test. Her reading score of 4.8 is more than one year below her expected reading level. Given the diagnosis of Developmental Reading Disorder, it is reasonable to regard the fighting and difficulty learning in a group as associated features of the Specific Developmental Disorder.

There is now considerable research evidence suggesting that early, chronic otitis may be associated with later learning or language difficulties.

DSM-III-R Diagnosis:

Axis I: V71.09 No Diagnosis or Condition
Axis II: 315.00 Developmental Reading Disorder (p. 44)

Brrr

K EVIN IS AN ATTRACTIVE six-year-old boy whose mother brought him to the emergency room because she was frightened that she could not prevent the child from setting fires, which he had done several times in the last year and a half. Although he had so far managed to put out all the fires he set himself, his mother was afraid that he would set the house afire while she and his sister were asleep. She complained that he was sneaky about setting the fires, making it impossible for her to control him or to know how many fires he had actually set.

Kevin says that he has set fires because a "man in my head tells me to do so." This "man" stays in his room when he is awake and "goes away" when he is asleep. The man makes a noise ("brrr"), which Kevin interprets as a command to "set fires." He is afraid to talk to anyone about the man or not to obey his commands, "because he might beat me up." His mother apparently does not take the voice seriously, stating that he has offered a variety of different reasons for setting fires, depending on to whom he was talking. Both agree that he sets fires in retaliation against his mother when he is angry with her.

Kevin has been fascinated with setting fires for the last two years. His mother remembers that he and a friend set the first fire by burning holes in the plastic sheets on his and his sister's beds. His mother found out about the incident later and reacted by hitting him on his hands and telling him how dangerous fires were. During the next fire-setting incident, Kevin used a lighter to try to burn a door frame that his mother had just painted. This time he was not hit, but was forbidden to ride his bicycle for a week. His mother was sleeping during a third episode, in which he set the garbage on fire with a table lighter. He then took a broom and beat out the fire. His mother awoke to a funny smell and remembers that he was running all over the house in a peculiar manner. She related this incident with amusement at the child's antics.

The last two fires had taken place three weeks previously, when Kevin first tried to burn a dishtowel on a gas flame. After he burned the fringe, he rolled up the towel and threw it in the garbage. His mother, who was just outside the apartment at the time, sent him to bed and later explained to him again about the dangers of fire-setting. During the last incident, he took a stretch monster toy that was kept in a styrofoam box and burned holes with a lighter on the sides of the box that corresponded to the monster's arms and feet.

Apart from these incidents, his mother remembers that Kevin would often find matches or go into the bathroom with a lighter and try to smoke. His mother has talked to him at length about fires, how they get bigger with alcohol, and can be put out with water. He becomes excited during these discussions, but then promises never again to play with fire.

At the present time, his mother reports, Kevin is unhappy in school and misses his former friends from the neighborhood the family moved from three months before admission. She says that he has made no new friends outside school, and that he and his sister complain frequently of boredom.

Aside from the fire-setting, there is no history of any other aggressive or antisocial behavior. His mother reports that Kevin has been difficult to discipline, but mainly because he ignores her. Kevin's schoolteacher was surprised to hear of his fire-setting. She described him as a lovely, bright, obedient child who played and worked well with both the teacher and his peers. Upon further inquiry, she could say only that at times he became a "little wild" in play.

Kevin lives with his 10-year-old sister and 26-year-old mother, who herself was hospitalized as an adolescent after she had been truant from school for seven months in retaliation for her mother's remarriage. In an initial discussion with the interviewer, she acknowledged that at times she becomes violently angry, to the point where she is unable to control herself.

The findings of Kevin's physical examination were within normal limits except for a second-degree burn on his hand, which his mother initially said came from her attempts to "teach him that fire hurts" by insisting that he put his hand in a gas flame. (She later denied this, but Kevin insisted that she had done it.)

When interviewed, Kevin was somewhat guarded and distrustful at first. This seemed to be a manifestation of shyness and fear of what his mother would say or do. Over the course of several evaluation sessions, Kevin's play revolved around themes of fires getting bigger and out of control. He knows that he can get burned and that a big fire could burn his house and "I would die." When talking about fires, his affect was either inappropriate (laughter) or blunted. When discussing the "man" and his command hallucinations, Kevin seemed to be genuinely frightened, as if he regarded the man as real and threatening. He denied suicidal ideation, although his mother reported that he had recently said that he wished to die.

Discussion of "Brrr"

Recurrent setting of fires may be a symptom of Conduct Disorder; Kevin, however, is described by his teacher as a lovely, bright, obedient child who plays and works well with both the teacher and his peers, and he apparently engages in no antisocial activities other than fire-setting. Political extremists may set fires to make a political statement. We doubt this is what Kevin is up to.

It does seem that Kevin has committed deliberate and purposeful fire-setting on several occasions, that he derives pleasure from the fire-setting, that he is very fascinated with fires, as evidenced by his excitement over his mother's discussions with him about the specifics of fires, and that there is no understandable goal, such as monetary gain from insurance. The diagnosis is therefore Pyromania, within the group of Impulse Control Disorders Not Elsewhere Classified.

Some readers may notice that the DSM-III-R diagnostic criteria for this disorder require "tension or affective arousal before the act." This feature can only be inferred from the available information, as this subjective experience is often not easily documented in a very young person.

Other readers may be bothered by the "command hallucinations." It is hard to reconcile his mother's evaluation that the "man" in his head is one of a number of stories that he provides to explain his behavior, with his behavior during the interview when he seemed genuinely frightened at thoughts of the "man." If the hallucinations were truly genuine, one would certainly expect other signs of disorganized or psychotic behavior, which have not been present. Therefore we do not add a diagnosis of a psychotic disorder.

DSM-III-R Diagnosis:

Axis I: 312.33 Pyromania (p. 326)

No Brakes

JEREMY, AGE NINE, is brought by his mother to a mental health clinic because he has become increasingly disobedient and difficult to manage at school. Several events during the past month convinced his mother that she had to do something about his behavior. Several weeks ago he swore at his teacher and was suspended from school for three days. Last week he was reprimanded by the police for riding his three-wheeler in the street, something his mother had repeatedly cautioned him about. The next day he failed to use his pedal brakes and rode his bike into a store window, shattering it. He has not been caught in any more serious offenses, though once before he broke a window when he was riding his bike with a friend.

Jeremy has been difficult to manage since nursery school. The problems have slowly escalated. Whenever he is without close supervision, he gets into trouble. He has been reprimanded at school for teasing and kicking other children, tripping them, and calling them names. He is described as bad-tempered and irritable, even though at times he seems to enjoy school. Often he appears to be deliberately trying to annoy other children, though he always claims that others have started the arguments. He does not become involved in serious fights, but does occasionally exchange a few blows with another child.

Jeremy sometimes refuses to do what his two teachers tell him to do, and this year has been particularly difficult with the one who takes him in the afternoon for arithmetic, art, and science lessons. He gives many reasons why he should not have to do his work, and argues when told to do it. Many of the same problems were experienced last year when he had only one teacher. Despite this, his grades are good, and have been getting better over the course of the year, particularly in arithmetic, art, and physical education, which are subjects taught by the teacher with whom he has the most difficulty.

At home Jeremy's behavior is quite variable. On some days he is defiant and rude to his mother, needing to be told to do everything several times before he will do it, though eventually he usually complies; on other days he is charming and volunteers to help; but his unhelpful days predominate. "The least little thing upsets him, and then he shouts and screams." Jeremy is described as spiteful and mean with his younger brother, Rickie; even when he is in a good mood, he is unkind to Rickie.

Jeremy's concentration is generally good, and he does not leave his work unfinished. His mother describes him as "on the go all the time," but not restless. His teachers are concerned about his attitude, not about his restlessness. His mother also comments that he tells many minor lies, though when pressed, is truthful about important things.

Discussion of "No Brakes"

Jeremy's defiant and reckless behavior suggests the possibility of both Conduct Disorder and Attention-deficit Hyperactivity Disorder. Though he has annoyed other children and adults, he has not violated their basic rights or displayed any of the more serious forms of behavior, such as stealing, cruelty, truancy, running away from home, or destroying property, that would justify a diagnosis of Conduct Disorder. His encounter with the police was over a petty violation, and the damage he caused to a shop window was not done with any destructive intent. Although Jeremy does quite well academically, he has problems with teachers and peers. He has a high energy level, but is not aimlessly hyperactive and does not appear to have the characteristics of Attention-deficit Hyperactivity Disorder.

The persistent argumentative, irritable, defiant, annoying, and resentful behaviors are characteristic symptoms of Oppositional Defiant Disorder. We note the severity as moderate.

Some clinicians consider Oppositional Defiant Disorder merely a mild form of Conduct Disorder, but many children with the disorder never develop any more serious behavioral problems.

DSM-III-R Diagnosis:

Axis I: 313.81 Oppositional Defiant Disorder, Moderate (p. 57)

Lady Macbeth

INTERVIEWER: TELL ME ABOUT when things were the hardest for you. When was that?

Patient: It was around Christmastime last year.

I: And you were how old then?

P: 13.

I: You're 14 now, right?

P: Yes.

I: When things were really at their worst, can you tell me what it was that was disturbing to you at that time?

P: Well, the major part about it was that, like all these things that I did, they were really stupid, and they didn't make any sense; but I'm still gonna have to do it and, it was sort of like being scared of what would happen if I didn't do it.

I: What were the things that you were doing?

P: In the morning when I got dressed, I was real afraid that there'd be germs all over my clothes and things, so I'd stand there and I'd shake them for half an hour. I'd wash before I did anything—like if I was gonna wash my face, I'd wash my hands first; and if I was gonna get dressed, I'd wash my hands first; and then it got even beyond that point. Washing my hands wasn't enough, and I started to use rubbing alcohol. It was wintertime and cold weather, and this really made my hands bleed. Even if I just held them under water, they'd bleed all over the place, and they looked terrible, and everyone thought I had a disease or something.

I: And when you were doing that much washing, how much time every day did that take if you added up all the different parts of it?

P: It took about six hours a day. In the morning I didn't have a whole lot of choice, because I had to get up at 6:00 and get ready for school. All I'd do was get dressed as best I could. I didn't even have time to brush my hair. At the time I never ate breakfast, so all these things—it was just so complex that I didn't have time to do anything.

I: You also told me about other things in addition to the washing and worrying about dirt: that you would have plans about how you would do other things.

P: Okay, well, they were like set plans in my mind that if I heard the word, like, something that had to do with germs or disease, it would be considered something bad and so I had things that would go through my mind that were sort of like "cross that out and it'll make it okay" to hear that word.

I: What sort of things?

P: Like numbers or words that seemed to be sort of like a protector.

I: What numbers and what words were they?

P: It started out to be the number 3 and multiples of 3 and then words like "soap and water," something like that; and then the multiples of 3 got really high, they'd end up to be 124 or something like that. It got real bad then . . .

I: At any time did you really believe that something bad would happen if you didn't do these things? Was it just a feeling, or were you really scared?

P: No! I was petrified that something would really happen. It was weird, because everyone would always say how sensible I was and intelligent. But it was weird because I tried to explain it in order to really make them understand what I was trying to say and they'd go, you know, like, "Well, that's stupid," and I knew it; but when I was alone, things would be a lot worse than when I was with this group, because if I was around friends, that would make me forget about most of this. But when I was alone it . . . like, my mind would wander to all sorts of things and I'd get new plans and new rituals and new ideas, and I'd start worrying more and more about people that could get hurt that I cared about and things that could really go bad if I didn't.

I: Who were the people you'd worry most would get hurt?

P: My family, basically my family.

I: Any particular people in your family?

P: Well, like my grandmother—she's 83, and you know, I was just worried that . . . I know that she's old and she's not gonna be around much longer, but I was worried that maybe something I did could cause her to get really, really sick or something.

I: Had anything like this ever been on your mind before you were 13, when this started?

P: Well, let's see . . . my mother, her family has always been mostly real neat people and extremely clean and so that could have affected it, because I was growing up in that sort of background. But I always like to be clean and neat, and I was never really allowed to walk around the house with muddy shoes or anything like that, so . . .

I: But your concerns about clean, about how many times you did things—have they ever gotten in the way of your doing things that you wanted to do?

P: Uh-huh. Many times. Like, I was supposed to go somewhere with a friend, and we were gonna leave at 11:00 and I wanted to take a shower before I left. So I had to get up about 6:00 in the morning, and sometimes I just won't even make it with five hours to do it . . .

I: And that was since you were 13. But what about any time in your life before that—had anything like this ever happened? Or as far as you know was this the first?

P: It was the first time.

I: Have you at any time felt that you had some other special idea about forces beyond you . . . about your being able to control things magically or be in control?

P: I'm really scared of supernatural things. I don't like to say that I believe in superstitions and things, but I guess I really do 'cause they frighten me. When I was little they weren't really bothering me or anything, but now I avoid it as much as I can. Like, the number 13 now, if it came up, you know, it wouldn't bother me, but I'd rather have the number 7 instead.

I: So you are superstitious, but you've never heard any special voice talking to you or . . .

P: Yeah, I have. It's like . . . if I tried to describe it, people would think that I saw little people dancing around or something, and that was wrong because all it was, it wasn't like a voice, it was just like a thought.

I: More like being able to hear yourself think?

P: Right.

I: Have you ever seen things that other people couldn't see?

P: No.

I: I know you are doing very well here in school and on the ward here at the hospital. Do you have any signs left of the problems that you used to have with your rituals and compulsions?

P: Well, everyone is compulsive to a point. I can see little things that I'll do. Like I will go over something twice, or three times, because that's a special number. Like, if I read something and I really don't understand it, maybe I would go over it one more time and then, say, one more time will make it three. But nothing really big. It's been really good, because I have gotten out and taken a shower, and gotten dressed, and washed my face and brushed my teeth, and all that stuff in like half an hour! That's really good for me because I wasn't able to do that before.

I: So, in general it's fair to say it's things that just you would notice now, and probably someone sharing the room with you wouldn't be able to tell the other things you are doing even though you know these little things are there. Good . . . Well, thank you very much.

Discussion of "Lady Macbeth"

This adolescent girl articulately and vividly describes what it is like to have a severe form of Obsessive Compulsive Disorder. This patient has both obsessions and compulsions, and both are a significant source of distress to her and interfere with her functioning.

The obsessions consist of ideas that (at least initially in the course of the illness) intrude themselves into her consciousness and are experienced as senseless. For example, she gets the idea that maybe she did something that could cause her grandmother to get sick. Another example is the thought that there are germs on her clothes. The need to neutralize such distressing thoughts has led to various compulsions that are repetitive, persistent, and performed according to certain rules or in a stereotyped fashion. For example, if she heard a word that suggested germs or disease, she had to undo it ("cross that out") by saying the number 3 and multiples of 3 or words like "soap and water." Although these behaviors were designed to prevent discomfort or some dreaded event, the activity was not connected in a realistic way to what it was designed to prevent and was clearly excessive. For example, she would wash her hands for hours to prevent becoming infected by the germs, to the point where her hands would bleed. Although emotionally she reacted as if the dangers were real ("I was petrified that something would really happen"), intellectually she always knew that her fears were irrational (her friends would say that it was stupid, and she *knew* that it was).

Obsessional thoughts need to be distinguished from auditory hallucinations. This patient recognized that if she described some of her obsessional thoughts to people, they might think that she was hallucinating ("if I tried to describe it, people would think that I saw little people dancing around or something"). However, she is quite clear that it was just her own thoughts, not a voice.

Obsessive Compulsive Disorder is sometimes associated with Obsessive Compulsive Personality Disorder. Whereas Obsessive Compulsive Disorder involves true obsessions and compulsions, Obsessive Compulsive Personality Disorder involves such personality traits as perfectionism, indecisiveness, and restricted ability to express warm and tender emotions. There is no evidence in this case of Obsessive Compulsive Personality Disorder.

People with Obsessive Compulsive Disorder also often have Major Depression, either before or during the course of Obsessive Compulsive Disorder. In fact, on further questioning, this patient did describe an episode of Major Depression that occurred early in the course of the Obsessive Compulsive Disorder.

DSM-III-R Diagnosis:

Axis I: 300.30 Obsessive Compulsive Disorder, Severe (p. 247)

Rocking and Reading

TWENTY-TWO-YEAR-OLD BETSY was referred for evaluation by the staff of her group home. She had been placed in the group home some three months previously, following court-ordered "deinstitutionalization" from a large residential facility for the retarded. The evaluation was requested because Betsy "didn't fit in" with other clients and had developed some problem behaviors, particularly aggression directed toward herself and, less commonly, toward others. Unlike other clients in the group home, she tended to "stay to herself" and had essentially no peer relations, although she did respond positively to some staff members. Her self-abusive and aggressive behaviors usually were triggered by changes made in her routine. Self-abusive behavior consisted of repeated pounding of her legs and biting of her hand.

Betsy had been placed in residential treatment when she was four years old, and had remained in some kind of residential setting ever since. Her parents had both died, and she had no contact with her only sibling. At the time of her transfer to the group home, she was reported to have had several abnormal EEGs, but no seizures or other medical problems had been noted. When last given psychological tests, she achieved a full scale IQ of 55, with comparable deficits in adaptive behaviors.

During the evaluation, Betsy spends much of her time reading a children's book she discovered in the waiting room. Her voice is flat and monotonic. She is unable to respond to any questions about the book she is reading and reacts to interruptions of her ongoing activity by pounding her legs with her fist. She rocks back and forth continually during the interview. She makes eye contact with the examiner initially, but otherwise seems oblivious of everyone around her. She neither initiates activities, imitates the play of the examiner, nor responds to attempts to interest her in alternative activities, such as playing with a doll. From time to time she repeats a single phrase in a monotonic voice, "Blum, blum." Physical examination reveals extensive bruises covering most of her lower extremities.

Betsy was the product of a normal pregnancy, labor, and delivery. She was noted to have been an unusually easy baby. Her parents had first become concerned when she failed to speak by age two. Motor milestones were delayed. Her parents initially thought that she might be deaf, but this was obviously not the case, as she responded with panic to the sound of a vacuum cleaner. As a young child, Betsy had been noted to "live in her own world," had not formed attachments to her parents, had idiosyncratic responses to some sounds, and always became extremely upset when there were changes in her environment.

By age four, Betsy was still not speaking, and placement in the state institution was recommended following a diagnosis of Childhood Schizophrenia. In the year after her placement, Betsy began speaking. However, she did not typically use speech for communication; instead, she merely repeated phrases over and over. She had an unusual ability to memorize and became fascinated with reading, even though she appeared not to comprehend anything she read. She exhibited a variety of stereotyped behaviors, including body rocking and head banging, requiring a great deal of attention from the staff.

Discussion of "Rocking and Reading"

Betsy has long-standing problems, including impairment in social interaction (lack of awareness of others and gross impairment in peer relations). Although she has some speech, it is markedly abnormal in its production (monotonic) and in its form and content (she repeats the same phrases over and over). She exhibits stereotyped behaviors (rocking), marked distress over environmental change and insistence on the same routines, and a markedly restricted range of interests. All of these, beginning in early childhood, establish the diagnosis of Autistic Disorder.

Although some cases of Autistic Disorder are associated with normal or, more rarely, high IQ, this case illustrates the frequent coexistence of Mental Retardation and Autistic Disorder.

At the time of Betsy's placement in the state institution, she was diagnosed as having Childhood Schizophrenia. That diagnosis assumed a continuity between the childhood disorder and adult psychosis. However, there is considerable evidence from family and longitudinal studies that Autistic Disorder and the adult psychosis are not related; therefore, in DSM-III-R, the childhood disorder is not referred to as "Schizophrenia."

DSM-III-R Diagnosis:

Axis I: 299.00 Autistic Disorder (p. 38)
Axis II: 317.00 Mild Mental Retardation (p. 31)

Wewwow Fwowers

BOB IS A FOUR-YEAR-OLD who is tall for his age and extremely good-looking. His mother reports that he has no physical health problems, gets along well at nursery school and at home, but seems restless, has trouble staying asleep, and has a "speech problem." The school reports that the boy is difficult to understand and has a short attention span.

Examination revealed a bright, pleasant youngster who played well and chatted happily while drawing and playing. Some of the boy's utterances included "Wook at the wewwow fwowers in duh gaden"; and "Zis is where I hurt my fumb on de hot tove."

Discussion of "Wewwow Fwowers"

Bob's speech difficulties are not part of impaired *language* development (as might be seen in Developmental Expressive Language Disorder, Mental Retardation, or a Pervasive Developmental Disorder), since they are apparently limited to problems in articulating certain speech sounds. Examination of his speech indicates difficulty pronouncing r, y, l, th, and s. This is quite characteristic of Developmental Articulation Disorder. There is no evidence of any other cause of his articulation difficulties, such as hearing impairment or dysarthria (articulation disturbance due to a disorder of the oral speech mechanism or to neurologic abnormalities).

The reference to trouble staying asleep, restlessness, and having a short attention span also suggests the possibility of Attention-deficit Hyperactivity Disorder, which should be ruled out or, at most, considered a "provisional" diagnosis on Axis I.

DSM-III-R Diagnosis:

Axis I: R/O Attention-deficit Hyperactivity Disorder
Axis II: 315.39 Developmental Articulation Disorder (p. 45)

Follow-up

As is not uncommon with children who have Developmental Articulation Disorder with no language disturbance, Bob was completely normal at follow-up when he was 12 years old. At that time there was no evidence of any speech, language, or learning problems.

Into Everything

EDDIE, AGE NINE, WAS REFERRED to a child psychiatrist at the request of his school, because of the difficulties he creates in class. He has been suspended for a day twice this school year. His teacher complains that he is so restless that the rest of the class is unable to concentrate. He is hardly ever in his seat, but roams around the class, talking to other children while they are working. He never seems to know what he is going to do next, and may suddenly do something quite outrageous. His most recent suspension was for swinging from the fluorescent light fitting over the blackboard, where he had climbed in the transition from one class to the next, and since he was unable to climb down again, the class was in an uproar.

His mother says that Eddie's behavior has been difficult since he was a toddler, and that as a three-year-old he was unbearably restless and demanding. He has always required little sleep and been awake before anyone else. When he was small, "he got into everything," particularly in the early morning, when he would awaken at 4:30 or 5:00 AM and go downstairs by himself. His parents would awaken to find the living room or kitchen "demolished." When he was four, he managed to unlock the door of the apartment and wander off into a busy main street, but, fortunately, was rescued from oncoming traffic by a passerby. He was rejected by a preschool program because of his difficult behavior; eventually, after a very difficult year in kindergarten, he was placed in a special behavioral program for first- and second-graders. He is now in a regular class for most subjects, but spends a lot of time in a resource room with a special teacher.

Psychological testing has shown Eddie to be of average ability, and his achievements are only slightly below expected level. His attention span is described by the psychologist as "virtually nonexistent." He has no interest in TV, and dislikes games or toys that require any concentration or patience on his part. He is not popular with other children, and at home prefers to be outdoors, playing with his dog or riding his bike. If he does play with toys, his games are messy and destructive, and his mother cannot get him to keep his things in any order.

Eddie is also quite disobedient, and in the last year or so has been provocative and defiant at school and, to some extent, at home. He has stolen small sums of money from home and school, and other children have complained because he has taken small toys that they have brought to school.

Eddie has been treated with a stimulant, methylphenidate, in small doses (5–10 mg a day); but this was discontinued in the past year, apparently because it was having no effect on his defiance and conduct problems. When he was taking the drug, he was much easier to manage at school in that he was less restless and possibly more attentive, even though other aspects of his behavior were unsatisfactory.

Discussion of "Into Everything"

Eddie's behavior graphically demonstrates the characteristic inattention, impulsivity, and hyperactivity of Attention-deficit Hyperactivity Disorder. He has difficulty remaining seated, fidgets, can't follow through on instructions, can't sustain attention, often doesn't seem to listen to what is being said to him, shifts from one activity to another, has difficulty playing quietly, and often engages in physically dangerous activities without considering the consequences. Because he almost certainly has the other symptoms of Attention-deficit Hyperactivity Disorder (such as difficulty waiting his turn, blurting out answers to questions, talking excessively and interrupting others), and because his symptoms significantly interfere with his functioning at home and at school, we note that the disorder is severe.

Eddie's disobedience, defiance, and stealing are not uncommon in older children with this condition, and may progress to full-blown Conduct Disorder. Unlike the symptoms of inattention, impulsivity, and hyperactivity, these behaviors do not respond to stimulants.

DSM-III-R Diagnosis:

Axis I: **314.01 Attention-deficit Hyperactivity Disorder, Severe (p. 52)**

Tim

TIM, SIX YEARS OLD, WAS REFERRED to the clinic by his general practitioner because of persistent soiling, for which no organic cause could be found.

Tim had never gained control of his stools. He was not constipated as an infant; but after a febrile illness at age two, he had become constipated. Six months later he had impacted feces, and was seen by a surgeon, who prescribed laxatives and suppositories. Following this, there was a pattern of alternating constipation, when he did not go to the toilet for several days, and runny diarrhea, when he soiled his pants many times a day. At age four, Tim took laxatives regularly, and his stool became softer and more regular. At about the same time, his mother first attempted to toilet train him. He was made to sit on the toilet every evening until he "performed." Although he usually managed this, producing a tiny amount or, rarely, a normal stool, he continued to soil his pants frequently during the day. His mother said that within half an hour of changing his pants, he would be soiled again, and this pattern has continued until the present time.

Tim himself has been distressed about the soiling since starting school. He hates taking his clothes off for gym or on the beach. He worries that people will notice if, as occasionally happens, feces drop out of his pants. He is anxious when sitting on the toilet in the evenings, and at first would do so only if bribed. Now he insists his mother stay in the bathroom with him.

Tim is also enuretic at night. He became dry by day at three and a half, but has continued to wet at night; and, as waking him at night has not prevented his wetting, his mother still puts him in diapers.

For the last month, since seeing a puppet show, Tim has awakened frequently with nightmares about witches. He often asks about witches, and his mother has tried to assure him that they do not exist. He has had a light on all night in his room for the past month. He never goes into his parents' bed, as they do not allow this because of his being wet.

His mother says that Tim has seemed rather preoccupied with death. He often asks why people have to die and if he or his parents will die first. He then works out how old he might be when his parents die. He has said that he doesn't want to be buried because then people would walk over him.

Apart from the problems of soiling and wetting, his mother feels he is a normal little boy who is happy and outgoing. He is very affectionate with his mother and likes to receive lots of kisses and hugs. His mother implied that this might be excessive for a boy. He is attached to his father, but not as much as to his mother. He likes to play and go out with his father, but with his mother he is clinging and likes to stay close to her.

Up until the age of four, Tim had worried his parents because of seeming rather effeminate. He liked to dress in girl's clothes and talked of "when I grow up to be a girl." Now when playing he likes to take traditionally male roles, such as policemen or bus conductors.

There was initially some difficulty in Tim's adjustment at school. He used to scream when his mother left him, and he was reported to be very timid and afraid of other children. This lasted most of the first term; but he eventually began "to stand up for himself," and has been quite happy at school since then. He has several friends there, and the school is satisfied with his progress.

Tim's developmental milestones were all a little behind those of his two older sisters, but his mother could not recall them exactly. He sat up at about 6 months, shuffled about on his bottom and did not crawl, and walked at about 18 months. He spoke his first words at about that same time.

Tim's mother is a smartly dressed, 35-year-old laboratory technician who seems timid and speaks quietly, but at the same time is quite forceful and articulate in what she says. She seems to feel unsure of herself with Tim and thinks that bringing up a boy is much more difficult than bringing up her daughters. She is embarrassed, as a professional person, not to have sought help earlier. She recalls how she, too, had in childhood hated to use lavatories away from home.

Tim's father is a 40-year-old, intelligent, distinguished-looking contractor. He was reticent during the interview. He readily admitted that he did not take an active part in the rearing of the children, but enjoyed them and was very fond of them. He explained that he was rather disgusted by the soiling and tried to keep out of the situation for fear of being too punitive.

In the interview Tim appeared rather small for his age and had a babyish, full face. At first he was very timid and shy and clung to his mother. However, he did allow his mother to leave the room after a short period and became much more assertive and outgoing once she had left. He played with family figures in the dollhouse and soon had the little boy figure on the toilet and all the other members of the family watching him. His speech was immature and difficult to understand, but his vocabulary was extensive.

Tim was also seen by a pediatrician. On physical examination, a fecal mass the size of a melon could be palpated in the lower abdomen, and soft feces could be felt in his rectum.

Discussion of "Tim"

Encopresis can sometimes be caused by physical disorders, such as aganglionic megacolon and anal fissure. Since these have been ruled out in Tim's case, the diagnosis of Functional Encopresis is appropriate. In addition, he continues to have nighttime wetting, warranting an additional diagnosis of Functional Enuresis. Since Tim's fecal and urinary incontinence was not preceded by a year of continence, both diagnoses are specified as Primary Type.

For the last month Tim has had nightmares about witches and has been scared of the dark and preoccupied with death. Since this is likely to be only a transient reaction, it does not warrant an additional diagnosis. If it persists or becomes more severe, however, then an additional diagnosis, such as Adjustment Disorder with Anxious Mood, should be considered.

Tim apparently went through a phase during which he showed some signs of possible disturbance in gender identity, but he now seems to have a clear sense of himself as a male.

DSM-III-R Diagnosis:

Axis I: 307.70 Functional Encopresis, Primary Type (p. 83)
            307.60 Functional Enuresis, Primary Type (p. 85)

A Child Is Crying

FIFTEEN-YEAR-OLD CINDY was brought to a mental health clinic by her father after he received a call from the counselor at school, who was concerned that Cindy was depressed and possibly suicidal. Her father had also been concerned about her because she had seemed sad and withdrawn for the past month.

The household consists of Cindy, her father, mother, and two younger siblings. According to Cindy, she has been depressed ever since she had a fight with her mother two years ago. During the fight her mother threw a pot of hot water and burned Cindy on the shoulder. She was taken to a nearby medical emergency room and treated for the burn. Since then, she stays out of her mother's way.

Cindy's mother has a long history of mental problems, with multiple hospitalizations and long-term outpatient treatment. She is reported by the father to be chronically "psychotic" and to have marked mood swings. There have been many conflicts in the marriage over the years, and the couple is now in the process of getting a divorce and selling their home. For the past two years, since the incident with the boiling water, Cindy's mother has occupied the third floor of their house and has had little contact with the family.

Before the incident with her mother, Cindy was very socially involved, taking dancing and music lessons and participating in both church and school activities. She was a straight-A student.

Cindy says that her mood has been much worse in the last six months. She feels depressed almost every day, all day long. She worries about her mother and feels that the fight was probably her fault. She has lost interest in school and social activities and has not really paid attention to her schoolwork for the last six months. Her grades have dropped from A's to B's and C's. She is tired all the time and takes a nap when she comes home from school. At night she has trouble falling asleep, and in the morning often has trouble getting up.

In the past three weeks, Cindy has become anxious and has had two experiences in which she felt "spacey and unreal." She often hears the voice of a young child crying for help; but when she looks to see if there is someone outside the door, there is never anyone there. At times, recently, especially when she feels guilty about the fight with her mother, she is convinced she doesn't deserve to live, and has considered killing herself. Three weeks ago, while she was washing dishes, she thought about cutting her wrists with a knife; but the thought of how upset her father would be kept her from doing anything.

The psychiatrist who evaluated Cindy recommended an elective admission to the hospital. However, both she and her father felt that she would be able to follow through with outpatient treatment. She was given the telephone number of the emergency room and the following day called to say that the voices were getting worse, and she was afraid she might hurt herself. She was directed to go immediately to the emergency room, and was subsequently admitted to the hospital.

Discussion of "A Child Is Crying"

Cindy has been depressed for two years, but in the past six months has had the characteristic symptoms of a Major Depressive Episode: unremitting depressed mood, loss of interest in most activities, decreased energy, insomnia, excessive guilt, and thoughts of suicide. More recently, she has had auditory hallucinations of a child crying, which is congruent with her depressed mood, and has experienced depersonalization (felt "spacey and unreal").

In the absence of either a history of a manic episode or of a known organic factor that initiated and maintained the disturbance, the diagnosis is Major Depression. It is further qualified as Single Episode (because there was no prior episode), and with Mood-congruent Psychotic Features (because of the hallucinations). This case illustrates that the characteristic symptoms of Major Depression do occur in children.

We do not know whether, prior to the onset of the Major Depressive Episode six months ago, Cindy had symptoms of Dysthymia, such as poor appetite and low energy. Thus we note the need to rule out this additional diagnosis.

DSM-III-R Diagnosis:

Axis I: 296.24 Major Depression, Single Episode, with Mood-congruent Psychotic Features (p. 229)
R/O Dysthymia

Cartographer*

A PSYCHIATRIC EVALUATION is requested by the teachers of C.B., a 13-year-old boy. He is of average intelligence, according to the Wechsler Intelligence Scale for Children (WISC), with better verbal than performance skills. He does well on tasks requiring rote learning, but his teachers are deeply puzzled and concerned about his poor comprehension of abstract ideas and his social naiveté. They find him appealing, but sadly vulnerable to the hazards of everyday life.

His mother dates her son's problems from the age of six months, when his head was accidentally bruised. From that time on, he became socially aloof and isolated and spent most of his time gazing at his hands, which he moved in complicated patterns before his face. At the age of one year, he began to watch the passing traffic, but still ignored people. He continued to be remote, with poor eye contact, until five years of age.

---

* Wing, Lorna: "Asperger's Syndrome. A Clinical Account." *Psychological Medicine*, 11:115-130, 1981

He passed his motor milestones at the usual ages and, as soon as he was physically able, began to spend hours running in circles with an object in his hand, and screamed if attempts were made to stop him. He performed many stereotyped movements as a young child, including jumping, flapping his arms, and moving his hands in circles.

At the age of three, C.B. was able to recognize letters of the alphabet, and he rapidly acquired skill in drawing; he drew the salt and pepper shakers, correctly copying the names written on them, over and over again. For a time this was his sole activity. Following this, he became fascinated with pylons and tall buildings, and would stare at them from all angles and draw them. C.B. did not speak till age four, and then for a long time used only single words. Later, he repeated phrases and reversed pronouns.

After age five, C.B.'s speech and social contact markedly improved. Until age 11, he attended a special school, where the staff tolerated a range of bizarre, repetitive routines. At one point, for example, he insisted that, before lessons could begin, all his class and the teacher should wear watches he made from plasticine. Despite all his problems, C.B. proved to have excellent rote memory, absorbed all he was taught, and could reproduce facts verbatim when asked. He was transferred to a regular public school at age 11.

C.B. uses good grammar and has a large vocabulary, but his speech is naive and immature and concerned mainly with his own special interests. He has learned not to make embarrassing remarks about other people's appearance, but tends to ask repetitive questions. He is not socially withdrawn, but prefers the company of adults to that of children his own age, finding it difficult to understand the unwritten rules of social interaction. He says of himself, "I am afraid I suffer from bad sportsmanship." He enjoys simple jokes, but cannot understand more subtle humor. He is often teased by his classmates.

C.B.'s main interest is in maps and road signs. He has a prodigious memory for routes and can draw them rapidly and accurately. He also makes large, complicated, abstract shapes out of any material that comes to hand and shows much ingenuity in ensuring that they hold together. He has never engaged in pretend play, but is deeply attached to a toy panda, to which he talks as if it were an adult when he needs comfort.

C.B.'s finger dexterity is good, but he is clumsy and ill-coordinated in large movements, and therefore is never chosen by the other children for sports and team games.

Discussion of "Cartographer"

C.B.'s many problems apparently began at an early age (six months), with severe impairment in several developmental areas.

He has shown grossly impaired social interaction, with a marked lack of awareness of the existence of others (totally ignoring the presence of others, watching only his hands or traffic) and no social play. Qualitative impairment in language development was indicated by his not speaking at all until age four, and then speaking only single words, progressing to the use of repetitive phrases and reversed pronouns. Finally, he showed a markedly restricted repertoire of activities and interests, as manifested by stereotyped body movements (e.g., jumping, flapping his arms, moving his hands in circles), unreasonable insistence on following routines in precise detail (e.g., insisting that his classmates wear plasticine watches), and preoccupation with a single narrow interest at a time (e.g., copying the names of the salt and pepper shakers). These characteristics indicate Autistic Disorder, a Pervasive Developmental Disorder.

Since age five, C.B.'s condition has improved considerably. He no longer exhibits bizarre behavior and gross distortions in language. Although he still retains some residual signs of the illness (his speech is naive and immature; he has difficulty understanding the unwritten rules of social interaction), the full syndrome of Autistic Disorder is no longer present. Hence, the diagnosis is Autistic Disorder, Residual State.

DSM-III-R Diagnosis:

Axis I: 299.00 Autistic Disorder, Residual State (p. 38)

Follow-up

In the seven years since his evaluation at age 13, C.B. has continued to make progress in practical and self care skills, and in the formal aspects of language (vocabulary and grammar). He still has an odd vocal intonation, a stilted, pedantic style of speech, and difficulty in initiating or taking turns in conversation. He retains his tendency to deliver monologues on the subjects that interest him. He has been unable to find work, and most of the time stays within his own home, where he lives with his parents. He has no friends with whom he associates, but he has become adept at using citizens' band radio, and regularly contacts a wide network of other radio enthusiasts. His circumscribed interests are now comprised of his radio, the progress of football teams, and maps. He remains somewhat clumsy and ill-coordinated in gross motor skills.

C.B.'s behavior is quiet and amenable, and he presents no problems for his parents or his sister, all of whom are very fond of him. The main concern is what will happen to him when his parents can no longer provide him with a home. They know that he is socially odd and naive and, despite the radio network, isolated, and that he lacks the ability to plan for himself and to cope with the demands of everyday life. Despite his skills, C.B. remains as innocent and vulnerable as a young child.

I'm Not Right Up Here*

PHILLIP, AGE 12, WAS SUSPENDED from a small town Iowa school and referred for psychiatric treatment by his principal. The following note came with him:

> This child has been a continual problem since coming to our school. He does not get along on the playground because he is mean to other children. He disobeys school rules, sasses the patrol children, steals from the other children, and defies all authority. Phillip keeps getting into fights with other children on the bus.
>
> He has been suspended from cafeteria privileges several times for fighting, pushing, and shoving. After he misbehaved one day at the cafeteria, the teacher told him to come up to my office to see me. He flatly refused, lay on the floor, and threw a temper tantrum, kicking and screaming.
>
> The truth is not in Phillip. When caught in actual misdeeds, he denies everything, and takes upon himself an air of injured innocence. He believes we are picking on him. His attitude is sullen when he is refused anything. He pouts and sasses. When asked why he does these things, he points to his head and says, "Because I'm not right up here."
>
> This boy needs help badly. He does not seem to have friends. His aggressive behavior prevents the children from liking him. Our school psychologist tested Phillip and the results indicated average intelligence, but his school achievement is only at the third and low fourth grade level.

The psychiatrist learned from Phillip's grandmother that he was an illegitimate child, born when his mother was a senior in high school. Her parents insisted that she keep the baby and help rear him; most of his upbringing has been by his grandparents, however.

Phillip was "three months premature," and a "blue baby," requiring oxygen for 24 hours. Shortly after his birth, Phillip's mother ran off with a man, married him, and had a second child. The marriage broke up, and she left this child with its father. Phillip has had no contact with his mother since she left him.

Phillip's toilet training was not successful, and he remained a bedwetter for some years. At the age of five years, his maternal grandpar-

---

* Jenkins, Richard L.: "Behavior Disorders of Childhood and Adolescence," Springfield, IL, Charles C. Thomas, 1973, pp. 60-64.

ents adopted him because they were afraid that his mother might some day claim him. He showed anxiety at separation from his grandmother when he began school.

He was then in a serious car accident, in which his grandmother was injured and one person in the other car killed. Phillip did not appear to be injured, but seemed to have some transient memory loss, probably a direct, immediate result of the impact. Subsequently, he suffered from nightmares, fear of the dark, and an exacerbation of his fear of separation from his grandmother.

Phillip's school progress was not good. He repeated third grade and then was in a special class for underachievers. His grandmother recalls that Phillip's teacher complained that he "could never stay in his seat."

A few months before the consultation, Phillip was seen in a mental health clinic and placed on some mild tranquilizers. A three-month return appointment was arranged, but the school suspended him before that date.

Discussion of "I'm Not Right Up Here"

Phillip's antisocial behavior began when he was in grade school, and a pattern of fighting, lying, and stealing has persisted for many years. In addition, he is disobedient and defies all authority and attempts to control his behavior. This disturbance of conduct, lasting more than six months, justifies the diagnosis of Conduct Disorder.

Unlike some children with this disorder, Phillip does not have a peer group with whom he engages in antisocial acts; in fact, he seems to have no relationships with his peers. Thus, the Conduct Disorder is specified as the Solitary Aggressive Type. Since his behavior problems do not cause serious physical harm to others and he does not have many of the other symptoms of Conduct Disorder, such as cruelty to animals or people, using a weapon, setting fires, or running away from home, the severity is noted as moderate.

DSM-III-R Diagnosis:

Axis I: 312.00 **Conduct Disorder, Solitary Aggressive Type, Moderate (p. 55)**

Follow-up

Phillip was admitted to the children's unit of a state mental hospital. After eight months he was discharged as having received "maximal hospital benefit," with a statement that "the prognosis is not favorable." He returned to school in his small community. Over the next two years, Phillip's behavior gradually deteriorated, with much involvement in name-calling, fights, and refusals to obey school personnel. He was suspended following the discovery in his locker of a tape recorder that was missing from a school office.

At this time his grandparents recognized that they could no longer cope with him and accepted his commitment for long-term treatment in the state mental hospital. Phillip's course in the hospital was stormy. He made himself unpopular with his peers by repeatedly stealing from them. When caught, he would lie or refuse to answer. He had a foul mouth and used derogatory, insulting language. As a result of his behavior, he spent much time in seclusion. While in seclusion he destroyed his mattress by cutting it with a piece of glass. He was generally hostile and uncooperative and, when crossed, would become combative. Hospital personnel controlled him only with difficulty and frequently had bruised shins to show for it. When Phillip lost control, he seemed to do so completely, and communication became impossible until he had been overpowered and had time to cool down.

His relations with staff began to improve as they persisted in showing interest and goodwill in spite of his assaultiveness. His relations with his peer group improved much more slowly. Real progress began when he was assigned to work with some of the maintenance staff. He enjoyed this work and often did a good job.

When Phillip was 16, he was transferred from the adolescent ward to a closed adult men's ward. Here his combativeness rapidly diminished, and his adjustment accordingly improved. Phillip ascribed this improvement to the fact that he was no longer in contact with other poorly controlled adolescents, who tended to stir him up and provoke him. After about three months, he was returned to the home of his grandparents and, when last seen (six weeks later), was making a satisfactory adjustment. He attended school in the morning, and worked in a gas station in the afternoon in a school-work program.

Note: The improvement in Phillip's behavior provides some hope that he will not be one of the many children with Conduct Disorder who go on to develop Antisocial Personality Disorder.

Refrigerator Raider

A LICE IS A SINGLE 17-YEAR-OLD who lives with her parents, who insisted that she be seen because of binge eating and vomiting. She achieved her greatest weight of 180 pounds at 16 years of age. Her lowest weight since she reached her present height of 5'9" has been 150 pounds, and her present weight is about 160 pounds.

Alice states she has been dieting since age ten and says she has always been very tall and slightly chubby. At age 12 she started binge eating and vomiting. She was a serious competitive swimmer at that time, and it was necessary for her to keep her weight down. She would deprive herself of all food for a few days and then get an urge to eat. She could not control this urge, and would raid the refrigerator and cupboards for ice cream, pastries, and other desserts. She would often do this at night, when nobody was looking, and would eat in one sitting, for example, a quart of ice cream, an entire pie, and any other desserts she could find. While binging, she would feel that her eating was totally out of control, and she would stop only when she felt physical discomfort. She would then become depressed and fearful of gaining weight, following which she would self-induce vomiting by sticking her finger deep into the back of her mouth until she gagged.

Alice has always been very concerned about the effect this behavior was having on her weight, and has constantly fretted about being over-weight, occasionally resorting to Dexedrine to help her lose weight. When she was 15, she was having eating binges and vomiting four days a week. Since age 13 she has gone through only one period of six weeks without gaining weight or eating binges or vomiting. She quit school this year (at age 17) for a period of five months, during which she just stayed home, binge eating and vomiting several times a day. She then went back to school and tried to do better in her schoolwork. She has obtained average or below-average grades in junior high and high school.

For the past two years Alice has been drinking wine and beer on weekends. She drinks mostly with girl friends; she dates infrequently. Alice states that she wants to date, but is ashamed of the way she looks. Several months ago she was hospitalized for two weeks to control her binge eating. During this time she was very depressed and cut her wrists several times while hospitalized.

Alice is neatly dressed, well oriented, and answers inquiries ratio-nally. During the interview she indicates that she realizes she has a serious problem with binge eating and vomiting, but feels rather hopeless about getting the behavior under control.

Discussion of "Refrigerator Raider"

Clearly, Alice has a gross disturbance in her eating behavior. She has recurrent episodes of binge eating, in which she rapidly consumes a large quantity of food over a discrete period of time. The food she eats during the binges is typically high in carbohy-drates (ice cream, pastries, and other desserts); she eats it in secret (at night when nobody is looking). During the binges, she experi-ences a feeling of lack of control over her eating behavior, so that only the physical discomfort caused by the binge allows her to stop eating. In order to keep from gaining weight as a result of this overeating, she regularly engages in self-induced vomiting and occasionally has used Dexedrine to help her lose weight. Because of her frequent fluctuations in weight due to the binges, dieting and control of her weight have been a chronic preoccupation. Her eating binges have been quite frequent, sometimes as often as several times a day, warranting the diagnosis of Bulimia Nervosa.

Although binge eating can be an associated feature of Anorexia Nervosa, there is no suggestion here of the severe weight loss characteristic of that disorder. As Major Depression is often associated with Bulimia, if the criteria are met for a full major depressive syndrome, the additional diagnosis of Major Depression may be warranted. Although it is mentioned that Alice was "very depressed" while in the hospital, apparently the depression lasted for less than two weeks, suggesting only a diagnosis of Adjustment Disorder with Depressed Mood, triggered, perhaps, by her hospitalization. Because depressive symptoms are typically associated with Bulimia Nervosa, we see no advantage in adding the nonspecific diagnosis of Adjustment Disorder to characterize the more recent depressive episode; but we would not quarrel with a clinician who added this diagnosis.

Mention is made of Alice's drinking wine and beer and using Dexedrine. There is, however, no clear pattern of maladaptive use or resulting impairment in social or occupational functioning to justify a diagnosis of Psychoactive Substance Abuse.

Finally, one or more Personality Disorders are frequently associated with this disorder. Alice's use of substances, binge eating, and wrist-cutting are suggestive of the diagnosis of Borderline Personality Disorder, but there is insufficient evidence at this point to warrant this additional Axis II diagnosis.

DSM-III-R Diagnosis:

Axis I: 307.51 Bulimia Nervosa (p. 68)

He Breaks His Toys

JOHNNY, AGE EIGHT, was brought to a clinic for evaluation by his mother, who said, "There is something wrong with his brain." When asked to be more specific, she replied with a vague litany of complaints that were frequently self-contradictory:

He was always slow to learn things, slower than any of my other children. But I know he's really very smart. Sometimes he just amazes me with what he remembers or can figure out. He doesn't do much, for example, at school or with activities outside school. Sometimes I think it's because he's lazy, and other times I think he's depressed, and other times I think maybe it's because he is sick a lot. He gets a lot of stomachaches. He's really such a sweet boy, I mean he's so nice with his four sisters and our pets. But sometimes he's so nasty I get afraid. For example, he gets frustrated with some of his toys, and then he gets destructive. He's broken more toys than all of my other three children put together. He seems to like people, but he only has one friend at school. He refuses to try out for soccer or anything like that where he could play with the other boys. Sometimes I think he just doesn't care about anything. He's always dropping dishes and things around the house.

A more detailed history revealed that the pregnancy, birth, and early medical history had been unremarkable, but minor problems had appeared in the first year of life. These included being slow to sit up, crawl, and walk. Since Johnny was the fourth child in the family, the mother had not "had time" to record the actual ages when these milestones were reached. She could only pinpoint that "he was much older than any of the other children when he did finally manage to do those things," adding that the pediatrician had nonetheless assured her that Johnny was not retarded. "A good thing he did," she laughed, "because later when Johnny had so much trouble learning to use the knife and fork, and to tie his shoelaces, and to button his shirts, I did worry about that."

Asked if there were any remaining concerns along these lines, the mother replied "none at all." Apparently, Johnny excelled in reading and did well in all his other school subjects, except for handwriting and physical education.

His medical history was also unremarkable. During the preschool years there had been only "the normal childhood illnesses" (chicken pox, earaches, and flu), and "an awful lot of bruises and scraped knees." The stomachaches had started "sometime around age seven," but again, the pediatrician had assured the mother that they were not cause for concern.

Examination revealed a pleasant, but rather quiet boy with appropriate affect, good concentration, and apparently normal cognitive skills. Although quiet and reserved, Johnny did not appear apathetic—indeed, he became quite enthusiastic when describing a book he had just read. During the interview, Johnny denied any problems in school or with peers. When specifically asked, he did admit to occasional stomachaches and to nonparticipation in group activities, which he attributed to simply "not liking that stuff."

Psychological testing performed in the school setting revealed above-average intelligence and academic performance. However, Johnny scored well below the norm on the Oseretsky Test of Motor Proficiency, a test of motor development requiring tasks involving running, balancing, coordination, and motor speed. The psychologist noted that he showed good concentration and attention during the testing.

Discussion of "He Breaks His Toys"

Many features of this case are typical of Coordination Disorder, which is coded on Axis II. These include: late gross motor milestones (standing, sitting, walking), early history of bruises (from bumping into things) and falls, reported "destructiveness" (dropping things or breaking toys when trying to manipulate them), difficulty with tasks requiring fine motor coordination (buttoning clothes, tying shoelaces, and handwriting) and with sports, such as ball games.

The stomachaches, "laziness," "depression," and "apathy" probably represent Johnny's efforts to avoid physical education class, tests in which handwriting is necessary, and the embarrassment of repeated failures in team sport situations. Similarly, Johnny's "bad temper" and "frustration" are probably not evidence of disturbance in attention or conduct, but rather a manifestation of his motor difficulties. As often happens, it is these secondary problems that have brought the problem to professional attention.

One may wonder why a disorder of physical coordination appears in a classification of mental disorders. It is true that the defining features of the disorder are more "physical" than "behavioral" or "psychological," and therefore one could argue that the disorder is more properly a physical, not a mental, disorder. However, it seems reasonable to classify it with the other developmental disorders of childhood because of the absence of a specific known organic cause and because the behavioral consequences of the disorder (e.g., irritability and avoidance behavior) are treated by mental health professionals.

DSM-III-R Diagnosis:

Axis I: V71.09 No Diagnosis or Condition
Axis II: 315.40 Developmental Coordination Disorder (p. 49)

Dolls

ROCKY IS A SIX-YEAR-OLD BOY for whom his parents seek treatment because "he wants to be a girl." The patient's major playmate is his younger sister; and although his parents are trying to foster friendships with other boys, Rocky prefers to play with girls or to be with his mother or a female baby-sitter. He particularly dislikes rough play with boys and physical fighting, although he is well built, above average in height for his age, and well coordinated. At home he engages in much role-playing, invariably assuming female roles. When playing house with his younger sister, he plays the "mother" or "big sister" role and leaves the male role to her. He likes to imitate female TV figures, such as the oldest daughter from the Cosby Show, the adult wives of the Flintstones, or Wonder Woman. Similarly, he likes to playact female characters from various children's books.

Rocky has never been interested in toy cars, trucks, or trains, but is an avid player with dolls (baby, Barbie®, and family dolls) and enjoys playing with kitchen toys. He also likes to play wedding, pregnancy, a female teacher, or a lady doctor. He is good at drawing and is very interested in drawing female figures. Although his parents try to restrict the activity, he engages in a lot of cross-dressing. Sometimes he uses a quilt or a towel around his middle for skirts, or a T-shirt or nightgown for a dress. He does not use any female underwear or bathing suits. He likes bows in his hair, and may use an underskirt or a veil on his head to imitate long hair. He loves dancing, preferably in dresses. He is very interested in jewelry, has plastic necklaces, and pretends at times to wear earrings. Also, he pretends to apply lipstick (with Chapstick®), and would use real lipstick and perfume if his mother would let him. He states, "I want to be a girl," often when he is unhappy—for instance, when he started kindergarten—or has felt in competition with his younger sister.

On examination, the boy is found to be clearly not effeminate. His intellectual development is apparently normal. Although somewhat reluctant, he is able to describe much of what his parents have related about his toy and game preferences. He says that he does not want to be a boy because he is afraid he will have to play with soldiers or play army with other boys when he grows bigger. He wishes a fairy could change him into a girl. What he likes about being a girl is wearing dresses, long hair, and jewelry. His drawings are all of female figures.

Family history, pregnancy, birth, and early development are all normal. The parents do not show any overt psychopathology. The patient's problems seem to have started with the birth of his younger sister, when he was two years old. For the first four months of her life, his sister suffered from digestive problems and required a great deal of parental attention and care. The patient then began to display definite signs of regression—played the baby role again, wanted to drink from a bottle, and to be held and carried. His mother gave in to some extent. Both parents and baby-sitters think that cross-dressing and wanting to be a girl date back to that time, although, before the birth of his sister, there were already some instances of the patient's imitating long hair by wearing a towel on his head. When the patient was four years old, his sister got a baby doll, which he took from her. Around this same time he spent a vacation with his sister at their grandparents' and complained that his sister got more attention than he, ending with the familiar "Why can't I be a girl? Why didn't God make me a girl? Girls get to dress up, get to wear pretty things."

From age three on, Rocky was enrolled in nursery school, and initially displayed much separation anxiety. He appeared more sensitive than the other children, always seemed to feel threatened by them, and did not stand up for himself. His teacher noted from the beginning that he dressed up very frequently, said that he wanted to be a mother when he grew up, and was reluctant to engage in rough-and-tumble activities. In the second grade he was so good at imitating a girl (batting his eyes, voice inflection, walking) that the teacher wondered if he were an intersex. In the third grade his classroom teacher closed off the doll corner because of his preoccupation with doll play.

Discussion of "Dolls"

There should be little question about the diagnosis in this case. This boy has a persistent and frequently stated desire to be a girl. He is preoccupied with female stereotypical activity, preferring to play with girls, and pretending that he is a girl, with frequent cross-dressing. He plays exclusively with stereotypically female toys such as dolls, rejecting male toys and activities. When imitating characters from books and TV, he always chooses female characters. He openly expresses a desire to be turned into a girl—not merely to play a female role.

These are the characteristic features of Gender Identity Disorder of Childhood as seen in a male. When this disorder is diagnosed in a female, the desire to be male, because of a profound discontent in being a female, needs to be distinguished from the desire merely to have the cultural advantages associated with being a male.

DSM-III-R Diagnosis:

Axis I: 302.60 Gender Identity Disorder of Childhood (p. 73)

Wild Child

A FRUSTRATED AND FRAZZLED MOTHER, on the advice of her pediatrician, brings her seven-year-old daughter, Wilda, to a genetics clinic of a large medical center. The little girl is exhibiting severe behavioral problems that her mother is unable to control. The problems consist of temper tantrums in which she stomps her feet, throws herself onto the floor, hurls objects across the room, and talks back to her mother. She steals, swears, runs away from the house, and gets into trouble at school. In addition, she exhibits certain bizarre behaviors, including grunting, repeating what is spoken to her, and touching herself repeatedly in the crotch.

Wilda's mother reports difficulties since infancy. The baby was colicky and cried whenever she was picked up. At six months of age, she had a febrile seizure. By three years of age, she was "constantly on the go" and "never stopped talking." Temper tantrums began at four. From the moment she entered kindergarten, she could not sit in her seat and appeared unable to concentrate. In the first grade she began to play pranks on her teacher and was frequently insolent. Although of good intelligence, by the second grade the little girl was behind in her skills. Telling lies became frequent. Grunting when playing and repetitious hiccuping began. She also developed difficulties sleeping, with frequent bad dreams and talking in her sleep.

Both at school and at home, Wilda never finishes what she starts, doesn't listen to instructions, and is easily distracted. She acts before thinking, moves from one activity to another, is completely disorganized in her approach to schoolwork or play, climbs on furniture, and needs constant supervision.

Wilda's mother does not know how to discipline her. The child's disobedience is deliberate and provocative; whenever her mother spanks her, she laughs. When her mother tries to talk to her about her misbehavior, Wilda typically says, "It was Debbie's fault!" or "Bobby made me do it!"

Wilda's father was killed while attempting to murder someone. Her mother did poorly in school, and has grunting tics. The mother's older brother has alcoholism and frequently beats his wife. Her younger brother "runs around the house like a wild animal" and has vocal tics. The mother's father has a history of a head-rolling tic, drinks heavily, and beats his wife. He also molested Wilda's mother when she was a child.

Discussion of "Wild Child"

One can only have compassion for Wilda's mother, who is faced with the problem of managing such an array of difficult behaviors!

Let us first consider Wilda's tics. She has many vocal tics in which she involuntarily grunts, hiccups, and repeats what has been said (echolalia). Some of her swearing may also be a vocal tic. The only motor tic that is suggested is her touching her crotch. If Wilda, in addition to the vocal tics, had *multiple* motor tics, the diagnosis would be Tourette's Disorder. The presence of vocal tics and the absence of multiple motor tics indicates the diagnosis of Chronic Motor or Vocal Tic Disorder.

Let us consider her behavior problems. As is often the case with children with Tic Disorders, there are many symptoms suggesting Attention-deficit Hyperactivity Disorder. In fact, we count 8 of the 14 symptoms that are included in the relevant diagnostic criteria, as either specifically mentioned or implied. Wilda is fidgety, has difficulty remaining seated, is easily distracted, often talks excessively, has difficulty sustaining attention, fails to finish projects, moves from one activity to another, and doesn't seem to listen to instruction. The eight symptoms are the minimum number required to make the diagnosis. Because there is more than minimal impairment in school and social functioning that can be attributed to these symptoms, we specify the severity as moderate.

Finally, let us consider Wilda's oppositional and defiant behavior. We count only two symptoms of Conduct Disorder: stealing and lying. At least three are required for the diagnosis. However, we count five symptoms of Oppositional Defiant Disorder (at least five are required): she loses her temper, argues with adults, blames others for her mistakes, swears, actively defies adult requests or rules (we assume this is probably how she gets into trouble at school), and deliberately does things to annoy other people (plays pranks on her teacher). Therefore, we diagnose Oppositional Defiant Disorder, of moderate severity.

It is common for patients with Tic Disorders to have family members who also have Tic Disorders. It is unusual, however, to find in one family as many people who apparently all have Tic Disorders as in Wilda's family.

DSM-III-R Diagnosis:

Axis I: 307.22 Chronic Motor or Vocal Tic Disorder (p. 81)
          314.01 Attention-deficit Hyperactivity Disorder, Moderate (p. 52)
          313.81 Oppositional Defiant Disorder, Moderate (p. 57)

Nailbiter

A 12-YEAR-OLD GIRL came for a consultation because of a one-year history of "nervousness." About a year before the consultation, her parents had separated. Their marriage had been apparently stable and outwardly satisfactory up until that time, and their child-rearing practices were unremarkable. Following her parents' separation, the patient developed several fears and a relatively persistent state of anxiety. She began to bite her nails and to worry about the quality of her school performance; she became afraid of the dark and appeared to live in a relatively constant state of apprehension. Her worries were mostly realistic, but greatly exaggerated. She was concerned about her appearance, felt awkward, and was extremely shy in social situations. She reported relatively constant feelings of nervousness and anxiety, which seemed to be exacerbated by almost any event in her life. She experienced no panic attacks and no specific fears upon separation from her parents, although she was occasionally worried, without good reason, about their safety.

The patient is a shy girl who often has difficulty making friends, though she has developed lasting and close relationships with several peers. Her school performance has ranged from adequate to outstanding and has not declined in the past year.

During the interview her palms were sweating, it was hard for her to look at the examiner, and she was rather inhibited and tense. She denied persistent feelings of sadness and lack of interest in her environment, and said she was able to enjoy things except for the times when her anxiety peaked. When questioned about guilt, she reported with difficulty that sometimes she felt that somehow she was responsible for her parents' separation or divorce, although she really couldn't say how.

Physical examination findings were unremarkable. Specifically, the patient had no goiter or exophthalmos, and thyroid indices were within normal limits. Neurologic findings were unremarkable except for a mild tremor of extended hands during the examination, but this did not interfere with fine-motor skills.

Discussion of "Nailbiter"

Anxiety and its various manifestations are the central features of this girl's illness. She has none of the circumscribed symptoms that would suggest such Anxiety Disorders as a Phobic Disorder, Obsessive Compulsive Disorder, or Panic Disorder. Even though the precipitating event was the separation of her parents and she "occasionally worried about their safety," she is not particularly concerned about separation from them. This would seem to rule out Separation Anxiety Disorder.

The patient displays a variety of symptoms of generalized anxiety: unrealistic worrying about her parents' safety, overconcern about her academic performance, marked self-consciousness, and inability to relax. These have all persisted for more than six months, and thus add up to a diagnosis of Overanxious Disorder. (The diagnosis of Generalized Anxiety Disorder is not considered because she is younger than 18.)

On Axis IV we should note the parents' separation as a moderate psychosocial stressor that apparently is related to the development of the Axis I disorder.

On Axis V we should code her highest level of functioning during the past year as 65, taking into account her good academic performance and several close friendships.

DSM-III-R Diagnosis:

Axis I: 313.00 Overanxious Disorder (p. 64)
Axis II: V71.09 No Diagnosis or Condition
Axis III: None
Axis IV: Psychosocial stressors: separation of parents
          Severity: 3 - Moderate
Axis V: Current GAF: 65
          Highest GAF past year: 65

Special Dinners

AT THEIR WITS' END, the parents of Jordan, a six-year-old boy, brought him to a child psychiatrist for evaluation. Their already shaky marriage was being severely tested by conflict over their son's behavior at home and at school. The mother complained bitterly that the father, frequently away from home on business, "overindulged" their son. In point of fact, the son would argue and throw temper tantrums and insist on continuing games, books, etc., whenever his father put him to bed, so that a 7:30 PM bedtime was delayed until 10:30, 11:00, or even 11:30 at night. Similarly, the father had been known to cook four or five different meals for his son's dinner if Jordan stubbornly insisted that he would not eat what had been prepared. At school several teachers had complained that the child was stubborn and spiteful, often spoke out of turn, and refused to comply with classroom rules.

On questioning by the psychiatrist, the parents denied that their son had ever been destructive of property, lied excessively, or stolen. When interviewed, the child was observed to be cheerful and able to sit quietly in his chair, listening attentively to the questions that were asked of him. His answers, however, were brief, and he tended to minimize the extent of the problems he was having with his parents and teachers.

Discussion of "Special Dinners"

Although disturbances in the functioning of this family unit may well have contributed to this child's difficulties, the child now shows a pattern of maladaptive behavior that is not limited to his interaction with his parents. Temper tantrums, breaking school rules, argumentativeness, annoying and provocative behavior, spitefulness, and stubbornness are all part of a persistent pattern of negativistic, hostile, and defiant behavior.

Since this boy's behavior does not involve violation of the basic rights of others or of major age-appropriate societal norms or rules (such as physical aggression or truancy), this is not a Conduct Disorder. Since there is no evidence of a more serious disorder, such as Schizophrenia or a Pervasive Developmental Disorder, the diagnosis Oppositional Defiant Disorder is made. We note the severity as mild, because there are no symptoms in excess of those required to make the diagnosis, and the interference with school and social functioning is minimal.

The specification of the V code condition for Parent–Child Problem is not made because the disturbance is not limited to interaction between the child and his parents: the disturbed behavior is also seen at school. Parent–Child Problem is not listed in *addition* to Oppositional Defiant Disorder because the disturbed parent–child interaction is symptomatic of the child's mental disorder.

DSM-III-R Diagnosis:

Axis I: 313.81 Oppositional Defiant Disorder, Mild (p. 57)

What's Happening?

THE PARENTS OF NINE-YEAR-OLD Benjamin consulted a pediatrician after he had awakened many nights, very frightened by what they assumed to be bad dreams. Beginning several months earlier, and several times a week thereafter, Benjamin would come downstairs, after having been asleep for only a short time, looking dazed and terrified, breathing rapidly, with widely dilated pupils and "goose pimples." At such times he kept asking, "What's happening?" It usually took 15 to 20 minutes to calm him down enough so that he could return to bed. He was never able to remember any bad dreams, but said that he just woke up feeling very strange and frightened that something terrible would happen.

The event that prompted the consultation occurred when Ben was home from school recovering from an ear infection. His mother had briefly left the house to do some shopping, and he apparently fell asleep on the couch, awoke in a state of terror, and ran out of the house, in winter, in his bare feet, and hitched a ride to a neighbor's house, where his frantic mother finally found him.

Discussion of "What's Happening?"

Benjamin's sleep disturbance is characterized by abrupt awakening after being asleep for only a short time, signs of extreme anxiety (rapid breathing, dilated pupils, piloerection), and relative unresponsiveness to the efforts of others to comfort him. Rapid eye movement (REM) sleep nightmares (Dream Anxiety Disorder) are ruled out by the occurrence of the episodes shortly after falling asleep (during non-REM sleep) and by Benjamin's inability to recall distinct and vivid dreams. Epileptic seizures during sleep with postictal confusion may present a similar clinical picture, but this diagnosis is unlikely as there is no mention of seizures during the day. Sleepwalking Disorder is suggested by Benjamin's running out of the house; but if there is any anxiety in Sleepwalking Disorder, it is mild and occurs only *after* the sleepwalking.

In fact, Benjamin's mother was happy to hear from her pediatrician that Benjamin suffered from Pavor Nocturnus, a relatively innocuous disorder that usually disappears in adolescence. In DSM-III-R it is called simply Sleep Terror Disorder and is classified as a Parasomnia, a sleep disorder in which the predominant disturbance is an abnormal event that occurs either during sleep or at the threshold between wakefulness and sleep.

DSM-III-R Diagnosis:

Axis I: **307.46 Sleep Terror Disorder (p. 311)**
Axis II: **V71.09 No Diagnosis or Condition**
Axis III: **None**
Axis IV: **Severity: 1 - None**
Axis V: **Current GAF: 65**
           Highest GAF past year: 0 - inadequate information

Down's Syndrome

A 15-YEAR-OLD BOY WAS BROUGHT to the emergency room by his mother, who, clutching the on-call resident's arm, pleaded, "You've got to admit him; I just can't take it anymore." The patient had been taken home from a special school by his mother six months previously. The mother showed the resident papers from the school that indicated that the patient's IQ was 45. He had had several placements, beginning at age eight. On visiting days, the boy always pleaded of his mother, "Mommy, take me home?" After a year or so away, the patient would be brought home by his mother, who had always been racked by guilt because of his retardation and her inability to manage him in the home. The patient was an only child whose parents had been divorced for the past four years. The father had moved to another city.

During the last six months at home, the patient had increasingly become a behavior problem. He was about 5'9" tall and weighed close to

200 pounds. He had become destructive of property at home—breaking dishes and a chair during angry tantrums—and then, more recently, physically assaultive. He had hit his mother on the arm and shoulder during a recent scuffle that began when she tried to get him to stop banging a broom on the apartment floor. The mother showed her bruises to the resident and threatened to call the mayor's office if the hospital refused to admit her son.

On examination, the boy was observed to have the typical signs of Down's syndrome, including thick facial features, slightly protruding tongue, epicanthal fold of the eyelids, and Simian crease of the palms of the hands. With indistinct and slurred speech, the boy insisted that he "didn't mean to hurt anybody."

Discussion of "Down's Syndrome"

This boy's IQ of 45 indicates significantly subaverage general intellectual functioning. The need for placement in special schools since age eight suggests that there have been severe concurrent deficits or impairments in adaptive behavior. These two features, with onset before the age of 18, indicate the Axis II diagnosis of Mental Retardation. Since the IQ level is between 35 and 55, the severity level is Moderate.

The diagnosis of Mental Retardation should be made when the criteria are met, regardless of the presence of another diagnosis. In the presence of significant Mental Retardation, the issue of a Specific Developmental Disorder is moot, since the specific deficit would have to be out of proportion to the deficits in other areas of development. A Pervasive Developmental Disorder can coexist with Mental Retardation; but unlike in this case, only when there is no interest or pleasure in social contact. Therefore, no additional diagnosis is warranted on Axis II.

This child, as is often the case, presents for admission because of destructive and aggressive behavior, not because of impairment in intellectual functioning. This aggressive behavior is presumably a persistent pattern; nevertheless, the additional diagnosis of Conduct Disorder is not justified because there are none of the other characteristic features of this disorder, such as stealing, lying, and running away from home.

In this case, Mental Retardation is apparently due to Down's syndrome, which would be noted on Axis III.

The possible contribution of psychosocial stressors to an exacerbation of this boy's behavioral problems is unclear from the available information. Perhaps returning home from the special school or a change in the mother's behavior, because of her guilt feelings, was a factor in triggering the boy's recent episodes of assaultive behavior. In the absence of more information, the Axis IV level of psychosocial stressors is noted as "0."

The patient's highest level of functioning in the past year is very poor, owing to marked impairment in all areas of functioning; therefore, an appropriate highest GAF rating is only about 20. Because of the increase in dangerous behavior recently, necessitating the visit to the emergency room, the current GAF is rated 10.

DSM-III-R Diagnosis:

Axis I: V71.09 No Diagnosis or Condition
Axis II: 318.00 Moderate Mental Retardation (p. 31)
Axis III: Down's syndrome
Axis IV: Psychosocial Stressors: Undetermined
           Severity: 0 - Inadequate information
Axis V: Current GAF: 10
           Highest GAF past year: 20

Silent Sister

A 16-YEAR-OLD HIGH-SCHOOL JUNIOR was referred by a teacher to a mental health clinic with the complaint that she was unable to make any verbal contributions in her classes. Her inability to speak had begun one year previously, following the death of her mother. It took school personnel some time to realize that the girl did not speak in any of her classes. She had kept up with her assignments, handing in all her written work and receiving better than average grades on tests.

The patient's father is a hardworking janitor in a large apartment building. He usually comes home late and is rather passive and indifferent toward the patient and her six younger siblings. He has never responded to school requests for visits to discuss his daughter's problems. Since her mother's death, the patient has assumed the mothering of her siblings: cooking the meals, cleaning, and listening to their requests and complaints.

When seen, the patient was a thin, neatly dressed girl who was alert, but initially responded with only brief nods of her head. With reassurance, she began to whisper monosyllabic answers to questions. Her responses were rational and logical, but she denied that her failure to speak was much of a problem. A younger sibling reported that the patient had no difficulty speaking at home.

Discussion of "Silent Sister"

Under ordinary circumstances this girl will not talk to anyone except her family, indicating a persistent refusal to talk in one or more major social situations (including at school), but intact ability both to comprehend spoken language and to speak. With considerable reassurance and coaxing, the interviewer manages to get whispered monosyllabic answers to questions.

Mutism may be a symptom of many mental disorders, such as Major Depression, Social Phobia, or Schizophrenia. In this case, however, it is the predominant—in fact, as far as we know, the only—symptom. Hence, the diagnosis is Elective Mutism.

DSM-III-R Diagnosis:

Axis I: 313.23 Elective Mutism (p. 89)

Follow-up

"Silent Sister" continued to do well in school. When the counselors and teachers became aware of her situation, she received more attention and support, and gradually started to talk at school.

Thin Tim

EIGHT-YEAR-OLD TIM WAS REFERRED by a pediatrician who asked for an emergency evaluation because of a serious weight loss during the past year. Tim is extremely concerned about his weight and weighs himself daily. He complains that he is too fat, and if he does not lose weight, he cuts back on food. He has lost ten pounds in the past year and still feels that he is too fat, though it is clear that he is underweight. In desperation, his parents have removed the scales from the house; as a result, Tim is keeping a record of the calories that he eats daily. He spends a lot of time on this, checking and rechecking that he has done it just right.

In addition, Tim is described as being obsessed with cleanliness and neatness. Currently he has no friends because he refuses to visit them, feeling that their houses are "dirty"; he gets upset when another child touches him. He is always checking whether he is doing things the way they "should" be done. He becomes very agitated and anxious about this. He has to get up at least two hours before leaving for school each day in order to give himself time to get ready. Recently, he woke up at 1:30 in the morning to prepare for school.

Discussion of "Thin Tim"

The emergency evaluation is because of Tim's recent weight loss. He has lost ten pounds in the last year, during which time a boy of his age might have been expected to gain about that amount. This means he has actually lost 20 pounds, which is undoubtedly more than the weight loss of 15% that is required for a diagnosis of Anorexia Nervosa. Although it is unusual to see this disorder in a male and in one so young, Tim also has the other characteristic features: fear of becoming fat, feeling fat even when obviously underweight, and refusal to maintain his weight in the normal range.

Although not the focus of attention, Tim's preoccupation with various recurrent thoughts concerning dirtiness causes him considerable distress. Moreover, he has to check whether he is doing things the way they "should" be done, and such activities apparently interfere with his normal functioning (he has to get up several hours before school in order to get ready). Although he does not describe these recurrent thoughts and repetitive acts as senseless, it is reasonable to assume that the thoughts do intrude into his consciousness and are beyond his control, and that his lengthy "getting ready" routines are performed in response to these thoughts. Thus, they represent true obsessions and compulsions. Because the content of these obsessions and compulsions is unrelated to Tim's Eating Disorder, an additional diagnosis of Obsessive Compulsive Disorder is made, and is listed second, since the initial focus of attention is the eating problem.

There is phobic avoidance (he won't visit friends' houses because they might be dirty), but the additional diagnosis of a Simple Phobia is not made because phobic avoidance is a commonly associated feature of Obsessive Compulsive Disorder.

DSM-III-R Diagnosis:

Axis I: 307.10 Anorexia Nervosa (p. 67)
           300.30 Obsessive Compulsive Disorder, Moderate
                  (p. 247)

Nighttime Visitor

TINA WAS EIGHT YEARS OLD when her guidance counselor at school referred her to the Family Treatment Center in Cleveland because of disruptive, aggressive behavior. Her 11-year-old brother, Don, and her 9-year-old sister, Sara, were also evaluated, together with their mother.

Several months earlier Tina had been admitted to the hospital with vaginal bleeding and a discharge. A diagnosis of vaginal warts (*condyloma acuminatum*) was made, and the vaginal culture proved to be positive for gonorrhea. When questioned by a social worker whom the pediatrician asked to see the children, Tina revealed that she and Sara had been sexually molested by their father for the past two years. According to her, he would come into their bedroom regularly at night and have vaginal intercourse with her, and, more rarely, with Sara. The girls noticed that if they were awake, their father often would not bother them. Nevertheless, Tina was so frightened that she would close her eyes and feign sleep during the molestation. Their father threatened them with beatings if they were to divulge the secret, so they had never told anyone.

Their brother, Don, after witnessing one of the molestations, told their mother. She did not believe him, told her husband, who then proceeded to beat Don. In fact, Don had often been beaten by his father. After Don's disclosure, Tina and Sara told their mother what had been happening, but she scolded them for "making up stories."

When the social worker talked with the mother about these events, she admitted that she had suspected that her children were telling the truth, but was afraid of confronting her husband about his sexual abuse because she feared his murderous rage. During their 12-year marriage, he had frequently beaten her, but she never thought of leaving him because her religion forbade divorce.

After the medical confirmation of the sexual abuse, the children were temporarily placed in foster care, the father was jailed, and the family court cited the mother for neglect because she had failed to intervene to protect the children from the father's sexual abuse. The children were subsequently placed with their maternal grandmother, and then returned to their mother after she agreed to a psychiatric evaluation and treatment for herself and her children.

When interviewed at the Family Treatment Center, Tina is a sad, unusually quiet child who rarely smiles. She describes nightmares about her father coming into her room. Tina has talked with the children in school about being molested, and now believes that they all dislike her because of it. When she testified in court, she was certain that she would be sent to jail because she had done something wrong. She also fears that her father will return and attack her. At home she often fights with Sara and Don, and feels "picked on" by her mother, whom she feels has always favored her siblings.

Discussion of "Nighttime Visitor"

Tina's reaction to having been sexually abused by her father and not protected (or even believed) by her mother has included depressed mood, nightmares about the trauma, anger, inappropriate self-reproach and guilt, and the feeling that schoolmates dislike her. There is no evidence that the depressed mood is accompanied by the characteristic symptoms of the depressive syndrome, other than self-reproach and guilt. Therefore, a diagnosis of Major Depression cannot be made. Although the sexual abuse has been going on for two years, there is no description of a persistent depressed mood that would justify a diagnosis of Dysthymia. In fact, during this time Tina seems to have been more frightened than depressed.

The reexperiencing of the trauma (nightmares of her father) suggest the diagnosis of Post-traumatic Stress Disorder. This diagnosis requires at least three symptoms indicating persistent avoidance of stimuli associated with the trauma or numbing of general responsiveness. We find evidence only for a feeling of estrangement from others (her classmates). In addition, the diagnosis requires persistent symptoms of increased arousal, and we find no evidence for this. We are therefore left with the residual diagnosis of Adjustment Disorder with Mixed Disturbance of Emotions and Conduct.

Although there is no specific DSM-III-R diagnosis that captures the clinical picture that Tina demonstrates, some have suggested that the syndrome, particularly the victim's inappropriate self-blame, is often seen in adults or children who have been sexually, physically, or psychologically abused. This syndrome might be called "Victimization Disorder," and could be considered for possible inclusion in DSM-IV.

DSM-III-R Diagnosis:

Axis I: 309.40 Adjustment Disorder with Mixed Disturbance of Emotions and Conduct (p. 330)

Follow-up

After the evaluation of the family, individual psychotherapy was recommended for Tina, Sara, and their mother. In addition, family treatment was instituted in order to improve the relationship between the children and their mother and to help establish structure and discipline in the home. Tina's mother was encouraged to allow the children to express their feelings of having been betrayed by her. At home Tina began to overeat and steal money from her mother's purse, as a way of expressing anger toward her mother and of getting more attention.

In the treatment setting, Tina acted frightened and needy, and she clung to her female therapist. She expressed her yearnings for nurturance and safety by caring for doll babies and stuffed animals. She was frequently involved in "traumatic play," in which she acted out various elements of the trauma. These dramas often involved a witch who poisoned children and devils and monsters who attacked them when they tried to run away.

Nathan

N ATHAN, A 14-YEAR-OLD BOY, was brought to a psychologist for consultation by his mother because of trouble in his special classroom, including restlessness, fidgeting, and being difficult to understand. He had been adopted from a Latin American country; little was known of his early history except that he had suffered from malnutrition. His mother provided a detailed history for the boy since the time of his adoption, noting that he sat up at age 19 months, stood at age 40 months, walked at age 4 years, 2 months, and said "bye-bye," his first word, at 30 months. An extensive medical workup, including an electroencephalogram, pneumoencephalograms, and chromosome studies, provided no clues to the etiology of the boy's delayed development.

Nathan's teacher described him as "meaning well, but causing a lot of problems." His mother reported that he was "very aware of relationships and vibes," but unable to deal with the abstract. She stated that he had very limited speech, daydreamed, became easily frustrated, and was difficult to take to stores because he liked to run up to people and touch them, often frightening them.

During examination the boy stared at the examiner, grabbed his hand, and tried to pull him to the toy chest. The boy made a few sounds—"da," "ah," and "wa"—but none could be considered real words. However, he used gestures to indicate his understanding of words, such as "telephone," "car," "cookie," and "spoon." He was able to follow four-step commands, but did not seem to comprehend questions, such as "How are you feeling?" His play was what might be expected of a much, much younger child.

Discussion of "Nathan"

Nathan has had markedly delayed developmental milestones and has current evidence of significantly subaverage intellectual functioning, as evidenced by his limited speech and ability to comprehend abstract questions. This is associated with markedly impaired adaptive functioning (troubles in school and in normal social interactions). These all indicate Mental Retardation. Since there is no mention of IQ testing, the level of retardation cannot be determined; hence, it is noted as Unspecified.

DSM-III-R Diagnosis:

Axis I: V71.09 No Diagnosis or Condition
Axis II: 319.00 Unspecified Mental Retardation (p. 33)

Follow-up

Nathan was seen again when he was 18 years old. He made little eye contact, showed limited attention for any testing tasks, and generally was uncommunicative. Testing suggested language comprehension at the two-year-old level. His mother reported that he had learned approximately 50 words in sign language. Nathan was in a prevocational school program, but was causing problems because of his immature behavior, short attention span, difficulty following rules, lack of guilt about misbehavior, inability to form peer friendships, and ritualistic behaviors. His mother reported serious problems with public masturbation.

No One Hits the Baby

FOUR-YEAR-OLD CAROL was referred for an evaluation when her teacher made a complaint to the state Central Registry for Child Abuse Reports. A family evaluation by a social worker revealed the following:

Carol is the older of two children, both of whom live with their parents in a two-bedroom apartment. Her problems began with the birth of her sister three months ago. Her teachers noticed a change in her behavior at school. She began pushing other children and hit a classmate with a wooden block, causing a laceration of the classmate's lip. When Carol's teacher took her aside to talk about her behavior, she noticed what seemed to be belt marks on Carol's abdomen and forehead.

Carol's sister was "colicky" and slept for only short periods throughout the day and night. She stopped crying only when her mother held her. Her mother therefore had little time for Carol, and Carol's father took over her care on evenings and weekends. He began to drink more than usual, half a bottle of wine each evening, and became increasingly irritable. He and his wife argued over her attention to the infant and the requirement that he take care of Carol. Carol, who was a bright, curious, talkative four-year-old, asked constant questions and often wanted to hold the baby. When refused, she would lie on the floor and have a tantrum. Since her sister's birth, she had begun to have difficulty falling asleep, and awoke repeatedly during the night.

Carol's father was unable to cope with her demands for attention and often told her to shut up and slapped her when she did not obey. On many occasions he responded to her tantrums or repeated questions by hitting her with his belt.

Carol is a lively and attractive little blue-eyed blond, dressed in jeans, T-shirt, and sneakers. She relates appropriately and warmly to the interviewer and easily separates from her parents in the waiting room. Her intelligence appears above average, as indicated by her fund of knowledge, vocabulary, and drawings of a person and of geometric forms.

About her sister, Carol says, "She's a bad girl. She cries all the time. I get hit when I cry, but no one hits the baby." When asked about fights at the day-care center, she replies, "I hit Robert (her playmate) because he pulls my hair." She says she is afraid to go to sleep because she has bad dreams of an old man killing her.

Discussion of "No One Hits the Baby"

We shall focus on the diagnosis of Carol's difficulties since she is the "identified patient," but should note that her problems are actually the consequence of her father's psychopathology. We assume that Carol's reaction to having a baby sister would not have been remarkable were it not for her father's physical abuse of her.

Researchers have only recently begun to study the psychological consequences of physical and sexual abuse of children. It would seem that children who are physically or sexually abused are at risk for developing several disorders. Major Depression, Separation Anxiety Disorder, Oppositional Defiant Disorder and Conduct Disorder are frequent initial reactions to sexual or physical abuse. In adolescents suicidal behavior and Psychoactive Substance Use are also frequent. It is unclear how often Post-traumatic Stress Disorder is an initial reaction. Major Depression, various personality disturbances and (more rarely) Multiple Personality Disorder are long-term consequences that are seen in adults. It is certainly clear that children who themselves have been physically or sexually abused are likely to abuse their own children. The cases in which this kind of multigenerational abuse has been identified have generally involved more serious and long-term abuse than Carol has experienced.

Carol's changed behavior includes temper tantrums at home, fighting with other children at school, and having trouble falling asleep. These few symptoms are not indicative of a syndrome that would justify the diagnosis of any of the above disorders. Therefore, we are left with the residual diagnosis of Adjustment Disorder with Mixed Disturbance of Emotions and Conduct.

DSM-III-R Diagnosis:

Axis I: 309.40 Adjustment Disorder with Mixed Disturbance of Emotions and Conduct (p. 330)
Axis II: None
Axis III: None
Axis IV: Psychosocial Stressor: Physical abuse
           Severity: 5 - Extreme (predominantly acute events)
Axis V: Current GAF: 55
           Highest GAF: 85

Follow-up

Carol, along with her mother and father, began a family therapy program that included parenting training and behavioral therapy for Carol, coordinated with the day-care center. Her father was persuaded to join Alcoholics Anonymous, has stopped drinking, and has been able to control his anger at his daughter. Six months later, Carol's aggressive behavior had ceased. She was doing well with peers and in her academic work, was sleeping throughout the night, and had stopped having temper tantrums.

Baby Susan

S USAN WAS ADMITTED to the hospital at six months of age, by an aunt, for evaluation of failure to gain weight. She had been born into an impoverished family after an unplanned, uncomplicated pregnancy. During the first four months of her life, she gained weight steadily. Regurgitation was noted during the fifth month, and increased in severity to the point where she was regurgitating after every feeding. After each feeding, Susan would engage in one of two behaviors: (a) she would open her mouth, elevate her tongue, and rapidly thrust it back and forward, after which milk would appear at the back of her mouth and slowly trickle out; or (b) she would vigorously suck her thumb and place fingers in her mouth, following which milk would slowly flow out of the corner of her mouth.

In the past two months Susan had been cared for by a number of people, including her aunt and paternal grandmother. Her parents were making a marginal marital adjustment.

Discussion of "Baby Susan"

Failure to gain weight or weight loss in an infant, once organic illnesses such as congenital anomalies have been ruled out, suggests either an Eating Disorder (Rumination Disorder of Infancy) or failure to thrive because of grossly inadequate care (Reactive Attachment Disorder of Infancy or Early Childhood). It is clear that in this case the child is not gaining weight because of the regurgitation after each feeding. This, plus the history of a normal period of weight gain, is characteristic of Rumination Disorder.

DSM-III-R Diagnosis:

Axis I: 307.53 Rumination Disorder of Infancy (p. 70)

She Wants to Be a Boy

K ELLY, A 16-YEAR-OLD Canadian girl from British Columbia, is referred to a gender identity clinic at the suggestion of her family physician and with her parents' agreement and participation. According to her mother, "Kelly wants a sex change. She wants to be a boy very desperately." Kelly echoes this, saying that she has wanted to be a boy "since I was two." The current referral was precipitated by Kelly's relationship with another girl, Anna, who has been living with the family for the past few months. Kelly's mother became agitated about the girls' relationship, feeling that it was sexual: "They always have their legs crossed, arms around each other, and once were lying naked with their breasts exposed reading dirty books."

Since reaching puberty, Kelly has continued to show a number of signs suggesting that she is very uncomfortable with being a female. She found her menstrual periods "horrible" and disliked having to wear a bra. Kelly has continued to say that she wants to be a boy, including having a penis. Last year, she learned of the possibility of sex-reassignment surgery. She knows that it would include a mastectomy, removal of her internal reproductive organs, and hormone injections. She is not sure whether she could have a penis surgically constructed.

During the interview, Kelly is asked why the idea of being a boy is so important to her, and why she cannot pursue her life goals and remain a girl. She then stated that at the present time her sole reason for wanting to be a boy was that she wanted to play in the National Hockey League. Kelly claims that a few months ago she had been asked to try out for a minor league team owned by the Los Angeles Kings. She felt that if she had a penis, she would have a better chance of getting on the team.

Kelly's physical appearance is ambiguous with regard to her biological sex. Her hair is short, she is dressed casually in blue jeans, and she wears no makeup. She does, however, wear one earring. Kelly says that she does not care if others perceive her as a male or as a female, preferring to be seen as a "human being." As she speaks, it becomes clear that she prefers that people not ask her if she is a male or a female, though she does not actually say that she wants others to perceive her as a male.

Kelly quit school after the seventh grade. She claims that she is now in a youth group, training to be in the military. She very much enjoys this because even though she is known to be a female, "They treat you like a buddy—the same as the other guys." She takes great delight in ordering around her cadet peers, relishing "being mean; they all hate me" when she demands that they do 500 pushups. Kelly spoke in great detail about using a submachine gun, and said she had been practicing weapon use for several years. She is attracted by "gory things, blood, and living dangerously." Kelly says that the thought of war appeals to her because "they push you so hard and you are down on your knees, begging them to stop."

Kelly's mother tried to find out about her sexuality by having her read a "pornographic" book and underline those passages that excited her or, as Kelly put it, gave her a "twingy" feeling, during which she felt "weird inside." The passages that elicited such a feeling involved love-making between women. Kelly says that she is not sure if boys or girls turn her on. She jogs whenever she begins to have "twingy feelings" and denies that she has ever masturbated. "I think it's sick."

She denies ever experiencing sexual images either in dreams or fantasy. She says she has never had any sexual experiences with another person and has no desire to marry. When asked about lesbianism, she claims not to want to know very much about the gay subculture: "It's their life."

When she appeared for the physical examination, she apologized for not having shaved her legs. An endocrine evaluation was performed and indicated that the sex chromosomes were XX, there were no abnormally elevated levels of testosterone, and there were no signs of physical hermaphroditism.

Discussion of "She Wants to Be a Boy"

Kelly's extreme discomfort with her assigned sex indicates a Gender Identity Disorder. Since she is past puberty, a current diagnosis of Gender Identity Disorder of Childhood is not appropriate. Because she is requesting a "sex change," the diagnosis of Transsexualism has to be considered. Kelly certainly has persistent discomfort and a sense of inappropriateness about her assigned sex. However, it is only recently that she has even considered the possibility of a sex-change operation. Therefore, she does not meet the stringent criteria for Transsexualism, which require that the person be persistently (at least two years) preoccupied with getting rid of his or her sex characteristics and acquiring the sex characteristics of the other sex.

DSM-III-R contains a new category for cases, such as Kelly's, in which there is discomfort about one's assigned sex and persistent cross dressing, but no persistent preoccupation with having a sex change: Gender Identity Disorder of Adolescence or Adulthood, Nontranssexual Type (GIDAANT). The disorder is further specified, as is Transsexualism, on the basis of the sexual-orientation history. Kelly denies a homosexual or heterosexual orientation, so we would specify, Asexual.

The psychologist who submitted this case notes that in all cases of female-to-male Transsexualism that have been studied, the sexual orientation is homosexual. This is in contrast to cases of male-to-female Transsexualism, in which some patients are heterosexual (the person being attracted to women). Because Kelly's case is so close to that of Transsexualism, the psychologist suspects that her sexual orientation is homosexual.

DSM-III-R Diagnosis:

Axis I: 302.85 Gender Identity Disorder of Adolescence or Adulthood, Nontranssexual Type (GIDAANT), Asexual (p. 77)

Follow-up

At four-year follow-up, Kelly remained preoccupied with changing her sex, yet she continued to live in an ambivalent gender role; for example, she was employed in a typically "masculine" occupation, but claimed that no one asked, or cared, if she was male or female. In the past year, Kelly made an application to an adult gender identity clinic with the hope that she would eventually be able to have a sex change operation. She failed to keep her appointment.

Tiny Tina

TINA, A SMALL, SWEET-FACED, freckled, ten-year-old, has been referred by a pediatrician who was unsuccessful in treating her for refusing to go to school. Her difficulties began on the first day of school one year ago when she cried and hid in the basement. She agreed to go to school only when her mother promised to go with her and stay to have lunch with her at school. For the next three months, on school days, Tina had a variety of somatic complaints, such as headaches and "tummy aches," and each day would go to school only reluctantly, after much cajoling by her parents. Soon thereafter she could be gotten to school only if her parents lifted her out of bed, dressed and fed her, and drove her to school. Finally, in the spring, the school social-worker consulted Tina's pediatrician, who instituted a behavior-modification program with the help of her parents. Because this program was of only limited help, the pediatrician had now, at the beginning of the school year, referred Tina to a psychiatrist.

According to her mother, despite Tina's many absences from school last year, she performed well. During this time she also happily participated in all other activities, including Girl Scout meetings, sleepovers at friends' houses (usually with her sister), and family outings. Her mother wonders if taking a part-time bookkeeping job two years ago, plus the sudden death of a maternal grandmother to whom Tina was particularly close, might have been responsible for the child's difficulties.

When Tina was interviewed, she at first minimized any problems about school, insisting that "everything [was] okay," and that she got good grades and liked all the teachers. When this subject was pursued, she became angry and gave a lot of "I don't know" responses as to why, then, she often refused to go to school. Eventually she said that kids teased her about her size, calling her "Shrimp" and "Shorty"; but she gave the impression, as well as actually stated, that she liked school and her teachers. She finally admitted that what bothered her was leaving home. She could not specify why, but hinted that she was afraid something would happen, though to whom or to what she did not say; but she confessed that she felt uncomfortable when all of her family was out of sight.

On the Rorschach there was evidence of obsessive rumination about catastrophic events involving injury to members of her family and themes concerning family disruption.

Discussion of "Tiny Tina"

All of Tina's problems involve a fear of going to school. The question is: Is it school that she is really afraid of, or is it separating herself from her parents? The evidence that she is really afraid of school is her claim that the other children tease her and her willing participation in other activities away from home, such as sleepovers and Girl Scout meetings. But Tina herself concludes that it is really her fear that something bad will happen when her family is out of her sight that is behind her refusal to go to school. We are inclined to accept this explanation. An enforced six hours away from her family every day is apparently more troubling to her than an occasional hour at a Girl Scout meeting or, surprisingly, a sleepover, usually with her sister.

In the absence of any more pervasive disorder, the excessive distress about separation from the family and unrealistic worry about harm befalling them, reluctance to go to school, and complaints of physical symptoms on school days, over a period of more than two weeks, all indicate Separation Anxiety Disorder. We should not quarrel with a clinician who wished to make this diagnosis provisional pending further clarification of Tina's distress about being teased. If she is excessively fearful of the possibility of being humiliated or embarrassed in public, then the diagnosis of Social Phobia should be considered as an alternative or as an additional diagnosis.

DSM-III-R Diagnosis:

Axis I: 309.21 Separation Anxiety Disorder (p. 60)

Exercises

J ENNY, AGE FOUR, WAS REFERRED by her pediatrician for a psychiatric evaluation. Her parents are concerned about the girl's "obsession" with her own and her father's genitals. This takes the form of spending a considerable amount of time every day masturbating, which she calls doing her "exercises," asking to see her father's genitals several times a day, and running upstairs with him to watch him urinate.

Her parents think that she has always been very interested in her genitals and began to masturbate for apparent pleasure when she was six months old. They did not think much of it, but became concerned when she increased the intensity and length of her masturbation at about one year of age. At that time she would spend up to three hours a day masturbating, often doing it while she was also playing with toys or watching her parents. The masturbation decreased somewhat at about 18 months, but flared up again when her baby sister was born 2 years previously. At that time she also began to soil again; she smeared feces on the wall. She was openly angry with the new baby, sometimes had to be forcibly restrained from hurting her (e.g., putting a pillow over her face), and could virtually never be left alone with the baby.

About eight months ago, she began spending more time masturbating and became fascinated with male genitals. She has approached other men to see their genitals, and two months ago asked a five-year-old boy to take his pants down. Although her parents did not consider this abnormal, the boy's parents were extremely upset, and have forbidden the boy to play with her. Currently, she masturbates mostly when she goes to bed, for about 20 to 30 minutes, and while she speaks to people or watches TV. There have also been times when she has masturbated by lying on the staircase sideways and rubbing her genitals against the stairs.

Jenny is the oldest of two children of an upper-middle-class family. The father comes from an island in the Mediterranean and is an outgoing, personable man. Her mother is from Australia, is much more reserved, and cannot show her feelings easily. They have a somewhat impoverished sexual relationship, the mother acknowledging that "Since the last baby I don't feel like it anymore." Regarding Jenny's problem, her father thinks that it is okay for him to let her look at his genitals, but he has tried to get her to stop asking to see other men's. The mother stresses that she "doesn't mind her doing her exercises," as she herself calls it, although she seemed quite upset and tense about it. The father, on the other hand, seems mainly concerned about the future of this behavior, especially when Jenny enters school.

Jenny has always been a very active child who has demanded much attention and generally has a hard time sticking to any activity for more than two or three minutes. Her mother says that she is impulsive and flits from activity to activity without seeming to enjoy herself at anything. When her mother confronts her about this, Jenny often has severe temper tantrums.

Jenny was evaluated for two hours, during which she played cheerfully and eagerly with the interviewer. She concentrated well on the tasks she set herself to do. Her drawings were of long snakes and race tracks for cars. Her mother found her attentiveness surprising and commented repeatedly that it was "the first time she had ever done that." Jenny's speech and general knowledge were quite advanced for her age. There were no signs of gross psychopathology.

Discussion of "Exercises"

It is now recognized that as part of normal development, many children engage in masturbation. However, the amount of time that Jenny spends every day masturbating and her preoccupation with her father's and other men's genitals seem outside the normal range. Excessive masturbation in a child may be a symptom of Mental Retardation or a Pervasive Developmental Disorder, but there is certainly no suggestion of either subaverage intellectual development or grossly bizarre behavior or gross impairment in social and language development in Jenny's case.

Her parents refer to her preoccupation with genitals as an "obsession," but there is no evidence either that this preoccupation is a true obsession or that her masturbation is a compulsion. Obsessions are persistent thoughts that intrude themselves into consciousness and are experienced as senseless or repugnant. There is no evidence that Jenny feels this way about them. A compulsion is a repetitive and seemingly purposeful behavior that generally does not include activities that are inherently pleasurable, such as eating or masturbation.

If the excessive masturbation and preoccupation with men's genitals developed after a specific psychosocial stressor, such as frequent arguments between the parents, this might be conceptualized as an Adjustment Disorder. However, there is no evidence of this here. One could make a case for considering this an atypical form of an Impulse Control Disorder. Presumably Jenny is unable to resist an increasing sense of tension, and experiences pleasure when she gives in to the impulse to masturbate. Generally, however, in Impulse Control Disorders, the resulting behavior has severely negative consequences for the patient and others. At the present time, except for the incident with the five-year-old boy and her parents' distress, there is no evidence of serious negative consequences. If the same behavior persists in school (her father's fear), then the consequences will undoubtedly be more significant.

Jenny is described as "a very active child" who is "impulsive and flits from activity to activity." This raises the question of Attention-deficit Hyperactivity Disorder, but there is no evidence of other symptoms of hyperactivity and attentional disturbance, such as inability to complete tasks.

Many readers will wonder if Jenny's behavior is best understood as a manifestation of a disturbance in the relationship between the parents and the child. More substantial evidence for this would suggest the appropriateness of the V code condition, Parent–Child Problem.

Since this unusual behavior does not conform to any of the specific mental disorders included in DSM-III-R, and since there is insufficient information to make a diagnosis of any of the mental disorders that are slightly suggested, we should recommend that the diagnosis be deferred until more information is available. In the introduction to the section on Disorders Usually First Evident in Infancy, Childhood, or Adolescence, it is acknowledged that certain disturbances in development are not easily classified. We should therefore not quarrel with a diagnosis of Unspecified Mental Disorder, Nonpsychotic. We should also not quarrel with the use of the V code condition, Parent–Child Problem, by clinicians who believe that, with the available information, it would be most useful to conceptualize the unusual behavior not as a symptom of a mental disorder, but rather as a symptom of a disturbed parent–child relationship, possibly requiring family intervention.

DSM-III-R Diagnosis:

Axis I: 799.90 Diagnosis Deferred

Bereaved

A 17-YEAR-OLD HIGH-SCHOOL JUNIOR was brought to the emergency room by her distraught mother, who was at a loss to understand her daughter's behavior. Two days earlier the patient's father had been buried; he had died of a sudden myocardial infarction earlier in the week. The patient had become wildly agitated at the cemetery, screaming uncontrollably and needing to be restrained by relatives. She was inconsolable at home, sat rocking in a corner, and talked about a devil that had come to claim her soul. Before her father's death, she had been a "typical teenager, popular, and a very good student, but sometimes prone to overreacting." There was no previous psychiatric history.

Discussion of "Bereaved"

Grief is an expected reaction to the loss of a loved one. This young woman's reaction, however, not only is more severe than would be expected (wildly agitated, screaming uncontrollably) but also involves psychotic symptoms (the belief that a devil has come to claim her soul). The sudden onset of a florid psychotic episode immediately following a marked psychosocial stressor, in the absence of prodromal signs of Schizophrenia or a Schizotypal Personality Disorder preceding onset of the disturbance, indicates the Axis I diagnosis of Brief Reactive Psychosis. Typically the psychotic symptoms last for more than a few hours, but less than one month. The diagnosis can be made before the one-month period—the maximum duration of symptoms consistent with the diagnosis—has elapsed, but it should be qualified as "provisional." It is anticipated that the symptoms will subside and that the patient will return to her usual level of good functioning. If the symptoms persist beyond that time, the diagnosis would be changed to another psychotic disorder, such as Schizophreniform Disorder.

Axis II indicates the absence of a Personality Disorder but the presence of the histrionic traits the patient's mother describes as "overreacting."

Axis III notes the absence of any physical disorder or condition.

Axis IV rates the severity of the father's death as an extreme psychosocial stressor.

Axis V: Because of the recent development of severe psychotic symptoms and the inability to function ("sat rocking in a corner"), the patient's current functioning is rated 20; on the basis of the limited information that she was a "typical teen-ager, popular, and a very good student, but sometimes prone to overreacting," the highest level of functioning during the past year is rated 80.

DSM-III-R Diagnosis:

Axis I: 298.80 Brief Reactive Psychosis (Provisional) (p. 206)
Axis II: Histrionic traits
Axis III: None
Axis IV: Psychosocial stressor: death of father
           Severity: 5 - Extreme (acute event)
Axis V: Current GAF: 20
           Highest GAF past year: 80

Seizure

A 16-YEAR-OLD, FEMALE junior-high-school student was hospitalized on the psychiatric service for behavior problems. She had been in trouble with school authorities since age 12 for truancy and petty thefts. More recently, she was expelled from junior high school when she and two friends were caught smoking marijuana in the locker room. Final series of thefts from neighborhood stores and an incident in which s and a companion set a fire in a vacant lot brought her into court and prompted a judge to remand her to a psychiatric ward for evaluation. Her parents said they were unable to control her, that she was a "born liar," and that when she became angry with them, she frequently had stayed out all night, without telling them where she had been.

On the ward, the girl befriended other adolescents. The staff found her to be demanding and affectively volatile. She frequently stormed out of community meetings when decisions were made that did not go her way. She tried to have the ward recreational activities revolve around her, was very enthusiastic about them at first, but later appeared angry and pouting when she was not permitted to monopolize the activity. Beneath her superficial bravado, however, the nursing staff found her to be insecure and dependent.

One evening about a week into her hospitalization, after being refused a pass to go out of the hospital, the patient stormed down the hall to her room. Minutes later, a scream was heard; and when the first nurse reached her, the patient was writhing on the floor on her back, making jerking movements of her pelvis, arms, and legs and rolling her eyes upward. When the staff and patients had congregated near her room, her violent shaking stopped. She lay nearly still, eyes closed, with a slight trembling visible over her body. She had not bitten her tongue or voided urine or feces. When her arm was raised above her face and dropped, it fell to the side of her head each time, rather than striking her face. Finally, the nurse, noting her to be fully alert, asked her some questions, which she answered appropriately, although she stated that she could not yet move. Fifteen minutes later, she walked to the examining room to be evaluated by the doctor on call.

Discussion of "Seizure"

The doctor on call would have no difficulty in making a diagnosis of the behavioral problems that led to this girl's hospitalization. For at least four years, she has been getting into trouble. She has repeatedly been truant, stolen from stores, and recently set a fire. She lies to her parents and stays out all night. This repetitive and pervasive pattern of violating the basic rights of others and major age-appropriate societal norms or rules indicates Conduct Disorder.

Conduct Disorder is subclassified as Group Type when most of the conduct problems occur as a group activity with peers, as in this case. This type generally has a better prognosis than the Solitary Aggressive Type in which the predominant disturbance is aggressive physical behavior, usually toward adults and peers, initiated by the

group activity. Since the number of conduct
has is more than enough to make the diagno-
others is not extremely harmful, we would
Conduct Disorder as moderate.

gnostic problem for the doctor on call is how
characterize her "fit." There are several features that suggest it was not a genuine epileptic seizure. During a genuine grand mal seizure, one would expect urinary, and possibly fecal, incontinence. One would also expect a period of postictal (postseizure) confusion during which the patient would not be fully alert and able to protect herself from hitting herself in the face when her hand was dropped.

Since there is a close temporal relationship between her being upset and the "fit," it is reasonable to assume that the fit is related to a psychological conflict or need. There are three diagnostic possibilities: Conversion Disorder, Factitious Disorder with Physical Symptoms, and the V code Malingering. Both Malingering and Factitious Disorder assume that the symptom is consciously faked. In this case, we do not see any evidence to support the notion that the patient was conscious of intentionally producing the symptom. Without additional evidence of her conscious production of the "seizure," we should prefer to give her the benefit of the doubt, assume that the symptom was not under her control, and diagnose it as Conversion Disorder. We should indicate our lack of certainty by qualifying the diagnosis as Provisional. If the patient were later to acknowledge that, angry with the staff, she decided to give them a hard time by faking the fit, we would change the diagnosis to the V code Malingering. In the unlikely event that she developed a pattern of exhibiting fake fits for no purpose other than to be a patient, we should change the diagnosis to Factitious Disorder with Physical Symptoms.

DSM-III-R Diagnosis:

Axis I: 300.11 Conversion Disorder, Single Episode (Provisional) (p. 259)
R/O Malingering
312.20 Conduct Disorder, Group Type, Moderate (p. 55)

No Friends

EMILY IS A SEVEN-YEAR-OLD GIRL who was brought to an outpatient mental health clinic for children by her mother because of difficulties with peer relationships. A recent telephone call from Emily's second-grade teacher convinced her mother that it was necessary to seek professional help for Emily. The teacher was becoming increasingly concerned about

Emily's reluctance to interact with the other children [?] recess, Emily stands off to the side of the playground w[?] looking extremely uncomfortable. In the classroom [?] conversation with the other children and has great di[?] even when approached by another child. It is now si[?] school year, and Emily's extreme discomfort around ...er peers has not improved at all. Indeed, she does not have a single friend in the classroom.

Emily's discomfort in interacting with peers dates back to kindergarten. Her teachers in kindergarten and first grade had commented on her report card that she was very withdrawn and nervous with the other children. However, her second-grade teacher was the first to take an active role in trying to get Emily the help she needed.

Emily's mother had tried repeatedly to get Emily involved with other children in the neighborhood. In fact, she would take Emily by the hand and lead her to neighbors' homes where there were children of the same age to try and make friends for her child. Unfortunately, when she did this, Emily would start to shake or cry and would not be able to say a word to the neighbor's child. Emily has never been asked to attend a birthday party for another child.

Her behavior at home is quite different. Emily is warm and outgoing with her family, in marked contrast to the withdrawn and anxious child observed by her teachers and peers.

Discussion of "No Friends"

Many children are socially reticent, that is, slow to warm up in an unfamiliar social situation. However, such children overcome their initial shyness and do not demonstrate the extreme and persistent social isolation that we see in Emily's case. In an adult, Emily's behavior would suggest the possibility of Avoidant Personality Disorder or Social Phobia, Generalized Type. However, because Emily is so young, the diagnosis of a personality disorder is not appropriate. We suspect that Emily, like people with Social Phobia, is afraid of doing or saying something that is embarrassing or humiliating. However, the classification provides us with a childhood version of Social Phobia, Generalized Type, called Avoidant Disorder of Childhood or Adolescence. The combination of excessive shrinking from contact with unfamiliar people for a period of at least six months, and satisfying relationships with members of her family, justifies this diagnosis.

DSM-III-R Diagnosis:

Axis I: 313.21 Avoidant Disorder of Childhood or Adolescence
              (p. 62)

Star Wars

S USAN, A 15-YEAR-OLD, was seen at the request of her school district authorities for advice on placement. She had recently moved into the area with her family and, after a brief period in a regular class, was placed in a class for the emotionally disturbed. She proved very difficult, with a very poor understanding of schoolwork at about the fifth-grade level, despite an apparently good vocabulary; and she disturbed the class by making animal noises and telling fantastic stories, which made other children laugh at her.

At home Susan is aggressive, biting or hitting her parents or brother if frustrated. She is often bored, has no friends, and finds it difficult to occupy herself. She spends a lot of time drawing pictures of robots, spaceships, and fantastic or futuristic inventions. Sometimes she has said she would like to die, but she has never made any attempt at suicide, and apparently has not thought of killing herself. Her mother says that from birth she has been different, and that the onset of her current behavior has been so gradual that no definite date can be assigned to it.

Susan's prenatal and parental history are unremarkable. Her milestones were delayed, and she did not use single words until four or five years of age. Ever since she entered school, there has been concern about her ability. Repeated evaluations have suggested an IQ in the low 70s, with achievement somewhat behind even that expected at this level of ability. Because her father was in the service, there have been many moves; results of her earlier evaluations are not available.

The parents report that Susan has always been difficult and restless and that several doctors have said she is not just mentally retarded, but suffers from a serious mental disorder. The results of an evaluation done at the age of 12, because of difficulties in school, showed "evidence of bizarre thought processes and fragmented ego structure." At that time she was sleeping well at night and was not getting up with nightmares or bizarre requests, though this apparently had been a feature of her earlier behavior. Currently she is reported to sleep very poorly and tends to disturb the household by getting up and wandering around at night. Her mother emphasizes Susan's unpredictability, the funny stories that she tells, and the way in which she talks to herself in "funny voices." Her mother regards the stories Susan tells as childish make-believe and preoccupation and pays little attention to them. She says that since Susan went to see the movie Star Wars she has been obsessed with ideas about space, spaceships, and the future.

Her parents are in their early 40s. Her father, having retired from military service, now works as an engineer. Susan's mother has many unusual beliefs about herself. She claims to have grown up in India and to have had a very bizarre early childhood, full of dramatic and violent episodes. Many of these episodes sound highly improbable. Her husband refuses to let her talk about her past in his presence and tries to play down this material and Susan's problems. The parents appear to have a rather restricted relationship, in which the father plays the role of a taciturn, masterful head of household and the mother bears the brunt of everyday family duties. The mother, in contrast, is loquacious and very circumstantial in her history-giving. She dwells a great deal on her strange childhood experiences. Susan's brother is now 12 and is an apparently normal child with an average school career. He does not spend much time in the house or with the family, but prefers to play with his friends. He is ashamed of Susan's behavior and tries to avoid going out with her.

In the interview Susan presents as a tall, overweight, pasty-looking child, dressed untidily and with a somewhat disheveled appearance. She complains vociferously of her insomnia, though it is very difficult to elicit details of the sleep disturbance. She talks at length about her interests and occupations. She says she made a robot in the basement that ran amok and was about to cause a great deal of damage, but she was able to stop it by remote control. She claims to have built the robot from spare computer parts, which she acquired from the local museum.

When pressed on details of how the robot worked, Susan became increasingly vague; and when asked to draw a picture of one of her inventions, drew a picture of an overhead railway and went into what appeared to be complex mathematical calculations to substantiate the structural details, but which in fact consisted of meaningless repetitions of symbols (e.g., plus, minus, divide, multiply). When the interviewer expressed some gentle incredulity, she blandly replied that many people did not believe that she was a supergenius. She also talked about her unusual ability to hear things other people cannot hear, and said she was in communication with some sort of creature. She thought she might be haunted, or perhaps the creature was a being from another planet. She could hear his voice talking to her and asking her questions; he did not attempt to tell her what to do. The voice was outside her own head, and was inaudible to others. She did not regard the questions being asked her as upsetting; they did not make her angry or frightened.

Her teacher comments that although Susan's reading is apparently at the fifth-grade level, her comprehension is much lower. She tends to read what is not there and sometimes changes the meaning of the paragraph. Her spelling is at about the third-grade level, and her mathematics, a little bit below that. She works hard at school, though very slowly. If pressure is placed on her, she becomes upset, and her work deteriorates.

Discussion of "Star Wars"

At the present time Susan exhibits several psychotic symptoms. She apparently is delusional in that she believes she has made a complicated invention and that she is in communication with "some sort of creature." She has auditory hallucinations of voices talking to her and asking her questions. The presence of delusions and hallucinations, in the absence of a specific organic factor that has initiated and maintained the disturbance, or of a full mood syndrome, raises the question of Schizophrenia.

The DSM-III-R criteria for Schizophrenia require that "During the course of the disturbance, functioning in such areas as work, social relations, and self-care is markedly below the highest level achieved before the onset of the disturbance (or when the onset is in childhood or adolescence, failure to achieve expected level of social development)." Certainly the onset of Susan's illness was in childhood, and she has failed to achieve the expected level of social development for someone her age. Therefore, our diagnosis of Susan's condition is Schizophrenia, Chronic. Since her delusions have many different themes, they are not systematized, ruling out the Paranoid Type; the absence of prominent catatonic features rules out Catatonic Type; and of flat or grossly inappropriate affect, the Disorganized Type; which leaves us with Undifferentiated Type.

Susan's IQ level above 70 mercifully spares her from the additional diagnosis of Mild Mental Retardation. One could argue for the V code Borderline Intellectual Functioning. However, it is not Susan's limited intellectual capacity, but rather her bizarre behavior that is creating difficulties at school.

DSM-III-R Diagnosis:

**Axis I: 295.92 Schizophrenia, Chronic, Undifferentiated Type
                    (p. 194)**

INTERNATIONAL CASES

CHAPTER THREE

INTERNATIONAL CASES

Africa

Two Cases from West Africa

Individual or mass dissociative phenomena often occur in Africa. From 1984 on, a mass spirit-possession movement has flourished in an ethnic group in Guinea-Bissau, West Africa. The movement first took hold in a socially marginal group of barren women. Later, more than a thousand young women and young men were "called by their highest being."

This calling is best understood as a dissociative phenomenon that occurs in two phases. During the first, a somnambulistic trance phase, the members of the movement run around and do "crazy" things until they establish contact with one of the leaders of the movement. They then talk about their personal problems, confess their sins, and start digging for medicinal roots while in a trance state. During the second phase, they hear voices inside their heads transmitting messages and orders from their "highest being." These messages have been interpreted as a form of rebellion on the part of the younger generation against their position of dependence within the male gerontocracy, as a rebellion of their ethnic group against the state, and as an economic and psychological revitalization.

The ideology of the movement is an amalgamation of traditional, Islamic, Christian influences and new, political, Western influences to which their culture has been exposed in recent decades. The following two cases are of individuals who were engaged in this movement.

The Leader of the Movement

THE 35-YEAR-OLD WOMAN who is a leader of the spirit-possession movement lives in a small village in the southern part of Guinea-Bissau. She tells her story to a psychiatrist who is interested in the movement.

> During the rice-planting season I became ill. I went to my father's house; but in spite of visits to several diviners, I was unable to discover the

365

cause of my illness. A year later I lost my only child, and within one month it happened: I felt pain all over my body. One afternoon I suddenly jumped up from my stool, ran around, and did not know what was happening to me. My head was shaking, and my body was thrown to all sides. While I was running around, our God opened my mouth and made me announce that he was calling me. Before that time I had had dreams that I can't remember anymore. But one dream I can still remember. A white man with white long hair, dressed in a white robe, visited me in my dream. He handed me a book like your writing pad, and a pen, and taught me how to write.

Then it also became clear to me that my strange sickness came from our highest being. It soon became clear to me that I should follow God. He guided me and gave me orders. He taught me and forced me to speak through my mouth. He told me that our people should get rid of their ancestor spirits and ancestor shrines. The people were not to hold big mourning feasts and slaughter their whole herd of cattle anymore. They were to stop beating the great slit drum during mourning feasts to praise or mock the cattle-stealing achievements of the guests. I was also to tell people that they were to refrain from witchcraft, not to eat pork and not to drink alcohol, and that they were to stop stealing and should work hard instead.

About once or twice a day, God forced me to rush around until I knelt down in a clearing He pointed out to me. Then He guided my hand, in which I was holding a digging knife, and made me dig a hole. There I found a root, the healing properties of which were explained to me by God. God gives me His orders by means of voices, which I hear in my head. Usually it is the voice of my father's dead younger brother, whom I took care of before his death. I loved that brother, but whether that sort of thing is mutual is difficult to tell. Once I heard the voice of one of my aunts. Sometimes God enters my body, which gets hot when I have visions. Mostly it happens when I lie in bed before I fall asleep, and sometimes during the day or in a dream. It is like a cinema. I see colored moving pictures, which come and go and which show God's way. These orders are more important than the voices; and if I don't accept them, my body hurts, and I feel like somebody who is very ill and who may die. If I accept, my body feels fine. But I can't see God's face. Sometimes when I see the pictures, He sits down in a long white garment, which covers His face. He can also give me an order just like that. For instance, as we sit here, He may tell me to stand up and clean the whole place.

The people here around me all hear things. But with some of them who say they hear things, it is not true. Then God's voice tells me that this or that person is not clairvoyant or that he or she is a witch. Apart from what my voices tell me, I can also see those things in a sort of dream, both during the day and before I fall asleep. Besides that I can smell a witch. That is our most important weapon against witchcraft.

Discussion of "The Leader of the Movement"

This woman has symptoms that would be considered psychotic if they were experienced by someone from a society that did not share the beliefs of her culture. She believes she has special powers, and she has auditory, visual, tactile, and olfactory hallucinations. In her local society, however, these phenomena are quite common. Her culture ascribes to her the role of healer and accepts her unusual experiences as normal for someone in that role. Indeed, she is a successful healer. She listed the names of 40 women who had tried unsuccessfully to conceive, but had become pregnant and given birth after she treated them.

In the Guinean *lingua franca*, Crioulo, this woman's behavior would be called *abri cabessa* (i.e., "open head"), an expression used to describe a variety of conditions, ranging from psychotic to culturally accepted religious experiences. Examples include when a clairvoyant or someone with intuitive gifts enters a state in which he or she can foresee the future, or when people enter into a trance during important ceremonies, meaning that their head "opens," and the soul of a deceased ancestor enters.

Local culture would assign her a role as a healer, and her behavior would not be seen as something to be treated. When an initiation as a healer does not end the complaints or the deviant behavior (e.g., the "healer" exhibits bizarre psychotic behavior, not in keeping with the role of healer), the culture could ascribe it to witchcraft or to a spell that has more power than can be neutralized by healers or doctors.

DSM-III-R lists trance states as an example of Dissociative Disorder Not Otherwise Specified. This is as close as we can come to a diagnosis of this puzzling case.

DSM-III-R Diagnosis:

Axis I: 300.15 Dissociative Disorder Not Otherwise Specified (p. 277)

International Spirit

IN A REGION OF GUINEA-BISSAU where the movement is active, a 20-year-old man, N'Daffa, is admitted to the hospital. He left his village the day before, swam across a turbulent bay, and then walked naked into the center of the city. When stopped by a policeman, he took a bite out of the policeman's hand, and then ran to the house of a doctor whom he knew. With the help of seven strong men, he was subdued so that a nurse could inject him with a tranquilizer. He was then carried off to the hospital. His family was called, and arrived at the hospital, where they observed him from a safe distance.

The patient is dressed by a nurse in the hospital and is interviewed by a doctor while lying on the bed tied in sheets. He tells the Dutch doctor that hundreds of people are going to die, and that he can kill people by pointing at them with his forefinger. The doctor now has to give him water and food, because he is the only one the young man trusts; he attacks anyone else approaching him.

The family says they want to take him to the woman leader of the "movement," but the police refuse and insist that he be taken to the mental health center in the capital. During the night the man develops a bronchopneumonia with high fever, for which he is given an antibiotic, ampicillin, in addition to the antipsychotic, chlorpromazine, already administered to him. The next morning N'Daffa is carried onto an airplane in a comatose state, accompanied by his brother. His brother stays with him during his hospitalization in the mental health center.

The brother gives the following history: N'Daffa was reared as the third child of a peasant family consisting of his father and his father's two wives, four sons, and three daughters. His father died when he was ten years old. N'Daffa took part in the funeral ritual without difficulties, as he did in other ceremonies, such as those celebrating passage from one age group to another. His calm and cheerful character always made him popular. He looked down somewhat on others, and did not care what they thought of him. He was not very interested in decorating his body with painting or beads, as is the custom, nor did he show much interest in competitive games with his peers.

N'Daffa's troubles apparently began suddenly two days before he was admitted to the hospital. He awoke during the night to urinate, and felt a slight earthquake (which all the people in the south had felt, but which is extremely rare for that area). He then started seeing strange things. He went to bed again, and when he woke up, he went out to fetch wood. During the course of the day he felt better. The next evening he felt worse, and he swam across the bay—normally nobody would dare to undertake such a thing—to find a healer. He was unable to find a healer and arrived in the city naked, where he eventually was taken to the hospital.

At the mental health center N'Daffa is again examined. He gives answers to questions that make no sense. He says he saw a spirit that looked like a white woman with long hair. He talks to himself and utters unintelligible phrases, calls the names of people he knows, and tells the other patient in his room that they are both "international spirits." He claims that he can still kill other people by pointing his finger at them, and that he is going to be a "scientist."

After three days in the mental health center, N'Daffa is back to his usual self. A normal conversation is possible; the "spirit has gone." He no longer has strange ideas. His temperature has dropped, and on auscultation his lungs are clear. The psychiatrist is skeptical about his total recovery from the effects of his experiences with the "movement." He nevertheless tries reducing his dosage of chlorpromazine, which produces an immediate return of N'Daffa's symptoms. The dosage is then increased, to 300 mg daily; and by the end of the fifth day, N'Daffa is again his old self. Both his brother and the visiting relatives urgently ask for his release because they still want to participate with him in a ceremony with one of the women in the "movement" in the south.

After one week N'Daffa leaves the mental health center and takes the plane back to the south. On his way home he participates in a "movement" ceremony. The woman leader of the "movement" concludes that his disease is an appeal by God for him to become a healer in the new movement.

Although N'Daffa takes a supply of chlorpromazine with him sufficient for four weeks (100 mg daily), he stops taking the medicine after two weeks. He does not show up for follow-up in the local hospital, which is one day's trip from his village. Three months later he says that he is immortal, that he speaks all languages, and that he can still kill people with his index finger. Three months after that, he is again back to normal, working in the fields, talking and behaving as he always has. He will soon be initiated as a healer.

Discussion of "International Spirit"

Although the psychiatrist has his doubts, the patient's deviant behavior, not seen in other members of the movement, make him inclined to diagnose a psychotic disorder. Unlike the healer in the previous case, N'Daffa's behavior is deviant even for those involved in the movement: he is incoherent, his behavior is bizarre (nudism, indiscriminate aggression), and his beliefs (e.g., that he can kill people by pointing his finger at them, and that he is going to be a "scientist") are not in keeping with the ideology of the movement.

It is not surprising that his symptoms are controlled with antipsychotic drugs, but return as soon as the drugs are withdrawn. Although N'Daffa describes his psychotic experiences in terms of the spirit-possession movement, his behavior is disorganized, and he is unable to function. Because his bizarre psychotic symptoms persist for less than six months, we, along with the local psychiatrist, diagnose Schizophreniform Disorder. Since the onset of the illness was abrupt and his social and occupational functioning before the episode were good, we specify "with good prognostic features."

DSM-III-R Diagnosis:

Axis I: 295.40 Schizophreniform Disorder, with good prognostic features (p. 208)

The Eleventh Pregnancy

NKECHI M. IS A 38-YEAR-OLD HOUSEWIFE from the middle belt area of Nigeria. She is admitted to the inpatient unit following referral by her half-brother, who is a surgeon.

She complains of heat, heaviness, and pain in the precordial and sternal areas of her chest. She also describes epigastric pain and a sensation of "something moving" in the suprapubic region. Other symptoms include intermittent crawling sensations in the head and legs and dizziness. These symptoms are of three months' duration. Her half-brother had examined her for duodenal ulcer by gastroscopy, but no ulcer was found. Symptomatic treatment of a possible duodenal ulcer, with antacids and cimetidine, a drug that inhibits gastric-acid secretion, was not helpful. Later, when an antianxiety agent, lorazepam, was given, she experienced short-lived relief. Gynecologic evaluation was normal.

Nkechi looked depressed on the ward, but denied any depressed feelings. When confronted with her depressed appearance, she listed all her symptoms and inquired from the examiner whether they were not enough to make anyone unhappy. When giving her history, she was irritable and demanded that she be given "pills" to eliminate her uncomfortable feelings, instead of being asked "all these questions."

Nkechi is one of 15 children from a polygamous family in which there are three wives. Her father died two years ago at a ripe old age. Her mother is the youngest wife, about sixty years old, and is now looking after Nkechi's children. She has five full siblings, three males and two females. She is the youngest, and has enjoyed a close relationship with her parents, especially her father. Her eldest sister, who lives in Lagos, has had a great influence on her.

Nkechi had the equivalent of a junior-high-school education, after which she went to typing school. She was employed as a government typist when she married a government driver, who was a Muslim. She gave up her job to raise her family, but refused to renounce her Christian upbringing. She regretted giving up her job, which she thought had more prospects than that of her husband. She had ten children, six girls and four boys, who were given Muslim names by their father, but were taken regularly to a Christian church by Nkechi.

She thought she had too many children, but did not discuss limiting the size of her family with her husband. She thought he would be outraged and blame it on their religious differences. When she "took in" (became pregnant) again earlier in the year of the consultation, she made clandestine and rather clumsy attempts at terminating the pregnancy, such as using abortifacients and presenting to several hospitals with symptoms suggestive of inevitable abortion. Eventually, she aborted.

When her husband and sister realized that she had had an abortion, they were very angry. Her sister demanded to know why "you have done this kind of thing . . . I didn't know you were that kind of person." Nkechi now regretted terminating the pregnancy, recalling that her eldest sister had 13 children. "Maybe," she said, "this eleventh child would have been a special gift from God. I believe that all this movement I am having inside my belly is a punishment from God for what I did." At times she thought that God wanted her life as well, especially when she found herself exhausted after very little exertion, or having palpitations for no apparent reason. She found it particularly terrifying to lie awake at night, unable to sleep or having "useless and bad dreams."

The medications were phased out. The lorazepam was switched to diazepam because the physician wanted Nkechi to give up the idea that pills for her stomach symptoms were a solution to her problems. Nkechi did not take to this approach easily. When she was upset—for example, when the physician was late for an appointment, or an expected visitor did not turn up—she demanded a reinstatement of the lorazepam prescription. When she was reminded of the disappointment that had preceded the exacerbation of symptoms, she charged that she was being accused of telling lies about sensations in her body. On one occasion she actually informed the doctor that she had been using a private stock of lorazepam. (The nurses disputed this and found no such tablets during a locker search.) On another occasion, when she was demanding discharge from the hospital on the grounds of desiring to go home to look after her children, confrontation with her weepy and miserable mood was more successful. She pointed out how long she had been in the hospital (four weeks), and how nobody was prescribing drugs that her brother promised her would be used in relieving her internal heat, palpitations, and other symptoms. Sympathetic comments changed her tirade into an account of how difficult it had been to bring up 10 children, the oldest of whom was only 22 years old and still dependent on her.

She achieved much symptom relief and was discharged with a prescription for night diazepam. She never kept any outpatient appointments, since she had traveled a long way to seek help. However, the half-brother confirmed that she never needed any more treatment for "ulcers" or similar complaints.

Discussion of "The Eleventh Pregnancy"

The Nigerian psychiatrist who contributed this case noted that complaints emphasizing somatic symptoms rather than feelings are common in African patients. Adjustment, Anxiety, Depressive, and Organic Mental Disorders often present with somatic symptoms as the chief complaint. Even cases of Schizophrenia have been missed because attention was focused only on the chief complaint of somatic symptoms.

The most common symptoms are internal heat (not fever), crawling sensations in parts or all over the body (e.g., worms, ants), peppery sensations on the skin, breathlessness, and dizziness. The sensations often are localized in parts of the body of current or dominant concern. Hence, students often complain of head or visual disturbances (sometimes referred to as "Brain Fag Syndrome"); infertile and menopausal women often present with suprapubic and back complaints.

The most common treatment approaches are the use of benzodiazepines or, more frequently, a combination of benzodiazepines and tricyclic antidepressants. Psychotherapy is not emphasized, as in the case presented. This case illustrates the kind of resistance that often discourages physicians from trying psychotherapeutic approaches. The patients are often given a prescription, to be renewed in two or three weeks; and patients then use their own support systems, which include religious organizations and traditional healers. This patient was admitted to the hospital because her significant relatives turned against her, and also because she had a physician half-brother who could arrange for modern psychiatric treatment.

We suspect that Nkechi has a Depressive Disorder, but she denies depressed mood, and there is no evidence of anhedonia or of the other symptoms that characterize the full depressive syndrome. Since her primary complaints are of physical symptoms for which there is no adequate organic explanation, and since the duration is less than six months, the diagnosis is Somatoform Disorder Not Otherwise Specified.

DSM-III-R Diagnosis:

Axis I: 300.70 Somatoform Disorder Not Otherwise Specified (p. 267)

Postpartum Piety

ZELA IS A 30-YEAR-OLD HIGH-SCHOOL TEACHER living in Lagos, Nigeria. She is married and has five children. The birth of her last child was complicated by hemorrhage and sepsis, and she was still hospitalized in the gynecology ward three weeks after delivery when her gynecologist requested a psychiatric consultation. Zela was agitated and seemed to be in a daze. She said to the psychiatrist, "I am a sinner. I have to die. My time is past. I cannot be a good Christian again. I need to be reborn. Jesus Christ should help me. He is not helping me." A diagnosis of Postpartum Psychosis was made. An antipsychotic drug, chlorpromazine, was prescribed, and Zela was soon well enough to go home.

Three weeks later, she was readmitted, this time to the psychiatric ward, claiming that she had had a "vision of the spirits" and was "wrestling with the spirits." Her relatives reported that at home she had been fasting and "keeping vigil" through the nights and was not sleeping. She had complained to the neighbors that there was a witch in her house. The "witch" turned out to be her mother.

Zela's husband, Peter, who was studying engineering in Europe, hurriedly returned and took over the running of the household, sending his mother-in-law away and supervising Zela's treatment himself. She improved rapidly on an antidepressant medication, and was discharged in two weeks. Her improvement, however, was short-lived. She threw away her medications and began to attend mass whenever one was given, pursuing the priests to ask questions about scriptures. Within a week she was readmitted.

On the ward she accused the psychiatrist of shining powerful torchlights on her and taking pictures of her, opening her chest, using her as a guinea pig, poisoning her food, and planning to bury her alive. She claimed to receive messages from Mars and Jupiter and announced that there was a riot in town. She clutched her Bible to her breast and accused all the doctors of being "idol worshipers," calling down the wrath of her God on all of them.

After considerable resistance, she was finally convinced to accept electroconvulsive treatment, and became symptom-free after six treatments. At this point, she attributed her illness to a difficult childbirth, the absence of her husband, and her unreasonable mother. She saw no further role for the doctors, called for her priest, and began to speak of her illness as a religious experience, similar to the experiences of religious leaders throughout history. However, her symptoms did not return, and she was discharged after six weeks of hospitalization.

Discussion of "Postpartum Piety"

The African psychiatrist who submitted this case says that the usual diagnosis for cases of this kind is Postpartum (Puerperal) Psychosis, Depressed Type. However, if the disturbance persisted well beyond the postpartum period, as it did in this case, the diagnosis would be changed to some other psychotic disorder. Most patients with Puerperal Psychosis seek treatment by traditional healers or spiritual church healers. Zela's case demonstrates the way in which the patient and family, even highly educated Nigerians, understand illness in terms of witchcraft or demonology.

This woman had recurrent, brief, psychotic episodes beginning shortly after the birth of her child. Her psychotic symptoms included delusions of guilt and visual and auditory hallucinations with a religious content. Although the diagnosis and successful treatment given by her African psychiatrist assumed the presence of depression, the case report actually does not describe depressed mood or anhedonia.

In discussing the diagnosis from the perspective of DSM-III-R, let us first consider the initial evaluation. At that time Zela was delusional, agitated, and in a daze. Psychotic symptoms and emotional turmoil shortly after, and apparently in response to, a markedly stressful event, that are not due to a known organic factor justify the diagnosis of Brief Reactive Psychosis. This diagnosis is noted as Provisional, pending the expected recovery within a month. (Many clinicians believe that organic changes associated with parturition are responsible for Postpartum Psychoses. However, DSM-III-R does not recognize the concept of Postpartum Psychoses because a specific organic factor has not been identified.)

The diagnosis of Brief Reactive Psychosis has to be changed when, after a month, Zela continues to have psychotic episodes. Because of the presence of both delusions and prominent hallucinations, the diagnosis of Schizophreniform Disorder is made, with the specification "with good prognostic features," because of the rapid onset of her psychotic symptoms, her good premorbid functioning, and the absence of blunted affect.

DSM-III-R Diagnosis:

Axis I: On admission: 298.80 Brief Reactive Psychosis (Provisional) (p. 206)
           At discharge: 295.40 Schizophreniform Disorder, with good prognostic features (p. 208)

Follow-up

During the following year, Zela had several brief relapses, with vivid and frightening dreams, which she described as a "loss of definition between reality and dream." Her priest believed that she was going through a difficult religious experience. Her mother thought that witchcraft might be the source of her difficulties, and proposed a traditional religious solution. However, it was her husband who prevailed, and each relapse was treated with medication.

Zela returned to the Psychiatry Department two years later to visit the staff and to offer condolences on the death of one of the professors who had treated her. She reported that she was well and living a full life. This was in spite of her having occasional experiences of "presences" and "spirits." She recalled that the first time she reported these experiences to her husband, Peter, his response was, "Oh my God! Where are those tablets? . . . " She herself, however, had a religious explanation of her experiences.

Although she is thought by some to be excessively religious, Zela has been able to function quite satisfactorily at her job and at home without any further psychiatric support.

Note: The DSM-III-R classification does not adequately deal with the recurrent and apparently brief psychotic experiences that Zela continues to have. We should not change the diagnosis to Schizophrenia, however, because she seems to be essentially well between these psychotic episodes.

Pseudocyesis

A 24-YEAR-OLD SINGLE XHOSA MAN from a small farm community in South Africa was referred for evaluation of his mental condition after murdering a male witch doctor.

According to the patient, he initially consulted the witch doctor for a cough, and was treated with "herbs." However, the witch doctor then had anal intercourse, with the patient as the passive partner, on three successive days. Over the next few days, the patient came to realize that he was pregnant by the witch doctor. He consulted the witch doctor again, and herbs were prescribed, apparently "to take away the baby." The patient fully complied with the prescription, but discovered that his "pregnancy" continued. He returned to the witch doctor a few weeks later—on the day of the murder. By this time, he believed he had developed a *linea nigra* (a line extending from the naval to the pubis that often becomes pigmented during pregnancy), and that his lower abdomen was slightly distended. This time, however, the witch doctor said he could not help him, and that he should see "the white man's doctor." The patient apparently then become incensed, and fatally stabbed the witch doctor.

On psychiatric examination, the patient was found to have a fixed, unshakeable belief that he was pregnant. He "proved" this to the examiner by pointing to his stomach, to demonstrate that something was moving inside. Other than the delusion that he was pregnant and its ramifications, he exhibited no other features of major psychopathology. He was well nourished and appropriately dressed. His speech was coherent and logical, and his affect and behavior were normal. He appeared to be intelligent, and related well. He expressed remorse for his actions and guilt about the homosexual affair. The psychiatrist was surprised to find that on physical examination the patient did have a *linea nigra*, and his lower abdomen was slightly distended. The remainder of the physical examination was normal.

The patient had no previous history of mental illness, and had been functioning well as a machine operator. He had always held witch doctors in high regard, as he believed they could effect cures others could not, but had never before consulted one. He had had several female sexual partners, but had never before had a male. There was no history of substance abuse, and no family history of mental illness.

Discussion of "Pseudocyesis"

A man's persistent belief that he is pregnant would be considered a bizarre delusion in most cultures and would therefore suggest the diagnosis of Schizophrenia or Schizophreniform Disorder. However, this man lives in a society in which the power of the witch doctor to perform miraculous acts is taken for granted. We therefore are reluctant to classify his belief that the witch doctor has impregnated him as a bizarre delusion. Furthermore, the diagnosis of Schizophrenia or Schizophreniform Disorder almost invariably involves other psychotic symptoms, such as hallucinations and marked impairment in general functioning, which are entirely absent in this case.

The presence of a nonbizarre somatic delusion, in the absence of hallucinations, bizarre behavior, or a mood syndrome, indicates a diagnosis of Delusional Disorder, Somatic Type. This presentation of Delusional Disorder is apparently rare in Africa, as it is in this country.

DSM-III-R Diagnosis:

Axis I: 297.10 Delusional Disorder, Somatic Type (p. 202)

Follow-up

The patient was judged to be not responsible for the murder because he was mentally ill. He remained in the hospital, and was treated with antipsychotic medication. At first, he steadfastly insisted that he was pregnant, although he did not know how far along in his pregnancy he was or whether the baby would ever come out. "Men don't generally get pregnant, but I am. This is so because God has willed it." When nine months went by and he had not delivered a child he began to wonder if he in fact was still pregnant. Shortly thereafter he concluded that a large bowel movement he passed was in fact the baby. He then no longer believed that he was pregnant, but it was unclear whether he still believed that he once was. The stigmata of pregnancy (*linea nigra*, abdominal distension) disappeared. The last follow-up was about a year and a half after the murder, at which time the patient exhibited no disturbance in ideation, mood, or behavior.

Central and South America

Boni Kinwi Seequit

P SYCHIATRIC CONSULTATION was requested by a thoracic surgeon for a 21-year-old Indian man from the Cuna tribe that inhabits the San Blas Islands on the Atlantic side of the Isthmus of Panama. The man had attempted to kill himself by shooting a bullet into his chest. When he was seen, he was already recovering from his wounds and was about to be discharged from the surgical ward.

The patient was cooperative and reported that on the day of the attempt, he felt well and had no particular preoccupations or concerns. He had performed his usual activities until noon, when he had lunch and then took a siesta in a hammock. He expected to visit a *nele* (a native healer) that afternoon for a medicinal bath. About half an hour later, he suddenly stood up, took the gun, and shot himself. At the time of this impulsive act, the patient was completely aware of his actions, but could do nothing to resist the urge. He said that he felt the shotgun was alive and overpowered him. He was taken to the nearest rural hospital, where the initial emergency treatment was provided before he was sent to a major hospital in Panama City.

When examined, the patient was alert, well oriented to time and place, and intellectually unimpaired. There was no evidence of thought disorder or hallucinations, and his mood was well modulated, without any symptoms of depression. Neurologic examination and EEG were normal. There was no history of alcohol or drug abuse.

When asked about the reason for shooting himself, the patient answered that he did not want to kill himself and that he was suffering the "illness of suicide" (*boni kinwi seequit*). The same explanation was given by his father and his *nele*, who explained that this illness affects only males and is usually apparent in childhood. The diagnosis is made when there is a history of the child's being aggressive and disrespectful toward his parents and having dreams of being killed. A diagnostic ritual is performed by the *nele*, and a series of medicinal baths are prescribed. It is believed that the illness is caused by possession by a spirit.

The patient's family had migrated to the jungle in an area west of the Panama Canal near the site of a hydroelectric plant. He lived in this area until age ten, when he was sent to Panama City to work as a servant. He also went to school, and seven years later finished junior high school, at which time his father insisted on taking him back to the village because he did not want his son to influenced by the alien culture of the city and lose his traditions and beliefs.

The patient returned to his village reluctantly, and two years later was forced to marry a girl he hardly knew, but who had been chosen for him according to tribal traditions. He remembered being angry, but compliant. Three months before the suicide attempt, his first child was born. The patient did not relate any of these events to the attempt, which was the first he had ever made, and insisted on the version of the "suicide illness" diagnosed shortly after his return from the city to his village.

Discussion of "Boni Kinwi Seequit"

A Latin American psychiatrist who commented on this case noted that "suicide illness" appears to be common among members of the Cuna tribe. Treatment varies; depending on the decisions made by the *nele*, patients may be ostracized, killed, or forced to take potions that occasionally kill them. The treatment also includes medicinal baths, a custom based on the theory that diseases enter the body through the skin, and are also cured through the skin.

There is no DSM-III-R category that adequately describes the puzzling situation in which a young man who is apparently living a normal, routine life suddenly picks up a gun and shoots himself. There is no suggestion of any of the disorders that are frequently associated with suicidal behavior, such as Major Depression, Alcoholism, a severe personality disorder, or a psychotic disorder.

What significance is there in the fact that while he was shooting himself, the patient felt that he could not resist the urge and that the shotgun was alive and overpowered him? The inability to resist the urge suggests an Impulse Control Disorder Not Otherwise Classified. However, patients with such disorders (e.g., Pathological Gambling, Kleptomania) are well aware that the impulses they have difficulty controlling are their own.

DSM-III-R does not recognize "spirit possession," but we believe the "suicide illness" can best be understood as a form of Dissociative Disorder in which part of the personality is split off and temporarily takes control of the person's behavior. Therefore, we reluctantly make the diagnosis of Dissociative Disorder Not Otherwise Specified. "Spirit possession" is not one of the examples given in DSM-III-R for this diagnosis, but we suspect that this patient's experience is similar to a trance state (altered state of consciousness with markedly diminished or selectively focused responsiveness to environmental stimuli), which is one of the examples.

DSM-III-R Diagnosis:

Axis I: 300.15 Dissociative Disorder Not Otherwise Specified (p. 277)

El Duende

U RSULINA IS A 14-YEAR-OLD GIRL living with her uncle and aunt in Cali, Colombia. On the day of the Assumption of the Holy Virgin Mary, they were startled by the sight and sound of rocks and sticks falling in their yard with great noise. They thought at first that the neighbors were throwing them, but discovered that this was not the case. The commotion continued well into the night and kept them awake. They gathered some rocks to keep inside the house as legal evidence, which they later produced. In the morning they were astonished to find that the rocks outside the house had disappeared. The next night they heard a whistle that seemed to come from all directions at once; it sounded "lugubrious" and "tired." The aunt said it might be a *duende* (ghost), which made Ursulina fearful, because she had recently heard about a *duende* in a nearby town.

Soon they discovered that the whistle followed Ursulina wherever she went. Once, when the girl got close to the door, a very forceful knock was heard; later, Ursulina felt that somebody touched her face with clammy hands, and the whistle turned into a whispered "sh sh sh sh. . . ." On the following morning, Ursulina was sent on an errand, and she felt her legs become heavy; she was almost unable to walk, and the distance to the store seemed enormous. She had the feeling that she was being accompanied by someone constantly, and that she was in an unfamiliar place.

Once, while having breakfast, Ursulina felt that someone with smooth and icy hands was embracing her, and then she felt the hands covering her eyes. She screamed in terror and called for help. Her aunt came and saw that Ursulina had something like an ointment of ashes and charcoal all over her face. Later that day, the girl was nauseated and vomited a good amount of toilet paper.

The *duende* centered his persecution on Ursulina; he began to cut locks of her hair and to pinch and scratch her arms and legs. Four days after the first incident, the *duende* appeared to Ursulina as a small black man wearing a huge hat, white shorts, black shirt, pointed boots, and long red socks. His feet were turned around, with heels in front and toes in back. He smiled at her, showing his big teeth; he called her and pointed to a little black doll he had with him. She felt as if a powerful force were pulling her upward. Then, she became dizzy and confused, failed to recognize people around her, and did not know where she was. The *duende* kept appearing, in a very gay mood; he danced and made fun of everybody. However, no one could see him but Ursulina. Once, he bit her on the hand and, later, on her right arm. When she prayed, he made fun of her. He knocked her crucifix from her hands and told her, "No matter how much they or you pray, I will never leave you, and you will be mine forever. Come on, let's go!" Some days later the *duende* grew in size. When Ursulina took a shower, the *duende* said with a grin, "Do you want me to rub you?" One day he squeezed her left breast with such strength that she fainted from pain. Another day he spit into her mouth and eyes, and the girl experienced a burning that lasted for days.

The *duende* changed shape frequently, and sometime appeared as a giant or a priest. Gradually he became bolder in his caressing; he touched Ursulina's legs and genitals while whispering "Please come with me." Often he passed wind with great noise and then looked at Ursulina with a malicious grin. On one of these occasions, when his stench was unbearable, he asked her, "How do you like my perfume?" When Ursulina showed him her crucifix, he made fun of it and showed her, in turn, a makeshift crucifix with a black doll as Christ, which he pulled out of a can full of mud. When she went to church, he became a nuisance, whistling and pulling her hair, encouraging impudent acts, and trying to force her to leave the church with him.

Some days later, while a Protestant service was being conducted in Ursulina's house, a noise like the shuffling of feet was heard, becoming louder and louder. Then several women in the audience felt that their breasts and genitals were being touched and fondled. This was particularly embarrassing at the moment of saying the final prayers, when a prolonged and loud whistle ("like a locomotive's") was heard by everyone present. At that moment Ursulina screamed, "Stop it, stop it! I am not going with you . . . leave me alone!" Then she revealed that the *duende* came to her bed every night and raped her savagely, despite all her struggling. The whole audience was petrified.

Ursulina began to experience levitation. Her aunt and uncle saw the girl rising from her bed, touching the ceiling, and then falling again to the floor, as if a great force were pulling her upward and then letting her fall. One day this was particularly awesome, since every time she reached the ceiling, she was dropped on top of a trestle. The whole sequence resembled a ride on a "wild horse."

The family first approached the parish priest after Ursulina had been troubled by the *duende* at mass. The priest advised the family to go to the bishop and ask him to appoint an exorcist. The bishop sent two nuns to investigate the case and make a report. During their visit the *duende* displayed frantic activity, whistling, scratching, and hitting Ursulina, singing obscene songs, passing flatus, and making profane remarks about the visitors, who, in spite of not seeing or hearing him, were terrified by all the gesticulations and wild activity exhibited by the girl.

Ursulina was then taken to a spiritualist center, where she was instructed in the use of appropriate formulas to "talk with the spirit." She tried the method, but it had no effect on the *duende*. The director of the center gave her a special ring to wear, but the ring disappeared on the spot. Later she was instructed to write the *duende* notes asking him to leave her alone. To these he answered verbally, "The words in your letter are nice, but I cannot answer them, since I am a dove and you are flesh."

Disappointed by the ineffectiveness of the spiritualists, her family decided that Ursulina had to go to confession and receive Holy Communion. The family reports that then, "All hell broke loose." The *duende* dragged Ursulina by the hair through the house, whipped, scratched, and bit her all night long and tormented her with threats and blasphemous language. The girl was in such a state the following morning that the priest refused to hear her confession and ordered her relatives to take her to the mental hospital.

Ursulina was brought to the hospital one month after the beginning of all these troubles. She was found to be "well oriented" and "rather indifferent about her problem," describing auditory and visual hallucinations, as well as delusions of being "chased by a spirit." She was treated with an antipsychotic medication. An EEG showed episodic discharges, particularly prominent in the frontal-temporal area of the right hemisphere. This was interpreted as evidence of a possible brain lesion in this area. However, neurologic and X-ray examinations did not disclose any focal neurologic disorder, and the diagnosis of temporal lobe epilepsy was made. While in the hospital, Ursulina continued to see and hear the *duende* for two days, but not thereafter. She stayed in the hospital for 20 days.

Meanwhile, her relatives were astonished that everything was quiet at home now. They realized that Ursulina was the center of all the problems. However, they were reluctant to accept the idea that she suffered from a mental disorder, since they had actually witnessed so many strange things. They were willing to believe that the persecution by the spirit had led to mental derangement, but not the other way around. As soon as Ursulina recovered from her severe condition, she was taken out of the hospital and never returned to the outpatient department to keep a follow-up appointment.

Discussion of "El Duende"

A psychiatrist from Latin America provided the following information about the cultural context in which Ursulina's problems developed. Creatures such as the "ghost" are part of the mythology of most Latin American countries. The typical *duende* is a small, pot-bellied individual, with a dark complexion, round face, flashing eyes, and large white teeth. He dresses eccentrically and in a very colorful way or occasionally is naked, but always wears a tall hat. His feet are turned around. He is agile and musical, plays jokes on his victims, is deceitful and mischievous, and is occasionally irritable and violent. He often falls in love with young women.

Religious as well as love-related events have been ascribed to the presence of the "ghost." Generally, his appearance is considered the result of a struggle between the victim and malignant forces. Hence, religious help is frequently sought, with requests for exorcism, blessings, and spiritual cures. Old formulas such as burning sulfur, placing holy water pots in rooms, aromatic fumes, and the crucial intervention of local healers, or *curanderos*, are used, with vigorous participation of the social group seemingly being a key ingredient in the therapy.

The concept of "poltergeist" describes phenomena such as rocks falling down, furniture being destroyed, and strange noises around the house, some of which Ursulina and her family experienced. Such phenomena have often been reported in several Latin American countries.

Ursulina experienced a variety of bizarre symptoms, including visual, auditory, tactile, and olfactory hallucinations (seeing, hearing, feeling, and smelling the *duende*) and delusional ideas about what was happening to her. In addition, she had a variety of physical symptoms (nausea, vomiting, heaviness in the limbs, and burning in the mouth and eyes). She also is described as experiencing "levitation" ("as if a great force were pulling her upward and then letting her fall"), which may have been the exaggerated way that her family described epileptic seizures she was having.

If we strictly apply the DSM-III-R criteria, without considering the cultural context, the persistence of bizarre delusions and hallucinations, in the absence of a clearly established organic factor that can account for the disturbance, leads to a diagnosis of Schizophreniform Disorder. This diagnosis is unsatisfactory for several reasons. First of all, virtually all of Ursulina's psychotic symptoms are exaggerations of beliefs that are shared by her family and neighbors. In fact, they claim to have observed many of the bizarre phenomena that she describes. Since, by definition, delusions are false beliefs that are not accepted by one's subculture, it is not even clear that Ursulina has delusions. Secondly, we suspect (but cannot prove) that some of her symptoms (the visual and olfactory hallucinations and the "levitation") may be due to temporal lobe epilepsy. Her bizarre symptoms may be a way in which she tries to make sense of the epileptic phenomena.

Forced to make a DSM-III-R diagnosis, we note, on Axis I, Psychotic Disorder Not Otherwise Specified, and on Axis III, complex partial seizures (temporal lobe epilepsy) (provisional diagnosis).

DSM-III-R Diagnosis:

Axis I: 298.90 **Psychotic Disorder Not Otherwise Specified**
           (p. 211)
Axis III: **Complex partial seizures (temporal lobe epilepsy) (Provisional)**

Follow-up

Ursulina's problems began again soon after she left the hospital. She was taken to a brotherhood of spiritualists, where she gained prompt notoriety because of her keen "sensitivity." The leader of the group showed special interest in developing her abilities and teaching her to communicate with the "spirits." Later, Ursulina became the center of a cult, and was given a prominent position in the group of spiritualists as an extraordinarily gifted "medium," under the name "Maria." She began to hold public seances during which she was able to go into a trance and make "astral trips." She "visited" several countries, the sun, the planets, and the stars.

As time went by, however, the spontaneous "trances" stopped altogether, and Ursulina felt herself free from persecution by "spirits." She gradually reduced the intensity of her spiritual activities, married, had a child and, for all practical purposes, led an uneventful, "normal" life.

Evil Spirits and Funeral Cars

A 28-YEAR-OLD WOMAN from Surinam, South America (Dutch Guiana), now living in Amsterdam, is referred to a psychiatrist. Her social worker and her family doctor are worried because she sees funeral cars everywhere and says she wants to commit suicide. Moreover, sometimes she suddenly starts to tremble violently, her eyeballs roll upward, her arms and hands twist, and she utters strange words and no longer understands Dutch. After five minutes she regains consciousness, and it is possible to get in contact with her. She does not remember anything that happens during these attacks, but behaves as if she has undergone an exhausting experience.

The patient tells the psychiatrist that since she came to the Netherlands seven years ago, she has been haunted four times by evil spirits, who push her "good spirits" aside and take over her body. Two of these spirits always come back during difficult periods and want her dead. One has the body of a frog, with a dog's head with horns; the other is a tall man with a white hat and white gloves. During these crises she also suffers from headache, back pain, abdominal pain, or chest pain. She also has sleeping problems and a lack of energy and appetite, and she broods. Occasionally she has "foam" in her mouth, which is an omen of death; at times she has "panting attacks."

At first the patient consulted her family doctor, who cured her panting attacks with a relaxation technique. She consulted two Surinamese diviners/healers in Amsterdam. A ritual was performed, after which her spirits were placated, and all her complaints disappeared. These episodes were apparently connected with problems concerning her family in Surinam, who made her feel she was badly needed there, or with disputes with her siblings in the Netherlands.

Since her arrival in the Netherlands, the patient has worked at cleaning jobs, and finally got a position in the linen room of a hospital. She became acquainted with a Dutchman working in the hospital; after she got pregnant, they decided to marry. Despite her taking birth-control pills meticulously after the delivery, she became pregnant again. Her request to work part-time was initially refused. She made an appeal to the personnel manager, who gave her a part-time job. However, by that time relations with her own supervisor were so disturbed that she was dismissed. For the first time since her arrival in the Netherlands she became economically dependent on her husband, who now forced her to justify all her expenses.

After the delivery of the unplanned baby, the patient again visited her family doctor, with a feeling of increasing fatigue in both arms, pain under her breasts, and pain behind her left breast, which at times radiated to her back. She felt too tired to take care of her children or to make love with her husband.

Now, three months later, she has pain everywhere, is frightened, cannot sleep, and feels feeble. She continually sees funeral cars following her, and she ruminates about killing herself.

Treatment with haloperidol results in a heavy and dizzy sensation, and has to be stopped after one day.

The patient tells the psychiatrist that she visited a Surinamese diviner and a Hindustani healer, who both told her that her soul had been robbed, that it was too late to do anything, and that she was going to die. Then her brother took her to a female diviner, a *lukuwoman*. This woman diagnosed her problem as the result of neglect of her ancestral spirits, who sought revenge; she gave the patient a bath with herbs, tore a white sheet into two parts over her body, smashed an egg on her head, and removed the mucus from her mouth, so that the evil spirits would leave her body. The treatment worked well. The patient felt much better, and could stand and walk again. The *lukuwoman* told her to go back to Surinam to strengthen her divining power by giving a family feast for the ancestral spirits. The patient also saw a Roman Catholic pastoral worker and a Rosicrucian.

The woman tells her psychiatrist that for the first time, the evil spirits walk about her house. The spirits resemble grey-red nebulous beings, who off and on present as a red eye or as the aforementioned frog with the dog's head. At other times she sees auguries of death, like a white floating sheet or the tall man with the white hat and white gloves. When she is scared, she cannot chase them away. She sees the cemetery where the funeral cars will take her; she hears the bell of her house chime; she cannot sleep because the frog changes into a little red ball with teeth that sucks her blood as soon as she goes to sleep. She eats the way she always has, but the spirits consume her, so that she has lost more than twenty-two pounds. Her menstruation has become irregular. Sometimes she feels as if her body is changed and that she smells bad, like death itself.

The tall man with the white hat wants to have intercourse, and sometimes lies upon her. Just when she dozes off, he tries to rape her. She wakes up, cannot move, and feels terribly scared. He presses heavily upon her heart (she indicates her breast bone), and sucks her nipples as if they were making love. He empties her breasts in the same way as a baby drinks milk. Her breasts have become totally flat; all that remains is a little piece of skin.

Once before, during one of her sick episodes, she had a similar experience. She had seen a diviner, who told her that somebody had cast a spell on her by sending a dwarf. Just when she was dozing off and her soul had left her body, the dwarf sat down heavily on her breast and tried to choke her by pressing her throat. But her soul was floating in the room, and saw her body lying on the bed. Her soul told her, "They have got your heart; hear how it bounces." She thought she was going to die; and when the episode passed, she was so scared that she wanted to sleep in her husband's arms.

In addition to the evil spirits who pester her and who threaten to harm her children, the patient hears her ancestors' voices encouraging her to stand up.

Her husband explains to the psychiatrist that he will not participate in the therapy. Over the past few years they have spent an enormous amount of money on diviners. He is fed up with her stories about spirits, her insistence that he has to enter his house backward, and her interpretation of every draft in the house as the presence of spirits.

Discussion of "Evil Spirits and Funeral Cars"

This woman is referred to a psychiatrist primarily because of her talk of suicide. She has apparently been depressed since the birth of her child three months earlier. She also has the full syndrome of a Major Depressive Episode; in addition to her preoccupation with suicide, she has no energy (is too tired to take care of her children), cannot sleep, and has lost twenty-two pounds. The somatic delusions and hallucinations (her breasts have shrunk, her body smells like death) indicate Major Depression with Mood-congruent Psychotic Features.

The unusual feature of this case is her bizarre psychotic symptoms: she believes that the spirits want her dead, and she has visions of a whole assortment of weird creatures, some of whom wish her ill, and others who are interested only in sex.

The Dutch psychiatrist who provided this case tells us that a member of her culture may have these experiences without being considered psychotic. The spirits walking around, sucking her blood; the funeral cars; and the tall man may be experienced as "visions." Whether such experiences should be considered as truly psychotic depends on the person's functioning when the visions are not present. In this case, such a judgment is difficult since, even apart from the visions, the patient has a Major Depression with Mood-congruent Psychotic Features.

There is insufficient information about her "panting attacks" to know whether they are full panic attacks, and we do not know how often they occur, so we cannot make an additional diagnosis of Panic Disorder.

Our diagnostic problems do not end here. This woman also has brief episodes during which she trembles violently, her eyeballs roll upward, she twists, utters strange words, and no longer understands Dutch. Because there is no loss of consciousness, an epileptic seizure is most unlikely. She interprets these episodes as possession by spirits, but we would see them as dissociative episodes that do not meet the criteria for a diagnosis of a specific Dissociative Disorder. We therefore make the diagnosis of Dissociative Disorder Not Otherwise Specified.

Finally, this patient has another kind of strange attack, occurring just when she falls asleep. She wakes up, cannot move, and feels terribly frightened. This would seem to be sleep paralysis, a benign neurologic phenomenon consisting of brief periods of inability to move or speak, usually occurring when awakening or, more rarely (as in this case), upon falling asleep. We note it on Axis III.

DSM-III-R Diagnosis:

Axis I: 296.34 Major Depression, Recurrent, with Mood-congruent Psychotic Features (p. 230)
            300.15 Dissociative Disorder Not Otherwise Specified (p. 277)
Axis III: Sleep paralysis

Follow-up

The psychiatrist saw this patient for eight one-and-a-half hour sessions. He allowed her to go into a trance whenever her spirits wanted to speak, but he suggested that she could get control over her "possession." Together they discussed the personal meaning of her different spirits in Surinamese and West-African cosmology. After this, the trances stopped. She felt relieved that somebody finally understood her experiences and, unlike her Surinamese family, was not afraid of the spirits.

After four sessions, one month later, she felt much better. However, her eating and sleeping problems continued, and she was given an antidepressant, amitryptiline, 50 mg/day. One month later she felt healthy again. She left for Surinam, where, during a big family ritual celebration, her "spirits danced for hours." During this ceremony one of her ancestor spirits entered her body. She saw another Hindustani healer, who liberated her from this evil spirit. A year and a half later she reported that, since that time, she has felt entirely well.

Continental Europe

Scarface

AN ANTWERP CORONER asks a psychiatrist to evaluate a 34-year-old single man who had murdered a prostitute. The man had been involved with the woman for several months, in what was apparently his first love affair. After she threatened to break off the relationship, he became frantic, stabbed her to death, and then made a serious, but unsuccessful, suicide attempt. He had no previous criminal record.

During several interviews in jail, the man's behavior is usually well controlled, but occasionally he breaks into tears and then immediately apologizes. He feels intensely sad and guilty about the murder. He reproaches himself, saying that he deserves the most severe sentence and does not deserve to have a lawyer: "Such an act cannot be defended, but must be punished." Although the man's sadness and sense of guilt are appropriate to what he has done, he describes the victim in a totally unrealistic and idealized way.

During the interview, the man surprises the psychiatrist by complaining about his physical appearance, specifically, ugly acne scars on his face. The psychiatrist can see only the faintest suggestion of old acne scars. The man claims that "because of these scars nobody wants my presence. I cannot be angry about that because they are right. The scars have ruined my life."

He describes himself as having been a well-adjusted, extroverted boy. With the appearance of acne during puberty, he consulted many physicians, but always felt they "minimized my illness, saying it will be better when I get older." He stopped seeing his school friends, avoided girls, and was afraid to be in public places because "people always made denigrating comments about my appearance."

In spite of superior intelligence and a strong interest in physics, he was not successful at the university. He felt lonely, remained socially isolated, and could not face the examinations. On several occasions he made suicidal gestures, but apparently never in the context of a full depressive illness. He tried several different kinds of medical treatment, and even consulted "healers," but all without success. He developed a painful itch on his face, which he treated with a special cream.

Engaged as an employee at a newspaper, the man asked for nightwork, "to go out only in the darkness like a cockroach." He remained distant from his colleagues because their silly conversations about soccer and other sports didn't interest him. During all these years he led a reclusive social life, always worried that other people were making fun of him and talking about his physical appearance.

At work he was well appreciated, and had lost only one day's work because of illness during the last ten years. His sex life was limited to masturbation and regular weekly contacts with prostitutes until, a few months previously, he met the victim, who displayed a personal interest in him.

During the interview, the man's speech is sometimes odd, repetitive, and unnecessarily detailed. Apart from his belief about his acne scars, there is no evidence of delusions. However, he sometimes expresses strange ideas. For example, "I put cotton wool in my ears because I don't like sharp sounds. I then lose my concentration and cannot think of her (the victim)." He says that during his leisure time he mainly reads English books on nuclear physics, astronomy, war, and weapons. He has written hundreds of pages of comments on these books.

Discussion of "Scarface"

In discussing this case, we must distinguish the chronic illness from the behavior that occasioned the psychiatric evaluation. This man has had a long-standing conviction that his face is so deformed as to be hideous to other people. If this conviction were only an overvalued idea, that is, if he could entertain the possibility that he exaggerated his ugliness, then the diagnosis of Body Dysmorphic Disorder would be appropriate. However, it would seem that his belief is held with delusional intensity, justifying the diagnosis Delusional Disorder, Somatic Type.

The murder of the prostitute can be understood as a consequence of his loss of judgment and control of his rage at being rejected. This would probably not have occurred were he not vulnerable as a consequence of his chronic psychotic illness. We are unsure whether the additional diagnosis of Adjustment Disorder with Mixed Disturbance of Emotions and Conduct should be made to describe his mental state at the time of the murder.

We considered a provisional diagnosis of Schizotypal Personality Disorder on Axis II because of his excessive social anxiety, ideas of reference, odd speech, paranoid ideation and social isolation. However, on further reflection, we believe these symptoms are probably related to his psychotic disorder.

Although an example of a mild stressor on Axis IV is "broke up with a girl friend," it seems to us that given the circumstances of the relationship, the rejection by his first lover is at least a moderate stressor in this case.

On Axis V the current rating of 15 reflects the loss of control that caused the man to commit murder (danger of hurting others). The highest level in past year, 35, takes into account his chronic impairment in reality testing.

DSM-III-R Diagnosis:

Axis I: 297.10 Delusional Disorder, Somatic Type (p. 202)
Axis II: V71.09 No Diagnosis or Condition on Axis II
Axis III: None
Axis IV: Psychosocial stressors: Rejection by first lover
           Severity: 3 - Moderate (acute event)
Axis V: Current GAF: 15
           Highest GAF past year: 35

Sleepless Housewife

OUR PATIENT IS A CHARMING 28-year-old lady from the Bavarian country-side, the mother of two children, who has been treated in a dermatology clinic for recurrent skin infections. She is referred to our psychiatric clinic five days after complaining to her dermatologist about insomnia, which started after she took her first dose of a new oral antibiotic, ofloxacine, that the dermatologist had prescribed.

Following her first sleepless night, the patient became unusually cheerful, social, and physically active. She played tennis for hours, saw friends she had not seen in years, and felt "tip-top." She awoke from only one hour of sleep feeling rested. After three days, she mentioned to her husband that "her thoughts were running away" and that "everything within her was vibrating." Two days later, the dermatologist, alarmed by her condition, discontinued the ofloxacine and prescribed an antianxiety drug, diazepam, with instruction to increase the dose over the next five days, and made an appointment for her to be seen in the psychiatric clinic that same day.

The woman reported no psychiatric history for herself or any family member. Other than the ofloxacine, she had not taken any medications during the four weeks preceding her illness. Her medical history was unremarkable except for previous hypothyroidism, which had been successfully treated. All laboratory data and medical, gynecologic, and neurologic findings were within normal limits. EKG, EEG, and a CT-scan of the head were all normal.

For the next week the woman complained of "feeling all mixed up."

On the one hand, she felt dysphoric and depressed, complained of loss of energy, indecisiveness, lack of interest, fatigue, and marked loss of appetite, with a 12-pound weight loss over the last few weeks. On the other hand, she experienced racing thoughts, felt restless and irritable, and was unable to concentrate. Her affect was labile, alternating between episodes of unprovoked crying and laughing. She also had four panic attacks, one of them witnessed by her private physician, during which she was suddenly apprehensive, trembled, turned pale, was short of breath, had tachycardia, and almost fainted. On another occasion during a panic attack, she mentioned to her physician that she feared that "something evil had happened" and was worried that he "might be hiding something" from her.

By the tenth day after the beginning of her troubles, the patient had developed a typical depressive syndrome with a markedly depressive mood, loss of energy, loss of interest in her children, marked loss of appetite, insomnia, and pronounced psychomotor retardation. Two weeks later her depression seemed to lift shortly after she slept for several consecutive hours for the first time. Within a few days her mood was back to normal.

Discussion of "Sleepless Housewife"

This woman, who had no prior psychiatric history, developed a variety of manic symptoms (insomnia, elevated mood, racing thoughts, increased activity) immediately following taking a drug. Soon after stopping the drug she developed a variety of depressive symptoms (dysphoria, loss of energy, lack of appetite, and loss of interest) that intermingled with the manic symptoms. This was followed by a period with only depressive symptoms.

Because of the absence of a history of mood disturbance in the patient or in her family, and because of the close temporal relationship between taking the drug and the mood disturbance, it is reasonable to conclude that the drug was an organic factor that initiated and maintained the manic and depressive disturbances. Therefore, in the absence of attentional disturbance suggesting a Delirium, we first make a diagnosis of Organic Mood Disorder, Mixed.

We assume that the panic attacks, which lasted for five days, were also triggered by the drug, so we add the diagnosis of Organic Anxiety Syndrome.

It is reasonable to assume that the patient's paranoid ideation (the doctor is hiding something from her) is also a reaction to the drug. However, this feature does not seem marked enough to warrant an additional diagnosis.

DSM-III-R Diagnosis:

Axis I: 292.84 Ofloxacine Mood Disorder, Mixed (p. 112)
           292.89 Ofloxacine Anxiety Disorder (p. 114)
Axis II: V71.09 No Diagnosis or Condition
Axis III: Ofloxacine ingestion
Axis IV: Severity: 1 - None
Axis V: Current GAF: 45
           Highest GAF past year: 85

The Champion and the Devil

TWO MONTHS PREVIOUSLY, a 31-year-old former boxing and wrestling champion was noticed by his friends to be undergoing a change in personality. They had always regarded him as shy and timid, but now he began to brag that he was becoming stronger, even "invincible." He told his friends that he was "a superior person" and that the whole world had turned into a "wonderful place." On the other hand, his friends noted that he sometimes had periods, lasting minutes to hours, when he seemed extremely anxious and depressed. During these times he spoke of being "controlled by Stalin and Hitler," and was convinced that the "CIA is spying on me." He believed that yellow cars were a "special sign of the devil."

After a fight with his landlady, the patient went out on his balcony and addressed her with a moving speech. He explained that the voices of Goebbels, Hitler, Stalin, Gandhi, and Jesus were talking through his mouth, one after the other. After this tirade, he walked to the church, where he asked for absolution and insisted on sharing the host with the priest. The priest accompanied him to the hospital, where he was admitted to the psychiatric service, talking endlessly about being threatened by the devil.

Upon admission, the champion is aggressive and agitated. His affect shifts rapidly from feelings of ecstasy to marked anxiety and perplexity. He talks on and on, and has difficulty keeping to the same topic. He describes his thoughts as being broadcast aloud, says he is Jesus, hears voices, sees "strange things," and addresses one of the physicians as the devil. He brags about his "telepathic" abilities, but is at times panic-stricken. Three days after admission, he takes one of the nurses on the floor as a hostage and locks her with him in a quiet-room for 12 hours.

The following history is obtained: Five years earlier, the patient had had his only other psychiatric hospitalization, for treatment of Alcoholism. During his military service, when he was 20, he had started to drink large amounts of beer and had developed a gastric ulcer. His drinking became even heavier as he needed to consume increasingly large amounts to feel intoxicated. Before that admission, he had been drinking 5 or 6 liters of beer daily, plus half a bottle of *Obstler* (hard liquor) and had suffered from withdrawal symptoms. He had lost his job because of frequently going to work intoxicated. His driver's license was suspended for six months after he had a fight with the police when they stopped him for driving while intoxicated. After the hospitalization he stayed "clean" (no drugs or alcohol). Subsequently, he became a truck driver.

The patient is treated during the current hospitalization with high doses of neuroleptic medication and gradually improves. He is discharged three months after admission. He is met by his friends, who are delighted that he is completely back to his usual self.

Discussion of "The Champion and the Devil"

The past diagnosis of Alcohol Dependence is justified by the history of heavy drinking with withdrawal symptoms, continuous drinking despite physical and job-related problems, and frequent intoxications during work and while driving. Because he has not used alcohol for the past five years, the Alcohol Dependence is "in Full Remission." (Some clinicians might prefer to give the patient the benefit of the doubt and not list the Alcohol Dependence diagnosis as current because of the long period of remission.)

The more difficult question is the differential diagnosis of the current psychotic episode. The following categories need to be considered: Schizophreniform Disorder, Schizoaffective Disorder, and Bipolar Disorder with Psychotic Features.

Schizophreniform Disorder requires the presence of a mood syndrome of brief duration relative to the duration of the illness. In this case, both of these disorders are ruled out because the mood syndrome persists throughout the disturbance. Schizoaffective Disorder is ruled out because there is no evidence of hallucinations and delusions in the absence of the mood disturbance.

Most of the time manic features were predominant, such as grandiosity, inflated self-esteem, excessive talkativeness, flight of ideas, and delusions of special power, of identity, and of a special relationship to God, the devil, and Stalin. The delusions were predominantly bizarre (e.g., thought broadcasting and believing that the voices of famous people were talking through his mouth) but they are also congruent with his manic mood. Therefore, a diagnosis of Bipolar Disorder, Manic, with Mood-congruent Psychotic Features seems appropriate. Since the current focus of clinical attention will be on Bipolar Disorder, it is listed first.

DSM-III-R Diagnosis:

Axis I: 296.44 Bipolar Disorder, Manic, with Mood-congruent
                   Psychotic Features (p. 217)
           303.90 Alcohol Dependence, in Full Remission (p. 167)

Vive la France

H ENRI, A 21-YEAR-OLD SCHOOLTEACHER, is brought to the emergency room by the police on July 13th, the eve of the French Fête Nationale (Bastille Day). He had caused a commotion in the lobby of a hotel, molesting staff and patrons, opening other people's luggage, moving furniture and flowerpots, and asking people what they thought about the government, Colonel Khadaffy, and the Berlin wall, all this accompanied by shouts of "Vive la France!"

On admission, Henri is almost totally mute. He appears frightened and looks around the room in a suspicious manner. Suddenly he begins talking in a rambling way, declaring that people are not what they seem to be, and that there are spies everywhere. He says that he is a spy himself, that his father was not his real father, that there are radiations everywhere, that he has a mission to accomplish, and that something either terrible or wonderful will happen. He then becomes euphoric as he confides that he can get hold of a lot of money and become as rich as the Rothschilds. Abruptly he begins to speak about his girl friend, wonders where she is, starts to cry, and accuses himself of having transmitted an incurable disease to her.

Henri has no psychiatric history. According to his parents, he was perfectly "normal" up to the day before he was admitted to the hospital. He did not drink, and had never been on drugs. He was liked by his pupils and respected by his colleagues. For the last six months he had had a steady girl friend, whom he intended to marry at the end of the year. During the night of the 12th to the 13th of July, he was unable to sleep, wandered around the house, and in the morning told his parents that the whole world was crazy. He asked a lot of bizarre questions, retired to his room, and refused to eat anything because he thought the food was full of "unnatural" ingredients. When his parents wanted to call a doctor, he left the house and disappeared.

Henri is transferred from the emergency room to the inpatient service. During the first week of hospitalization, his behavior keeps changing. He is oriented in time and space, but wonders whether the hospital is a "real" hospital and the doctors, "real" doctors. When asked about his job, he seems perplexed at the idea of being a schoolteacher, although he can give the address of the school where he was working. His speech is, for the most part, incomprehensible, because he either does not finish his sentences or shifts unpredictably from one subject to another.

At times Henri laughs and tries to talk to everyone who is nearby. At other times he is withdrawn, stays in his room, and cries. On yet other occasions he becomes agitated and anxious. For several days he puts toilet paper in his ears to "keep the voices away," wears sunglasses to "avoid seeing things," and gloves to "prevent my hands from betraying me." He keeps away from radiators because of radiations that "block my mind, confuse my thoughts, and penetrate my body, giving me some kind of disease, possibly AIDS." He is afraid to sleep in his room, and on several occasions takes his blankets and covers and tries to sleep in the middle of the corridor. He wakes up several times each night and falls asleep for two or three hours during the course of the day.

The physical examination and all laboratory tests are negative. Henri is treated with a combination of two antipsychotics: haloperidol, 30 mg, and levomepromazine, 100 mg during the first week, and with half this dosage for the next two weeks. By the third week of his illness, all of his symptoms have disappeared, and he is discharged on medication. He is seen once a week in the outpatient department for another month, during which the medication is progressively reduced and then stopped completely. Now, two months after the onset of his illness, he is considered "as before" by his family and colleagues. During the next year he is seen by a psychiatrist every three months, and on each occasion is considered completely well.

Discussion of "Vive la France"

The significant features of this man's disorder are acute multiple delusions of rapidly changing content accompanied by symptoms of psychotic turmoil, including momentary shifts from elation to depression and fear, agitation to withdrawal, and pressure of speech to mutism. In addition, there are incoherence, hallucinations, and perplexity in the absence of disorientation. The disorder developed to its peak in less than 24 hours, and resolved in a few weeks, with complete recovery within 2 months. There was no psychiatric history, and the onset of the disturbance was not preceded by a significant psychosocial stressor.

The psychiatrist who provided this case explained that the French classification of mental disorders led to a diagnosis of *Bouffée Délirante*. This diagnosis had its origin in the theories of the French psychiatrist Magnan. Current views correspond closely to the original description and emphasize (1) the acute onset of the disorder, which develops "like a bolt from the blue," in the absence of a psychosocial stressor; (2) the presence of unsystematized delusions of a polymorphic nature; (3) the presence of emotional turmoil, with intense and changing feelings of anxiety, happiness, or sadness; (4) the presence of perplexity, depersonalization, or derealization without impairment of consciousness; and (5) resolution of the disorder, with complete recovery within 2 months.

About two of three patients hospitalized in France with an acute psychosis are given an admission diagnosis of *Bouffée Délirante*. Usually the diagnosis is changed at discharge—often to Schizophrenia if the patient has not fully recovered. The treatment described in this case is the usual treatment for *Bouffée Délirante*.

According to DSM-III-R, the differential diagnosis should include Schizophreniform Disorder, Bipolar Disorder, and Schizoaffective Disorder. There are many features suggesting a Manic Episode, such as the recurrent periods of euphoric mood, grandiosity, gregariousness, and overactivity. Although these periods are not sustained, one could argue that they alternate with depressive symptoms and thus constitute the picture of an episode with both manic and depressive features. However, according to DSM-III-R, Bipolar Disorder, Mixed requires that the depressive symptoms last a full day, which does not seem to be the case with Henri. Thus, we are not convinced that a full mood syndrome has been present, and we therefore rule out a diagnosis of Bipolar Disorder or Schizoaffective Disorder.

The presence of the characteristic symptoms of Schizophrenia (bizarre delusions and hallucinations) in an illness of less than six months' duration leads to a DSM-III-R diagnosis of Schizophreniform Disorder. In addition, the disorder has all four of the good prognostic features: abrupt onset, confusion or perplexity, good premorbid functioning, and absence of blunted affect.

DSM-III-R Diagnosis:

Axis I: 295.40 Schizophreniform Disorder, with good prognostic features (p. 208)

The Witch

MADAME DUBOIS, A 48-YEAR-OLD WOMAN, was admitted to the hospital. Her husband reported that she had apparently been well until about two months ago, when she became anxious, suspicious, and convinced that people in the neighborhood were spying on her and talking about her. She became withdrawn, refused to go outside her home, and on several occasions was observed talking to herself. She neglected her household duties and spent her days wandering through the house, entering one room after the other, opening and closing cupboards and closets, or looking out of windows from behind closed curtains.

On admission, the patient declared that she could no longer stay at home because "something frightening is going on." She described how, for the last two months, she had been hearing voices without being able to determine where they came from or to whom they belonged. The voices bothered her all the time, except at night when she was asleep. Most of the time she slept well; but whenever she woke up during the night, the voices were there, and prevented her from falling asleep again. At times, two or three voices would talk among themselves, telling each other nasty things about her, saying she was a witch who had to be "destroyed." Then again, one or several voices would talk to her directly, telling her obscene things, interrupted by shouts of "Witch, Witch," or insisting that she disappear, or else something terrible would happen. The voices would sometimes require her to say aloud "bomb alert" over and over again. At other times they would simply echo her thoughts or keep up a sarcastic running commentary on what she was doing.

On several occasions Madame DuBois declared that she need not give any further details, since the attending clinician, like everybody else, was already aware of what she was thinking. She emphasized the fact that many of those thoughts were, in fact, not her own, but imposed on her by something or somebody she could not identify, perhaps through radiation, waves, or electricity, and that she did, in fact, sometimes feel "electrical discharges" in her body, especially in the genital area. In some way, her neighbors were probably involved in all this, although she could see no reason why they would be, since she had always been on friendly terms with everybody.

At the beginning of her difficulties, Madame DuBois had not felt depressed; but in the last two weeks, she had felt low and "down," stating that anyone who was going through what she was experiencing would, of necessity, become depressed. She did not feel guilty about anything, and was not aware of anything she might have done wrong in the past. She did not wish to die, and had never contemplated suicide, but was afraid that the voices might somehow harm or even kill her.

Madame DuBois discussed her problems in a perfectly coherent and understandable way, without ever losing the thread of her thoughts. There was no evidence from the physical examination or laboratory tests of any physical illness or of alcohol or drug use.

The patient was treated with an antipsychotic, haloperidol, 30 mg daily. The voices completely disappeared in about two weeks. At discharge, a few weeks later, the dosage of haloperidol was reduced to 15 mg. The patient left the hospital in good spirits, looking forward to resuming her household duties and to working in her garden. She was not quite convinced, however, that her voices had been due to some disturbance in her brain; she remained suspicious about her neighbors, and hardly ever left her home. In addition, she developed an interest in telepathy, clairvoyance, and other similar beliefs she had always regarded as "humbug" in the past. During the following 12 months, she discontinued her medication on two occasions, and the voices reappeared about two weeks later. On both occasions the voices disappeared again shortly after she resumed taking antipsychotic medication.

Discussion of "The Witch"

The significant features of Madame DuBois's disorder are prominent auditory hallucinations of voices keeping up a running commentary on her behavior and thoughts, or conversing with each other, and bizarre delusions, including thought broadcasting and thought insertion. The delusions are elaborated and related by Madame DuBois to a single theme (persecution). Her affect is full and appropriate, and there is no disturbance in the form of her thought. Although she became depressed in response to her psychotic experiences, there is no evidence that she ever had a full depressive syndrome.

Using the French classification of mental disorders, this patient was given a diagnosis of Chronic Hallucinatory Psychosis. This diagnosis is given at discharge in about 2% of hospital admissions for mental disorder, about half as often as a diagnosis of Schizophrenia, Paranoid Type. The concept of Chronic Hallucinatory Psychosis was introduced by the French psychiatrist Ballet and further developed by De Clérambault as a nonschizophrenic chronic delusional state with predominantly hallucinatory symptoms. Current French views on the nosologic independence of the disorder from Paranoid Schizophrenia emphasize that Chronic Hallucinatory Psychosis has a better prognosis, occurs at a later stage of life, is not accompanied by incoherence or loosening of associations, and is accompanied by delusions that are related by the person to a single event or theme.

According to DSM-III-R, a diagnosis of Delusional Disorder is ruled out by the prominent hallucinations and bizarre delusions. The bizarre delusions, prominent hallucinations of voices, persistence of a residual phase characterized by social isolation and odd beliefs, and the recurrence of both delusions and hallucinations after discontinuation of medication confirm the diagnosis of Schizophrenia. The subtype is classified as Paranoid because of the prominent persecutory delusions and the absence of flat or disturbed affect or incoherence, and Late Onset is specified because the disturbance developed after age 45.

DSM-III-R Diagnosis:

Axis I: 295.31 Schizophrenia, Paranoid Type, Late Onset (p. 194)

Far East

Shrinking Problem

MR. CHIN, A 28-YEAR-OLD married worker in Hunan, People's Republic of China, comes to a psychiatric clinic complaining of repeated episodes over the past ten years of his penis "shrinking." He seeks treatment now because someone recently told him that if his penis retracts into his abdomen, he will die, and he is very frightened about this.

The first episode occurred one evening when he was 18. He suddenly became convinced that his penis was retracting into his abdomen. He became extremely tense, felt his heart beat loudly, broke out into a sweat, and felt he was about to die. After he had held his penis for a few minutes, the episode passed. Since that time, he has had similar episodes about twice a year, each lasting about 15 minutes. These episodes do not seem to follow any psychosocial stressor or to be preceded by any prodromal symptoms.

Though the patient has often been told that his penis does not actually retract, he continues to believe that it really has happened. Between episodes, he functions well, with no signs of social or emotional disturbance. He has always been ashamed to talk about these experiences with other people.

Mr. Chin was born to a middle-class family and reared by his grandmother in a southern province of the country. As a boy he often thought his penis was very much smaller than those of other boys, and for this reason he was very anxious and afraid of bathing in any public bath. His childhood was in other ways unremarkable. After graduation from high school, he lived in a countryside village for two years, and then became a worker. He married at age 26 and had his first child the next year.

A physical examination, including an examination of his sexual organs and secondary sex characteristics, revealed no abnormality.   When interviewed, Mr. Chin gave a clear account of his difficulties. He exhibited no psychotic symptoms. He appeared to be mildly depressed, but otherwise asymptomatic. There were no signs of personality disturbance.

Discussion of "Shrinking Problem"

Mr. Chin is suffering from *Koro*, a syndrome that occurs in southern China and in islands in the South Pacific. *Koro* is usually described as an anxiety reaction in which a man fears that his penis is shrinking and may disappear into his abdomen, with death following. More rarely, the syndrome occurs in women, in which there is a fear that the breasts or vulval labia are disappearing.

A Western-trained clinician might consider that Mr. Chin has not only an anxiety reaction but a delusion, since even between episodes he is convinced that his penis actually did shrink. However, it is common for family members to share the anxiety and the conviction that the event is actually happening. Thus, strictly speaking, the belief is a culturally shared idea and, by definition, not a delusion. For this reason, the diagnosis of a Delusional Disorder, Somatic Type is not given. The central feature of the syndrome is recurrent and episodic unrealistic anxiety about a physical symptom in the absence of organic findings, suggesting a Somatoform Disorder. In Body Dysmorphic Disorder there is preoccupation with some imagined defect in appearance in a normal-appearing person. This would seem to apply to our case but ordinarily that disorder is chronic and does not involve acute episodes of disturbance. Similarly, the diagnosis of Undifferentiated Somatoform Disorder requires a duration of the disturbance of at least six months. We are therefore left with Somatoform Disorder Not Otherwise Specified, hardly as specific as the term *Koro.*

DSM-III-R Diagnosis:

Axis I: 300.70 Somatoform Disorder Not Otherwise Specified
           (p. 267)

Tired Technician

M R. WU, A 36-YEAR-OLD married technician, came to an outpatient psychiatric clinic in Hunan, People's Republic of China, complaining of easy fatigability. He also had insomnia, and his ability to work had decreased because of persistent weakness and tension headaches.

These symptoms began about twelve years ago, without any evident cause. Mr. Wu noticed that he began to tire easily and felt weak after exerting any mental or physical effort. He also had difficulty falling asleep and awakened many times during the night. He felt that his mental energy was insufficient during the day. He could not read or watch television for more than half an hour without feeling weary. Though he could perform his occupational tasks, he had difficulty concentrating and his memory was poor. In the past twelve years he has hardly ever been free of these symptoms, but they fluctuate in intensity over time. When his condition is really bad, he feels distressed, irritable, and "nervous." It is not clear why he now comes for help.

Mr. Wu does not spontaneously complain about depression. However, when asked specifically about depressed mood, he says that sometimes he feels depressed and is unable to enjoy anything, which he attributes to his difficulty concentrating and his physical exhaustion. When he is feeling depressed, he experiences guilt, slowed thinking, appetite disturbance, or motor retardation. The periods of depression never last more than two weeks and occur about five or six times a year.

Mr. Wu has gone to the local hospital on many occasions, and has been treated with Chinese herbs and Western medicines. Once he went to see a psychiatrist, and amitriptyline was prescribed, 100 mg every day for a month. All of these treatments were without effect.

Mr. Wu describes himself as an "introverted person" since puberty, always preferring to stay home by himself. He obtained above average-grades in school. After graduating from college, he was hired as a technician in a factory. At the present time he is still working at his job.

In the interview, Mr. Wu looks exhausted. There is no evidence of prominent anxiety or depression. Physical examination and laboratory tests are within normal limits.

Discussion of "Tired Technician"

Chinese-trained clinicians would have no difficulty in making a diagnosis of Mr. Wu's condition since he has the characteristic features of Neurasthenia, one of the most commonly diagnosed disorders in the People's Republic of China. Mr. Wu expresses almost all of his complaints in terms of somatic symptoms. For many years he has not had the energy and strength to function adequately. He also complains of difficulty sleeping and headaches.

Although these symptoms, plus his poor concentration and memory, suggest a depressive syndrome, Mr. Wu denies persistent depression or anhedonia. Therefore, the diagnosis of Dysthymia, which a Western-trained clinician might consider, cannot be made. The rarity of the typical picture of Neurasthenia in the United States and the relative rarity of Major Depression and Dysthymia in China are probably due to the Chinese use of physical symptoms as a metaphor for expressing unpleasant mood states, whereas in this country it is common for patients to report unpleasant mood states. There is also evidence, however, that when Chinese patients with Neurasthenia are systematically interviewed about depressed mood, their symptoms usually meet the criteria for Major Depression or Dysthymia. (For further discussion of the Chinese use of physical symptoms to express dysphoria, see "Comrade Yen," p. 407).

We suspect that had a Western-trained clinician evaluated Mr.

Wu, he or she might well have described him as appearing "depressed" rather than "exhausted," and would therefore have made a diagnosis of Dysthymia. However, if we accept the Chinese psychiatrist's description of Mr. Wu, then, according to DSM-III-R, his chronic physical complaints without any organic basis, and without a complaint of sustained depressed mood or anhedonia, indicate a diagnosis of Undifferentiated Somatoform Disorder.

DSM-III-R Diagnosis:

Axis I: 300.70 Undifferentiated Somatoform Disorder (p. 267)

Menstrual Madness

MRS. NEE, A 21-YEAR-OLD married woman, was hospitalized in the Hunan Province of the People's Republic of China, complaining of recurrent episodes of "madness."

The first episode occurred when she was 15 years old, a year after her menarche. A week before her menses were expected, she began to have difficulty sleeping and became emotionally upset and irritable. She had palpitations and "hot flashes" in her face and extremities. When menstruation began, she suddenly started talking to herself in a rambling and incoherent way—for example, " . . . make up mind, the sun in the West will down and the sun in the East will rise. . . . you are one of my friends. . . ." She became aggressive, threw furniture around, and tore her clothes. Sometimes she laughed loudly, and then abruptly began to cry. At night she was unable to fall asleep and jumped up and down on the bed. She was sexually seductive, grimaced, and ignored attempts to calm her down.

Eight days after the beginning of menstruation, she recovered, suddenly and completely, but remembered all the symptoms of the episode. In subsequent premenstrual and menstrual periods, the same symptoms returned, and she was then referred to a local hospital. Upon examination the doctors found symptoms of autonomic nervous system and endocrine disturbances, including tachycardia, flushes, sweating, excessive menstrual flow, and secretion of milk. Eight days after the beginning of this menstrual period, she recovered completely, as before.

Mrs. Nee has had six to eight attacks of this kind each year, always beginning in the premenstrual period and persisting for about a week after the beginning of menstruation. In the intervals between menstruation, she shows no symptoms of emotional disturbance.

Treatment programs over the years have included an antipsychotic, chlorpromazine, 600 mg/day, and electroconvulsive therapy, neither of which has helped.

Discussion of "Menstrual Madness"

The Chinese psychiatrist who submitted this case noted that the unofficial DSM-III-R diagnosis Late Luteal Phase Dysphoric Disorder was not appropriate since this woman's symptoms were most severe in the menstrual phase and did not remit until a week or more after menstruation began. In contrast, in Late Luteal Phase Dysphoric Disorder, the symptoms are most marked in the late luteal phase and quickly remit when menstruation begins. Furthermore, the characteristic symptoms of Late Luteal Phase Dysphoric Disorder are depressed mood, irritability, and anger, but do not include psychotic symptoms such as those in this case. Therefore, the Chinese psychiatrist made a diagnosis of Periodic Psychosis, a category that is not recognized by DSM-III-R even though there is a bit of literature describing brief psychotic episodes associated with the menstrual cycle. (It should be noted that the diagnosis of Late Luteal Phase Dysphoric Disorder is not ruled out by the presence of psychotic symptoms; however, in this case, the temporal pattern of symptoms is not consistent with the DSM-III-R criteria for that disorder.)

The only appropriate DSM-III-R diagnosis is the residual category Psychotic Disorder Not Otherwise Specified, as the illness does not meet the criteria for any specific psychotic disorder. Although an organic factor related to the menstrual cycle is undoubtedly involved in the development of this psychotic condition, a specific organic factor cannot be established; hence, the diagnosis is not an Organic Mental Disorder.

DSM-III-R Diagnosis:

Axis I: 298.90 Psychotic Disorder Not Otherwise Specified
                    (p. 211)

Follow-up

At her next menstrual period, Mrs. Nee's mental status was normal. Following discharge, she was given maintenance estrogen and progesterone to reduce the intensity of the hormonal changes throughout the menstrual cycle. This treatment seemed to work, since at the nine-month follow-up she was entirely well and had had no return of her previous symptoms.

Frigophobia

MR. LIN IS A 63-YEAR-OLD, separated, former military officer and native of Suchuang province in the People's Republic of China. Currently living in Taiwan, he has long suffered from *pa-leng*, fear of cold.

One day in October 1952, when Mr. Lin had diarrhea after eating a watermelon, he experienced a strange cold sensation on his abdomen. This frightened him and caused him to visit an herb doctor, who told him that watermelon and other fruits would cause deficiency of vitality. Mr. Lin recalled that his father had warned him in his childhood that he would eventually die of "cold" disease. To protect his abdomen and head and to feel secure, he started to wear heat retainers such as blankets, coats, towels, heavy clothes, and a hat. Eventually he wore all of these heat retainers all day long, even in hot weather. They weighed over thirty kilograms (66 pounds).

He received treatment, from the herb doctor, based on the principle of *shenn-kuei* (vital deficiency) for six months, but without any effect. He then visited various internists and finally came to the psychiatric clinic in March 1953. On arrival, he wore many clothes and blankets and a hat, and was in a panic state. He moved very slowly to avoid losing the warmth from his clothes.

Mr. Lin was given insulin subshock therapy for three months, and was given electroconvulsive therapy twenty times; but he did not improve. In April 1954, he was admitted to the psychiatric ward and received prolonged sleep therapy for three weeks. He said that this therapy, which entailed absolute rest, was quite similar to *chin-tsuo* (quiet sitting), the Buddhist treatment that had cured his father. It was effective; subsequently, he discarded his heat retainers. On discharge he obtained a job in an insurance company as an adviser.

In 1957, Mr. Lin was again seized by fear of cold, without any obvious precipitating factor. He was readmitted, received prolonged sleep therapy again, and improved. The third admission was in June 1963. This time he was depressed about his mother's death on the mainland. Prolonged sleep therapy was once again effective. However, there was a relapse two months afterward. One more month of hospitalization was needed for a full course of sleep therapy and psychotherapy, which started in October 1963. The fifth and last hospitalization was from July 1965 to July 1980. None of the treatments were effective: his condition remained the same, with regression and social withdrawal. Finally, he was transferred to a veterans' hospital.

Mr. Lin was born in 1917, the second of four siblings and the only son in an old-fashioned scholar's family. His father was a *shiu-tsai* (scholar of the Ching Dynasty), and dominated the home. He paid much attention to his son because he was often ill, but brought him up very strictly. His mother, a typical, taciturn Chinese woman, loved him very much. However, his aunt, an unmarried enthusiastic Buddhist, bore most of the responsibility for the child's upbringing. He slept with her until he was 14.

Neither his mother nor his aunt ever disciplined him. They did not let him get up at night, to prevent his catching cold. He wet his bed until he was 15 years old.

The boy started masturbating, sometimes twice a day, when he was 15. When his father discovered this, he scolded him severely. At that time, his father also suffered from fear of cold on the abdomen and other emotional difficulties, which caused him to give up his job. Deeply steeped in traditional Chinese medicine, he then received the Buddhist therapy, *chin-tsuo* (quiet sitting).

Despite his poor records in school, which Mr. Lin attributed to his brain's being weakened by masturbation, he graduated from high school in 1935 and entered college to study politics. His father's affiliation with influential people facilitated his admission to a good school. Immediately after graduation from college, he became a high-ranking military officer—again, with his father's help.

In 1943, at the age of 26, Mr. Lin married a domineering woman, a college graduate, 2 years older than himself. They had three children. He began to suffer from sexual difficulties and gained much weight. He gradually lost his sexual desire, and frequently ejaculated prematurely.

In 1949, while still on the mainland, Mr. Lin was a director of a section of military supplies and transport, and in this capacity, had a good income. He moved to Taiwan in 1950, without his family, but accompanied by a girl friend, an attractive dancer. He then lived with this girl friend, surviving on his capital without working. Two years later, after most of his money had been spent, his girl friend left him. He attributed her departure to his sexual inadequacy. He worried a good deal about his general lack of physical vitality. At about this time, he was informed that his father had been killed, his mother was seriously ill, and his wife had been forced to marry another man on the mainland. He became very depressed and soon had his first episode of fear of cold.

During his long hospitalizations, Mr. Lin has been described as "immature and overdependent," "extremely rigid, demanding, and overpolite." He initially insisted that his illness was a physical defect that he had inherited from his father. Later he came to believe that it was related to *shenn-kuei* (vital deficiency) and loss of sexual power.

Discussion of "Frigophobia"

The Chinese psychiatrist who contributed this case noted that the clinic staff agreed on a diagnosis of Frigophobia, an extreme form of a marked fear of cold. It represents a culture-bound disorder that is closely related to the traditional Chinese concepts of vitality and the *yin yang* principle. It is often associated with depression, Obsessive Compulsive Disorder, or Histrionic Personality. Using the

International Classification of Diseases, the Chinese psychiatrist's diagnosis would be Phobic Neurosis, Other Type.

In order to make a DSM-III-R diagnosis, the first question to consider is whether Mr. Lin's experience of coldness is best understood as a delusion, a somatic hallucination, or merely preoccupation and anxiety about his physical condition. Delusions generally involve phenomena that are subject to consensual validation or disproof. Who is to say how cold Mr. Lin actually feels? We therefore prefer to regard his problem as chronic preoccupation with a physical symptom for which there is no organic basis. Thus, we make the diagnosis Undifferentiated Somatoform Disorder, recognizing that this particular presentation of the disorder may be seen only in China, because of its compatibility with Chinese cosmology.

There are several references in the case to long-standing personality problems, and one might speculate on the role that identification with his father played in the development of Mr. Lin's disturbance. However, there is insufficient information to make a specific personality-disorder diagnosis.

DSM-III-R Diagnosis:

Axis I: 300.70 Undifferentiated Somatoform Disorder (p. 267)

Hot-tempered Elder

MRS. CHEN, A 70-YEAR-OLD Beijing housewife, was brought to the clinic by her husband. According to him, her sons, and her sons' wives, her behavior at home had gradually and increasingly become "abnormal" over the past ten years. They all suspected that she had some "nervous illness," despite the fact that she remained quite normal in her contact with neighbors and friends and was energetic in the care of her house and unchanged in her loving relations with her many grandchildren.

The patient had married at 19 and had lived with her husband's extended family for several decades. She had been a meek, docile, deferential, and industrious housewife of the younger generation and a considerate, kind, and modest member of her peer group. She never became angry or complained about anything. She had been regarded by the entire family as virtuous, showing good sense and reason, although her husband's mother was quite strict and hypercritical toward her. Her husband's parents had died one after the other about twenty years ago. After that, Mrs. Chen became the housekeeper and authority of the family.

The family dates the patient's change in personality as beginning about ten years previously. She had become increasingly domineering and dogmatic, always speaking in a commanding tone to everyone in the family. If any family member fails to obey her, she flares up, pouring out a stream of abuse and shouting at the top of her voice. In recent months the house has become more crowded as her youngest son's bride has come to live with the family and her second son and his wife have had a new baby. The rearrangement of rooms was not in accordance with Mrs. Chen's wishes, and she complains bitterly and incessantly to any family members who will listen. The whole family suffers from her imperviousness to reason and her loud complaining.

Mrs. Chen is in good physical health. There are no signs of intellectual impairment. Her memory is good, and no psychotic symptoms are observed. The consulting psychiatrist found it easy to make contact with her. She did not deny being a "hot-tempered elder," but touched upon the "quarrels" lightly, saying that the younger members of her family were "disobedient and concerned only about themselves."

Discussion of "Hot-tempered Elder"

We had many questions for the Chinese psychiatrist who provided this case and offered the unofficial diagnosis of "morbid development of personality in later life." First, we wondered if there might be cultural reasons to expect this kind of personality change in an older person. We were told that it is the cultural tradition in China for the young to "be obedient and heed what an elder says . . . and that the eldest woman of the family is the matriarch in dealing with the household affairs while her retired husband has practically no right to interfere." Therefore, there is cultural support for the eldest woman to take over the household in a way that would have been considered inappropriate when she was younger.

Given this cultural context, we asked if the family regarded her change of personality as pathological, and were told that her case was so extreme that the family members all suspected that she had some "nervous illness." Finally, we wondered if the personality change might be caused by frontal-lobe damage or some other chronic organic mental disorder. We were told that a thorough neurological examination was negative.

With all this information, we prefer the Chinese psychiatrist's diagnosis to anything that is available in DSM-III-R. In DSM-III-R, Personality Disorders are defined as beginning by early adulthood, and the only other personality disturbance that is recognized is Organic Personality Disorder, which is not supported by the normal neurological examination.

DSM-III-R Diagnosis:

Axis I: 300.90   Unspecified Mental Disorder (Nonpsychotic) (p. 363)

Comrade Yen*

COMRADE YEN IS A 40-YEAR-OLD teacher in a rural town in China, interviewed in 1982. She is intelligent, articulate, and deeply depressed. She sits immobile on the wooden stool opposite us, looking fixedly at the floor. Her black hair, wound tightly in a bun, is streaked with white; her handsome, high-cheekboned face is deeply lined with crow's feet radiating outward from each eye. She slowly recounts for us the story of her chronic headaches:

> There are several sources. Before the Cultural Revolution [approximately 1966-1976] I was outgoing, active, and had high self-regard. As a teen-ager I had been secretary of the local Communist Youth League. I dreamed of advanced education and a career with the Party. My family and friends all expected great achievements. I had ambition and high goals. Then, during the Cultural Revolution, I was severely criticized. I had to leave my position in the Youth League. I went to the distant countryside to a very poor place. I couldn't adjust to the conditions. The work was too hard; there was too little to eat. Bad smells were everywhere, and nothing was clean. Terrible living conditions!

All of this was made worse by the realization that Comrade Yen's career aspirations were no longer tenable, that even a return to an urban environment was unlikely. The daughter of intellectuals, with several generations of professionals in the family, Comrade Yen felt deeply the lost opportunity for a university education and career in the Communist Party, sources of social mobility in China. Cut off from family and friends, books and newspapers, yet not well accepted, at least initially, by the peasants among whom she lived, she became aloof and solitary.

As the Cultural Revolution accelerated, Comrade Yen occasionally bore the brunt of self-criticism sessions. On one occasion she was denied an injection by a nurse at a rural county hospital, who accused her of being a "stinking intellectual." She began to experience a change in personality. She constantly felt demoralized; and instead of her former optimism, she felt a hopelessness that generalized to all aspects of her life. Comrade Yen expected only the worst to happen. She became introverted and sensitive to what she perceived as the rejecting and critical eyes of peasants and cadres. She first began to depreciate her goals, then herself.

Hesitant where she had once been assertive, lacking confidence where she once had radiated it, Comrade Yen regarded herself as inadequate and coped by further narrowing her behavioral field and already limited options. She stayed to herself. Eventually she obtained a post as a primary-school teacher in a rural town. When her native abilities became apparent to her fellow teachers, they wanted to elect her the principal; but Comrade Yen declined because she feared the responsibility and did

---

*Taken from: Kleinman, A. Social Origins of Distress and Disease: Neurasthenia, Depression and Pain in Modern China. New Haven: Yale University Press, 1986

not want to expose herself again to a situation in which she might well fail
and suffer further losses.

Comrade Yen married a native of the region, who is presently a
peasant, but was previously a cadre in a mine. They live apart, and it is
clear she prefers it this way. He resides with a distant production team,
while she lives in the small commune town. They have three children,
two adolescent sons who live with their father, and one daughter who still
lives at home with her mother. Comrade Yen is angry that her husband
has not been rehabilitated and given back his post as a cadre. It is ag-
gravating to her that her husband has given up, declaring that he will
never regain his former status. This is a chronic source of frustration,
another difficulty about which she feels nothing can be done.

Comrade Yen's third source of anger is her daughter. "I really did not
want to have her. I wanted to be alone. We already had enough children.
When I was very pregnant, I hit myself several times quite hard against the
wall, hoping I might abort. But my husband wanted a child, and I could
not decide on an abortion at the hospital. Thus, I blamed myself when I
gave birth to a baby girl with a withered arm. I felt I caused it." The
daughter grew up to be beautiful and very bright, an outstanding student.
But her mother grieved for her because of her deformity. "In China
normal people don't marry cripples. Even though she can do everything—cook, clean, play sports—I knew she would have trouble marrying."

At this point in our interview, the patient silently cried, her gaze fixed
on the cement floor beneath the table separating us. Her husband, who
had accompanied her, looked much older than Comrade Yen. He was
wide-eyed at being in a provincial capital he had visited only a few times
before. His coarse peasant features contrasted with his wife's more re-
fined face, but he joined her in weeping openly when she continued on
about their daughter:

> There is no hope for her. Even though she is one of the best students in
> the senior middle school, she cannot take the examination to go to the
> university. Her school principal and the secretary of the local branch of the
> party decided that only completely healthy, normal children can take the
> examination. We appealed to the county authorities, but they upheld the
> decision. Nothing can be done. Our daughter will live at home and do what
> work she can.

There followed several minutes during which the patient could not
go on, but sobbed and wept. Finally, she told us how she and her husband had arranged for their daughter to meet another "cripple" in a
nearby town. But her daughter decided she would not marry someone
else who was deformed; she preferred to remain single.

Comrade Yen shared her complete hopelessness with us. Often she
thinks it would be preferable to be dead. Her headaches keep her to
herself. She cannot face any more "stress": it is too upsetting. "My health
is too uncertain. I cannot do too much. I think only of my headaches, not

of the future or the past." Comrade Yen severely restricts her world. She withdraws from all but essential responsibilities. She cannot plan any outing "because of bad influences on my health: the weather, the noise . . . the crowds. . . . "

Because of her feelings of inadequacy, failure, hopelessness, and despair, Comrade Yen has limited her life to school and dormitory room. Only on occasional weekends does she visit her husband. Her daughter stays with her. They appear to be like two recluses, each grieving about somewhat different losses. Comrade Yen's world is now that of pain: experiencing her hurt, waiting for it, fearing it, talking about it, and blaming her problems on it. It is the pain (and related complaints) that legitimizes her withdrawal at work and in family life, sanctions her isolation, her demoralization and depression. Her chronic pain is an unavailing expression of her multiple losses. Before we departed, she sent us a letter:

> I feel always sad about being ill for such a long time. I feel headaches, dizziness, don't like to talk, take no pleasure in things. My head and eyes feel swollen. My hair is falling out. My thinking has slowed down. Symptoms are worse when I am with others, better when I am alone. Whenever I do anything, I have no confidence. I think because of the disease I have lost my youth and much time and everything. I grieve for my lost health. I must work a lot every day just like the others, but I have no hope in what lies ahead. I think there is nothing you can do.

Discussion of "Comrade Yen"

[The following discussion was prepared by Dr. Arthur Kleinman, who submitted this case.]

Comrade Yen was one of more than 150 cases with the diagnosis of Neurasthenia whom I studied in 1980 and 1983 in the outpatient psychiatry clinic of the Hunan Medical College. Her case, like the others I studied, was referred by the clinic's psychiatrists to a research team consisting of several Chinese psychiatrist trainees in a postdoctoral research training program; my wife, who is a China scholar; and me. We interviewed Comrade Yen and our other subjects for over two to three hours. This interview was repeated five weeks later, and again at three-year follow-ups (in both of which Comrade Yen declined to take part).

Comrade Yen is quite representative of the group we studied and of patients in China's psychiatric clinics generally. Her symptoms can be traced to a major social source of stress, the turmoil of the Cultural Revolution. Her initial illness was an episode of Major Depression, which was neither recognized nor appropriately treated. Over time she suffered both several recurrences of Major

Depression and chronic demoralization (Dysthymia, according to DSM-III-R), or what has been called "double depression."

During periods of depression, her chief complaints have been physical symptoms of headaches, dizziness, and lack of energy. Although she looks depressed, neither she nor her doctors focus on dysphoria or any other emotion. This is in keeping with traditional cultural norms that orient Chinese to regard emotional display as unseemly, stigmatize any behavior suggesting mental illness, authorize a disabled role only for physical complaints, and provide an elaborate and subtle somatic semantic system for expressing psychosomatic and social problems. Moreover, headaches and dizziness and a weakness-exhaustion cluster of complaints have long held salience in Chinese culture as signs of real disease requiring Chinese medical treatment and deserving all of the benefits of the sick role.

During the Cultural Revolution—China's decade-long historical whirlwind—many people under great social pressure, especially those with personal vulnerability, were diagnosed as having Neurasthenia. At present, although this cross-cultural difference in diagnostic styles is still true, psychiatrists in China increasingly diagnose patients like Comrade Yen as cases of Depressive or Anxiety Disorders.

DSM-III-R Diagnosis:

Axis I: 296.32 Major Depression, Recurrent, Moderate (p. 222)
            300.40 Dysthymia, Primary Type, Late Onset (p. 232)

Fear of Thinking Aloud

MS. MURA, A 48-YEAR-OLD, unmarried woman in Tokyo, consults a psychiatrist with the complaint that she is "thinking aloud unconsciously and hurting the feelings of other people around me." She lives with her 78-year-old mother; her 43-year-old unmarried brother, a bank employee; and her 37-year-old unmarried sister, who is a government clerk. When she spoke to her sister about her problem, her sister assured her that no one at home hears her speaking her thoughts out loud. However, Ms. Mura insists that she often does, and that her sister is a "foggy head" and other family members are unobservant.

Five years ago, Ms. Mura's brother started to talk to himself while bathing at home. This annoyed her, and she started to worry that she might someday do the same thing. Three years later, she began to feel that she was expressing her thoughts aloud without realizing it. She feared that other people's feelings were hurt when they heard her critical thoughts being spoken aloud.

She says she is never aware of thinking aloud or of speaking ill of others. When questioned about how she knows that this is actually happening, she says that she has received several telephone calls during which no one spoke. She is sure they were made by somebody who knows her habit of thinking aloud, and who has attempted to evoke her habit while she was holding the phone receiver. When a new bill-collector appeared a few weeks ago, she concluded that the previous collector had heard her think ill of him, even though she had no memory of this. When a store clerk smiled at her yesterday, she considered it a response to her thinking ill of the store when she passed by some days ago.

Ms. Mura believes that her habit of thinking aloud is known to everybody in her neighborhood. She hesitates to go out shopping, fearing that people will avoid her or look back or turn their heads away from her. Whenever she leaves the house, she believes that her neighbors come out of their homes and stand at their gates or on the street, watching her and saying she is a "queer woman."

Ms. Mura had an apparently unremarkable childhood. She graduated from high school with a good record. She worked for many years, first as an assistant teacher at a primary school, then as a cartographer and in various clerical jobs. For the last few years she has stayed at home doing housework, and sometimes has taken part-time jobs.

She describes herself as always having been reserved, prudent, conscientious, and tender in sentiment. She was never overly sociable, but has had some close friends. She has been sensitive to the feelings of others, and always desired the acceptance of those around her.

During the interview Ms. Mura's mood is appropriately sad. When she speaks of her habit of thinking aloud, she has tears in her soft eyes. She says she would rather die than live with such pain and misery.

Discussion of "Fear of Thinking Aloud"

This patient is seriously distressed by her belief that she must have hurt the feelings of other people around her by unconsciously thinking ill of them aloud. She interprets various trivial actions and behaviors of other people as responses to her unintended malicious messages spoken to them while she was "thinking aloud." She believes this in spite of her sister's reassurance that she never thinks aloud at home.

This clinical picture is not rare in Japan, where it is called *Taijin-kyofu*, which can be translated as "fear of other people" or "anthropophobia." In this disorder, the predominant disturbance is an unrealistic interpretation of trivial actions and behaviors of people around the patient, leading to the preoccupation or belief that the patient is causing unpleasant feelings in the other people. In mild cases patients are aware that their fears are excessive and unreasonable.

Patients with *Taijin-kyofu* complain of varying worries, such as fear of body odor (*Taishu-kyofu*), in which the patient believes that he or she emits rank odors from the body, often from the axilla, mouth, anus, or genital area; fear of glancing (*Shisen-kyofu*), in which the patient believes that he or she glances at other people unintentionally and gives them unpleasant feelings; fear of blushing (*Sekimen-kyofu*), in which the patient is fearful about blushing in front of others; or fear of ugly facial expressions (*Shubou-kyofu*), such as grinning, or showing the whites of the eyes; or fear of thinking aloud (*Dokugo-kyofu*). In Japan, *Taijin-kyofu* is usually considered a type of neurotic disorder appearing in a person with a "sensitive personality."

In diagnosing Ms. Mura, the first judgment that must be made is whether her belief that she offends people by "thinking aloud" is a delusion, an overvalued idea, or only an unrealistic fear. It seems clear that in this case we are dealing with a delusion. Since this is the only psychotic symptom, the next issue is whether the delusion is bizarre, that is, involves a phenomenon that the person's culture would regard as totally implausible. This is clearly not the case, since it is possible to speak one's thoughts aloud inadvertently. Therefore, Schizophrenia is ruled out and the diagnosis of a Delusional Disorder is appropriate.

Whereas some of the delusions associated with *Taijin-kyofu* are observed in the United States (for example, delusions of having a bad odor), Ms. Mura's delusion that she has inadvertently offended other people is virtually never seen, and seems to be culture-specific and an expression of the extreme concern with issues of shame found in Japanese culture.

DSM-III-R Diagnosis:

Axis I: 297.10 Delusional Disorder, Unspecified Type (p. 202)

India

Fits

MRS. CHATTERJEE, A 26-YEAR-OLD patient, attends a clinic in New Delhi, with complaints of "fits" for the last four years. The "fits" are always sudden in onset, and usually last 30-60 minutes. A few minutes before a fit begins, she knows that it is imminent, and she usually goes to bed. During the fits she becomes unresponsive and rigid throughout her body, with bizarre and thrashing movements of the extremities. Her eyes close and her jaw is clenched, and she froths at the mouth. She frequently cries, and sometimes shouts abuses. She is never incontinent of urine or feces, nor does she bite her tongue. After a "fit" she claims to have no memory of it.

These episodes recur about once or twice a month. She functions well in between the episodes and reports no prominent depressive or anxiety symptoms.

Both the patient and her family believe that her "fits" are evidence of a physical illness and are not under her control. However, they recognize that the fits often occur following some stressor, such as arguments with family members or friends.

Mrs. Chatterjee comes from a middle-class, urban family. She has been married for five years to a clerk in a government office. They have two children. Her mother-in-law and father-in-law live with the family, and this has sometimes led to conflicts.

She is described by her family as somewhat immature, but "quite social" and good company. She is self-centered, craves attention from others, and often reacts with irritability and anger if her wishes are not immediately fulfilled. She handles routine household tasks well.

On physical examination, Mrs. Chatterjee was found to have mild anemia, but was otherwise healthy. A mental status examination did not reveal any abnormality in her speech, thought, orientation, perception, or intellectual functions. She did not display any sustained mood change, and her memory was normal. An electroencephalogram showed no seizure activity. A skull X-ray was also normal.

Discussion of "Fits"

The Indian psychiatrist who contributed this case, using the ninth revision of the International Classification of Diseases (1978), made a diagnosis of Hysteria. He noted that this kind of presentation is quite common in India, Pakistan, and neighboring countries; in fact, Hysteria is diagnosed in from 5% to 8% of all patients seen in the psychiatric unit of his general hospital.

The predominant symptom resembles an epileptic seizure; however, the absence of such typical features of organic seizures as incontinence and biting of the tongue strongly suggests a nonorganic etiology of the seizures. This is further substantiated by the normal electroencephalogram.

We see no evidence of intentional feigning of the symptoms, as in Factitious Disorder with Physical Symptoms. Since the predominant symptom suggests a physical disorder (epilepsy), and the symptoms seem to recur in response to stressful situations, we diagnose Conversion Disorder, Recurrent. However, we would not quarrel with a clinician who diagnosed a Dissociative Disorder, viewing the "fits" as a disturbance of the normally integrative functions of memory and consciousness.

DSM-III-R Diagnosis:

Axis I: 300.11 Conversion Disorder, Recurrent (p. 259)
Axis III: Mild anemia

Follow-up

The patient was treated, with her husband, in family sessions over the next two months. The couple was taught that the patient's fits were not evidence of a serious physical illness. In addition, the husband was urged to take a more active role in handling problems that arose between the patient and her in–laws and to pay more attention to the patient in general, but not during her fits. The couple stopped therapy after two months, during which time the patient had no more fits.

Polynesia

Cultural Healing

A 26-YEAR-OLD POLYNESIAN female bus driver was brought to the emergency room of a local hospital in New Zealand following an incident in which the bus she was driving knocked the arm of a pedestrian, resulting in a loud thump against the bus, but not injuring the pedestrian. She was brought to the emergency room by witnesses to the accident who said she was in a state of "emotional shock." When seen by the emergency-room doctor she had an unfocused stare and was holding up one finger on each hand and softly repeating "One, killed," very slowly. She would not respond to questions, but did not resist passive movement of her arms. She seemed to be preoccupied rather than depressed, suspicious, or anxious.

Six weeks before the accident, the patient had married a European man. Three years earlier she had left her Polynesian husband, with whom she had two children, aged nine and five years. She had joint custody of the two children; but her new husband was moving to a job in a different city, and she was fearful about the changes in custody arrangements that this might cause. Her family was pressuring her to return to her home islands with her new husband, but financing this posed further problems, particularly as she felt her job was threatened because of some disciplinary proceedings at her workplace. She viewed these as portents of misfortune for her family.

The patient came from a "high-born" Pacific Island family, and had come to New Zealand ten years previously. Before the incident she had a happy, friendly, outgoing disposition, had many friends, and was regarded as a conscientious worker by her employers.

In the emergency room, the patient's mental state improved slightly over several hours. She then spoke in a slow, monotonous tone, expressing fears of coming to further harm. She was responsive to reassurance and showed no evidence of delusions or hallucinations. She was released to her husband's care; but the next day he found her hiding under a blanket, clutching a kitchen knife, and in her previous mute state. He brought her back to the hospital, where she was given diazepam, an antianxiety drug, and an attempt was made to get her to talk about her problems. This resulted in only transient improvement.

Because her symptoms had a clear relationship to the accident, her Polynesian relatives encouraged her husband to take her to a cultural healer, who gave her massage and a drink. She refused the latter, bit the glass, and broke it. The healer interpreted this as indicating that she was possessed by the ghost of her Polynesian ex-father-in-law, who had recently died and who was (allegedly) angry that she had deserted his son. (When next seen at the hospital, the patient acknowledged that she saw some resemblance between the man involved in the accident and her father-in-law.) Within a few hours after visiting the healer, all of the patient's symptoms disappeared.

Discussion of "Cultural Healing"

The psychiatrist who contributed this case made the diagnosis of a Dissociative Disorder Not Otherwise Specified, and noted that similar kinds of cases are seen in psychiatric units of general hospitals in New Zealand in approximately one in a hundred admissions. He suspects that many such patients never come to the hospital, and that this woman came primarily because her episode occurred in a public place.

We would agree with the diagnosis of Dissociative Disorder Not Otherwise Specified, because, when examined, the patient seemed to be in a "trance" state, with selective responsiveness to the environment. It is less clear what to make of her extreme fearfulness (hiding under a blanket clutching a kitchen knife) and her belief that there had been portents of her misfortune. We give her the benefit of the doubt and do not add a diagnosis of psychosis.

DSM-III-R Diagnosis:

Axis I: 300.15   **Dissociative Disorder Not Otherwise Specified** (p. 277)

Follow-up

Ten days after her recovery following her visit to the healer, the thought that she might be responsible for causing a car or bus accident kept intruding into her mind (obsession?). She became terrified of going near a bus, and was twice stopped by the traffic police for driving too slowly and with excessive caution. Her family brought her back to the hospital, where she was treated with an intensive behavioral program consisting of relaxation training and graded exposure to buses. Within two weeks she had totally recovered, and was still well one year later.

Scandinavia

Factory Worker

JORGEN, A 35-YEAR-OLD, married factory worker in Oslo, has asked for a psychiatric consultation because of pressure from his wife. Together they have had some joint sessions of marital counseling, in which the main problem has been identified as his difficulty in expressing any feelings. For example, he hardly ever talks to his wife about anything other than tasks that need to be done. When they make love, his wife feels that he is mechanical and does it without any tenderness. The marriage counselor suggested that he be seen in individual psychotherapy. Jorgen acknowledges general dissatisfaction with his life, and admits that his wife's complaints may be justified. Her complaints about him have increased considerably since she had a passionate affair with another man, and began her own psychotherapy about a year ago.

During the two evaluation sessions, Jorgen is timid, hesitant, and seldom makes eye contact with the psychiatrist. His posture is stiff, and he is quite formal. He tells his story slowly and in great detail, with few gestures or expressions of emotion.

He is the only child of working-class parents. His father was abroad as a sailor for a year when Jorgen was three years old, during which time he lived with his mother and her parents. He remembers feeling uncomfortable when his father returned. During his childhood he believed that his parents did not love him. They gave him food, shelter, clothes, and money, but took no interest in him emotionally. He is still bitter because of this and has little contact with them now.

Although he was intellectually bright in elementary school, he recalls being scolded by his teachers because he was noisy and domineering in class. Gradually, he became more silent and timid at school. His favorite sport was sailing a small boat. He did a lot of racing, but, he says, "For some reason I was always second best." He had a few friends and dated occasionally.

Jorgen did well in high school and college and later studied science at the university. While he was finishing his physics thesis, he got an assistantship as a science teacher at a senior high school in the upper-class part of the city. The students there made fun of his accent. He became quite anxious and tense because of this, and had to leave the job. While at the university he had been politically active in the Marxist party. Partly because of party ideology and because of the above-mentioned teaching experience, he left the university without finishing his thesis.

He started to work on an assembly line in a big factory. He tried to influence the other workers politically and had moderate success. His fellow workers understood that he was intelligent and chose him to negotiate with the board of directors concerning working conditions. He became quite anxious in this situation. He felt "fuzzy" in his head and was unable to make his points except when he specifically could point to laws and agreements.

Although he was preoccupied with sex and wanted a close relationship with a girl, he rarely dated. In his relations with girls he was shy, passive, and helpless. When he was in his mid-20s, he met his future wife, a nurse, who was also shy. They married after one year, although their sexual adjustment was poor. It seemed that the relationship helped both of them overcome their loneliness. His wife seemed to tolerate the lack of intimacy in their marriage and their poor sex life, until her affair and her own psychotherapy. Her increasing demands on him caused Jorgen to realize that he was emotionally inhibited, and he discovered that a few drinks made him feel freer. He developed a pattern of taking a couple of drinks each night, but denies that this has ever caused any problems.

Discussion of "Factory Worker"

The Norwegian psychiatrist who contributed this case notes that in his country such a patient would be given the diagnosis of Character Neurosis, a term used to describe "inhibitions of the personality" that restrict the person's enjoyment of life and the use of his abilities and talents. Restrictions in the expression of love, intimacy, anger, and the competitive display of one's talents are common, as in this case. People given this diagnosis often have a rigid posture and inhibition of spontaneous use of their bodies, and they often present themselves to others as formal, reserved, and lacking vitality. "A patient with a character neurosis drives through life with the brakes on."

The clinical picture seen in this Norwegian patient is no different from that seen in many patients receiving outpatient psychotherapy in the United States. Some traits are characteristic of several personality disorders (Obsessive Compulsive, Dependent, and Avoidant), but the full diagnostic criteria are not met for any one disorder. It is nevertheless apparent that this man does suffer from a pervasive pattern of inflexible and maladaptive behavior that has caused him significant functional impairment. Therefore, we diagnose Personality Disorder Not Otherwise Specified.

DSM-III-R Diagnosis:

Axis I: 301.90   **Personality Disorder Not Otherwise Specified** (p. 358)

Student Nurse

MARLIS IS A 21-YEAR-OLD Norwegian nursing student who is admitted as an emergency to the acute ward. She is agitated, intensely anxious, and feels that she is being persecuted, sometimes by her fellow students, sometimes by the nursing supervisor, and sometimes by a male relative. She is desperate, and alternately cries and asks for comfort, then becomes aggressive and threatens the attendants on the ward. Her difficulties began a week previously.

Marlis started nursing school two years ago. She had no difficulty with the academic courses; but this year, when she started to care for sick patients, she became anxious, particularly when she saw blood, wounds, or someone dying. In the last few weeks she has cried easily, lost her appetite, and had difficulty sleeping at night. She has felt an increasing pressure in her head. She has become emotionally labile and yelled at several of her fellow students. She has gradually become convinced that they are against her and will force her to leave nursing school. She believes they have complained about her to the nursing supervisor. When a male relative came to visit her last week, she believed that he tried to seduce her, although there was no evidence for this.

On admission, Marlis acknowledged being ill, saying, "I have become so peculiar." However, she was very guarded and suspicious of the true intentions of the interviewer. She asked for help to stop "the persecution."

Marlis lived with her maternal grandparents as a child because both of her parents died before she was five. They were overprotective of her, and she made few friends as a child. She was always seen as "the poor child who had lost her parents." As a child she easily became anxious, especially when someone quarreled or shouted aggressively. She was scrupulous and conscientious in her schoolwork. After school, she worked as an assistant in a kindergarten and later on in a nursing home.

Her grandmother died when Marlis was 11 years old, and she lived on with her grandfather. He was a Pentecostal and took her to religious services. Her religious interests, however, vanished after he died, two years ago. She has always been physically well. She has sometimes dated, but has never had a serious relationship with a boy.

Discussion of "Student Nurse"

The Norwegian psychiatrist who contributed this case said that it illustrated the Scandinavian concept of Reactive Psychosis, a diagnosis given to nearly half of the psychotic patients on first admission to a hospital. Reactive psychoses are assumed to result from the action of a psychological trauma on a vulnerable person. The concept of Reactive Psychosis emphasizes the vulnerability of the individual who experiences the stress; therefore, it does not require a precipitant that would be markedly stressful to almost anyone, as does the corresponding DSM-III-R concept of Brief Reactive Psychosis. DSM-III-R does not require evidence of vulnerability and specifically excludes cases in which there is evidence of Schizotypal Personality Disorder or any of the prodromal symptoms of Schizophrenia.

According to DSM-III-R, Brief Reactive Psychosis has a maximum duration of one month. If the symptoms persist, the diagnosis is changed to some other psychotic disorder. In contrast, the Norwegian diagnosis of reactive psychosis does not place any limit on the maximum duration of the illness, although in most cases recovery is expected within a few months.

Our initial DSM-III-R diagnosis was Brief Reactive Psychosis, but on further reflection we realized that the caring for seriously ill and dying patients, although stressful, would not be "markedly stressful" to almost anyone in her circumstances. Therefore, in the absence of Schizophrenic-like psychotic symptoms, we are left with Psychotic Disorder Not Otherwise Specified.

DSM-III-R Diagnosis:

Axis I: 298.90   Psychotic Disorder Not Otherwise Specified (p. 211)

Follow-up

Gradually, without medication, the patient's anxiety, emotional turmoil, and persecutory delusions vanished over a month. She left the hospital after five weeks. She did not continue her studies at nursing school, deciding that nursing was too stressful for her. At follow-up seven years later, she was working as a kindergarten teacher, and reported that she had been well since leaving the hospital.

The Lumberman

A NORWEGIAN LUMBERMAN was admitted to the psychiatric ward of a hospital shortly after starting his required military duty at the age of 20. During the first week after his arrival at the military base, he thought the other recruits looked at him in a strange way. He watched the people around him in order to see whether they were out "to get" him. He heard voices calling his name several times. He became increasingly suspicious, and after another week had to be admitted to the Psychiatric Department, University of Oslo. There he was guarded, scowling, skeptical, and depressed. He gave the impression of being very shy and inhibited. His psychotic symptoms disappeared rapidly when he was treated with an antipsychotic drug, chlorpromazine. However, he had difficulties in adjusting to hospital life. Transfer to a mental hospital was considered; but after three months, a decision was made to discharge him to his home in the forests. He was judged unfit to continue his military service, and was struck from the military lists.

The patient, the eldest of five siblings, was the son of a farm laborer in one of the valleys of Norway. His father was an intemperate drinker who became angry and brutal when drunk. The family was very poor, and there were constant quarrels between the parents. As a child, the patient was inhibited and fearful, and often ran into the woods when troubled. He had academic difficulties and barely passed elementary school.

When the patient became older, he preferred to spend most of his time in the woods, where he worked as a lumberman from the age of 15. He had his own horse, lived in log cabins, and disliked being with people. He sometimes took part in the youth dances in the village. Although never a heavy drinker, he often got into fights in the village when he had a drink or two. At the age of 16, he began to keep company with a girl one year his junior who sometimes kept house for him in the woods. They eventually became engaged.

Discussion of "The Lumberman"

The Norwegian psychiatrist who provided this case made the Scandinavian diagnosis of Reactive Psychosis, Paranoid Type. The patient displays the typical features of the disorder: reaction to extreme stress that exacerbates underlying psychological conflicts, in which the prognosis for full recovery is very good. In order to label a psychosis reactive, the psychic trauma must be considered of such significance that the psychosis would not have appeared in its absence. There must be a temporal connection between the trauma and the onset of the psychosis, and the content of the psychotic symptoms must reflect the traumatic experience. In this case, for an extremely shy and isolated man, military service was a much more serious stressor than for an ordinary person of the same age.

According to DSM-III-R, the differential diagnosis would include Brief Reactive Psychosis, Delusional Disorder, and Psychotic Disorder Not Otherwise Specified. The appearance of delusions soon after the stress of entering military service suggests the diagnosis Brief Reactive Psychosis. However, many would question whether entering military service would be markedly stressful to almost anyone in similar circumstances. In addition, there is no evidence of emotional turmoil, which is also required for that diagnosis. The nonbizarre delusion that he was being persecuted suggests Delusional Disorder, Persecutory Type; but Delusional Disorder requires a duration of at least one month, and this patient apparently recovered from his psychotic symptoms within a few weeks. We are therefore left with the residual diagnosis Psychotic Disorder Not Otherwise Specified. The importance of the stressor would be indicated on Axis IV.

Although the lumberman has had a tendency towards social isolation and difficulties with peers as an adolescent, there is insufficient information to justify a Personality Disorder diagnosis. Therefore, we shall simply note the presence of Schizoid personality traits on Axis II.

DSM-III-R Diagnosis:

Axis I: **298.90 Psychotic Disorder Not Otherwise Specified (p. 211)**
Axis II: **Schizoid personality traits**
Axis III: **None**
Axis IV: **Psychosocial Stressor: Entering military service**
          Severity: 3 - Moderate (acute event)
Axis V: **Current GAF: 35**
          Highest GAF past year: 55

Follow-up

The patient was reinterviewed by hospital personnel at 4 years, 7 years, and 23 years after his admission. He has had no recurrences of any psychotic symptoms, and has been fully employed since six months after he left the hospital. He married the young woman to whom he was engaged, and at the last follow-up, he had two grown children.

After leaving the hospital, the patient worked for two years in a factory, and then as a lumberman. For the last 20 years, he has managed a small business, which he has run well. He has been happy at work and in his family life. He has made an effort to overcome his tendency toward isolation and has several friends. Among other duties, he has been chairman of a sheep-rearing association in the county. He is well-liked in the village.

The patient believes that his natural tendency is to be socially isolated and that his disorder was connected with the fact that in the military situation, he was forced to deal with other people.

The Woodcarver

IN NOVEMBER OF 1946, a 30-year-old woodcarver was admitted to the inpatient psychiatric unit of the Oslo University Hospital. Two months before admission he had moved to Oslo to attend an arts and crafts school; he lived with relatives. He soon began to behave in an odd manner, thought people were persecuting him, and often had to get off the tram because of this. He became increasingly introverted, and started to hear voices. He noticed "radiations" from other people that caused him to become sexually excited. He thought his food was poisoned and noticed that his surroundings had mysteriously "changed." He read things in the newspaper that indicated to him that he was going to be kidnapped.

In the hospital his behavior was odd; his mood was labile, with swings between laughter and weeping. He felt "currents" in his body, especially in his genitals. Electroconvulsive therapy was given, but had no effect. After five months, he was transferred to a mental hospital, where he stayed for three months, adapted well, and took part in all the therapeutic activities. When discharged, he was without symptoms.

The patient was a farmer's son, the third of six siblings who grew up in a stable family without obvious emotional difficulties. He passed rural elementary school with slightly above average grades, then worked on his father's farm, developing carpentry and wood-carving skills. He was industrious, but touchy, usually keeping to himself and shy of the opposite sex. He never had a girl friend. He lived in his village until he moved to Oslo.

Discussion of "The Woodcarver"

According to Scandinavian diagnostic concepts, this patient would be given an admission diagnosis of Schizophreniform Psychosis, which would be changed to Schizophrenia, Paranoid Type, at discharge. The DSM-III-R diagnoses would be virtually the same. Schizophreniform Disorder would be diagnosed on admission to account for the bizarre delusions and hallucinations in the absence of a mood syndrome and with a duration of less than six months. Because of the apparently acute onset and the absence of blunted or flat affect, the disorder would be further qualified as with good prognostic features. At discharge the diagnosis would have to be changed to Schizophrenia, Paranoid Type, because the symptoms persisted beyond the minimal six-months duration.

DSM-III-R Diagnosis:

Axis I: On admission: 295.40 Schizophreniform Disorder, with
                                Good Prognostic Features (p. 208)
Axis I: At discharge: 295.31 Schizophrenia, Paranoid Type,
                                Subchronic (p. 194)

Follow-up

The patient was seen by a psychiatrist intermittently over 17 years. He has had no psychotic symptoms during these years, but has remained shy and reserved. On follow-up visits, the psychiatrist noted that his affect was not blunted or flat, and there was no loosening of associations.

The patient is still single. After his father's death, he took over the farm, which he now runs, together with his mother. It is a large farm, and is very well managed. He is a clever woodcarver, has a workshop, and has popular products to sell. He remembers his psychosis and reflects on the details with a smile. He believes the reason for his disorder was that he felt isolated in the big city after having spent all his life in a simple, rural environment.

The woodcarver at follow-up had the same shy and reserved personality traits that he had always had before his psychosis. We do not regard these symptoms as either prodromal or residual symptoms of Schizophrenia. We believe that the follow-up demonstrates that although the DSM-III-R diagnosis of Schizophrenia is generally associated with a poor outcome, complete recovery does sometimes occur.

Union of Soviet Socialist Republics

Alexi

A LEXI, A SOMEWHAT OVERWEIGHT 23-year-old man, who looks more like 17, is brought to the Moscow District Mental Health Center by his father for an evaluation. Alexi's father had been estranged from his wife and child since the patient was five years old. He is a retired army officer who knows about Alexi mostly from his wife's letters. Until four weeks ago, Alexi lived with his mother in a single room, sharing kitchen and bath with three other families in a communal apartment. Four weeks ago, his mother died suddenly of a heart attack. A neighbor, who had known both Alexi and his mother for years, somehow found means to communicate this news to the father, who came to bury his wife, and who had spent the last four weeks with his son.

The father is alarmed by Alexi's condition. According to the father, Alexi spends all of his time alone at home. He sleeps during the day and spends his nights reading and taking copious notes from "strange books." He is a vegetarian, and amazes his father by his total lack of interest in any food other than boiled potatoes and sweet tea. According to the neighbor, on the morning following his mother's death, Alexi shaved his head, referring vaguely to some Eastern rites of mourning. This was incomprehensible to the father until he explored Alexi's bookshelves, where he discovered numerous books on Eastern religion, natural healing, and astronomy.

The father has tried to engage his son in talking about the future, but Alexi has no interest in education, work, or the "things all young people should be interested in." Over the last four weeks, all the father's attempts to discuss his son's future have caused Alexi to become irritable and either withdraw to his bed or leave the apartment, to wander the streets until his father was asleep.

The young man is interviewed by a young psychiatrist, who starts the interview with great enthusiasm and a friendly attitude. Soon, the psychiatrist is amazed at failing to make any connection with the patient, who remains impassive, virtually silent, and answers the psychiatrist's questions only when presented with the same question at least twice. Most of his answers are monosyllabic, and his face betrays no emotion. He is informed that he will be admitted to the hospital for "further evaluation." He greets this news with only one comment: "Will you allow my father to bring me some of my books?"

In the hospital, the young man's psychiatrist and other members of the staff fail to make any emotional contact with him, and describe him as "cold, but not hostile." He appears to be profoundly disinterested in his surroundings, and shows some air of contentment only when he is allowed to read one of the books his father has brought from home.

On further investigation of school records, information from the patient's pediatrician and elementary- and secondary-education teachers is located. The young man is described as having been a "perfect infant"; he could play in his crib for hours alone, and was "not demanding on his mother." His mother once remarked to the pediatrician, "this kid never even tried to climb out of the playpen." Elementary- and secondary-school teachers described the young man as a loner who stayed away from other children and who was able to work academically with an average level of achievement up until the 7th grade. At that time, he gradually lost interest in his studies, but was never defiant when scolded by his teachers or teased by his classmates, who called him "retard." He absolutely refused to take physical education and, only after being confronted by the principal, mumbled, "I don't want to undress."

Throughout most of the young man's life, his mother worked the night shift at a factory and slept most of the day. The boy never complained about being left alone most of the time. At the age of 11, he was given a pet, a little hamster, to which he became attached in a matter of hours. He took great care of his pet; but when the pet died three months later, he showed an astonishing lack of emotion. When his mother bought him several tropical fish to console him, he never looked at the aquarium, refused to feed the fish, and impassively watched them die one by one.

In the hospital, where the patient remained for four weeks, he was given small doses of neuroleptics, to which he immediately developed an acute dystonic reaction. A senior physician from another department was called as a consultant. Having evaluated the record, and having failed to elicit more than a few monosyllabic responses from the patient over a 40-minute attempted interview, the consultant suggested eliminating all medication. A diagnosis that qualified the patient for permanent disability was established, and he was referred to a sheltered workshop. Several days following his discharge, when his father came to the ward to collect some of the things his son left behind, one of the nurses remarked: "I already have difficulty remembering his name. I'm sure we will not remember his face in a week or so."

Discussion of "Alexi"

In the Soviet Union this patient was given the diagnosis of "Simple Schizophrenia" because he displayed no psychotic symptoms throughout his illness, but demonstrated a relatively rapid development of a host of negative symptoms (symptoms of "personality deficit"). A Soviet psychiatrist would note the characteristic premorbid personality that is believed to be almost specific to Schizophrenia with onset in late childhood or early adolescence. The diminished "psychic activity" expressed in worsening academic performance, with presumed diminution of cognitive abilities, is believed to be one of the specific symptoms of this form of Schizophrenia. A history of steadily developing "affective impoverishment of personality" with attendant episodes of irritability, primarily to ward off interpersonal engagement, is believed to be an expression of the developing illness process. Increased social isolation, the lack of expected affectionate responses to family members, and the absence of such responses following losses, described as "emotional coldness," are progressively increasing symptoms of the disorder. The peculiarities of thought, "odd logic," and "strange preoccupations," accompanied by increasingly intense interest in abstract and obscure questions, referred to as "philosophical intoxication," complete the clinical picture of an inexorably developing schizophrenic process that, according to the Soviet concept of the disorder, will inevitably result in a "residual state," which will be indistinguishable from other forms of Schizophrenia.

DSM-III-R requires psychotic symptoms for the diagnosis of Schizophrenia; hence, it does not recognize the traditional "Simple Schizophrenia" subtype. Alexi's illness has many of the features of DSM-III-R's Schizotypal Personality Disorder, e.g., odd beliefs, eccentric behavior, constricted affect, and marked social isolation. The difficulty with this diagnosis, however, is that ordinarily one would expect a stable course in a personality disorder, whereas in Alexi's case (and central to the concept of "Simple Schizophrenia"), there was a marked deterioration in overall functioning, beginning in early adolescence.

We recognize that a child psychiatrist might wonder, given the history of odd behavior and markedly impaired social relations as a child, why the diagnosis of Pervasive Developmental Disorder Not Otherwise Specified is not appropriate. According to DSM-III-R, that diagnosis is ruled out by the presence of Schizotypal Personality Disorder, a more specific diagnosis. This case illustrates the lack of a precise boundary between severe Schizotypal Personality Disorder and the concept of a Pervasive Developmental Disorder.

DSM-III-R Diagnosis:

Axis I: **V71.09 No Diagnosis or Condition**
Axis II: **301.22 Schizotypal Personality Disorder, Severe (p. 341)**
Axis III: **None**
Axis IV: **Severity: 1 - None**
Axis V: **Current GAF: 28**
           Highest GAF past year: 28

Crimes Against the State

GREGOR, A 40-YEAR-OLD ECONOMIST, is brought to the maximum security ward of the Moscow Central Institute for Forensic Psychiatry from the KGB prison. Four months earlier, while searching the house of a friend, the KGB agents discovered a book, written by Gregor, that was critical of the Soviet economic system. In this book Gregor defined himself as a "Marxist economist" and a patriot of his country. He used language indistinguishable from that of the "official" and "approved" concepts current in Soviet economic and political thought. However, the book is an impassioned argument for reform of the state economy in order to bring about greater prosperity and economic stability in the country.

Gregor was arrested and charged with "antigovernment propaganda and agitation harmful to the interests of the Socialist state." Because he was uncooperative during his detention, he has now been referred for a psychiatric evaluation by a KGB investigator, who writes in the referring document that "There are strong reasons to suspect that this detainee suffers from chronic mental illness, which is responsible for his behavior and has resulted in serious crimes against the state, with which he is charged."

The prisoner arrives in handcuffs, looking anxious and fearful. At the beginning of his admission report, the forensic psychiatrist takes note of "burning and penetrating eyes, and a Christlike beard."

During the interview the prisoner insists on his right to take notes and to write down the questions asked him; when this is denied, he refuses to participate in the evaluation interview. On the ward, surrounded by seriously ill offenders, he keeps to himself, and is described as "withdrawn, with long staring spells, and persistent refusal to discuss his thoughts and feelings." The ward staff is puzzled by his "excessive attention" to food served in the hospital, and his concern that medication has been put into his food is described in ward notes as "paranoid."

By the end of the first week, the prisoner is demanding to see the medical director of the hospital; when the director obliges, the prisoner confronts him with an accusation of "corroborating in crimes against humanity." The doctor is reminded of the fate of the Nazi doctors during the Nuremberg Trials. The prisoner categorically denies the criminal nature of his activity and claims that he pursued his chosen profession in writing a book about the state economy.

From the information provided by the secret police investigator and summaries of treatment obtained from the local health center and the district mental health clinic, the forensic psychiatrist learns that the patient had a "stormy adolescence," during which he pursued, with abandon, the study of his country's history, literature, and art. He was described by his teachers as "stubborn, oppositional, and obsessed with his ideas." His principal wrote: "This young man is far too sensitive and intense for his age. He is negative about everything our country stands for, and his tastes in art and music are bizarre. However, he is a great mathematician, and with proper guidance and education, can be an asset to our country."

The records of the local draft board revealed that the prisoner was relieved from compulsory military duty because of a diagnosis of "psychoneurosis" established by a psychiatrist at the district mental health clinic. The records from the clinic described a young man who was "moody, preoccupied with his interest in history and mathematics, precise and compulsive in his habits, with some excessive concern about his health." Apparently, the prisoner was seen at the mental health clinic only three times, and never requested any treatment.

The forensic psychiatrist makes no attempt to contact, or interview by telephone, Gregor's wife, parents, or friends and colleagues (he is under strict orders not to reveal the prisoner's whereabouts because of the KGB's insistence on keeping Gregor incommunicado before the trial). Failing to do that, the forensic psychiatrist never learns that the prisoner was a "star student" in the department of economics of a leading state university, or that he was universally admired by his peers and faculty. Most of his professors later became his colleagues, when Gregor was invited to remain in the department to continue his research. The forensic psychiatrist also never learns that the prisoner has written several articles approved for publication in respected professional journals, that he has been married for 18 years, maintains numerous close and enduring friendships, and has adopted two children, after having been extensively interviewed by the state adoption agency before being approved as an adoptive parent. Finally, the forensic psychiatric was also denied an opportunity to read Gregor's book, which presumably was a product of a disturbed mind.

By the end of the third week, the prisoner was forcibly given small doses of a neuroleptic. He became weak and apathetic, complained of dryness of the mouth, increased appetite, and grogginess throughout the day, and an increasingly troublesome tremor. Each time the prisoner was given medication, he offered resistance. This was described in the record as "paranoid refusal to believe in the good intentions of the medical personnel, and inability to develop insight into his condition and his own needs."

When medication produces no change in the prisoner's attitude except for obvious side effects, it is discontinued. One week after this, the prisoner is looking more cheerful, and finally agrees to cooperate with the expert committee, consisting of three forensic psychiatrists. When the committee sees the prisoner, none of its members has had a chance to read the manuscript that brought the man to the attention of the authorities. During the interview, the prisoner is attentive and guarded, and later is described by one of the members as "hypervigilant, with obvious ideas of reference." The committee unanimously agrees on the diagnosis offered by the forensic psychiatrist, Sluggish Schizophrenia. (Sluggish Schizophrenia is considered by Soviet psychiatrists to be the mildest form of the continuous subtype of Schizophrenia. It is roughly equivalent to the concepts of "pseudoneurotic" and "pseudopsychopathic" Schizophrenias that were used by clinicians in the United States in previous decades. It is presumed to have a more favorable course than the other types of Schizophrenia.) The committee recommends compulsory psychiatric treatment for Gregor "because of his inability to have a critical attitude toward his own condition and circumstances and failure to cooperate with necessary medical treatment."

Discussion of "Crimes Against the State"

The Soviet psychiatrist (now living in the United States) who provided this case suggests that the KGB investigator knew that the state would have considerable difficulty in prosecuting Gregor since it would have had to prove that he had a malicious intent to "undermine and harm the interests of the Socialist State." Because Gregor is articulate and persuasive, a public trial would have been embarrassing to the government. Knowing that Gregor had been given a psychiatric diagnosis that exempted him from the draft, the KGB investigator reasoned that a trial would be unnecessary and that the credibility of Gregor's ideas would be undermined if his behavior could be attributed to a mental disorder.

The forensic psychiatrist was given inadequate and biased information, had no access to his "patient's" family or colleagues, and had to deal with a frightened and unwilling man. Practicing within a social system with an extremely narrow range of "permissible" behavior and within a profession that uses an extraordinarily broad concept of Schizophrenia, the forensic psychiatrist could very well have been sincere in considering Gregor mentally ill. It is also possible that the psychiatrist was cynically using his power to make diagnoses, hospitalize, and treat in order to satisfy an implicit request from the KGB to take this "troublesome" man off their hands.

Whether or not the forensic psychiatrist actually believed that Gregor was ill, he probably justified his diagnosis as follows: The onset of Gregor's Schizophrenia was, as is usual in this illness, at the time of adolescent transition to adult life. He exhibited overvalued ideas, instability of mood, inappropriately intense and single-minded pursuit of interests unusual for boys of his age, and obsessive compulsive personality traits. He developed a system of rationalized obsessive preoccupations with seeking reforms in Soviet society. His tragic world view is evidence of chronic dysphoria and anhedonia. His belief that he can make a contribution to the economic theory and well-being of his country is evidence of an overvalued idea that has progressed into a fantastic delusion of reform.

His cautious attitude toward authorities and state-appointed physicians is an expression of paranoid and self-referential perception.

In contrast to the Soviet forensic psychiatrist, we see absolutely no justification for making a psychiatric diagnosis in Gregor's case. His difficulties are certainly a result of the interaction between his personality traits and an oppressive society. However, in a freer society these personality traits might not cause any particular difficulties—indeed, might even be rewarded.

DSM-III-R Diagnosis:

Axis I: **V71.09 No Diagnosis or Condition**
Axis II: **V71.09 No Diagnosis or Condition**

CHAPTER FOUR

HISTORICAL CASES

CHAPTER FOUR
HISTORICAL CASES

Emil Kraepelin (1856–1926)

Kraepelin, a professor of psychiatry in Germany, provided the basis for modern classification of mental disorders. He used the natural history of the illness—its onset, course, and outcome—and its clinical picture as the basis for classification. Thus, he differentiated Maniacal-Depressive Insanity from Dementia Praecox (later renamed Schizophrenia by Bleuler). He subdivided Dementia Praecox into three types: catatonic, hebephrenic, and paranoid.

Kraepelin's major textbook was first published in 1883, and went into nine editions. The following cases are taken verbatim from his Lectures in Clinical Psychiatry,* first published in 1904. They provided generations of clinicians with detailed illustrations of his diagnostic concepts.

Music Student

Y OU SEE BEFORE you a student of music, aged nineteen, who has been ill for about a year. The highly-gifted patient, without any tangible cause, while studying music, became depressed, felt ill at ease and lonely, made all manner of plans, which he always gave up, for changing his place of residence and his profession, for he could come to no fixed resolutions. During a visit to Munich, he felt as if people in the street had something to say to him, and as if he were talked about everywhere. He heard an offensive remark at an inn at the next table, which he answered rudely. Next day he was seized with the apprehension that his remark might be taken as lèse majesté. He heard that students asked for him at

---

*Kraepelin E: *Lectures in Clinical Psychiatry.* Translated by Thomas P. Johnstone, New York, Hafner Publishing Co., 1968. "Music Student," p. 74; "Schoolmaster," p. 262; "Wicked Young Lady," p. 265; "Innkeeper," p. 97; "Stately Gentlemen," p. 140; "Widow," p. 157; "Farmer," p. 4; "Oberrealschul Student," p. 77; "Suffering Lady," p. 252; "Onanistic Student," p. 21; "Factory Girl," p. 83.

the door, and he left Munich post-haste with every precautionary measure, because he thought himself accompanied and followed on the way. Since then he overheard people in the street who threatened to shoot him, and to set fire to his house, and on that account he burned no light in his room. In the streets voices pointed out the way he ought to go so as to avoid being shot. Behind doors, windows, hedges, pursuers seemed everywhere to lurk. He also heard long conversations of not very flattering purport as to his person. In consequence of this, he withdrew altogether from society, but yet behaved in such an ordinary way that his relatives, whom he visited, did not notice his delusions. At last the many mocking calls which he heard at every turn provoked the thought of shooting himself.

After about six months he felt more free, "comfortable, enterprising, and cheerful," began to talk a lot, compose, criticized everything, concocted great schemes, and was insubordinate to his teacher. The voices still continued, and he recognized in them the whisperings of master spirits. Hallucinations of sight now became very marked. The patient saw Beethoven's image radiant with joy at his genius; saw Goethe, whom he had abused, in a threatening attitude; masked men and ideal female forms floated through his room. He saw lightning and glorious brilliancy of colours, which he interpreted partly as the flowing out of his great genius, partly as attestations of applause from the dead.

He regarded himself as the Messiah, preached openly against prostitution, wished to enter into an ideal connection with a female student of music, whom he sought for in strange houses, composed the "Great Song of Love," and on account of this priceless work was brought to the hospital by those who envied him, as he said.

The patient is quite collected, and gives connected information as to his personal circumstances. He is clear as to time and place, but betrays himself by judging his position falsely, inasmuch as he takes us for hypnotizers, who wish to try experiments with him. He does not look upon himself as ill; at the most as somewhat nervously overexcited. Through diplomatic questions we learn that all people know his thoughts; if he writes, the words are repeated before the door. In the creaking of boards, in the whistle of the train, he hears calls, exhortations, orders, threats. Christ appears to him in the night, or a golden figure as the spirit of his father; coloured signs of special meaning are given through the window. In prolonged conversation the patient very quickly loses the thread, and produces finally a succession of fine phrases, which wind up unexpectedly with some facetious question. His mood is arrogant, conceited, generally condescending, occasionally transitorily irritated or apprehensive. The patient speaks much and willingly, talks aloud to himself, and marches boisterously up and down the ward, interests himself more than is desirable in his fellow-patients, seeking to cheer them and to manage them. He is very busy, too, with letter-writing and composing, but only produces fugitive, carelessly jotted down written work, with numerous marginal notes.

Kraepelin's Diagnosis: Maniacal-Depressive Insanity

Discussion of "Music Student"

There are two phases of this illness. In the first, the patient is described as depressed and indecisive (" . . . he could come to no fixed resolutions"), and had suicidal ideas (" . . . thought of shooting himself"). We suspect that this is a Major Depressive Episode; but we do not have enough information about other depressive symptoms, such as loss of appetite and sleep disturbance, to make a firm diagnosis.

The psychotic features during this period consisted of mood-incongruent persecutory delusions and hallucinations; they apparently had no relation to typical depressive themes such as deserved punishment, personal inadequacy, or guilt. There were persecutory delusions ("Behind doors, windows, hedges, pursuers seemed everywhere to lurk.") and hallucinations ("He . . . heard long conversations of not very flattering purport as to his person."). There were ideas of reference ("He heard that students asked for him at the door, and he left Munich post–haste with every precautionary measure, because he thought himself accompanied and followed on the way.").

Currently the patient is clearly in a Manic Episode. There is an elevated mood with grandiosity ("He regarded himself as the Messiah . . . "), hyperactivity (" . . . [he] marches boisterously up and down the ward . . . "), overtalkativeness, and poor judgment (" . . . [he] interests himself more than is desirable in his fellow-patients, seeking to cheer them and to manage them."). There is a suggestion of loose associations and, possibly, flight of ideas ("In prolonged conversation the patient very quickly loses the thread, and produces finally a succession of fine phrases, which wind up unexpectedly with some facetious question."). Most of the other psychotic features are mood-congruent in that they are associated with themes of inflated worth, knowledge, and identity. Hallucinations ("The patient saw Beethoven's image radiant with joy at his genius . . . ") and delusions (" . . . [he] composed the 'Great Song of Love,' and on account of this priceless work was brought to the hospital by those who envied him . . . ") are present. In addition, there are illusions ("In the creaking of boards, in the whistle of the train, he hears calls, exhortations, orders, threats.").

It is interesting to note the presence of certain psychotic symptoms such as possible thought-broadcasting (" . . . all people know his thoughts; if he writes, the words are repeated before the door."). Even though many clinicians have regarded such symptoms as indicative of Schizophrenia, both Kraepelin and DSM-III-R do not regard these as incompatible with a Mood Disorder.

If, during the first phase of the illness, the patient had psychotic symptoms in the absence of a full depressive syndrome, then the diagnosis would be Schizoaffective Disorder, Bipolar Type. Since we suspect that he may have had a full depressive syndrome, we note the need to rule out Bipolar Disorder, Manic, with Psychotic Features (Mood-congruent).

DSM-III-R Diagnosis:

Axis I: 295.70 **Schizoaffective Disorder, Bipolar Type (p. 210) R/O Bipolar Disorder, Manic, with Psychotic Features (Mood-congruent)**

The Schoolmaster

F IRST YOU SEE A SCHOOLMASTER, aged thirty-one, who came to the hospital of his own accord four weeks ago in order to be treated here. The patient was, in fact, violently agitated when he had to come here, sank down on his bed, and said that the discussion in the hospital would cost him his life. He begged to be allowed to sit in the hall before the lecture began, so that he could see the audience come in gradually, as he could not face a number of people so suddenly.

The patient is quite collected, clear, and well-ordered in his statements. He says that one of his sisters suffers in the same way as himself. He traces the beginning of his illness back to about eleven years ago. Being a clever lad, he became a schoolmaster, and had to do a great deal of mental work to qualify. Gradually he began to fear that he had a serious disease, and was going to die of heart apoplexy. All the assurances and examinations of his doctor could not convince him. For this reason he suddenly left his appointment and went home one day seven years ago, being afraid that he would die shortly. After this he consulted every possible doctor, and took long holidays repeatedly, always recovering a little, but invariably finding that his fears returned speedily. These were gradually reinforced by the fear of gatherings of people. He was unable to cross large squares or go through wide streets by himself. He avoided using the railway for fear of collisions and derailments, and he would not travel in a boat lest it might capsize. He was seized with apprehension on bridges and when skating, and at last the apprehension of apprehension itself caused palpitations and oppression on all sorts of occasions. He did not improve after his marriage three years ago. He was domesticated, good-natured, and manageable, only "too soft." On the way here, when he had finally made up his mind to place himself in our hands, he trembled with deadly fear.

The patient describes himself as a chicken-hearted fellow, who, in spite of good mental ability, has always been afraid of all sorts of diseases—consumption, heart apoplexy, and the like. He knows that these anxieties are morbid, yet cannot free himself from them. This apprehensiveness came out in a very marked way while he was under observation in the hospital. He worried about every remedy, whether it was baths, packs, or medicine, being afraid it would be too strong for him, and have a weakening effect. He always wished to have a warder within call in case he got agitated. The sight of other patients disturbed him greatly; and when he went for a walk in the garden with the door shut, he was tormented by the fear of not being able to get out of it in case anything happened. At last he would hardly venture in front of the house, and always had to have the door open behind him so that he could take refuge indoors in case of necessity. He begged to have a little bottle of "blue electricity" that he had brought with him to give him confidence. Sometimes he was seized with violent palpitation of the heart while he was sitting down. Some little acne spots gave him so much alarm that he could neither go for a walk nor sleep. It struck him that his look had got very gloomy, and he thought it was the beginning of a mental disturbance which would certainly seize upon him while he was here.

Kraepelin's Diagnosis: Insanity of Irrepressible Ideas

Discussion of "The Schoolmaster"

The patient demonstrates three significant diagnostic features. First of all, there is a morbid preoccupation with a fear of having a serious physical disease (" . . . he began to fear that he had a serious disease, and was going to die of heart apoplexy. All the assurances and examinations of his doctor could not convince him."). This, in the absence of a physical disorder that can account for the disturbance, justifies the diagnosis of Hypochondriasis.

Secondly, there is a strong suggestion of recurrent panic attacks ("Sometimes he was seized with violent palpitation of the heart while he was sitting down. . . . He trembled with deadly fear."). Perhaps because Kraepelin did not recognize recurrent panic attacks as a distinct clinical syndrome, there is no mention of other characteristic symptoms such as shortness of breath, dizziness, and sweating.

Finally, there is an irrational avoidance of being in public places ("He was also unable to cross large squares or go through wide streets by himself. . . . He was seized with apprehension on bridges. . . ."). This suggests Agoraphobia, avoidance of public places from which escape might be difficult or help unavailable in case of sudden incapacitation. Most likely the recurrent panic attacks led to the Agoraphobia, indicating the diagnosis of Panic Disorder with Agoraphobia. (There is not enough information to record the current severity of the panic attacks and the agoraphobic avoidance.)

Some clinicians might wish to make the additional diagnosis of a Simple Phobia to account for the fear and avoidance of trains and boats, because the patient attributes his anxiety to concern that an accident might occur rather than to the possibility that he might be incapacitated while alone. We do not add this diagnosis because we are not sure that he is markedly distressed by this fear or that it causes significant impairment in social or occupational functioning.

DSM-III-R Diagnosis:

Axis I: **300.21 Panic Disorder with Agoraphobia (p. 237)**
          300.70 Hypochondriasis (p. 261)

Wicked Young Lady

A YOUNG LADY, AGED TWENTY-SIX. . . . The slightly-built, ill-nourished, sickly-looking girl has an expression of pain and trouble. Her hands and fingers are always in slight movement, reflecting her mental restlessness. She is quite collected and clear, but only gives monosyllabic answers. . . . She was constitutionally healthy herself, lively, and cheerful, but fell ill ten years ago of chronic inflammation of the tarsal joint, which brought her under medical treatment for a year. Even now walking is made difficult and slightly painful by the stiffness of the joint. In answer to our questions, the patient says that she is not insane, but only a wicked person who would be sent to the devil if people knew how continually she sins. She does not deserve to be well treated, and she cannot bear that people should look on her as an invalid, when in reality she is only pretending. It is impossible to get any details from her, as she evades every attempt to extract information. We can only learn that she has been to confession unworthily, and so could find no rest, even if she went to the end of the world. She must go away, anywhere, only not to her home, where she has lied and deceived. She cannot stay here either, as people are far too good to her.

So far as we know this state of depression has developed quite gradually in the last year or two. It struck the patient's relations that her mood changed quickly and abruptly. She occasionally expressed religious doubts, on account of which she was sent to the priest, and also to a place of pilgrimage. But this only produced an aggravation of her condition each time. The restlessness increased, and the patient's sleep and appetite became worse and worse, her strength gradually becoming very much reduced in consequence. She felt burdened with grievous sins, of which she could not properly repent, and so has fallen into the power of the devil. She had neither wishes nor will; everything had become indifferent to her. Her whole previous life, with all her transgressions, stood out clearly before her, so that she was surprised at her own memory. She could not help brooding and having unclean thoughts, which broke her heart. Hence she worked feverishly, just to avoid thinking, although everything was very difficult for her.

After great reluctance, she has informed me of the purport of her tormenting thoughts. She was almost continually haunted by ideas associated with the reproductive organs of the opposite sex, which need not be detailed here. Thoughts of this kind, concerned in different ways with the same object, persecute her unceasingly without her being able to ignore them. Hence she says that she must really wish to have such thoughts; she must find pleasure in them, or they would not come. It is very difficult to divert the patient's mind from her painful self-torture; she always returns to it. She is quite unable to read, or to occupy herself mentally in any other way, as these sexual ideas attach themselves, by the most remarkable connections, to her course of thought, however remote it may be. In her general thinking the patient is clumsy and slow. She has always to overcome great disinclination, even when she has to write a simple letter. She generally obeys the doctor's orders, but has a number of peculiarities. The baths give her pains; meat is not good for her; she must follow certain paths in her whole way of life if she is not to grow worse. No physical disturbances have appeared except stiffness, swelling, and pain in the left instep, and a tendency to constipation, which has existed for many years. She sleeps badly.

Kraepelin's Diagnosis: Maniacal-Depressive Insanity

Discussion of "Wicked Young Lady"

What apparently disturbs this patient most are the sexual ideas that force themselves into her awareness against her will. As Kraepelin notes in his discussion of the case, even though she says that she must really "wish" to have such ideas, " . . . it is clear that she has a strong desire to be freed from her tormenting thoughts, but cannot refrain from them." These thoughts have all the characteristics of obsessions, or what Kraepelin referred to as "irrepressible ideas": The thoughts are recurrent and persistent. She recognizes them as products of her own mind and unsuccessfully attempts to suppress them. Because the obsessions cause her marked distress, a diagnosis of Obsessive Compulsive Disorder is warranted.

In addition to the Obsessive Compulsive Disorder the patient has an episode of illness that meets the criteria for Major Depression. In addition to the depressed mood there are guilt, disturbed sleep, decreased appetite and energy (". . . sleep and appetite became worse and worse, her strength gradually becoming very much reduced . . . "), loss of interest ("She had neither wishes nor will; everything had become indifferent to her"), difficulty concentrating, and, possibly, psychomotor agitation ("restlessness").

The patient's guilt is of psychotic proportions—she believes that she has "fallen into the power of the devil." This delusion is mood-congruent in that it involves the theme of guilt and deserved punishment.

Do the prominent obsessions justify a separate diagnosis in addition to the diagnosis of Major Depression? As Kraepelin notes ". . . a single symptom, however characteristic it may be, never justifies a definite diagnosis by itself, and only the whole picture can ever be decisive of the clinical hypothesis." DSM-III, following Kraepelin's approach, instructed the clinician to make only one diagnosis, assuming that the obsessions were best understood as an associated feature of the Major Depression. In DSM-III-R, this hierarchic relationship has been suspended, and the clinician is instructed to make both diagnoses.

DSM-III-R Diagnosis:

**Axis I: 296.24 Major Depression, Single Episode, with Psychotic Features (Mood-congruent) (p. 229)
300.30 Obsessive Compulsive Disorder (p. 247)**

The Innkeeper

THE INNKEEPER, AGED THIRTY-FOUR, whom I am bringing before you today was admitted to the hospital only an hour ago. He understands the questions put to him, but cannot quite hear some of them, and gives a rather absentminded impression. He states his name and age correctly. . . . Yet he does not know the doctors, calls them by the names of his acquaintances, and thinks he has been here for two or three days. It must be the Crown Hotel, or, rather, the "mad hospital." He does not know the date.

. . . He moves about in his chair, looks round him a great deal, starts slightly several times, and keeps on playing with his hands. Suddenly he gets up, and begs to be allowed to play on the piano for a little at once. He sits down again immediately, on persuasion, but then wants to go away "to tell them something else that he has forgotten." He gradually gets more and more excited, saying that his fate is sealed; he must leave the world now; they might telegraph to his wife that her husband is lying at the point of death. We learn, by questioning him, that he is going to be executed by electricity, and also that he will be shot. "The picture is not clearly painted," he says; "every moment someone stands now here, now there, waiting for me with a revolver. When I open my eyes, they vanish." He says that a stinking fluid has been injected in his head and both his toes, which causes the pictures one takes for reality; that is the work of an international society, which makes away with those "who fell into misfortune innocently through false steps." With this he looks eagerly at the window, where he sees houses and trees vanishing and reappearing. With slight pressure on his eyes, he sees first sparks, then a hare, a picture, a head, a washstand-set, a half-moon, and a human head, first dully and then in colours. If you show him a speck on the floor, he tries to pick it up, saying that it is a piece of money. If you shut his hand and ask him what you have given him, he keeps his fingers carefully closed, and guesses that it is a lead-pencil or a piece of India rubber. The patient's mood is half apprehensive and half amused. His head is much flushed, and his pulse is small, weak, and rather hurried. His face is bloated and his eyes are watery. His breath smells strongly of alcohol and acetone. His tongue is thickly furred, and trembles when he puts it out, and his outspread fingers show strong, jerky tremors. The knee-reflexes are somewhat exaggerated.

. . . Our patient has drunk hard since he was thirteen years old. . . . At last, by his own account, he drank six or seven litres of wine a day and five or six stomachic bitters, while he took hardly any food but soup. Some weeks ago he had occasional hallucinations of sight—mice, rats , beetles, and rabbits. He mistook people at times, and came into his inn in his shirt. His condition has grown worse during the last few days.

Kraepelin's Diagnosis: Delirium Tremens

Discussion of "The Innkeeper"

This is a classic case of Delirium Tremens, which in DSM-III-R is called Alcohol Withdrawal Delirium to differentiate it from Delirium caused by withdrawal from other drugs, such as barbiturates.

The delirium is evidenced by reduced ability to maintain attention to external stimuli ("He understands the questions put to him, but cannot quite hear some of them, and gives a rather absent-minded impression . . . begs to be allowed to play the piano . . . looks eagerly at the window . . . "); rambling speech; perceptual disturbances ("... he sees houses and trees vanishing and reappearing [hallucination].... If you show him a speck on the floor, he tries to pick it up, saying that it is a piece of money" [illusion]); increased psychomotor activity ("He moves about in his chair ... and keeps on playing with his hands"); and disorientation (" ... he does not know the doctors ... [nor] the date").

In addition, the patient displays the autonomic hyperactivity that characteristically accompanies a delirium due to Alcohol Withdrawal ("His head is much flushed, and his pulse is small, weak, and rather hurried."). He also demonstrates persecutory delusions (" ... he is going to be executed by electricity"), which are often present.

Although the case description makes no mention of a recent reduction in alcohol ingestion, it is reasonable to assume that the delirium resulted from alcohol withdrawal in a person who has been dependent on alcohol for a long period of time.

DSM-III-R Diagnosis:

Axis I: **291.00 Alcohol Withdrawal Delirium (p. 131)**
           303.90 Alcohol Dependence (p. 173)

Stately Gentleman

THE STATELY GENTLEMAN, aged sixty-two, who presents himself before us with a certain courtly dignity, with his carefully-tended moustaches, his eye-glasses, and his well-fitting if perhaps somewhat shabby attire, gives quite the impression of a man of the world. He is somewhat testy at first because he has to allow himself to be questioned before the young gentlemen, but soon enters into a long, connected conversation in a quiet and positive manner. We learn from him that as a young man he went to America, and there went through many vicissitudes, finally settling in Quito, where as a merchant he made a small fortune. With this he returned home twenty-one years ago, but on the dissolving of his business connections he was done out of considerable sums. At home he lived at first on his money, spending his time in amusements, reading the newspaper, playing billiards, going for walks, and sitting about in cafes. At the same time he occupied himself with all sorts of schemes from which he hoped for recognition and profit. Thus, he submitted to the leading Minister the plan (with a map) whereby Germany could lay claim to a lot of still unpossessed land.... A short time after that same Minister travelled to Berlin, and now began the German Colonial Policy, without ... due thanks falling to the lot of the real originator.... Then our patient drew up a plan for the cultivation of cinchona and cacao in our colonies; he also made several inventions for the better connection of railway metals, by which the jolting, an important cause of derailment, would be done away with. Finally, he applied for a number of situations which seemed suited to him, including that of the consulship at Quito, but had always only failures to record.

. . . He was enticed into a district asylum, under the false pretext that he would be given a post, and there he assisted in the management till it became evident to him that they had no intention of paying him for his services. When, on that account, he tried hard for other situations, they sent him, also under false pretenses, to the hospital, where he is now illegally detained. That, he concluded with bitterness, was the thanks which the Fatherland bestowed upon him for his services.

. . . [He] then relates, little by little, that a woman whom he calls by the nickname Bulldog, and who was the daughter of the English Consul at Quito, had persecuted him for twenty-three or twenty-four years with her plans for marriage, and sought in every way to cross his steps in order to reduce him to submission. Even in America things ultimately never went as he wished, and a hundred stuffed birds had, out of spite, been stolen from him by means of a skeleton key; everywhere he noticed the frauds of the Bulldog and her accomplices. "If people do everything differently from what I should have wished, there must be something more than meets the eye." The half-crazy American also travelled home after him, had insinuated herself into this neighbourhood, had the impudence to dress herself up in man's clothes, and to force marriage by preventing him from finding a post, and by these means brought him to want. This artful person had approached him under various names, though he had always told her that one did not win a man's love through such chicanery. He would perhaps be the richest man in California if the Bulldog had not prevented it. She was also to blame for his being brought to the asylum. "Who else, then, could it possibly be?" Both at home and abroad he was eternally meeting her. . . . All objections that one raises to these ideas are received by the patient in a superior, incredulous manner, and glance off from his steadfast conviction without leaving the slightest impression.

Kraepelin's Diagnosis: Paranoia

Discussion of "Stately Gentleman"

This is a classic example of the traditional notion of Paranoia. The patient demonstrates an elaborate system of persecutory delusions: his contributions to German foreign policy are not acknowledged; he is employed by the district asylum—without pay; he is pursued by the "Bulldog," who dresses in men's clothes and prevents him from obtaining employment. As is frequently the case in patients with Paranoid Disorders, there is associated grandiosity. For example, his ideas were incorporated into German colonial policy; he would "... perhaps be one of the richest men in California if the Bulldog had not prevented it."

This condition is distinguished from Paranoid Schizophrenia by the absence of such characteristic symptoms as delusions that are patently absurd, prominent hallucinations, marked loosening of associations, or incoherence. Furthermore, whereas in Schizophrenia continued deterioration in social functioning is common, in Delusional Disorders it is generally absent, as in this case. In the traditional concept of Paranoia, the illness has an insidious onset and a chronic course of many years, as is true in this patient. All such cases fall within the more inclusive DSM-III-R category of Delusional Disorder, which does not require an insidious onset and requires a duration of only one month. Because the predominant theme in this case involves delusions of being malevolently treated, the Delusional Disorder is further specified as Persecutory Type.

DSM-III-R Diagnosis:

Axis I: **297.10 Delusional Disorder, Persecutory Type (p. 202)**

The Widow

THE WIDOW, AGED THIRTY-FIVE, whom I will now bring before you ... gives full information about her life in answer to our questions, knows where she is, can tell the date and the year, and gives proof of satisfactory school knowledge. It is noteworthy that she does not look at her questioner, and speaks in a low and peculiar, sugary, affected tone. When you touch on her illness, she is reserved at first, and says that she is quite well, but she soon begins to express a number of remarkable ideas of persecution. For many years she has heard voices, which insult her and cast suspicion on her chastity. They mention a number of names she knows, and tell her she will be stripped and abused. The voices are very distinct, and, in her opinion, they must be carried by a telescope or a machine from her home. Her thoughts are dictated to her; she is obliged to think them, and hears them repeated after her. She is interrupted in her work, and has all kinds of uncomfortable sensations in her body, to which something is "done." In particular, her "mother parts" are turned inside out, and people send a pain through her back, lay ice-water on her heart, squeeze her neck, injure her spine, and violate her. There are also hallucinations of sight—black figures and the altered appearance of people—but these are far less frequent. She cannot exactly say who carries on all the influencing, or for what object it is done. Sometimes it is the people from her home, and sometimes the doctors of an asylum where she was before who have taken something out of her body.

The patient makes these extraordinary complaints without showing much emotion. She cries a little, but then describes her morbid experiences again with secret satisfaction and even an erotic bias. She demands her discharge, but is easily consoled, and does not trouble at all about her position and her future. Her use of numerous strained and hardly intelligible phrases is very striking. She is ill-treated "flail-wise," "utterance-wise," "terror-wise"; she is "a picture of misery in angel's form," and "a defrauded mamma and housewife of sense of order." They have "altered her form of emotion." She is "persecuted by a secret insect from the District Office. . . ." Her former history shows that she has been ill for nearly ten years. The disease developed gradually. About a year after the death of her husband, by whom she has two children, she became apprehensive, slept badly, heard loud talking in her room at night, and thought that she was being robbed of her means and persecuted by people from Frankfort, where she had formerly lived. Four years ago she spent a year in an asylum. She thought she found the "Frankforters" there, noticed poison in the food, heard voices, and felt influences. After her discharge she brought accusations against the doctors of having mutilated her while she was there. She now thought them to be her persecutors, and openly abused the public authorities for failing to protect her, so she had to be admitted to this hospital two months ago. Here she made the same complaints day after day, without showing much excitement, and wrote long-winded letters full of senseless and unvarying abuse about the persecution from which she suffered, to her relations, the asylum doctors, and the authorities. She did not occupy herself in any way, held no intercourse with her fellow-patients, and avoided every attempt to influence her.

Kraepelin's Diagnosis: Dementia Praecox, Paranoid

Discussion of "The Widow"

This patient demonstrates numerous characteristic symptoms of Schizophrenia. The most conspicuous are bizarre persecutory delusions (" . . . voices . . . must be carried by a telescope or a machine from her home. Her thoughts are dictated to her; she is obliged to think them . . . "; " . . . persecuted by a secret insect from the District Office"), some of which are also somatic (" . . . her 'mother parts' are turned inside out . . . "). She also has persecutory hallucinations (" . . . she has heard voices, which insult her and cast suspicion on her chastity."). Her speech is at times incoherent (" . . . she is . . . a defrauded mamma and housewife of sense of order."), with neologisms ("flail-wise, utterance-wise, terror-wise"). Her affect is both flat ("The patient makes these extraordinary complaints without showing much emotion.") and inappropriate ("She . . . describes her morbid experiences again with secret satisfaction and even with an erotic bias.").

In addition, common associated features of Schizophrenia are described: apathy ("does not trouble at all about her position and her future"); lack of insight (" . . . says that she is quite well . . . "); and social withdrawal (" . . . held no intercourse with her fellow-patients . . . ").

These characteristic symptoms, the marked impairment in multiple areas of functioning, and the ten-year duration of the illness, in the absence of a significant mood disturbance, justify the diagnosis of Chronic Schizophrenia. According to DSM-III-R, incoherence or flat affect rules out the Paranoid Type. Therefore, given the presence of prominent delusions, hallucinations, and incoherence, the type is noted as Undifferentiated.

DSM-III-R Diagnosis:

Axis I: 295.92   **Schizophrenia, Undifferentiated Type, Chronic (p. 194)**

The Farmer

I WILL PLACE BEFORE YOU A FARMER, aged fifty-nine, who was admitted to the hospital a year ago. The patient looks much older than he really is, principally owing to the loss of teeth from his upper jaw. He not only understands our questions without any difficulty, but answers them relevantly and correctly; can tell where he is, and how long he has been here; knows the doctors, and can give the date and the day of the week. His expression is dejected. The corners of his mouth are rather drawn down, and his eyebrows drawn together. . . . On being questioned about his illness, he breaks into lamentations, saying that he did not tell the whole truth on his admission, but concealed the fact that he had fallen into sin in his youth and practiced uncleanness with himself; everything he did was wrong. "I am so apprehensive, so wretched; I cannot lie still for anxiety. O God, if I had only not transgressed so grievously!" He has been ill for over a year. . . . It began with stomach-ache and head troubles, and he could not work any longer. "There was no impulse left." He can get no rest now, and fancies silly things, as if someone were in the room. Once it seemed to him that he had seen the Evil One: perhaps he would be carried off. . . . As a boy, he had taken apples and nuts. "Conscience has said that that is not right; conscience has only awakened just now in my illness." He had also played with a cow, and by himself. "I reproach myself for that now." It seemed to him that he had fallen away from God. . . . His appetite is bad, and he has no stools. He cannot sleep. "If the mind does not sleep, all sorts of thoughts come. . . ." He fastened his neckerchief to strangle himself, but he was not really in earnest. Three sisters and a brother were ill too. The sisters were not so bad; they soon recovered. "A brother has made away with himself through apprehension."

The patient tells us this in broken sentences, interrupted by wailing and groaning. In all other respects, he behaves naturally, does whatever he is told, and only begs us not to let him be dragged away—"There is terrible apprehension in my heart." Except for a little trembling of the outspread fingers and slightly arrhythmic action of the heart, we find no striking disturbances at the physical examination. As for the patient's former history, he is married, and has four healthy children, while three are dead. The illness began gradually seven or eight months before his admission, without any assignable cause. Loss of appetite and dyspepsia appeared first, and then ideas of sin. . . .

Kraepelin's Diagnosis: Melancholia

Discussion of "The Farmer"

This patient is clearly suffering from a Major Depressive Episode. There is a pervasive depressed mood ("I am so apprehensive, so wretched"; "His expression is dejected."). In addition there are the typical associated features: loss of interest ("There was no impulse left."), self-reproach for earlier sexual activities ("He had also played with a cow, and by himself."), insomnia, poor appetite, weight loss, thoughts of suicide, and excessive guilt. There is a suggestion of a hallucination ("Once it seemed to him that he had seen the Evil One . . . "); however, in the context of his culture, this may not have great pathological significance. Similarly, in the context of his culture, it is difficult to decide if his guilt is of delusional proportions.

This is a severe depression that, with additional information, probably would also meet the criteria for the Melancholic Type. The loss of interest would appear to be pervasive. It seems likely that his severely depressed mood is unresponsive to environmental events. In addition, there are several other characteristic features of Melancholia: psychomotor agitation (". . . I cannot lie still for anxiety."), significant anorexia, and weight loss. What we do not know is whether his depression is regularly worse in the morning, whether he has early morning awakening, and whether there is a history of significant personality disturbance.

DSM-III-R Diagnosis:

Axis I: 296.23 Major Depression, Single Episode, Severe (p. 229)
          R/O Melancholic Type

Oberrealschul Student

THE PATIENT I WILL SHOW YOU to-day has almost to be carried into the room, as he walks in a straddling fashion on the outside of his feet. On coming in, he throws off his slippers, sings a hymn loudly, and then cries twice (in English), "My father, my real father!" He is eighteen years old, and a pupil of the Oberrealschul [high school], tall, and rather strongly built, but with a pale complexion, on which there is very often a transient flush. The patient sits with his eyes shut, and pays no attention to his surroundings. He does not look up even when he is spoken to, but he answers, beginning in a low voice, and gradually screaming louder and louder. When asked where he is, he says, "You want to know that too; I tell you who is being measured and is measured and shall be measured. I know all that, and could tell you, but I do not want to." When asked his name, he screams, "What is your name? What does he shut? He shuts his eyes. What does he hear? He does not understand; he understands not. How? Who? Where? When? What does he mean? When I tell him to look, he does not look properly. You there, just look! What is it? What is the matter? Attend; he attends not. I say, what is it, then? Why do you give me no answer? Are you getting impudent again? How can you be so impudent? I'm coming! I'll show you! You don't turn whore for me. You mustn't be smart either; you're an impudent, lousy fellow, an impudent, lousy fellow as stupid as a hog. Such an impudent, shameless, miserable, lousy fellow I've never met with. Is he beginning again? You understand nothing at all–nothing at all; nothing at all does he understand. If you follow me now, he won't follow, will not follow. Are you getting still more impudent? Are you getting impudent still more? How they attend, they do attend," and so on. At the end he scolds in quite inarticulate sounds.

The patient understands perfectly, and has introduced many phrases he has heard before into his speech, without once looking up. He speaks in an affected way, now babbling like a child, now lisping and stammering, sings suddenly in the middle of what he is saying, and grimaces. He carries out orders in an extraordinary fashion, gives his hand with the fist clenched, goes to the blackboard when he is asked, but, instead of writing his name, suddenly knocks down a lamp, and throws the chalk among the audience. He makes all kinds of senseless movements, pushes the table away, crosses his arms, and turns round on his axis, chair and all, or sits balancing, with his legs crossed and his hands on his head. Catalepsy can also be made out. When he is to go away, he will not get up, has to be pushed, and calls out loudly, "Good-morning, gentlemen; it has not pleased me."

. . . The patient himself was always quiet and very industrious, but of moderate mental endowment. Seven months ago, during the holidays, he suddenly began to learn in a quite senseless way, and then became confused, thought he was laughed at for being dirty, and washed himself all day long, was afraid his effects would be taken, broke the windows, seemed to hear voices, attacked his mother without any cause, became wet and dirty in his habits, and would not speak a word. In the hospital he was almost dumb, was cataleptic, gave his hand stiffly and jerkily, and almost entirely refused to eat. His expression was generally indifferent, though sometimes cheerful, and visits from his relations made no impression at all on him.

The patient understood quite well what was taking place around him, but as a rule he did not obey orders; indeed, he sometimes did the exact opposite of what was wanted. Thus, he shut his eyes when his pupils were mentioned, covered his face with his handkerchief if you wished to see it, and drew his hand back when he ought to have stretched it out. He was often dirty, and also smeared faeces about, and rolled them into little balls—a sign diagnostic of great emotional dullness. After refusing food for a long time, he suddenly asked for Swiss cheese and then for chocolate, and devoured them both greedily. From this we can plainly see the senseless and impulsive nature of his refusal of food. Once he laid his outstretched leg on the next bed, and remained in that position when the bed was moved away. In the seventh month of the illness the patient began to be excited, after having sung occasionally during the period of dumbness. In the middle of the night he threw away his bedding, rocked rhythmically up and down on the bedstead, and screamed incessantly, "Now, I want to know where my brother is." Since then he has been in a continual state of excitement, is destructive and abusive, and talks in a confused way. He briefly informed his relations, from whom he takes the eatables they bring when they come to see him, without talking to them much, that he was going to travel by Gibraltar to the Cameroons and by Constantinople to Bucharest.

Kraepelin's Diagnosis: Catatonic Excitement

Discussion of "Oberrealschul Student"

In the absence of any known organic factor, the combination of marked incoherence and catatonic behavior (stupor and excitement) clearly suggests the diagnosis of Schizophrenia. The diagnosis is further confirmed by the history of onset of symptoms seven months previously and a clear deterioration in functioning. Although the hyperactivity, confused speech, and irritability might suggest a Manic Episode, there is no description of a period with a persistent and predominant elevated, expansive, or irritable mood. Although he often is irritable and even violent, his mood seems to fluctuate unpredictably. When irritability is seen in mania, it usually is a response to frustration of grandiosity or hyperactivity.

Although delusions and hallucinations have been present, the most prominent and persistent features are the disorganization of speech and behavior. The patient's frequent incoherence and grossly disorganized behavior are characteristic of the Disorganized Type of Schizophrenia. However, there are numerous prominent examples of classic catatonic behavior: he exhibits negativism (refuses to do what is asked of him or does the opposite), catatonic excitement (senseless movements while ignoring his surroundings), and posturing (kept his leg in an awkward position). In DSM-III-R the Disorganized Type is not diagnosed if the clinical picture is dominated by catatonic symptoms, which represent more specific forms of disorganized behavior.

Since, according to the history, the illness began suddenly seven months before the examination, the course should be noted as Subchronic. The patient demonstrates, over the course of his relatively brief illness, alternation between catatonic stupor (became wet and dirty in his habits, and would not speak a word) and his current catatonic excitement.

DSM-III-R Diagnosis:

Axis I: 295.21 Schizophrenia, Catatonic Type, Subchronic
          (p. 196)

The Suffering Lady

THE YOUNG LADY, AGED THIRTY, carefully dressed in black, who comes into the hall with short, shuffling steps, leaning on the nurse, and sinks into a chair as if exhausted, gives you the impression that she is ill. She is of slender build, her features are pale and rather painfully drawn, and her eyes are cast down. Her small, manicured fingers play nervously with a handkerchief. The patient answers the questions addressed to her in a low, tired voice, without looking up, and we find that she is quite clear about time, place and her surroundings. After a few minutes, her eyes suddenly become convulsively shut, her head sinks forward, and she seems to have fallen into a deep sleep. Her arms have grown quite limp, and fall down as if palsied when you try to lift them. She has ceased to answer, and if you try to raise her eyelids, her eyes suddenly rotate upwards. Needlepricks only produce a slight shudder. But sprinkling with cold water is followed by a deep sigh; the patient starts up, opens her eyes, looks round her with surprise, and gradually comes to herself. She says that she has just had one of her sleeping attacks, from which she has suffered for seven years. They come on quite irregularly, often many in one day, and last from a few minutes to half an hour.

Concerning the history of her life, the patient tells us that . . . she was educated in convent schools, and passed the examination for teachers. As a young girl, she inhaled a great deal of chloroform, which she was able to get secretly, for toothache. She also suffered from headaches, until they were relieved by the removal of growths from the nose. She very readily became delirious in feverish illnesses. Thirteen years ago she took a place as governess in Holland, but soon began to be ill, and has passed the last seven years in different hospitals, except for a short interval when she was in a situation in Moravia.

It would appear from the statements of her relations and doctors that the patient has suffered from the most varied ailments, and been through the most remarkable courses of treatment. For violent abdominal pains and disturbances of menstruation, ascribed to stenosis of the cervical canal and retroflection of the uterus, recourse was had five years ago to the excision of the wedge supposed to cause the obstruction, and the introduction of a pessary. At a later period loss of voice and a contraction of the right forearm and the left thigh set in, and were treated with massage, electricity, bandaging, and stretching under an anaesthetic. Heart oppression and spasmodic breathing also appeared, with quickly passing disablements of various sets of muscles, disturbances of urination, diarrhoea, and unpleasant sensations, now in one and now in another part of the body, but particularly headaches. Extraordinarily strong and sudden changes of mood were observed at the same time, with introspection and complaints of want of consideration in those about her and in her relations, although the latter had made the greatest sacrifices. Brine baths, Russian baths, pine-needle baths, electricity, country air, summer resorts, and finally, residence on the Riviera—everything was tried, generally with only a brief improvement or with none at all.

The immediate cause of the patient being brought to the hospital was the increase in the "sleeping attacks" two years ago. They came on at last even when the patient was standing, and might continue for an hour. The patient did not fall down, but simply leaned against something. The attacks continued in the hospital, and spasmodic breathing was also observed, which could be influenced by suggestion.

After spending eight months here, the patient went away at first to her sister's. But after a few months she had to be taken to another asylum, where she stayed about a year, and then, after a short time spent with her family, came back to us.

During her present residence here, so-called "great attacks" have appeared, in addition to her previous troubles. We will try to produce such an attack by pressure on the very sensitive left ovarian region. After one or two minutes of moderately strong pressure, during which the patient shows sharp pain, her expression alters. She throws herself to and fro with her eyes shut, and screams to us loudly, generally in French, not to touch her. "You must not do anything to me, you hound, *cochon, cochon!*" She cries for help, pushes with her hands, and twists herself as if she were trying to escape from a sexual assault. Whenever she is touched, the excitement increases. Her whole body is strongly bent backwards. Suddenly the picture changes, and the patient begs piteously not to be cursed, and laments and sobs aloud. This condition, too, is very soon put an end to by sprinkling with cold water. The patient shudders, wakes with a deep sigh, and looks fixedly round, only making a tired, senseless impression. She cannot explain what has happened.

The physical examination of the patient shows no particular disturbances at present, except the abnormalities already mentioned. There is only a well-marked weakness, in consequence of which she often keeps to her bed or lies about. All her movements are limp and feeble, but there is no actual disablement anywhere. She often sleeps very badly. At times she wanders about in the night, wakes the nurses, and sends for the doctor. Her appetite is very poor, but she has a habit of nibbling between her meals at all kinds of cakes, fruit, and jam, which are sent at her request, by her relations.

With her growing expertness in illness, the emotional sympathies of the patient are more and more confined to the selfish furthering of her own wishes. She tries ruthlessly to extort the most careful attention from those around her, obliges the doctor to occupy himself with her by day or by night on the slightest occasion, is extremely sensitive to any supposed neglect, is jealous if preference is shown to other patients, and tries to make the attendants give in to her by complaints, accusations, and outbursts of temper. The sacrifices made by others, more especially by her family, are regarded quite as a matter of course, and her occasional prodigality of thanks only serves to pave the way for new demands. To secure the sympathy of those around her, she has recourse to more and more forcible descriptions of her physical and mental torments, histrionic exaggeration of her attacks, and the effective elucidation of her personal character. She calls herself the abandoned, the outcast, and in mysterious hints makes confession of horrible, delightful experiences and failings, which she will only confide to the discreet bosom of her very best friend, the doctor.

Kraepelin's Diagnosis: Hysterical Insanity

Discussion of "The Suffering Lady"

Although Somatization Disorder was a new diagnostic category in DSM-III, this nineteenth-century case is a classic example of the disorder. There is a history of many physical symptoms and complaints, not adequately explained by a physical disorder or injury, that go back to the patient's adolescence. The DSM-III-R criteria for the disorder require 13 symptoms from 6 groups of symptoms. We count 13 in this case history: loss of voice, loss of consciousness, memory loss, seizures, trouble walking, muscle weakness, urinary problems, abdominal pain, diarrhea, menstrual problems, shortness of breath, chest pain, and pain "now in one and now in another part of the body." There is no mention of her psychosexual functioning; it seems likely that on inquiry she would acknowledge symptoms in that area, such as sexual indifference.

As is commonly the case, genuine physical problems coexist, but are hardly adequate to explain the myriad physical complaints.

Although the "sleeping attacks" represent periods of dissociation—that is, temporary, nonorganic alterations of consciousness—in this case they are better thought of as pseudoneurologic symptoms of Somatization Disorder. Thus, the additional diagnosis of a Dissociative Disorder Not Otherwise Specified is not made.

Although Kraepelin's description of the way in which this woman relates to others is based on his observations of her current condition, it is reasonable to assume that it is characteristic of her long-term functioning. The vivid portrayal of the patient as someone who is self centered, expresses emotion with inappropriate exaggeration, displays rapidly shifting and shallow expression of emotions, and needs to be the center of attention is sufficient evidence for a diagnosis of Histrionic Personality Disorder. Several features of Narcissistic Personality Disorder are also present: a sense of the uniqueness of her problems, the need for constant attention, entitlement, and interpersonal exploitation, but not the five symptoms required for a diagnosis. Nevertheless, we would have no quarrel with an additional provisional diagnosis of Narcissistic Personality Disorder based on the suspicion that the patient might well have fantasies of ideal love with "her very best friend, the doctor."

DSM-III-R Diagnosis:

Axis I: 300.81 Somatization Disorder (p. 263)
Axis II: 301.50 Histrionic Personality Disorder (p. 349)

Onanistic Student

YOU HAVE BEFORE YOU TODAY a strongly-built and well-nourished man, aged twenty-one, who entered the hospital a few weeks ago. He sits quietly looking in front of him, and does not raise his eyes when he is spoken to, but evidently understands all our questions very well, for he answers quite relevantly, though only slowly and often only after repeated questioning. From his brief remarks, made in a low tone, we gather that he thinks he is ill, without getting any more precise information about the nature of the illness and its symptoms. The patient attributes his malady to the onanism he has practiced since he was ten years old. He thinks that he has thus incurred the guilt of a sin against the sixth commandment, has very much reduced his power of working, has made himself feel languid and miserable, and has become a hypochondriac. Thus, as the result of reading certain books, he imagined that he had a rupture and suffered from wasting of the spinal cord, neither of which was the case. He would not associate with his comrades any longer, because he thought they saw the results of his vice and made fun of him. The patient makes all these statements in an indifferent tone, without looking up or troubling about his surroundings. His expression betrays no emotion; he only laughs for a moment now and then. There is occasional wrinkling of the forehead or facial spasm. Round the mouth and nose a fine, changing twitching is constantly observed.

The patient gives us a correct account of his past experiences. His knowledge speaks for the high degree of his education; indeed, he was ready to enter the University a year ago. He also knows where he is and how long he has been here, but he is only very imperfectly acquainted with the names of the people round him, and says that he has never asked about them. He can only give a very meager account of the general events of the last year. In answer to our questions, he declares that he is ready to remain in the hospital for the present. He would certainly prefer it if he could enter a profession, but he cannot say what he would like to take up. . . . The patient makes his statements slowly and in monosyllables, not because his wish to answer meets with overpowering hindrances, but because he feels no desire to speak at all. He certainly hears and understands what is said to him very well, but he does not take the trouble to attend to it. He pays no heed, and answers whatever occurs to him without thinking. No visible effort of the will is to be noticed. All his movements are languid and expressionless, but are made without hindrance or trouble. There is no sign of emotional dejection, such as one would expect from the nature of his talk, and the patient remains quite dull throughout, experiencing neither fear nor hope nor desires. He is not at all deeply affected by what goes on before him, although he understands it without actual difficulty. It is all the same to him who appears or disappears where he is, or who talks to him and takes care of him, and he does not even once ask their names.

. . . He broods, staring in front of him with expressionless features, over which a vacant smile occasionally plays, or at the best turns over the leaves of a book for a moment, apparently speechless, and not troubling about anything. Even when he has visitors, he sits without showing any interest, does not ask about what is happening at home, hardly even greets his parents, and goes back indifferently to the ward. He can hardly be induced to write a letter, and says that he has nothing to write about.

But he occasionally composes a letter to the doctor, expressing all kinds of distorted, half-formed ideas, with a peculiar and silly play on words, in very fair style, but with little connection. He begs for "a little more allegro in the treatment," and "liberationary movement with a view to the widening of the horizon," will "ergo extort some wit in lectures," and "nota bene for God's sake only does not wish to be combined with the club of the harmless." "Professional work is the balm of life."

The development of the illness has been quite gradual. Our patient . . . did not go to school till he was seven years old, as he was a delicate child and spoke badly, but when he did he learned quite well. He was considered to be a reserved and stubborn child. Having practiced onanism at a very early age, he became more and more solitary in the last few years, and thought that he was laughed at by his brothers and sisters, and shut out from society because of his ugliness. For this reason he could not bear a looking-glass in his room. After passing the written examination on leaving school, a year ago, he gave up the viva voce, because he could not work any longer. He cried a great deal, masturbated much, ran about aimlessly, played in a senseless way on the piano, and began to write observations "On the Nerve-play of life," which he cannot get on with. He was incapable of any kind of work, even physical, felt "done for," asked for a revolver, ate Swedish matches to destroy himself, and lost all affection for his family. From time to time he became excited and troublesome, and shouted out of the window at night. In the hospital, too, a state of excitement lasting for several days was observed, in which he chattered in a confused way, made faces, ran about at full speed, wrote disconnected scraps of composition, and crossed and recrossed them with flourishes and unmeaning combinations of letters. After this a state of tranquility ensued, in which he could give absolutely no account of his extraordinary behavior.

Kraepelin's Diagnosis: Dementia Praecox (Insanity of Adolescence)

Discussion of "Onanistic Student"

The most prominent features of the illness are delusions of guilt (his onanism has caused his illness), persecutory delusions ("he thought [his comrades] saw the results of his vice and made fun of him"), incoherence, and flat and inappropriate affect ("His expression betrays no emotion; he only laughs for a moment now and then."). These features, plus the chronic nature of the illness, establish the diagnosis of Schizophrenia.

If this patient were seen at the time that he "chattered in a confused way, made faces, ran about at full speed," the appropriate subtype might be Catatonic or Disorganized. At the point at which he was presented by Kraepelin, he was neither frequently incoherent nor excited; the appropriate subtype is therefore Undifferentiated.

The initial description of the patient might lead some clinicians to consider the possibility of a Major Depressive Episode: psychomotor retardation, delusions of guilt, and hypochondriacal preoccupation are present. However, as Kraepelin later notes, "There is no sign of emotional dejection, such as one would expect from the nature of his talk."

DSM-III-R Diagnosis:

Axis I: 295.92 Schizophrenia, Undifferentiated Type, Chronic (p. 198)

Factory Girl

THE FACTORY GIRL, AGED THIRTY-TWO, who now comes into the room with an awkward and very deep curtsy, presents an entirely different aspect from the last patient. She declines to sit down to talk to us, thanks us for the "honour," goes up and down with affected, waddling steps, and begins to declaim and recite verses, and to interpolate witty remarks in our discussion of her condition. Her name is what the parson christened her, and she is as old as her little finger. She knows her position, the date, where she is, and the people around her, and can give the most exact information about her past experiences. She does not consider herself insane. She often interweaves her disconnected talk with scraps of bad French and senselessly altered quotations, such as "Ingratitude is the world's praise"; "Many hands, many minds." She rides single phrases to death in uninterrupted repetition—"Devil's dung on the soul's foot, the soul's foot in devil's dung." She often uses very strange and almost incomprehensible compound words and phrases.

Her mood is silly, cheerful, sometimes erotic, and then again irritable. She takes pleasure in the most indecent sexual allusions, and occasionally in outbursts of the wildest abuse. She does not obey orders, and refuses to give her hand on the ground that they are her hands. She will not write, and pertly refuses to do anything she is asked. She chatters continually, and will not let anyone get in a word. Her speech is extremely laboured. She cuts the separate syllables sharply asunder, accentuates the final syllables sharply, pronounces g like k, and d like t, talks like a child, in imperfectly formed sentences, distorts words, inserts senseless expletives and strangely-formed words, and constantly changes the subject. All her movements and gestures are clumsy, angular, and stiff, and are very lavishly employed, but monotonous; she hops about, bends down, claps her hands and makes faces. She has ornamented her clothes in an extraordinary way with embroidery and crochet-work of startlingly bright wool. From her talk it appears that she looks on herself as the mistress of the house; she pays the nurses and appoints them, and will get herself better doctors. Moreover, she complains of being exposed to sexual assaults, and says that her lungs, heart, and liver have been taken out. She says she is engaged to a doctor in the asylum where she was before. She tells her name with the prefix "von." She also seems to have heard voices, but will only make evasive statements about them.

... The patient ... was considered very selfish and obstinate ... from her youth up. She was first a servant girl and then a factory hand, had two illegitimate children, and then aborted once. About six months later, two years ago now, she saw gray men and women's heads, and heard knocking and voices which called abusive words to her. Later on she wrote a love-letter to the proprietor of her factory, and was dismissed and picked up helpless on the street. When taken to an asylum, she was quiet and collected at first, but soon had brief attacks of the most violent excitement, during which she undressed herself completely, hit out round her in a senseless way, and bit. Later on she showed a repellent, discontented disposition and a tendency to stereotypism and impulsive actions. When she was brought here a year and a quarter ago she presented the same picture as now in all essential features. It should perhaps be added that she showed echopraxis, followed the same track—a figure of eight, for instance for hours in the garden, and was very refractory. For a long time she had to be kept quite alone in the garden and in her room, because, though quite collected and free from great emotional excitement, she was very dangerous to the other patients.

Kraepelin's Diagnosis: Catatonic Excitement

Discussion of "Factory Girl"

This case indicates how difficult it is to distinguish the excitement seen in the Catatonic Subtype of Schizophrenia from that seen in a Manic Episode. This woman has many symptoms that suggest the manic syndrome. Her mood is described as alternately silly, cheerful, and irritable. There are pressure of speech ("She chatters continually, and will not let anyone get in a word") and hyperactivity ("she hops about, bends down, claps her hands ... "). She is also grandiose (" ... she looks on herself as the mistress of the house; she pays the nurses and appoints them ... ") and sexually provocative.

We are told that for some unspecified period before the excitement began, there were persecutory hallucinations, apparently not accompanied by any disturbance in mood. Assuming that this period was longer than two weeks, according to DSM-III-R this would rule out the diagnosis of a Manic Episode and would suggest the diagnosis of Schizoaffective Disorder or Schizophrenia. Whether the diagnosis of Schizophrenia is made depends on the duration of the mood syndrome in relation to the total duration of the illness. If the mood syndrome is brief, the diagnosis is Schizophrenia; if not, it is Schizoaffective Disorder. Since we are told that this patient is pretty much the same now as she has been for the year that she has been in the hospital, we should conclude that the manic syndrome has not been brief and diagnose Schizoaffective Disorder, Bipolar Type. An important implication now for such a diagnosis is that it would suggest the advisability of a trial of lithium therapy.

Kraepelin notes the primary disturbance as one of behavior rather than mood. He emphasizes the negativism ("She does not obey orders . . . and pertly refuses to do anything she is asked."), stereotypism ("she . . . followed the same track—a figure of eight, for instance—for hours in the garden"), and mannerisms ("All her movements and gestures are clumsy, angular, and stiff, and are very lavishly employed."). These features, plus the "attacks of the most violent excitement," disorganized speech, and lack of any deep emotion led him to make a diagnosis of Catatonic Excitement.

Many clinicians (particularly those trained before DSM-III), would agree with Kraepelin's diagnosis of Schizophrenia because they would question the description of the patient's excitement as a manic syndrome, considering the mood as more shallow and silly than elevated or expansive. They would also point to the incoherence, grossly disorganized behavior, hallucinations, and inappropriate affect in an illness that has lasted continually for more than two years (unusual in Bipolar Disorder) and that represents a distinct change from the patient's usual level of functioning.

Catatonic symptoms without an organic etiology used to be regarded as pathognomonic of Schizophrenia. It is now recognized that catatonic symptoms may also be seen in a manic syndrome (as in this case, we think) and in a Manic Episode of Bipolar Disorder (see "A Praying Athlete," p. 161).

DSM-III-R Diagnosis:

Axis I: 295.70 Schizoaffective Disorder, Bipolar Type (p. 210)

Eugen Bleuler (1857-1939)

Bleuler, a Swiss psychiatrist, coined the term Schizophrenia to describe what he considered to be the fundamental disturbance—a splitting of the psychic functions that, in extreme cases, leads to disorganization of the personality. Whereas Kraepelin by and large limited himself to describing the clinical picture and course of the illness, Bleuler attempted to understand the underlying psychopathologic process as well. He differed from Kraepelin in maintaining that deterioration was not characteristic of the illness. He added a subtype, Simple, which he believed occurred as frequently as the other subtypes, although it was rarely seen in hospitals.

The following case is taken verbatim from a translation of his major work, Dementia Praecox or the Group of Schizophrenias,* first published in 1911.*

Domestic Tyrant

A NORMAL, INTELLIGENT GIRL marries at twenty and lives happily for more than five years. Very gradually she becomes irritable, gesticulates while talking, her peculiarities continue to increase; she cannot keep a servant anymore; she is constantly quarreling with her neighbors. Within her own family group, she has developed into an unbearable domestic tyrant who knows no duties, only rights. She is unable to manage the household or do the housework anymore because she makes all kinds of silly, stupid, and useless purchases and is proving herself utterly impractical. During the many years in which she is in the hospital, she exhibits the same behavior only in increasing measure, so that it is only possible to keep her either in her own room or outdoors where there are very few people. However, after some ten years of hospitalization, she can be released although she still causes trouble by her gossiping and disagreeableness. She complains continually of some vague nervous troubles because, as she says, she was not properly treated in the hospital. Yet she is entirely indifferent to important things such as her relations to her family, etc. She has no love for her children. She is incapable of pulling herself together although she knows quite well that she could have a very decent life if she were less of a nag and a scold. There were no traces of paranoid or catatonic symptoms.

Bleuler's Diagnosis: Simple Schizophrenia

Discussion of "Domestic Tyrant"

According to the information available, this woman functioned well until she was 25. She then developed a progressively incapacitating illness characterized by poor judgment, irritability, and indifference to others. No psychotic symptoms, disorders of mood, or

---

*Bleuler E: *Dementia Praecox or the Group of Schizophrenias.* Translated by Joseph Zinkin. New York, International Universities Press, 1950, p. 238.

symptoms suggesting an Organic Mental Disorder are described. This peculiar picture corresponds to no DSM-III-R Axis I disorder! Many of the features of her illness suggest a severe Personality Disorder, but Bleuler's description of her as living "happily" until her illness began at age 25 suggests a distinct change in functioning. This is inconsistent with the concept of a Personality Disorder, since manifestations of a Personality Disorder are generally recognizable by adolescence or earlier. We are therefore left with the rather unsatisfying but accurate diagnosis of Unspecified Mental Disorder (Nonpsychotic).

Bleuler was able to diagnose this patient as having Schizophrenia because he emphasized the "primary symptoms" (disturbances of association and affect, ambivalence and autism) and did not require, as does DSM-III-R, the presence of psychotic symptoms, such as delusions or hallucinations. We suspect that a clinician interviewing this patient today would uncover either evidence of some period with psychotic symptoms, suggesting Schizophrenia, or an earlier onset, suggesting a severe Personality Disorder, or perhaps both.

DSM-III-R Diagnosis:

Axis I: 300.90 Unspecified Mental Disorder (Nonpsychotic)
**   (p. 363)**

Alois Alzheimer (1864-1915)

Alzheimer was a German neuropathologist who investigated the relationship between anatomic changes in the brain and mental disorder. In 1907 he described a deceased patient from the insane asylum in Frankfurt-am-Main whose nervous system had been given to him for investigation because the patient presented with an unusual clinical picture that could not be categorized under any of the known diseases.*

Perplexed Woman

A WOMAN, 51 YEARS OLD, showed jealousy toward her husband as the first noticeable sign of the disease. Soon a rapidly increasing loss of memory could be noticed. She could not find her way around in her own apartment. She carried objects back and forth and hid them. At times she

---

*Wilkins, RH, Brody, IA, "Alzheimer's Disease." *Archives of Neurology*, July 1969, 21:109-110.

would think that someone wanted to kill her and would begin shrieking loudly.

In the institution her entire behavior bore the stamp of utter perplexity. She was totally disoriented to time and place. Occasionally she stated that she could not understand and did not know her way around. At times she greeted the doctor like a visitor, and excused herself for not having finished her work; at times she shrieked loudly that he wanted to cut her, or repulsed him with indignation, saying that she feared from him something against her chastity. Periodically she was totally delirious, dragged her bedding around, called her husband and her daughter, and seemed to have auditory hallucinations. Frequently, she shrieked with a dreadful voice for many hours.

Because of her inability to comprehend the situation, she always cried out loudly as soon as someone tried to examine her. Only through repeated attempts was it possible finally to ascertain anything.

Her ability to remember was severely disturbed. If one pointed to objects, she named most of them correctly, but immediately afterwards she would forget everything again. When reading, she went from one line into another, reading the letters or reading with a senseless emphasis. When writing, she repeated individual syllables several times, left out others, and quickly became stranded. When talking, she frequently used perplexing phrases and some paraphrastic expressions (milk-pourer instead of cup). Sometimes one noticed her getting stuck. Some questions she obviously did not comprehend. She seemed no longer to understand the use of some objects. Her gait was not impaired. She could use both hands equally well. Her patellar reflexes were present. Her pupils reacted. Somewhat rigid radial arteries; no enlargement of cardiac dullness; no albumin.

During her subsequent course, the phenomena that were interpreted as focal symptoms were at times more noticeable and at times less noticeable. But always they were only slight. The generalized dementia progressed however. After 4½ years of the disease, death occurred. At the end, the patient was completely stuporous; she lay in her bed with her legs drawn up under her, and in spite of all precautions she acquired decubitus ulcers.

Alzheimer's Diagnosis: A Peculiar Disease of the Cerebral Cortex

Discussion of "Perplexed Woman"

The first sign of the illness was apparently delusional jealousy. Persecutory delusions, and possibly auditory hallucinations, developed later. However, the more significant disturbance is the gradual development of a progressive Dementia. The patient has marked impairment in immediate and recent memory, is disoriented to time and place, and shows many signs of disturbed higher cortical functioning. For example, her use of "paraphrastic expressions" (milkpourer instead of cup) indicates aphasia, and her inability to understand the use of some objects indicates agnosia.

Although Alzheimer refers to her as periodically being "totally delirious," he may have been referring more to periods of agitation and excitement than to reduced ability to maintain attention to external stimuli, a requirement for the DSM-III-R concept of Delirium. In any case, her usual state is not characterized by this inability to maintain attention to external stimuli.

The evidence of a Dementia with insidious onset and a generally progressive deteriorating course, plus the exclusion of all other specific causes of the Dementia, indicate Primary Degenerative Dementia of the Alzheimer Type. Because the illness began before the patient was 65, the onset is presenile. The presence of delusions is indicated in the fifth digit.

The historical significance of this case is that it was the first one in which microscopic examination of the brain revealed the characteristic histopathologic changes of what has become known as Alzheimer's disease: senile plaques, neurofibrillary tangles, and granulovacuolar degeneration of neurons. The neurologic disorder Alzheimer's disease is recorded on Axis III.

DSM-III-R Diagnosis:

Axis I: **290.12 Primary Degenerative Dementia of the Alzheimer Type, Presenile Onset, with Delusions (p. 121)**
Axis III: **Alzheimer's disease**

Josef Breuer (1842-1925)

Breuer was a Viennese physician who collaborated with Freud in using hypnosis to treat patients with hysteria. The case of "Anna O." was abstracted from Breuer and Freud's Studies in Hysteria,* *published in 1895. Anna O. was treated and her case reported by Breuer. It was the case that suggested to Freud the possibility of a "talking cure"—later known as psychoanalysis.*

---

*Breuer J, Freud, S: *Studies in Hysteria*. Translated by AA Brill. Boston, Beacon Press, 1937, p. 14.

Anna O.

A NNA O. WAS THE ONLY DAUGHTER of a wealthy Viennese Jewish family. She became ill when she was 21, in 1880.

Up to the onset of the disease, the patient showed no sign of nervousness, not even during pubescence. She had a keen, intuitive intellect, a craving for psychic fodder, which she did not, however, receive after she left school. She was endowed with a sensitiveness for poetry and fantasy, which was, however, controlled by a very strong and critical mind. . . . Her will was energetic, impenetrable and persevering, sometimes mounting to selfishness; it relinquished its aim only out of kindness and for the sake of others. . . . Her moods always showed a slight tendency to an excess of merriment or sadness, which made her more or less temperamental. . . . With her puritanically-minded family, this girl of overflowing mental vitality led a most monotonous existence.

She spent hours daydreaming, making up fanciful plots in what she called her "private theatre." She was at times so engrossed in fantasy that she did not hear when people spoke to her.

In July, 1880, her father, whom she admired and "loved passionately," developed tuberculosis. From July through November Anna was his night nurse, sitting up with him every night, observing his pain and deterioration, with the knowledge that he would not recover.

Her own health eventually began to decline:

. . . she became very weak, anemic, and evinced a disgust for nourishment, so that despite her marked reluctance, it was found necessary to take her away from the sick man. The main reason for this step was a very intensive cough about which I [Breuer] was first consulted. I found that she had a typical nervous cough. Soon, there also developed a striking need for rest, distinctly noticeable in the afternoon hours, which merged in the evening into a sleep-like state, followed by strong excitement. . . . From the eleventh of December until the first of April the patient remained bedridden.

In rapid succession there seemingly developed a series of new and severe disturbances.

Left-sided occipital pain; convergent strabismus (diplopia), which was markedly aggravated through excitement. She complained that the wall was falling over (obliquus affection). Profound analyzable visual disturbances, paresis of the anterior muscles of the throat, to the extent that the head could finally be moved only if the patient pressed it backward between her raised shoulders and then moved her whole back. Contractures and anesthesia of the right upper extremity, and somewhat later of the right lower extremity. . . .

It was in this condition that I took the patient under treatment, and I soon became convinced that we were confronted with a severe psychic alteration. There were two entirely separate states of consciousness, which alternated very frequently and spontaneously, moving further apart during the course of the disease. In one of them she knew her environment, was sad and anxious, but relatively normal; in the other, she hallucinated, was "naughty"—i.e., she scolded, threw the pillows at people whenever and to what extent her contractures enabled her to, and tore with her movable fingers the buttons from the covers and underwear, etc. If anything had been changed in the room during this phase, if someone entered, or went out, she then complained that she was lacking in time, and observed the gap in the lapse of her conscious ideas. . . . In very clear moments she complained of the deep darkness in her head, that she could not think, that she was going blind and deaf, and that she had two egos, her real and an evil one, which forced her to evil things, etc. . . . there appeared a deep, functional disorganization of her speech. At first, it was noticed that she missed words; gradually, when this increased her language was devoid of all grammar, all syntax, to the extent that the whole conjugation of verbs was wrong; . . . In the further course of this development she missed words almost continuously, and searched for them laboriously in four or five languages, so that one could hardly understand her. . . . She spoke only English and understood nothing that was told her in German. The people about her were forced to speak English. . . . There then followed two weeks of complete mutism. Continuous effort to speak elicited no sound.

About ten days after her father died, a consultant was called in whom she ignored as completely as all strangers, while I demonstrated to him her peculiarities. . . . It was a real "negative hallucination," which has so often been reproduced experimentally since then. He finally succeeded in attracting her attention by blowing smoke into her face. She then suddenly saw a stranger, rushed to the door, grabbed the key, but fell to the floor unconscious. This was followed by a short outburst of anger, and then by a severe attack of anxiety, which I could calm only with a great deal of effort.

The family was afraid Anna would jump from the window, so she was removed from her third-floor apartment to a country house where, for three days " . . . she remained sleepless, took no nourishment, and was full of suicidal ideas . . . " She also broke windows, etc., and evinced hallucinations [of black snakes, death's heads, etc.] without absences [dissociated periods].

Breuer treated Anna by asking her, under hypnosis, to talk about her symptoms, a technique she referred to as "chimney sweeping." As the treatment proceeded, she had longer periods of lucidity and began to lose her symptoms. After 18 months of treatment, as Anna prepared to spend the summer in her country home, Breuer pronounced her well and said he would no longer be seeing her. That evening he was called back to the house, where he found Anna thrashing around in her bed, going through an imaginary childbirth. She insisted that the baby was Breuer's. He managed to calm her by hypnotizing her. According to Ernest Jones, Breuer then "fled the house in a cold sweat" and never saw her again.

Anna remained ill intermittently over the next six years, spending considerable time in a sanatorium, where she apparently became addicted to morphine. She was often fairly well in the daytime, but still suffered from hallucinatory states toward evening.

By 30 she had apparently completely recovered, and moved to Frankfort with her mother. There she became a feminist leader and social worker. She established an institution for "wayward girls" and spoke out against the devaluation of women that she believed was inherent in orthodox Judaism.

Anna never married, but was said to be an attractive and passionate woman who gathered admirers wherever she went. She had no recurrences of her illness and never spoke about it—in fact, apparently asked her relatives not to speak of it to anyone. In her later years her attitude toward psychoanalysis was clearly negative, and she became quite angry at the suggestion that one of her "girls" be psychoanalyzed.

Anna died at 77, of abdominal cancer.

Breuer's Diagnosis: Hysteria

Discussion of "Anna O."

Anna O. presents a clinical picture that was apparently seen with some frequency in consulting rooms in the Victorian period. We doubt that many clinicians at the present time see patients quite like Anna O. For this reason DSM-III-R does not have a single category that would encompass the variety of symptoms and the often chronic course that correspond to the traditional concept of Hysteria. Anna O. is therefore a diagnostic enigma for today's clinician.

Following her father's death Anna becomes depressed—"she remained sleepless, took no nourishment, and was full of suicidal ideas." Since this severe condition apparently lasted for only a few days, we are reluctant to make a diagnosis of a Major Depressive Episode.

The most striking features of Anna's illness, and the reason for Breuer's being called in on the case, were the numerous physical symptoms: cough, left-sided occipital pain, convergent strabismus, visual disturbance, weakness of throat muscles, contractures, and anesthesia of the extremities. If we assume that Breuer had correctly ruled out an organic etiology for these symptoms, they indicate a Conversion Disorder.

Her "sleep-like state[s]," going through an imaginary childbirth, and alternating states of consciousness all indicate a Dissociative Disorder; but since the description does not correspond to any of the specific DSM-III-R Dissociative Disorders, the diagnosis must be Dissociative Disorder Not Otherwise Specified.

Anna had many other symptoms that suggest a psychotic disorder—incoherence ("her language was devoid of all grammar, all syntax, to the extent that the whole conjugation of verbs was wrong"), hallucinations of black snakes and death's heads, and possible delusions ("she complained . . . that she had two egos, her real and an evil one, which forced her to evil things").

Because of these seemingly psychotic symptoms, rigid use of

the DSM-III-R criteria might lead to a diagnosis of Schizophrenia. However, this diagnosis fails to capture the essence of Anna O.'s illness. The problem is that DSM-III-R does not recognize "hysterical" psychotic symptoms, with the exception of Factitious Disorder with Psychological Symptoms. Did Anna O. intentionally produce her symptoms, as in a Factitious Disorder? Certainly Breuer and Freud did not think so. We also doubt that Anna O. "decided" to produce her various symptoms.

If forced to give a DSM-III-R diagnosis that would account for these "psychotic" symptoms, we would add Psychotic Disorder Not Otherwise Specified, thereby indicating the unusual nature of her psychotic disorder. Admittedly, the approach taken here fragments Anna O.'s illness into several different diagnoses, each of which describes a different phase.

DSM-III-R Diagnosis:

Axis I: **300.11 Conversion Disorder (p. 259)**
298.90 Psychotic Disorder Not Otherwise Specified (p. 211)
300.15 Dissociative Disorder Not Otherwise Specified (p. 277)

Sigmund Freud (1856-1939)

Sigmund Freud, the originator of psychoanalysis, attempted to explain the mechanisms by which unconscious conflicts result in the clinical manifestations of psychopathology. The cases that follow have been edited to focus on the descriptive features rather than on the psychodynamic explanations of the symptoms. These cases, first published between 1909 and 1911, were abstracted from Volume III of Freud's Collected Papers.*

Little Hans

L ITTLE HANS' PARENTS were friends and early followers of Freud who had agreed to bring up their first child with " . . . no more coercion than might be absolutely necessary for maintaining good behavior. And, as the child developed into a cheerful, good-natured, and lively little boy, the

---

*From *The Collected Papers of Sigmund Freud*, ed. by Ernest Jones, M.D., authorized translation by Alix and James Strachey. Published in the U.S.A. by arrangement with The Hogarth Press, Ltd., and the Institute for Psychoanalysis, London. New York, Basic Books, Inc., 1959. "Little Hans," p. 149; "The Rat Man," p. 296; "Dr. Schreber," p. 390.

experiment of letting him grow up and express himself without being intimidated went on satisfactorily."

Freud asked Hans' father to collect observations on the sexual life of his child, and received frequent letters reporting on Hans, beginning just before his third birthday. All went well until Hans was nearly five, at which time Freud received the following letter from his father:

> My dear Professor, I am sending you a little more about Hans—but this time, I am sorry to say, material for a case history. As you will see, during the last few days he has developed a nervous disorder, which has made my wife and me most uneasy, because we have not been able to find any means of dissipating it. . . . No doubt the ground was prepared by sexual over-excitation due to his mother's tenderness; but I am not able to specify the actual exciting cause. He is afraid *that a horse will bite him in the street,* and this fear seems somehow to be connected with his having been frightened by a large penis. . . . I cannot see what to make of it. Has he seen an exhibitionist somewhere? Or is the whole thing simply connected with his mother? It is not very pleasant for us that he should begin setting us problems so early. Apart from his being afraid of going into the street and from his being depressed in the evening, he is in other respects the same Hans, as bright and cheerful as ever.

It was some months later that Hans remembered an incident which had, in fact, occurred just before his symptoms began. He had been walking with his mother and had been frightened when a large horse pulling a bus had fallen down and kicked its feet around violently.

The first evidence of the disturbance was noticed in the first few days of January (1908): "Hans woke up one morning in tears. Asked why he was crying, he said to his mother: 'When I was asleep I thought you were gone and I had no Mummy to cuddle with.' " Several days later, on January 7:

> . . . he went to the Stadtpark with his nursemaid as usual. In the street he began to cry and asked to be taken home, saying that he wanted to "cuddle" with his Mummy. At home he was asked why he had refused to go any further and had cried, but he would not say. Till the evening he was cheerful, as usual. But in the evening he grew visibly frightened; he cried and could not be separated from his mother, and wanted to "cuddle" with her again. Then he grew cheerful again and slept well.
>
> On January 8 my wife decided to go out with him herself, so as to see what was wrong with him. They went to Schonbrunn, where he always likes going. Again he began to cry, did not want to start, and was frightened. In the end he did go, but was visibly frightened in the street. On the way back from Schonbrunn he said to his mother, after much internal struggling: "I was afraid a horse would bite me." (He had, in fact, become uneasy at Schonbrunn when he saw a horse.) In the evening he seemed to have had another attack similar to that of the previous evening, and to have wanted to be "cuddled." He was calmed down. He said, crying: "I know I shall have to go for a walk again tomorrow." And later: "The horse'll come into the room."

On Freud's instructions, Hans' father had some discussion with the little boy about his desire to be taken into his mother's bed and his excessive interest in "widdlers"—his own and everyone else's.

There ensued a fairly quiet period during which Hans could be persuaded to walk in the park, but felt compelled to look at the horses: "I have to look at horses, and then I'm frightened."

After two weeks in bed with influenza, and then a tonsillectomy, his phobia became much worse. "He goes out on to the balcony, it is true, but not for a walk. As soon as he gets to the street door he hurriedly turns round."

In late March, with some persuasion, he consented to go to the zoo with his father. There he was afraid of the large animals but not the small ones, and would not even look at the elephant or the giraffe. "During the next few days it seemed as though his fears had again somewhat increased. He hardly ventured out of the front door, to which he was taken after luncheon."

It was during this period that there was much discussion between father and son about Hans' masturbation, about the nature of the female sexual apparatus, and about Hans' desire to get into bed and "cuddle" with his mother.

Freud had one session with Hans, during which he made a connection between the white horses that Hans was particularly afraid of and Hans' father, and explained to Hans that he was afraid of his father " . . . precisely because he was so fond of his mother."

In subsequent weeks Hans alluded to his fear that his mother and father would go away and leave him.

Over a period of some months, Hans' symptoms disappeared, and he became closer to his father. Freud saw Hans only once again, when he was "a strapping youth of nineteen" who "suffered from no troubles or inhibitions." He had no memory of the anxiety, the phobia, or the analysis.

Freud's Diagnosis: Phobia

Discussion of "Little Hans"

There can be little doubt that Hans has a phobia. He has a persistent excessive fear of and compelling desire to avoid horses. Since the dreaded object does not involve a fear of having a panic attack, of being in situations or public places from which escape is impossible, or being in social situations with the possibility of public humiliation or embarrassment, this is a Simple Phobia.

There are other important features. Hans has nightmares about being separated from his mother ("When I was asleep I thought you [his mother] were gone and I had no Mummy to cuddle with."). In the evenings, when anticipating going to bed, he is extremely distressed, perhaps to the point of panic, and cannot be separated from his mother. Finally, he has an unrealistic fear that his parents will "go away and leave him." These are all expressions of excessive anxiety concerning separation from his parents, and together support the additional diagnosis of Separation Anxiety Disorder.

DSM-III-R Diagnosis:

Axis I: 300.29 Simple Phobia (p. 244)
**   309.21 Separation Anxiety Disorder (p. 60)**

The Rat Man

A YOUNGISH MAN of university education introduced himself to [Freud] with the statement that he had suffered from obsessions ever since his childhood, but with particular intensity for the last four years. The chief features of his disorder were *fears* that something might happen to two people of whom he was very fond—his father and a lady whom he admired. Besides this he was aware of *compulsive impulses*—such as an impulse, for instance, to cut his throat with a razor; and further he produced *prohibitions*, sometimes in connection with quite unimportant things. He had wasted years, he told me, in fighting against these ideas of his, and in this way had lost much ground in the course of his life. He had tried various treatments, but none had been of any use to him. . . .

The experience that precipitated this patient's first visit to Freud occurred when he was on maneuvers with a military unit. An officer had described to him a form of torture in which the prisoner was tied up, a pot of rats was turned upside down on his buttocks, and the rats bored their way into his anus. He reported: "At that moment the idea flashed through my mind *that this was happening to a person very dear to me*" [in fact, to the lady he loved, and to his father, who had actually died nine years before]. When the officer had spoken of this ghastly punishment, and the obsessions had come into his head, he had warded them off by employing a particular "formula." He said to himself, "But," accompanied by a gesture of repudiation, and then "Whatever are you thinking of?"

> That evening, he continued, the same Captain had handed him a packet that had arrived by the post and had said: "Lt. A. has paid the charges for you. You must pay him back." . . . At that instant, however, a "sanction" had taken shape in his mind, namely, *that he was not to pay back the money* or it would happen—(that is, the fantasy about the rats would come true as regards his father and the lady). And immediately, in accordance with a type of procedure with which he was familiar [to make sure

the fantasy would not come true], there had arisen a command in the shape of a vow: *"You must pay back the 3.8 crowns to Lt. A."* He had said these words to himself almost half aloud.

The necessity of obeying his vow sent him on a complicated journey during which he went in search of Lt. A. He discovered that Lt. A. was not, in fact, the one who had paid the charges. He therefore devised numerous complicated schemes in order to follow the exact wording of his vow (that is, pay back the 3.8 crowns to Lt. A.) even though it was now clear that he did not owe the money to Lt. A.

The first instances of obsessive thoughts had occurred when the patient was six or seven. As he grew older, they waxed and waned, but they had now persisted since his father's death. Freud describes the "exciting cause" of his incapacitation as follows: After his father's death the patient's mother proposed that he marry a wealthy cousin, thus ensuring . . . a business connection with the firm [that] would offer him a brilliant opening in his profession. This family plan stirred up in him a conflict as to whether he should remain faithful to the lady he loved in spite of her poverty, or whether he should follow in his father's footsteps and marry the lovely, rich, and well-connected girl who had been assigned to him. And he resolved his conflict, which was in fact one between his love and the persisting influence of his father's wishes, by falling ill; or, to put it more correctly, by falling ill he avoided the task of resolving it in real life . . . the chief result of this illness was an obstinate incapacity for work, which allowed him to postpone the completion of his education for years. . . .

Freud relates numerous examples of his patient's obsessions and compulsions in relation to his "lady":

> . . . as they were sitting together during a thunderstorm, he was obsessed, he could not tell why, with the necessity for *counting* up to forty or fifty between each flash of lightning and its accompanying thunder-clap. On the day of [the lady's] departure he knocked his foot against a stone lying in the road, and was *obliged* to put it out of the way by the side of the road, because the idea struck him that her carriage would be driving along the same road in a few hours' time and might come to grief against this stone. But a few minutes later it occurred to him that this was absurd, and he was *obliged* to go back and replace the stone in its original position in the middle of the road. After her departure he became a prey to an *obsession for understanding*, which made him a curse to all his companions. He forced himself to understand the precise meaning of every syllable that was addressed to him, as though he might otherwise be missing some priceless treasure. Accordingly he kept asking: "What was it you said just then?" And after it had been repeated to him he could not help thinking it had sounded different the first time, so he remained dissatisfied.

Freud's analysis focused on the patient's ambivalence toward his father and his lady, originating in his precocious and intense sexuality and early feelings of rage against his father—both of which had been severely repressed. The rat symbol led Freud and his patient through a series of associations that included anal eroticism, the patient's having been beaten by his father at age four for biting someone, the father's early problems in gambling [in German a gambler is a *Spielratte*—or "play-rat"], the infantile notion of anal birth, and the patient's own real childhood experience of having worms. After a year of analysis, the patient was cured of his symptoms and, in Freud's words, "the rat delirium disappeared."

Freud's Diagnosis: Obsessive Compulsive Neurosis

Discussion of "The Rat Man"

The Rat Man is plagued by both obsessions and compulsions. The obsessions are recurrent, persistent ideas (e.g., that something terrible will happen to his sweetheart), impulses (e.g., to cut his throat), and images (e.g., that a rat is boring into the anus of his father). He experiences them as intrusive and senseless (ego-dystonic) and evolves complicated formulas in an effort to neutralize them (e.g., He said to himself: "But," accompanied by a gesture of repudiation, and then, "Whatever are you thinking of?"). He recognizes that the obsessions are products of his own mind.

The compulsions are repetitive, purposeful, and intentional behaviors that are performed according to certain rules and are designed to prevent some future event (e.g., he had to remove a stone from the road and replace it so that his sweetheart's carriage would not "come to grief against this stone"). As with the obsessions, he recognizes that the behavior is senseless, in that it is not connected in a realistic way with what it is designed to prevent. In addition, he derives no pleasure from carrying out the compulsion, other than the release of tension.

Minor obsessions and compulsions that do not cause significant distress or interfere with social or role functioning do not warrant a diagnosis. However, the Rat Man has "wasted years . . . in fighting against these ideas." Thus, a diagnosis of Obsessive Compulsive Disorder is indicated. Although Obsessive Compulsive Disorder is often seen in people with Obsessive Compulsive Personality Disorder, in this case there is no description of the patient's personality functioning, apart from the symptoms of his Obsessive Compulsive Disorder.

DSM-III-R Diagnosis:

Axis I: 300.30 Obsessive Compulsive Disorder, Severe (p. 247)

Dr. Schreber

I N 1903 A GERMAN JUDGE, Dr. Daniel Paul Schreber, published his own case
history, translated as *Memoirs of a Neurotic*. Freud made his analytic
interpretations of the connection between unconscious homosexuality
and paranoia on the basis of this document and a report prepared by Dr.
Schreber's physician for a mental competency hearing. Freud quotes at
length from both.

All we know about Dr. Schreber's first illness, in 1884, is that it was
diagnosed as an "attack of severe hypochondria," from which he recovered completely after six months, and returned to his wife and his judicial
position. It is unclear how old he was at this time; but since he was already
married and had some status in his profession, he cannot have been very
young. Subsequent to this illness he was elected to a high judicial position.

The second illness, in 1893, began with the idea that he was to be
transformed into a woman. In Dr. Schreber's words:

> . . . a conspiracy against me was brought to a head. . . . Its object was to
> contrive that, when once my nervous complaint had been recognized as
> incurable or assumed to be so, I should be handed over to a certain person
> in a particular manner. Thus my soul was to be delivered up to him, but my
> body . . . was to be transformed into a female body, and as such surren-
> dered to the person in question with a view to sexual abuse, and was then
> simply to be "left where it was"—that is to say, no doubt, abandoned to
> corruption.

Dr. Weber, the director of the Sonnenstein Sanatorium in which
Schreber was a patient, described his condition as follows:

> . . . he was chiefly troubled by hypochondriacal ideas, complained
> that he had softening of the brain, that he would soon be dead, etc. But
> ideas of persecution were already finding their way into the clinical picture,
> based upon sensorial illusions which, however, seemed only to appear
> sporadically at first, while simultaneously a high degree of hyperaesthesia
> was observable—great sensitiveness to light and noise. Later, the visual and
> auditory illusions became much more frequent. . . . He believed that he
> was dead and decomposing, that he was suffering from the plague; he
> asserted that his body was being handled in all kinds of revolting ways; and,
> as he himself declares, to this day, he went through worse horrors than any
> one could have imagined, and all on behalf of a sacred cause. The patient
> was so much occupied with these pathological phenomena that he was
> inaccessible to any other impression and would sit perfectly rigid and mo-
> tionless for hours. . . . On the other hand, they tortured him to such a
> degree that he longed for death. He made repeated attempts at drowning
> himself in his bath, and asked to be given the cyanide of potassium that was
> intended for him. His delusional ideas gradually assumed a mystical and
> religious character; he was in direct communication with God, he was the
> plaything of devils, he saw "miraculous apparitions," he heard "holy mu-
> sic," and in the end he even came to believe that he was living in another
> world.

It may be added that there were certain people by whom he thought he was being persecuted and injured, and upon whom he poured abuse. The most prominent of these was his former physician, Flechsig, whom he called a "soul-murderer." The voices he heard during this period mocked him and jeered at him.

Over the next few years there was a gradual change in Dr. Schreber's condition, as his distress about being transformed into a "strumpet" developed into a conviction that it was all part of a divine plan, and that he had a mission to redeem the world. In Schreber's words:

> Now, however, I became clearly aware that the order of things imperatively demanded my emasculation, whether I personally liked it or not, and that no *reasonable* course lay open to me but to reconcile myself to the thought of being transformed into a woman. The further consequence of my emasculation could, of course, only be my impregnation . . . by divine rays to the end that a new race of men might be created.

And, Schreber elaborates:

> The *only thing* which could appear unreasonable in the eyes of other people is the fact, already touched upon in the expert's report, that I am sometimes to be found, standing before the mirror or elsewhere, with the upper portion of my body partly bared, and wearing sundry feminine adornments, such as ribbons, trumpery necklaces and the like. This only occurs, I may add, when I am by myself, and never, at least so far as I am able to avoid it, in the presence of other people.

Dr. Weber, in a report dated 1900, described Schreber's changed condition as follows:

> Since for the last nine months Herr President Schreber has taken his meals daily at my family board, I have had the most ample opportunities of conversing with him on every imaginable topic. Whatever the subject was that came up for discussion (apart, of course, from his delusional ideas), whether it concerned events in the field of administration and law, or of politics, or of art, or of literature, or of social life—in short, whatever the topic, Dr. Schreber gave evidence of a lively interest, a well-informed mind, a good memory and sound judgment; his ethical outlook, moreover, was one which it was impossible not to endorse. So, too, in his lighter talk with the ladies of the party, he was both courteous and affable, and if he touched upon matters in a more humorous vein, he invariably displayed tact and decorum. Never once, during these innocent talks round the dining-table, did he introduce subjects which would more properly have been raised at a medical consultation.

Dr. Schreber made numerous appeals to regain his liberty. In Freud's words:

> . . . he did not in the least disavow his delusion or make any secret of his intention of publishing [his memoirs]. On the contrary, he dwelt upon the importance of his ideas to religious thought, and upon their invulnerability to the attacks of modern science; but at the same time, he laid stress upon the absolute harmlessness of the actions, which, as he was aware, his delusions obliged him to perform. Such, indeed, were his acumen and the

cogency of his logic that finally, and in spite of his being an acknowledged paranoiac, his efforts were crowned with success. In July 1902 Dr. Schreber's civil rights were restored. . . .

Freud's Diagnosis: Dementia Paranoides

Discussion of "Dr. Schreber"

Dr. Schreber's illness is characterized by bizarre delusions (involving a phenomenon that the person's culture would regard as totally implausible), which begin as persecutory (that he will be transformed into a woman, "with a view to sexual abuse"), and later become somatic ("softening of the brain"), nihilistic ("he was dead and decomposing"), religious (he was "in direct communication with God"), and, finally, grandiose (he had a "mission to redeem the world"). What Dr. Weber refers to as "hypochondriacal ideas" are, in fact, somatic delusions. This leads one to suspect that the original illness, diagnosed as "attack of severe hypochondria," also involved somatic delusions. The delusions were accompanied by auditory hallucinations (holy music), visual hallucinations (seeing miraculous apparitions), and, probably, tactile hallucinations as well (his body being handled in all kinds of revolting ways). His sitting "rigid and motionless for hours" suggests catatonic stupor, that is, marked decrease in reactivity to the environment and reduction in spontaneous movements and activity. The same behavior might suggest depressive stupor; but, apart from the suicidal ideas, there is no other reference to characteristic depressive symptoms.

Although the predominant psychotic symptoms are paranoid delusions, the diagnosis of a Delusional Disorder is not made because of the prominent hallucinations and the bizarre nature of the delusions.

The presence of bizarre delusions and prominent hallucinations, with functioning in many areas that is markedly below the highest level achieved before the onset of the disturbance, suggests a diagnosis of Schizophrenia. Although persecutory delusions are prominent, since they do not relate to a single theme, the Paranoid Type is ruled out. Although catatonic symptoms are present, they do not dominate the clinical picture, thus ruling out the Catatonic Type. Therefore, the subtype of Schizophrenia is Undifferentiated. The course is considered chronic because the disturbance lasted for more than two years.

DSM-III-R Diagnosis:

Axis I: 295.92 Schizophrenia, Undifferentiated Type, Chronic
                (p. 194)

Jacob S. Kasanin (1897-1946)

*Kasanin provided a bridge between Schizophrenia and Affective Disorder by first proposing, in 1933, the term Schizoaffective. According to Kasanin, this disorder occurs in "fairly young individuals, quite well integrated socially, who suddenly blow up in a dramatic psychosis and present a clinical picture which may be called either schizophrenic or affective, and in whom the differential diagnosis is extremely difficult." The following cases have been extracted from his article "The Acute Schizoaffective Psychoses."**

Suspicious Wife

S. R., FEMALE, WHITE, MARRIED, age 25, admitted to the hospital February 25, 1927. . . . Diagnosis: *dementia praecox*. Chief complaint[:] The patient was sent to a psychiatric hospital from the [city] hospital where she was restless, excited and showed a "schizophrenic reaction type."

Personal History[:] The patient was always an active, energetic, industrious person. She was ambitious, full of life, was very much interested in her house and held several positions after marriage. She was extremely affectionate, demonstrative and romantic. . . . The patient has one child, a boy of 6 years, to whom she was extremely devoted. . . .

Present Illness[:] [Six months before admission] when the little boy began to attend school, the patient felt that she ought to escort him to school. Her husband [a policeman] ridiculed her anxiety about the boy. She became upset and told the husband that if anything ever happened to the boy she would be through with him. [A month before admission] a policeman in their neighborhood committed suicide. The husband came home, told his wife about the incident and said that such work would drive anybody to suicide. This seemed to have affected the patient and she became depressed afterward. When the husband asked the patient about the cause of her depression she told him that somebody was coming between them and complained about the interference of his parents. . . . The patient cried a good deal and [a week later] she said that her heart was bad and that she was going to die. [A few days] later she became very upset, said something was going to happen in the house, said the peddler who came to the door was going to hurt her and had a feeling that the chimney was going to fall down and kill her. She said that her house was a house of ill omen. . . . [Five days before admission] the patient suddenly got up in the middle of the night, dressed, packed her suitcase and said that she was going to her parents. The husband helped his wife to do it. Immediately on her arrival at her father's home the

---

*Kasanin J: "The Acute Schizoaffective Psychoses." *American Journal of Psychiatry*, 13:97-126, 1933.

patient commenced to accuse her father and mother of being in league to influence her husband against her. She stayed there that day and the next night the sleeplessness was repeated. She got up and went into her brother's room. She accused him of intending to poison her husband and that he was trying to come between them. Suddenly she left the house, called up the police and asked them to come to her parents' house and rescue her, as something dreadful was going to happen. The husband succeeded in preventing the police from coming, and took her over to the city hospital.

When the husband came to see the patient at the city hospital she accused him of trying to wean the boy away from her and complained of all kinds of peculiar noises in the hospital. She felt that the other patients in the ward were discussing her affairs, swore at her, said that her husband was unfaithful to her and that he was going to steal the boy away from her. The other patients also said that her husband was "four in one," intimating that he was of mixed blood and part Negro. She thought that these voices were "rayed" from someone who was in a trance in one of the other rooms. When her husband visited her at the hospital he appeared "funny"—his eyes were glassy and had a peculiar staring expression in them.

[She was then transferred to a psychiatric hospital.] She said that she felt sad, unhappy and depressed. The intellectual functions were intact. She expressed a large number of ideas, revolving around her relationship to her husband. She complained that there was a good deal of interference in their home life. She also felt that she was going to be harmed, thought that her husband was going to shoot her rather than shoot himself. She said that when she was at the city hospital she heard her name being called out over the loud speaker. She denied any hallucinations in the psychiatric hospital. She also said that while at the city hospital she smelled many and various odors. [Two weeks after admission] she was transferred to a state hospital. There she was sullen, morose and made very little attempt to get interested in the ward. She was mildly depressed and was quite embarrassed when asked about her illness. She spoke freely about her illness and said that while she was in the psychopathic hospital she saw "studies" of her husband from childhood to manhood. She saw him as a boy, a sailor, and a police officer. She said that she had had many somatic sensations before she came to the hospital and had "funny impressions which seem to spell danger." She could not help but feel that something dreadful was going to happen to her child, and that her husband would blame her if anything happened to him. She had the suspicion that her husband was unfaithful to her, and that he had begun to take "dope," as he seemed very dull and stupid. She intimated that her gastric symptoms may have been due to poison. Within a few weeks the patient changed a great deal. She began to laugh, appeared happy, talked very freely and spoke a great deal about "radio hypnotism," to which she attributed all her troubles.

[She was discharged after two months, and at a six-month follow-up]

. . . appeared perfectly well, resumed her care of the house and got a job in a department store during the Christmas rush. [Two years later] She, herself, analyzed the whole situation and described the conditions which led to her breakdown. . . . The patient [had] moved into a new house which she bought with her own savings. She had a great deal of work to do putting the house in order, as it was an old house. . . . She was troubled by the fact that the furnace was not working properly and she could smell gas in the house. She lost her appetite, could not sleep and felt very badly. . . . Things did not go very well with her personal life. Her husband loved and adored her, but he was under the influence of his mother who disliked the patient. One night while she was in bed she saw three bright stars from her window. She could not fall asleep. The stars were bright red in color. She did close her eyes, but when she opened them again the stars would still be there. She felt that something terrible was going to happen.

A review of the family situation brought out the fact that there was a real foundation for some of the patient's beliefs. Both her family and her husband's family were doing everything possible to estrange the patient and her husband. . . . The patient said that the psychosis was a good thing, as somehow it has helped to straighten out the various tangles in her life, and gave her courage, confidence in herself. The patient is doing very well now and handles unusually well the affairs which are just as complicated as they were before.

Kasanin's Diagnosis: Schizoaffective Schizophrenia

Discussion of "Suspicious Wife"

Less than four months elapsed from the onset of the first definite symptoms (after the suicide of her husband's friend) until this patient apparently completely recovered. The illness is characterized by depressed mood and a variety of changing persecutory delusions, some of which are bizarre. In addition, there are auditory hallucinations (or at least illusions) with a persecutory content, and problems with appetite and sleep and thoughts of her own death.

Although the patient is frequently described as depressed and unhappy, the persistence of a prominent depressed mood is not established. In fact, within a few weeks, "She began to laugh, appeared happy, talked very freely and spoke a great deal about 'radio hypnotism,' to which she attributed all of her troubles." This indicates that even if there were a sustained depressed mood and the associated symptoms of the depressive syndrome, the psychotic symptoms apparently were present when she was no longer depressed. For this reason the diagnosis of a Major Depressive Episode cannot be made, and the differential diagnosis is thus between Schizoaffective Disorder and Schizophreniform Disorder. Because there is no specific evidence of the full depressive syndrome, we prefer the diagnosis of Schizophreniform Disorder, a disorder with all of the characteristics of Schizophrenia except that the duration is less than six months. We specify "with good prognostic features" because of the onset of psychotic symptoms within four weeks of the first noticeable change in the patient's behavior, her good premorbid functioning, and the absence of flat or blunted affect.

DSM-III-R Diagnosis:

Axis I: **295.40 Schizophreniform Disorder, with good prognostic features (p. 208)**

Magnet Man

E. F., MALE, AGE 20, SINGLE LABORER, white [was] admitted to the hospital March 15, 1929. . . . Diagnosis: *dementia praecox.*

Chief Complaint[:] The patient was sent to the hospital by his family because about two weeks before admission he became overactive, exhibited queer behavior and spoke a great deal about his theories of life. Finally he became so excited that he was taken to the out-patient department from which he was referred to the hospital.

Personal History[:] The patient did well in the various positions in which he was employed. . . . He was a model employee but very quiet and shy. . . . As far as his personality is concerned he was quite an average young man. . . . His outside interests were mostly athletic. He took part in several sports and played baseball with amateur groups. . . . Several months prior to admission he fell in love with a girl who worked in the same factory where he worked and told his family about it. He wanted to bring the girl to the house, but his mother told him he was too young to go out with girls. Although the patient spoke about having dates with the girl, she told her foreman that their acquaintance was very casual.

Present illness[:] Two weeks before admission the co-workers in the factory noticed that the patient began to talk a great deal and that he began to sing very loudly. Quite suddenly he declared that he was going on the stage or else would join a professional baseball team. The same behavior was observed at home. He sent a telegram to a Boston baseball team which was at that time playing in the South, asking the manager for a position. He told his family that he was going to make a great deal of money and they should finance him for the trip. He slept very poorly and was very restless at night. A week before admission he went to one of the Harvard physicians and offered him his body for scientific purposes. The latter referred him to the hospital. He was quite excited for several days and spoke a great deal about scientific experiments on his brain and the cure of insanity. Finally he was brought to the out-patient clinic. . . .

For several days the patient was quite active and restless, but responded very well to continuous baths. He was very cooperative and talked freely to the physician. He took a fair amount of interest in the ward routine and was friendly with other patients. His speech was relevant, but at times incoherent and he spoke about a great many things. The patient spoke a great deal about his philosophy of life giving several variants of his theory of personal magnetism. For some time the patient has had a conflict over auto-eroticism which he has practiced since childhood. He also had sex relations with a nine-year-old girl when he was of the same age and it disturbed him. The conflict was intensified by the fact that he was quite religious. He met a girl a year ago and fell in love with her, but it took him a long time before he was introduced to her. Finally he asked her for a date, about four months ago. She refused. He felt badly but he asked again three months ago, and she told him she was going to the beach with her parents. He finally got a date about a week prior to his admission to the hospital, they went to her house after the movies, and they "got to loving on the sofa." He felt magnetism go over him when he kissed her, and when he passed his hand over her hair he "felt the flow of magnetism just like in a wet dream."

. . . He began speculating about causes of this and thought he had made a new discovery. The patient said that he was able to solve all his conflicts by this discovery. He found that the brain controlled the fluid which traveled throughout the whole body and could be drawn from mouth, teeth, roof of the mouth, lips and nose, if touched. This fluid would travel throughout the whole body, producing a magnetic feeling passing over him, the same as a sexual act. . . . Not only did he get this magnetic feeling when he touched an animate object, but an inanimate object as well. When in church he felt that the holy images might be alive and that God was in communication with him. He stated that when he expectorated, the saliva was equivalent to spermatic fluid. . . . [He felt this power came to him from God.] The patient said that he could see God if he closed his eyes. He could see God moving about, saw Him moving His fingers and saw His features. He saw God sitting on the throne, pointing His fingers and controlling the movement of the world. God never talked to him. At one time he saw God mold clay and blow the breath of life into it.

Clinical Course[:] Within a few days the patient became quiet, cooperative but still insisting on elaborating his ideas. Commitment to a state institution was recommended, but nine days after the patient entered the hospital he was taken home by his family. Within a few weeks he joined one of the branches of the governmental service and has been doing very well in his field of service.

Kasanin's Diagnosis: Schizoaffective Schizophrenia

Discussion of "Magnet Man"

This brief illness is characterized by elevated and expansive mood, pressure of speech, grandiosity, and hyperactivity. The patient is described as sleeping "very poorly" and being "very restless at night." We assume that this represents the characteristic decreased need for sleep seen in a Manic Episode. In addition, there are many delusions, all of them involving grandiose themes, and hallucinations of God. Thus, his psychotic symptoms are all congruent with his elevated mood.

Kasanin undoubtedly made a diagnosis of Schizoaffective Schizophrenia because he believed that the prominent bizarre delusions were incompatible with a diagnosis of Mania; but in recent years, in this country, the concept of mania has broadened. Hence, in DSM-III-R even the most bizarre delusions do not necessarily exclude a diagnosis of mania. Because of the rather clear evidence of the full manic syndrome and no evidence that the psychotic symptoms were present at a time when there was no mood disturbance, the diagnosis in this case is Bipolar Disorder, Manic, with Psychotic Features (Mood-congruent).

DSM-III-R Diagnosis:

Axis I: 296.44 Bipolar Disorder, Manic, with Psychotic Features
            (Mood-congruent) (p. 217)

Paul Hoch (1902-1964) and
Philip Polatin (1905-1980)

Drs. Hoch and Polatin, from the New York State Psychiatric Institute, proposed in 1949 the concept of Pseudoneurotic Schizophrenia. According to them, this diagnosis applies to patients who have "the basic mechanisms of schizophrenia" yet, because of their "subtle" manifestations, "there is no way to demonstrate it clinically." Many of the patients in question had been analyzed "for a considerable period of time; and the suspicion [had] never been raised that they were not psychoneurotic." The following case is abstracted from their article "Pseudoneurotic Forms of Schizophrenia."*

*Hoch P, Polatin P: "Pseudoneurotic Forms of Schizophrenia." *Psychiatric Quarterly* 23:248-76, 1949

Fearful Girl

S. S. IS A 21-YEAR-OLD-GIRL who was hospitalized because she had not improved after a year of outpatient psychotherapy.

On admission, she stated, "I have fears of food; I have fears of something happening to my family; I cannot sleep; I get depressed; I become tense, anxious and agitated."

She was cooperative and pleasant, gave a coherent and reasonably complete history, and denied delusions or hallucinations (although she had sometimes been afraid that she might someday have hallucinations). Her affect was labile, with a shallow quality.

At times she speaks of feeling very hopeless and of feeling that suicide is the only answer in the end; but usually she does not appear to feel this way, and more often seems rather to enjoy the uniqueness which she feels her illness possesses. Occasionally a really depressing thought will strike her; at such times she will appear truly depressed, with ready tears and a more convincing attitude of despair. Ideas suggesting irreparable organic damage or deficits in the field of emotional experience seem most capable of provoking these markedly depressed moods which are usually short-lived.

S.S. dates the beginning of her illness to a night in her 15th year when she overheard her parents having intercourse. She became sexually aroused and describes

> . . . feeling there was something wrong with me, like I was going up in an elevator, and I thought it would never go away; I thought maybe I couldn't experience any sexual feeling. Soon afterward, the word "fuck" was popping in my mind and kept going over and over, and not for a minute could I get it out of my thoughts. A couple of months later it was still going over in my mind, and then I told myself, "Why should you think such a word like that, that you cannot tell to anyone, if they asked you what is wrong," so I changed it to "worry." . . . I don't know how I ever got through school. Ever since I was 15, "worry" kept rotating in my mind continually. I got so I couldn't swallow; I couldn't eat. Food did not agree with me because I was worried. The word "fuck" made me feel nauseated; I couldn't sleep. I would lie there with agitation, with the idea of the word going over and over.

Since that time, she has had a number of similar preoccupations—the fear that she would some day be so concerned about the cleanliness of food that she would be able to eat only kosher food; the fear that she would come to believe in Christ and thus upset her orthodox Jewish family; the worry that she might upset her sisters so much that they would become insane. She also had some compulsions, such as having to turn off the light six times each night and having to leave her shoes in a parallel line when she went to bed; but these were not elaborate or time consuming.

She has had many crushes on boys, but no sexual relationships. She has stated, in an amytal interview, that she does not know whether she is male or female, that she fears she cannot lead a normal life or be happy. She appears to have had no close girl friends, but to have been intensely and ambivalently involved with her extended family.

She finished high school and a one-year business course and was able to work as a clerk until a year ago, when she came home from work with a dazed appearance and refused to talk to anyone, saying "You wouldn't understand." It was at that time that she was referred for outpatient treatment. She spent the year at home, doing very little except trying to "understand" her illness.

On the ward she is described as careless and listless, staying in bed all day, with no initiative. "She manifests a belief in thought magic and also shows a fluctuating appraisal of reality and, at times, depersonalization."

Hoch and Polatin's Diagnosis: Pseudoneurotic Schizophrenia

Discussion of "Fearful Girl"

This woman suffers from a variety of symptoms: morbid fears of possible future events, labile but "shallow" affect, obsessions (thinking about the words *fuck* and *worry*), compulsions (turning off the light and lining up her shoes), identity disturbance (that she might be male or become a Christian), difficulties in interpersonal relations (no close girl friends), magical thinking, depersonalization, and markedly impaired functioning (spending the last year at home thinking about her illness). Undoubtedly, this plethora of chronically disabling symptoms was a major factor in Hoch and Polatin's diagnosis of Schizophrenia. However, the absence of delusions, hallucinations, flat affect, and loosening of associations or incoherence rules out a DSM-III-R diagnosis of Schizophrenia.

An Axis I diagnosis of Obsessive Compulsive Disorder is justified by the prominence of the obsessions and compulsions and the degree of distress and interference in functioning they cause the patient. She probably does not recognize the morbid fears as senseless, and they are therefore ego-syntonic, not true obsessions. However, they are best understood as an associated feature of the Obsessive Compulsive Disorder.

The Axis I diagnosis does not account for the patient's chronic maladaptive pattern of relating to and thinking about her environment and herself. Some of her symptoms are characteristic of Borderline Personality Disorder: identity disturbance and affective instability. Others are characteristic of Schizotypal Personality Disorder: magical thinking, no close friends, and shallow affect. It is likely that other features of these disorders were present, although not noted. In the absence of positive evidence that the criteria for these specific personality disorders are met, a diagnosis of Personality Disorder Not Otherwise Specified is appropriate.

DSM-III-R Diagnosis:

Axis I: 300.30 Obsessive Compulsive Disorder, Severe (p. 247)
Axis II: 301.90 Personality Disorder Not Otherwise Specified
**   (with Borderline and Schizotypal features) (p. 358)**

Albert Hofmann (1906-)

Dr. Hofmann, a chemist working in a large Swiss pharmaceutical company, had been studying the synthesis of various natural ergot alkaloids. In April 1943 he described the following experiences.*

Dr. Hofmann

L AST FRIDAY, APRIL 16, 1943, I was forced to stop my work in the laboratory in the middle of the afternoon and to go home, as I was seized by a peculiar restlessness associated with a sensation of mild dizziness. On arriving home, I lay down and sank into a kind of drunkenness, which was not unpleasant and which was characterized by extreme activity of imagination. As I lay in a dazed condition with my eyes closed (I experienced daylight as disagreeably bright) there surged upon me an uninterrupted stream of fantastic images of extraordinary plasticity and vividness and accompanied by an intense, kaleidoscope-like play of colors. This condition gradually passed off after about two hours.

[Dr. Hofmann suspected that his strange experiences were the result of accidentally ingesting the drug that he had been working on. Three days later he conducted an experiment on himself by taking the smallest dose of the substance that he believed could be expected to have any effect. After 40 minutes, in his laboratory notes he reported "slight dizziness, unrest, difficulty in concentration, visual disturbances, marked desire to laugh. . . ." At this point, his laboratory notes are discontinued. Later he describes what happened.]

I asked my laboratory assistant to accompany me home as I believed that I should have a repetition of the disturbance of the previous Friday. While we were cycling home, however, it became clear that the symptoms were much stronger than the first time. I had great difficulty in

---

*Ayd FJ, Blackwell B: *Discoveries in Biological Psychiatry.* Philadelphia, JB Lippincott Co., 1970, p. 91.

speaking coherently, my field of vision swayed before me, and objects appeared distorted like images in curved mirrors. I had the impression of being unable to move from the spot, although my assistant told me afterwards that we had cycled at a good pace. . . . Once I was at home the physician was called.

By the time the doctor arrived, the peak of the crisis had already passed. As far as I remember, the following were the most outstanding symptoms: vertigo; visual disturbances—the faces of those around me appeared as grotesque, colored masks; marked motoric unrest, alternating with paralysis; an intermittent heavy feeling in the head, limbs and the entire body, as if they were filled with lead; dry, constricted sensation in the throat; feeling of choking; clear recognition of my condition, in which state I sometimes observed, in the manner of an independent, neutral observer, that I shouted half insanely or babbled incoherent words. Occasionally I felt as if I were out of my body.

The doctor found a rather weak pulse but an otherwise normal circulation. . . . Six hours after ingestion of the [drug] my condition had already improved considerably. Only the visual disturbances were distorted like the reflections in the surface of moving water. Moreover, all objects appeared in unpleasant, constantly changing colors, the predominant shades being sickly green and blue. When I closed my eyes, an unending series of colorful, very realistic and fantastic images surged in upon me. A remarkable feature was the manner in which all acoustic perceptions (e.g., the noise of a passing car) were transformed into optical effects, every sound evoking a corresponding colored hallucination constantly changing in shape and color like pictures in a kaleidoscope. At about one o'clock I fell asleep and awoke next morning feeling perfectly well.

Dr. Hofmann's Diagnosis: an "Extraordinary Disturbance" caused by the ingestion of a hallucinogen

Discussion of "Dr. Hofmann"

The many symptoms, predominantly perceptual changes, clearly are related to the ingestion of a drug. In fact, the drug that Dr. Hofmann was working with was lysergic acid diethylamide, better known now as LSD. His description of his own reaction illustrates the characteristic features of a Hallucinogen Hallucinosis: illusions (faces appeared grotesque), depersonalization (". . . I felt as if I were out of my body."), hallucinations (". . . colored hallucination constantly changing in shape and color . . ."), and synesthesias (". . . acoustic perceptions . . . were transformed into optical effects . . ."). He also describes another characteristic feature: all of the symptoms occur during a state of full wakefulness and alertness and with full recognition that the symptoms are the effect of the drug ("... clear recognition of my condition, in which state I sometimes observed, in the manner of an independent, neutral observer...").

The DSM-III-R criteria for Hallucinogen Hallucinosis also require certain physical symptoms, such as pupillary dilation, tachycardia, tremors, and incoordination. Although these are not reported by Dr. Hofmann, we should assume that some of them were present. Needless to say, the inability of Dr. Hofmann to continue working while experiencing the effect of the drug is evidence of maladaptive behavioral effects, also required to make the diagnosis.

DSM-III-R Diagnosis:

Axis I: 305.30 Hallucinogen Hallucinosis (p. 145)

Hervey Cleckley (1905-)

In The Mask of Sanity,* *published in 1955, Cleckley attempted to clarify the confusing and paradoxical nature of Psychopathic Personality. According to him, people with this disorder are "outwardly intact, showing excellent peripheral function, but centrally deficient or disabled in such a way that abilities ... cannot be utilized consistently for sane purposes or prevented from regularly working toward self-destructive and other seriously pathological results." The following case is extracted from his book.*

Tom

THIS YOUNG MAN, twenty-one years of age, does not look at all like a criminal type or a shifty delinquent.... Tom looks and is in robust physical health. His manner and appearance are pleasing.... There is nothing to suggest that he is putting on a bold front or trying to adopt any attitude or manner that will be misleading. Though he knows the examiner has evidence of his almost incredible career, he gives such an impression that it seems for the moment likely he will be able to explain it all away.

... This poised young man's immediate problem was serious but not monumental. His family and legal authorities were in hope that if some psychiatric disorder could be discovered in him he might escape a jail sentence for stealing.

*Cleckley H: *The Mask of Sanity*, 5th ed., St. Louis, C.V. Mosby, 1976, p. 64.

... Evidence of his maladjustment became distinct in childhood. He appeared to be a reliable and manly fellow, but could never be counted upon to keep at any task or to give a straight account of any situation. He was frequently truant from school. . . . Though he was generously provided for, he stole some of his father's chickens from time to time, selling them at stores downtown. Pieces of table silver would be missed. These were sometimes recovered from those to whom he had sold them for a pittance or swapped them for odds and ends which seemed to hold no particular interest or value for him.

... Often when truant from high school classes Tom wandered more or less aimlessly, sometimes shooting at . . . chickens, setting fire to a rural privy around the outskirts of town, or perhaps loitering about a cigar store or a pool room, reading the comics, throwing rocks at squirrels in a park, perpetrating small thefts or swindles. He often charged things in stores to his father, stole cigarettes, candy, cigars, etc. . . . He lied so plausibly and with such equanimity, devised such ingenious alibis or simply denied all responsibility with such convincing appearances of candor that for many years his real career was poorly estimated. . . . Though he often fell in with groups or small gangs, he never for long identified himself with others in a common cause.

... At fourteen or fifteen, having learned to drive, Tom began to steal automobiles with some regularity. . . . After he had tried to sell a stolen car his father consulted advisers and, on the theory that he might have some specific craving for automobiles, bought one for him as a therapeutic measure. On one occasion while out driving he deliberately parked his own car and, leaving it, stole an inferior model which he left slightly damaged on the outskirts of a village some miles away. . . . Meanwhile Tom continued to forge his father's name to small checks and steal change, pocketknives, textbooks, etc., at school. Occasionally, on the pretext of ownership he would sell a dog or a calf belonging to some member of the community.

... Tom was sent to a federal institution in a distant state, where a well-organized program of rehabilitation and guidance was available. He soon impressed authorities at this place with his attitude and in the way he discussed his past mistakes and plans for a different future.

... He found employment in a drydock at a nearby port and talked modestly but convincingly of the course he would now follow, expressing aims and plans few could greatly improve. . . . His employers found him at first energetic, bright, and apparently enthusiastic about the work. Soon evidence of inexplicable irresponsibility emerged and accumulated. Sometimes he missed several days and brought simple but convincing excuses of illness. As the occasions multiplied, explanations so detailed and elaborate were made that it seemed only facts could have produced them. Later he sometimes left the job, stayed away for hours, and gave no account of his behavior except to say that he did not feel like working at the time.

... Reliable information indicates that he has been arrested and imprisoned approximately fifty or sixty times. It is estimated that he would have been put in jails or police barracks for short or long periods of detention on approximately 150 other occasions if his family had not made good his small thefts, damages, etc., and paid fines for him.

Sometimes he was arrested for fomenting brawls in low resorts, provoking fights, or for such high-handed and disturbing behavior as to constitute public nuisance. Though not a very regular drinker or one who characteristically drank to sodden confusion or stupefaction, he exhibited unsociable and unprepossessing manners and conduct after taking even a few beers or highballs. In one juke-joint imbroglio he is credited with having struck a fellow reveler on the head with a piece of iron.

. . . Tom's mother had over years suffered special anxiety and distress through his unannounced absences. After kissing her goodbye, saying he was going downtown for a Coca-Cola or to a movie, he might not appear for several days or even for a couple of weeks! . . . This young man has, apparently, never formed any substantial attachment for another person. Sexually he has been desultorily promiscuous under a wide variety of circumstances. A year or two earlier he married a girl who had achieved considerable local recognition as a prostitute and as one whose fee was moderate. He had previously shared her offerings during an evening (on a commercial basis) with friends or with brief acquaintances among whom he found himself. He soon left the bride and never showed signs of shame or chagrin about the character of the woman he had espoused or any responsibility toward her.

Cleckley's Diagnosis: Psychopathic Personality

Discussion of "Tom"

Tom illustrates all of the features required for a DSM-III-R diagnosis of Antisocial Personality Disorder: current age over 18 (to distinguish it from Conduct Disorder), onset of antisocial behavior before age 15 (truancy, stealing, lying, vandalism, delinquency, chronic violations of rules at home), and since age 18, pervasive manifestations of the disorder (failure to hold a job, multiple arrests, fights, and abandonment of his wife).

One of the controversies regarding the DSM-III criteria for Antisocial Personality Disorder was that they did not require evidence of a lack of socialization, that is, absence of guilt feelings, loyalty to others, and empathy. Tom certainly demonstrates these characteristics, which Cleckley also believed were central to the concept of Psychopathic Personality. These features were not included in the DSM-III criteria for Antisocial Personality Disorder for two reasons. First of all, they require more inferential judgments than do the largely behavioral symptoms listed in the criteria. Second, it seemed likely that, for the most part, people who met the behavioral criteria for Antisocial Personality Disorder in DSM-III would, like Tom, be undersocialized.

DSM-III-R addressed the criticisms of the DSM-III criteria by including the symptom "lacks remorse" in the diagnostic criteria. It is hoped that the revised criteria will better discriminate people with the disorder from those without it who regularly engage in criminal activity.

DSM-III-R Diagnosis:

Axis I: **V71.09 No Diagnosis or Condition**
Axis II: **301.70 Antisocial Personality Disorder (p. 344)**

APPENDIX A

Index of Case Names

Cases by Special Interest

Forensic
- Beasts
- Binoculars
- Brrr
- Child Psychiatrist
- End Times
- Heavenly Vision, The
- Heiress, The
- Loan Sharks
- Martial Arts
- Mr. Macho
- Parental Rights
- Perfect Relationship
- Sam Schaefer
- Something Happened
- Supply Sergeant
- Underground Sex
- Worthless Wife

Difficult or Unusual Differential Diagnosis
- Bully, The
- Disabled Vet
- Eggs
- Enigma, The
- Exercises
- Fidgety
- First Baby
- Fix It
- Foggy Student
- Former Pilot
- Foster Mother

- Gloria
- He Breaks His Toys
- Heavenly Vision, The
- Hungarian Opera Singer
- Jerk, The
- Minister's Daughter
- Outdoorsman, The
- Perpetual Patient
- Procrastinator, The
- Roman
- Slim and Trim
- Socialite, The
- Something Happened
- Three Voices
- Traction
- Triple Divorcée
- Vertigo
- Wild Child

Multiaxial
- Agitated Businessman
- Bereaved
- Down's Syndrome
- High Strung
- Nailbiter
- Outdoorsman, The
- Radar Messages
- Roman
- Sickly
- Sniper
- What's Happening?
- Worthless Wife

DSM-III-R Classification: Axes I and II Categories and Codes

All official DSM-III-R codes are included in ICD-9-CM. Codes followed by a * are used for more than one DSM-III-R diagnosis or subtype in order to maintain compatibility with ICD-9-CM.

Numbers in parentheses are page numbers.

A long dash following a diagnostic term indicates the need for a fifth digit subtype or other qualifying term.

The term *specify* following the name of some diagnostic categories indicates qualifying terms that clinicians may wish to add in parentheses after the name of the disorder.

NOS = Not Otherwise Specified

The current severity of a disorder may be specified after the diagnosis as:

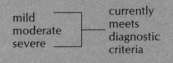

in partial remission
   (or residual state)
in complete remission

DISORDERS USUALLY FIRST EVIDENT IN INFANCY, CHILDHOOD, OR ADOLESCENCE

DEVELOPMENTAL DISORDERS
Note: These are coded on Axis II.

Mental Retardation (28)
317.00	Mild mental retardation
318.00	Moderate mental retardation
318.10	Severe mental retardation
318.20	Profound mental retardation
319.00	Unspecified mental retardation

Pervasive Developmental Disorders (33)
299.00	Autistic disorder (38) *Specify* if childhood onset
299.80	Pervasive developmental disorder NOS

Specific Developmental Disorders (39)

Academic skills disorders
315.10	Developmental arithmetic disorder (41)
315.80	Developmental expressive writing disorder (42)
315.00	Developmental reading disorder (43)

Language and speech disorders
315.39   Developmental articulation disorder (44)
315.31*   Developmental expressive language disorder (45)
315.31*   Developmental receptive language disorder (47)

Motor skills disorder
315.40   Developmental coordination disorder (48)

315.90*   Specific developmental disorder NOS

Other Developmental Disorders (49)
315.90*   Developmental disorder NOS

Disruptive Behavior Disorders (49)
314.01   Attention-deficit hyperactivity disorder (50)

Conduct disorder, (53)
312.20   group type
312.00   solitary aggressive type
312.90   undifferentiated type
313.81   Oppositional defiant disorder (56)

Anxiety Disorders of Childhood or Adolescence (58)
309.21   Separation anxiety disorder (58)
313.21   Avoidant disorder of childhood or adolescence (61)
313.00   Overanxious disorder (63)

Eating Disorders (65)
307.10   Anorexia nervosa (65)
307.51   Bulimia nervosa (67)
307.52   Pica (69)
307.53   Rumination disorder of infancy (70)
307.50   Eating disorder NOS

Gender Identity Disorders (71)
302.60   Gender identity disorder of childhood (71)
302.50   Transsexualism (74)
          Specify sexual history: asexual, homosexual, heterosexual, unspecified
302.85*   Gender identity disorder of adolescence or adulthood, nontranssexual type (76)
          Specify sexual history: asexual, homosexual, heterosexual, unspecified
302.85*   Gender identity disorder NOS

Tic Disorders (78)
307.23   Tourette's disorder (79)
307.22   Chronic motor or vocal tic disorder (81)
307.21   Transient tic disorder (81)
          Specify: single episode or recurrent
307.20   Tic disorder NOS

Elimination Disorders (82)
307.70   Functional encopresis (82)
          Specify: primary or secondary type
307.60   Functional enuresis (84)
          Specify: primary or secondary type
          Specify: nocturnal only, diurnal only, nocturnal and diurnal

Speech Disorders Not Elsewhere Classified (85)
307.00*   Cluttering (85)
307.00*   Stuttering (86)

Other Disorders of Infancy, Childhood, or Adolescence (88)
313.23   Elective mutism (88)
313.82   Identity disorder (89)
313.89   Reactive attachment disorder of infancy or early childhood (91)
307.30   Stereotypy/habit disorder (93)
314.00   Undifferentiated attention-deficit disorder (95)

ORGANIC MENTAL DISORDERS (97)

Dementias Arising in the Senium and Presenium (119)

Primary degenerative dementia of the Alzheimer type, senile onset, (119)

290.30	with delirium
290.20	with delusions
290.21	with depression
290.00*	uncomplicated

(Note: code 331.00 Alzheimer's disease on Axis III)

Code in fifth digit:
1 = with delirium, 2 = with delusions, 3 = with depression, 0* = uncomplicated

290.1x   Primary degenerative dementia of the Alzheimer type, presenile onset, _____ (119) (Note: code 331.00 Alzheimer's disease on Axis III)

290.4x   Multi-infarct dementia, _____ (121)

290.00*   Senile dementia NOS
Specify etiology on Axis III if known

290.10*   Presenile dementia NOS
Specify etiology on Axis III if known (e.g., Pick's disease, Jakob-Creutzfeldt disease)

Psychoactive Substance-Induced Organic Mental Disorders (123)

Alcohol
303.00	intoxication (127)
291.40	idiosyncratic intoxication (128)
291.80	Uncomplicated alcohol withdrawal (129)
291.00	withdrawal delirium (131)
291.30	hallucinosis (131)
291.10	amnestic disorder (133)
291.20	Dementia associated with alcoholism (133)

Amphetamine or similarly acting sympathomimetic
305.70*   intoxication (134)

292.00*	withdrawal (136)
292.81*	delirium (136)
292.11*	delusional disorder (137)

Caffeine
305.90*   intoxication (138)

Cannabis
305.20*	intoxication (139)
292.11*	delusional disorder (140)

Cocaine
305.60*	intoxication (141)
292.00*	withdrawal (142)
292.81*	delirium (143)
292.11*	delusional disorder (143)

Hallucinogen
305.30*	hallucinosis (144)
292.11*	delusional disorder (146)
292.84*	mood disorder (146)
292.89*	Posthallucinogen perception disorder (147)

Inhalant
305.90*   intoxication (148)

Nicotine
292.00*   withdrawal (150)

Opioid
305.50*	intoxication (151)
292.00*	withdrawal (152)

Phencyclidine (PCP) or similarly acting arylcyclohexylamine
305.90*	intoxication (154)
292.81*	delirium (155)
292.11*	delusional disorder (156)
292.84*	mood disorder (156)
292.90*	organic mental disorder NOS

Sedative, hypnotic, or anxiolytic
305.40*	intoxication (158)
292.00*	Uncomplicated sedative, hypnotic, or anxiolytic withdrawal (159)
292.00*	withdrawal delirium (160)
292.83*	amnestic disorder (161)

Other or unspecified psychoactive substance (162)
305.90*   intoxication

292.00*	withdrawal
292.81*	delirium
292.82*	dementia
292.83*	amnestic disorder
292.11*	delusional disorder
292.12	hallucinosis
292.84*	mood disorder
292.89*	anxiety disorder
292.89*	personality disorder
292.90*	organic mental disorder NOS

Organic Mental Disorders associated with Axis III physical disorders or conditions, or whose etiology is unknown. (162)

293.00	Delirium (100)
294.10	Dementia (103)
294.00	Amnestic disorder (108)
293.81	Organic delusional disorder (109)
293.82	Organic hallucinosis (110)
293.83	Organic mood disorder (111) *Specify*: manic, depressed, mixed
294.80*	Organic anxiety disorder (113)
310.10	Organic personality disorder (114) *Specify* if explosive type
294.80*	Organic mental disorder NOS

PSYCHOACTIVE SUBSTANCE USE DISORDERS (165)

	Alcohol (173)
303.90	dependence
305.00	abuse
	Amphetamine or similarly acting sympathomimetic (175)
304.40	dependence
305.70*	abuse
	Cannabis (176)
304.30	dependence
305.20*	abuse
	Cocaine (177)
304.20	dependence
305.60*	abuse

	Hallucinogen (179)
304.50*	dependence
305.30*	abuse
	Inhalant (180)
304.60	dependence
305.90*	abuse
	Nicotine (181)
305.10	dependence
	Opioid (182)
304.00	dependence
305.50*	abuse
	Phencyclidine (PCP) or similarly acting arylcyclohexylamine (183)
304.50*	dependence
305.90*	abuse
	Sedative, hypnotic, or anxiolytic (184)
304.10	dependence
305.40*	abuse
304.90*	Polysubstance dependence (185)
304.90*	Psychoactive substance dependence NOS
305.90*	Psychoactive substance abuse NOS

SCHIZOPHRENIA (187)
Code in fifth digit: 1 = subchronic, 2 = chronic, 3 = subchronic with acute exacerbation, 4 = chronic with acute exacerbation, 5 = in remission, 0 = unspecified.

	Schizophrenia,
295.2x	catatonic, _____
295.1x	disorganized, _____
295.3x	paranoid, _____
	Specify if stable type
295.9x	undifferentiated, _____
295.6x	residual, _____
	Specify if late onset

DELUSIONAL (PARANOID) DISORDER (199)

| 297.10 | Delusional (Paranoid) disorder |

Specify type: erotomanic
grandiose
jealous
persecutory
somatic
unspecified

PSYCHOTIC DISORDERS NOT ELSEWHERE CLASSIFIED (205)

298.80   Brief reactive psychosis (205)
295.40   Schizophreniform disorder (207)
          Specify: without good prognostic features or with good prognostic features
295.70   Schizoaffective disorder (208)
          Specify: bipolar type or depressive type
297.30   Induced psychotic disorder (210)
298.90   Psychotic disorder NOS (Atypical psychosis) (211)

MOOD DISORDERS (213)

Code current state of Major Depression and Bipolar Disorder in fifth digit.
1 = mild
2 = moderate
3 = severe, without psychotic features
4 = with psychotic features (specify mood-congruent or mood-incongruent)
5 = in partial remission
6 = in full remission
0 = unspecified

For major depressive episodes, specify if chronic and specify if melancholic type.

For Bipolar Disorder, Bipolar Disorder NOS, Recurrent Major Depression, and Depressive Disorder NOS, specify if seasonal pattern.

Bipolar Disorders

          Bipolar disorder, (225)
296.6x   mixed, _____
296.4x   manic, _____
296.5x   depressed, _____
301.13   Cyclothymia (226)
296.70   Bipolar disorder NOS

Depressive Disorders

          Major Depression, (228)
296.2x   single episode, _____
296.3x   recurrent, _____
300.40   Dysthymia (or Depressive neurosis) (230)
          Specify: primary or secondary type
          Specify: early or late onset
311.00   Depressive disorder NOS

ANXIETY DISORDERS (or Anxiety and Phobic Neuroses) (235)

          Panic disorder (235)
300.21   with agoraphobia
          Specify current severity of agoraphobic avoidance
          Specify current severity of panic attacks
300.01   without agoraphobia
          Specify current severity of panic attacks
300.22   Agoraphobia without history of panic disorder (240)
          Specify with or without limited symptom attacks
300.23   Social phobia (241)
          Specify if generalized type
300.29   Simple phobia (243)
300.30   Obsessive compulsive disorder (or Obsessive compulsive neurosis) (245)
309.89   Post-traumatic stress disorder (247)
          Specify if delayed onset
300.02   Generalized anxiety disorder (251)
300.00   Anxiety disorder NOS

SOMATOFORM DISORDERS (255)

300.70*   Body dysmorphic disorder (255)
300.11   Conversion disorder (or Hysterical neurosis, conversion type) (257)
          Specify: single episode or recurrent
300.70*   Hypochondriasis (or Hypochondriacal neurosis) (259)
300.81   Somatization disorder (261)

307.80 Somatoform pain disorder (264)
300.70* Undifferentiated somatoform disorder (266)
300.70* Somatoform disorder NOS (267)

DISSOCIATIVE DISORDERS (or Hysterical Neuroses, Dissociative Type) (269)
300.14 Multiple personality disorder (269)
300.13 Psychogenic fugue (272)
300.12 Psychogenic amnesia (273)
300.60 Depersonalization disorder (or Depersonalization neurosis) (275)
300.15 Dissociative disorder NOS

SEXUAL DISORDERS (279)

Paraphilias (279)
302.40 Exhibitionism (282)
302.81 Fetishism (282)
302.89 Frotteurism (283)
302.20 Pedophilia (284)
 Specify: same sex, opposite sex, same and opposite sex
 Specify if limited to incest
 Specify: exclusive type or nonexclusive type
302.83 Sexual masochism (286)
302.84 Sexual sadism (287)
302.30 Transvestic fetishism (288)
302.82 Voyeurism (289)
302.90* Paraphilia NOS (290)

Sexual Dysfunctions (290)
Specify: psychogenic only, or psychogenic and biogenic (Note: If biogenic only, code on Axis III)
Specify: lifelong or acquired
Specify: generalized or situational

 Sexual desire disorders (293)
302.71 Hypoactive sexual desire disorder
302.79 Sexual aversion disorder

 Sexual arousal disorders (294)
302.72* Female sexual arousal disorder

302.72* Male erectile disorder

 Orgasm disorders (294)
302.73 Inhibited female orgasm
302.74 Inhibited male orgasm
302.75 Premature ejaculation

 Sexual pain disorders (295)
302.76 Dyspareunia
306.51 Vaginismus

302.70 Sexual dysfunction NOS

Other Sexual Disorders
302.90* Sexual disorder NOS

SLEEP DISORDERS (297)

Dyssomnias (298)
 Insomnia disorder
307.42* related to another mental disorder (nonorganic) (300)
780.50* related to known organic factor (300)
307.42* Primary insomnia (301)
 Hypersomnia disorder
307.44 related to another mental disorder (nonorganic) (303)
780.50* related to a known organic factor (303)
780.54 Primary hypersomnia (305)
307.45 Sleep-wake schedule disorder (305)
 Specify: advanced or delayed phase type, disorganized type, frequently changing type
 Other dyssomnias
307.40* Dyssomnia NOS

Parasomnias (308)
307.47 Dream anxiety disorder (Nightmare disorder) (308)
307.46* Sleep terror disorder (310)
307.46* Sleepwalking disorder (311)
307.40* Parasomnia NOS (313)

FACTITIOUS DISORDERS (315)
 Factitious disorder
301.51 with physical symptoms (316)
300.16 with psychological symptoms (318)
300.19 Factitious disorder NOS (320)

IMPULSE CONTROL DISORDERS NOT ELSEWHERE CLASSIFIED (321)

312.34	Intermittent explosive disorder (321)
312.32	Kleptomania (322)
312.31	Pathological gambling (324)
312.33	Pyromania (325)
312.39*	Trichotillomania (326)
312.39*	Impulse control disorder NOS (328)

ADJUSTMENT DISORDER (329)

Adjustment disorder

309.24	with anxious mood
309.00	with depressed mood
309.30	with disturbance of conduct
309.40	with mixed disturbance of emotions and conduct
309.28	with mixed emotional features
309.82	with physical complaints
309.83	with withdrawal
309.23	with work (or academic) inhibition
309.90	Adjustment disorder NOS

PSYCHOLOGICAL FACTORS AFFECTING PHYSICAL CONDITION (333)

316.00	Psychological factors affecting physical condition *Specify* physical condition on Axis III

PERSONALITY DISORDERS (335)
Note: These are coded on Axis II.
Cluster A

301.00	Paranoid (337)
301.20	Schizoid (339)
301.22	Schizotypal (340)

Cluster B

301.70	Antisocial (342)
301.83	Borderline (346)
301.50	Histrionic (348)
301.81	Narcissistic (349)

Cluster C

301.82	Avoidant (351)
301.60	Dependent (353)
301.40	Obsessive compulsive (354)
301.84	Passive aggressive (356)
301.90	Personality disorder NOS

V CODES FOR CONDITIONS NOT ATTRIBUTABLE TO A MENTAL DISORDER THAT ARE A FOCUS OF ATTENTION OR TREATMENT (359)

V62.30	Academic problem
V71.01	Adult antisocial behavior

V40.00	Borderline intellectual functioning (Note: This is coded on Axis II.)

V71.02	Childhood or adolescent antisocial behavior
V65.20	Malingering
V61.10	Marital problem
V15.81	Noncompliance with medical treatment
V62.20	Occupational problem
V61.20	Parent–child problem
V62.81	Other interpersonal problem
V61.80	Other specified family circumstances
V62.89	Phase of life problem or other life circumstance problem
V62.82	Uncomplicated bereavement

ADDITIONAL CODES (363)

300.90	Unspecified mental disorder (nonpsychotic)
V71.09*	No diagnosis or condition on Axis I
799.90*	Diagnosis or condition deferred on Axis I

| V71.09* | No diagnosis or condition on Axis II |
| 799.90* | Diagnosis or condition deferred on Axis II |

MULTIAXIAL SYSTEM

Axis I   Clinical Syndromes
          V Codes

Axis II   Developmental Disorders
          Personality Disorders

Axis III Physical Disorders and
          Conditions

Axis IV   Severity of Psychosocial
          Stressors

Axis V   Global Assessment of
          Functioning

APPENDIX D

Index of Cases by Diagnosis